Gertrude Hildreth

2nd Edition 1961

In his short span of
professional years - to 1962
Russell did 2 editions of
this book, vocabulary studies,
a reader series, articles,
bulletins & monographs

On 1st meeting him at
Lincoln School in the 1930s
I said you'll go far Mr Russell
because you have the ability
and - your name's Russell
(same as the Doctor)

A big fault of this book -
Readiness is chart work
Learning to read begins with
the use of his reader series

CHILDREN LEARN TO READ

The Modern Child Must Read
A California Boy Looks at his Required Reading in the First Eight Grades. (His Recreational Reading is not included.) (Courtesy of Hayward Public Schools, Hayward, California)

CHILDREN LEARN TO READ

Second Edition

DAVID H. RUSSELL
University of California, Berkeley

GINN AND COMPANY
BOSTON NEW YORK CHICAGO ATLANTA DALLAS
PALO ALTO TORONTO LONDON

Library of Congress Catalogue Card Number 61-14660

161.5
A

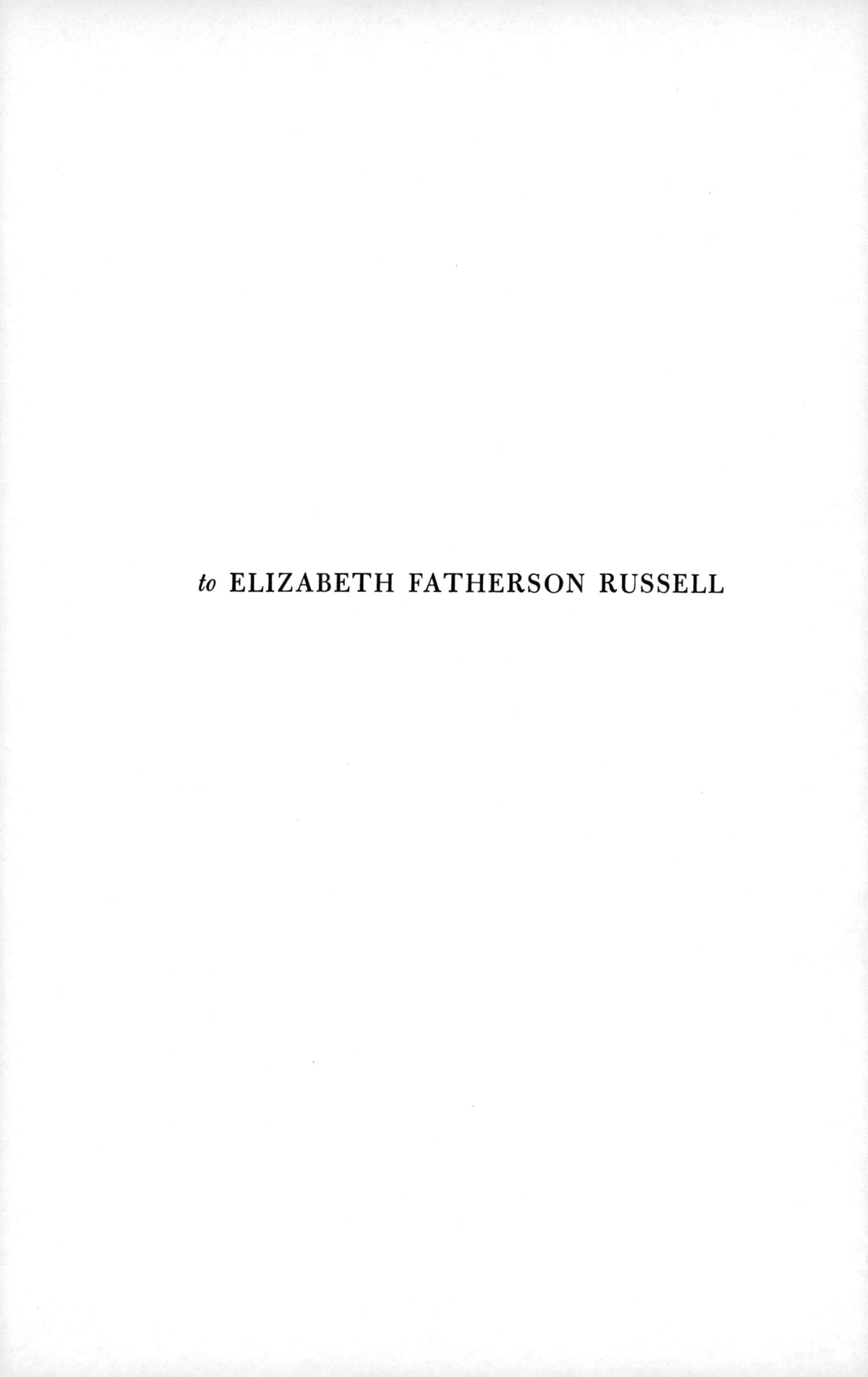

to ELIZABETH FATHERSON RUSSELL

Preface to Second Edition

The first edition of *Children Learn to Read* has been read by many teachers and used as a text in courses given in over 150 teachers colleges and universities. This response to the book prompts me to bring some of the materials up to date and to add certain sections to a second edition. In this new edition Chapter 1, on the role of reading in American life, has been completely rewritten and minor changes have been made in Chapters 2, 3, and 4 on the various backgrounds of the teaching of reading. These chapters have not been planned as immediate, practical guides to a teacher's day-by-day procedures, but they are attempts to put reading instruction in its setting. They seek to provide the foundation on which a true *profession* of teaching is built, for they give a little of the history, research, and knowledge of childhood which are the soundest bases for teaching procedures.

In Part II of the second edition the careful reader will find a number of changes in all chapters. The overview of reading instruction in Chapter 5 has been brought up to date, and Chapter 7 on the primary program has been considerably enlarged. So much new material has been appearing on reading in both the primary and upper elementary grades that the former chapters have been changed in many places. It has never been the intention of the author to present reading instruction at the whole secondary school level since other books do this well.

All of the chapters in Part III have been revised and enlarged, but the most extensive additions have been made in the new Chapter 10 on the word recognition program, because of the current interest in phonics, and in Chapter 14, on creative reading, an emphasis which was originally unique to this book. Many new references on children's literature are included. Part III is not planned to give help on diagnostic and remedial work with retarded readers because this large topic has been presented so fully in separate books such as Gates' *Improvement of Reading* and Harris's *How to Increase Reading Ability*. The section ends, however, with a completely new chapter on how teachers and parents may work together to achieve the best possible reading program in their own schools.

In making changes in the volume I should like to acknowledge specific aid from Elizabeth F. Russell, David R. Russell, and the typing contribution of Marjorie Bruce. Marion A. Anderson read all the revised manuscript and made helpful suggestions on it. Once again I should also like to acknowledge the help of colleagues and of many teachers in my classes and in their own classrooms. In the twelve years since the first edition was written, we have had the rise of television, a controversy over phonics, a fresh look at methods emphasizing individual activities, an increasing concern for understanding ideas which goes beyond literal comprehension to creative and critical thinking, and a general realization of the value of expert reading in tougher academic and international competition. During this time I have received countless suggestions from research reports, from my students, and from teachers and children at work together. I hope these are reflected in a sound philosophy, in a clear program of instruction, and in many practical suggestions throughout this revised volume.

Berkeley, May, 1960.

Contents

Part III DEVELOPMENTAL PHASES OF THE READING PROGRAM

Part I

BACKGROUNDS FOR THE WHOLE READING PROGRAM

Chapter 1

SOCIOLOGICAL BACKGROUNDS: READING ABILITIES AND HABITS IN AMERICAN LIFE

This book is concerned with the questions, "How do children acquire reading abilities?" and, "Do they read?" It is written that children may learn to read better and to love doing it. If children and adults can learn these two things, their personal lives may be enriched and their behavior as participants in community and national affairs strengthened. As individuals and as citizens they are better people.

In the world today about half the people are hungry, unable to read or write, and expect to die by the age of thirty-five. Although the present book can do nothing directly about food or health, it does attempt to aid the cause of learning to read and write, especially in schools. It concentrates on procedures in the United States but should be an aid to instruction in reading English anywhere. It is based on the belief that the act of reading can be both skillful and rewarding. Its aim is to increase the number of children who can read competently and who will continue to read throughout their lives.

Reading abilities and habits have social significance as well as individual value. Most teachers want Tom in the second grade or Alice in the sixth grade to be better readers for the children's own sakes. If they read skillfully and habitually Tom and Alice will do better school work[1] and, in terms of their all-round development, they will usually be more successful in their jobs and more effective as individuals. But, in addition, we want all the Toms and Alices in our schools to read well for the sake of their communities and our demo-

[1] Ruth C. Penty, *Reading Ability and High School Drop-outs.* Bureau of Publications, Teachers College, Columbia University, New York, 1956.

cratic institutions. An informed and enlightened citizenry is essential to the survival of the democratic way of life in community, state, or nation. When children learn to read better they contribute to the potential of their group; they eventually become better citizens who understand more about the events and problems which all groups of people must face in the modern world.

But we want more than boys and girls who can read well; we want them to value reading in their lives. An Elmo Roper Poll published in 1960 reported answers of typical Americans to the question, "If you could keep only one means of communication which would you select?" The replies were: television 42 per cent, newspapers 32 per cent, radio 19 per cent, and magazines 4 per cent. Perhaps parents and teachers need to do more to make reading an important and rewarding activity for children.

If reading abilities and reading habits have both personal and social significance, we must help children not just to read well but to read habitually. Only as he develops a habit of reading, can a person achieve some of the independence of thought and action that goes with true individuality. Only then can he become a useful member of a functioning group, a well-informed worker in his particular occupation, and a citizen competent to think and act about basic social issues. Both reading abilities and reading interests are essential to individual development and to society's health.

This fact suggests the need of development of reading abilities and habits not only in elementary and secondary schools but perhaps through college and graduate school. If habits are important, perhaps there should be systematic planning for the life-long reading of adults. The educated adult with literary interests may spurn a cut-and-dried program and will plan his own reading excursions, but it may be that most of us might be helped by some such plan as suggested in *Good Reading*[2] or in Fadiman's[3] *The Lifetime Reading Plan*. We still have little factual evidence about the best way of encouraging lifetime reading habits. Not everyone will become a "constant reader" but perhaps more people can be helped in this direction.

Much of this book accordingly deals with improving the reading

[2] J. Sherwood Weber, ed., *Good Reading*. Committee on College Reading, National Council of Teachers of English. Bowker, New York, 1960. Paperback, New American Library, New York, 1960.

[3] Clifton Fadiman, *The Lifetime Reading Plan*. World, Cleveland, 1960.

skills of the individual, but it is also concerned with patterns of reading activity in relation to other concerns. The present chapter is concerned largely with people's habits of reading or what may be called sociological aspects of reading. As school staffs know more about what people read, and why they read or do not read, they have one sound basis for improvements in elementary and secondary school reading programs. This chapter suggests that goals in the school's reading program should be set not only in terms of immediate activities in classroom learning but also in light of the behavior patterns of individuals after they have left school.

FREEDOM TO READ

In both personal and sociological senses, reading is an integral part of the process of communication of ideas. Communication is such an important part of all human activities that teachers and parents alike must be concerned with freedom to read and speak. "Freedom of speech," the first of the Four Freedoms of the Atlantic Charter, dedicated to all the peoples of the world, included freedom to read. As an elementary teacher struggles to help a small boy with the recognition of the *at* phonogram or finding the main idea of a paragraph, the teacher and boy probably have little time for abstract ideas of freedom or the national good. Yet it is still true that teacher and child are working as small parts of a large whole concerned with human welfare, human dignity and human liberty. Highly developed reading skills are of little value if one's reading is restricted to one type of material prescribed by some government official. Freedom to read may sometimes be infringed by censorship, however well-meaning it may be. It is doubtful if young children should be allowed to read everything printed, such as the pornographic or the sadistic in some of the worst of books or horror comics, but it is still a dangerous practice to say that such-and-such material should be banned. One question is, "Who decides?" Another is, "What about other books or magazines just a little better?" And so the censor may arrive at a place where many books or stories are made unavailable and a real threat to freedom of ideas has arisen.[4] As suggested in Chapter 12, the school's job is not to ban so much as to raise stand-

[4] Richard McKeon, R. K. Merton, and W. Gellhorn, *The Freedom to Read.* Sponsored by National Book Committee. Bowker, New York, 1957.

ards of taste, to create interests so that children want to read worth-while things.

Many people believe that the threat to freedom of exchange of ideas in the western world is a real one. In a world where perhaps 75 per cent of all persons live under some sort of government censorship, the people of the United States and a few other democracies must protect their first freedom, the freedom of speech. The Bill of Rights in 1791 guaranteed to the press of the United States freedom from government interference, and that freedom has never been seriously threatened since. Some people believe that the chief threat to freedom of ideas in the newspapers and other media of communication lies, not in government domination, but in the controls exercised by a relatively small group of people over newspapers, magazines and radio and television programs. For example, Morris L. Ernst, a New York lawyer, has written, "The pipelines of thought to the minds of the nation are being contracted and squeezed. About thirty men realistically dominate the conduits of thought through the ether, the printing presses and the silver screen. . . . The cartelization of the mind of America is well on the way."[5]

There is some evidence to support this frightening statement. Although readership of daily newspapers continues to rise, the number of different newspapers has been going down rather steadily over the last fifty years. Many small cities and towns of the United States do not have competing papers. Even where two papers are published they may be owned by the same person or persons and the owners may also control the local radio or television station. Between 1920 and 1950 the population of the United States increased 43 per cent whereas the circulation of daily newspapers increased 69 per cent, and in these years radio and television became widespread means of communication. But, in the same period, the number of different daily newspapers went down steadily through amalgamation or cessation of publishing. Furthermore, newspaper content during this period became more standardized through increased use of press services and the syndicating of columnists. For example, Alistair Cooke,[6] the newspaper correspondent and television commentator, suggested that the steelworker in Gary, Indiana, and the date farmer

[5] Morris L. Ernst, *The Best is Yet,* p. 90. Harper, New York, 1945.

[6] Alistair Cooke, "The Press and the Common Man," *Saturday Review,* Vol. 37, pp. 9-10, 55-56, March 13, 1954.

in Indio, California, get their foreign news in the same package—from the same agency man in Berlin or Washington. Not only the ideas made available but newspaper reading habits of adults, discussed in the next section, are pertinent to the topic of freedom. Similarly, the sources of ideas, the materials available and the habits of using magazines suggest some dangers in monopoly of ideas. A small group of mass circulation and women's magazines dominates the newsstands in terms of number of sales and home reading in relation to subscription figures. The *Reader's Digest* with a domestic circulation over 12 million in 1960 and seventeen other regional and language editions, plus such magazines as *Life, Saturday Evening Post, Ladies Home Journal,* and *McCall's,* represent a few sources for the ideas many persons receive from reading. Movie-making, too, has been characterized by the domination of three or four big companies, and even when many "independents" are producing pictures, they must still be booked into theatres and drive-ins by a limited number of circulation agencies.

In radio and television there may also be some threat to freedom in the number of ideas presented to the American people, again not because they are circumscribed by the federal government or its agency, the Federal Communications Commission, so much as because of the more subtle pressures by the owners of facilities and the control of programs by sponsors and advertising agencies. There are only three large television networks in the country, the National Broadcasting Company, the Columbia Broadcasting System, and the American Broadcasting Corporation, each of which establishes certain "standards" for news broadcasts and other programs. No advertiser can afford to alienate any large segment of the population for the sake of a poignant or challenging drama on TV. Controversial areas may be too "sensitive" for commercial programs. One columnist[7] quotes Rod Serling, the television writer, as follows:

"If the trend toward censorship continues the next few years in the same direction and to the same degree it has, there'll be a new citizenry evolving in this country. They will be very selective in terms of their cereals and automobiles, but they'll have forgotten how to read books, make a decision and, probably, in the long run, to even think a thought.

"It's a little disheartening to look on the last two or three years of TV

[7] Bill Fiset, "TV Drama: Antiseptic Oatmeal," *Milwaukee Journal,* June 28, 1958. (Also other newspapers.)

and note that there has been no marked improvement in quality or any appreciable trend toward innovations in programing.

"Programing, by and large, remains unimaginative, static and very much uninspired. It's my contention that the apparent stultification of creativity among this country's 3,000 writers is not an evidence of diminishing talent. It's a net and direct result of an increasing specter of censorship which hangs heavy over the typewriters of every writer currently laboring in the vineyards of TV.

"The long list of taboos has grown from its initial area of simply politics to embrace a much more vast set of dogma that dictate what he can and cannot write about. The TV drama is evolving as such an innocuous, oversimplified, rigidly stainless, antiseptic dish of oatmeal that any relation of a dramatized conflict to an existing real life conflict becomes highly coincidental."

Serling's pointed remarks seem most pertinent in relation to network programs and may not apply to many local programs or to educational television. It is important to note that during the late 1940's and the 1950's network radio's income was halved and its maximum audience dropped from 25 million to 1.5 million families[8] but at the same time independent stations were flourishing and radio became more localized and stabilized. Furthermore, in less than a decade after the Federal Communications Commission granted TV channels to non-commercial, educational stations over fifty such stations representing an investment of over 50 million dollars were "on the air." Such diversity in stations and ownership can be one safeguard for the freedom of ideas.

Nor is the situation completely monopolistic in regard to radio and television stations, which carry heavy loads of network programs. Government agency and private ownership have developed the idea that chains must give some place to divergent ideas or "both sides of a question." Guinzberg[9] has summarized the point as follows:

"In the course of regulating radio, a principle startlingly new in its implications to traditional American concepts has been introduced—an extension, if you like, of the principle of free speech. This is the doctrine that when certain controversial subjects are discussed over the air, both sides must be given an equal amount of time. To be sure, in some cases it is impossible to exercise this right, since, if time has been paid for by one side, the other side may not have money enough to meet the high

[8] *Newsweek,* Vol. 48, p. 61, August 20, 1956.

[9] H. K. Guinzberg, R. W. Frase, and T. Waller, *Books and the Mass Market.* University of Illinois Press, Urbana, 1953.

cost of radio time. But in general the very notion presents a definite enlargement of the concept of free expression. It says, in effect, that we are no longer merely concerned, as we were in the eighteenth century, lest some authority prevent a man from saying what he wants to. It says, in addition, that those who control limited channels for reaching the public have an obligation to present both sides of controversial issues."

Compared to radio and television, the range of ideas available in books is tremendous and the sources of ideas are numerous. So sharp is the contrast that a teacher or school staffs may well consider not the general problem of developing better reading but of producing better readers of books. The number of publishers of books in the United States has risen rapidly in the last forty years. In 1957, for example, over 13,000 hard-cover book titles and 4,500 paperback titles were published. The mass-marketing of books and the rapid rise of the various paperback books, including children's books, has greatly extended the range of ideas available in books. The drug stores and supermarkets may be dominated by mystery stories and Westerns, but the fact remains that most of the great classics of world literature as well as recent works of fiction and nonfiction are easily accessible to most urban dwellers of the United States. As suggested below, the country is not a nation of book readers, but at least the materials are available in books. Americans in the middle of the twentieth century had at their elbows more tools and methods of communication and more sources of ideas in newspapers, magazines, and books than ever before.

Some implications for elementary- and secondary-school teachers seem clear. First, there is no longer a scarcity of reading material as in Colonial times, and so it is seldom necessary to go over a selection again and again pondering the meaning of every word. Instead, the teacher's and pupil's reading problem is one of selection. From all the reading materials available how shall we choose the most helpful and most important? Second, young people need help in working out a balance in their use of the mass media. If a child reads only comic books or looks only at TV Westerns, he is missing many good things and not really enjoying the freedom that is his. In the second half of the twentieth century children increasingly need help in the wise use of the different resources available. Third, with the tremendous amount of material available, it becomes even more important that children and youth develop standards of excellence. They must gradually be helped in distinguishing between the vicious and pernicious in some comics or paperbacks, the mediocre in some television, magazines, and books, and the excellent in most of these sources. This means that they must develop tastes, as suggested in Chapter 12, and be able to think critically about what they read and hear, as discussed in Chapter 14. In other words, the freedom of ideas found today in books and the other mass media implies responsibility—responsibility for developing standards of judgment and use of the rich supply of contemporary materials. Some of the ways children and adults are currently using these materials are discussed below.

READING HABITS IN THE UNITED STATES

Freedom to read is worthless if children and adults never bother to read. The values of books can be destroyed by their neglect as surely as by their burning. If the peoples of the United States have the freedom to read, how are they using that freedom? Do your neighbors or the typical families in your community read magazines, newspapers, and books, or only tabloids and comics, or nothing? The test of the success of reading programs in American schools is not so much the scores made by their pupils on reading tests but the reading habits of their students and graduates. What sort of reading activities do we find in American communities today?

The reading picture in the United States is a puzzling, paradoxical one to sociologists and to school people alike. For example:

In 1955 a poll by the American Institute of Public Opinion (the Gallup Poll) of a cross-section of American adults found that 60 per cent did not remember reading a single book, other than the Bible, during the whole preceding year.

In contrast, scores of book clubs flourished. In 1955 their members bought 65 million books, over twice the number sold in regular bookstores.

In 1956 nearly one billion comic books were published in the United States. One study[10] estimated that the amount spent on these comics was about $100,000,000 annually, or about four times the annual book budget of all United States public libraries.

In the late 1950's paperback books had good years and sold about 300 million copies annually, but an earlier Gallup poll estimated that 9 per cent of their buyers accounted for 78 per cent of all copies sold.

[10] Edward Feder, *Comic Book Regulation*. Bureau of Public Administration, University of California, Berkeley, 1955.

In regard to newspapers, the United States has some 11,200 dailies and weeklies. Their circulation has been going up rather steadily and has been increasing more rapidly than the general population. Between 1920 and 1950, for example, the population increased 43 per cent whereas the average circulation of daily newspapers increased 69 per cent.

In the late 1950's Americans spent about one-third as much on books as on newspapers and magazines and about one-quarter as much on books as on keeping radio and television sets in repair.

These few selected items indicate (1) that Americans generally are not habitual book readers, (2) that they do read magazines and newspapers fairly regularly, and (3) that the amount of reading they do, if not the quality, has been going up rather steadily. These facts are discussed here in more detail and then possible reasons for the facts are given. Both the facts and the influences affecting them are of immediate concern to all school people.

Newspaper Reading

Different investigations, made at different times and places, have found that most Americans, young and old, urban and rural, are newspaper readers. One study[11] made at the University of Minnesota found that over 95 per cent of people in both rural and metropolitan areas read local newspapers and listened to the radio. In contrast, about three-quarters of the group read magazines but only one-half of the people in large cities read books and this number declined further in less populous areas with four out of ten farmers reading no books. Other studies have shown that most rural people read at least a local weekly newspaper and often a metropolitan daily. In a study of the newspaper reading of children from grades three through eleven in Des Moines, Iowa, Lyness[12] found that 85 per cent of the youngest children read some parts of the newspaper and that the amount of attention given all mass media, including newspapers and magazines, increased somewhat with age. In contrast, the amount of book reading declined at the adolescent age levels. Boys spent more time reading newspapers than girls did. To a greater extent than girls, boys preferred to read about violence and adventures as in robberies and accidents. Girls showed a marked preference for

[11] Malcolm S. MacLean, "Mass Media Audiences: City, Small City, Village and Farm," *Journalism Quarterly*, Vol. 29, pp. 271-282, Summer, 1952.

[12] Paul I. Lyness, "The Place of the Mass Media in the Lives of Boys and Girls," *Journalism Quarterly*, Vol. 29, pp. 43-54, Winter, 1952.

love affairs, private life, and glamor. Interest in comic strips and in books was highest around the fifth and seventh grades respectively and varied widely among individuals.

A more recent study by the Gilbert Youth Research Company, dealing with habits and tastes of teen-agers and syndicated in many newspapers, showed a higher amount of book reading, at least equal to the 76 per cent of the groups that regularly read a daily newspaper. The top category in newspaper interests was "front page news," listed by 36 per cent of the group. Other reader interest was shown by the following "Most Liked" choices: comics and cartoons, 28 per cent; sports, 17 per cent; society news, 8 per cent; movie, radio, and television news, 6 per cent. The least liked features of newspapers were advertisements at 27 per cent and editorials at 14 per cent. Other continuing studies by the Gallup Poll indicate almost 100 per cent reading of news stories by both men and women but considerable differences in subject interests of the two groups.[13]

Since children and young people read newspapers regularly, they should be given some help in the understanding and use of the daily and weekly press. For example, they should know that about three-fourths of the income of the newspaper is from advertising and only one-fourth from subscriptions and newsstand sales. They should learn that newspapers often represent a particular point of view in matters political, social, and religious and in other areas. They can be helped to understand that all papers work under terrific time pressures to select what goes into one issue and that sometimes important items or long-range views are lost in daily deadlines. They can understand that editors make mistakes in judgment as when the story of the first plane flight by the Wright brothers was put in a short column on page 12 of the *Dayton Daily Herald* with space equal to an advertisement "Rheumatism is Caused by Bad Blood."

Dale[14] has given an excellent summary of what the mature newspaper reader can do:

"He can get a quick overview of the news by reading news summaries, by reading the headlines which summarize the stories they head.

"He can learn to adjust his speed of reading, learn to change gears. An

[13] Lester Asheim, "What Do Adults Read?" *Adult Reading,* Fifty-fifth Yearbook, Part II, National Society for the Study of Education, University of Chicago Press, Chicago, 1956.

[14] Edgar Dale, "How to Read a Newspaper," *The News Letter,* Vol. 22, pp. 1-4, December, 1956.

occasional editorial, quotation, or serious piece of writing may deserve slow, careful reading. But we should read most of the newspapers at speeds of not less than three hundred words a minute. Many readers plod through chaff and wheat at exactly the same halting pace.

"He can compare the treatment of stories in different newspaper sources. He can see how the *Toledo Blade* covered a story as compared with the *New York Herald-Tribune* or the *Berkshire Eagle*. He can pit his judgment against the editor as to whether certain stories were over-played or under-played.

"He can check the radio and television news against the news in the press for adequacy, depth, and quality of treatment. He can turn to an atlas, an encyclopedia, a pamphlet, a magazine, a book to supplement the news story he has read in the newspaper.

"Finally, the critical reader can apply his critical judgment to the press as it touches all phases of his life. He can use standards of evidence that he has picked up in good history courses. He can apply the critical standards learned in courses on logic or propaganda analysis.

"Indeed, everything we learn in school and out of school will have its daily counterpart in the press. Every day a fresh book of life is laid on nearly every doorstep in the United States. How can readers and writers learn to give this book the respect and intelligent attention it deserves?"

Paperbacks

Changes in the reading habits of the American people are illustrated most dramatically in the rise of the inexpensive, "pocket book" type of publication. It is probably proper to speak of "the paperback revolution." The modern period of the paperback began in the United States in 1939 with the publishing of Pocket Books and the importation of Penguin Books from England. In the twenty-year period following it was estimated that Americans consumed some 2,600,000,000 paperbacks. As can be seen in any corner newsstand, the lurid adventure story, the crime or detective story, and what has been termed "bosomy fiction" outnumber other types of books, but it is also true that the various publishers of paperbacks include most of the world's great books ranging at least from the Greek dramatists to modern classics. The paperbacks have made accessible to most people the entertaining, the serious, and the great writing of all time.

Of course, the paperback idea is not new. As Schick[15] points out in his history of the paperbound book, chapbooks and pamphlets were read in both England and United States at least as early as

[15] Frank L. Schick, *The Paperbound Book in America.* Bowker, New York, 1958.

Cotton Mather's popular denunciation of "foolish Songs and Ballads" published in 1713. It was in 1860 that Beadle & Co. issued its first dime novel in orange paper covers. By 1960 there were about one hundred firms in the business of producing paperbacks with titles being added at the rate of about 120 a month.

The modern paperback means that everyone has access to excellence. The quality paperbound book is already used widely in colleges and universities, and its use will probably grow in elementary and secondary schools, especially for supplementary and individual reading. As suggested above, the wide range of possibilities in the field makes it imperative that schools help children develop standards and employ critical judgment in the selection of such books. The rise of children's and adolescents' book clubs, mentioned in Chapter 13, is in some cases an example of a selected use of paperbacks. Most of the discussion in this chapter applies to paperbacks as well as to other books.

Comic Books

In the late 1950's nearly one billion comic books a year were published in the United States. As one speaker put it, "The children read almost as many of them as the adults did." During the latter part of the decade, however, there was a decline in the purchase of comic books, which has usually been attributed to the influence of television.

Comic strips are one of the most popular parts of the newspaper. Studies by Witty[16] and others have shown that most children read some comic books or strips regularly and that the amount of such reading reaches a peak somewhere around eleven or twelve years of age. Thereafter, like other recreational reading, it declines generally. Its persistence in the case of individual adolescents and adults is probably related to low reading ability. One reads comics if one can't read other things.

The problem of the comics is considered more fully in Chapter 12, which deals with children's interests in reading. In relation to the sociology of reading, it seems important to suggest that comic books and strips vary widely—that some may be interesting and useful and others may be vicious in content and harmful to young chil-

[16] Paul A. Witty and R. A. Sizemore, "Reading the Comics: Summary of Studies and an Evaluation," *Elementary English*, Vol. 31, pp. 501-506, December, 1944; Vol. 32, pp. 43-49, 109-114, January, February, 1955.

dren. Wertham[17] has attempted to make a case for comics as the cause of juvenile delinquency but it seems doubtful, from the point of view of scientific evidence, that they can be considered a sole cause. Combined with such social factors, for example, as slum living conditions, lack of parental control, broken home, and few recreational opportunities, and with certain individual factors such as personality and mental ability, the reading of comics may be associated with delinquency. However, the primacy of comic-book reading in causation is not thereby established. On the positive side, some of the more wholesome comics may provide children with humorous and informative materials. In general, teachers and parents should probably distinguish between the comic strips, over which newspapers have some control, and the comic book which may be published by some small and irresponsible firm. An association of comic book manufacturers attempts some voluntary censorship of materials, but not all comics are checked closely enough. The annual evaluations of the Cincinnati committee[18] are examples of what a group of parents, teachers, and librarians can do in evaluating the qualities of the various comic books. Burton[19] has illustrated how a teacher may analyze the basic appeals of the comics and steer pupils to other materials with related content and more enduring values.

A study of the content of comic strips was made by Spiegelman and others,[20] who analyzed a group of comics published over a three-week period and seen by an estimated audience of 60 million people. Analysis was made in terms of characters depicted, caricature, humor, and situation. The analysis disclosed that "100 per cent Americans" hold a dominant place and that most minority groups are ignored. Animals occupy an important position, especially if humor is intended. A suggested definition of comic-strip humor is to "place an anthropomorphized animal in an incongruous situation with or at the expense of humans." Adventure, on the other hand, is serious business. The authors believe the comics are "skewed toward reality" in terms of situations but that unreality of situation and reality of

[17] Frederick Wertham, *Seduction of the Innocent*. Rinehart, New York, 1954.

[18] Committee on the Evaluation of Comic Books, *Annual Reports*. Cincinnati, Ohio. See also *Parents' Magazine*.

[19] Dwight L. Burton, "Comic Books: A Teacher's Analysis," *Elementary School Journal*, Vol. 56, pp. 73-75, June, 1955.

[20] Marvin Spiegelman, Carl Terwiliger, and Franklin Fearing, "The Content of Comic Strips: A Study of a Mass Medium of Communication," *Journal of Social Psychology*, Vol. 25, pp. 37-57, February, 1952.

characters go together and vice versa. As suggested in Chapter 12, it may often be useful for teachers, parents, and children to attempt some simple analyses of comic books or comic strips in an attempt to develop critical judgment about the content and to move to more valuable materials. One such informal analysis suggested the following stereotypes:

> People in authority are often stupid.
> People in authority are either good or bad and you can tell which by their appearance.
> The end justifies the means.
> Romantic love and money are at the heart of life's problems.

Such clichés are obviously not confined to comic books, but there and elsewhere they need examination and criticism by boys and girls as well as adults.

Magazines

The people of the United States are a magazine-reading population. The circulation of magazines went up steadily during the first half of the twentieth century, and one survey in the 1950's, for example, showed that nine major magazines reached a total of some 60 million readers ten years of age and older on an average-issue basis. A study made by the Gilbert Youth Research Company in 1959, and syndicated in newspapers, found that 72 per cent of teenagers read magazines each week. It is true that in the magazine field the "pulps" still outnumber the "slicks," but perhaps due to the prevalence of easy entertainment in television, the 1950's were also marked by an upgrading in quality of some of the mass circulation magazines.

In his introduction to an anthology of magazine writing Clifton Fadiman[21] commented on the situation as follows:

> "The tripe magazines that teem on the newsstands seek with great success a lower and lower level. On the other hand, the so-called middlebrow magazines, at least some of them, have slowly, steadily upped their standards."

For the American public, frequency of magazine reading comes

[21] Clifton Fadiman, Introduction to *Ten Years of Holiday*, pp. vii, viii. Simon and Schuster, New York, 1956.

between newspaper reading and book reading. One report[22] estimates that over 80 per cent of adults read one or more newspapers a day, about 70 per cent read one or more magazines regularly, and only about 50 per cent read one or more books a year. The magazine market is dominated by the "big" magazines such as *Life, Look,* the *Saturday Evening Post,* and *Reader's Digest,* and by such women's magazines as *Ladies Home Journal, McCall's,* and *Good Housekeeping.* A newer group of magazines aimed largely at the feminine market and sometimes called the supermarket magazines include *Family Circle, Woman's Day,* and *Everywoman's,* with a combined circulation in the late 1950's of over 9 million copies. At the same time *Seventeen,* for teenage girls, had a circulation of about one million.[23] Such women's magazines, with a combined circulation of over 20 million, far outsell what have been called the magazines of ideas such as the *Atlantic, Harper's, The Saturday Review, The Reporter,* and *The Nation,* whose combined circulation is about three-quarters of a million.

It depends largely on one's point of view whether one is encouraged or discouraged by the tremendous readership of the mass circulation magazines. In recent years the magazines have included less saccharine fiction and more factual articles than they did twenty or thirty years ago. Wolseley[24] says the women's magazines are "leagues ahead of the literature for ladies available a century ago." They often deal in important ideas, skillfully presented. On the negative side, they have been criticized for "the cult of the beautiful," stress on conformity in clothes, hairdos, and furniture, and the stimulation through advertising of a desire for new objects and services. Fiction is still stereotyped, but nonfiction often deals ably with the arts, current affairs, and even controversial issues.

The place of magazines in the school program varies widely from school system to school system. Most secondary schools and some elementary school libraries make current and back issues of selected magazines available on their shelves. Social studies teachers find in them worthwhile materials on current topics. Some publications such as *My Weekly Reader* (a newspaper in graded editions), *Read,* and

[22] Daniel Katz and others, eds., *Public Opinion and Propaganda,* p. 238. Dryden, New York, 1954.

[23] Roland E. Wolseley, "Women's Magazines—Dope or Dynamite," *Niemann Reports,* Vol. 11, pp. 31-34, April, 1957.

[24] *Ibid.*

Junior Scholastic are definitely aimed at school uses. Unfortunately there are few magazines especially planned for children which seem able to survive in a competitive market. Such exceptions as *Jack and Jill,* produced by the Curtis Publishing Company, *Boys' Life,* supported by the Boy Scouts of America, and *Children's Digest,* sponsored by *Parents' Magazine* and including much reprint material, are more enduring than most because they have outside means of support. Advertisers who provide most of the revenue for the mass circulation magazines do not ordinarily believe in the effectiveness of a juvenile magazine as an advertising medium, and such magazines have difficulty in surviving on subscriptions alone. Many adult magazines such as *Life, National Geographic,* and *Look* have appeal for children, at least after the primary grades, but it is doubtful how much actual reading of them is done by younger children.

The adolescents interviewed in the Gilbert survey (mentioned above) cited interesting stories about important people as their primary reason for liking magazines. Other reasons were better articles than other media, good pictures, and fiction and nonfiction stories. Their chief objection to magazines was too many advertisements. There seems little reason to doubt that the chance to discuss and use magazine articles, both in elementary and secondary schools, can be an important part of a child's total reading, just as it is for his parents, and that it can help develop skill and taste in handling magazine materials.

Books and Libraries

As mentioned above, Americans are not book readers to the extent they are newspaper and magazine readers, and yet, in recent years, the production and consumption of books has gone up enormously. Perhaps the situation can best be described as "mixed": on the unfavorable side, a Gallup Poll of the 1950's found that only 17 per cent of the adults interviewed were actually reading a book at the time they were interviewed. Over half of the adults in the United States lived within a mile of a public library, yet only one-fifth of them visited it during the year and only one-tenth of them averaged as much as one visit a month to the library.[25] Some 27 million children and adults in the United States were found to be without any library service in a survey made by the American Library Associa-

[25] A. Campbell and C. A. Metzner, "Books, Libraries and Other Media of Communication," in D. Katz and others, eds., *Public Opinion and Propaganda, op. cit.* p. 235.

tion in 1956. Ninety per cent of these people were in rural areas.

On the other hand, the number of books sold in the United States in 1947, including textbooks and encyclopedias, was over 487 million. In 1954, the number was 770 million, an increase of about 60 per cent in seven years.[26] Similarly, in the children's field, both hard-cover books and the inexpensive series, often sold in supermarkets, have boomed. In the middle 1950's over 30 million copies of the *Little Golden Books* and 25 million copies of the *Wonder Books* were sold annually. Over a five-year period, one publisher sold 6 million copies of one series alone, the *Landmark Books.* Apparently young Johnny Q. Public was reading, and books were found not only in privileged homes.

Although such figures are encouraging, it should be noted that Americans spent very little of their total incomes, after taxes, on books. A report of the United States Department of Commerce on "Personal Consumption Expenditures" suggested that the American people put nearly one-third of personal expenditures into food, tobacco, and alcoholic beverages, about one-tenth into clothing, one-fourth into housing, one-eighth into transportation, and only about one-twentieth into recreation, including "books and maps." Of the recreation dollar about 10 cents goes to automobiles and of the 5 or 6 cents for recreation nearly one cent goes to foreign travel, one cent for radio, television and records, about two-thirds of a cent for magazines and newspapers, and only one-fifth of a cent for books.[27]

As in the case of other reading statistics, these figures can be viewed with optimism or with foreboding. Book clubs distribute many millions of books yearly, but the total number of full-fledged bookstores is under 1,500. The number of hard-back and paperback books published is going up faster than the population, but on a per capita basis Americans read fewer books, for example, than the people of England, Australia, and Canada. From most points of view the findings are "mixed."

Book-reading habits should be a concern of all school people. The best test of a school's reading program may be not the scores made on measures of reading achievement, but the reading habits which children have when they leave school—habits which may persist for

[26] U. S. Bureau of the Census, *Statistical Abstract of the United States, 1959,* p. 523. Superintendent of Documents, Washington, D.C., 1959.

[27] "Books Continue to Take 1/5 cent of U. S. Consumer Dollar," *Publishers Weekly,* Vol. 172, p. 46, September 9, 1957.

the rest of their lives. The problem of reading interests and tastes is discussed in more detail in Chapter 12. Reading instruction in both elementary and secondary schools can be aimed not only toward skillfull reading but toward developing a love of reading in nearly every child.

FACTORS AFFECTING READING HABITS

School people can be aware of national and community habits of reading newspapers, paperbacks, comics, magazines, and books, but they also need insights into reasons back of these phenomena. Why do we read as we do? How does one develop lifetime reading habits? There are many reasons why we read or don't read. Five of the more compelling factors in a people's reading may be described briefly.

Level of Reading Skills and Abilities

A man doesn't read much if he can't read well. A 1960 report of the United States Census indicated that the average reading ability today of the American adult (over twenty-five years) is probably that of the typical tenth-grade student. This corresponds roughly to average schooling. But the Census also indicated that about 4 million adults in this country are "functionally illiterate"—that they have completed less than five years of schooling and can't read and write sufficiently well to carry on the ordinary business of living. An earlier Census report revealed that there were three times as many functional illiterates as college graduates in the country, but this figure has been reduced in recent years. (See illustration, page 21.)

There are, of course, variations in literacy by states, but no people of any state can afford to be smug. In New York State alone in the 1950's there were about a million functional illiterates and Illinois and California each had over 400,000 of them. These states rank high in educational achievement, but in them and other states there are illiterates by the hundred thousand. Illiteracy is associated with such conditions as poverty, disease, low wages, occupational deficiency, and Selective Service rejections. Functional illiteracy is highest in our Southern states but is obviously not confined to this area—migration alone would take care of that. If one lives in a typical town in the United States and walks down the street on a typical day, he will meet some adults who are "functionally illiterate." Is it surprising that they read little or not at all?

MR. DAY

Mr. Day works in a factory.

He has a car.

Mr. Day will go to work in the car.

At night he will go to school.

He will walk to school.

Mr.	Day	has
he	will	factory

Page from reader in a literacy program for adults (Federal Textbook on Citizenship, *The Day Family,* Book I, United States Government Printing Office, Washington, D.C., 1942)

Dark as this picture is, it is better than it used to be. Census reports indicate improving educational achievement since the late 1800's. In a study of a cross-section of adults in the Chicago area made about 1930, Gray and Leary from the University of Chicago found that average reading ability was only about the sixth-grade level. As children stay longer in school, they learn to read better and may continue to improve their reading abilities after they leave school. A comparison of the educational attainments of hundreds of thousands of young men, statistically a good sample, in World War I and World War II leaves no doubt as to the improvement of the reading abilities of people over the last forty years. The results are still not good enough but they are much better than they used to be. Furthermore, there is hope for illiterates, as illustrated by their training in World War II[28] and because of their importance today in the mobilization of manpower. Ginzberg and Bray[29] have analyzed the extent and problems of illiteracy and reported army programs in which 89 per cent of the men were rehabilitated for useful service.

But what about Bill Smith, the big boy in the next block who can't read or never reads for himself? Such mass statistics or army training may not affect a younger boy who is having trouble with reading—the boys with this problem outnumber the girls at least four to one. Occasionally, then, an irate parent raises the cry "Why don't the schools teach reading?" An occasional book has a transient success by maintaining that the schools don't teach reading as well as they once did. The weight of evidence about the huge majority of the cases is against such a parent or author—careful studies indicate that children do read as well or a little better than they did thirty or fifty years ago, given the same general ability and opportunity. Reading achievement is much the same as it used to be at the fourth- or ninth-grade levels, for example, but school children are younger than they used to be at corresponding stages and, age for age, they are somewhat better readers now than fifty years ago.

Of course this fact about most children may not apply to the individual Bill or Michael who is having trouble with reading and perhaps with school generally. Studies of the Bills and Mikes show

[28] Samuel Goldberg, "Army Training of Illiterates in World War II," *Teachers College Contributions to Education,* No. 966. Bureau of Publications, Teachers College, Columbia University, New York, 1951.

[29] Eli Ginzberg and Douglas Bray, *The Uneducated.* Columbia University Press, New York, 1953.

that causes of reading difficulty, like those of delinquency or any socially disapproved behavior, are often subtle and complex. Furthermore, they occur in some sort of constellation or syndrome of causes rather than a single, isolated cause. Accordingly, simple and single remedies such as more phonics, retardation in school, or word drill at home are not usually an answer. Bill or Mike usually needs some individual help for a period of months, the kind he can get in a clinic but not in a class of thirty-five or more youngsters. More school systems, in Europe as well as in North America, are gradually developing the facilities to give such individual help. With this special help the children need, at least for a while, reading materials which are for them high in level of interest but low in level of difficulty.

Perhaps the outstanding fact which parents and others need to recognize more clearly is the wide range of reading abilities found in any group of children of any one age. Every test of every school population that has ever been given suggests that children spread out widely in reading ability. If Bill and Michael are in the fourth grade but only reading at second-grade level, it is also true that in their class will be other youngsters reading above their grade, with fifth- or sixth-grade, or even higher, abilities. A group of ninth graders normally range in reading ability from that of third graders to that of average college freshmen or sophomores. Such differences are perfectly usual and normal. The better the school teaches reading the farther it spreads children apart in reading abilities. This means that the good school gives the poor reader the special help he needs and challenges the gifted reader to do even better than he has been doing.

Such facts and such aims for schools have helped to raise the level of reading skills and abilities in this country. In some countries of the world, the literacy programs have not been too effective because, after people learn to read, there is practically nothing for them to read. In the United States, most people get a good start on their reading in school, but they too need continuing help in finding some good things to read, not just the pulps, if they are to grow in their reading comprehension and tastes.

Educational and Socio-Economic Level

The amount of a person's reading is partly determined by his education and the class of people to which he belongs. The magazine that boasts of the executives among its readers, the journal that claims its audience constitutes a class market, even the woman's magazine that advocates the power of womankind in purchasing choices, all have a point. Different people with different educational backgrounds read different kinds of materials—if they read at all.

Undoubtedly some adults read the comics because they can't unravel print without the help of pictures. Some read the picture magazines for reasons other than the quality of photographs—"a picture is worth a thousand words" only when you can't decipher some of the words. Educational status and socio-economic status are closely related to one another and to the amount and kind of reading done.

This is just one way of saying that if a person graduated from only the sixth grade in school the chances of his reading many books are much less than they are if he graduated from college. This is not surprising, and it could even be argued that college doesn't make serious readers of as many people as it should. It is still true, however, that circulation figures from public libraries and other counts all indicate that college families read more and use more of a variety of media for news, facts, and entertainment. This close relationship between educational level and cultural and living standards more generally seems to be true not only of different cities and regions of the United States but also among the countries of Europe and the Americas. The amount of reading done cannot be shown to be causal, but it is closely associated with such factors as per capita income, mean annual manufacturing wage, life insurance per capita, relative number of physicians, dentists and nurses, and retail sales per capita. More reading goes along with more education, more income, and other status factors.

The Mass Media

Radio and television, and to a lesser extent movies, compete for people's reading time. Reading habits are necessarily affected by other means of getting information and spending leisure time. In some backward countries today it may be better to concentrate on good radio for all the people than to spend time and money on reading instruction in small groups. Here in the United States the potential reader is affected, not only by his level of reading abilities and his economic condition, but by radio, movies, television, and other media which give him some of the same benefits as reading—or which he thinks give him such benefits.

In 1949, before television was as prevalent as today, Asheim[30] estimated that:

> About 25 to 30 per cent of the population read one or more books a month.
> About 45 to 50 per cent of the population see a motion picture once every two weeks or oftener.
> About 60 to 70 per cent of the population read one or more magazines more or less regularly.
> About 85 to 90 per cent of the population read one or more newspapers more or less regularly.
> About 90 to 95 per cent of the population listen to the radio fifteen minutes a day or more.

Today the figure for television would seem to be much the same as the one quoted for radio (in places where there is television coverage), and in these areas the amount of radio listening has dropped sharply but not disappeared.

Some beginning studies show that television affects radio time most, movie time next, and reading time the least of the three. On the other hand, studies by Witty[31] suggest that elementary-school-age children who have TV in the home spend at least three hours a day looking at it, and this persists beyond the "honeymoon period" of the first months the set is in the house. With three hours a day spent on the Westerns, crime, space travel, and the like, something has to give, and reading is probably part of the something.

We should not make the mistake, however, of saying that the effects of movies, radio and television on reading are all bad. For example, in a study of children in grades four to twelve in Ann Arbor, Michigan, Battin[32] found that about one-third of the group believed television had not influenced their reading habits. About 20 per cent said they read more books and magazines and less than 15 per cent said they read less than before TV.

Just as some movies send people back to buy and read a certain book, so televiewing is not the complete undoing of reading habits.

[30] Lester Asheim, "Portrait of the Book Reader as Depicted in Current Research," *Mass Communications*, pp. 424-429, University of Illinois Press, Urbana, 1949.

[31] Paul A. Witty, "Children's Interest in Comics, Radio, Motion Pictures and TV," *Educational Administration and Supervision*, Vol. 38, pp. 138-147, 1952. Paul A. Witty, "Some Results of Eight Yearly Studies of TV," *School and Society*, Vol. 86, pp. 287-289, Summer, 1958.

[32] T. C. Battin, *Television and Youth*. Television Information Commission, National Association of Radio and Television Broadcasters, Washington, D.C., 1954.

There does come a time in their lives when many children become conscious of the repetition and scarcity of ideas in comics, the pulps, or certain television programs. Then it is to be hoped that they will also discover some of the breadth and depth of ideas found in good books and other printed materials.

Personal Needs

People will read if reading helps them with their problems. By reading, some people can learn to make a model airplane or a bookcase, or some can escape from the workaday world. Perhaps some reading has subtler effects on personality, as in the case of the teenager who sees the members of her own family in a new light as she reads through a novel of family life. The story of courage on a mountain-top or in the business group may inspire courage, physical or social, in child or adult. The story of adolescent emancipation may encourage a youth's growing independence of his family; the account of triumph over disease may inspire one to social service or a life devoted to science.

Child or adult, a person will continue to read if reading fulfills some of his deepest psychological needs. A casual interest in a topic does not make for continued reading. The kind of a community one lives in, the friends one has or does not have, the kind of jobs one holds—all these affect the amount and kind of reading one does. If a person needs prestige, he reads to feel superior or to relieve feelings of inferiority. If he needs respite, he reads for relaxation and escape. If he needs greater competence or more beauty, he reads for practical solutions or for aesthetic experiences in fine literature.

Personal needs have been stated in many ways by psychologists and others. For example, Carlsen[33] gave insightful examples of how reading materials contribute to personal needs of the fourteen- to eighteen-year-olds. He listed three needs of this age-level, (1) "assurance of status as human beings"—hence animal, adventure and hero stories; (2) "assurance of his own normality"—hence stories of adolescent life, high school, or even of possible abnormality, as in *Of Human Bondage;* (3) "need for role-playing"—hence possible pictures of themselves from the inside in vocations or in Selective Service. Stories which contribute to these may add to the "self-concept" of boys and girls today.

[33] G. Robert Carlsen, "Behind Reading Interests," *English Journal,* Vol. 43, pp. 7-12, January, 1954.

One of the trends in book publishing in the late 1950's was the decline of the light, romantic novel of the escape variety. One suggestion frequently made for the rise of more serious nonfiction was that most people can find their light fiction in the TV program. One other possibility was the changed character of our lives, especially feminine lives. The somewhat apocryphal, Victorian young lady had lots of time to moon over long romantic novels. Today, in a country where 23 million women were working in 1960[34] (a full one-third of the adult female population) there may be more need for something in the book line that is shorter and more factual.

What children and adults will read in their free time, then, depends upon the amount of their free time but also upon their interests and their more fundamental personality characteristics. Much reading is not for a specific purpose, and therefore newspapers, magazines, and books should be readily accessible so that the busy person may read. But an important part of the school's work in developing permanent reading habits is not only building reading skills but providing reading materials that fill fundamental human needs. We all need to discover that reading will help us solve some of *our* problems, whether we call them that or not.

Social factors, such as the mass media and one's socio-educational level, and personal factors, such as reading skills and psychological needs—these four are identifiable factors affecting the amount and kind of reading we or our neighbors do. Many other interlocking influences such as availability of materials, the demands of one's job or one's family, competing interests, friendship patterns, community activities, and a hundred other factors, many of them subtle or deep-rooted, undoubtedly affect the adult's reading.

Permanent Habits of Reading

The four factors above tend to culminate in a fifth influence on the adult's reading activities. This is the development of the *habit* of turning to books, magazines, and newspapers many times during the week, and especially on weekends. Some people develop the habit of reading and others, almost equally estimable people, never do. Studies of children's reading interests show that many of them reach a peak in reading activity somewhere around eleven, twelve, or thirteen years. Thereafter sports, friends, homework, and a thousand

[34] Statement by Mrs. Alice K. Leopold, Director of the Women's Bureau of the U. S. Department of Labor.

influences conspire against much thoughtful, voluntary reading. If a child does not have the *habit* of reading by the time he is twelve years old, the chances are pretty good that he is lost as a regular reader. It would seem, then, that homes and schools cannot do too much in developing permanent interests in reading, striking hard especially around the upper elementary and junior high school levels. It isn't much help to a parent or a school faculty, or to children themselves, if they make good scores on reading tests but never open a book of their own accord. Reading skills are important, but the joy and usefulness of books and magazines probably affect reading habits more completely and permanently. The implications for the teacher are clear and direct.

READING AROUND THE WORLD

Problems of illiteracy and low levels of reading habits and tastes are not confined to the United States and may be said to be world wide. The amount of book reading and general literacy is reported to be higher in Great Britain and the Scandinavian countries, although statistics are not always strictly comparable. Elsewhere in Europe and the other parts of the world, literacy and reading habits tend to be at a level somewhat below and, in many cases far below, the levels in the United States. Low levels are particularly characteristic of much of South America and most of the native populations of Africa. Certain countries such as Russia, Indonesia, and China have been making strenuous efforts to improve national standards of literacy. In underdeveloped regions of the world, illiteracy is closely related to economic factors and health. One UNESCO report describes the problem as follows:

> "More than half the people of the world are illiterate. This means that 1,200 million men and women can neither read nor write.
>
> "More than half the people of the world are also desperately poor. Their earnings are so low that their daily caloric diet is barely enough to keep them alive. Moreover, in the countries of Asia and Africa where illiteracy is most prevalent, a child at birth can expect to live no more than 30 years, whereas in Europe where a high proportion of the people are able to read and write, a child can expect to live 55 years or more.
>
> "Illiteracy is part of a tragic circle of underproduction, malnutrition and endemic disease.
>
> "The circle cannot be broken by an attack on only one of these elements. It is useless to concentrate on improving health if inefficient farm-

ing methods and soil erosion are left unchecked and entire populations remain undernourished. It is equally useless to teach people to read and write unless they have an incentive to learn and use this knowledge. The incentive can only be an improvement in their daily lives. . . ."[35]

Various terms such as "mass education" and "community development" have been used to describe the type of educational program needed as part of a general effort to raise standards of living. The United Nations Educational, Scientific and Cultural Organization (UNESCO) uses the description "fundamental education." UNESCO workers are conscious that other media of communication such as radio and television may short-cut the work of getting information to illiterates. Its bulletin *World Communication* reported that by 1956 the number of radio receivers exceeded the number of copies of daily newspapers in the world. The use of radio expanded most rapidly in some of the countries mentioned above as highly illiterate. In another UNESCO report Gray[36] has described the teaching of reading in different countries of the world.

In addition to the work of the United States and local governments, other drives against illiteracy have been led by Dr. Frank Laubach, described by the *New Yorker*[37] as "perhaps the most ambitious pedagogue of his time." Dr. Laubach has worked for thirty years, beginning with a remote section of the Philippines, to construct lessons in over seventy countries and in some 250 languages and dialects, many of which had never been written down before. The *New Yorker* estimated that he has been responsible for over 15 million people learning their A.B.C.'s and more recent estimates are higher. He has devised methods based on (1) the invention or simplification of a method of recording symbols either in the Roman alphabet or an adaptation of existing systems of writing, (2) the use of a system of simple key-words and drawings by means of which people learn to associate one symbol with one sound, and (3) the power of individual instruction with its tenet of "each one teach one." (See charts, page 31.) It is not always clear whether Laubach's pupils achieve "functional literacy" or reading skills necessary to carry on the ordinary business of living. His methods and campaigns are de-

[35] *Learn and Live,* p. 7. UNESCO, Paris, 1951.

[36] William S. Gray, *The Teaching of Reading and Writing.* Monographs on Fundamental Education, No. 10. UNESCO, Paris, 1956.

[37] February 16, 1952, Vol. 27, p. 38.

scribed for older boys and girls in Medary's *Each One Teach One*.[38] Perhaps his point of view is best revealed in the following:

> "The most bruised people on this planet, the naked, the hungry, the fallen among thieves, the sick, the imprisoned in mind and soul, are the twelve hundred million illiterates. More than half the human race is hungry, driven, diseased, afraid of educated men in this world and of the demons in the next."[39]

As the world daily grows smaller, with more and faster jet planes and improved communications, the conditions of which Laubach writes become more and more a concern to all people. Perhaps most teachers in the United States are not prepared to cope with the literacy problems of Southeast Asia or Central Africa, but these conditions in different parts of the world differ only in degree from the problems at home. When Miss Smith teaches reading in her fourth grade or Mr. Jones helps a poor reader in the seventh grade, they are working for higher literacy and higher-grade persons partly in the way Dr. Laubach or a teacher in New Guinea or Nyasaland are working on their problems. In the United States as elsewhere the improvement of reading abilities may be regarded as part of the attempt to defeat illiteracy and create a better world.

READING HABITS AND THE TEACHER

The teacher of reading in the 1960's is working with children who live in a world very different from that of the 1900's or even the 1930's. Children live in an environment of television, radio, motion pictures, comic books, newspapers, youth service agencies, and recreational activities, all of which compete for time they might otherwise give to reading. Studies have shown, for example, that some children give four or five hours a week to free reading but over twenty hours a week to watching television. In this competitive world, it would seem that reading can survive only as it has important uses and unique values for the individual. Children will continue to read regularly only as reading provides satisfactions and gives answers to problems in a way no other medium does so well. If the custom of reading books is to survive, it is not enough that the mechanics of

[38] Marjorie Medary, *Each One Teach One: Frank Laubach, Friend to Millions*. Longmans, Green, New York, 1954.

[39] Frank C. Laubach, *The Silent Billion Speak*. Friendship Press, New York, 1945.

CHART-3

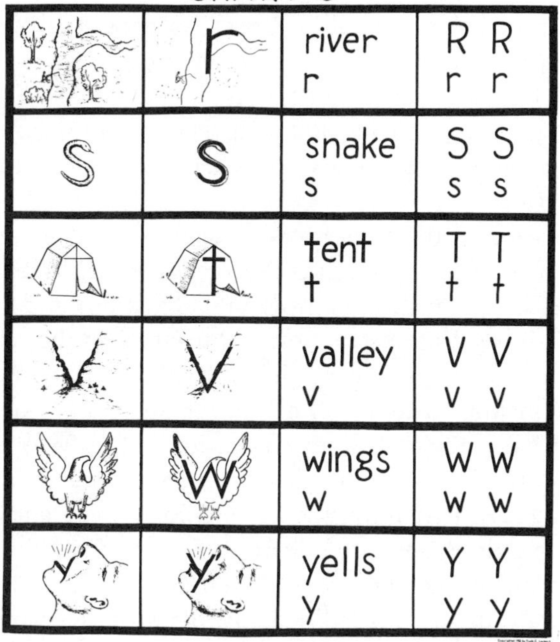

river r	R R r r
snake s	S S s s
tent t	T T t t
valley v	V V v v
wings w	W W w w
yells y	Y Y y y

Story 3

Here is a river.
Here is a snake.
Here is a tent.
Here is a valley.
Here are a bird's wings.

The man is in the tent.
The girl is in the tent.
The bird is in the tent.

The man looks at the bird's wings.
The girl looks at the bird's wings.

The tent is in the valley.
The river is in the valley.

The man goes to the river.
The girl goes to the river.

The man sees a snake.
The girl sees a snake.
The man yells: "Here's a snake."
The girl yells: "Here's a snake."

Pages from Laubach's Streamlined Reading Series (copyright 1955 by Frank C. Laubach) reading be well taught, but that boys and girls discover that books can play important roles in their lives. Permanent habits of reading will be developed only when children and youth discover that books contain worlds of valuable information and works of imagination which all the radio, movies, and television cannot hope to match. The relative values of these activities are discussed further in Chapters 12 and 13.

Such goals for reading instruction mean, of course, an increasing variety of good books and magazines in school libraries and classrooms. They mean careful planning to match a boy and a book. They mean a shift in reading instruction to emphasis on the relation of the content of ideas to the life of the individual. They mean that in reading lessons the teacher will ask fewer questions like, "What was the color of Bill's dog?" and more questions like, "Was Bill the kind of a boy you would like to have for a friend?" Increasingly, reading must be taught so that most people find in it some answers to their important questions, some application to their daily lives, and some solutions to their deepest needs. Then reading goes beyond mere literacy, important as this is in many parts of the world, to make reading habits an enduring part of individual behavior and of our culture.

SELECTED REFERENCES

BANNING, EVELYN I. "Social Influences on Children and Youth," *Review of Educational Research,* Vol. 25, pp. 36-47, February, 1955.

BURT, CYRIL. "The Education of Illiterate Adults," *British Journal of Educational Psychology,* Vol. 15, pp. 20-27, February, 1945.

BUSWELL, GUY T. *How Adults Read.* Supplementary Educational Monographs, No. 45, especially Chap. 3. University of Chicago Press, Chicago, 1937.

Commission of Freedom of the Press. *A Free and Responsible Press.* University of Chicago Press, Chicago, 1947.

DALE, EDGAR. "Let Us Rise Up and Build," *The Newsletter,* Ohio State University, Vol. 23, pp. 1-4, October, 1957.

ERNST, MORRIS L. *The First Freedom.* Macmillan, New York, 1946.

GINZBERG, ELI, and BRAY, DOUGLAS W. *The Uneducated.* Columbia University Press, New York, 1953. 246 p.

GOLDBERG, SAMUEL. *Army Training of Illiterates in World War II.* Teachers College Contributions to Education, No. 966. Bureau of Publications, Teachers College, Columbia University, New York, 1951. 302 p.

GRAY, WILLIAM S. *The Teaching of Reading and Writing.* Monographs on Fundamental Education, No. 10. UNESCO, Paris, 1956. 281 p.

GRAY, WILLIAM S., and MONROE, RUTH. *Reading Interests and Habits of Adults.* Macmillan, New York, 1929.

GRAY, WILLIAM S., and ROGERS, BERNICE. *Maturity in Reading: Its Nature and Appraisal.* University of Chicago Press, Chicago, 1956.

HACKETT, ALICE P. *Sixty Years of Best Sellers.* Bowker, New York, 1955.

HART, JAMES D. *The Popular Book: A History of America's Literary Taste.* Oxford, New York, 1950.

HOVLAND, CARL I. "Effects of the Mass Media of Communication," in Gardner Lindzey, ed., *Handbook of Social Psychology,* Vol. 2, Chap. 28, pp. 1062-1103. Addison-Wesley, Reading, Mass., 1954.

HUNNICUTT, CLARENCE W., and IVERSON, WILLIAM J., eds. *Research in the Three R's,* Chap. 1. Harper, New York, 1958.

LAUBACH, FRANK. *Thirty Years with the Silent Billion: Adventuring in Literacy.* Revell, Westwood, N.J., 1960.

LEWIS, M. M. *The Importance of Illiteracy.* Harrap, London, 1953.

LUKE, ROBERT A. "The Cost of Adult Undereducation," *National Education Association Journal,* Vol. 45, pp. 428-429, October, 1956.

LYNESS, PAUL I. "The Place of the Mass Media in the Lives of Boys and Girls," *Journalism Quarterly,* Vol. 29, pp. 43-54, Winter, 1952.

MCKEON, RICHARD; MERTON, R. K.; and GELLHORN, W. *The Freedom to Read.* Sponsored by the National Book Committee. Bowker, New York, 1957.

MOTT, FRANK L. *The News in America.* Cambridge University Press, London, New York, 1952.

National Society for the Study of Education. "Adult Reading," Fifty-fifth Yearbook, Part II. University of Chicago Press, Chicago, 1956.

New York Board of Education. *Manual for Teachers of Adult Elementary Classes.* Curriculum Bulletin, 1949-1950, No. 2. The Board, New York, 1950.

NORBERG, KENNETH D. "Our Children and Mass Media of Communication," *Elementary School Journal,* Vol. 51, pp. 301-308, February, 1951.

Radio and Television Bibliography. U. S. Office of Education Bulletin, 1956, No. 2. Superintendent of Documents, U. S. Government Printing Office, Washington, D.C., 1956.

SCHICK, FRANK L. *The Paperbound Book in America.* Bowker, New York, 1958.

SCHRAMM, WILBUR. *Responsibility in Mass Communication.* Harper, New York, 1957.

SELDES, GILBERT. *The Public Arts.* Simon and Schuster, New York, 1956.

SHAYON, ROBERT L. *Television and Our Children.* Longmans, Green, New York, 1951.

SIMPSON, RAY H. "Reading: In School Goals and Out-of-School Behavior," *School Review,* Vol. 58, pp. 147-152, March, 1950.

SQUIRE, JAMES R. "Literacy and Literature," *English Journal,* Vol. 49, pp. 154-160, March, 1960.

WAPLES, DOUGLAS; BERELSON, BERNARD; and BRADSHAW, FRANKLYN R. *What Reading Does to People.* University of Chicago Press, Chicago, 1950.

Chapter 2

HISTORICAL BACKGROUNDS: MAN DEVELOPS WRITING AND READING ABILITIES

A teacher of history must know history and a teacher of science must know science. Similarly, the teacher of language must know something about language. Because reading is one of the language arts, the teacher of reading must also be informed about the development and use of language. To the teacher this knowledge may not be as functional as knowledge of history and science which are taught directly as facts, concepts, or generalizations, but it is still important background. Since the English language arts taught in school are usually categorized as reading, writing, speaking, and listening, the teacher of English more generally, and reading more specifically, must understand our language as a language. Because of their complexity, the historical facts and linguistic principles of the language are not taught directly to young children, but they may guide the teacher's work in primary grades and be studied, at least in part, by older school children.

Current problems in the sociology and teaching of reading and other forms of communication gain added meaning as they are considered in a historical setting. As indicated in Chapter 1, the teaching of reading to the Bills, the Toms, the Alices, and the Mary Lous of the second grade or the tenth grade takes on additional importance when considered in terms of the need for an enlightened citizenry in a democratic state. Similarly, the daily and weekly activities of the reading program have increased meaning for the teacher and parent when viewed in terms of the structure of his language and of man's development and use of language down through the ages. The child reading from the primer or the adolescent browsing through a new book in geography or science has behind his activities many centuries of the arts of language, of writing, of bookmaking, and of using libraries. A brief account of the development of these arts may enrich the meaning and place of reading in the elementary school and in men's lives.

The development of various phases of language must be considered at once as one of man's great achievements and one of his recurrent problems. As Thorndike said, "It [language] is more important than all the physical tools invented in the last two thousand years."[1] Because the school is concerned with the cultural heritage, it will emphasize the gradual development of the language arts. But not only the past is involved. Language is part of the lives of all people every day. It includes all of men's efforts to convey ideas to others and most of their attempts to formulate thoughts for themselves. It reflects how men live and the sort of persons they are. As such it represents not only achievements but problems. The reading phase of the language arts can be understood only in the larger setting of the development of these arts as described below.

THE STUDY OF LANGUAGE

Before man began to read, he had to have written records; before he had written records, he had to have speech and ideas to record. How long speech has been used no one knows. The appearance of written records is of comparatively recent date in man's long history, but even that is so long ago that the first use of written language is lost in the obscurity of prehistoric times. Writing was developed well past the pictorial stage in Babylon by 6000 B.C. Egypt had a partially alphabetic system of writing seven thousand years ago and probably had used some system of records for thousands of years before that. Undoubtedly man had used some form of speech for a very long time before he attempted to record his ideas, even in the roughest way.

A number of guesses have been made about the way man first developed speech abilities, but none of them completely accounts for the development of complex modern languages. We know only that part of any modern language is very, very old and that in its gradual development certain words become definitely associated with specific objects or ideas. The objects or ideas may be the same in different countries, but the spoken and written symbols which rep-

1 Edward L. Thorndike, *Man and His Works*. Harvard University Press, Cambridge, 1943.

resent them may be very different. In any one language the words themselves have changed markedly in the course of transmission. Thus the vocabulary of any language is simply a collection of symbols or conventionalized auditory and visual patterns which people speaking or writing that language agree to use. In English the symbol *artichoke* stands for one thing and the symbol ÷ for something else. Often the symbol is far removed from the object or idea it represents. Accordingly, young children particularly have difficulty in associating words or sentences with the reality behind them.

The account above suggests that the use of words is at once one of the most complex and one of the most fascinating of human activities. It is complex because it is as old a form of behavior as drilling for fire or chipping stone and because since earliest times it has developed in an unplanned way. Men have used language for a very long time, but it is only with a high degree of civilization that they have begun to study its complex structure and to organize it. A teacher of reading and other communication arts may understand these processes better in terms of the ways of studying languages and in the light of the characteristics of language given below.

WAYS OF STUDYING LANGUAGE

The teacher of reading is usually aware that the study of language may be made from several different points of view. An excellent summary of various approaches may be found in Carroll's *The Study of Language,*[2] a volume recommended to teachers concerned with language as language. Some of the disciplines involved in the study of the growth, structure, and use of languages are:

History, especially social history, deals with such topics as the extent of literacy and the consequent use of written materials in different civilizations. Because of lack of precise tools for analysis, the historical method has not been very useful in the analysis of language structure in different civilizations.

Etymology is concerned with the origins and derivations of words as shown by analysis of their parts. Thus it deals with such topics as the roots of English words in Greek or Latin and changes in word

[2] John B. Carroll, *The Study of Language.* Harvard University Press, Cambridge, 1953.

usage over the years. Teachers should beware of a pseudo-science of etymology in a number of popular books.

Philology is concerned with literary and cultural studies which focus on the use of language. The student of literature, the historian, and the archaeologist may work with cultural and social documents and thus be concerned with both the structure of language and the humanities. In England, *philology* is often a synonym for *linguistics* as the term is used in the United States.

Semantics is concerned with the varied meanings of words. As such, it deals with the relationship between words and the ideas for which they stand, between verbal symbols and their referents. Thus it is concerned with variations in meaning depending upon such things as the occasion, the experience of the receiver, and the intention of the speaker. The several "schools" of semantics have somewhat different approaches to "the science of meaning," but all are concerned with educational procedures somewhat more than with experimental investigations.

Communication Engineering is the application of scientific findings to the improvement of efficiency in communication. It has developed from concern with equipment for the transmission of speech (telephones, etc.) to wider problems involving science of sound, medium of transmission, the psychological set of the person receiving, and interferences such as noise. While few applications to education have been made, the field has potential values, especially in the teaching of speech, oral reading, and listening.

Psycholinguistics, as the term implies, is the study by psychologists of language behavior. As such it may be involved with such topics as the physiology of hearing and seeing and influences on the perception of, and response to, any language stimulus. It is sometimes concerned, then, with reasons underlying behavior, not just surface usage of language.

Linguistics is the study of languages as systems of sound symbols or codes or vocal habits useful in human interaction. Linguistic scientists, accordingly, carefully observe language behavior and seek to establish general theories and principles about language which can be checked by further observation and testing.

Because the study of linguistics has advanced rapidly in recent years but has so far had only few applications to school language learning, a brief description of some of its methods and findings may be given. The applications of linguistics to specific methods of teaching reading have yet to be made. Bloomfield[3] and Soffietti[4] have attempted such applications, but as Buswell[5] has pointed out, reading involves many visual as well as auditory factors. Furthermore, there are real difficulties in applying the beliefs and theories of the specialized scholar to the everyday work of the class teacher. In the last hundred years linguistics has been concerned, in order, with comparative studies (the "families" of languages), with historical changes in languages, with linguistic geography, and with structural analysis of language. Its two main branches today may be said to be *comparative* linguistics and *descriptive* linguistics. The latter seems to have more direct applications for the teaching of speech, usage in writing, and foreign languages than for the teaching of reading, but some further mention of its findings may be relevant, for example, to the second-grade teacher teaching "phonics" or word-attack skills.

The modern work in linguistics stems from the development of the concept of the *phoneme* shortly before 1900 and the development of techniques of *structural analysis* in the 1920's and 1930's. The idea of the phoneme made possible the usual checks on scientific accuracy by unprejudiced observers and thus contributed to a "science" of language. Structural analysis was a new approach to larger language units and as such had applications to pupils' understanding and phrases and writing of sentences. Both are based on the assumptions that the spoken language is *the* language, that linguistic activities are largely matters of habit, that languages change in time and space, and that language can be analyzed into identifiable parts of phonological, morphological, or syntactical units.

The last assumption may be illustrated by listing the units used in descriptive linguistics to analyze a language passage. These are:

1. The *phoneme*—a speech-sound in a specific language at its most elementary, distinctive level. It is not to be confused with the letters of the alphabet or their combinations. The English language contains thirty-five phonemes, other languages from ten to seventy. English has three

[3] Leonard Bloomfield, "Linguistics and Reading," *Elementary English Review,* Vol. 19, pp. 125-130, 183-186, April, May, 1942.

[4] James P. Soffietti, "Why Children Fail to Read: A Linguistic Analysis," *Harvard Educational Review,* Vol. 25, pp. 63-94, Spring, 1955.

[5] Guy T. Buswell, "Perceptual Research and Methods of Learning," *Scientific Monthly,* Vol. 64, pp. 521-526, June, 1949.

letters which are not really needed (c, f, x) since other letters perform the same function, but it has no single letters to represent single sounds such as /ʃ/⊃ / usually written *sh* and *ng*. The word "poppy" contains the (p) sound with two spellings and what is usually called the *ch* sound /tʃ/ is written five ways in *ch*eap, pa*tch*, righ*te*ous, ques*ti*on and na*tu*ral.

2. The *morpheme*—the smallest linguistic unit with a lexical or relational meaning of its own. It is composed of one or more phonemes usually in the form of stems and affixes. (*I* and *aye* are one phoneme and one morpheme; *at* is two phonemes but one morpheme). *Lexical* meaning possessed by morphemes (and words and utterances) occurs in linguistic references to organisms, things, events, or their parts. *Relational* meaning refers to time, place, and number relations. (We know that the word "does" refers to present tense, singular number). In addition to morphemes, the speaker of English makes use of word order, intonation, and stress to convey meanings.

3. The *word*—the smallest linguistic unit that stands alone. In English it is usually composed of two or more morphemes but may consist of one as in "bad." The word "book," however, consists of two morphemes because it conveys both sound and singular meaning.

4. The *utterance* is a "bit of talk" usually involving a speaker and a hearer, i.e., the encoder and the decoder. It may consist of practically any number of words and may be analyzed not only into phonemes and morphemes but in terms of intonation, rhythm, and stress. The study of how words are arranged in utterances is called syntax, or the grammatical arrangements in speech and writing. Fries[6] speaks of grammar as all the devices that signal structural meanings.

All these four units may not seem directly applicable to the work of the third-grade teacher, but both Carroll[7] and Soffietti[8] have suggested some relationships to the teaching of reading. Carroll, for example, contrasted the approaches of Bloomfield, who advocated the early introduction of phonemes, and of Gray, who emphasized beginning with word wholes. He supported early attention to letter cues in words and also suggested applications to speech and to spelling. Soffietti states that the lack of consistency between the letter and the phoneme it spells reduces the letter's reliability in representing a specific sound and thus causes spelling and reading difficulties. Because English letters are not always primary cues to word pronunciation, Soffietti believes that reading becomes a more complex process of word and sentence analysis for secondary cues, meaning, and struc-

[6] Charles C. Fries, *The Structure of English,* p. 56. Harcourt, New York, 1952.
[7] Carroll, *op. cit.*
[8] Soffietti, *op. cit.*

ture and then proposes a system, adapted from Bloomfield, which might simplify the process of learning to read in its early stages.

Teachers who wish to explore the science of linguistics further will find help in the book by Carroll and the article by Soffietti. A good introduction to the linguistic point of view in educational terms may be found in a chapter by Horn.[9] Other sources dealing with language and linguistics are the books by Henle[10] and by Gleason,[11] and an article by Hill.[12] Further applications to education may be found in the book by Smith,[13] the review by Carroll,[14] and the book edited by Allen.[15] The next section gives a general description of language which also forms a background for reading instruction.

SEVEN CHARACTERISTICS OF LANGUAGE

Language Is a Human Tool

The first characteristic of language is that it is a human activity. Every child knows that animals have forms of communication with one another, but these are not flexible and complete enough to be language in the sense in which man uses language. By making a series of recordings in the London zoo, Huxley found that lions make six distinct sounds which ranged from a hunting call to a grumble of satisfaction after the kill. But this is not really language as man knows it. As Huxley put it, "Plenty of animals can express the fact that they are hungry; but none except man can ask for an egg or a banana."[16] After a long study of anthropoid apes Yerkes concluded: "Everything seems to indicate that their vocalizations do not constitute true language. . . . Apparently the sounds are primarily

[9] Ernest Horn, "Language and Meaning," *The Psychology of Learning,* Forty-first Yearbook, Part II, National Society for Study of Education, University of Chicago Press, Chicago, 1942.

[10] Paul Henle, ed., *Language, Thought and Culture.* University of Michigan Press, Ann Arbor, 1958.

[11] Henry A. Gleason, *An Introduction to Descriptive Linguistics.* Holt, New York, 1955.

[12] Archibald A. Hill, "Linguistics Since Bloomfield," *Quarterly Journal of Speech,* Vol. 41, pp. 253-260, October, 1955.

[13] Henry L. Smith, *Linguistic Science and the Teaching of English,* Inglis lecture series. Harvard University Press, Cambridge, 1956.

[14] John B. Carroll, "Communication Theory, Linguistics and Psycholinguistics," *Review of Educational Research,* Vol. 28, pp. 79-88, April, 1958.

[15] Harold B. Allen, ed., *Readings in Applied English Linguistics.* Appleton-Century-Crofts, New York, 1958.

[16] Julian S. Huxley, *Animal Language,* with two records. Country Life, London, 1938.

innate emotional expressions."[17] It seems to be man alone who uses true language as a tool to help to accomplish what he wants.

Language Is One of Man's Most Important Activities

Language is a basis for all group living. It is difficult to imagine a modern world without language; without books, telephones, letters, or speech our civilization would soon perish. Children only three or four years old speak as many as twelve thousand words a day and are engaged linguistically in as much as fifty-five minutes out of every hour of their waking day. Older children and adults are daily bombarded with words from newspapers, magazines, books, radio programs, television programs, movies, lectures, or sermons. Modern living demands basic skills in reading, listening, speaking, and writing; modern democracy demands abilities to sift, weigh, and interpret ideas out of all this welter of words. Accordingly language activities are among the most important parts of any school curriculum; every child must first develop basic language skills and, later, methods and habits of using these, which will enable him to participate as a responsible citizen in his social group. The use of his mother tongue, in the form of reading and the other language arts, must be an important part of the home and school activities of every child.

Language Is a Form of Behaving

While we have canned language in phonograph records or in literature, language is essentially doing something in such ways as speaking, reading, interpreting, or listening. Jespersen, world-famed Danish authority on language, said, "The essence of language is human activity—activity on the part of one individual to make himself understood by another, and activity on the part of the other to understand what was in the mind of the first." Since language is behaving, its problems are psychological rather than mechanical. In reading, as in other behavior, the child's language activities are reactions to the stimuli of the environment or parts of his interaction with that environment; that is, they can be studied only with reference to their surroundings or psychological field. This means that emphasis on the mechanics of language, as isolated bits of behavior, such as drill on word families or on correct verb forms, has been largely misplaced in

[17] Robert M. Yerkes and Ada M. Yerkes, *The Great Apes. A Study of Anthropoid Life.* Yale University Press, New Haven, Conn., 1929.

many schools in the past. Many teachers have failed to place language in its setting. They have not distinguished between the formal language of the English classics and the everyday language of conversation, or the reading of such classics and the reading of the newspaper. These are used in two quite different situations, but most teachers have tried for the same standards in each. Language is a form of behavior and as such must be considered as part of a child's total activity in certain social situations.

Since reading is behaving, the form of which is determined by the circumstances in which it is used, it must be studied in relation to other forms of behavior. Teachers and parents may well pay more attention to a child's feelings about reading to a group for the first time, or having a foreign accent, or being unable to give a short book review rather than to his oral use of the past participle of the verb *go* or his overuse of *and* or *er* or his spelling of *Schenectady*. We are interested in what the child actually produces in oral or written activities, so that exactness and lucidity of expression are important; but, even more, the wise parent or teacher is concerned with the effects of language behavior on the child and the circumstances surrounding his use of language rather than the bits of language themselves. As Koffka said, "The teacher, if he wants to teach accurate and refined language, should try to make his pupils accurate and refined persons."[18] Alert parents and teachers see language activities in relation to personality traits, emotional outlets, and reactions to everyday affairs.

Language Is an Acquired Form of Behavior

Language is not a native, inborn human skill; it is something which must be learned. Cases of "wolf children" have never been authenticated in a scientific sense, but such accounts as we have agree that these children did not possess a true language. Children who have been out of human society from infancy, such as the Wild Boy of Aveyron[19] or Kamala, the Wolf Girl,[20] all learned some form of locomotion, but none developed a complex form of communication. Language is universal, but it is one of the most variable of all human institutions. In very different civilizations, parts of the cultures, such as religious beliefs, the decorative arts, and kinship systems, may have

[18] Kurt Koffka, *The Growth of the Mind: An Introduction to Child Psychology*. Harcourt, New York, 1924.

[19] Wliliam Boyd, *From Locke to Montessori*, Chap. 6. Harrap, London, 1914.

[20] Arnold L. Gesell, *Wolf Child and Human Child*. Harper, New York, 1941.

some common features. The speech of these different groups, however, in terms of words, forms, and methods of articulating may be almost infinitely variable. The variety is a product of different environments. A Chinese boy brought up from infancy in an English-speaking home would speak, read, and write English, not Chinese, and a French boy brought up in a Zulu tribe would speak Zulu, not French. As Sapir put it, "Language is a purely human and non-instinctive method of communicating ideas, emotions and desires by means of a system of voluntarily produced symbols."[21] But children not only learn different languages in different countries; they may learn different varieties of the same language. These variations may be patterned after local speech customs or may reflect the educational status of parents or friends. Children learn the language they hear and see.

The influence of a child's early language environment on his use of language has an important implication. It underlines the importance of considering the child as an individual user of language, not only when he enters school but in the later grades. Owing to their early environments, children in school differ in their use of correct language, their interest in words, their familiarity with books and newspapers, their knowledge of children's stories and rhymes, and any phase of the language arts in which they can be measured. Spending time on such constructions as "There *are* pupils" or reading *Little Bo-Peep* may be not only a waste of time but sheer boredom to pupils who have had these experiences many times. The child's language and reading needs are, above all, an individual matter.

Language Is Based on Symbols and Conventions

If we see an object with four legs, a back, and a seat on which a person sits, we call it "chair" because that is the conventional thing to do; but we could call it "cow" just as well if everyone agreed to that name or symbol. There is no essential reason why "f" should be the sixth letter of the alphabet and should be sounded with an outgoing rush of air. There is no essential "chairness" about a chair which means that it must be called "chair" rather than "cow," "umbrella," or "Carl Sandburg"; we simply have adopted that symbol for the object, and it would be confusing to others if we kept changing round. The written word "chair," in turn, is simply a con-

21 Edward Sapir, *Language: An Introduction to the Study of Speech.* Harcourt, New York, 1921.

ventional way of writing the sounds that go to make up the spoken word "chair." One of the reasons behind difficulty in learning to read or write English is the fact that the basic language, the spoken form, can be represented in so many different ways in alphabetic symbols. Both the spoken and written words "chair" represent a certain piece of furniture only because all men agree that they are suitable symbols for that particular object. In the same way all words we use are symbols for concrete or abstract ideas.

Why we use the particular speech sounds *ch, a,* and *r* in combination when we want to refer to a chair is a more difficult problem; the word comes from the Middle English *chayer,* derived from old French *chaiere,* probably derived from Latin *cathedra* (a seat or chair held by a bishop or professor). The Latin word in turn comes from something else, which takes us back in time to the origin of language.

The artificiality of language symbols is shown further in the fact that one word may stand for many different objects or ideas. For example, *race* may signify a competition, a water course, a division of mankind, a slot for ball bearings, or a flavor of wine. According to Webster there are thirteen ways of being *false* and at least one hundred and five uses of the word *set.* Symbols are very arbitrary affairs, indeed, in representing the objects or ideas behind them. The shifting meanings of words studied in semantics are based on our language system of artificial symbols.

There are, of course, ways of conveying ideas other than by words. If one boy puts his fist within an inch of another's nose, there is usually no mistaking his meaning. The hard of hearing read lips or use hand signs. The Morse code conveys ideas directly to the practiced listener. It is based, however, on the usual language symbols; in fact, we may say a Morse word is "a symbol of a symbol of a symbol." Even gestures become conventionalized: pointing a finger in the open mouth with the head well back would mean "hunger" or "thirst" to most people. So far no other method has developed symbols of such scope as language.

The fact that language is based upon conventionalized symbols gives rise to important educational problems. We do not want a child to say *meat* when he should say *milk,* and we want him to read, write, and spell a word or sentence so that others will recognize it. Not only must the child use the right symbols to convey his meaning but he must be able to recognize the reality behind the symbols of others. In general he develops ideas around a word or phrase very slowly. In other words a concept is a slow growth involving deeper and wider meanings. To the small child the word *chair* may first mean his own little wooden chair; the large stuffed object in which his father sits is something quite different. Gradually he sees that chairs have certain common and certain variable elements; he generalizes his idea of chair and so understands the concept. As Huxley put it, "The faculty of recognizing objects as members of a class provides the potential basis for the concept." Many persons add meaning to abstract concepts such as *justice* or *democracy* all their lives. Our language system, then, is not a natural activity. It is based on a system of symbols and conventions which present difficulties to the young child but which allow for continued growth in language power up through the adult years.

Language Is Essentially a Social Activity

The most commonly mentioned use of language is the communication of ideas. De Laguna believed that speech performs the "fundamental function of *co-ordinating the activities of the members of the group.*"[22] As a result of his observations of small children in the Maison des Petits, Institut Rousseau, Geneva, Piaget believed that young children's speech is egocentric rather than social and that it is not until about the age of seven years that the child does much thinking in the adult sense of seeing relations.[23] Other studies, such as those summarized by McCarthy,[24] find less egocentricity in speech, even in young children, and more use of speech to accomplish purposes involving one or more other people. It seems safe to assume that in elementary-school days and even long before, the child's use of language is largely social. For this reason the teacher usually plans the language work of the class in a natural social setting.

Kennedy[25] pointed out that an important purpose of language is to make an impression on others and influence their conduct. He believed that as people rise in the social scale they watch more and more the effects they produce in language and that high-school and college instruction is largely motivated by the impression that will be made on others. Not only spoken language but written language in adver-

[22] Grace A. de Laguna, *Speech: Its Function and Development,* p. ix. Yale University Press, New Haven, Conn., 1927.

[23] Jean Piaget, *Judgment and Reasoning in the Child.* Harcourt, New York, 1928.

[24] Dorothea McCarthy, "Language Development in Children," in Leonard Carmichael, ed., *Manual of Child Psychology,* rev. ed., Chap. 10, pp. 476-581. Wiley, New York, 1954.

[25] Arthur G. Kennedy, *Current English.* Ginn, Boston, 1935.

tising and propaganda may be used to influence conduct. This is a different use, but still a social use, of language.

A third social use of language is the transmission of the cultural heritage. Writing and reading are key activities here. In primitive tribes speech makes possible the transmission from father to son of the knowledge, attitudes, mores, and customs of the tribe. In more complex civilizations written language makes possible the handing down of various types of documents which in themselves contain large amounts of knowledge and opinion. In these oral and written communications children and adolescents have a great store of ready-made solutions; instead of attempting to solve them all for themselves, they acquire mastery of social problems which will henceforth cease, or largely cease, to be problems. If a boy wants to know the best way to fish, his father or, in some cases, a book will offer information about such things as bait, hooks, nets, and locations. If a girl wants to know how to cook a particular dish she may consult a cookbook or even texts in home economics or science which explain changes in food during cooking. Other children find out about neighboring communities or parts of their country which they have never seen. Thus, through language, boys and girls become a part of the modern world and do not need to repeat in their own lives some of the struggles of the race in achieving its present control of the physical world.

Language Has Individual as Well as Social Significance

Language skills are social in use, but from the earliest months they become important to the child as an individual. Speaking and, later, reading and writing are so important socially that they early assume a prominent place in the individual's adjustments. If he learns to speak readily, he acquires more control over his environment and so achieves a better status with others. The small child who cannot communicate his wants is a well-known picture of frustration. If he does not acquire language skills easily, especially after he begins school, the child usually suffers loss of prestige with parents and teachers. Just acquiring these or other valuable skills seems to have a direct influence on the adjustment of the whole child. In the play, *The Miracle Worker,* the story is told of Helen Keller that at the age of six years, before her systematic instruction in language activities, she displayed a furious and uncontrollable temper. Later her emotional outbursts were brought under control, perhaps partly because she acquired mastery of language skills. Research shows a close relationship between learning difficulties and personality maladjustments.[26] Language learning may be especially subject to the influence of personality.[27]

Language is important for the individual not only in relation to his personality adjustments but as his basis for thinking. Every child and teacher has had the experience of having something to say but not being too sure of the idea until he attempts to express it. In thinking, people use language constantly without uttering a single word; it is equally true that trying to formulate thought in written or spoken form often has the effect of clarifying the pattern of thinking. Otto Jespersen quoted a girl as saying, "I talk so as to find out what I think, don't you?" As children mature they seem to have many thoughts occurring in advance of their expression in words or even without such expression. They learn to keep some of their thoughts to themselves. But, particularly if they are thinking in fresh or creative ways, it helps to "talk it out." In either reproductive or creative thinking, words are usually needed. Some mastery of language is important to the child as an individual if he is to think through his problems and make adjustments necessary to successful living with his group.

The seven characteristics of language have been stated generally to apply to any language and with references to many phases of language behavior. A few characteristics of English, as determined in the study of linguistics, have been mentioned. Space does not permit a similar account of the development of the English language. The exciting story of how our own language has developed through the Old English period, the Middle English period or Age of Chaucer, the modern English period (from 1500), and in America has been well told elsewhere.[28] The general characteristics described above

[26] John E. Anderson, "The Relation of Emotional Behavior to Learning," *The Psychology of Learning,* Forty-first Yearbook, Part II, Chap. 9, National Society for the Study of Education, Public School Publishing Company, Bloomington, Ill., 1942.

[27] David H. Russell, "Interrelationships of the Language Arts and Personality," *Child Development and the Language Arts,* Bulletin of National Conference on Research in English, National Council of Teachers of English, Champaign, Ill., 1953.

[28] Charles C. Fries, *American English Grammar.* D. Appleton-Century, New York, 1940. Arthur G. Kennedy, *op. cit.,* especially Chap. 5. Otto Jespersen, *Growth and Structure of the English Language,* 4th ed. D. Appleton, New York, 1923. Henry C. K. Wyld, *A Short History of English,* 3d ed., revised and enlarged. Dutton, New York, 1927. Henry L. Mencken, *The American Language,* 4th rev. ed. Knopf, New York, 1937. Henry L. Mencken, *The American Language,* Supplement I. Knopf, New York, 1945. Supplement II, Knopf, New York, 1948.

give backgrounds for language behavior and help to show how the acts of oral or silent reading are related to other phases of language activity. The following sections concentrate more on the historical development of actual writing and reading rather than the whole gamut of the language arts.

DEVELOPMENT OF WRITING

The origins of man's writing are as obscure as the beginnings of his speech. Long after he was able to communicate by means of gestures and simple speech, man felt the need of making some sort of record of his activities or giving ideas to others who were distant in space or time. The idea of making records by means of marks on stone, wood, bone, and other materials did not originate in any one place. Signs of them are found in most parts of the world, wherever primitive man has existed. For example, pictures of animals and cup and ring markings (a small hole in a rock surrounded by cut rings) are found in many places.[29] It is only in comparatively recent times that various kinds of record-keeping have been unified and true writing has emerged.

The earliest marks made by man that still exist are rock markings or carvings, because these were often in protected places where the weather could not destroy them. Notable for their beauty and fidelity of detail are the representations of animals in the cave of Altamira, in northern Spain. In other caves in Spain and southern France figures of old-time horses, very different from ours, of mammoths, of bison, and of reindeer are scratched or cut, drawn or painted, on the walls of the caves or on the handles of tools. In many cases the location of the drawings suggests that they were records rather than decoration, and the representation has a simplified line or design which was the first approach to writing.

The variety of early records is almost unlimited. Well-known examples of the use of stone are the Ten Commandments, which were engraved on tablets of stone, and the Rosetta stone, an example of trilingual inscription now in the British Museum. Dating back to the second century before the birth of Christ, this stone bears an inscription in hieroglyphic, demotic, and Greek; and, since the Greek

[29] Cyril Davenport, *The Book. Its History and Development.* Van Nostrand, Princeton, N.J., 1907.

was understood, it gave at once the key to the interpretation of the other languages. In India inscriptions were made on jewels, in China on jade. A more primitive form of record was the notches cut on sticks. As Davenport[30] suggested, "A savage warrior of a literary turn of mind would naturally wish to keep some record of the number of enemies he had killed and perhaps eaten, and an obvious way of doing this would be to cut or scratch marks on his war club." In Scandinavia and Great Britain in early times almanacs were cut on flat pieces of metal, bone, horn, or wood. The blade bones of buffalo in North America and the shoulder blades of sheep raised by the Arabs were equally convenient for inscribing. The Incas of Peru had a regular system of keeping records and government statistics by means of quipus, or colored pieces of string knotted in special ways. The beads of the rosary and those of the abacus used by the Greeks and Chinese may have a similar origin. Wampum belts of North America were ordinarily used as money, but sometimes they were made also to record historical events.

In the development of writing as we know it today, four stages are evident: pictographs, ideographs, phonograms, and the alphabet. Some examples of the first of these have already been mentioned.

Pictographs

From rather complete pictures the economy of sketching a few details developed; for example, a whole animal could be represented by a part, such as a paw or head. Gradually these pictures became conventionalized, as in the well-known signs for the sun or rain in Amerindian writing. In addition, the pictures and the writing were affected by the instruments used for recording (see illustration, page 50). The Chinese brush pen affected Chinese characters, and the cuneiform writing of the Assyrians was largely determined by the wedge-shaped stylus used to press their clay tablets. These two systems represent a transition from pictographs to ideographs, as do the well-known hieroglyphics of the Egyptians. The term *hieroglyphics* means "sacred writing cut in stone" and was first used by the Greeks to describe Egyptian writing, which, incidentally, was by no means all sacred nor all cut in stone. In early Egyptian hieroglyphic writing the picture is often easily recognizable; but in time the pictures were changed, just as in other writing, and the symbols began to stand for

30 *Ibid.*, p. 6.

more general or even abstract ideas. For example, the sun might represent day or a horse might stand for travel in a corresponding stage of development in North America. Thus the pictograph gradually developed into the ideograph.

Old and more recent Chinese characters for sun, moon, and mountains (Committee on Materials of Instruction, *The Story of Writing*, American Council on Education, Washington, D.C., 1932)

Ideographs

The ideograph is a conventionalized character substituted for the pictograph. The Dakota Indians symbolized *plenty* by a buffalo head, a pit, and a forked stick denoting support for the drying pole. The meaning of the tomahawk or the calumet (or pipe of peace) is well known. With the ideograph the direct relationship or origin of the symbol becomes difficult to trace. In complex languages, such as the Egyptian and Chinese, combinations of symbols were used to express new ideas. As men began to live in communities they had to write about such things as friendship, hatred, trading, and government, and ideographs were not always available to record such concepts.

Phonograms

Since men could not find symbols to represent all the ideas they wished to express, they gradually developed a system of making symbols stand for sounds. To complete this change, which Mason[31] called "the most signal intellectual achievement ever attained by man," required several thousand years. McMurtrie[32] suggested that this extremely slow emergence of a phonetic system may be due to the

[31] William A. Mason, *A History of the Art of Writing*. Macmillan, New York, 1920.
[32] Douglas C. McMurtrie, *The Book. The Story of Printing and Book-Making*, 3rd rev. ed. Oxford University Press, Fair Lawn, N.J., 1943.

fact that writing from the very beginning seems to have been the prerogative of the priestly and ruling classes, who may not have wished the mysterious process to become too well known to the masses. Another block to rapid progress was undoubtedly the fact that many

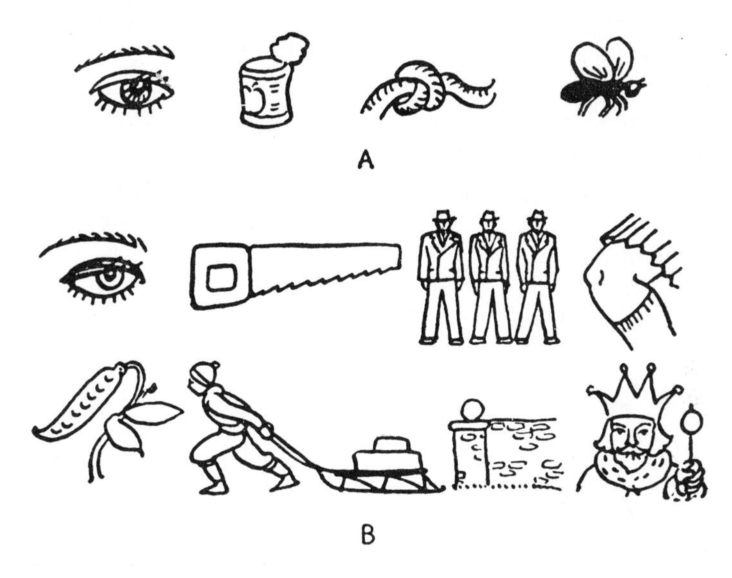

Two sentences written as rebuses

A. I cannot fly. B. I saw many ("men knee") people ("peapull") walking ("wall king") (Committee on Materials of Instruction, *The Story of Writing,* American Council on Education, Washington, D.C., 1932)

words in a language like Egyptian contained the same sound but very different meanings. It was like obtaining a symbol for the word *run* in English, which might mean the action in one case and a salmon run in another.

The actual development of phonetic writing from ideographs seems clear. The idea was something like the type of riddle we call a *rebus.* In English the word *football* would be represented by separate pictures of a foot and a ball. The illustration shown above gives two sample sentences which show the process and some of the difficulties in it. Inherently, phonographic writing has no advantage over ideographic writing. Just as the earlier ideograph required as many signs as there were ideas, so the phonographic systems required at least as many separate characters as there were words. It was a long time before men came to realize that all the words used in speaking, or all that ever could be used, could be expressed in a few elementary sounds. The Chinese, Chaldeans, Assyrians, and Egyptians progressed from the pictograph to the ideograph to phonograms and syllabary, but they never developed a true alphabetic writing. The Egyptians had the key to the simplified system for several thousand years, but never got farther than combining alphabetic writing with their system of ideographs and phonograms. As a result the Chinese, until the recent simplification of their writing, did not master reading and writing until they were adults, and in other ancient civilizations these arts remained the possession of the privileged few.

The Alphabet

The invention of the alphabet is one of the great intellectual achievements of all time. The fact that the 600,000 words of the English language can be written with twenty-six letters is proof of its economy of effort.

The modern alphabet is usually credited to the Phoenicians but was actually developed by their forefathers, the Seirites, who modified what they had learned from the Egyptians. The Seirites lived in Seir, a rough mountain region between the Dead Sea and the Red Sea. They came in contact with Egyptians and Egyptian writing during the prosperous reign in Egypt of Amenemhet III, who ruled from about 1850 to 1800 B.C. At this time the wealthy Egyptians mined copper and turquoises in the Sinai peninsula and employed the Seirites as workmen and foremen. Borrowing from the Egyptian scribes, over a period of time the Seirites developed twenty-one symbols, corresponding to our letters of the alphabet, which represented single sounds of consonants. The first of their inscriptions was found on Sinai in 1868. One inscription has been found which reads, "I, miner Shahmilat, am foreman, from mine shaft number four."[33] The Seirites never dreamed that they had made one of the great inventions of civilization; but modern alphabets come from theirs, and, indeed, the word *alphabet* comes from the first letters of the two Seirite words *alpha* and *bet* meaning *ox* and *house* respectively. Some of the Seirites migrated south with their alphabet, and over the centuries the language changed to South Arabic, which still exists in Abyssinia. Others moved northward, lived in the great cities of Tyre and Sidon on the Mediterranean, and came to be called Phoenicians.

33 Committee on Materials of Instruction, *op. cit.*, p. 45.

The Phoenicians were the traders of their day and carried their alphabet over most of the then known world. In such travels the system of writing was changed still more, but was confined largely to simple business records and inscriptions on tombstones. Among the first people to use the alphabet for important writings were the Hebrews, who collected poems, stories, and speeches into one of the great books of all time, the Old Testament. The Yiddish alphabet is the same as the ancient Hebrew. In the East the Hindus learned to produce similar books, but these have been known in the Western world only recently. Beginning at least as early as 1000 B.C., the Greeks developed the alphabet much more fully as signs representing sounds, not as pictures of anything. Probably by accident they hit on the idea of writing vowels as well as consonants. Eventually they used the alphabet to produce a great literature, perhaps the truest contribution to the art of writing. Our modern English alphabet came to us from the Greeks, through the Etruscans and the Romans, who simplified it in the process. The figure on page 55 represents a simple history of our alphabet and shows that a few forms have not changed much from those used nearly four thousand years ago on the Sinai peninsula.[34]

DEVELOPMENT OF THE MATERIALS OF READING AND WRITING

Not every child who picks up an attractive book in school today realizes that behind such features as good paper, readable type, and interesting illustrations there is a long and colorful story. The above summary of the development of writing suggests that its form was often influenced by the tools men used in writing. Inscribing stone as the only method of writing would not make it a very rapid or easy process. In advancing from stone inscriptions to modern silk-screen color processes, men have evolved many kinds of writing materials.

The considerable development of writing in Egypt, outlined above, was due in part to the invention of papyrus made from the papyrus plant, which, in those days, flourished in the Nile region. Two layers of the split pith of the stalk were laid at right angles to one another, treated with a gum solution, and pressed, pounded, and smoothed

[34] Martin Sprengling, *The Alphabet: Its Rise and Development from the Sinai Inscriptions*. Oriental Institute Communications, No. 12, 72 p. University of Chicago Press, Chicago, 1931.

until the surface was suitable for the brush pen used in writing. For long manuscripts the papyrus was made into rolls, so that it was possible in ancient Egypt to read a book a hundred feet long. Papyrus was damaged easily by water or dampness, so that it was suitable for a dry climate such as Egypt, but could not be preserved in Greece.

Parchment, made from the skins of the sheep and the calf, was known as early as 500 B.C., but did not come into common use until some seven hundred years later. By the fourth century A.D. it had become the chief writing material in Europe; and accordingly a broad pointed pen, made of reed or quill, came into use, thereby affecting the form of writing. The Chinese had invented a rag paper before this time (it is credited to Ts'ai Lun in the year 105 A.D.), but its use moved westward slowly. It seems to have arrived in Egypt before the year 900, in Germany in 1390, in England in 1494, and finally was manufactured for the first time on the American continent at Philadelphia in 1690.[35] In other words, before paper became common in the Western world, it had been used in spreading and mingling Eastern cultures for centuries. It was a Chinese monopoly for some six hundred years, passed into the control of the Moslems for five hundred years, and was adopted slowly in a Western world where there was little demand for books and considerable suspicion of a Moslem or Jewish product. The process used today for the mass production of paper was invented in 1798 by Louis Robert, who worked in a paper mill in France.

Books as we know them, made up of leaves bound at the side, did not come into general use until about the fourth Christian century. In the *codex,* as a book in this form was called, the parchment sheets, instead of being rolled, were folded to make two sheets each and then fastened together along the folds. The codex, as well as the roll, was written by hand. After the "fall of Rome," in 476 A.D., during the so-called Dark Ages, scholarship and books flourished only in the monasteries. There in the *scriptorium,* or "writery," the monks produced the beautiful volumes which can still be seen in museums and certain libraries. In many monasteries the scriptorium was closely guarded, and the scribes could not use artificial light because of the danger of fire. Outside of the Egyptian papyri the oldest manuscripts which now survive were copied and recopied in the monastery. To these writers we owe our present knowledge of the Bible and of Homer, Plato, Aristotle, and Euclid. Credit for preservation and

[35] Douglas C. McMurtrie, *op. cit.,* p. 63.

copying of books at a somewhat later date must be given also to certain kings, such as Charlemagne, to other princes and nobles, and to

Seirite-Sinaitic	Canaanite-Phoenician-Aramaic	Greek	Latin
		A	A
		B	B
		ΓC	CG
		ΔD	D
		F E	E
		F Y	FVUWY
		I	Z
		H	H
		I	IJ
		K	K
		ΛL	L
		M	M
		N	N
		+Ξ	X
		O	O
		ΠΓ	P
		Ϙ	Q
		PR	R
		Σ S	S
		T	T

Our alphabet and its ancestors (Committee on Materials of Instruction, *The Story of Writing,* American Council on Education, Washington, D.C., 1932)

the early universities, such as those of Bologna and Paris, the university mothers.

Like the invention of paper, the development of printing occurred much earlier in China than in the West. The oldest known printed book, now in the British Museum, was discovered by an archaeologist in 1907 as part of materials found in a cave in the desert of Turkestan. Here again caves and climate helped to preserve a book which contains part of the Buddhist scriptures and, at the end of the text, the startling statement that it was "printed on May 11, 868, by Wang Chieh, for free general distribution, in order in deep reverence to perpetuate the memory of his parents."[36]

Although printing was widely used in the East, including printing with movable type, in western Europe printing seems to have been an independent discovery. It was made possible by the availability of paper, of suitable ink, of presses, and of a metal alloy which could be cut in molds for casting. It was further encouraged by the temper of the times, the beginning of the Humanist movement, with its interest in classical literatures, and the beginnings of the intellectual awakening which was to be called the Renaissance. The invention of printing from movable type has usually been credited to Johann Gutenberg of Mainz, Germany, or to Lourens Koster of Haarlem, Holland, between 1430 and 1450. It seems possible that the first book printed from movable wooden type should be credited to Koster about 1430, or about twenty years earlier than the Bible of Gutenberg, but that Gutenberg should be credited with the real development of the process through his use of movable metal type, produced by casting, and improvements in the mechanism of the hand presses then in use.[37] In either case the invention may be regarded not so much as the result of individual inspiration but as the almost inevitable consequence of a long series of experiments conducted where persons were interested in the multiplication of literature.

The first printing in English was done not in England but by an Englishman living at Bruges, now in Belgium. William Caxton translated into English the *Recueil des histoires de Troies,* a collection of stories about Troy, and printed them about 1475. A copy of the book is now in the Huntington Library, San Marino, California. Caxton soon took his type to England, began printing in London about 1477, and issued a 374-page edition of Chaucer in 1478.

The first printing in the New World was done in Mexico and later in Peru, a full century before it was begun in English-speaking North America. The first English printing press arrived in Mas-

[36] Douglas C. McMurtrie, *op. cit.*, p. 88.

[37] George H. Putnam, *Books and Their Makers during the Middle Ages.* Putnam, New York, 1896.

sachusetts in 1638, eighteen years after the landing of the Pilgrims on Plymouth Rock; and the first book (published in 1640) was *The Whole Booke of Psalmes faithfully Translated into English Metre,* now usually called the Bay Psalm Book. Ten copies of the book are known to be in existence. Further study of the development of printing in North America can be made in the writings of Lehmann-Haupt,[38] McMurtrie,[39] and Thomas.[40]

No account of the development of the materials of reading would be complete without mention of libraries. The earliest libraries were mainly private and confined to the upper classes. As indicated above, they were composed of tablets of clay, wax, and stone and later of rolls of papyrus, vellum, or parchment. The use of rolls marked an important advance in libraries, because rolls were much more economically stored than clay or stone tablets. Despite the difficulties of storage, libraries were developed in the ancient civilizations of the Sumerians, the Babylonians, the Chaldeans, and Assyrians. The library in Nineveh probably contained ten thousand documents. Most of the citizens of Athens (less than half the total population) could read at the height of Greek civilization. There was a state collection of books, but there did not exist any system for the general production and distribution of books. The first libraries in the modern sense were founded in Alexandria, Egypt, and Pergamum, Asia Minor, during the second century B.C. The number of volumes in the Alexandrian library has been estimated anywhere from 100,000 to 700,000. Plutarch mentions that the library in Pergamum had 200,000 volumes. It later had considerable influence on education at Rome. The formation of these libraries encouraged the output of books, and, for the first known time in history, reading became an activity of the masses of the people. In Alexandria such Greek classics as Homer were known as a best seller is known today.

Roman education and literature were strongly influenced by Greek literature. By the first century Greek literature and books were well known in Rome and the other principal cities of the Roman Empire. Reading, however, can go no farther than education, and this was still confined to a limited class. Well-known Romans such as Cicero,

[38] Hellmut Lehmann-Haupt, *The Book in America.* A History of the Making, the Selling and the Collecting of Books in the United States. Bowker, New York, 1939.

[39] Douglas C. McMurtrie, *A History of Printing in the United States.* Bowker, New York, 1936.

[40] Isaiah Thomas, *The History of Printing in America,* 2nd ed., 2 vols. J. Munsell, Albany, N.Y., 1874.

Lucullus, and Caesar owned libraries. Public libraries were first founded in the reign of Augustus, with Greek and Latin sections. By the fourth century A.D. there were about thirty public libraries in Rome and several in the provinces. During the first Christian century private libraries became common, and Seneca vehemently denounced the ostentatious accumulation of books not for learning but for show.[41] He objected that a library was considered as essential an adornment of a house as a bathroom.

The fall of Rome and the anarchy which followed wiped out libraries and literacy except in the monasteries. As the relations of the Church and the nobility grew closer, the nobles became more literate; and by the eleventh and twelfth centuries they generally knew some Latin and possessed a few books. The rise of the universities stimulated the collection of books once again, the Renaissance stimulated reading in all forms, and the Reformation, with its emphasis on individual salvation, spurred people to read the Bible.

In England the universities of Oxford and Cambridge had early libraries. The first library of the former institution was in existence in 1337, but it and another library perished before the founding of the famous Bodleian Library in 1598. English church libraries contained chained books as late as the eighteenth century. The British Museum, founded in 1753, contains one of the great libraries of the world, with a collection of 6,000,000 printed books and other materials. It is equalled in size by the French Bibliothèque Nationale.

In Colonial America the first libraries were private, because books were expensive to import and printing did not begin until about 1640. The Harvard College library dates from 1638, and the first subscription library was projected by Benjamin Franklin nearly one hundred years later. The Library of Congress, the largest in the United States, was established in 1800; but its real beginning came fifteen years later, when Thomas Jefferson's library of seven thousand volumes was purchased. In 1958 it had about 12,000,000 printed volumes and other materials. It was not until 1905 that public-school libraries came into existence.

RISE OF LITERACY IN THE WESTERN WORLD

Even with a free public educational system and hosts of available books some of the population of the United States may be termed

[41] Frederic G. Kenyon, *Books and Readers in Ancient Greece and Rome.* Oxford, New York, 1932.

illiterate in the modern sense of the word. In comparison with earlier times, and with other countries today, the record is better. In ancient and medieval times there was no question of complete or nearly complete literacy. For thousands of years writing was confined to rulers, nobles, and the priestly class. By the time of the Phoenicians reading and writing were known to the commercial classes, but they formed a limited system chiefly involved with tallies. Even in so brilliant a civilization as that of Athens the number of copies of any work of literature was extremely limited, and the authors of works later regarded as masterpieces had no notion of what we should regard as practical measures for the preservation or circulation of their writings. The widespread knowledge of Greek literature was undoubtedly due to dramatic performances and public recitations. In Athens of the fourth century B.C. a habit of reading was growing up; but general opinion did not rate reading highly as mental training, in comparison with the interplay of minds in oral discussion.[42] By the time of Aristotle, however, the educated Greek world had passed from the habit of oral instruction to the habit of reading.

The first widespread literacy coincided with the founding of the libraries in Alexandria. At the time of the Ptolemys it was estimated that 60 per cent of the men and 40 per cent of the women wrote Greek, and more still wrote Egyptian. Athens and Alexandria, however, were exceptions in the ancient world.

In Rome there were many schools (*ludi*), with general dependence on the familiarity of the written word. Laws, treaties, and decrees were written on stone, bronze, and wooden slabs. Pottery-makers put their names on their wares. But, despite the fact that there were some thirty libraries, there was no real attempt to spread literacy among all the people,[43] and with the break-up of the Roman Empire literacy disappeared except in the isolated monasteries.

It is interesting to note that the ancient and medieval mind made a clear distinction between the reader and the writer. In early times and up through the fifteenth and sixteenth centuries many more could read than write. In these latter times it was proper for a woman (of the upper classes) to read, but not genteel to write. With the rise of Italian universities and the growth of trade about the time of Columbus, literacy spread beyond the ruling classes to the commer-

[42] *Ibid.*, p. 24.

[43] Helen Sullivan, "Literacy and Illiteracy," E. R. A. Seligman, ed., *Encyclopedia of Social Sciences*, Vol. 9, pp. 511-523. Macmillan, New York, 1937.

cial groups. By 1400 there is some evidence that German and English artisans could write, and Thomas More (1478-1535) estimated that "not three fifths of English people" could read in his day. The increase of literacy, of course, was dependent on the inventions of printing and cheap paper, and from the days of Luther and John Wesley it was always connected with religious literature. In Europe reading expanded enormously in the eighteenth century in terms of periodicals, newspapers, and novels, but even then did not reach below the middle class. Illiteracy is still high in some European countries, such as Spain and Bulgaria. It is even higher in most Asiatic, African, and South American countries.[44]

In North America the "logic of democracy," the humanitarian point of view stemming from England and France, and the importance of reading for religious purposes brought an early emphasis upon developing a literate citizenry. However, there was opposition to literacy in some places even in the 1700's. Resistance of the propertied classes to opening of the frontier delayed efforts toward general literacy until the first quarter of the nineteenth century.[45] Then followed the period of rapid growth in compulsory elementary schools throughout the country. The first United States census of literacy was made in 1840, and by 1900, even with extensive immigration, illiteracy had declined to about 10 per cent. As one example of the importance of literacy to the people of the United States, it may be mentioned that in 1917 the United States Congress, over the President's veto, passed a law to give a literacy test to all immigrants.

WRITING AND READING IN THE UNITED STATES

Michael Pupin in his autobiography tells how he stood before an immigration official declaring that he had three friends in America. "What friends?" asked the official. "Benjamin Franklin, Abraham Lincoln, and Harriet Beecher Stowe," answered the boy stoutly. Children and adults have had many book friends in America from colonial times to the present.

The dominance of religious purposes in colonial times is illustrated by the famous beginning school book of the time, *The New*

[44] James F. Abel and Norman J. Bond, *Illiteracy in the Several Countries of the World.* United States Bureau of Education, Bulletin No. 4. United States Government Printing Office, Washington, D.C., 1929.

[45] Helen Sullivan, *op. cit.*

England Primer (see sample below). This combination of religious manual, catechism, and speller was published about 1690, and for over a hundred years was the chief school and reading book. Every home possessed copies of the book, it was for sale at all bookstores, and

As runs the Glaſs,
Man's life doth paſs.

My Book and Heart
Shall never part.

Job feels the rod,
Yet bleſſes God.

Kings ſhould be good
No men of blood.

The Lion bold
The Lamb doth hold.

The Moon gives light
In time of night.

A page from *The New England Primer* (Reproduced from a copy in the George A. Plimpton Collection)

over 3 million were sold in various editions. In general, people were so busy wresting a living from the new land that little energy was given to literature during this period. The Revolutionary War helped to pave the way for artistic and literary development and opened a new period in history.

The period of the Revolutionary War was the period of the pamphleteer, the orator, the essayist, and the statesman. Probably the best literature of the time is contained in the Declaration of Independence and the Constitution. The writings of Thomas Jefferson, Benjamin Franklin, Tom Paine, and similar figures were the best-known general literature. Another schoolbook, Noah Webster's *Elementary Spelling Book,* familiarly known as the *Blue-back Speller,* was published in 1783 and dominated the school field for many years. It is estimated that 100,000,000 copies of the book have been sold. Although the royalties were less than one cent a book, Webster was able to support his family from them for the twenty years he was work-

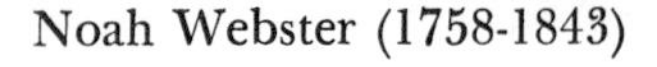

Noah Webster (1758-1843)

William Holmes McGuffey (1800-1873)

Two Pioneers in Preparing Reading Materials (Photo above left courtesy of G. & C. Merriam Co., Publishers of the Merriam-Webster Dictionaries; above right from The American Book Company)

ing on his *Dictionary of the English Language,* itself a milestone in American writing. The first edition of the dictionary contained about seventy thousand words and sold for twenty dollars. When Noah Webster died, in 1843, the publishing rights were bought by G. & C. Merriam Company for only three thousand dollars. The Second Edition of *Webster's New International Dictionary* (copyright, 1959) contained 600,000 entries and cost $1,300,000 to produce.

The other great publishing success in the school-text field was the famous McGuffey readers, the first complete set of which appeared between 1836 and 1844 (see page 63). They retained their great popularity for at least forty years and were sold until recently. Through the McGuffey readers poems like "Twinkle, twinkle little star," "The Old Oaken Bucket," and "Casabianca" became part of the folk literature of America. As Sullivan[46] said,

> These books were, to the average American, the storehouse of the fables, stories, mottoes, proverbs, adages and aphorisms which constituted

[46] Mark Sullivan, *Our Times,* 6 vols. Scribner's, New York, 1926-1935.

the largest body of ethical teaching he had, except the Bible, and the teaching of the Bible was overlapped by that of the Readers.

McGuffey's books were successful partly because they were the

THE ECLECTIC SERIES. 21

LESSON IV.

blest	guide	tar'dy	teach'er
learn	wrong	les'sons	school'-boy
haste	i'dler	end'less	knowl'edge

HASTE THEE, SCHOOL-BOY.

1. HASTE thee, school-boy, haste away,
Far too long has been thy stay;
Often you have tardy been,
Many a lesson you 've not seen;
Haste thee, school-boy, haste away,
Far too long has been thy stay.

2. Haste thee, school-boy, haste away,
Join no more the idler's play;
Quickly speed your steps to school,

A page from the *McGuffey Third Reader,* the first edition of which was published in 1837

first attempt to present a graded series consisting of one reader for each grade of the elementary school. Although McGuffey graded his readers only by a feeling for what children could do, modern methods[47] of checking readability bear out the fact that they increased gradually in difficulty. In comparison with typical modern readers they contained small amounts of material at different levels of difficulty, and they omitted any beginning step corresponding to the

[47] Edward W. Dolch, "How Hard Were the McGuffey Readers?" *Elementary School Journal,* Vol. 46, pp. 97-100, October, 1945.

modern primer or primers. The material in the various readers has usually been accorded praise for its ethical content. An evaluation by Mosier[48] suggested that the social and political ideas of the books were solidly on the side of the conservatives in the conflict between the Jeffersonian and Hamiltonian proponents of democracy. For example, "the McGuffey readers adopted Blackstone's explanations for the origin of private property and found with him that property was bestowed on the few in order that a leisure and ruling class be created, and that time . . . might be devoted by society's ruling groups to the cultivation of the arts." The successive editions of the McGuffey books changed with the times, but never quite accepted the democracy of the frontier and the Mid-West. One modern analysis suggested that the McGuffey books actually contained less material on "moral and spiritual values" than was found in representative present-day readers.[49] They were gradually supplanted by more carefully graded and more attractive texts.

In 1820 Sydney Smith, an English divine and essayist, wrote in the *Edinburgh Review* a famous article entitled "Who Reads an American Book?" This criticism of the cultural contributions of the United States aroused resentment and hot argument and may have helped to initiate a literary movement which was to produce such writers as Washington Irving, William Cullen Bryant, James Fenimore Cooper, and, a little later, Edgar Allan Poe and Nathaniel Hawthorne. At about the time of the War between the States, New England culture and creative power were at their height, producing—besides Hawthorne—Emerson, Longfellow, Lowell, Whittier, and Holmes. Then as now, literature reflected the life of the country and was influenced by the development of the South, the westward movement, the machine age, and later wars.

This book is concerned with reading rather than literary writing, and it may be well to record what people have been reading. The best-selling book of all time is the Bible, and the works of Shakespeare probably come second. The best-selling book of fiction since 1880 is *In His Steps,* by Charles M. Shelden, first published in 1897. Margaret Mitchell's *Gone with the Wind* sold over 3,600,000 copies between 1936 and 1946. The most popular novels written during the

[48] Richard D. Mosier, *Making the American Mind. Social and Moral Ideas in the McGuffey Readers.* King's Crown Press, Columbia University, New York, 1947.

[49] Paul S. Anderson, "McGuffey vs. the Moderns in Character Training," *Phi Delta Kappan,* Vol. 38, pp. 53-58, November, 1956.

latter half of the nineteenth century were *Ben Hur* (Lew Wallace), *Huckleberry Finn* (Mark Twain), *Looking Backward* (Edward Bellamy), *Tom Sawyer* (Mark Twain), *Little Lord Fauntleroy* (Frances Hodgson Burnett), and *Trilby* (George du Maurier). Hackett's *Sixty Years of Best Sellers*[50] and Mott's *Golden Multitudes*[51] gave the most popular books by decades in the United States over the years.

A few of the popular books mentioned by Hackett are as follows:

In the 1910's: *The Rosary,* by FLORENCE BARCLAY; *The Harvester,* by GENE STRATTON PORTER; *The Inside of the Cup,* by WINSTON CHURCHILL; *The Eyes of the World,* by HAROLD BELL WRIGHT; *Penrod,* by BOOTH TARKINGTON; *The Lone Star Ranger,* by ZANE GREY; *The Tree of Heaven,* by MAY SINCLAIR; *The Four Horsemen of the Apocalypse,* by V. BLASCO IBAÑEZ.

In the 1920's: *The Man of the Forest,* by ZANE GREY; *Main Street,* by SINCLAIR LEWIS; *Black Oxen,* by GERTRUDE ATHERTON; *So Big,* by EDNA FERBER; *The Private Life of Helen of Troy,* by JOHN ERSKINE; *Elmer Gantry,* by SINCLAIR LEWIS; *The Bridge of San Luis Rey,* by THORNTON WILDER; *All Quiet on the Western Front,* by E. M. REMARQUE.

In the 1930's: *Cimarron,* by EDNA FERBER; *The Good Earth,* by PEARL S. BUCK; *Magnificent Obsession,* by LLOYD C. DOUGLAS; *Anthony Adverse,* by HERVEY ALLEN; *So Red the Rose,* by STARK YOUNG; *Green Light,* by LLOYD C. DOUGLAS; *Of Time and the River,* by THOMAS WOLFE; *Gone with the Wind,* by MARGARET MITCHELL; *The Citadel,* by A. J. CRONIN; *The Grapes of Wrath,* by JOHN STEINBECK; *All This and Heaven Too,* by RACHEL FIELD.

In the 1940's: *The Robe,* by LLOYD DOUGLAS; *How Green Was My Valley,* by RICHARD LLEWELLYN; *Kitty Foyle,* by CHRISTOPHER MORLEY; *For Whom the Bell Tolls,* by ERNEST HEMINGWAY; *Song of Bernadette,* by FRANZ WERFEL; *Forever Amber,* by KATHLEEN WINSOR; *Mrs. Miniver,* by JAN STRUTHER; *Berlin Diary,* by WILLIAM SHIRER; *The White Cliffs,* by ALICE DUER MILLER; *See Here, Private Hargrove,* by MARION HARGROVE; *The Egg and I,* by BETTY MACDONALD; *One World,* by WENDELL WILKIE; *Peace of Mind,* by JOSHUA L. LIEBMAN; *The Power of Positive Thinking,* by NORMAN VINCENT PEALE.

In the early 1950's: *The Silver Chalice,* by THOMAS COSTAIN; *Not As A Stranger,* by MORTON THOMPSON; *A Man Called Peter,* by CATHERINE MARSHALL; *From Here to Eternity,* by JAMES JONES; *The Caine Mutiny,* by HERMAN WOUK; *The Sea Around Us,* by RACHEL CARSON.

These lists of best sellers indicate trends in writing and reflect, to some extent, the mood or needs of the people. Wars, prosperity, and depressions affect the kind of reading done by different groups. The

[50] Alice P. Hackett, *Sixty Years of Best Sellers.* Bowker, New York, 1955.

[51] Frank L. Mott, *Golden Multitudes, the Story of Best Sellers in the United States.* Macmillan, New York, 1947.

sales record of a book does not indicate its quality or long-term importance. Many of the books named above are regarded now as trivial or even worthless by literary or psychological standards. A group of writers put out a series of essays on what they regarded as important books, *Books That Changed Our Minds.*[52] These books would not be read by most people, but they may actually affect their lives. Among the books listed are *The Interpretation of Dreams* (Freud); *The Frontier in American History* (Turner); *Folkways* (Sumner); *Main Currents in American Thought* (Parrington); and *The Decline of the West* (Spengler). Another editor or group would undoubtedly list other books.

A few trends in reading in the United States were discussed in Chapter 1. These trends and the short account above give a partial picture of how writing and reading have developed in the United States. The early settlers of the country were fortunate in bringing religious traditions and later receiving ideas, especially from France, which assumed that ability to read was a usual and natural thing. Conservatism of propertied groups and the difficulties of opening up the frontier delayed the spread of literacy, but the democratic spirit of the New World and faith in education were sufficient to overcome such obstacles. Although literacy is neither as complete nor at as high a functioning level as one might wish, it is still true that the United States is a reading nation. While the quality of what people read should never be confused with quantity, as more people read more things the chances for improved tastes and a better-informed citizenry should increase. That is where the reading program in the school takes over part of the task.

CONCLUSIONS

The long, slow growth of man's abilities in writing and reading makes these arts seem even more precious today. When boys and girls, and their parents, take it for granted that all children should learn the various language arts, they do not always realize the vast heritage of early struggle and discovery which lies behind the simple process of opening a book for a few moments' enjoyment. The first use of speech, the invention of writing and the alphabet, the development of the materials of writing and reading, the effort to keep great

[52] Malcolm Cowley, ed., *Books That Changed Our Minds.* Doubleday, New York, 1939.

literature from perishing, and more recent ventures in writing and publishing are all part of the great tradition behind the reading program in the elementary school. As teachers and other curriculum workers review a few of these achievements in this chapter, they gain perhaps some sense of the inheritance with which they work. Clarence Day expressed the feeling as follows:

THE WORLD OF BOOKS
IS THE MOST REMARKABLE CREATION OF MAN
NOTHING ELSE THAT HE BUILDS EVER LASTS
MONUMENTS FALL
NATIONS PERISH
CIVILIZATIONS GROW OLD AND DIE OUT
AND AFTER AN ERA OF DARKNESS
NEW RACES BUILD OTHERS
BUT IN THE WORLD OF BOOKS ARE VOLUMES
THAT HAVE SEEN THIS HAPPEN AGAIN AND AGAIN
AND YET LIVE ON
STILL YOUNG
STILL AS FRESH AS THE DAY THEY WERE WRITTEN
STILL TELLING MEN'S HEARTS
OF THE HEARTS OF MEN CENTURIES DEAD

CLARENCE DAY[53]

SUPPLEMENTARY READINGS

ALTICK, RICHARD D. *The English Common Reader: A Social History of the Mass Reading Public, 1800-1900.* University of Chicago Press, Chicago, 1957.

BLOOMFIELD, LEONARD. "Lingustics and Reading," *Elementary English Review,* Vol. 19, pp. 125-130, 183-186, April, May, 1942.

CARROLL, JOHN B. *The Study of Language.* Harvard University Press, Cambridge, 1953.

CARROLL, JOHN B. "Communication Theory, Linguistics and Psycholinguistics," *Review of Educational Research,* Vol. 28, pp. 79-88, April, 1958.

CLODD, EDWARD. *The Story of the Alphabet.* Appleton, New York, 1917.

Committee on Materials of Instruction. *The Story of Writing.* Achievements of Civilization, No. 1. American Council on Education, Washington, D.C., 1932.

ESPER, E. A. "Language," in C. Murchison, ed., *Handbook of Social Psychology,* pp. 417-460. Clark University Press, Worcester, Mass. 1935.

FORD, PAUL L. *The New England Primer.* Dodd, New York, 1897.

GLEASON, HENRY A. *An Introduction to Descriptive Linguistics.* Holt, New York, 1955.

HACKETT, ALICE P. *Sixty Years of Best Sellers.* Bowker, New York, 1955.

HENLE, PAUL, ed. *Language, Thought and Culture.* University of Michigan Press, Ann Arbor, 1958.

[53] Reproduced by permission of Yale University Press from Clarence Day's *The Story of Yale University Press Told by a Friend.* 1920.

HOGBEN, LANCELOT. *From Cave Painting to Comic Strip*. Dufour, Chester Springs, Pa., 1959.

IRWIN, KEITH G. *The Romance of Writing*. Viking Press, New York, 1956.

JESPERSEN, OTTO. *Language: Its Nature, Development and Origin*. Holt, New York, 1922.

LEHMANN-HAUPT, HELLMUT. *The Book in America. A History of the Making, the Selling and the Collecting of Books in the United States*. Bowker, New York, 1939.

MASON, WILLIAM L. *A History of the Art of Writing*. Macmillan, New York, 1920.

MAXWELL, MARJORIE. *The Story of Books Up through the Ages*. Harper, New York, 1928.

MCMURTRIE, DOUGLAS C. *The Book. The Story of Printing and Bookmaking*, rev. ed. Oxford University Press, New York, 1943.

MILLER, GEORGE A. *Language and Communication*. McGraw-Hill, New York, 1951.

MINNICH, HARVEY C. *Old Favorites from the McGuffey Readers*. American Book, New York, 1936.

MINNICH, HARVEY C. *William Holmes McGuffey and His Readers*. American Book, New York, 1936.

MOSIER, RICHARD D. *Making the American Mind. Social and Moral Ideas in the McGuffey Readers*. King's Crown Press, Columbia University, New York, 1947.

MOTT, FRANK L. *Golden Multitudes. The Story of Best Sellers in the United States*. Macmillan, New York, 1947.

PEI, MARIO. *All About Language*. Lippincott, Philadelphia, 1954.

SAPIR, EDWARD. *Language, an Introduction to the Study of Speech*. Harcourt, New York, 1921. Also Harvest Books, paperback edition.

SHOEMAKER, FRANCIS, ed. *Teachers College Record*, Vol. 57, No. 2, November, 1955. Issue on "Communication and Communication Arts."

SMITH, HENRY L. *Linguistic Science and the Teaching of English*. Harvard University Press, Cambridge, 1956.

SMITH, NILA B. *American Reading Instruction*. Silver Burdett, New York, 1934.

SOFFIETTI, JAMES P. "Why Children Fail to Read: A Linguistic Analysis," *Harvard Educational Review*, Vol. 25, pp. 63-94, Spring, 1955.

SULLIVAN, HELEN. "Literacy and Illiteracy," in E. R. A. Seligman, ed., *Encyclopedia of Social Sciences*, Vol. 9, pp. 511-523. Macmillan, New York, 1937.

THORNDIKE, EDWARD L. *Man and His Works*, Chaps. 4, 5. Harvard University Press, Cambridge, 1943.

UNESCO. *Progress of Literacy in Various Countries*. Monograph on Fundamental Education, No. 6. UNESCO, New York, 1953.

WEBBER, WINSLOW L. *Books about Books*. Hale, Cushman & Flint, Boston, 1937.

Chapter 3

CHILD-DEVELOPMENT BACKGROUNDS: INTERRELATIONSHIPS OF READING AND CHILD DEVELOPMENT

ONE INFLUENCE ON READING PROGRAMS

This chapter discusses one of the most significant trends in modern education as its affects the reading program. It relates research in child development to the reading curriculum. The first two chapters suggest that one cannot thoroughly understand a modern reading program unless one knows something of the historical and current sociological conditions affecting reading. The present chapter suggests an even more important factor in determining a reading program—the nature of the child himself.

The child-development emphasis has been a comparatively late influence on reading programs. The 1949 Yearbook on Reading of the National Society for the Study of Education,[1] for example, gave data on child development considerably more place than did the corresponding 1936 yearbook. With an even greater emphasis on child development, the 1961 Yearbook had as its theme "Development In and Through Reading." In the past, reading programs often were organized in terms of skills or abilities supposedly appropriate for various grade levels and determined by tradition or a philosophy of education or community demands on the school. Since the early 1940's the characteristics and needs of children have been used more than before in planning the reading program, and teachers and other curriculum workers have become more aware of the influences of reading upon the child's total development. This book, and especially Chapters 12, 13, and 16, is concerned not only with children's growth *in* reading abilities but with children's development *through*

[1] National Society for Study of Education, *Reading in the Elementary School,* Forty-eighth Yearbook, Part I, University of Chicago Press, Chicago, 1949.

reading activities. For example, the following chapter contains a section on the effects of reading, a topic usually disregarded in books on reading instruction.

The growth of the child study movement after the First World War was one of the outstanding events in educational history. During this time an enormous amount of research contributed to knowledge of the nature, needs, experiences, and growth patterns of childhood. This research has still not covered all phases of child growth and is more complete for the preschool child and the adolescent than it is for the elementary-school child. Despite gaps in knowledge of childhood it is no longer possible for curriculum-makers to go blithely on, producing reading programs without referring to the results of research on childhood. The modern point of view arising out of the child-study movement sees reading not only as the mastery of a body of skills but as a part of the well-rounded development of children and adults. The curriculum group working out a reading program must now ask themselves what experiences in reading will contribute most to the development of individual children who share in these activities.

In the modern reading program, then, reading is regarded as a means rather than an end in itself. It is a means to greater knowledge of a topic that is interesting to the child or greater understanding of his own or others' behavior rather than a program for producing rhythmic eye movements or accurate blending ability. This does not mean that reading skills are of no consequence. Instead it implies that because the emphasis in the reading program is not on the isolated skill but on the purposes involved, the skills and habits acquired will be more meaningful and more efficient. In addition, reading abilities will contribute to some of the more subtle aspects of personality development in a way they never would in a program emphasizing only the mechanics of reading.

DIFFICULTIES IN USING CHILD DEVELOPMENT DATA

Although the Child Study movement has influenced education in many ways, there are various difficulties in applying research knowledge of children and youth to classroom situations. Succeeding sections suggest possible bridges from child development data to school learning activities in reading but the connection is never a simple one-to-one relationship. In other words, we cannot take a study of peer relationships or one of the declared interests of a group of children such as boarding-school stories and say, in isolation, that these specified books are the ones a child in this group should be reading for recreational purposes. Rather the social behavior and verbalized interest of his group must be considered in relationship to many other things we know about the child and about his total reading activities.

Some of the difficulties in applying child development data to the curriculum have been indicated by Ausubel.[2] He says that child development data offer "important insights about the changing intellectual and emotional capacities of children as developing human beings." Child study may "legitimately be considered one of the basic sciences underlying education" but he goes on to state that "at present our discipline can offer only a limited number of very crude generalizations and highly tentative suggestions"[3] about the curriculum. For example, Ausubel is particularly critical of the "going-togetherness" idea somewhat as developed by Olson in his "organismic age" concept, an approach that has also been criticized by Tyler.[4] Blommers and Stroud[5] go so far as to conclude that "there are neither theoretical nor empirical bases for believing that organismic age predicts school achievement." These and other writers warn against "premature and wholesale extension of developmental principles to educational theory and practice."

One reason that child development data must be interpreted cautiously in making applications to the reading program lies in the nature of the data. Much of our information about children and adolescents may be characterized as follows:[6]

1. It has been collected in research institutes attached to universities and in laboratory situations rather than in ordinary school classrooms.

2. The volume of research data contains more studies of preschool

[2] David P. Ausubel, "Viewpoints from Related Disciplines: Human Growth and Development," *Teachers College Record,* Vol. 60, pp. 245-254, February, 1959.

[3] *Ibid.,* p. 245.

[4] Fred T. Tyler, "Organismic Growth, Sexual Maturity and Progress in Reading," *Journal of Educational Psychology,* Vol. 46, pp. 85-93, February, 1955.

[5] Paul Blommers and J. B. Stroud, "Note on the Organismic Age Concept," *Journal of Educational Psychology,* Vol. 46, pp. 142-150, March, 1955.

[6] David H. Russell, chm., *Child Development and the Language Arts.* Research Bulletin of National Conference on Research in English. National Council of Teachers of English, Champaign, Ill., 1953.

children and adolescent youth than of elementary-school-age children.

3. Many researches present data on individual children or on small groups tested individually rather than involving the typical classroom interactions of groups of thirty or more children.

4. Studies in child development give few leads to the content of the curriculum. Instead of *what* and *why*, they help give answers on the *how* and *when* level.

5. Studies of individual children in laboratory situations tend to give maximum results rather than typical results for an age group. For example, in a study of children's concepts done by individual interview with an adult, the child may be stimulated beyond his average performance.

Such difficulties in using child development data can be overcome, in part, by more studies in normal classroom situations. At the present time however, there may be dangers in attempting to apply developmental data, such as children's perceptual abilities recorded in a laboratory, to groups of children in classrooms and schools. With this warning in mind, the reader will find several hundred examples of *possible* uses of developmental data in the sections below.

CONTRIBUTIONS OF READING TO CHILD DEVELOPMENT

Children have many needs which have been given different names by different writers. For example, they need security with parents and teachers, status with their peers, and the opportunity for activity and for achievement or success in meeting some of their problems. Adults would say that they need to increase some worth-while skills, to grow in understanding of their environments and in their attitudes connected with good citizenship in a democracy. The reading program can contribute to these needs in the quality of the ideas it deals with, in the way the total program is organized, and in the various methods the teacher uses in reading situations.

A reading program may make an important contribution to a child's personal and social needs through its content, through the manner in which it is conducted, and through a careful organization and gradation of materials which will help toward successful activity and desirable attitudes toward reading. More specifically, some of the possible contributions of a reading program to child development are these:

A. *Through Content*

1. The reading program may add to the understanding and enjoyment of life in the pupil's immediate environment, his home, and his community.
2. It may give an understanding and appreciation of life in modern America and in an interdependent world.
3. It may make children's lives more meaningful through stories and descriptions of earlier days.
4. It may present ideas and suggest attitudes associated with worthy citizenship and sound character.
5. It may help to satisfy curiosity about specific topics in such fields as science, social studies, the arts, and health.
6. It may suggest possibilities for constructive and creative activities.
7. It may refer to specific related experiences available in such forms as songs, recordings, radio programs, and club activities.
8. It may contribute to mental health by offering opportunities for fun and recreation.
9. It may give the child some insight into his own and others' adjustment and behavior.

B. *Through Organization*

1. The reading program may provide for gradual and complete growth in reading skills, habits, and attitudes. These are important for their own sake. They are important also because of the effect of successful achievement on social and emotional adjustments.
2. It may provide for exploration in broad areas or centers of interest related to children's activities at different developmental levels. By providing a variety of materials centered in one theme or topic, a well-organized program of reading can provide both breadth and depth of understanding.

C. *Through Method*

1. The reading program may cultivate personal interests and tastes in a wide variety of good literature. Methods which stress reading for enjoyment rather than minute dissection of the text help to develop desirable reading interests.
2. It may contribute to group skills and habits through planning, sharing, and other group activities.
3. It may contribute to and enrich other forms of language development. In so doing it may help to provide freer communication of ideas.
4. It may help to develop thoughtful interpretation and critical thinking about current problems important to the individual or group.

5. It may provide for optimum individual growth at different rates and along different lines suggested in the items above to produce unique personal traits, such as those needed by leaders and creative artists.

These sixteen items are only some of the contributions a reading program may make to individual development. However, they indicate the varied possibilities inherent in a modern conception of the reading curriculum. In one sense they represent a set of objectives teachers or school systems can have for their reading programs. As contributions or objectives they can be utilized fully only when the facts of pupil development in related areas are known. Accordingly there follows a summary of child development in areas closely allied to the reading program. This summary is organized by preschool, primary, intermediate, and junior-high-school levels, not because these are separate stages of development but because references to school activities are facilitated.

LANGUAGE DEVELOPMENT IN EARLY CHILDHOOD

Few children learn to read before they enter school, but the reading program cannot be considered in a developmental way without reference to the early language development on which reading skills will largely be based.

The story is told of Thomas Carlyle, eminent English writer, that as a young child he spoke for the very first time upon hearing a baby cry. He asked, "What ails wee Jock?" Carlyle's language development is hardly typical; most children don't begin speech by saying complete sentences. What, then, are the typical sequences in a child's language development?

McCarthy[7] has summarized about 700 studies of language development in childhood and suggested the type of development that usually occurs. One of the first responses of the new-born infant is a vocal one, namely, the birth cry. This and other vocal efforts appearing soon after birth, of course, are not true speech, but they are undoubtedly valuable to the child, particularly as practice in motor skills. Language as communication begins between the ages of twelve and eighteen months and develops so rapidly that by the age of four years a child is saying ten or twelve thousand words in a single day;

[7] Dorothea McCarthy, "Language Development in Children," in Leonard Carmichael, ed., *Manual of Child Psychology*, rev. ed., Chap. 10, pp. 476-581. Wiley, New York, 1954.

and by the age of six years he has a huge understanding vocabulary,[8] has a speaking vocabulary of at least 2500 different words,[9] and uses every part of speech and every form of sentence. When a child enters school, if he adjusts easily to the new situation, he normally will speak rather well; for, as Anderson[10] suggested, he has had millions of specific bits of practice in his preschool years. Some of the important facts in general development and in related language development of the preschool years are given on pages 76-77.

The chart illustrates some of the typical items in the general and language development of the preschool child. It suggests that there is an orderly sequence of development which runs through various types of language into the reading programs of most schools. The sequence forms into a pattern somewhat like this:

1. The child learns to listen to oral language—to differentiate speech noises and to relate them to facts within the immediate environment.

2. He learns to use speech noises to communicate with others. These change from simple sounds to naming, to one-word sentences, and to more complex organizations of words.

3. The child's speech ordinarily develops in at least three stages of egocentric speech, parallel speech, and socialized speech. Authorities do not agree entirely on the proportions of these at different age levels.

4. With a wide background of oral language the child learns to differentiate somewhat between visual symbols as presented in pictures or in simple stories on charts.

5. The child learns to associate printed words with concrete objects and more abstract ideas and to use them arranged in sentences and short paragraphs.

6. Along with or after some experience with verbal symbols in reading situations he begins to reproduce these in writing situations. The handwriting and later the spelling may help to reinforce some reading habits.

[8] Mary K. Smith, "Measurement of the Size of General English Vocabulary through the Elementary Grades and High School," *Genetic Psychology Monographs,* Vol. 24, pp. 311-345, 1941.

[9] Madorah E. Smith, "An Investigation of the Development of the Sentence and Extent of Vocabulary in Young Children," *University of Iowa Studies in Child Welfare,* Vol. 3, No. 5, 1926.

[10] John E. Anderson, "Principles of Growth and Maturity in Language," *Elementary English Review,* Vol. 18, pp. 250-254, November, 1941.

GROWTH CHARACTERISTICS AND LANGUAGE DEVELOPMENT OF THE PRESCHOOL CHILD[11]

Age	*General Growth Characteristics*	*Language Development*
Birth to One Year	First two weeks—adjustment to new environment. Tremendous physical and mental growth. Birth weight doubled by 5 months, trebled by one year. [11][10] Brain gains in size about 130 per cent. [11] Rapid growth in muscular co-ordination—child sits with support at 4 months [17] and walks when led at 11 or 12 months [17]. Diffuse emotional patterns of pleasure and pain which change by individuation and conditioning into more definite patterns. By second month he smiles at adults; after 6 months reacts to other children [11]. By one year he shows most forms of social behavior.	Random gestures and vocalization; vowel sounds—first, *a* and *u;* later, consonant sounds, first *m,* by two months *p, b, g, ng,* and *k.* [17] Bodily needs shown by crying. By 4 to 6 months all vowel and consonant sounds have appeared spontaneously. In third month syllabic utterances like *ma, ba, goo, boo.* [15] Between 6 and 10 months the "babbling stage"—repetition of syllables such as *oddle-oddle* and *a-bah-bah.* [17] Between 8 and 17 months first word appears. [1] Median age 60 weeks [17] or 52 weeks [10].
One Year to Three Years	Continues rapid physical and mental growth at a slightly decreasing rate. Differential rate of growth of different body organs. Brain size increases about 25 per cent the second year and 10 per cent the third year. [11] Growth in motor co-ordination continues—he stands alone at about 14 months and walks at about 15 months. Emotional behavior begins to develop from an egocentric to a social frame of reference. Variety of social behavior patterns increases. Language growth means that he understands names of objects and can obey commands. Resistance and negativism reach a peak between 2½ and 3 years. Friendships and co-operation often begin at about 3 years.	After beginning of speech new words added slowly for about 6 months; then, between eighteenth and twenty-fourth months, the "naming" stage—extensive use of nouns. By 3 years child has spoken vocabulary of at least 900 words. [18] First uses one-word sentences. True sentences appear between fifteenth and twenty-eighth months. Average length of sentence by three years between 3 and 4 words. [15, 18] Mental development is sufficient to see clear relationships. Social contacts are increased greatly by increasing facility in conversation.

Growth Characteristics and Language Development of the Preschool Child

Age	*General Growth Characteristics*	*Language Development*
The Later Preschool Period	Rapid physical and mental growth, but at decreasing rates. Bodily proportions change. By age of 5 most of basic motor skills (running, handling, jumping, etc.) have been acquired. [11] Child learns to feed himself, using spoon and fork, and to adjust own clothing, except possibly shoe laces. Handedness increases rapidly between third and fifth birthdays. Clear-cut patterns of emotional behavior appear. Emotions occur as responses to words as well as situations. Play changes from egocentric to social basis. Child begins to identify self with group. Increase of individual differences in social reactions—social and emotional habits being established.	Increased motor co-ordination shows in improved ability in articulation, larger vocabulary, increased ability in drawing. Child draws what he knows rather than what he sees. [11] Vocabulary increases to about 2500 words. Of the total number of word concepts used by children aged 2 to 5, one third refer to mother, father, sibling, or home. [17] Conversations contain fewer nouns, proportionally, and have longer sentences. Sentences often contain 6 to 8 words; they are usually simple in structure, but complex ones are sometimes used. [1] Language used is less egocentric, more social in tone. Five-year-old may use questions for sake of holding attention of parent or teacher, as well as out of curiosity. [16] Dramatic play may involve much verbal activity.

11 Numbers in brackets indicate sources of statements as listed in the research bibliography at the end of this chapter.

7. The child continues to develop in various reading abilities required by his curricular and extraschool experiences. These developmental stages are discussed below. They are introduced by an account of developmental difficulties in the language arts experienced by some children when they enter school.

LANGUAGE PROBLEMS ON ENTERING SCHOOL

The chart on pages 76-77 presents the usual picture of language growth in preschool years. However, it does not cover the cases of individual boys and girls on that milestone in their lives, the day they enter school. Even this normative picture suggests how individuals vary; for example, the first sentences may be used anywhere between the fifteenth and twenty-eighth months. The primary teacher knows, however, that she has thirty boys and girls at very different stages of language development and with quite different language problems. Some of the problems these boys and girls may face, a number of them suggested by Harrison[12] and by Heffernan,[13] are these:

1. The child is ill at ease in a new social situation. He knows how to talk to adults, particularly if he comes from a small family; but he does not know how to communicate with classmates of his own age, many of whom come from homes of a different social-economic level. This may be particularly true of a bright child whose big words and long sentences make him an object of fun in classroom or playground situations.

2. The child may use baby talk or a private language. His parents understand these efforts at communication, but his teacher can only guess at his meaning. Consequent difficulties hinder his adjustment to the school situation. Mary Ellen Chase, in *Windswept,* told how Philip Marston got into difficulties in a boys' school because he wrote of how to "haskell" a task. The family had this private word for "cleaning up" because of their former housekeeper, a Mrs. Haskell, who insisted upon everything's being left neat and tidy. Somewhat similarly, private words for the bodily functions may embarrass a pupil after he uses them in public. A private language may embarrass the child in a number of ways and hinder his free participation in reading-readiness activities.

3. The child may have articulation difficulties. Inability to sound

[12] M. Lucille Harrison, *Reading Readiness,* rev. ed. Houghton Mifflin, Boston, 1939.
[13] Helen Heffernan, ed., *Guiding the Young Child.* Heath, Boston, 1951.

a few consonants or a slight lisp are probably no handicap in the ordinary first grade; but if the defect is serious, perhaps with a physical basis, the alert teacher takes immediate steps for the correction of the physical defect and special help in speech activities. Minor defects of articulation in the primary grades seem to respond best to practice in informal word games rather than formal speech exercises. If the defect is very serious, a speech expert may advise definite exercises and treatment of physical disabilities.

4. The child does not understand the language used by the teacher. School always involves a vocabulary that is partly new to the child. In addition, the school may prescribe certain forms of speech not used in the home. Such grammatical or phonetic difficulties add to the child's burden of adjustment. This situation arises in some schools in London, for example, where Cockney children must learn standard English almost as a foreign language.

Speech work in Great Britain and America attempts to break down barriers between home and school speech so that children may keep the spontaneity of home and play conditions and still speak in a generally acceptable manner. As suggested in Chapter 1, language activities grow out of other activities, so that the alert primary teacher encourages free expression in the children and in her own speech recognizes the pupils' types of language development. By giving the child many opportunities for informal speaking the teacher is preparing the way for informal reading of the child's own sentences and early charts.

5. The child may be required to do formal reading and writing too early in his school career. As suggested above, reading and writing are simply formalized extensions of early language abilities. Some writers estimate that the average child speaks thirty thousand running words a day before entering public school, so that no pupil can be switched immediately from relatively free and informal language experiences to entirely new activities with distinct limitations on what one can do. It seems important, then, that teachers replace the "We don't talk in school" attitude with a positive approach to utilizing speech in reading and in other related language activities.

The wide acceptance of the principle of readiness programs for children means that fewer pupils today are required to go through the processes of reading and writing before they are prepared to do them successfully. Good teachers are realizing more than formerly, however, that a readiness program is not a period of inactive waiting for maturation to take place, but a planned series of stimulating experiences leading up to the more formal procedures of reading or writing. In this way reading and writing are put on a more individual basis, and instead of being hindrances to learning are enriching and joyful activities.

Language growth, then, is usually not retarded if an effective reading-readiness program is in operation in a school. At a slightly later stage in the first grade, however, there are still some dangers. Harrison[14] summarized research to show that from the fifth year on into the early school years there is a falling off in vocabulary gains, although in later school years very rapid gains again take place. This may be due to the fact that early reading uses only simple sentences, and these are based on very common experiences. Later in the year the first handwriting employs even simpler forms. Both writing and reading, therefore, may be limiting factors in language growth. The importance of a rich variety of language and concrete, nonverbal experiences in the child's first years in school cannot be overestimated if general vocabulary growth and the development of the whole child are the aim. In the first months of a child's school life the teacher cannot depend upon reading to enrich the child's living.

This discussion of possible difficulties of the child's first months in school stresses some of the developmental factors involved. Actually the child's growth is continuous, and he may also face many of these problems at later stages of his school career. For example, readiness for reading is a factor in learning throughout all the grades of elementary and secondary school. The characteristics and needs of children at various age levels must always influence the materials and methods used in the reading program. The following sections suggest some possible relationships between developmental traits and reading activities at ages corresponding roughly to the primary, intermediate, and junior-high-school periods. Applications to reading are usually based on knowledge of the child's total development rather than on a specific developmental trait.

CHILD DEVELOPMENT AND THE READING OF SIX-SEVEN-EIGHT-YEAR-OLDS

Just as there are certain relationships between general development and language development in the preschool years, so there are

[14] M. Lucille Harrison, "The Need for an Adequate Oral Language Program," *Elementary English Review,* Vol. 18, pp. 99-102, March, 1941.

interrelationships of general growth factors and reading abilities during the primary grades. These growth factors are described very briefly below in three sections which, however, overlap one another and which tend to be related to reading achievement in integrated rather than isolated ways.

Physical Factors

Physical growth and activities are an important part of a child's development up to the age of five or six. In the preschool years the child has learned a large number of general motor skills and uses a wide variety of large-muscle activities. Gradually, from the age of six to that of eight, the child begins to place less emphasis on these activities for their own sake. Instead of manipulation and construction as an end in themselves, these skills become useful for other purposes, often in the social context. From six to eight the child also undertakes an increasing number of activities involving finer muscular co-ordinations. These are developed gradually and at different ages by different children. A third characteristic of the period is the tremendous amount of physical activity in which the child engages, often without a place for what adults regard as proper rest. Girls at this age are approximately one year more mature than boys [24].

The applications of this physical development to the primary reading program are rather direct. Children in the first grade should engage in many physical activities and thus need a program involving something more than just sitting. The fine muscular co-ordinations required in reading must be developed gradually by the teacher with reference to the varying abilities of different children in this regard. The primary teacher will plan short periods of concentration on charts or other materials, followed by opportunities to engage in physical activity involving large-muscle skills. Since the span of attention is generally rather short, lessons dealing with one activity or one topic must also be short. This is particularly true if a teacher uses some rather formal approaches to reading, such as phonetic analysis. Such mechanical activities should probably never last over ten or twelve minutes, even in the third grade.

Mental Factors

Children of the primary age group are essentially interested in the here and now. During this period their interests broaden so that eight-year-olds may be interested in people and things removed from the immediate environment. However, for these children experiences must be real and related to past experiences if they are to become part of the child's living. [3] Similarly, their spontaneous interests are concerned with themselves or topics close to themselves. Thinking in general shows this personal bias, but probably cannot be regarded as entirely egocentric. Emphasis in a group, for example, swings back and forth from impersonal to personal experiences. [2]

Primary children are realistic. They insist upon telling the whole story with details. As they grow older they gradually begin to see the importance of detail in the total concept, but at this age they are largely engrossed in detail. [2, 6] Their language is generally factual, direct, and specific. [2] The thinking of primary-school children is evolving from the concrete toward some abstract. At five or six most questions are of the "What is it?" sort, but how and why questions appear more frequently from seven on. The seven-year-old can reason about differences. In general these can be told before similarities. [8] Responses to similarities and differences develop earlier than the ability to verbalize such distinctions. [21] Seven-year-olds thus see some relationships which are not checked by perception. They have some understanding of cause and effect. [5] Their conversation may include some abstract words, such as *idea* or *responsibility,* but they usually reach conclusions on the basis of a limited examination of facts. [2]

The applications of mental development to the reading program relate to both method and content. In regard to method it is important to have the reading period grow out of the child's immediate environment and experiences. Not until the third grade is the child ordinarily ready for many reading materials somewhat remote from his other activities in and out of school. The closer the teacher can tie the reading to other activities through the use of experience charts, bulletin boards, daily newspapers, and similar devices the greater the chances of a successful program.

Similarly, the teacher will have as one of her early objectives the development of fairly concrete ideas rather than abstract generalizations. As the children think over the materials read, the teacher will evaluate growth in specific information dealing with home, farm, or community rather than generalizations about their places in modern society. The teacher must always be alert for inadequate concepts, even of rather common objects or events. However, the children of these ages are growing in ability to see relationships, including cause and effect, so that questioning on a passage may involve these types of response among the more mature members of the six-to-eight group.

Content and method affect one another, so that content of early reading materials is rather definitely indicated. Most basic reading programs and successful books for young children at this level are concerned with childlike experiences in home and community. They enjoy Mother Goose, animal-talking stories, and easy fairy tales. [20] Although reading interests are more realistic than certain early writers indicated, it is also true that older children of this group are interested in poetry, fairy tales, and the strange and bizarre. Dramatic play reflects these imaginative interests. Many children fail to distinguish between the real and the make-believe, usually because of lack of experience in the matter concerned.

The concern of children for the immediate should not limit the materials of reading to this area, especially in the upper half of the third grade. Children's curiosity at this age is one of the great sources of motivation of their conduct. This resource can be used in expanding interests to wider fields. Although the children have little conception of time in the historical sense, or of distance, their curiosity leads them to read of children, adventures, and conditions of far-off times and places.

Social Factors

From the sixth to the eighth year an ordinary child's individual pursuits are gradually abandoned to make way for more social enterprises. His self-assertion dwindles in the face of some desire for group approval. Individualistic play gives way to more organized and competitive play. Imitation of others, especially adults, is usually superseded by competition for one's place in the sun. Much of the bickering and arguing at this level, disturbing to parents who may overhear a ball game, for example, is an attempt to gain status with the group. [3] Spontaneous language activity is direct and specific, with short sentences and few subordinate clauses. [2] In the early parts of the period much of speech is a monologue, but later most pupils generally develop ability to participate in discussion. Toward the end of the period, boys and girls often divide themselves into distinct groups for games or other activities.

These social characteristics naturally influence a teacher's planning and executing of the reading program. Much of the early work must necessarily emphasize group membership and participation. Informal circles in which the group listens to one child read may aid this socialization process. By the end of the third grade the language and ideas of a book or basic reader may affect directly the language and ideas of some child to whom they appealed. About the end of the period a beginning of diverging interests in content may appear between girls and boys. The teacher is alert for this beginning in her recommendation of books for free reading periods.

The six-to-eight-year period is one of the most important for the whole child and probably the most important for his reading abilities. In general development he is in a transition period from large-muscle skills to finer co-ordinations, from home security to competition with his peers, from considerable language facility without background experiences to a more deeply rooted experience, and from individualistic to group interests. All these are important general phases of growing up. In actual reading activities too the child is laying a foundation for all his skills, habits, and attitudes. The importance of this period is emphasized in Part II (see page 139).

CHILD DEVELOPMENT AND THE READING OF NINE-TEN-ELEVEN-YEAR-OLDS

As with younger children, it is valuable for teachers of older children to sense a few of the possible relationships between general developmental factors and reading abilities. The general factors are again subdivided below for convenience rather than with the intention of suggesting discrete areas.

Physical Factors

The period from nine to eleven years is usually a continuation of the growth patterns of the previous period. A few girls may experience the onset of puberty, but this change is more characteristic of the later period. In general boys and girls of this period enjoy a healthy, vigorous life. There is usually a rapid development of ability to make finer co-ordinations; such skills have important psychological, as well as physical, values for children.

The development of finer co-ordinations and resistance to fatigue means that children of this age group can read longer and with greater skill than they were capable of doing previously. This ability, linked with their good health and other activities, means that the period is one in which the child does a large amount of reading if materials are accessible.

Mental Factors

Caswell and Foshay stated that this period is one of "(1) a specialization and differentiation in interests, (2) a differentiation between work and play, (3) uninhibited creative work, and (4) distinctly more mature intellectual ability." [3:114] The period is marked by rapid growth in vocabulary. Children begin to organize memory around clues instead of attempting to recall wholes. [6] They increase in ability to see similarities and differences and causal relationships. [21] They make simple generalizations on the basis of concrete experiences and will examine a limited number of facts in making a judgment.

The differentiation of interests expresses itself as a sex difference and in terms of individuals. [20, 22] Boys are more interested in nonfiction and tend to do more magazine and newspaper reading. Girls, however, read more than boys in terms of total time spent in reading. They like stories of home and school life, often written in series, whereas boys may read a little more science and biography. More important, children now begin to use reading to satisfy their own interests, and individual children may read widely to satisfy curiosity. This is the stage at which the teacher will find many children eager to learn the use of encyclopedias and other reference books. It is a period also when the child will profit by practice in work-type reading situations with emphasis upon study skills.

Since this is often a period of uninhibited creative work, the teacher can use reading as a foundation for many expressive activities. Reading may contribute to vicarious experiences which can be translated into writing, music, drama, rhythms, or other forms of expression. Here the teacher has a particularly good opportunity to make reading one of the group of language arts.

Social Factors

Social changes from the age of nine to that of eleven years are usually more significant than physical ones. Most children of this age favor activities shared with a "best friend" or a group above individual pursuits. Most boys and girls belong to a group, or gang, of their own sex. This group may exercise a greater influence on activities, ambitions, and qualities of character than the home. The group, especially if it is a boys' group, often revolves round a recognized leader. Boys in general avoid participation in any activities with girls.

The influence of the group may be felt in the child's reading. He may read certain books or comics just because it is being done. Boys will avoid a book that has been labeled "sissy." The good teacher works to establish good group standards of reading, because these probably have more influence than any adult standard. The reading group now has an authentic basis in terms of the needs and friendships of the children involved. The skillful teacher uses hobby clubs, such as a reading club, a library committee, or a newspaper staff, to stimulate interest in reading and other language activities. Furthermore, she can help the group in co-operative activities related to reading, such as dramatization, radio skits, and team games involving verbal abilities.

The nine-to-eleven-year period, then, is one of steady progress in physical development and rather important changes in mental and social activities. The influence of the group is all-important, but at the same time individual interests are appearing. Boys and girls begin to develop separate interests in reading, and varied materials must be available. The teacher can use the period as one for extending experience, developing good work habits while reading, encouraging creative activities, and employing co-operative methods to give desirable experiences in language arts. In some respects this period is the best of a child's life for reading. Some studies indicate that the child reads more at about eleven or twelve years of age than at any other period. He seems to have time for it at this stage that he will never have from middle adolescence to old age. The importance of reading in his life at this age level should be reflected in the place given to reading activities in the total school program.

GENERAL DEVELOPMENT AND THE READING OF TWELVE-THIRTEEN-FOURTEEN-YEAR-OLDS

The twelve-to-fourteen-year period is usually regarded as the beginning of that indefinite stage of development known as adolescence. More is known about development at this level than at the nine-to-eleven level. The attainment of puberty, which marks the early stages of adolescence, has always been of considerable interest to man. It was marked by the pubic rites of quite primitive tribes and was one of the earliest studies of beginning psychology in America. Study of the adolescent period on this continent dates back at least to the work of G. Stanley Hall, whose *Adolescence* was published in 1904. Since that time much more research has revealed a large collection of important facts about the early adolescent, who is usually found in the senior grades of the elementary school or in the junior high school. Accordingly it is possible to state rather clearly some of the characteristics of growth in the twelve-to-fourteen-year period which may be related to the reading program.

Physical Factors

Unlike the previous period early adolescence is marked by many physical changes. Anatomic and physiological changes may be far-reaching, with consequent effect on metabolism, motor skills, and organization of physical traits. Maturation of the sex organs and growth of the secondary sex characteristics are usually important to the person involved. Growth curves of large numbers of early adolescents are gradual, but there is general agreement on a prepubertal spurt in growth. It seems to be largely an individual matter whether or not this spurt continues into middle adolescence. Indeed, many experts regard the chief characteristic of the period as the differential growth rate. It is impossible to overemphasize the importance of teachers', parents', and adolescents' understanding that (1) different individuals mature at very different times and (2) different body parts of any one individual grow at very different rates. Accordingly clumsiness or glandular imbalance or other physical difficulties may result for some adolescents but not for others. Malnutrition and lowered resistance to infection may result. One constant factor in differential growth rates is the fact that girls ordinarily achieve puberty from one and a half to two years earlier than boys. Girls often gain height rapidly between eleven and thirteen years, but many boys gain most rapidly between thirteen and fifteen years.

The child of eleven or twelve is typically a healthy, active child who does considerable reading. As suggested above, more reading seems possible at about twelve years of age than at any other time. [20] Most boys of twelve and thirteen are still prepubescent and retain these interests in physical activities, the gang, hoarding, and collecting (possibly comic books). They read books of mystery and adventure, often in series. Many girls of these ages, however, are pubescent and more mature in their interests. They continue to read more than boys; but they read more novels, love stories, women's magazines, and other so-called adult magazines. These reading interests probably reflect changing social factors as much as physical ones, but they are none the less important for teachers who advise and direct the preadolescent or adolescent about reading.

Mental Factors

Most writers agree that the rate of intellectual growth diminishes only slightly from the age of eight years to that of fifteen or sixteen years. Teachers and parents can expect more mature performance in application of intellect such as work-type reading, problem-solving, and creative situations. Data from the same children over a ten-year period indicate that individual differences with respect to the rate and form of the mental growth curve are very large. [7]

The preadolescent period was characterized by Averill[15] as one of "a general thirst after information" and therefore of popularity for books of knowledge and children's encyclopedias. In the twelve-to-fourteen-year period this interest may continue, especially for boys. Associated with general mental development and language development, the abilities to generalize and to reason about personal and social problems improve. The ability to memorize increases, as does organizing ability. Although difficult to measure, imaginative powers also seem to increase. [4]

This general growth in mental ability means that the teacher can begin to place more reliance on reading as a learning situation. Without eliminating concrete, first-hand experiences teachers can use readings that demand organization and generalization. At this stage they may further, for example, the beginnings of broad social insights in pupils' thinking—feelings for justice, ideas about international affairs or problems created by scientific advances. Many of the early adolescent group, and particularly the immature, will be largely concerned with personal interests, or fiction by writers they know, or in styles with which they are familiar. However, teachers have the opportunity of stimulating more mature reading interests and using reading to broaden understanding of people and the modern world.

Social Factors

The influence of the gang in the lives of ten- and eleven-year-olds continues into the early adolescent period. During these years the individual becomes increasingly aware of self, but he sees himself in the world of his peers. "The fundamental adolescent drive is to be acceptable to like-age companions of both sexes." [19] The most

[15] Lawrence A. Averill, *Adolescence. A Study in the Teen Years*, p. 10. Houghton, Boston, 1936.

admired qualities in boys at the eleven- and twelve-year level seem to be competence in group games, readiness to take chances, not too much attention to cleanliness, and a certain aggressiveness and boisterousness, on playground or in classroom. At this age a very different pattern appears for girls. Aggressive, noisy behavior is disapproved, but prestige attaches to being friendly, pretty, tidy, enthusiastic, and good-humored. [23]

During the twelve-to-fourteen- or fifteen-year period the values for girls change markedly, but those of boys' groups remain much more constant. By fourteen or fifteen years of age boys still emphasize physical skill and daring; but attention-getting devices are regarded as rather childish, and more place is given to social poise, likableness, and grooming. Girls are more concerned with establishing social contacts with friends of the opposite sex, usually in groups. Approved conduct changes from an emphasis on quiet, docile behavior to rather dominating activity in groups and the attractive, glamour-girl type of personality. [24] There is some evidence to suggest that this change occurs earlier in the west-coast group studied by Tryon than with Midwest or Eastern girls.

These changing social values and activities of the early adolescent group have implications for the reading program, although some of them are negative implications. The increasing importance of group activities, such as dances and spectator sports, means that the mature person of the twelve-to-fourteen-year group has less time for individual pursuits such as reading. Some individuals of the group, especially younger boys, will often pursue specific interests and hobbies with great enthusiasm and concentration. This may involve reading on a high level of efficiency and difficulty of material. In general, however, interest in reading begins to wane in this period, crowded out by social activities and interests.

The period is not one to be viewed negatively, however, by teacher or parent. While adult authority has become much less important than peer-group sanctions, the adult can still guide the early adolescent in experiences in worth-while literature. Indeed, the greater intellectual abilities and the increased emotional sensitivity of the period make possible esthetic experiences which would have been appreciated by only a few children in previous years. Early adolescence often has a romanticism and sensitivity to beauty which result in heightened appreciation of selections such as Kipling's *Ballad of East and West* or William Allen White's *Mary White*. This appreciation may be heightened by combining reading procedures with group activities such as dramatization and choral speaking. The total amount of reading done in the latter half of the twelve-to-fourteen-year period may be less, but the reading may still be very significant in the emotional, social development of the young adolescent.

The contribution of reading to the emotional life of the early adolescent may be extended to a contribution to the whole personality. For example, La Brant and Willis[16] suggested how seventh-, eight-, and ninth-grade pupils may develop more sense of security, gain a better understanding of themselves, and achieve a growing independence through reading literature and related activities. Adolescence is no longer regarded as necessarily a period of storm and stress, but it is true that problems may arise at this time which require special guidance by the teacher or counselor. Shy and also overeager pupils may find their places in a co-operative group project such as a class-written play. A group which consistently reads below its ability level, for example, in simple adventure material, may profit by books about their own development such as Keliher's *Life and Growth* and McLean's *Knowing Yourself and Others.* Reading can mean a facing of reality as well as a retreat from it. Certain books of fiction can often influence children greatly; here the teacher or librarian can do some direct guidance of reading choices followed by some nondirective counseling. The use of literature for the improving of psychological insights and adjustments is discussed further in Chapter 13.

FIVE GENERALIZATIONS ABOUT CHILD DEVELOPMENT AND READING

The foregoing sections mention some results of research in child development which may be related to the reading program of the elementary school and the junior high school. Many pertinent findings have been omitted; but perhaps enough evidence has been presented to permit a few generalizations, of which the teacher can be reasonably sure, about such development and its applications to the reading curriculum. These are as follows:

1. Children's Development of Reading Abilities is Continuous and Gradual Rather than Intermittent and Saltatory

The patterns of general development and reading development

[16] Lou La Brant and Margaret Willis, "Some Problems of Adolescents," *Mental Health in the Classroom,* Thirteenth Yearbook, Chap. 12, pp. 174-187, Department of Supervisors and Directors of Instruction, National Education Association, Washington, D.C., 1941.

here described are not stages but sequences. Reading ability does not suddenly appear in the first grade. It is based upon a number of factors associated with readiness and is an expansion of abilities acquired earlier rather than an abrupt step upward. Similarly, the ability to read materials on the fourth-grade level or the eighth-grade level emerges gradually instead of being a sudden transformation resulting from promotion to these grades. Any reading program must be planned as a continuous developmental program with no sharp breaks from grade to grade. (See Part III, page 259.)

2. Most Children Go through the Same Patterns of Development with an Orderly Emergence of Reading Abilities

The order in which various developmental traits appear varies but little from one child to another. For example, every normal child develops speaking and listening abilities before reading abilities. More specifically, his development in perception as illustrated in mental testing suggests that a child can copy a square (Year 4 on the Stanford Binet Scale) before he can reproduce a diamond (Year 7). As a child's reading ability develops, his eye movements ordinarily become more rhythmic, with fewer regressions. Children can comprehend simple materials based on their concrete experiences before they can read materials containing many abstract words. Certain reading interests are typical of various age levels (for typical stages in reading ability, see Chapter 5). Curriculum workers who plan reading programs or authors of basic readers have general sequential patterns to follow in the content of materials and in the teaching and learning methods advocated.

3. Although Development Is Orderly, It May Proceed at Different Rates at Various Times

Studies of child development all agree on the rapid growth of the new-born child in nearly every way children grow. This development generally slows down, but may spurt again later, as in adolescence. Similarly, various reading abilities have different growths at different times. Buswell[17] showed that progress in fundamental habits of recognition, involving rate, span, and rhythmical progress, is very rapid in the first four grades and relatively slow and irregular in the upper grades. On the other hand, ability to interpret difficult passages and to read for different purposes is low in the primary grades, but in-

[17] Guy T. Buswell, *Fundamental Reading Habits: A Study of Their Development*, Supplementary Educational Monographs, No. 21, Chap. 2, Department of Education, University of Chicago, Chicago, 1922.

creases throughout the upper grades, high-school, and college. A teacher of any one grade cannot expect equal development of all reading abilities during the year a pupil is in the grade. Not only do pupils vary among themselves but any one pupil changes in the amount and type of reading growth he is making during a certain period of time.

4. There Is Great Variation in the Ages at Which Different Children Reach the Various Developmental Stages

Children may normally say their first word any time between ten months and three years; the range of age at which puberty is achieved is at least five years. Similarly in reading, children entering the first grade differ in background experiences, interest in books, visual perception, auditory discrimination, ability to follow directions, and any measurable factor which is related to success in reading. Furthermore, educational experiences tend to increase rather than decrease these differences among children. Pupils in the third grade vary more widely in reading abilities than those in the first grade; pupils in the seventh grade have an even greater range of abilities. It seems obvious, then, that no reading program can be planned to use the same methods and the same materials with all the pupils of any one grade. Providing for individual differences is one of the great problems of the teacher of reading. It is discussed more fully in Chapter 15.

5. There Seems to Be a Positive Correlation between the Patterns of Physical, Mental, Social, and Emotional Development and Their Relations to Children's Reading Activities

In general, good physique, superior intelligence, and good social and emotional adjustments seem to be associated. People are prone to comment on outstanding individual exceptions to this rule; but although further research is needed, compensation in the form of a particular strength to balance a particular weakness is not usual. Some relationships between reading interests and physical, mental, and social development have been mentioned above. The child who has a good mind, a happy home, and a wide variety of concrete and verbal experiences is generally a high-grade reader of good materials. If individual exceptions occur which necessitate remedial instruction, the chances of success are usually greater with this type of child than with one of limited background and abilities. The reading program, however, must not neglect the latter child. Rather it must be designed to overcome his background deficiencies, promote more successful social adjustments, and give him success in certain reading situations. With all children, because positive developments are related, successful reading has the function of providing worth-while mental, social, and emotional experiences and thus contributing to a wholesome all-round development.

CONCLUSIONS

Reading and child development are related in two ways: (1) the developmental traits and needs of children help to determine what and how they should be taught in reading; and (2) reading activities may influence children's growth by developing new abilities and interests and by changing attitudes and values related to personality patterns. The first relationship suggests that teachers should study their pupils as persons; some suggestions for doing this in relation to reading are given in Parts II and III of this book. The second relationship involves the uses and effects of reading in the teaching of literature and is considered more fully in Chapter 13. The interrelationships of developmental characteristics and reading activities, here described, illustrate one of the most important trends in modern curriculum-making. An understanding in general of the characteristics of children, and especially of the particular group with which he or she is working, plus some knowledge of what reading can do for children, is indispensable to the successful teacher of reading.

SUPPLEMENTARY READINGS

A. Research References Mentioned in Chapter 3

1. ANDERSON, JOHN E. "The Development of Spoken Language," *Child Development and the Curriculum,* Thirty-eighth Yearbook, Part I, pp. 211-224, National Society for the Study of Education. Public School Publishing Company, Bloomington, Ill., 1939.
2. BIBER, BARBARA; MURPHY, LOIS B.; WOODCOCK, LOUISE P.; and BLACK, IRMA S. *Child Life in School. A Study of a Seven-Year-Old Group.* Dutton, New York, 1942.
3. CASWELL, HOLLIS L., and FOSHAY, A. W. *Education in the Elementary School,* rev. ed. American Book, New York, 1950.
4. COLE, LUELLA. *Psychology of Adolescence.* Farrar, New York, 1936.
5. DEUTSCHE, JEAN M. *The Development of Children's Concepts of Causal Relations.* University of Minnesota Press, Minneapolis, 1937.
6. DRISCOLL, GERTRUDE. *How to Study the Behavior of Children.* Bureau of Publications, Teachers College, Columbia University, New York, 1941.

7. Freeman, Frank N. *Mental Tests,* rev. ed., Chap. 11. Houghton Mifflin, Boston, 1939.
8. Gesell, Arnold. *Infancy and Human Growth.* Macmillan, New York, 1928.
9. Gesell, Arnold, and Ilg, Frances L. *The Child from Five to Ten.* Harper, New York, 1946.
10. Gesell, Arnold, and Thompson, H. *Infant Behavior.* McGraw-Hill, New York, 1934.
11. Goodenough, Florence L. *Developmental Psychology.* Appleton-Century, New York, 1934.
12. Goodenough, Florence L. *Developmental Psychology,* 2nd ed. Appleton-Century, New York, 1945.
13. Jersild, Arthur T. *Child Development and the Curriculum.* Bureau of Publications, Teachers College, Columbia University, New York, 1946.
14. Jersild, Arthur T. *Child Psychology,* 4th ed. Prentice-Hall, Englewood Cliffs, N.J., 1954.
15. McCarthy, Dorothea. "Language Development in Children," *Manual of Child Psychology,* 2nd ed., Chap. 9. Wiley, New York, 1954.
16. Murphy, G.; Murphy, L. B.; and Newcomb, T. M. *Experimental Social Psychology,* rev. ed. Harper, New York, 1937.
17. Shirley, Mary M. "Common Content in the Speech of Pre-School Children," *Child Development,* Vol. 9, pp. 333-346, December, 1938.
18. Smith, Madorah E. *An Investigation of the Development of the Sentence and the Extent of Vocabulary in Young Children.* University of Iowa Studies in Child Welfare, Vol. 3, No. 5, 1926.
19. Stoddard, George D. "An Evaluation of the Yearbook," *Adolescence,* Forty-third Yearbook, Part I, Chap. 18, p. 350, National Society for the Study of Education. University of Chicago Press, Chicago, 1944.
20. Terman, Lewis M., and Lima, Margaret. *Children's Reading.* Appleton-Century, New York, 1935.
21. Terman, Lewis M., and Merrill, Maud A. *Measuring Intelligence, A Guide to the Administration of the New Revised Stanford-Binet Tests of Intelligence.* Houghton, Boston, 1937.
22. Thorndike, R. L. *Children's Reading Interests. A Study Based on a Fictitious Annotated Title Questionnaire.* Bureau of Publications, Teachers College, Columbia University, New York, 1941.
23. Tryon, Caroline. *Evaluation of Adolescent Personality by Adolescents.* Monograph of the Society for Research in Child Development 4, No. 4. National Research Council, Washington, D.C., 1939.
24. Tryon, Caroline. "The Adolescent Peer Culture," *Adolescence,* Forty-third Yearbook, Part I, pp. 217-239, National Society for the Study of Education. University of Chicago Press, Chicago, 1944.

B. General References on Reading and Child Development

Almy, Millie C. *Ways of Studying Children: A Manual for Teachers.* Bureau of Publications, Teachers College, Columbia University, New York, 1959.

Anderson, J. E. "The Development of Spoken Language," *Child Development and the Curriculum,* Thirty-eighth Yearbook, Chap. 10, National Society for the Study of Education. Public School Publishing Company, Bloomington, Ill., 1939.

Anderson, J. E. "Principles of Growth and Maturity in Language," *Elementary English Review,* Vol. 18, pp. 250-254, 1942. Also *Education Digest,* Vol. 7, pp. 24-26, February, 1942.

BETTS, EMMETT A. *Foundations of Reading Instruction,* Part IV, especially Chap. 17. American Book, New York, 1957.

BRECKENRIDGE, M. E., and VINCENT, E. L. *Child Development,* 4th ed., especially Chaps. 6, 9, and 11. Saunders, Philadelphia, 1960.

BRUECKNER, L. J. "Language: The Development of Ability in Oral and Written Composition," *Child Development and the Curriculum,* Thirty-eighth Yearbook, Part I, Chap. 11, pp. 225-240, National Society for the Study of Education. Public School Publishing Company, Bloomington, Ill., 1939.

BURTON, WILLIAM H., and others. *Reading in Child Development.* Bobbs-Merrill, Indianapolis, Ind., 1956.

California State Department of Education. "The Child Development Approach to Curriculum," *Teachers' Guide to Education in Early Childhood,* Chap. 2. State Department, Sacramento, 1956.

Commission on the English Curriculum, "Child Development and Its Relationship to the Language Arts Program," *Language Arts for Today's Children,* Chap. 2. National Council of Teachers of English, Champaign, Ill., 1954.

DOLCH, E. W. "How Much Word Knowledge Do Children Bring to Grade One?" *Elementary English Review,* Vol. 13, pp. 177-183, May, 1936.

GATES, ARTHUR I. "Role of Personality Maladjustment in Reading Disability," *Pedagogical Seminary,* Vol. 59, pp. 77-83, September, 1941.

GESELL, ARNOLD, and ILG, FRANCES. *The Child from Five to Ten,* Chap. 18. Harper, New York, 1946.

GOODENOUGH, FLORENCE L. *Developmental Psychology,* 2nd ed., Chaps. 11, 13, 14. Appleton-Century, New York, 1945.

GORDON, I. J. *The Teacher as a Guidance Worker.* Harper, New York, 1956.

GRAY, WILLIAM S., ed. and comp. *Promoting Personal Social Development through Reading.* Supplementary Educational Monographs, No. 64. University of Chicago Press, Chicago, 1947.

GRAY, WILLIAM S. "Reading," *Child Development and the Curriculum,* Thirty-eighth Yearbook, Chap. 9, National Society for the Study of Education. Public School Publishing Company, Bloomington, Ill., 1939.

GRAY, WILLIAM S. *Reading and Pupil Development.* Supplementary Educational Monographs, No. 51. University of Chicago Press, Chicago, 1940.

HURLOCK, ELIZABETH. *Child Development,* 3rd ed., Chaps. 6, 11. McGraw-Hill, New York, 1956.

JERSILD, ARTHUR T. *Child Development and the Curriculum.* Bureau of Publications, Teachers College, Columbia University, New York, 1946.

JERSILD, ARTHUR T. *Child Psychology,* 4th ed., Chaps. 12, 13, 14. Prentice-Hall, Englewood Cliffs, N.J., 1954.

LA BRANT, L. "The Relations of Language and Speech Acquisition to Personality Development," in P. A. Witty and C. E. Skinner, eds., *Mental Hygiene in Modern Education,* Chap. 12, pp. 324-352. Farrar, New York, 1939.

LA BRANT, L. *A Study of Certain Language Developments of Children in Grades Four to Twelve Inclusive.* Genetic Psychology Monographs, Vol. 14, No. 5. 105 p. Clark University Press, Worcester, Mass., 1934.

LACEY, JOY. *Social Studies Concepts of Children in the First Three Grades.* Contributions to Education, No. 548. Teachers College, Columbia University, New York, 1932.

MCCARTHY, D. "Language Development in Children," in Leonard Carmichael, ed., *Manual of Child Psychology,* 2nd ed., Chap. 9. Wiley, New York, 1954.

MARTIN, WILLIAM E., and STENDLER, CELIA B. *Child Behavior and Development,* rev. ed., especially Chap. 15. Harcourt, Brace, New York, 1959.

MUNN, N. L. *Psychological Development: An Introduction to Genetic Psychology,* Chap. 12. Houghton, Boston, 1938.

Ohio State University, Faculty of University School. *How Children Develop.* Ohio State University, Columbus, 1946.

PRESCOTT, DANIEL A. *The Child in the Educational Process.* McGraw-Hill, New York, 1957.

RUSSELL, DAVID H., chm. *Child Development and the Language Arts.* Research Bulletin of National Conference on Research in English. National Council of Teachers of English, Champaign, Ill., 1953.

SAYLOR, J. GALEN, and ALEXANDER, WILLIAM M. "The Pupil as a Factor in Curriculum Planning," *Curriculum Planning,* Chap. 5. Rinehart, New York, 1954.

SMITH, DORA V., "Growth in Language Power as Related to Child Development," *Teaching Language in the Elementary School,* Forty-third Yearbook, Part II, Chap. 4, pp. 52-97, National Society for the Study of Education. University of Chicago Press, Chicago, 1944.

Chapter 4

PSYCHOLOGICAL BACKGROUNDS: THE READING PROCESS AND ITS IMPLICATIONS FOR INSTRUCTION

READING PROGRAM DETERMINED PARTLY BY THE READING ACT

Instruction in reading is determined in part by the nature of the act of reading. To guide children's learning of word recognition skills or meaning vocabulary or speed or comprehension in reading a teacher must know something of the processes involved in these activities. As suggested in Chapter 2, the character of the writing of the Chinese was determined in part by the brush and paper with which they worked. Similarly, improvement in reading must be based on the materials used and on ways of using them. A child's reading will be affected by his own physical equipment for reading, such as visual structure and control, the kinds of materials he uses, such as size of type and length of line, and by the conditions under which he reads, such as lighting and noise. Whatever we know about the eye and eye-movements helps set goals in reading speed, and what we know about materials may help control reading fatigue. An important question today concerns the best use of learning aids, whether they be books, films, filmstrips, tape recordings, or television programs. The reading act itself and the physical materials used in it are two of the important determinants of the nature of instruction in reading.

Chapters 1, 2, and 3 have pointed out other influences which shape a program of instruction in reading. For example, Chapter 1 stresses the importance of a literate, thoughtful citizenry if a democracy is to be strong and vigorous. Chapter 2 sketches the nature of language and the development of some of the tools of reading and writing. Chapter 3 emphasizes that most reading programs involve children and that they are therefore determined, in part at least, by the characteristics of children at different age levels. As stated above, the nature of reading instruction must be partly directed by the character of the process of reading itself and the materials involved in it.

The present chapter gives a few hints about the nature of the reading act and about reading materials and their implications for instruction. The psychology of reading is developed in a number of basic researches such as the classic study of Judd and Buswell[1] and the later group of three studies by Morse, Ballantine, and Dixon.[2] In recent years some of the most successful attempts to apply knowledge of the psychology of reading to reading instruction have been presented in volumes dealing with diagnosis and remediation of retarded readers.

Examples of such books are those by Blair,[3] by Bond and Tinker,[4] by Gates,[5] by Harris,[6] and by Robinson.[7] Somewhat more specialized volumes are that of Anderson and Dearborn[8] which concentrates on reading instruction in the primary grades and the volume by Carmichael and Dearborn[9] entitled *Reading and Visual Fatigue.* The availability of most of these volumes makes it unnecessary here to describe all the technical details of reading behavior. A complete description of the structure of the eye or some experiments on blinking as a measure of reading effectiveness, for example, may not seem close to the work of a third-grade teacher in developing smooth oral reading. One compilation of experimental studies in psychology, for example, has seven chapters of detailed reports dealing with visual and auditory perception and their physical basis.[10] Teachers cannot know all this background but they should be aware that a large body

[1] Charles H. Judd and Guy T. Buswell, *Silent Reading: A Study of the Various Types,* Supplementary Educational Monographs, No. 23. University of Chicago Press, Chicago, 1922.

[2] William C. Morse, Francis A. Ballantine, and W. Robert Dixon, *Studies in the Psychology of Reading.* Van Arlson, University of Michigan Press, Ann Arbor, 1951.

[3] Glenn M. Blair, *Diagnostic and Remedial Teaching.* Macmillan, New York, 1956.

[4] Guy L. Bond and Miles A. Tinker, *Reading Difficulties: Their Diagnosis and Correction.* Appleton-Century-Crofts, New York, 1957.

[5] Arthur I. Gates, *The Improvement of Reading,* 3rd ed. Macmillan, New York, 1947.

[6] Albert J. Harris, *How to Increase Reading Ability,* 3rd ed. Longmans, Green, New York, 1956.

[7] Helen M. Robinson, *Why Pupils Fail in Reading.* University of Chicago Press, Chicago, 1946.

[8] Irving H. Anderson and William F. Dearborn, *The Psychology of Teaching Reading.* Ronald, New York, 1952.

[9] Leonard Carmichael and William F. Dearborn, *Reading and Visual Fatigue.* Houghton Mifflin, Boston, 1947.

[10] S. S. Stevens, ed., *Handbook of Experimental Psychology.* Wiley, New York, 1951.

of basic research on the reading process is also available to the student. It is the purpose of this chapter only to give a brief summary of some of the well-known facts about reading behavior and materials.

ANALYSIS OF READING BEHAVIOR

Reading is a subtle and complex act. It involves, more or less simultaneously, the following: sensation of light rays on the retina of the eye reaching the brain, perception of separate words and phrases, functioning of the eye muscles with exact controls, immediate memory for what has just been read, remote memories based on the reader's experience, interest in the content read, and organization of the material so that finally it can be used in some way. These various features operate more or less concurrently; but they can be analyzed in at least four overlapping stages: sensation, perception, comprehension, and utilization.

Sensation

Sensation is unlearned. It is the first reaction to some stimulus in the environment involving some receptor of the organism which is equipped to respond, however fleetingly. The child does not learn to see or hear, although he must later learn the meaning of what he sees and hears. For example, the infant can see the word *calabash* or *Saskatchewan* in black ink on white paper before him or hear them spoken, but he doesn't see or hear a gourd or a province. The adult sees the word, the young child has only the sensation. Woodworth and Marquis[11] suggested that "when we speak of sensation we are thinking of stimuli and investigating the relationship of the individual's experiences to the various stimuli which reach his receptors." They pointed out that sensation is usually the first in a series of responses, followed by recognition and the utilization of the information so acquired.

From the point of view of reading, accordingly, sensation is important in terms of the structure of the eye and of the stimuli in the immediate environment. In regard to eye structure and functioning, research workers have achieved little agreement in different studies as to the importance of such visual functions as visual acuity, refractive errors, binocular co-ordination, fusion, and size of visual fields

[11] Robert S. Woodworth and Donald G. Marquis, *Psychology*, 5th ed., p. 439. Holt, New York, 1947.

in relation to reading achievement.[12] Stimuli involve questions of readability in terms of the physical factors needed, such as strength of illumination, size and variety of type, length of line, type of paper used, and quality and amount of picture material included. Research data on these topics have been summarized by Luckiesh and Moss,[13] by Paterson and Tinker,[14] and by others.

Proper conditions for reading involve good posture, proper illumination, acceptable physical format for the printed materials, and occasional rest periods. Neglect of any of these may result in eyestrain, fatigue, and less efficient reading. In regard to posture, reading material should be held in the lower half of the field of vision, about fifteen to eighteen inches from the eyes. The material should be centered directly in front of the eyes, the left edge should not be tilted above or below the right edge, and correct posture should contribute to these conditions. Reading in bed, for example, may disturb some of them. If a person is reading steadily, the eyes should be rested briefly by looking at some distant object approximately every fifteen minutes.[15]

Proper illumination requires sufficient light without glare. The standard of measurement is the foot-candle, the light cast by a source of one candle power one foot away. Most plain hundred-watt electric bulbs give an illumination of one hundred foot-candles one foot away, twenty-five foot-candles two feet away, and about eleven foot-candles three feet away. The eyes are capable of adjusting to wide differences in illumination, but reading ordinarily requires between fifteen and twenty foot-candles for efficient work and may need much higher intensity for detailed or prolonged work. The intensity of illumination may be measured on the principle of the photoelectric cell by a very simple device usually called a light-meter or sight meter. (See page 101.) The glare of strong, direct light on a page, reflection from a glossy page, and strong contrasts in illumination within a room should be avoided.

[12] Lois B. Bing, "A Critical Analysis of the Literature on Certain Visual Functions Which Seem to be Related to Reading Achievement," *Journal of the American Optometric Association,* Vol. 22, pp. 454-463, March, 1951. William H. Edson, Guy L. Bond, and Walter W. Cook, "Relationships Between Visual Characteristics and Specific Silent Reading Abilities," *Journal of Educational Research,* Vol. 46, pp. 451-457, February, 1953.

[13] Matthew Luckiesh and Frank K. Moss, *Reading as a Visual Task.* Van Nostrand, Princeton, N.J., 1942.

[14] Donald G. Paterson and Miles A. Tinker, *How to Make Type Readable.* Harper, New York, 1940.

[15] Conrad Berens, *The Eye and Its Diseases,* pp. 1163-1171. Saunders, Philadelphia, 1936.

The best physical format for printed materials has been studied by publishers and research workers. The quality and color of the paper used, the form, size, and spacing of type, the arrangement of the text on the page, and the quantity and quality of pictures and

The light meter (General Electric Company)

other illustrations are involved. The best paper is white with a little tinge of gray or cream in it. Type should be simple and clear. Its size is measured in terms of the "point," which is about one seventy-second of an inch. Adults do their best reading with ten- or twelve-point type; children beginning to read find less strain in reading fourteen- to eighteen-point type. Reading is made easy by increasing space between lines through "leading" or inserting thin strips of metal between lines. The typography of this book has been designed for ease of reading. The lines are four and one-half inches long. The text type is 11 point Baskerville, leaded 2 points, with footnotes in 8 point. The sample on page 102 is suitable for the first grade. It is 18 point Century Schoolbook, leaded with 12 points.

Since most books and other printed materials used in the elementary school have been carefully checked for these physical features, the chief duty of the teacher is to observe whether or not the classroom is properly lighted, say on winter afternoons, and whether the pupils observe hygienic conditions such as good posture and avoidance of direct sunlight when they read. She should verify an illumination of at least twenty foot-candles, as measured by a light-meter, and take steps to increase natural or artificial illumination if needed. The teacher should also be alert for signs of eyestrain, such as much

Mother said, "Come and look.
This is something Pony wants.
Look and see, Susan."

"Look, Tom, look!" said Susan.
"Here is something red.
Here is something big and red."

Sample of part of preprimer page (*My Little Blue Story Book,* rev. ed., p. 27. Ginn, Boston, 1956)

blinking, watering eyes, frequent headaches, and books held in an unusual position. Children with such symptoms must be referred to the school physician or some other competent diagnostician.

Perception

Perception, like sensation, is partly unlearned, but it is very susceptible to the influence of learning. The figure or pattern of words seen among other stimuli is unlearned, but what the figure or pattern means is learned. Children perceive the peculiar form or shapes that make up a word pattern, and learn that a particular word is *Tom* and not *Nancy* or *Bob*. They learn to direct their attention to certain parts of words or phrases that are most valuable as cues, to integrate these, and to cut down close attention to unimportant parts. Adults reading such a sentence as "A large black crow sat on the old wood fence" may see it as "A . . . crow . . . sat . . . fence."

The integrative act of word perception in which certain blends of sensation are combined to give a "percept" of a meaningful unit of language is possible because of rather complicated eye movements. These are discussed in the sources quoted above and in the research literature of Buswell,[16] Gilbert,[17] Tinker,[18] and others. The eye movements of second and sixth grade pupils as recorded on film are shown on page 104. The vertical lines indicate the time the eyes are not moving (fixations), and the horizontal or diagonal lines represent movements across the page and return movements to a new line. The following terms help to describe the total process of eye movements in reading:

1. Number of fixations per line—good adult reader three to five, poor child reader nine to fifteen.
2. Number of regressions (backward movements) per line—good adult one every three or four lines, poor child three per line.
3. Return sweeps to next line—left-to-right diagonal sweep to a fixation at beginning of next line.
4. Average length of fixations when words are seen—one-eighth to one-quarter second.
5. Interfixation movement during which vision blurs—one twenty-fifth of a second each; only about 6 per cent of total time of reading is spent in movement.
6. Reading span—distance between two fixations—good reader thirteen or fourteen spaces, poor reader six spaces.
7. Rhythmic movements—the two eyes working together in a regular pattern line after line. Rhythm is broken by irregular fixations and by regressions.

Eye movements depend upon the general reading ability of the subject, his purpose in reading, and the difficulty of the material.

In addition, Morse[19] has stressed the wide individual differences found in eye movements which seem to be the result not so much of

[16] Guy T. Buswell, *Fundamental Reading Habits: A Study of Their Development,* Supplementary Educational Monographs, No. 21. Department of Education, University of Chicago, Chicago, 1922.

[17] Luther C. Gilbert and Doris W. Gilbert, "Reading before the Eye-Movement Camera versus Reading Away from It," *Elementary School Journal,* Vol. 42, pp. 443-447, February, 1942.

[18] Miles A. Tinker and Donald G. Paterson, "Effect of Typographical Variations upon Eye Movements in Reading," *Journal of Educational Research,* Vol. 49, pp. 171-184, November, 1955.

[19] Morse, *op. cit.*

the difficulty of the passage read or the general maturity of the child (fifth grade versus seventh grade) but of some other unexplained, individual factor. Morse believed that individual variations in reading the same passage are more important than differences between

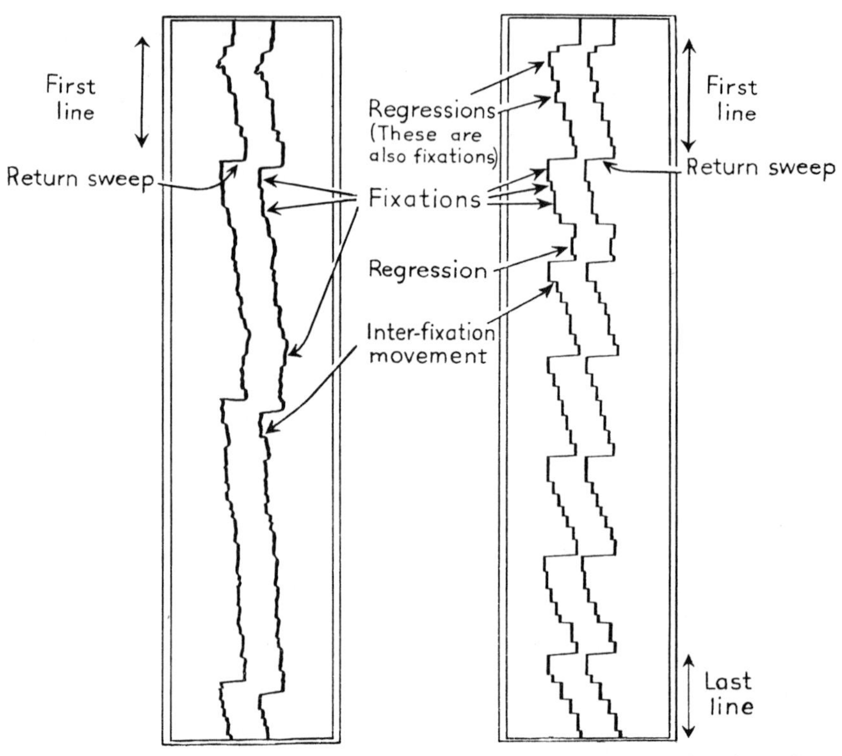

Eye movements of typical second and sixth grade pupils (American Optical Company)

passages, and that the most efficient eye movements are not necessarily identical with the highest comprehension. In general, poor eye movements should be regarded as symptoms rather than causes of poor reading. If a teacher notes poor eye movements she should look for causes in the pupil's early training, in the size of his sight vocabulary, in his ability to work out new words, and possibly in the physical structure of the eye. The last factor requires, of course, an examination by a well-trained physician. In general, practicing eye movements is not a particularly effective way of improving general reading.

A number of studies of word perception[20] suggest how word recognition takes place in reading. The first step seems to be observation of the whole word or phrase in terms of general shape, or configuration. The arrangement of the consonants determines the general shape and serves as a primary perception clue. The length of the word is important for whole-word recognition. Perception clues of the beginning and end of words, and especially the beginning, are more important than those in the middle of words. The relation of the word to the rest of the sentence or paragraph, the context clue, helps to determine recognition. When the general shape of the word fails to bring recognition and when the context clue is vague, the reader may resort to some form of word analysis. He will probably first attempt to break the word into major units such as *auto-mobile* or *select-man*. The next step may involve sounding the first letter, or dividing into syllables, or attempting phonetic analysis, depending upon previous teaching methods and practice. Such analysis must be followed by synthesis of the word parts.

The child's recognition of a word is accordingly a combination of perception on the one hand and verbal learning and language behavior on the other. Postman and Rosenzweig[21] have shown that familiarity, as determined by frequency of usage, is a major determinant for older students of the ease of recognition in hearing as well as in vision. They point out that word frequencies as determined by a scientifically prepared word list indicate the practice of the population as a whole, not of the specific individual. They suggest that responses to auditory stimulation tend to be in larger units than response to visual stimulation and finally that, with increasing familiarity of a word or phrase, the individual tends to use reduced cues (some letters rather than all letters) in word recognition. This does

[20] Curt Berger, "Grouping, Number and Spacing of Letters as Determinants of Word Recognition," *Journal of General Psychology,* Vol. 55, pp. 215-228, October, 1956. Arthur I. Gates, "Implications of the Psychology of Perception for Word Study," *Education,* Vol. 75, pp. 589-595, May, 1955. Jean T. Goins, *Visual Perceptual Abilities and Early Reading Progress,* Supplementary Educational Monographs, No. 87. University of Chicago Press, Chicago, 1958. Robert E. Mills, "Evaluation of Techniques for Teaching Word Recognition," *Elementary School Journal,* Vol. 56, pp. 221-225, January, 1956. Arthur V. Olson, "Growth in Word Perception Abilities as it Relates to Success in Beginning Reading," *Journal of Education,* Vol. 140, pp. 25-36, February, 1958. Muriel C. Potter, *Perception of Symbol Orientation and Early Reading Success,* Contributions to Education, No. 939. Teachers College, Columbia University, New York, 1949. Magdalen D. Vernon, *Backwardness in Reading: A Study of its Nature and Origin.* Cambridge University Press, New York, 1957.

[21] Leo Postman and Mark R. Rosenzweig, "Perceptual Recognition of Words," *Journal of Speech and Hearing Disorders,* Vol. 22, pp. 245-253, June, 1957.

not mean, however, that children necessarily rely on individual or dominant letters in words. As Buswell[22] has noted, work with tachistoscopes (devices for timed presentation of words on a screen) and eye-movement cameras has shown that large words are recognized as wholes and that the span of recognition may be two or more words. The greater efficiency of silent reading has been clearly demonstrated in terms of such factors as number of fixations per line and duration of fixations. This realization resulted in less oral work and more emphasis on silent reading in the decade 1915-1925.

Finally, the evidence is clear from the studies quoted and others that words familiar in meaning are learned more readily than unfamiliar words. Frequent observation of a word does little good unless meaning is attached to it.

Recognition literally means *knowing again,* and previous experience must be associated with a word or phrase before retention is complete. This association is considered in the next step of comprehension.

Comprehension

Comprehension carries the understanding of a word or phrase beyond recognition to the understanding of the meaning intended by the author. Building such an understanding is not simple; sometimes the author is not clear, and authors and speakers can twist the meanings of words around to suit their own purposes. Sometimes the reader has no background to project into the situation presented by the author. Comprehension is such an essential part of the reading process that it is considered more fully in Chapter 9, on "Vocabulary Building," Chapter 11, on "Work-Type Reading," and in various other parts of this book.

Comprehension is usually described as being largely a central process, or an activity of the brain closely related to intelligence or mental maturity. As early as 1917, Thorndike[23] wrote of "reading as reasoning." His analysis of errors made by children in reading a fairly simple paragraph showed that comprehension involved the same sort of "organization and analytic action of ideas as occurs in thinking of supposedly higher sorts." In this classic study, he also

22 Guy T. Buswell, "Perceptual Research and Methods of Learning," *Scientific Monthly,* Vol. 64, pp. 521-526, June, 1947.

23 Edward L. Thorndike, "Reading as Reasoning: A Study of Mistakes in Paragraph Reading," *Journal of Educational Research,* Vol. 8, pp. 323-332, June, 1917.

stressed the importance of set or purpose in comprehension and of the influence of certain dominant words on the meanings derived by children. In 1922 Judd and Buswell[24] also found that the eye movements of the reader were affected by his purposes in reading various materials. In a later study Larsen and Feder[25] found that it makes little difference whether material is presented orally or visually, although most people prefer a visual presentation. They concluded that comprehension is largely a centrally determined function operating independently of the mode of presentation of material, and they said, "Reading seems to be largely language or thought activity." It is still true, however, that intelligence, or mental maturity, is only one factor in comprehension. Correlations between reading tests measuring different types of comprehension in different curricular areas often correlate only .20 or .30. In a study of ninth-grade reading, Bond[26] found negative relationships between tests of reading comprehension in history and in science. In each case the same brains were at work, but the comprehension scores differed markedly because of the past experiences and other abilities of the pupils. Intelligence is important in comprehension, but it is not the whole story.

Most teachers are aware that comprehension operates on different levels. The simplest level is very close to perception. It is an identification of the symbol or idea in its primary, literal sense. Somewhat deeper comprehension involves memory: the idea is compared and associated with similar ideas. Out of some relating and classifying activities the child goes on to generalize. He develops a concept, or generalized understanding, of a word or statement. At first the concepts are rather meager; with experience they take on added meaning. The young prairie child's first concept of *boat* probably involves a limited number of toys in his own home. By the time he finishes elementary school he knows something about many types of boats, their development in early times from simple logs, their place in transportation today, house boats, junks, yachts, and clippers. Another child who lives near a busy harbor will probably have more accurate and broader concepts of boats. In other words, any child's

24 Judd and Buswell, *op. cit.*

25 Robert P. Larsen and Daniel D. Feder, "Common and Differential Factors in Reading and Hearing Comprehension," *Journal of Educational Psychology*, Vol. 31, pp. 241-252, April, 1940.

26 Eva Bond, *Reading and Ninth Grade Achievement*, Contributions to Education, No. 756. Bureau of Publications, Teachers College, Columbia University, New York, 1938.

concept of boats may be enriched by both concrete and verbal experiences.

Finally, comprehension of a statement about boats or a selection on any other topic can be on the level of interpretation and judgment. The child is now disposed to think over the statement, to compare it with previous related experiences, and to come to some decision about its truth or value. If he reads a statement "Boats are a better means of transportation than trains," he may see reasons both for and against the statement. The possibilities of comprehension here are practically unlimited. In the elementary school such comprehension cannot be fully matured, but sound foundations for it can be laid.

The child learning about *boats* illustrates partly what research workers down through the years have attempted to analyze in comprehension. Some of these attempts have been outlined in a historical setting by Gray.[27] After the findings of Judd and Buswell of the effect of purpose on the reading process, teachers and research workers during the twenties and thirties tried to identify, to test for, and to improve various types of comprehension such as getting the main idea, noting specific details, and following a sequence of ideas or events. In 1943 Artley[28] showed that most comprehension tests were concerned with some form of fact-getting rather than interpretive or critical abilities. Similarly, most teachers find it easier in a reading lesson to ask questions like "Where did they go?" or "What was the color of Mary's dress?" rather than "Was this the right thing to do?" or "Why was Mary the kind of a girl you would like to have for a friend?" At about the same time Bell[29] showed that a group of Scottish fifteen-year-olds found comprehension questions to range from easy to difficult in the following order:

1. Questions of direct reference—answers found in the text in the same words.
2. Questions of indirect reference—answers found in the text in slightly different words.

[27] William S. Gray, "New Approaches to the Study of Interpretation in Reading," *Journal of Educational Research,* Vol. 52, pp. 65-67, October, 1958.

[28] A. Sterl Artley, "The Appraisal of Reading Comprehension," *Journal of Educational Psychology,* Vol. 34, pp. 55-60, January, 1943.

[29] H. Bell, "Comprehension in Silent Reading," *British Journal of Educational Psychology,* Vol. 12, pp. 47-55, February, 1942.

3. Easy inferences—not directly stated in the text but could be inferred easily.
4. Use of qualifying phrases—when grasp of a passage depended upon such phrases as *largely, alone, chief, only,* and *full.*
5. Difficult inferences—deriving ideas not found in the passage through various forms of relational thinking.

From the 1930's onward a large number of studies of reading comprehension have also been concerned with factors related to comprehension. Most of these show that general intelligence (especially if measured by a verbal test) and size of vocabulary are closely related to most reading comprehensions. Many other factors also correlate positively with various comprehension tests[30]. McCullough[31] has also shown the positive relationships, at the second- and fourth-grade levels, among tests of main idea, facts or details, sequence, and the more "creative reading" of drawing conclusions, passing judgments, and seeing relationships. Correlations among these tests ranged from .26 to .63 with a median of .47.

Such work on specific comprehensions led to the attempt to analyze such abilities more sharply through the statistical technique of factor analysis. For example, from a variety of sub-tests, Davis[32] believed that he identified factors of "knowledge of word meaning," "ability to reason," "ability to identify the writer's intent," "ability to grasp the detailed statements in a passage," and "knowledge of literary devices and techniques." Using another method of analysis on the same data, however, Thurstone[33] found only one common factor in the tests, which he simply called reading ability. The results of factor analysis are necessarily limited by the nature of the tests used, and it should be added that Thurstone wrote of the need of further evidence about "the components of the complex that we call reading ability."

For example, the complexity of comprehension at the teachers'

30 Lyman B. Hunt, "Can We Measure Specific Factors Associated with Reading Comprehension?" *Journal of Educational Research,* Vol. 51, pp. 161-172, November, 1957.

31 Constance M. McCullough, "Responses of Elementary School Children to Common Types of Reading Comprehensions," *Journal of Educational Research,* Vol. 51, pp. 65-70, September, 1957.

32 Frederick B. Davis, "Fundamental Factors of Comprehension in Reading," *Psychometrika,* Vol. 9, pp. 185-197, September, 1944.

33 L. L. Thurstone, "Note on a Reanalysis of Davis' Reading Tests," *Psychometrika,* Vol. 11, pp. 185-188, September, 1946.

college level was illustrated by Black[34] who combined subjective and objective measures and found such difficulties in reading prose as (1) failure to understand the writer's intention; (2) failure to detect irony; (3) vocabulary; (4) difficult allusions; (5) inadequate background of information; (6) failure to use context clues; and (7) the reader's preconceptions. Probably most of these factors also operate, often in combination, at the elementary and secondary school level.

More recently in the study of comprehension there has been a return to the method used by Thorndike of analyzing pupils' verbal and written responses while engaged in reading. For example, Piekarz[35] analyzed responses of sixth-grade pupils which showed that the type of comprehension used by a reader depends upon his competence. The better readers made a greater number and variety of responses fairly equally divided into literal meanings, implied meanings, and evaluations. The poorer readers confined their answers largely to literal meanings. The good readers tended to be objective in their interpretations, but the poorer readers were more personal and emotional in their responses.

Both early and recent research suggests, therefore, that reading comprehension is a complex of various abilities. Teachers cannot work on it for two or three weeks and then leave it for the rest of the year. In the primary grades continuous attention must be given to literal understanding of main ideas, specific facts, and sequence. Some primary children and most intermediate children are ready to go beyond these to other literal interpretation, such as following directions or describing persons and events. All must be helped also to go beyond literal interpretation to critical judgment and "reading between the lines" to develop new ideas. Teaching these aspects of reading is considered more fully in Chapter 14.

Utilization

Utilization is usually the final phase of the reading act from the pupil's and the teacher's point of view. It comes in making use of what one reads. Not all teachers and psychologists care to include this phase of reading in a description of the reading act. It seems difficult, however, to separate some final activity from comprehension as such.

[34] E. L. Black, "The Difficulties of Training College Students in Understanding What They Read," *British Journal of Educational Psychology*, Vol. 24, pp. 17-31, February, 1954.

[35] Josephine A. Piekarz, "Getting Meaning from Reading," *Elementary School Journal*, Vol. 56, pp. 303-309, March, 1956.

In work-type reading a pupil or adult is reading in order that he may carry out some project which seems of value to him. Even in recreational reading he is doing something: continuing to laugh or enjoy, noting parts of the story that can be told to others, thinking of a similar adventure that happened or might happen to himself, or reading more rapidly to discover the climax. The variety of activities that grow out of reading, both in and out of school, suggests that utilization is an essential part of most reading.

The inclusion of thinking and doing in the reading act does not mean that they originate only in reading. Obviously thinking and doing may follow listening, observing, participating in construction, seeing movies, and other activities. Other school activities, such as arithmetic, social studies, art, and music, may be equally important bases for thinking and doing. Kindergarten and first-grade children are often busy thinking and doing without reading as a stimulus to their activity. At a later stage, however, their activities become more varied, partly at least because they are stimulated by reading; and at all grade levels reading is one of the widest possible stimuli to thinking.

Using what one is reading must be regarded as the high point of the reading act. Into such use come the processes of memory, reasoning, and judgment, in which past experience is called upon to round out the reading activity. From the first, children use reading naturally and easily. They may follow a simple direction from the teacher, written on the blackboard, such as "Color the apple red." When they laugh at the first line of the jingle "I never saw a purple cow," they are using past experience in one interpretation of what they read. When they follow instructions for making a map or sketching a medieval costume, there is no sharp break between the perception, comprehension, and utilization of the material. When they are discussing or critically evaluating the material read, they are engaging in the final creative aspects of the reading process. Teachers cannot be content with developing factual readers.

One article[36] has suggested that the thinking that goes on in a reading lesson may exist on at least four levels. If a teacher or group is tired or if the material is dull it may only function at the first level. If conditions are right it may occasionally operate at the third or fourth levels. Here is what children, under teacher guidance, may do:

[36] David H. Russell, "The Child's Reading and Thinking," *Chicago Schools Journal*, Vol. 36, pp. 105-108, January-February, 1955.

1. Talk over details given and the relationships between them as stated in the printed page.
2. Express personal feelings about the individual's behavior or statements in a story or factual selection.
3. Give illustrations and analogies from their personal experiences which support or criticize conclusions about what happened and why.
4. Make inferences concerning the events of the story in terms of either cause or effect, with special reference to the human motivations involved.

The discussion of comprehension and utilization suggests that reading never can be taught as mere recognition of words or even ideas. Rather it is regarded as a thoughtful process of adding to one's experience. Children cannot rely upon concrete, first-hand experiences for all the information they need in working on a problem or for evidence on a controversial issue. They cannot always be within the sound of a parent's or teacher's voice telling them what to do. As they grow in general independence they normally use reading as a guide to action more than ever before. Accordingly, the reading program will emphasize their careful comprehension, thoughtful interpretation, and planned execution of the ideas with which they are dealing. Teachers can help children to:

Think before reading
Think while reading
Think after reading
Think beyond reading

The Effects of Reading

Although most teachers do not include a consideration of the effects of reading among their conscious aims, even a brief account of the psychology of reading should include this topic. One reason teachers do not emphasize this phase of the reading act is that its psychology has been largely neglected. We have hundreds of good studies of eye movements and instructional methods but little solid data on what reading does to boys and girls. In an age of movies, easy travel, and television we need to know the personal values in reading for children and youth, not the joys of the literary critic nor the values, if any, of the comic book, but the intrinsic worth of reading for each person in a group or class. These rewards may come to the group reading a good story in a basal text or to the child reading individually in his library book.[37]

The meager research about the impact of reading on the individual has been summarized in terms of (1) the characteristics of the material read; (2) the content of ideas communicated; (3) the traits of the person reading; and (4) the overt responses that may be made.[38] Put another way, some children in a class will respond enthusiastically to a story read by themselves or the teacher but others will be uninterested in that particular type of story. Second, to get at the important ideas in a story or passage, teacher and pupils must then go below the surface or superficial aspects of a story to get at underlying themes and values, such as the meaning of courage or the "right thing" to do. Third, responses to a story will depend upon the needs and personality characteristics of the person reading. A child in an unhappy, broken family situation may reject a story of happy family life. Fourth, children, and especially young children, may be encouraged to interpret the meaning of a story in dramatization, conversation, drawing, and other activities. In the elementary school the teacher can help draw out overt physical, verbal, musical and other responses.

In regard to the characteristics of the reader, Crossen[39] has shown that attitudes affect critical judgment while reading. The more intense the feeling of the reader, the greater the barrier to accurate interpretation. Similarly Groff,[40] in a study of fifth- and sixth-graders, found that their attitude toward certain specific types of material was related to critical reading abilities. There were differences between boys and girls in their attitude toward, and critical reading of, materials in such areas as sports, airplanes, and interpersonal relationships. As a result of a study of the responses of an eighth-grade class to books and stories, Taba[41] believed that children at this level may be divided into four types of readers: (a) those who enter into a story freely and fully without generalizing about it; (b) egocentric readers

[37] David H. Russell, "Personal Values in Reading," *The Reading Teacher,* Vol. 12, pp. 3-9, October, 1958.

[38] David H. Russell, "Some Research on the Impact of Reading," *The English Journal,* Vol. 47, pp. 398-413, October, 1958.

[39] Helen J. Crossen, "Effects of the Attitudes of the Reader upon Critical Reading Ability," *Journal of Educational Research,* Vol. 42, pp. 289-298, December, 1948.

[40] Patrick J. Groff, *Children's Attitudes Toward Reading and Their Critical Reading Abilities in Four Content-Type Materials.* Unpublished doctoral dissertation, University of California, Berkeley, 1955.

[41] Hilda Taba, *With Perspective on Human Relations: A Study of Peer Group Dynamics in the Eighth Grade.* American Council on Education, Washington, D.C., 1955.

who find meaning only in light of their own experience; (c) egocentric readers who make prescriptive judgments about story characters; and (d) readers who project and generalize and thus find new experiences in their reading. Such types are probably overlapping.

A few studies in the fourth area of overt responses to reading suggest the wide variety of activities evoked by the printed page. For example, Boyd and Mandler[42] studied the responses of eight- and nine-year-olds to stories and pictures of people and animals. They found that (a) stories with human characters elicit more personal identification and involvement than animal stories; (b) socially disapproved behavior elicits demands for punishment and socially approved behavior stimulates more projection of the self; and (c) socially disapproved behavior in human beings may arouse anxiety in the young child. Squire[43] made a careful study of reactions of fourteen- and sixteen-year-olds to four short stories with themes of personal development. He found a wide variety of responses to the same story. By coding over fourteen thousand response statements, he found the most frequent reaction was one of interpretation, followed in decreasing order of frequency by narrational, associational, and self-involvement comments, and literary and prescriptive judgments. Similarly, Loban[44] found that adolescents rated as most sensitive have the most to say about a story, while those rated as less sensitive tend to attach blame to someone in the story. He felt that many young people by themselves miss important implications in stories and tend to respond with superficial concepts. This and other research suggests the importance of leading children to thoughtful consideration of ideas, character, and values without imposing on their varied judgments a single "right" answer which may be the teacher's best analysis, but which in turn might not be accepted as final or best by other adults.

This brief discussion of the effects of reading on children relates closely to their motivation for reading. As stated earlier, the aim of reading instruction is not only to have children read skillfully but to develop individuals who love to read. In competition with the

[42] Nancy A. Boyd and G. Mandler, "Children's Responses to Human and Animal Stories and Pictures," *Journal of Consulting Psychology*, Vol. 19, pp. 367-371, October, 1955.

[43] James R. Squire, *The Responses of Adolescents to Literature Involving Selected Experiences of Personal Development*. Unpublishd doctoral dissertation, University of California, Berkeley, 1956.

[44] Walter Loban, *Literature and Social Sensitivity*. National Council of Teachers of English, Champaign, Ill., 1954.

many distractions of modern life, reading will persist in a child's or youth's behavior patterns only as it is useful to him and as it helps him fill some basic needs, whether for recreation, for mental stimulus, or for answers to personal problems. Although the research is sparse to guide them, many teachers can gain some knowledge of the impact of a story or book on an individual child. Such knowledge will help suggest other stories for the child and other children who may profit from reading the same story. Thus the teacher is intelligently matching child and book.

OTHER ANALYSES OF READING

The description of reading in the above section in terms of sensation, perception, comprehension, utilization, and effect is only one of the possible ways of analyzing reading behavior. For example, Thorndike's classic study[45] emphasized reading as reasoning, as a process of continuous evaluation of the relative importance and interrelation between words, phrases, and sentences as one reads.

In a later discussion Betts[46] suggested that reading may be viewed in at least four ways. "Reading is a language process rather than a subject. In a psychological sense, reading is a thinking process. In another sense, reading is a 'social process' that 'relates the reader to his environment and conditions that relationship.' Psychophysiological factors, such as seeing and hearing, also are embraced by an adequate concept of reading as a process." Of all these processes Betts emphasizes most the idea of evaluation, or "of reconstructing the facts behind the symbols."

In a study by factorial analysis of reading abilities at the college-freshman level, Langsam[47] identified four factors in reading ability: (1) a verbal factor relating to ideas and to meanings of words, (2) a perceptual factor involved in rapid observation and selection of the correct words from among other words, (3) a word factor of fluency in dealing with words rather than vocabulary as in (1), and (4) a factor tentatively named as seeing relationships. The factorial analyses, based on test results, must be regarded as fairly good guesses of what is involved in the process of reading.

45 Thorndike, *op. cit.*

46 Emmett A. Betts, *Foundations of Reading Instruction*. American Book, New York, 1946.

47 Rosalind S. Langsam, "A Factorial Analysis of Reading Ability," *Journal of Experimental Education*, Vol. 10, pp. 57-63, September, 1941.

In another type of study of the reading of college students which has implications for the elementary school, Robinson and Hall[48] found that reading in the different subject fields of art, fiction, geology, and history is not highly related even when selections are written under one editorship (in an encyclopedia intended for school use), but that reading different topics in the same field (history) is quite consistent. They believe that the lowest level of reading ability is the same word-by-word method for all reading, that a second level (achieved by most adults) is adjustment of speed to comprehension-difficulty level, and that a third level appears in the reading of fiction by using earlier parts of a story to facilitate comprehension of later parts of the story.

In one of the most complete analyses of reading ability from items mentioned in the literature Burkart[49] found 214 reading abilities. These were grouped and ranked for importance by specialists in reading. The results giving the rank order of importance of eighteen of these groups of abilities are given on page 117. This list of abilities is obviously overlapping. The placement of some items, such as putting comprehension under observation, may be questioned. However, the article gives a definite impression of the large number of abilities included in the complex act of reading.

A more inclusive point of view about reading than is usual, and a more comprehensive definition than used in this volume, are expressed by Spencer[50] in some of the Claremont Reading Conferences. He said that "Reading is performed whenever one experiences sensory stimulation. . . . Consequently we may treat of reading which is visual, or aural, or tactile, gustatory, olfactory, thermal, kinesthetic, etc. as regards the sensory basis." Accordingly, reading cannot be confined to printed materials and involves use of such sensory cues as those of social situations, the "sign language" of trainmen, the gestures of the orchestra conductor, movies, rocks, and plants.

In his definition Spencer equated reading with observation and interpretation of the sensations received. The definition has some value in emphasizing the fact that much learning is nonverbal learn-

48 Francis P. Robinson and Prudence Hall, "Studies of Higher Level Reading Abilities," *Journal of Educational Psychology,* Vol. 32, pp. 241-252, April, 1941.

49 Kathryn H. Burkart, "An Analysis of Reading Abilities," *Journal of Educational Research,* Vol. 38, pp. 430-439, February, 1945.

50 Peter L. Spencer, "The Reading Process and Types of Reading," *Claremont College Reading Conference,* Eleventh Yearbook, pp. 17-22, Claremont College Library, Claremont, Calif., 1946.

ing and that, particularly for slow-learning students, the school has a responsibility for providing a wide variety of stimuli to learning. Spencer explores the various reading patterns—social, aural, tactile, etc. Whether or not one accepts his definition of reading, there is no question about the value of further studies in these areas. Since the

RANK ORDER OF MAJOR READING ABILITIES CONSTITUTING THE GENERIC READING ABILITIES (FROM BURKART)

ABILITY	RANK ORDER
I. Observation	
A. Visual ability	6
B. Auditory ability	18
C. Comprehension	2
D. Speed	4
E. Attention	1
F. Reproduction	3
G. Perception	14
II. Research abilities	
A. Ability to locate data	12
B. Ability to select data	7
C. Ability to organize data	11
D. Ability to be stimulated creatively	13
III. Vocabulary abilities	
A. Ability to acquire increased vocabulary	5
B. Phonic abilities	15
C. Ability to "unlock" words	8
IV. Aesthetic abilities	
A. Emotional appreciation	9
B. Literary appreciation	17
V. Hygienic abilities	16
VI. Oral reading abilities	10

field of reading is already rather complex, and since most schools conceive of reading as work with printed materials, that viewpoint is taken in this book.

Recent research has made more specific analysis of the abilities which make up reading and other abilities which are positively related to reading achievement. In summary, the work of Goins[51] and

[51] Jean T. Goins, *Visual Perceptual Abilities and Reading Progress.* University of Chicago Press, Chicago, 1957.

of Freeburne[52] are examples of studies which emphasize the importance of visual perception in beginning readers and older students. Durrell[53] and his colleagues stress the significance of auditory perception in beginning reading and for remedial cases, although there is some doubt that this ability is as important for average pupils of the fourth grade and later as it is for younger children.[54] Such writers as Chall,[55] Burks,[56] Raymond,[57] and Sheldon[58] have shown, respectively, the relationships of reading to previous knowledge, intelligence scores, memory span and associative learning, and characteristics of the home. Holmes[59] has attempted to account for underlying factors affecting reading by his "substrata-factor theory" which provides an orderly arrangement of causal factors both of speed and power in reading. At the first depth Holmes found that such perceptual factors as word discrimination, word sense, and span of recognition contribute 56 per cent of the variance in speed and power of reading. Such factors as vocabulary-in-context, intelligence, and understanding of verbal relationships contribute 77 per cent of the variance found in power of reading. The analysis then goes on to underlying abilities contributing to each of these factors. For example, the factor of word sense which partly determines speed of reading is itself affected by phonetic association, vocabulary-in-context, and span of recognition. Further work on patterns of relationships may reveal more about the reading process but, at the present stage, the study again shows "the complex interrelated causal framework which affects the reading ability of an individual."

[52] C. M. Freeburne, "Influence of Training in Perceptual Span and Perceptual Speed," *Journal of Educational Psychology,* Vol. 40, pp. 321-352, October, 1949.

[53] Donald D. Durrell and Helen A. Murphy, "The Auditory Discrimination Factor in Reading Readiness and Reading Disability," *Education,* Vol. 73, pp. 556-560, May, 1953.

[54] Maynard C. Reynolds, "Study of the Relationships between Auditory Characteristics and Specific Silent Reading Abilities," *Journal of Educational Research,* Vol. 46, pp. 439-449, February, 1953.

[55] Jeanne S. Chall, "Influence of Previous Knowledge on Reading Ability," *Educational Research Bulletin,* Vol. 26, pp. 225-230, December, 1947.

[56] H. F. Burks and P. Bruce, "Characteristics of Good and Poor Readers as Disclosed by the Wechsler Intelligence Scale for Children," *Journal of Educational Psychology,* Vol. 46, pp. 488-493, December, 1955.

[57] Dorothy M. Raymond, "Performance of Reading Achievers on Memory Span and Associative Learning Tests," *Journal of Educational Research,* Vol. 48, pp. 455-465, February, 1955.

[58] William D. Sheldon and Warren G. Cutts, "Relation of Parents, Home and Certain Developmental Characteristics to Children's Reading Ability," *Elementary School Journal,* Vol. 53, pp. 517-521, May, 1953.

[59] Jack A. Holmes, *The Substrata-Factor Theory of Reading.* California Book, Berkeley, 1953.

The results of many research workers, and the analysis in the early part of this chapter indicate that reading is not a simple ability. Because of the complexity of the process, teachers, parents, and administrators are warned against early pressure on the young child to learn to read and against expectation of rapid progress in early grades. Teachers and other curriculum workers cannot fail to be impressed with the need of reading instruction throughout the whole school. In view of the nature of the process it may be called a modern miracle that children learn to read as easily and as well as they do in the primary grades of a good, modern school.

TYPES OF READING

The reading act may be described not only through a psychological analysis but in terms of the types and purposes of reading in which children and adults engage. It seems unwise, particularly for teachers, to think of reading as a single act which covers all enterprises with printed materials. Research shows clearly that what is good reading in one situation may be poor reading in others. Reading some material in science to get exact facts is not at all the same activity as reading some social-studies material to get an impression of the author's viewpoint. The nature of the reading act changes with the various settings in which it may occur.

General Types

In *The Teaching of Reading: A Second Report,*[60] Gray classified reading as follows:

1. With respect to its general form—silent reading and oral reading.
2. Based on the reader's general attitude—work-type reading and recreational reading.
3. Based on the specific purposes of the reader—to find answers to specific questions, to determine the author's aim or purpose, to find the central thought of a selection, to enjoy the story—a total of fourteen purposes listed.
4. Based on the relation of the ideas involved—reading in the areas of geography, of history, of fiction, of drama, of science, etc., with possible subdivisions under each.

[60] William S. Gray, "The Nature and Types of Reading," *The Teaching of Reading: A Second Report,* Thirty-sixth Yearbook, Part I, Chap. 2, pp. 23-38, National Society for the Study of Education, University of Chicago Press, Chicago, 1937.

The second, third, and fourth categories are developed in Chapters 11, 12, 13, and other sections of this book. As background for the whole reading program a brief discussion of the place and use of silent reading and oral reading is given below. The more specialized types of reading are considered as developmental programs in the later chapters.

Silent Reading

Silent reading is ordinarily much more useful than oral reading, and accordingly both children and adults do more of it. The elementary school therefore stresses instruction in silent reading more than instruction in oral reading. A hundred years ago books were often in short supply and most reading was oral. Research such as the studies of Judd and Buswell and of Thorndike mentioned above (pages 98 and 106) show some of the dangers of extreme emphasis on oral reading. By the 1920's there was a tendency in some schools to omit instruction in oral reading after the first two or three grades. By the 1940's the values of oral reading were recognized again, and the use of some oral work was re-established in most lessons directly guided by the teacher. Current opinion suggests that there are certain uses for oral reading which require some practice, but that silent reading should be emphasized more, particularly in the intermediate and upper grades as the child matures in reading abilities and tastes.

In developing silent-reading abilities the teacher is usually concerned with (1) comprehension, (2) vocabulary, (3) speed, and (4) accuracy. Each of these factors is obviously related to the other three. For example, comprehension will depend upon the size of one's recognition vocabulary and the rate and accuracy of reading the textual materials.

Comprehension, discussed more fully in Chapter 11, involves both *type* of comprehension and *level* of comprehension. As suggested above, one child may develop habits of painstaking reading which means high accuracy and good comprehension of detail but a slow rate and an inability to organize a selection in main and subordinate facts. He is therefore good at some types of comprehension and not others. Level of comprehension, on the other hand, refers to the difficulty of the material a child can read with understanding. Most reading tests are partly power tests: they measure how far a child can go in reading paragraphs or selections graded from easy to difficult. The teacher must know a child's level of comprehension so that she may place him in the proper reading group and give him materials which challenge his abilities without discouraging him by their difficulty. It is also important for teachers to note that the level of material a child can read is not fixed. On a standardized test he may obtain a reading-grade score of 4.3 (equal to that of the average child who has spent three months in the fourth grade), but at times he can read only materials at the third-grade level and at other times he can read materials well into the fifth-grade level of difficulty, according to his interest in the material and the way the teacher has helped to develop purposes for reading the material.

Vocabulary is an important part of silent reading (see Chapter 10). Most silent-reading tests contain some sort of vocabulary section, and the size of the child's vocabulary is closely related not only to his reading success but to his achievement in other areas. Children seem to find words difficult (a) when they have never met them before, (b) when they cannot select the correct meaning of a multiple-meaning word, and (c) when the word is technical, as in *sonic boom,* or obsolescent, as when Aunt Polly goes after Tom Sawyer with a *switch.*

Speed is often a desirable characteristic of the reading of older children and adults. Its value in covering a wide range of materials is obvious. Ordinarily it should not be stressed as such in the primary grades, when children are concentrating on learning the basic techniques of left-to-right eye movements, return sweeps, the association of symbols with meaning, work patterns with books, and the use of work-type materials and similar skills. Furthermore, an undue emphasis upon speed in the upper grades may affect comprehension unfavorably, particularly when reading to note details or to follow closely a sequence of ideas or events. However, a moderate speed of reading average materials is better than a slow one for most types of comprehension, perhaps because it gives less time in which to forget the earliest details read.[61]

Without placing undue stress upon speed, the teacher should be aware of the usual rates at which children read at various ages. Results have been summarized by Harris[62] in terms of the average rates

[61] James B. Stroud and Margaret Henderson, "Rate of Reading and Learning by Reading," *Journal of Educational Psychology,* Vol. 34, pp. 193-205, April, 1943. R. Carlson, "Relationship between Speed and Accuracy of Comprehension," *Journal of Educational Research,* Vol. 42, pp. 500-512, March, 1949. Charles T. Letson, "Speed and Comprehension in Reading," *Journal of Educational Research,* Vol. 52, pp. 49-53, October, 1958.

[62] Albert J. Harris, *How to Increase Reading Ability,* 2nd ed., p. 449. Longmans, Green, New York, 1947.

required by various reading tests. He stated the following median rates in terms of words per minute: grade two, 86; grade three, 116; grade four, 155; grade five, 177; grade six, 206; grade seven, 215; and grade eight, 237. The results are not comparable from grade to grade, because more difficult tests are used in the upper grades to measure speed. It would seem that most adults read about 250 words per minute with average materials, but this figure fluctuates widely with purpose and with type of materials read. Older children occasionally enjoy checking their own rates of reading in a speed test. Speed of reading is sometimes associated with skimming. Grayum[63] studied skimming practices of good and poor readers from fourth grade through adulthood on social studies materials. She found that the techniques, employed at all age-grade levels, were as follows: (1) skipping in various degrees, (2) marked changes in regular reading rate, (3) pausing, (4) regressing, (5) looking back, and (6) looking ahead. The techniques of the superior skimmers were marked by flexibility and individuality. Skimming required ability in fundamental reading skills together with power to evaluate and constant awareness of purpose.

Accuracy of reading is similarly a product of a number of factors, such as difficulty of the material and purpose in reading. Ordinarily the child should be expected to read with complete accuracy; otherwise he will get entirely wrong ideas from what he reads. On the other hand, it is probably not worth while to be absolutely sure of every word spoken or every object described in recreational reading, such as magazines and comic books. Accuracy in reading a whole chapter is wasteful if the child needs only one or two facts from the chapter, such as a name or a correct date. In general, then, accuracy can be considered a desirable factor in silent reading; but it should not be applied to all materials read, and particularly those which lie outside the special purpose in reading a selection.

Oral Reading

Oral reading, like silent reading, involves comprehension, vocabulary, speed, and accuracy. In it knowledge of vocabulary and accuracy are almost synonymous. Comprehension and speed, however, operate differently in oral reading and in silent reading, because in oral reading it is chiefly the comprehension of the listener that counts, so that

63 Helen S. Grayum, *An Analytic Description of Skimming: Its Purpose and Place as an Ability in Reading.* Doctoral dissertation, Indiana University, Bloomington, 1952.

speed becomes undesirable beyond a certain point, perhaps a rate of 150 words a minute. In general there is considerable contrast between oral and silent reading, particularly in the case of good readers. Oral reading has a longer fixation, a shorter reading span between two fixation points, and more regressions, the latter because the eye often moves far ahead of the voice (the eye-voice span) and so the reader has to retrace his steps to a point near where his voice is following. As he begins to read, the child's silent reading is much like his oral reading: he may vocalize his silent reading, and fixations and regressions are frequent. As he improves his silent reading, however, it takes on the characteristics of greater speed and fluency, and he should not be required to follow on the page silently while another child haltingly reads the same page orally.[64] A study by Bridges[65] indicated that with average and below-average readers in the fourth and fifth grades, practice that emphasizes comprehension and takes no account of speed is more effective than practice that emphasizes speed over a period of time, in developing both speed and comprehension. Too much emphasis on speed tended to inhibit growth in reading at these levels, although good readers in the sixth grade were not affected by practice with emphasis upon rapid reading.

There are certain additional characteristics of oral reading which are of little importance in silent reading. These exist because oral reading is a process of sharing ideas with others. In earlier days, when schools paid much attention to oral reading, teachers sometimes developed complex systems of interpreting literature.[66] Today oral reading is chiefly confined to a number of practical situations, such as reading a report, giving directions for the class to follow, quoting verbatim from a book or article, and recreational reading for enjoyment of the beauty or humor of the selection. Although oral reading is used less frequently, it still involves certain new factors; like silent reading it includes recognition, association, and thinking, but it also requires expressing the thought in such a way that the listener will think with the reader. There are accordingly a number of factors in

[64] Luther C. Gilbert, "The Effect on Silent Reading of Attempting to Follow Oral Reading," *Elementary School Journal,* Vol. 40, pp. 614-621, April, 1940.

[65] Lucile H. Bridges, "Speed Versus Comprehension in Elementary Reading," *Journal of Educational Psychology,* Vol. 32, pp. 314-320, April, 1941.

[66] Ada V. Hyatt, *The Place of Oral Reading in the School Program. Its History and Development from 1880-1941.* Contributions to Education, No. 872, 140 p. Bureau of Publications, Teachers College, Columbia University, New York, 1943. M. Margaret Robb, *Oral Interpretation of Literature in American Colleges and Universities,* 242 p. Wilson, New York, 1941. Helen M. Robinson, ed., *Oral Aspects of Reading.* Supplementary Educational Monographs, No. 82. University of Chicago Press, Chicago, 1955.

oral reading which may or may not be aids to good listening. These additional factors may be classified roughly as (1) voice factors and (2) techniques of oral reading.

Research indicates that speech difficulties are related to reading difficulties, in both oral and silent reading.[67] Teachers who are especially interested in speech may wish to check the speech of their pupils with reference to such characteristics as the following:

1. *Delayed speech.* The child who begins to talk much later than the average age.
2. *Articulatory disorders.* Production of improper sounds because of structural or environmental defects—lisping, lolling, clumsy speech, sound substitutions, "baby talk," foreign accents.
3. *Rhythmic disorders.* Poor co-ordination in operation of speech apparatus, giving rise to stuttering.
4. *Voice disorders.* Huskiness, nasality, shrillness, weakness, and monotony.
5. *Symbolic disorders, or aphasias.* Difficulty not in the formation of sounds but in putting words in acceptable grammatical relationships.[68]

One teachers' manual for reading in the primary grades suggests the speech chart shown on page 125. The improvement of speech habits that have been built up in the child for five or six years is not a simple process. Most teachers should attempt speech-correction work in simple mispronunciations, rate, volume, and "giving the thought"; but correction of the more complex difficulties should be attempted only by teachers with supervisory help or by teachers who are thoroughly familiar with such books as those of Anderson,[69] Ogilvie,[70] and the National Association of Teachers of Speech.[71]

In addition to improving the speech components of oral reading, the good teacher is alert to possibilities of helping the child to improve his techniques of oral reading. Perhaps in too many groups the teacher still merely hears the child read orally, occasionally helping with a hard word. If children read with high-pitched voices or at a

[67] Gertrude H. Hildreth, "Speech Defects and Reading Disability," *Elementary School Journal,* Vol. 46, pp. 326-332, February, 1946. Jeanette G. Yedinack, "A Study of the Linguistic Functioning of Children with Articulation and Reading Disabilities," *Journal of Genetic Psychology,* Vol. 74, pp. 23-59, March, 1949.

[68] C. M. Louttit, *Clinical Psychology of Children's Behavior Problems,* rev. ed., Chap. 12. Harper, New York, 1947.

[69] Virgil A. Anderson, *Improving the Child's Speech.* Oxford University Press, New York, 1953.

[70] Mardel Ogilvie, *Speech in the Elementary School.* McGraw-Hill, New York, 1954.

[71] National Association of Teachers of Speech, *Guides to Speech Training in the Elementary School.* Expression, Magnolia, Mass., 1944.

monotonous rate, without changes to give expression to ideas, some specific helps can be given. In the area of techniques of oral reading many teachers help certain of their reading groups by providing opportunities for work in the following:

INDIVIDUAL SPEECH–ANALYSIS CHART

CONSONANTS

Directions: Show the child a picture representing a word below and ask him to name or tell about the picture. If a word cannot be pictured, ask the child to repeat a sentence containing the word. If the sound being checked is indistinct, draw a line through the word; if a substitution is made, write the substituted form above the word; if the sound is omitted, circle the word.

	Initial	Medial	Final		Initial	Medial	Final
b	boat	cabbage	tub	sh	ship	machine	dish
d	dog	puddle	hand	ch	chicken	teacher	match
f	father	muffin	knife	t	tie	mitten	gate
g	girl	wagon	frog	th	thumb	nothing	tooth
h	house	behind		~~th~~	them	mother	with
k	key	turkey	book	v	vine	river	stove
l	lamb	collar	ball	w	wood	twins	
m	mouse	hammer	farm	wh	white		
n	nose	pencil	barn	y	yellow	barnyard	
ng		singer	ring	z	zoo	magazine	rose
p	pig	apple	cap	zh		treasure	garage
r	rabbit	shirt	car	j	jacket	engine	page
s	sun	postman	horse				

VOWELS

Directions: Note words in which the child makes vowel substitutions, or nasalizes, or flattens vowel sounds. Typical examples are listed below.

Substitutes—jist for just, kin for can, becuz for because, etc.

Nasalizes—dinner, fence, flame, man, light

Flattens—house, round, town

Suggestions for Improvement

Notes on Progress

Speech check list (*Manual for Teaching the Primer Program* to accompany *The Little White House,* rev. ed., p. 63. Ginn, Boston, 1957)

1. *Pronunciation.* In work-type periods on word recognition, teachers will develop with children such methods as analyzing words and using context clues. In oral reading in the audience situation it is better not to interrupt the thought; thus the teacher or a pupil gives a correct pronunciation, and oral reading proceeds. The teacher usually makes a note of the difficult word and helps the child or group to study it later.

2. *Use of punctuation marks and capital letters.* Over a period of time, teachers can develop the idea that there are "starters" and "stoppers" in reading, that periods mean a somewhat longer pause than commas, and that breaks do not necessarily come at the ends of lines.

3. *Phrasing.* Closely allied to the use of punctuation marks is the matter of phrasing as one reads orally or talks. Most boys and girls would not say, "Thecowscameoverthehilltothebarnbesidethebigwillowtree," giving equal accent to each word and equal spacing between them. Rather they would say, often without being conscious of the phrasing, "The cows came over the hill to the barn beside the big willow tree." In such reading the words *the, over, to, beside,* would run easily into the succeeding words. Some teachers use the device of separating the phrases to encourage such reading. If pupils practice with material in separated form, they should immediately go back to the same material in the usual spacing, to repeat the phrasing with regular text.

4. *Varying the voice to indicate changes of meaning.* Most children enjoy changing tone or volume or rate to indicate changes in meaning. The three voices of the bears in "The Story of the Three Bears" offer an easy opportunity for variation. Many children's poems deliberately change their tempo to indicate changes in meaning. In oral reading from a text the teacher or group may ask, "Did Susan read the page the way the person in the story would say it?" Dramatization encourages changes in voice to indicate changes in meaning and, under the guidance of the teacher, may transfer to the oral-reading situation.

This introduction to the components and use of silent and of oral reading indicates that the two are rather different processes, particularly from the third grade upward. As such they must each be given a place in the whole reading program and taught in somewhat different ways. In determining what part of the reading activities of a group should be oral and how much time should be given to silent reading, the teacher can be guided by the needs of the group rather than by any general statement. For example, a fourth grade containing many children from non-English-speaking homes may need more work in speech and oral reading than a group of equal ability from English-speaking homes. In general the tendency is to give less time to oral reading as children mature. In his discussion of the reading program Harris[72] stated time divisions as follows:

[72] Albert J. Harris, *op. cit.*

In the first term of reading instruction, oral reading (including chart and blackboard exercises) should take up more than half of the time devoted to reading. After the children are well started on book reading, the proportion of time devoted to silent reading should be gradually increased and the time spent on oral reading should be decreased. In the second and third grades less than half of the time should be given to oral reading, decreasing to not more than one-third in the fourth grade, and to not more than one-quarter in the fifth grade and above.

Above the first grade Harris is careful to set upper limits rather than exact times to be spent on oral reading. His suggestions should be considered as general indications rather than specifications for the program of any particular class or group within a class.

NATURE OF READING AT DIFFERENT ACHIEVEMENT LEVELS

Chapter 3 indicates that the different characteristics of children at different age levels help to determine the form of the reading program—what types of reading shall be stressed, what materials shall be used, and similar concerns. It follows naturally that the characteristics of the reading act also differ at different levels throughout the school.

In one sense, reading skill begins about the age of eighteen months, when the child learns to talk. In a more restricted sense it begins somewhere about six years of age, when the child learns that certain peculiar symbols stand for certain words. At first he may say that the pattern of letters making up the symbol *boy* is "dog." There is no essential "boyness" about the word *boy,* and it would be perfectly right to call that word "dog" if everyone else did so. However, the child soon learns that the particular pattern *boy* can mean only a boy or that *We saw the fire-engine* means only that and not *We went to the farm.* If the child recognizes most of the words and gets them into correct sequence, their meaning is apparent to him, because he has met all the words in his previous experience.

Word-recognition abilities continue to develop as the child reads more. He builds up an ever-larger sight vocabulary of words which he recognizes instantly. He recognizes not only single words but also common phrases and short sentences which occur frequently in his reading materials. Sometimes he knows the larger unit, such as the sentence, before he knows its parts well. As he reads much familiar material he does not have to say every word orally or even to himself.

That is, he begins to read silently, without vocalization or even lip movement, and still gets the meaning of what he reads.

As the child grows into the stage of automatic recognition of many words he also develops his ability to work out new or partly known words for himself. Methods of teaching these abilities are considered in Chapter 7, on the primary-grade program, and in Chapter 10, on the program of developing word-recognition abilities. At this stage, too, the materials of reading become more complex. The child learns to read longer sentences which run over into the next line or lines. Paragraphs are longer and introduce ideas with which so far he has had no direct contact. In the third grade, for example, he may be reading about the wheat farms of the prairies, although he has seen only dairy farms and market gardens near an Eastern city.

As the child meets reading materials of greater variety, he finds he must vary his style of reading. Sometimes he has to read slowly, with attention to nearly every word. At other times he wants to skim rapidly, to find one or two exact facts. At other times he reads rather rapidly, for enjoyment of the plot of a story, or more slowly, to distinguish major from minor points, to outline, or to summarize. In other words, he develops *differential* reading abilities and various study habits. With his greater maturity the child is able increasingly to interpret, evaluate, and use what he reads. Under the proper stimulus he develops habits of critical thinking as he reads. The development of these creative reading abilities is considered further in Chapter 14.

The developmental nature of reading abilities is illustrated in the widely quoted six stages in reading development enunciated by the National Committee on Reading of the National Society for the Study of Education.[73] These may be described as follows:

1. The pre-reading stage (birth to sometime in grade one)
2. The beginning reading stage (grade one)
3. The initial stage of independent reading (grade two)
4. The transition stage (grade three and early grade four)
5. The intermediate or low-maturity stage (grades four to six)
6. Advanced stages of reading (grade seven and later)

The twenty-fourth and thirty-sixth and forty-eighth yearbooks of the National Society for the Study of Education all develop these stages

[73] *Reading in the Elementary School,* Forty-eighth Yearbook, Part II, Chap. 2, National Society for the Study of Education, University of Chicago Press, Chicago, 1949.

in detail and give many suggestions for activities in each. Many teachers and school systems feel that the five or six stages are very rough descriptions, and they prefer to develop their program by as many as ten or twelve different levels. These may be given such names as readiness level, initial reading level, preprimer level, primer level, first-reader level, etc. Such an arrangement may give teachers more specific help in planning for children in different groups in the same classroom, but it increases the difficulties always present in any attempt to group pupils in stages or levels.

Although a child may reach a certain stage in reading development at a particular time, the teacher must always bear in mind that there are no hard-and-fast stages in reading abilities which divide children automatically and finally from one another. A stage in reading is merely one spot in a continuous growth ranging from infancy at least to adulthood. Not only do children differ widely from one another at any one level but an individual child varies greatly in his different reading abilities. A boy in the fifth grade may be able to read comics at the sixth-grade level, adventure stories at the fifth-grade level, and exacting factual material at the third-grade level. A first-grade child may know rhymes at the third-grade level and recognize words at the preprimer level. At best, then, any one of the six stages above or any one of the levels adopted by a school system can be only a general description of the child's reading abilities. Because distinct changes and reorganization of his patterns of reading appear at different times, some reference to his stage of reading development can be made.

CHARACTERISTICS OF READING MATERIALS

Throughout the preceding descriptions of reading in various situations, frequent mention has been made of the materials which may affect a child's speed and comprehension. The development of printed materials has been considered from a historical point of view in Chapter 2. Reading matter can also be analyzed from the psychological point of view in terms of the interest of reader or the characteristics of the material itself. Since reading interests are discussed further in Chapter 12, the present section deals only with the nature of printed materials.

Most of the recent work in this area has been concerned with the "readability" of printed materials, an important fact to the teacher who does not want a text to be so hard that it dismays everyone or so easy that few children are challenged to read better. The authors and editors of most basal reader series, and of some other texts, attempt to control the difficulty of reading materials, especially at the primary levels, by careful introduction of new words, planned repetition of these words, the use of short sentences, accompanying illustrations, and a content of ideas familiar to most children. These factors are also taken into account in the intermediate-grade materials but here vocabulary seems to be only one of a group of factors which make materials hard or easy. The experimental analysis of mechanical qualities (rather than ideas or concepts) which affect difficulty has led to the development of readability formulas or quantitative checks on the difficulty of materials. Many of these stem from pioneer work on vocabulary by Thorndike[74] and the first major measures of readability developed by Gray and Leary[75] and by Washburne and Morphet.[76] Improved statistical analyses have simplified the Gray-Leary materials and added other items to be included in a count of factors which affect the difficulty of a passage. Some of the better-known formulas, the grade levels at which they seem to measure difficulty most accurately, and their bases of measurement are given below:

Spache[77] (grades 1, 2, 3), average sentence length and number of hard words beyond Dale list of 769 words.

Lorge[78] (grades 4 to 9), average number of words per sentence plus words not on a list of 769 plus relative number of prepositional phrases.

Dale-Chall[79] (grades 7 to 12), average number of words per sentence plus hard words beyond a list of 3,000 words.

Flesch[80] (adult), average number of words per sentence plus hard words plus "human interest" indicated by personal pronouns and words (1943 formula).

[74] Edward L. Thorndike and Irving Lorge, *Teacher's Word Book of 30,000 Words.* Bureau of Publications, Teachers College, Columbia University, New York, 1944.

[75] William S. Gray and Bernice Leary, *What Makes a Book Readable?* University of Chicago Press, Chicago, 1935.

[76] Carleton Washburne and Mabel U. Morphet, "Grade Placement of Children's Books," *Elementary School Journal,* Vol. 38, pp. 355-364, January, 1938.

[77] George Spache, "New Readability Formula for Primary Grade Materials," *Elementary School Journal,* Vol. 53, pp. 410-413, March, 1953.

[78] Irving Lorge, "The Lorge and Flesch Readability Formulae: A Correction," *School and Society,* Vol. 67, pp. 141-142, February 21, 1948.

[79] Edgar Dale and Jeanne S. Chall, "A Formula for Predicting Readability," *Educational Research Bulletin,* Vol. 27, pp. 11-20, 37-54, January 21, February 17, 1948.

[80] Rudolf Flesch, "A New Readability Yardstick," *Journal of Applied Psychology,* Vol. 32, pp. 221-233, June, 1948.

This summary suggests that the two quantitative factors which most affect difficulty are vocabulary and sentence structure. Accordingly, the different formulas are accompanied by lists of easy words, with all other words counted difficult; such factors as average sentence length and frequency of prepositional phrases are included in the numerical calculation which usually gives a grade-level score of difficulty. It should be noted that no formula so far developed attempts to use the concept load or the difficulty of ideas to arrive at the difficulty of a passage; the calculations are strictly numerical ones. Chall[81] has summarized a wide variety of studies using readability measures and has stated some of the advantages and disadvantages of formulas in current use.

Teachers are busy people and ordinarily do not need to use the formulas unless they are making a study of the use of materials in the school in the form of action or operational research. As stated above, most reading texts have been checked for ease of reading and gradual growth in difficulty. Some of these procedures should be applied more widely to texts in such areas as science and social studies. However, a librarian-teacher or a curriculum committee may wish to use one of the formulas in selecting books to recommend, for example, for a group of retarded readers. A curriculum committee in one large school system checked the social studies texts in use and found the ninth grade book was as difficult as the eleventh grade text. Sometimes the readability of materials sent from school to inform parents about the school program should be checked.

In addition to the mechanical measures of difficulty included in readability formulas, some attempts have been made to analyze the more subtle ideas and underlying assumptions in reading materials. This procedure is sometimes called "content analysis." For example, in one study of the third readers of basic reading series Child[82] found a dominance of what he labelled middle-class values in the books. In another analysis Anderson[83] found more material in modern readers on "moral and spiritual values" than he did in the famous old McGuffey readers. Perhaps both these findings are related to those of

[81] Jeanne S. Chall, *Readability: An Appraisal of Research and Application.* Bureau of Educational Research, Ohio State University, Columbus, 1957.

[82] Irvin L. Child and others, "Children's Textbooks and Personality Development: An Exploration in the Social Psychology of Education," *Psychological Monographs* 60, No. 3, 1946.

[83] Paul S. Anderson, "McGuffey vs. the Moderns in Character Training," *Phi Delta Kappan,* Vol. 38, pp. 53-58, November, 1956.

McConnell[84] who discovered in twenty-four biographies for children that achievement in life was said to be related to (a) individuality, (b) persistence, (c) friendly personal relationships, and (d) attitudes to the self and one's work characterized by modesty, simplicity, and idealism. Such analyses of content do not guarantee that the young reader will grasp these ideas, but they indicate possible effects of reading books. Much work remains to be done in this area, and some teachers will enjoy getting pupils' reactions to certain types of stories which go more deeply than a few sentences on "Why I like (or dislike) this story." Given the proper materials and encouragement, many pupils will state candidly just what a passage meant to them. Some of their interpretations must be regarded not as "wrong" but as individual interpretations growing out of specific preconceptions and needs. Consideration of such characteristics as these means that a teacher or group of teachers is exploring this neglected dimension of the reading process.

OTHER AUDIO-VISUAL AIDS

The large amount of research on the use of printed materials is in contrast to what we know about other audio-visual aids. A few schools have experimented with the use of the film strip in teaching beginning reading,[85] and some publishers have made available film strips to accompany basal materials, which reproduce pages of a basic text or offer opportunities for practice in word-recognition techniques.[86] In addition, there is some research literature on the use of machines in improving reading ability although most of this is concerned with remedial work or with adult reading improvement courses. Interest in tachistoscopic devices for flashing words under controlled rates involving very rapid visual perception was stimulated by the work of Renshaw[87] in training airplane spotters during World War II. Renshaw questioned the "span of perception" concept of some educational workers and preferred the Gestalt term of speed in perceptual field structuring—seeing the mass or whole and then proceeding to specific differentiations. The other research on

[84] Gaither A. McConnell, "Achievement Factors in Juvenile Biographies," *Elementary English,* Vol. 32, pp. 240-244, April, 1955.

[85] Glenn McCracken, "New Castle Reading Experiment," *Elementary School Journal,* Vol. 54, pp. 385-390, March, 1954.

[86] Houghton Mifflin; Row-Peterson; Scott, Foresman.

[87] Samuel Renshaw, "The Visual Perception and Reproduction of Forms by Tachistoscopic Methods," *Journal of Psychology,* Vol. 20, pp. 217-232, October, 1945.

the value of machines in school work has shown that there is usually rapid improvement in rate of reading scores, but there is little evidence about the permanence of such improvement.

Perhaps most important for the teacher's work, the research that is available tends to suggest that under classroom conditions reading practice on machines is not so effective as teacher guidance with ordinary books.[88] For example, Cason[89] found for third-grade pupils a program emphasizing wide library reading was more effective than one using a metronoscope (a phrase flashing device) in developing reading speed. However, it should be noted that certain types of tachistoscopes and reading accelerators have produced good results with some high school students and with remedial cases. The mechanical device may act as a stimulus to interest in reading, especially in the beginning stages of improvement.[90]

Similarly at the college freshman levels where reading courses are increasingly being given, Westover[91] compared results of five weeks' practice in using Strang's *Study Type of Reading Exercises* in their regular form with a mechanical device for controlling speed in reading the same materials. Westover found gains in both groups but no significant difference favoring either plan in immediate results or gains six months later. There seems to be some evidence, accordingly, that building up a library of materials or improving teaching methods may pay at least as many dividends as the purchase of expensive machines.

Despite this somewhat negative judgment, the gains from practice on the machines such as the tachistoscope and the reading-rate controller are often considerable. Accordingly, these may have value for the school's remedial reading program, especially for boys who have been failing on other kinds of reading materials. The late 1950's and early 1960's saw a rapid development of different kinds of "teaching machines" including some adapted to certain aspects of reading in-

88 Constance M. McCullough, "What Does Research Reveal about Practices in Teaching Reading?" *What We Know About High School Reading.* Bulletin of the National Conference on Research in English. National Council of Teachers of English, Champaign, Ill., 1958.

89 Eloise B. Cason, *Mechanical Methods for Increasing the Speed of Reading,* An Experimental Study at the Third Grade Level. Contributions to Education, No. 878. Bureau of Publications, Teachers College, Columbia University, New York, 1943.

90 Robert Karlin, "Machines and Reading: A Review of Research," *Clearing House,* Vol. 32, pp. 349-352, February, 1958.

91 Frederick Lee Westover, *Controlled Eye Movements versus Practice Exercises in Reading.* Contributions to Education, No. 917. Bureau of Publications, Teachers College, Columbia University, New York, 1946.

struction. In a review of their possibilities Porter[92] pointed out that many of these were adapted from the ideas of Pressey and of Skinner and that the devices most frequently studied in reading improvement were the tachistoscope, the accelerator, and the reading film. Studies are lacking on problems of pupil satiation and of transfer of reading skills to other media. The whole question of mechanical devices as an aid to reading needs further study. Experimentation would seem to be particularly desirable in adapting television programs to certain types of reading instruction. Davis,[93] as early as 1952, listed films for teaching reading at various grade levels and added suggestions for use of flannelboards, tape recorders, and other devices. Shortly afterward Leestma[94] compiled a useful hundred-page booklet of audio-visual materials for teaching reading. The availability of this material suggests the need of further experiments to evaluate its usefulness at various school levels and with different kinds of children.

IMPLICATIONS OF THE NATURE OF THE READING ACT AND READING MATERIALS FOR INSTRUCTION

When a curriculum committee is attempting to produce a guide to the reading program at any or all levels or when a teacher is planning the reading activities of one of her groups for the following week, they take into account the nature of reading itself. If the committee or teacher feels that reading is both difficult and important at a particular level, they will suggest more time for it than for easier or less important learnings. If they feel that reading is usually well mastered at a particular level, say the seventh grade, they will suggest less time for it in the school program as such and look for opportunities to use reading in various ways in several subject-matter areas, thereby strengthening the growth of differential reading abilities. In other words, the reading program depends, partly at least, upon the nature of reading behavior at various levels. Some of the general implications of this fact for a teacher's or other curriculum worker's planning may be summarized from the foregoing discussion as follows:

1. A reading program is determined by such factors as the char-

[92] Douglas Porter, "Critical Review of a Portion of the Literature on Teaching Devices," *Harvard Educational Review,* Vol. 27, pp. 126-147, Spring, 1957.

[93] Herbert J. Davis, "Teaching Reading the A-V Way," *Educational Screen,* Vol. 31, pp. 417-419, December, 1952.

[94] Robert Leestma, comp., *Audio-visual Materials for Teaching Reading.* Slater's Book Store, Ann Arbor, Mich., 1954.

acteristics of children, the aims of the school system, the community demands on the school, and the nature of the reading process itself.

2. Reading is not a simple, single process that applies to all situations involving printed materials. Rather, it is a highly skillful, complex process which includes many different abilities that vary in importance in different reading situations.

3. Since reading is often a subtle and complicated procedure, it seems unwise to require rapid growth in it of the young and immature children who enter first grade in many parts of the country. In adhering to this principle a primary teacher may have to resist pressures from the parent or the community in general.

4. Since reading is a varying process, it seems important that the teacher and school system provide a wide variety of reading situations and materials in the total program, even in the primary grades. The use of such a diversity of materials is explained in Chapter 5.

5. Since perception, like other parts of the reading act, is a varying procedure, the teacher will help pupils to develop four or five ways of recognizing words independently. These methods are described in Chapter 10.

6. In planning a range of situations that go beyond a basic reader and the use of subject-matter texts, the teacher will always plan how reading can be used. Since the reading act involves not only recognition, association, and interpretation but also "putting the reading to work," the relating of reading activities to all parts of the day's activities is a vital part of all work in reading.

7. The teacher controls only a few of the physical conditions involved in reading. Beyond the usual requirements for a healthful environment the teacher is responsible for referring a child to a competent authority if she suspects visual difficulties and for checking the strength of illumination in a classroom where reading is in progress.

8. Reading activities may be described as silent or oral, recreational or work-type, or as related to some ten or fifteen different purposes. In general the curriculum of reading activities maintains a balance between these various types, with emphasis given to the needs of the particular group of children involved.

9. Oral-reading abilities can be developed as definitely as comprehension in silent reading. It is not enough to hear children read orally, correcting an occasional mispronunciation. Definite guidance in voice production, phrasing, observing punctuation marks, and similar activities must be included in an oral reading program.

10. The developmental nature of reading ability and its relationship to general maturity suggest that some guidance in reading growth be continued at least through all the high-school grades.

11. Although all children go through similar patterns of reading development, as suggested in Chapter 3, they may reach any one stage of development at quite different chronological ages. Accordingly one of the chief tasks of any teacher is to meet the needs of children in any one class who have wide variations in their reading patterns and abilities. Ways of providing for a wide range of individual differences in reading behavior are considered in Chapter 15.

12. Some teachers speak of having pupils work on either speed or comprehension in reading as if these were different things. Research reveals that they are positively related, that the faster reader will be the more comprehending reader, especially on fairly easy materials. The relationship depends upon the measures of speed and comprehension used and decreases for more difficult materials. Most readers tend to maintain a reading rate independent of difficulty or purpose and so need help in making their speed more flexible.

13. Since reading is a process of continuous growth, since children vary greatly in their rate of development, and since many factors may affect growth in various reading behaviors, some systematic evaluation of children's development in reading should be made in all school systems. The complex nature of the reading process suggests that this evaluation should be on a broad basis.

14. Part of the evaluation of the reading program should be concerned with the effects of reading on individual children. Potential effects may be explored by "content analysis" of the ideas in stories or passages, but it seems unlikely that the expert's view of content will be the same as most children's idiosyncratic responses.

15. Another type of analysis of reading materials includes numerical counts of such factors as number of hard words, and average sentence length. Such analyses may give clues to the level of difficulty or the readability of the material. Other factors such as interest in the topic and the level of abstraction of the passage may also affect its readability.

16. New types of "teaching machines" may contribute to children's reading development when they have been tested experimentally and improved. At the beginning of the 1960's they seemed best adapted to certain associative aspects of learning to read such as choosing the correct word to go with a picture or the right answer in a multiple-

choice list of responses. Future developments may increase their usefulness, especially in individual practice.

SUPPLEMENTARY READINGS

ANDERSON, IRVING H., and DEARBORN, WALTER F. *The Psychology of Teaching Reading.* Ronald, New York, 1952.

BLIESMER, EMERY P. "Reading Abilities of Bright and Dull Children of Comparable Mental Ages," *Journal of Educational Psychology,* Vol. 45, pp. 321-331, 1954.

CARMICHAEL, LEONARD, and DEARBORN, WALTER F. *Reading and Visual Fatigue.* Houghton Mifflin, Boston, 1947.

CHALL, JEANNE S. *Readability: An Appraisal of Research and Application.* Bureau of Educational Research, Ohio State University, Columbus, 1957.

DALE, EDGAR, and CHALL, JEANNE. "A Formula for Predicting Readability," *Educational Research Bulletin,* Vol. 27, pp. 11-20, 37-54, January 21, February 17, 1948.

DARBY, O. N. "Place of, and Methods of Teaching Oral Reading in the Elementary School," *Elementary School Journal,* Vol. 51, pp. 380-388, March, 1951.

DURRELL, DONALD D. *Improving Reading Instruction.* World Book, Yonkers, N.Y., 1956.

FLESCH, RUDOLF. *How to Test Readability.* Harper, New York, 1951.

GOINS, JEAN T. *Visual Perception Abilities and Early Reading Progress.* Supplementary Educational Monographs, No. 87. University of Chicago Press, Chicago, February, 1958.

GRAY, WILLIAM S., ed. *Promoting Growth Toward Maturity in Interpreting What is Read.* Supplementary Educational Monographs, No. 74. University of Chicago Press, Chicago, 1951.

HARRIS, ALBERT J. *How to Increase Reading Ability,* 3rd ed. Longmans, Green, New York, 1956.

HOLMES, JACK A. *The Substrata-Factor Theory of Reading.* California Book, Berkeley, 1953.

HYATT, ADA. *The Place of Oral Reading in the School Program: Its History and Development from 1880-1941.* Contributions to Education, No. 872. Bureau of Publications, Teachers College, Columbia University, New York, 1943.

LETSON, CHARLES T. "Speed and Comprehension in Reading," *Journal of Educational Research,* Vol. 52, pp. 49-53, October, 1958.

OLSON, ARTHUR U. "Growth in Word Perception Abilities as it Relates to Success in Beginning Reading," *Journal of Education,* Vol. 140, pp. 25-36, February, 1958.

POSTMAN, LEO, and ROSENZWEIG, MARK R. "Perceptual Recognition of Words," *Journal of Speech and Hearing Disorders,* Vol. 22, pp. 245-253, June, 1957.

POTTER, MURIEL C. *Perception of Symbol Orientation and Early Reading Success.* Contributions to Education, No. 939. Bureau of Publications, Teachers College, Columbia University, New York, 1949.

RAYMOND, DOROTHY M. "Performance of Reading Achievers on Memory Span and Associative Learning Tests," *Journal of Educational Research,* Vol. 48, pp. 455-465, February, 1955.

Russell, David H. "Some Research on the Impact of Reading," *The English Journal,* Vol. 47, pp. 398-413, October, 1958.

Spache, George. "A New Readability Formula for Primary Grade Reading Materials," *Elementary School Journal,* Vol. 53, pp. 410-413, March, 1953.

Townsend, Agatha. "Interrelationships between Reading and Other Language Arts Areas," *Elementary English,* Vol. 31, pp. 99-109, February, 1954.

Vernon, Magdalen D. *Visual Perception.* Cambridge University Press, New York, 1937.

Vernon, Magdalen D. *Backwardness in Reading: A Study of its Nature and Origin.* Cambridge University Press, New York, 1957.

Part II

LEARNING TO READ AT VARIOUS LEVELS

Chapter 5

OVERVIEW OF THE WHOLE READING PROGRAM: METHODS AND MATERIALS

Part I has given some attention to the considerable social, historical, and psychological influences which have operated on the modern reading program. Parts II and III discuss the reading program, respectively, in terms of levels or grades (the horizontal approach) and in terms of developmental sequences of various phases of reading (the vertical approach). Before going on to the organization of specific activities in these two parts, a look at the whole reading program may be of value. Current trends, aims, practices, and materials help to give an overall picture of the reading program. The details of this picture will then be filled in more completely in succeeding chapters.

TRENDS IN READING PROGRAMS

The newer demands of daily living on reading together with scientific research on children and on the reading process, as discussed in Part I, have combined to revolutionize the reading program since about 1920. Many parents of children now in school were taught to read by entirely different methods and accordingly are puzzled by or critical of modern methods. School people therefore must take active steps to make parents acquainted with new developments in reading by means of demonstrations, discussions, and other procedures (see Chapter 17). Some of the trends of which teachers should be aware and about which parents may need explanation are given below. A number of these have been given by Hildreth[1] in the two editions of her book *Learning 3 R's* and in an article by Anderson.[2]

[1] Gertrude Hildreth, *Learning the 3 R's: A Modern Interpretation*, pp. 110-121. Educational Publishers, Minneapolis, 1936. Also 2nd ed., Chap. 6, 1947.

[2] Irving H. Anderson, "Current Trends in the Teaching of Reading," *University of Michigan School of Education Bulletin*, Vol. 24, pp. 49-52, January, 1953.

1. Children read for some use. Reading is considered a functional skill instead of an isolated exercise; emphasis is on the purpose rather than the process. The way the reading is to be used will determine partly how it is done.

2. Reading is a part of many of the school day's activities. It is integrated with the activities of the entire school program. Thus reading is not just something done out of a reader in a reading period.

3. Reading is often used and practiced as children have need of it. In this way, a better balance is achieved between reading and other school activities.

4. There is more recognition of the way children in a single class may vary in reading interests and abilities. Reading achievement goals are set for children in terms of individual capacities and learning aptitudes rather than by rigid class standards.

5. The good teacher uses a combination of methods, with greater emphasis than formerly upon "whole" methods using thought units. Synthetic methods starting with word parts are used with known or with meaningful material.

6. There is a tendency toward flexibility in methods and varied instructional techniques. A good teacher does not repeat the same reading activity day after day.

7. More materials naturally accompany wider activities. A single basic text has less place in the reading program than formerly and is supplemented by other printed materials.

8. As suggested in Chapter 4, the teacher stresses meanings rather than the mechanical features of the reading act. Mechanics, such as eye movements, are interpreted in relation to the maturity and purposes of the pupil reader.

9. Since children in the first grade are younger than they were, reading is delayed in the primary grades until children are mature enough to profit by instruction in it. On the other hand, television and the use of many inexpensive books in homes may help make some children more ready to read at an earlier age.

10. Readiness is emphasized at all levels. A more informal and natural introduction to reading is provided than was the case formerly. This includes not only the primary grades but also new reading situations in higher grades.

11. A more gradual approach to reading tasks is provided in the primary grades through controlled introduction of new words, providing adequate repetition of these words, gradually increasing

sentence and paragraph length, and like devices. These controls are worked out most carefully in basic reading series but the teacher also applies them in chart work and other reading experiences.

12. Reading instruction is more individualized. Teachers attempt more instruction in small groups and with a single child. Individualized reading programs may be a larger part of the total reading activities of a class.

13. The teacher plans for a balance between oral and silent reading in terms of the needs of the group. Oral reading is recognized as having certain values and some place in the program, although this place is usually smaller than that of silent reading.

14. Phonics activities are viewed as one technique of word analysis, not as a complete system of learning to read. The skillful reader can employ a number of techniques in unlocking new words.

15. Vocabulary work concentrates on meaning and use rather than isolated word drills.

16. The teacher gives more place to reading for enjoyment and for satisfaction of individual motives. She sets the stage in the hope that reading will influence the child's personality in desirable ways.

17. Teacher and pupils do not hurry to "cover" a book. The teacher sees reading as a thinking process, encourages related enrichment activities, and helps children find ethical values in stories.

18. The teacher attempts a continuous diagnosis of strengths and weaknesses and evaluates the program, not only in terms of reading achievement but in relation to the children's interest in and use of reading in their daily lives.

AIMS OF READING INSTRUCTION

Trends in reading programs usually bear a close relationship to the accepted aims of instruction. As indicated by the trends above, these aims are wider than they were in former times. The main aim of reading instruction is not to have pupils acquire some mechanical facility in recognizing words or understanding sentences so much as it is to contribute to the wholesome growth of the child. Some of the personal values in reading come in children's literature, as discussed in Chapter 13. But in addition to personal values the modern teacher considers reading a means of developing social habits and attitudes which contribute to good citizenship in a democracy. As suggested in Chapter 1 and Chapter 14, these aims also go beyond mere literacy.

More specifically, the modern teacher in reading tries to achieve the following goals:

1. To make provisions for determining and developing reading readiness at all levels.

2. To encourage strong motives for and permanent interests in reading as an activity of value in both work and recreational situations.

3. To acquaint children with ideas that will extend and enrich their experiences of life in modern America and an interdependent world.

4. To present ideas and develop attitudes associated with good citizenship and worthy character.

5. To cultivate tastes and interests in a wide variety of good literature in books, other current publications, songs, recordings, and radio and television programs.

6. To provide for the gradual increase in skills and acquisition of valuable habits in silent and oral reading.

7. To develop abilities associated with the use of books and other study activities.

8. To provide a basis for successful reading of printed materials in the various subject-matter areas of the curriculum, with special stress on the contribution of reading to other language-arts activities.

These aims imply that the teacher helps the child *to learn to read* and *to read to learn.* They suggest that the child grows *in* and *through* reading. They underline the fact that he develops not only reading skills but also permanent habits and attitudes. Reading is important to the child, as it can contribute to the solution of his basic problems and needs. Sometimes its significance may be falsely exaggerated because of the pressure of a parent or teacher upon the child to learn to read. The purposes set forth above indicate that reading can do much for the child, but it can do so only if instruction is planned and executed not in the light of adult ambitions but in terms of the child himself.

READING ACTIVITIES

The trends and aims outlined above may idealize the picture of much reading instruction. In reading, as in other school activities, there is often a considerable gap between theory and practice. Unfortunate practices still exist, such as emphasis upon drills with isolated words in situations of no meaning to the child, or much oral reading from one book while the other pupils follow in their books, waiting for their turn. These and related procedures are unfortunate. Their frequency is probably decreasing as the results of research and successful practice illustrate improved methods and materials.

In a typical class the following types of activities often make up the reading program:

1. *Reading the basic reader selections* with guidance by the teacher, some emphasis upon vocabulary development, group discussion, and evaluation.

2. *Independent reading of supplementary readers and other books,* with occasional guidance by the teacher and direct application to social studies and other class activities.

3. *Guided reading of texts and materials in content fields,* with the amount of guidance varying according to the difficulty of the reading task.

4. *Work-type periods emphasizing skills* and involving workbooks, reading games, teacher-prepared materials, and other activities related to specific needs of the group.

5. *Creative activities growing out of reading* to extend enjoyment or to reinforce the larger ideas of a selection or unit through dramatization, drawing a picture, playing a game, or expressing ideas in rhythms.

6. *Free reading,* often outside of class, of books at home or from the library which are related to the interests and purposes of the child.

As suggested above, reading practices in classrooms do not always include the above aims and activities. For example, in a study of elementary schools, previously chosen as outstandingly good ones, Gregg[3] recorded the reading activities he observed in seventy-three visits to classrooms. The most frequently observed activities, in descending order, were: pupils read text at seats; teacher questions and pupil answers; pupils read aloud from book; pupils work with workbooks at seats; and pupils study materials other than books at seats.

In another study of materials in 474 schools, in all states but Alaska and Hawaii, Staiger[4] found that 69 per cent of the schools used one

[3] George H. Gregg, *Some Characteristics of Instruction in the 3 R's as Observed in 242 Classrooms in 65 Schools in 28 States.* M.A. Thesis, University of California, Berkeley, 1954.

[4] Ralph C. Staiger, "How are Basal Readers Used?" *Elementary English,* Vol. 35, pp. 46-49, January, 1958.

series of readers basally but that many variations in related materials existed. Twenty per cent of the respondents reported using two series co-basally, and various combinations of two or more sets were used. Forty per cent of the schools reported shifting to different sets of books at opportune times which varied from preprimer level to the completion of third-grade readers. Ninety-two per cent of the respondents approved of using basal readers other than the adopted series for supplementary reading. Fifteen per cent of the respondents thought of teachers' manuals as prescribed courses and more than two-thirds of them approved of manuals as guides to teaching. Less than one per cent suggested that manuals are useful only occasionally.

Methods of guiding the six reading activities listed above are described more fully in Parts II and III. However, a few general ideas about these methods may be summarized here as follows:

1. The reading period is an enjoyable experience undisturbed by competition between individuals or by undue pressure from the teacher on particular pupils.

2. The methods used lend themselves to individualization of teaching and learning. Teachers work with small groups and, for a few minutes each day, with a few pupils who need individual help.

3. Pupils are encouraged to try a number of different methods of word recognition—by sight, by context clues, by phonetic analysis, by comparisons with similar words, and other methods. Some pupils will use certain of these methods; others will use other methods.

4. Pupils are encouraged to use reading material so that understanding and interpretation, not mere verbalization, are involved.

5. The purpose of reading is always clear to the children doing it and often grows out of other class activities.

6. The methods of instruction encourage the creative abilities of the children. Stories may be interpreted in various art forms, additional books and magazines consulted independently, items for school programs devised, and other materials written in original form.

7. The methods suggested provide for other educational activities related to reading habits and attitudes—language, art, drama, and construction activities are easily incorporated in the day's program.

8. The methods employed make it easy for children to know their own progress.

9. The methods tend to be economical of pupils' and teachers' time and energies.

10. The methods are adapted to the content of the material read; a clear distinction is made between recreational reading and work-type reading in various curricular fields.

11. The methods give large place to different types of silent reading, but they also give guidance to oral reading procedures in the first grade and in succeeding grades.

This summary suggests that in the modern program there is no one best method of teaching reading. Despite a great number of research studies and descriptions of procedures filling many volumes, no one has yet discovered an infallible method by which every child learns to read well. Probably no such method ever will be devised. Good teachers today use a variety of approaches and procedures in developing power in the reading task. So much is known about how children differ from one another in every possible ability related to reading that every good teacher includes in her planning a rich variety of learning activities adaptable to the needs of individual children. Her instructional program sees the individual as an interacting, unified whole. It aims toward reading as meaningful behavior, not in isolated responses but as a basic factor in adjustment to different aspects of living. Teaching methods are based on the assumption that reading can be one of the most significant forms of learning for individual and social development.

PLACE OF BASIC READERS IN THE WHOLE PROGRAM

In some schools of former days reading was done only from readers, and one reader made up the materials of the program for a year, or at least one-half year. Influenced by their parents' attitude, some children today think they have not had a reading period unless they have read orally to the group from a reader. Sometimes it is necessary for a teacher to explain to her pupils or a group of their mothers that reading exists outside basic readers in many ways. The modern program consists of much more than reading from one book; but here, as in other school practices, tradition often dies hard. Although the use of a basic series is only part of the complete reading program, sets of basic readers are so commonly used in most schools that a few suggestions about their use are important for an overview of reading activities.

Within recent years basic readers have been changed and improved in content, format, and mechanics of writing perhaps more than any other schools texts.[5] In fact, ideas first developed in readers have often been adopted later in other school books. In general the modern basic reading series is constructed on four main principles:[6]

1. It provides *continuity of growth* in reading skills, habits, and attitudes by means of a carefully graded series of reading materials. The basic series starts with the simplest reading materials and very gradually introduces new words, longer lines, broken lines, the "said" phrase, complex sentences, longer paragraphs, unfamiliar concepts, and a different style of writing. So gradually do the materials increase in difficulty that most pupils can advance through the successive stories and books without the discouragement of facing too many difficulties at one time.

2. It provides for a *wide variety of reading activities.* Older reading programs stressed word recognition and reading for details. The modern basic series is written on the assumption that children have to read many different kinds of materials for many different purposes. Accordingly it includes both recreational and work-type reading activities, with a wide variety of the latter. For example, since most children have to read to get a general impression, to follow a sequence of events or ideas, to follow directions, to skim for one or two specific facts, to find answers to specific questions, and to give pleasure to others, basal readers contain materials and suggestions for these activities. The basic series is a foundation program upon which a variety of reading activities can be built.

3. It provides a *complete organization of reading experiences.* Research shows that learning to read is a developmental process in which children build upon certain knowledge and skill in developing new knowledge and skills. Accordingly a good basic series avoids gaps in learning experiences and provides in an organized way for the different reading abilities children acquire. It includes not only stories which may be read for a general impression, but those which may be read for specific details or for information in connection with social-studies activities. It often includes a variety of materials, in-

[5] Agnes G. Gunderson, "Types of Reading Matter Contained in Readers Published over a Period of Twenty Years," *Educational Methods,* Vol. 17, pp. 226-230, February, 1938. George Spache, "New Trends in Primary Grade Readers," *Elementary School Journal,* Vol. 42, pp. 283-290, December, 1941.

[6] David H. Russell, *The Basic Reading Program in the Modern School,* rev. ed., Contributions to Education, No. 1. Ginn, Boston, 1957.

cluding factual material and some poetry, since these are suitable bases for the different types of reading in which an older child engages. Further, it shows how the different ways of reading are related and can be combined in an organized pattern. Thus reading becomes, not a series of separate skills, but a group of related, organized abilities.

4. It provides for a *worth-while content of ideas.* The elementary curriculum must always select, out of the vast accumulation of human knowledge and behavior patterns, only a few of the ideas and types of conduct that are most important for junior citizens of a democracy. Accordingly basic readers contain materials selected for their intrinsic value. Stories about family living, the community, boys and girls of other parts of America and other lands, food, shelter, and communication and transportation will be included. More factual materials in these areas in science and in biography are usually included. Many selections illustrate high ideals and strong character. In other words, the basic series includes a content of ideas important for children, individually and collectively, in the modern world. (See illustration, page 150.)

Although modern basic readers have been carefully written for *gradation, variety, organization,* and *content,* the good teachers uses them as only part of her whole reading program. As indicated by the six types of activities listed on page 145 other materials may have considerable value. Charts made co-operatively by teacher and pupils can capture some of the fun and excitement of other class activities in social studies or related fields. No classroom is complete without a "library table" or bookshelf. Other books, on a level which the children can read, enlarge and enrich the materials of the basic books. Current newspapers, pamphlets, and magazines help older children to develop ability to think about current events and problems. Some pupils who develop reading abilities slowly need supplementary reading materials which give additional practice on habits and skills developed in the basic program. The modern teacher, then, gives considerable place to a basic series in her program (reports indicate that about 95 per cent of teachers use basic series[7]), but she never hesitates to use other materials as well. With the concept of "reading for use," materials from other curricular fields will naturally take their place, alongside the basic series, as part of the materials of the reading program.

[7] Staiger, *op. cit.*

Aborigines of Northern Australia (*The Bush Books,* Book I, p. 12. Commonwealth Office of Education, Australia)

Primer from Thailand (*Cooperation,* K. Sawatipanich, ed., Ministry of Education, Education Printing Office, Bang-Rum-Poo-Bon, Bangkok, Thailand, 1958)

Basic reading materials adapted to lives of boys and girls

The trend has been toward a wider variety of materials, along with an increased amount of material in a basic series. A typical modern series of readers may include the following:

A reading-readiness book
Two or three preprimers
A primer and first reader
Two second readers
Two third readers
One or two each of fourth, fifth, and sixth readers
Teachers' manuals to accompany each of the above
Pupil workbooks to accompany the above (except the readiness book)
Supplementary or enrichment books related to the basic books
Supplementary materials such as word cards, charts, and tests of related content

Information about books in different basic series may be obtained from the publishers of them. Selection committees often study different series in terms of their mechanical features, such as vocabulary control, but an examination of content and organization as suggested in the four principles above should be given at least equal weight. Beginning teachers, and teachers-in-service who plan to add new books to their shelves, will enjoy the actual examination and reading of these books and their accompanying materials.

PROVIDING A BALANCE BETWEEN BASIC READERS AND OTHER MATERIALS

The teacher and a reading group can enjoy together many pleasant experiences in a basic reader. However, just because such books are usually available, there is a danger that they may become too prominent a part of the reading program. The following are a few dangers in the use of basic books which can be overcome by careful planning:[8]

1. The children of any one class cannot all profit by the same book of a basic series. It is common for children of the primary grades to vary two or three years in reading ability; in the fifth grade it is not uncommon to have children of third-grade reading ability and of seventh- or eighth-grade ability. Accordingly the practice of assigning only one book to one grade level (as is done in some state and city

[8] David H. Russell, *op. cit.*, p. 5.

adoptions) is not in harmony with the known facts. Schools must be careful to provide basic readers on different levels of difficulty for any one class.

2. A basic series of readers cannot capitalize upon the community environment of a particular school or the interesting news events (local, national, and international) which occur every week. The teacher must be careful to extend the reading program beyond basic books by using materials of community and current interest, thus stimulating her pupils to read materials important to them.

3. A basic series of readers should not be used to make reading something apart from the rest of the school program. After children have established some of the basic skills in reading, it is particularly important to have reading situations which grow out of the other meaningful activities of the class. Reading is not so much getting experience from the printed page as bringing experience to it. Therefore reading materials and situations must be related to the children's other activities. This is particularly important for children who have difficulty with abstract symbols.

4. A basic series of readers may not provide all the reading situations needed by some children. The modern child needs help in reading maps, charts, and graphs. Out of school he reads signs, scans electric meters, spots airplanes, and interprets movies. If one accepts reading as involving something more than word symbols, growth in such abilities must ordinarily be encouraged in ways outside a basic series of books. Children need guidance in selecting from the wide range of reading materials available today. Such guidance will come best in actual use of various materials.

METHODS OF USING BASIC READERS

The teacher who is aware of such dangers as the above is best equipped to plan for the correct use of basic books in reading activities. It would be unwise, as well as impossible, to suggest one method of using basic readers which would apply to children of all maturity levels and to all types of reading materials. The sixth and seventh trends listed early in this chapter suggest that there is no single best way of teaching reading. It is still true, however, that the teachers' manuals accompanying basic books usually suggest a rather fundamental plan of using the readers in directed-reading activities. This plan varies from lesson to lesson, with greater or less emphasis on certain parts of it in any one lesson. The plan should never be regarded as a prescribed form for any reading lesson. However, it is of value for teachers, supervisors, and principals to generalize about the large number of specific suggestions made in manuals. A plan for the use of basic readers that can be found in different manuals looks essentially something like this:

A. Developing readiness for reading
   1. Through a check on adequate background of experiences
   2. Through developing a meaningful vocabulary or concepts
   3. Through stimulating interest and setting up worthy reading purposes

B. Guiding the first silent (or survey) reading
   1. To stimulate interest in the selection
   2. To develop understanding of the whole
   3. To develop the habit of reading for a purpose
   4. To promote versatility in approaching selections for different purposes
   5. To foster understanding of sequence and organization
   6. To discover words, concepts, and larger ideas which require further study

C. Rereading for specific purposes
   1. To prepare for some worth-while activity based on the selection, such as story-telling, dramatization, finding an interesting word, discovering a well-liked character, and answering questions

D. Building essential habits and skills
   1. To develop word-recognition abilities through the use of accurate perception, picture clues, context clues, phonetic analysis, structural analysis, and related techniques
   2. To increase comprehension of important ideas in words, sentences, paragraphs, or complete selections
   3. To give practice in oral, silent, or audience reading, as needed by the group
   4. Use of charts, blackboards, workbooks, and teacher-prepared materials related to the content of the selection
   5. Evaluation of pupils' progress by means of observations, informal tests, word games, and the reading of related materials
   6. To help the individual child as time allows

E. Enrichment activities
   1. Following up certain activities begun under *C* and *D*
   2. Encouraging discussion, organization of ideas, critical thinking about the materials, further reading of an independent and research nature, and other language activities
   3. Using reading in planning construction, excursions, dramatic play, and other art activities.

In most modern schools children engage in a rather wide range of reading activities. This implies a variety of reading materials, but does not lessen the primary importance of making the best use of basal reading materials. The outline above is a generalized statement of what a teacher will find in many manuals or guides. It points out some of the essential procedures in most lessons using basic books.

In addition to methods a further approach to the wise use of basic readers is suggested below in that they are one, but only one, of the important types of material used in complete reading programs.

THE INDIVIDUALIZED READING PROGRAM

Learning to read is usually an individual matter. The description of the use of basic readers given above assumes that children will usually be taught in small groups, with some individual activities growing out of the group lessons. Surveys show that grouping for reading instruction is most common in the primary grades. They indicate that the usual number of groups is three, although Stendler[9] and Smitter[10] point out that there is no special magic in three and that children should be grouped in various ways for different purposes throughout any school day. McCullough[11] has given positive suggestions for various types of grouping, and these and related problems are considered more fully in Chapter 15. Because of certain difficulties in grouping, including the fact that children within a sub-group are still very different in reading achievements, interests and learning abilities, there has been a revival in recent years of interest in making reading more of an individual activity. The "individualized reading program" has been tried out and described by a number of teachers.[12]

Methods of individual instruction are not new; perhaps as long as

[9] Celia B. Stendler, "The Ritual of Primary Reading," *Elementary English,* Vol. 25, pp. 153-160, March, 1948.

[10] Faith Smitter, "The Pros and Cons of Grouping," *The Reading Teacher,* Vol. 7, pp. 74-78, December, 1953.

[11] Constance M. McCullough, *Meeting Individual Needs by Grouping,* Ginn Contributions in Reading, No. 19. Ginn, Boston, 1957.

[12] A few sample references are: Mary A. Daniel, "You can Individualize Your Reading Program Too," *Elementary English,* Vol. 33, pp. 444-446, November, 1956. Marian Jenkins, "Self-Selection in Reading," *The Reading Teacher,* Vol. 11, pp. 84-90, December, 1957. Harold Kaar, "An Experiment with an Individualized Method of Teaching Reading," *The Reading Teacher,* Vol. 7, pp. 174-177, February, 1954. F. Maib, "Individualizing Reading," *Elementary English,* Vol. 29, pp. 84-89, February, 1952. Alice Miel, ed., *Individualizing Reading Practices.* Bureau of Publications, Teachers College, Columbia University, New York, 1957. Mary C. Wilson, "Individualizing Reading Instruction," *Peabody Journal of Education,* Vol. 26, pp. 195-201, January, 1949.

there has been teaching, good teachers have tried to help children with their individual problems. For many years, teachers in England have used considerable self-help, and individual material in the form of games and exercises.[13]

Most American teachers, in an ordinary school day, try to give some time to helping a few children, by themselves, on specific reading problems as well as working with groups or the whole class. The increased interest in the topic during the 1950's, however, has helped to clarify some of the procedures and requirements for successful individualization. For example, Evans[14] suggested that if an individualized program is to be successful, children must learn to assume considerable self-direction and develop the ability to work independently. The classroom must be stocked with a wide variety of books including a number of basic readers and fiction and non-fiction on different levels of difficulty. Pupils must have in their possession at all times a book of their own choice and keep accurate records in notebooks of their reading. Evans indicated also that the teacher must help the child through both individual and group conferences and instruction.

Jacobs[15] pointed out that "individualized reading is not a single method, with predetermined steps in procedure to be followed." He stated also that individualized reading does not eliminate group reading and that it must not be used to support a laissez-faire attitude toward instruction in which the child merely does what he wants to do. Evans[16] also does not prescribe specific procedures but recommends the following seven activities for a good individualized program:

1. Individual conferences (of three to ten minutes) between teacher and child.
2. Silent reading in books of the child's own choice.
3. Group instruction in which help is given in all types of reading skills.
4. Grouping of children who have selected the same story for reading and discussion.
5. A whole class discussion of reading the children have enjoyed.

[13] David H. Russell, "Primary Reading Programs in England and Scotland," *Elementary School Journal,* Vol. 57, pp. 446-451, May, 1957.

[14] N. Dean Evans, "Individualized Reading Program for the Elementary School," *Elementary School Journal,* Vol. 54, pp. 157-162, November, 1953.

[15] Leland Jacobs, "Individualized Reading is Not a Thing," *Teachers College Record,* Vol. 59, pp. 319-329, March, 1958.

[16] N. Dean Evans, *op. cit.*

6. Provision of time for some children to work on individual vocabulary lists.
7. Provision of time for small groups to engage in creative work growing out of common reading, such as preparing a play.

Such activities do not make the individualized program a unique or specialized method of teaching so much as they provide a desirable emphasis in a total reading program. The published accounts of individualized reading programs have usually been descriptive, and sometimes hortatory, rather than strictly evaluative. They show that under the stimulus of "new" procedures pupils and teachers achieve as high or somewhat higher reading scores and enjoy the process more than the routine or "old" ways of doing things. Whether superior achievement can be attributed to individualization of reading or to enthusiasm and interest of teacher and pupil is not usually spelled out. Problems in the program such as the difficulty of helping many individuals in a limited school day, of organizing the classroom, of providing a wide range of materials, and of keeping adequate records also need to be considered. The results available are perhaps not so much an argument for individualized reading as they are evidence of the importance of teachers' and pupils' trying new things occasionally and engaging in action or operations research in reading. Further analysis of some of the problems and activities involved in individualization is given in Chapter 15 on "Providing for Individual Differences."

MATERIALS FOR A COMPLETE READING PROGRAM

The reading program is now better equipped with learning materials than any comparable division of the curriculum. The variety of materials may occasionally cause overemphasis on reading, to the exclusion of other worth-while activities, but a forward-looking school system will plan to increase materials in other fields rather than reduce them in reading. There seems some basis for the opinion that teachers in the future may look to as complete help in arithmetic or social studies as now exists for reading. In an overview of the reading program, accordingly, a brief appraisal of these reading materials should be made, as is done above for basic reading series.

The following sections summarize a few guides to teachers in planning a wide variety of reading experiences in terms of teacher-prepared materials, workbooks, visual aids, and the school library. With basic readers these constitute, in the narrow sense, the usual materials for reading as such.

Teacher-Prepared Materials

No reading program can prosper unless it carries the warmth and interest of some materials prepared by the teacher herself. Primary children especially are pleased when the teacher "makes up a story" of her own rather than reading one from a book. This story may be told, hectographed, or reproduced on a chart. Even greater interest and enthusiasm are generated when the children themselves have a chance to share in preparing the story. Work-type materials, such as word cards, or word games, reading exercises, vocabulary-practice material, and similar devices have value only as they are adapted to the particular needs of a child or small group. Such materials must be prepared or adapted by one who knows intimately the child's status, and the teacher is usually the only one who combines this knowledge of the child and of the school's reading program.

Teacher-prepared materials have a relationship to the child's needs at a particular time and to other events in his daily life which no other materials can achieve. They are essential, accordingly, in making reading something more than "book larnin'." On the other hand, indiscriminate use of teacher-prepared materials may overbalance a program. Children soon tire of filling blanks in rather dim mimeographed or hectographed exercises unless these are related to other worth-while activities. If the materials are prepared with little relation to reading need or interest, the teacher might well have avoided taking the time and effort by using commercially prepared materials. Particularly in the early stages of learning to read, the materials must be scanned for vocabulary control and other possible difficulties if they are to be effective helps to learning.

Another possible disadvantage of teacher-prepared materials is the difficulty of getting the lettering pens, india ink, tagboard, and other tools necessary for constructing reading games and devices. Some school systems overcome this difficulty when the principal or supervisor plans a series of workshop sessions which teachers may attend. To these sessions each teacher brings two or three types of material which have been useful to some of her pupils. Ideas are exchanged, and the actual construction of materials proceeds in an informal atmosphere.

Some elementary teachers in one city exchanged ideas in such a workshop session and then put their ideas together into a bulletin for others unable to attend the work meetings.[17] Two samples of their suggestions are as follows:

Prepare on paper a list of words which can be separated into two or more general classifications. The child arranges the words in proper groupings by writing the word in the proper column, as

	Food	*Clothing*	*Transportation*
car			
horse			
potatoes			
sweater			
cabbage			
etc.			

Write or type children's individual stories and paste them on cardboard. Develop a library of these. On the back write a sentence or two giving some directions for something to do after reading the story. Number these cards. Have a set of cards numbered containing the answers for the child to check. One might have a check list so that the child may sign his name upon correct completion of a card.

Samples of directions:

1. Prepare this story to read to the class.
2. Draw John's dog.
3. Cut out the ball, wagon, and house in Mary's story.

Further suggestions for the use of such devices are made in Chapter 15, because they are helpful in meeting children's individual needs. Sources for obtaining suggestions for literally hundreds of such activities are given in the books listed on pages 504-505.

Workbooks

Opinion about the place of workbooks in the reading program is often sharply divided. Some of the opinions of teachers and others about the advantages and disadvantages of workbooks were assembled by Goodykoontz[18] in chart form, as shown on page 159.

17 Pasadena City Schools, *Reading Activities Used in the Pasadena Elementary Schools*, Curriculum Guide Reading Bulletin, No. 2. Pasadena City Schools, Pasadena, Calif., September, 1946.

18 Bess Goodykoontz, "Current Uses and Effects of Workbooks," *Curriculum Journal*, Vol. 6, pp. 30-35, April 22, 1935.

Summary of Opinions

VALUES OF WORKBOOKS

In developing desirable learning techniques

1. Stimulate interest in reading
2. Establish learning situation quickly
3. Provide for self-competition
4. Allow pupils to work out their own problems
5. Provide diagnostic testing program
6. Provide for developing good study habits and skills
7. Create favorable pupil reactions
8. Encourage pupil activity

In presenting desirable subject matter

1. Provide good amount and quality of drill material, better than teacher selection
2. Provide sufficient supplementary material
3. Build up specific vocabularies
4. Provide suitable material for home study

In providing individualized instruction

1. Pupils progress at their own rate
2. Pupils check up on their own progress
3. Variety of material provides for individual rates, interests, etc.

In efficiency of classroom management

1. Saves teacher's time for supervision
2. Saves pupils' time in having materials ready to use
3. Simplified assignment
4. Allows for more scientific grading

WEAKNESSES OF WORKBOOKS

In theory underlying their use

1. Reduce learning to a matter of doses
2. Make children mechanical memorizers
3. Reduce teacher's initiative, originality, and creativeness for specific problems

In their content

1. Faulty analysis of processes or subject matter, not based on research
2. Too many trivial, unrelated facts
3. Poorly graded, exercises not cumulative in difficulty
4. Ill-adapted to courses or textbooks
5. Inflexible
6. Formal
7. Lack of extra units for bright pupils

In their use

1. Teachers tend to use exercises in consecutive order or to follow too closely
2. Teachers frequently fail to check the exercises and to follow up

In mechanical make-up

1. Too large and cumbersome
2. Illustrations poor
3. Expensive

A later study by the Association for Childhood Education[19] verified the widespread use of reading workbooks and found that more would be used in the primary grades if they were available. Although 12 per cent of the primary teachers questioned would not use workbooks, the majority of the 543 teachers believed that workbooks contribute to learning to read, are valuable for review, and are better in detecting reading difficulties than in correcting them. The chief objection to the books is the expense of time and effort and the consequent displacement of other varied experiences appropriate to wholesome development of young children.

Two other studies[20] of the opinions of experts in reading found that workbooks for the primary grades were favored by over half the group for all or most pupils, but that, for the intermediate grades, only about 40 per cent of those giving opinions approved workbooks. A wide variety of values of workbooks, such as maintaining new skills, developing and checking comprehension, and teaching study skills, were given.

The teacher of reading, accordingly, must think through carefully whether workbooks are desirable for her class and, if so, how her pupils can best use them. If workbooks are used to reduce the amount of oral instruction, they are valuable, as the teacher substitutes other worthwhile educational services. If they help the teacher to provide for individual differences among her pupils and if they develop independence in reading, their use is probably justified. On the other hand, they are not a substitute for direct, first-hand experiences and for charts describing them. They are not as closely adapted to the needs of an individual child as materials specially prepared for that child would be. Assigned lessons to be learned and stereotyped tests are not substitutes for experiences contributing to desirable child growth. Reading workbooks can be helpful or harmful. The important factor is the way they are used.

Visual Materials

The modern reading program involves more than books, teacher-prepared materials, and workbooks. The use of experience charts has been mentioned and will be discussed further in Chapter 7. The

[19] Association for Childhood Education, *A Study of Reading Workbooks,* Bulletin of the Association, 40 p., Washington, D.C., 1939.

[20] David H. Russell, "Opinions of Experts about Primary-Grade Basic Reading Programs," *Elementary School Journal,* Vol. 44, pp. 602-609, June, 1944. David H. Russell and Marion A. Anderson, "Professional Opinions about Basic Reading Programs in the Middle and Upper Grades of the Elementary School," *Elementary School Journal,* Vol. 46, pp. 81-88, October, 1945.

teaching value of pictures is particularly important in the primary grades. In preprimers and primers where the vocabulary has been greatly simplified, the text requires pictures to round out the meaning of the story. One of the best-known criteria for pictures to be used in primary grades is "Does the picture tell a story?" Accordingly many teachers use picture cards. These may contain only a picture for stimulating language or developing readiness. Often they contain a picture accompanied by a word, phrase, or sentence. The cards may be used many times until recognition of the word symbols is possible without using the identifying pictures. Pictures are also valuable for helping to clarify concepts or ideas to be met in later reading.

Many teachers, especially in the primary grades, use word cards as another form of learning materials. These should not be regarded as flash cards in most circumstances, since emphasis upon speed of reading is seldom made at the primary level. At higher levels the cards may occasionally stress some values of speedy and accurate perception. The best method of use is probably to hold the cards behind a blank card and then show one for approximately a fifth of a second before replacing it behind the blank card. In an exercise, more difficult words or longer phrases may be introduced gradually.

Some publishers of basic readers issue large books, suitable for placing on an easel, which reproduce the early pages of the first preprimer. Such books seem to have value as transitional materials between experience charts and the books themselves.

A number of audio-visual materials and mechanical devices have been prepared which may be used in the reading program. These include films[21] which emphasize successive phrases in a page of reading material, which direct eye movements across a series of lines by means of the "bouncing Ball" device, a "flash meter,"[22] and a metronoscope,[23] which flashes phrases of various sizes at controlled speeds across a space corresponding to a line of print. As suggested in Chapter 4, the values of these devices have not been fully established,[24]

[21] Walter F. Dearborn, H. Anderson, and J. R. Brewster, "A New Method for Teaching Phrasing and for Increasing the Size of Reading Fixations," *Psychological Record,* Vol. 1, pp. 459-475, December, 1937.

[22] Manufactured by the Keystone View Company, Meadville, Pa.

[23] Manufactured by the American Optical Company, Southbridge, Mass.

[24] Eloise B. Cason, *Mechanical Methods for Increasing the Speed of Reading: An Experimental Study at the Third-Grade Level,* Contributions to Education, No. 878. Bureau of Publications, Teachers College, Columbia University, New York, 1943. Arthur E. Traxler, "Value of Controlled Reading: a Summary of Opinion and Research," *Journal of Experimental Education,* Vol. 11, pp. 280-292, June, 1943. Robert Karlin, "Machines and Reading: a Review of Research," *Clearing House,* Vol. 32, pp. 349-352, February, 1958.

and their use is not common in different school systems. Perhaps of more value are simple tachistoscopes,[25] or devices for controlling the length of exposure of words or phrases, and also the reading-rate controller or reading accelerator in which a solid plate covers successive lines of print at controlled rates. Such devices may be large and elaborate, or they may be simple and inexpensive, like the cardboard one designed by Durrell.[26] These devices and the use of films and film strips may increase interest in reading, especially among pupils who have not succeeded in it previously. The more complex, expensive machines do not always justify their cost in use by the classroom teacher. However, teachers themselves can make films or film strips with captions to be read by pupils.[27] Another example of materials much like the usual small booklets but carefully graded for reading difficulty are the *SRA Reading Laboratories,* one for elementary and one for secondary school students.[28] These were planned in part for remedial work with retarded readers but they may have other uses in regular classroom reading activities.

In addition to commercially prepared materials many teachers feel their reading program must always include visual materials specially prepared for a particular group or individual in it. Sometimes the pupils themselves write them; they are then reproduced by hectograph or mimeograph, so that all pupils can use them. Sometimes the teacher adapts materials to the reading levels of her class, often in the form of tests or informational matter. Sometimes these visual aids are those mentioned in the preceding section, such as word games, reading exercises, and other practice materials, which are placed on a special shelf available to pupils who have free time. These visual materials are often related to the work-type periods emphasizing skills and are changed frequently by the teacher. They are valuable as independent reading and work-type activities emphasizing visual methods only as the pupils have been carefully prepared for their use.

The School Library

No overview of the reading program in the elementary school is

[25] Various tachistoscopes are described in A. S. Harris, *How to Increase Reading Ability,* 3rd ed., pp. 525, 526. Longmans, Green, New York, 1956.

[26] Distributed by World Book Co., Yonkers, N.Y.

[27] Esther L. Berg, "Use of Filmstrip to Assist Retarded Readers," *Educational Screen,* Vol. 20, p. 281, September, 1941.

[28] Science Research Associates, Chicago.

complete without mention of the school library. If the teacher accepts as one of the aims of reading instruction the encouragement of "strong motives for and permanent interests in reading," she must rely on the school library, however large or small it may be. All studies of children's reading preferences indicate that they will read what is accessible to them. Making a variety of books and other reading materials available to all children is one of the first responsibilities of the teacher and other school authorities. The usual way of making such provision is, of course, in the school library.

The elementary-school library usually exists as a central collection and, in schools with more than one classroom, as a series of changing room collections. The latter are placed on a library table, on an easily reached shelf, or in an attractive book corner decorated with book covers, a chart of books read by pupils, pupils' pictures based on materials they have read, and similar objects. Some of these books contain information needed in social studies, science, health, and other activities in which the class is engaging. Others are individual story books for recreational reading in the children's free time throughout the day.

School libraries are still not as common as they should be, especially in rural areas; but many schools have a central library around which much of the work of the school revolves. These libraries contain, in addition to books and magazines, such materials of instruction as pamphlets, maps, pictures, slides, films, and recordings. The librarian is a regular member of the school staff working with pupils, other teachers, and the community. The library is used as a place of instruction in the use of library materials and as a source of material in curriculum revision and planning in the school system. A delightful account of how a modern library works as an integral part of the school program is given in Fenner's *Our Library*.[29]

Too few school libraries can meet all the tests involved, but the following criteria by Wilson[30] make one of the best statements of a modern school-library program:

(*a*) Adequate collections of material to support the curriculum and to provide for free reading by pupils; (*b*) proper rooms and equipment to ensure easy access to materials and library personnel; (*c*) provision in the school budget for the maintenance of materials and the operation of the

[29] Phyllis R. Fenner, *Our Library*, 172 p. Day, New York, 1942.

[30] Louis R. Wilson, "Introduction: Purposes and Scope of the Yearbook," *The Library in General Education*, Forty-second Yearbook, Part II, p. 8, National Society for Study of Education, Department of Education, University of Chicago, Chicago, 1943.

library, (*d*) formal or integrated programs of instruction for students in the use of materials; and (*e*) library personnel competent to organize and direct service in accord with the concepts of the modern school.

Library facilities which meet these criteria and a teaching staff which shares its own enjoyment of literature with children every day can be the most important factor in developing permanent reading habits and interests.

SUMMARY: CHECK LIST OF MATERIALS

The activities of the modern reading program are described in the following chapters of Part II and in Part III of this book. One way of summarizing the overview of the whole program given here is to list some of the materials which teachers and pupils use in the program. These lists for the primary and the postprimary grades are given as a check list against which a teacher, principal, or administrator may evaluate the adequacy of the reading program of a particular school. Yoakam[31] summarized some suggestions for the purchase and use of materials such as given in the check list. He recommended:

1. Buy several small sets of six to twelve copies of a number of different textbooks planned for the same level instead of one large set.
2. Obtain books of several different difficulty levels on the same topic but useful at the same grade level.
3. Start a subject catalogue of references to different topics found in available books. Add the readability levels to each title. The Rue Indexes[32] may be models here.
4. Catalogue history, geography, health and science books as well as readers.
5. Collect clippings from many sources, mount and catalogue.
6. If no library card index is available, catalogue books for free reading, perhaps marking for slow, average and fast readers.
7. Check reading lists of children's books from time to time to add to the card index.

Yoakam is conscious of the large amount of work suggested in this list and believes that teachers may reduce it somewhat by organizing it as a school staff or in some other co-operative fashion. As suggested in Chapter 17, sometimes parents can give efficient help in building

31 Gerald A. Yoakam, "Providing for the Individual Reading Needs of Children," *Education Digest*, Vol. 20, pp. 47-50, October, 1954.

32 Eloise Rue, *Subject Index to Books for Primary Grades*. American Library Association, Chicago, 1943. Eloise Rue, *Subject Index to Books for Intermediate Grades*, 2nd ed. American Library Association, Chicago, 1950.

Check List of Materials for the Reading Program

PRIMARY GRADES	INTERMEDIATE GRADES
( ) Concrete objects such as bells, water glasses, and wires for auditory discrimination	( ) Several basic series of readers at different grade levels corresponding to pupils' abilities
( ) Concrete visual materials such as different-shaped blocks and varied pictures	( ) Texts in arithmetic, social studies, etc. at levels of difficulty which pupils can read
( ) Concrete materials used in drawing, writing, and other kinesthetic experiences	( ) Workbooks related to a basic series of readers for certain pupils who seem to profit by their use
( ) Readiness books containing activities preparatory to formal reading	( ) Charts based on pupil experiences (science, vocabulary, standards for discussion, etc.)
( ) Charts based on experiences of the children	( ) Tests and exercises based on materials read in different parts of whole curriculum program
( ) Transition materials from charts to booklets	( ) Teacher-made materials for additional practice in reading skills—exercises, games, devices
( ) Preprimers related to charts or other group experiences	( ) Pupil-made materials related to reading, social studies, and other fields[33]
( ) Primers; first, second, and third readers	( ) Encyclopedia
( ) Tests and exercises based on these readers	( ) Dictionaries
( ) Workbooks and teacher-made practice materials	( ) A few standard reference books such as the *World Almanac*
( ) Individual "story books" suitable for each of the first three grades	( ) Individual library books related to children's interests and needs
( ) Picture dictionaries	( ) Some hectographed or mimeographed materials on the use of the specific library in the school
	( ) A few books on how to study[34]
	( ) Current periodicals adapted to levels of reading abilities and interests
	( ) Pamphlets, bulletins, and government reports related to curricular activities

[33] Lucile F. Fargo, *Activity Book for School Libraries,* 208 p. American Library Association, Chicago, 1940. Contains hundreds of suggestions for activities related to library books, vocabulary-development games, work-type exercises, and similar activities.

[34] For example, Robert W. Frederick, *How to Study Handbook.* Appleton-Century, New York, 1938.

up such good reference materials for a school's total reading activities.

A reading program which provides these materials, used in conjunction with the aims and methods described in this chapter, may be considered an adequate or superior reading program in a modern school.

SUPPLEMENTARY READINGS

ADAMS, FAY; GRAY L.; and REESE, D. *Teaching Children to Read,* rev. ed. Ronald, New York, 1957.

ANDERSON, IRVING H., and DEARBORN, W. F. *The Psychology of Teaching Reading.* Ronald, New York, 1952.

BETTS, EMMETT A. "Directed Reading Activities," *Educational Administration and Supervision,* Vol. 30, pp. 449-489, 532-559, November, December, 1944.

BETTS, EMMETT A. *Foundations of Reading Instruction,* rev. ed. American Book, New York, 1957.

BOND, GUY L., and WAGNER, EVA B. *Teaching the Child to Read,* 3rd ed. Macmillan, New York, 1960.

DURRELL, DONALD D. *Improving Reading Instruction.* World Book, Yonkers, N.Y., 1956.

GATES, ARTHUR I. *The Improvement of Reading,* 3rd ed., Chaps. 2, 5. Macmillan, New York, 1947.

GATES, ARTHUR I. "The Place of Basal Books in a Reading Program," *Teachers' Service Bulletin in Reading,* Vol. 1, No. 6, February, 1940.

HARRIS, ALBERT J. *How to Increase Reading Ability,* 3rd ed., Chaps. 1, 3. Longmans, Green, New York, 1956.

HILDRETH, GERTRUDE H. *Learning the Three R's,* 2nd ed., Chaps. 1, 5, 6, 11. Educational Publishers, St. Louis, Mo., 1947.

HILDRETH, GERTRUDE H. *Teaching Reading.* Holt, New York, 1958.

KOPEL, DAVID, and O'CONNOR, J. F. "Criteria for Evaluating Reading Textbooks," *Journal of Experimental Education,* Vol. 12, pp. 26-33, September, 1943.

McKEE, PAUL G. *The Teaching of Reading in the Elementary School,* Chaps. 1-6. Houghton Mifflin, Boston, 1948.

McKIM, MARGARET. *Guiding Growth in Reading.* Macmillan, New York, 1955.

National Society for Study of Education. *Teaching Reading in the Elementary School,* Forty-eighth Yearbook, Part II, Chaps. 1, 4, 8. University of Chicago Press, Chicago, 1949.

ROBINSON, HELEN M. *Materials for Reading.* Supplementary Educational Monographs, No. 86. University of Chicago Press, Chicago, 1958.

RUSSELL, DAVID H. *The Basic Reading Program in the Modern School.* Contributions to Reading, No. 1. Ginn, Boston, 1947.

WITTY, PAUL A., and KOPEL, DAVID. *Reading and the Educative Process,* Chaps. 1, 2, 10. Ginn, Boston, 1939.

YOAKAM, GERALD A. *Basal Reading Instruction.* McGraw-Hill, New York, 1955.

Chapter 6

THE READINESS PROGRAM

CONCEPT OF READINESS

In recent years the concept of readiness has influenced many school practices. The idea is largely an outgrowth of the child-study movement. It suggests that there is an optimum time for any particular learning and that attempts at instruction before this stage is reached are usually laborious and unsuccessful.

As Gates suggested,[1] readiness means somewhat different things to different people. Some regard it only as an expression of interest or purpose. Others describe it with emphasis upon general maturation which occurs in rather regular physical, mental, and other ways in most individuals. Some teachers and writers stress maturation in specific matters such as visual equipment or emotional security in a peer group. Still others believe that readiness depends upon information or abilities developed during educational experiences. It seems probable that readiness is usually a composite of all these, with the influence of any one factor depending upon the type of activity involved. Certainly all these factors seem involved in reading readiness.

A large body of information has been collected about reading readiness in the first grade.[2] Most writers agree that it depends upon (1) physical factors such as the child's ability to see words clearly, (2) mental factors such as the ability to follow an easy sequence of events in a story, (3) social-emotional factors such as the ability to work with the group, and (4) psychological factors such as interest in reading. Every primary teacher must diagnose her pupils' development in these areas. Suggestions for this are given below. Actually, however, the idea of readiness cannot be confined to first-grade or even primary-grade levels. Readiness is undoubtedly a factor in successful

[1] Arthur I. Gates, "Basal Principles in Reading Readiness Testing," *Teachers College Record,* Vol. 40, pp. 495-506, March, 1939.

[2] M. Lucille Harrison, *Reading Readiness,* rev. ed. Houghton Mifflin, Boston, 1939. Emmett A. Betts, *Foundations of Reading Instructions,* rev. ed. American Book, New York, 1957. Gertrude H. Hildreth, *Readiness for School Beginners.* World Book, Yonkers, N.Y., 1950.

reading at the intermediate and upper-grade levels. The same four main factors apply here as in the primary grades, except at higher levels of accomplishment. The teacher in the intermediate grades and the teacher of any subject such as history or mathematics in the high school must also be prepared to help pupils develop readiness for reading tasks at these levels.

A thorough understanding of the reading-readiness program is important for teachers and principals because of modern conditions of teaching. At the turn of the century, particularly in rural areas, children often did not go to school regularly until they were seven or eight years old. Nowadays children start school at an earlier age, particularly in urban areas. This means that primary teachers are working with children who are often immature and not ready for the rather complex task of reading from books. Few primary teachers still believe that all children should begin rather formal reading as soon as they enter school. All teachers know, however, that many children come to school expecting to learn to read in the first few weeks of their school life. These expectations receive little support from scientific knowledge of childhood and of learning. It is important, therefore, that all the personnel of a school system have an understanding of the problems of readiness and a clear-cut policy concerning it.

The need for such a policy is evidenced by the rather conflcting demands made on the school by parents of young children. Many parents expect their children to begin reading from books when they enter the first grade. Irrespective of the ability and maturity of the children, these ideas are often held by child and parent alike. Teacher and principal must assume some responsibility for interpreting the modern program of readiness work to both child and parent. Most parents who have been out of elementary school fifteen or twenty years need help in understanding the modern program. Through arranging for parents to visit the classroom, interviews with the teacher, talks at Parent-Teacher Association meetings, and other means teacher and principal must acquaint parents with the aims and procedures of the reading-readiness program. As Chapter 7 suggests, children are learning to read when they are learning to recognize rhymes or discriminate between two similar pictures which are somehow different, for they are building skills which will be useful in working with words.

The modern concept of readiness is that it is based on a combination of physical, mental, social, and psychological factors. General and specific maturation are important, but so are information, attitudes, and abilities gained through experiences. The teacher cannot just wait for readiness to be achieved. General maturation is important, but the teacher must also provide experiences which contribute to the growth of reading readiness.

FIRST-GRADE CHILDREN

On that milestone in their lives, the first day they enter school, children differ in every way we can measure them. They differ in such physical factors, for example, as height, weight, and strength of grip. More directly related to reading, every child in the first-grade class will differ in his vocabulary, his knowledge of stories, his ability to look at sentences or words to see details, his ability to express his ideas in a sentence, and his ability to distinguish between words which sound alike. Varying experiences with television programs and advertisements may further affect visual abilities and interests. With this large spread in abilities it is obvious that the first-grade teacher cannot have all children begin at the same place in learning to read. The old teaching rule of beginning at the child's level or building upon what is already known must be observed here as in other learning activities. In general, then, the first-grade teacher has three main tasks in regard to the reading program: (1) how to discover readiness or lack of it, (2) what experiences will compensate for lack of readiness, and (3) how to organize the classroom program and adjust it to the different needs and maturation levels of all the pupils.

DIAGNOSING READING READINESS

A teacher may discover readiness or lack of it in her pupils by three main methods:

1. The use of a reading-readiness test
2. The use of a general-ability or intelligence test
3. Directed observation of pupils' behavior

Readiness Tests

Readiness tests followed achievement and mental tests in first-grade programs, but some school systems now use them instead of mental tests to help teachers to place pupils in the group where they will make most progress. Where possible a combination of both a reading-readiness test and an intelligence test is probably a better diagnosis. Probably, however, the observation of behavior by the skilled teacher with some system of recording these observations is more important than either a reading test or a mental test at the beginning stages of reading. Henig[3] found that teachers' estimates of ninety-eight first graders after only three weeks of observation were just as accurate as a single readiness test in predicting reading achievement.

The following readiness tests are valuable:

Classification Test for Beginners in Reading. CLARENCE R. STONE and C. C. GROVER. Webster, St. Louis, Mo., 1933. [Picture-picture visual association. Picture-word visual association. Word-word visual association.]

Gates Reading Readiness Tests. A. I. GATES. Bureau of Publications, Teachers College, Columbia University, New York, 1939. [Picture directions, word matching, flash-card perception and word matching, rhyming, and individual letter- and number-reading tests. Different parts may be given at different times. Group tests with some individual attention for certain children.]

Lee-Clark Reading Readiness Test, rev. ed. J. MURRAY LEE and WILLIS W. CLARK. California Test Bureau, Los Angeles, Calif., 1951. [Match letter symbols. Understand concepts in oral English and identify common objects. Identify letters and words by making comparisons. May be given to 10-15 kindergarten or first-grade children.]

Metropolitan Readiness Test. G. H. HILDRETH and N. L. GRIFFITHS. World Book, Yonkers, N.Y., 1950 [Designed for kindergarten and grades 1 and 2. Six parts to the test. Requires approximately 70 minutes to give, but may be given in three sections. May be given to from 15 to 20 children, but it is recommended that it be made as individual as possible.]

Monroe Reading Aptitude Tests. MARION MONROE. Primary form. Houghton Mifflin, Boston, 1935. [For prediction and analysis of reading abilities. Visual, auditory, motor, articulation, and language tests. Group and individual items. Time: about 50 minutes.]

Murphy-Durrell Diagnostic Reading Readiness. HELEN A. MURPHY and DONALD D. DURRELL. World Book, Yonkers N.Y., 1949. [Tests of auditory discrimination, visual discrimination, and learning rate.]

[3] Max S. Henig, "Predictive Value of a Reading Readiness Test and of Teachers' Forecasts," *Elementary School Journal,* Vol. 50, pp. 41-46, September, 1949.

Van Wagenen Reading Readiness Tests. M. J. VAN WAGENEN. Educational Test Bureau, Minneapolis, 1932. [Word-word visual association. Word-knowledge auditory association.]

In addition to the seven standardized tests mentioned there are available to principals and teachers a number of reading-readiness tests each connected with a basic series of readers. These tests are composed of subtests similar to the ones mentioned above. (See illustration, page 172.) They differ from the general standardized test in that some of the particular test items relate to the materials to be found in the basic books. For example, they may test children's acquaintance with some of the words in the books or their knowledge of concepts which will be met later. Since one of the chief purposes of a reading readiness test is to predict later success in reading, the similarity in items between tests and books usually gives the teacher considerable information of value in helping the child. Such a test may have general predictive value, but it is most useful when the child is going to use the materials on which some of the test items have been based. As such, it may be for levels other than the first grade as well as for beginners. For example, the test of suffixes illustrated on page 173 includes words specifically used in the fourth-grade reader which the child will meet later.

All the tests named above, both general ones and those related to particular series, contain subtests which the authors believe will help to predict success in beginning stages of reading. Accordingly they include such items as tests of familiarity with words and phrases; seeing likenesses and differences in words and phrases; the ability to interpret pictures and drawings; the ability to follow teachers' directions; and the grasp of story structure. (See illustrations, pages 174 and 175.)

Some of the tests give a critical score above which the child is likely to succeed in reading and below which he definitely needs a program of activities leading to reading readiness. It seems unlikely that any test can arrive at a specific score which divides the good prospects from the poor ones. But in a more general way the scores may be interpreted to help the first-grade teacher (or a teacher of higher grades) in studying her pupils. Even more important, the pupils' abilities or disabilities as revealed on the specific items of the test may give the teacher a number of clues for definite help which a child needs or methods which he will find easy in beginning reading. In other words, the reading-readiness test may be used as an instru-

PRE-READING TEST 5 **Comprehension Readiness** SCORE--------

1. Find Tom and Betty.

2. Find Tom and Betty racing with Flip.

3. Find the one who came first.

4. Find what happened when they ran too fast.

9

Page from pre-reading test (David Russell and Constance McCullough, rev. ed., p. 9. Ginn, Boston, 1957)

ment of specific diagnosis for individual strengths and weaknesses, as well as a prediction of early progress in reading.

Intelligence Tests

A mental test may give some indication of a child's probable success in beginning reading. In general it will not give the teacher the specific suggestions for methods or work with the individual which

TEST 2. WORD ANALYSIS: c. Structural (Endings; Suffixes) Score-----

1. The old king ruled -----.	wisest	wiser	wise	wisely
2. Of the two roots, this is the -----.	deeper	deep	deepen	deeply
3. The money was taken by several -----.	thief	thieves	thieving	ex-thief
4. Try always to speak ---- to everyone.	kind	kindness	kindly	unkind
5. After the crash, the tug lay there -----.	helpless	helping	helper	helped
6. All the children were talking at once. They were very -----.	noisy	noise	noiseless	noisily
7. When Joe rode in an airplane, he thought he was the ---- boy in the world.	happy	happier	happiest	happiness
8. Over the mountains flew the plane. It was a ---- ride.	wondering	wonderful	wonder	wondered
9. We play outdoors when the sun is -----.	shine	shining	shines	shiny
10. The lake ---- in the sunshine.	sparkle	sparkly	sparkling	sparkled

Page from fourth-grade readiness text (David Russell and Constance McCullough, p. 5. Ginn, Boston, 1953)

she may get from a readiness test. However, the score on a mental test may be one of a number of indications of probable success or failure. A number of studies have shown that mental test scores and early success in reading have coefficients of correlation ranging from about .40 to about .55, depending on the tests used.[4] These are not high enough to predict later achievement of young children; but the

[4] Arthur I. Gates, Guy L. Bond, and David H. Russell, *Methods of Determining Reading Readiness*. Bureau of Publications, Teachers College, Columbia University, New York, 1939. Department of Educational Research, *Predicting Reading Achievements in First Grade*. Ontario College of Education, University of Toronto, Toronto, 1945.

mental test, particularly if it is an individual Stanford-Binet test, may give considerable information. It may indicate, for example, the size

Sample page from a reading-readiness book (*Fun with Tom and Betty,* rev. ed., p. 58. Ginn, Boston, 1957)

of the child's vocabulary, his memory for words and numbers, his ability to see relationships, and some of his visual-perception abilities. Particularly if a child seems to be having difficulties, a discussion of his test results between teacher and psychologist or psychometrist may have great value in increasing insight into his abilities.

A number of writers have claimed that a mental age of 6.5 is needed for success in beginning reading.[5] This statement should be

[5] Mabel U. Morphett and Carleton Washburn, "When Should Children Begin to Read?" *Elementary School Journal,* Vol. 31, pp. 496-503, 1931. Sam Duker and Thomas P. Nally, *The Truth About Your Child's Reading,* pp. 78-85. Crown, New York, 1956.

interpreted with the greatest caution. If true, it can guide practices generally rather than specifically. As in the case of a total score on a readiness test there is probably no one critical point on a test above

Understanding story sequence (Whitman Tell-a-Tale, *Little Red Riding Hood,* illustrated by Stella. Whitman, Racine, Wis., 1953)

which a child will succeed in reading and below which he will fail. However, given an average teacher with average equipment and an ordinary type of school program, there is some indication that a mental ability of approximately 6.5 is needed if a child is to achieve success in reading. This should not be interpreted to suggest that work in reading must be postponed until the child achieves such a mental test score. As Gates[6] pointed out, the important thing is probably not the mental test score of the child but the type of educational program in which he is participating. In Gates's study, children of mental ages about five years had reasonable success in reading where skillful teachers provided with a considerable amount of reading materials gave individual attention to the pupils. On the other hand, another group where the quality of instruction and materials was not as good required a mental age a full year in advance of that used in the first group for reading success. In other words, the important thing is not the mental age of the child but the quality of teaching and instructional materials, especially with reference to their adaptation to the needs of the individual child. Teachers cannot do much about a mental-test score, but they can capitalize on mental abilities in a well-planned program.

Observation of Pupil Behavior

Probably the best way of determining whether or not a child is ready to read from charts or preprimers is directed observation of the child's behavior in various situations in the classroom and on the playground. His reactions in situations involving books, charts, and words will give the most valuable clues to his possible reading success. However, the teacher must diagnose more widely than in such a situation as determining the child's ability to follow two or three simple sentences on the blackboard. As suggested above, reading readiness is a rather complex matter, and the teacher will often get hints for her work by watching other behaviors. Rather complete charts for determining readiness are given by Harrison,[7] by Bond and Wagner,[8] and in a bulletin issued by the New York Board of Education.[9] A summary of factors related to readiness which may be made into an individual problem chart or check list is given on the following pages.

[6] Arthur I. Gates, "The Necessary Mental Age for Beginning Reading," *Elementary School Journal,* Vol. 37, pp. 497-508, March, 1937.

[7] M. Lucille Harrison, *Reading Readiness,* rev. ed. Houghton Mifflin, Boston, 1939.

[8] Guy L. Bond and Eva Wagner, *Teaching the Child to Read,* 3rd ed. Macmillan, New York, 1960.

[9] J. Wayne Wrightstone, *Determining Readiness for Reading,* Educational Research Bulletin of the Bureau of Reference, Research and Statistics, pp. 27-31. Board of Education of City of New York, New York, September, 1943.

CHECK LIST FOR READING READINESS[10]

Physical Readiness

		Yes	No
1. Eyes			
a. Does the child seem comfortable in the use of his eyes (does not squint, rub eyes, hold materials too close or too far from eyes)?	1.	☐	☐
b. Are the results of clinical tests or an oculist's examination favorable?	2.	☐	☐
2. Ears			
a. Is it apparent through his response to questions or directions that he is able to hear what is said to the class?	3.	☐	☐
b. Does he respond to a low-voice test of 20 feet, a whisper test of 15 inches?	4.	☐	☐
c. Do the results of his audiometer test indicate normal hearing ability?	5.	☐	☐
3. Speech			
a. Does he articulate clearly?	6.	☐	☐
b. Does he speak in a group with some confidence?	7.	☐	☐
c. Does he speak without gross errors in pronunciation?	8.	☐	☐
d. Does he respond to suggestions for speech improvement?	9.	☐	☐
4. Hand-Eye Co-ordination			
Is he able to make his hands work together in cutting, using tools, or bouncing a ball?	10.	☐	☐
5. General Health			
a. Does he give an impression of good health?	11.	☐	☐
b. Does he seem well nourished?	12.	☐	☐
c. Does the school physical examination reveal good health?	13.	☐	☐

Social Readiness

		Yes	No
1. Co-operation			
a. Does he work well with a group, taking his share of the responsibility?	14.	☐	☐
b. Does he co-operate in playing games with other children?	15.	☐	☐
c. Can he direct his attention to a specific learning situation?	16.	☐	☐
d. Does he listen rather than interrupt?	17.	☐	☐

[10] Reprinted from pages 55-57 of the *Manual for Teaching the Reading-Readiness Program,* rev. ed. Ginn, Boston, 1957, by David H. Russell, Odille Ousley, and Grace B. Haynes.

2. Sharing

a. Does he share materials, without monopolizing their use? 18. ☐ ☐

b. Does he offer help when another child needs it? 19. ☐ ☐

c. Does he await his turn in playing or in games? 20. ☐ ☐

d. Does he await his turn for help from the teacher? 21. ☐ ☐

3. Self-reliance

a. Does he work things through for himself without asking the teacher about the next step? 22. ☐ ☐

b. Does he take care of his clothing and materials? 23. ☐ ☐

c. Does he find something to do when he finishes an assigned task? 24. ☐ ☐

d. Does he take good care of materials assigned to him? 25. ☐ ☐

Emotional Readiness

1. Adjustment to Task

a. Does the child see a task, such as drawing, preparing for an activity, or cleaning up, through to completion? 26. ☐ ☐

b. Does he accept changes in school routine calmly? 27. ☐ ☐

c. Does he appear to be happy and well adjusted in schoolwork, as evidenced by relaxed attitude, pride in work, and eagerness for a new task? 28. ☐ ☐

d. Does he follow adult leadership without showing resentment? 29. ☐ ☐

2. Poise

a. Does he accept a certain amount of opposition or defeat without crying or sulking? 30. ☐ ☐

b. Does he meet strangers without displaying unusual shyness? 31. ☐ ☐

Psychological Readiness

1. Mind-Set for Reading

a. Does the child appear interested in books and reading? 32. ☐ ☐

b. Does he ask the meanings of words or signs? 33. ☐ ☐

c. Is he interested in the shapes of unusual words? 34. ☐ ☐

2. Mental Maturity

a. Do the results of the child's mental test predict probable success in learning to read? 35. ☐ ☐

b. Can he give reasons for his opinions about his own work or the work of others? 36. ☐ ☐

c. Can he make or draw something to illustrate an idea as well as most children of his age? 37. ☐ ☐

d. Is his memory span sufficient to allow memorization of a short poem or song? 38. ☐ ☐

e. Can he tell a story without confusing the order of events? 39. ☐ ☐

f. Can he listen or work for five minutes without restlessness? 40. ☐ ☐

3. Mental Habits

a. Has the child established the habit of looking at a succession of items from left to right? 41. ☐ ☐

b. Does his interpretation of pictures extend beyond mere enumeration of details? 42. ☐ ☐

c. Does he grasp the fact that symbols may be associated with spoken language? 43. ☐ ☐

d. Can he predict possible outcomes for a story? 44. ☐ ☐

e. Can he remember the central thought of a story as well as the important details? 45. ☐ ☐

f. Does he alter his own method to profit by another child's example? 46. ☐ ☐

4. Language Patterns

a. Does he take part in class discussions and conversations? 47. ☐ ☐

b. Is he effective in expressing his needs in classroom situations? 48. ☐ ☐

c. Are the words used in the preprimers and the primer part of his listening and speaking vocabulary? 49. ☐ ☐

d. Does he understand the relationships inherent in such words as *up* and *down, top* and *bottom, big* and *little?* 50. ☐ ☐

e. Does he listen to a story with evidence of enjoyment and the ability to recall parts of it? 51. ☐ ☐

f. Is he able to interpret an experience through dramatic play? 52. ☐ ☐

Not all the foregoing items may be pertinent for any one child. However, in general the primary teacher will help the child to make a good start if she watches children carefully in terms of behavior related to the overlapping categories of their physical, social, emotional, and psychological readiness. Some teachers make these items into a check list with one sheet for each pupil, followed by a few notes on teaching procedures which seem best for that pupil.

EXPERIENCES TO COMPENSATE FOR LACK OF READING READINESS

Children come to school with different backgrounds of experience, as well as different abilities. Some will have traveled extensively; others may not have been more than ten miles away from their homes in all their lives. Some children will have shared many books and stories with their parents and other adults; others come from homes where little or no reading of any sort is done. Some children may have "half concepts" or partial understandings as a result of television programs. Even children who have had a rather rich background may not have understood all they have seen. The teacher's work is to build up an understanding of certain ideas or developed concepts. The first-grade program must be planned to give children some common experiences which they can use as background for their discussions and later their reading. Someone has remarked that reading is not so much getting experience from the printed page as bringing experience to the printed page. In this sense, experiences of children in the kindergarten and first grade are a basic foundation for any future reading.

Building concepts is usually a slow process. A two-year-old acquiring speech will first attach the word *picture* to a particular object in his home. It is some time before he can associate "pictureness" with a large variety of objects ranging from story illustrations to large oil paintings. In general the concept of even so concrete a thing as a picture is built up through a considerable variety of experiences. Some of the most abstract ideas considered suitable for the first grade, such as *tall* and *short* or *above* and *below* used in describing letters, will take an even longer time and greater variety of experience before the concept is established. Most first-grade programs involve some time spent in studying the home. Homes vary greatly in their physical characteristics, in the people who are there, in the types of work done by parents and children, and in the whole pattern of family relationships, especially the place of the child. Even in such common experiences as *home* and *family,* then, considerable discussion, use of pictures, visits to homes, and making up stories about one's family may be needed. In other first-grade programs where some phase of the community or the farm may be studied, there is even greater need of building up common understandings. Such understandings involve more than being able to say a few words. The primary teacher, and indeed all teachers, should never confuse the ability to verbalize with real knowledge. A child may imitate a teacher or book in saying that "An island is a body of land completely surrounded by water" without ever having seen an island or a model of one. Any concept requires considerable variety of experience before it is really understood.

The first-grade teacher in a readiness program, accordingly, will plan a wide variety of experiences. The aim of these experiences will be to improve personal and social relationships in the group, build new concepts and abilities to express them, develop an interest in books, and lead up to simple reading skills. Actual experiences for the program include the following:

1. *Trips*—round the school building and yard, to places of interest in the community.
2. *Follow-up activities after trips*—discussions and reports, dramatic play, making a scrapbook, recording experiences on simple charts, listening to stories and poems on related topics.
3. *Experiences with pictures*—a picture file, scrapbooks made by the children, picture charts grouped around certain ideas such as animals or vegetables, story books with pictures, illustrated nursery rhymes, bulletin-board displays.
4. *Play*—experiences in play in classroom and playground, on week ends and holidays; dramatic play involving home or community activities.
5. *Language experience*—conversations, storytelling, dramatizations, discussion, planning, vocabulary-building, simple reporting.
6. *Library experiences*—visiting the library, borrowing simple books, storytelling in the library.
7. *Games and devices*—listening to sounds and words, looking at objects and words for differences and similarities, rhythmic activities associated with poems and nursery rhymes, exercises for building concepts of color, left and right, top and bottom, language games to encourage sentences and clear enunciation.
8. *Preliminary reading experiences*—discovering that charts may record ideas, learning one's own name and simple labels around the classroom, learning to use a readiness book in connection with basic readers, learning to relate blackboard stories to charts and to mimeographed or hectographed pages.

Most modern series of basic readers begin with a readiness book. These books are designed to foster abilities and interests such as those listed in the four categories given in the previous section. They do not require formal reading; but they stimulate discussion, develop concepts, foster understanding of sequence in a story, and give practice in simple visual and auditory perception, all of which are needed for success in early reading activities. As in the case of readiness tests related to a basic series, the readiness book often contains material which will reappear in preprimers in a somewhat different form. Working with a readiness book can never be considered as an adequate total program of readiness work because of the nature of readiness as outlined in this chapter. However, the use of readiness books, along with other activities, gives children practice in handling books, in working in a group, and in habits and skills which will be valuable in later reading activities.

The foregoing list is a mere indication of what the teacher may do to build readiness for reading. In general these activities are concerned with the child's adjustment to school and to his group, with building concepts which he will meet in his early reading and social-studies experiences, developing an interest in reading, and building some specific habits and skills, such as auditory and visual discrimination, which will be of value in early reading tasks. Even at the readiness level a broad program of developmental activities will do more than a narrowly conceived program to foster initial reading activities.

ORGANIZING THE CLASSROOM PROGRAM

The first-grade teacher usually finds it convenient to divide her class into about three different groups. This first division is usually a tentative one based on some of the diagnostic procedures outlined above—results of tests and her observations of the pupils' behavior. In an average class the more mature pupils will be ready for reading from books with very little preliminary preparation. They may require a short time to make the adjustments to school and a larger group of children. They must be able to share in trips, picture study, and other language experiences; but they are probably ready to read from charts almost as soon as they enter school, and they can make the transition from charts to preprimers very easily.

The second, or average, group of pupils in the class will take longer in making the adjustment to school and the work of reading from charts, teacher-made booklets, and preprimers. It is impossible to state any general rules which apply to all groups of children; but ordinarily the teacher will plan for this group a program of readiness activities such as that outlined above, which stretches from about one month to three months. There can be no general prescription in terms of time. Older children may require less; young, immature children usually should have more. During this period the children are learning to read in the best sense of the term. They are learning at the level at which they can succeed and from which they can progress toward more formal reading activities. Their readiness activities will merge so gradually into actual reading that few of them will realize they have accomplished the first important hurdles of the task.

The third, or low, group in the class ordinarily will require a longer preparation for reading. Again it is impossible to state a program for any group without studying the individuals in that group carefully. The program of reading readiness for this group may run anywhere, on the average, from three to six months. There are two or three children in most first-grade classes who are not ready to read at the end of a year's program. Usually the low group will need a large amount of direct guidance by the teacher. When she can arrange it, a few minutes' work with individual pupils or two or three pupils will be of much profit to them. The teacher ordinarily will need a large variety of materials for the group. Since time is often limited, she may find it of value to use readiness books and supplementary materials directed toward developing readiness for reading.

The good modern teacher plans the reading program in a general sort of way before a new term opens. She attempts to get what information she can about her pupils as individuals, and she knows what reading materials of various types are available. In addition, she plans the reading program on a weekly basis. She must arrange to give direct guidance to each group in the class. Such guidance will probably be given to the best group at least once a day, and for the average and low groups it may be twice a day. As important as planning direct readiness activities or actual reading is the fitting in of the readiness or reading activities with the rest of the school program. Sometimes children in the first grade (and their parents) do not feel a child has read unless he has read orally to a group from a reader. Experienced teachers know that even in the first grade reading activities exist in many forms. Work in language and social studies will contribute much to the reading program. All these factors go into preliminary plans.

The planning of specific lessons in first-grade reading will depend upon the children involved and the materials selected by the teacher or the school for the reading program. In general, teachers will find it helpful to consult the manuals accompanying basic sets of readers now used in schools (see illustration, page 184). These manuals have

Telling stories

1. Cut out pictures from magazines of activities that the story Father might do to help around home—moving, building, repairing toys, and the like. Have the children tell

Making a display

stories about the pictures. Then post them on a large chart or on the bulletin board. Lead the children to suggest a title for the display; for example, "What Father Does."

Drawing

2. Give each child a paper with the word *Father* on it. Ask each child to draw a picture of some activity he enjoys doing with his father.

Talking together

3. As an outcome of the drawing activity, encourage the children to tell about the work that their fathers do, and about what their fathers do to play with them.

Telling a Story about Father

Making word blocks

4. Provide manuscript copies of the words *Father* and *Mother* with dashed lines around each word for tracing and blocking. After the word blocks have been traced and lightly filled in, lead the children to observe the similarities and differences in the word forms and in the words themselves.

Page of manual to accompany a basic reader (*Manual for Teaching the Reading-Readiness Program,* rev. ed., p. 194. Ginn, Boston, 1957)

been prepared by competent teachers and other experts in the teaching of reading. They ordinarily represent good practices in terms of the material in the particular series of books involved. As a teacher knows her class thoroughly and gains experience she will always adapt the suggestions in the manuals to the needs of her particular group. Many teachers, however, after years of experience still refer to the manuals for some specific suggestions which they may use in planning their lessons. They may not adopt these completely, but they use them as a basis for their procedures.

Dunklin[11] listed some of the essential qualities of the first-grade program which summarize teaching during this period:

1. Instruction is characterized by an appreciation of individual problems.
2. Definite objectives guide the instruction.
3. The child's status with relation to his attainment of these objectives is known at the beginning.
4. It is also known continuously throughout the course of instruction.
5. Provision is made for the child's constitutional and other limitations.
6. Progress of instruction is adjusted to the child's ability.
7. At each step sufficient reading experience is provided to ensure success.
8. Special reading activities are provided with guidance by the teacher to meet specific needs.
9. The instruction engages the child's interest and effort.
10. The adjustment is evidenced by daily success.

WHEN TO BEGIN FORMAL READING

The preceding section indicates that different children begin reading from books at different times. No specific rule can be laid down for any child without knowing him as an individual. However, the whole problem is such an important one that a few general suggestions on the whole question should be considered by primary teachers and principals. Some teachers believe that postponing actual reading is coddling the child. Other writers have suggested that formal reading should be postponed until as late as eight or nine years of age.[12] What are a few points to be considered in determining when the child should begin formal reading?

[11] H. T. Dunklin, *The Prevention of Failure in First Grade Reading*, Teachers College Contributions to Education, No. 802. Bureau of Publications, Teachers College, Columbia University, New York, 1940.

[12] Edgar A. Doll, "Psychological Moments in Reading," *Baltimore Bulletin of Education*, Vol. 23, pp. 46-53, November, 1945. Also *Education Digest*, Vol. 11, pp. 5-7, November, 1945.

Gates said that the determination of the optimum time of beginning reading seemed a problem of determining the maximum general and social returns from learning to read at any given time.[13] In other words, the problem is not only one of determining at what age the child can learn to read easily and effectively but also one of the value of reading in comparison with other activities. In some modern families the number of children is small, and in preschool years children in certain urban communities and in some rural areas have little opportunity for gaining experience in work and play with a group of their peers. In some first-grade classes, accordingly, the chief problem of the first-grade teacher at the beginning of the year is promoting adjustment to school and to the group. Only as these adjustments are achieved can the child begin to develop successfully certain academic abilities. If much stress is placed upon learning some words and little attention is paid to general preparation for school life, the first-grade program must be considered a failure.

Another factor in determining the optimum time for beginning reading is, of course, the nature of the reading program itself. Davidson[14] showed that bright three-year-olds can learn to read if they have a large amount of individual attention and many materials adapted to their particular needs. It seems probable, however, that three-year-olds can be doing more profitable things than learning to read. If the teacher finds herself in the school system with few materials and incentives for reading, she may be wise to postpone the program until with the co-operation of her principal and other teachers she can provide some of these materials and incentives.

As indicated above, the nature of the child himself must be considered in determining when to begin formal reading. A study by Gates and Russell[15] indicated that a group of dull-normal, underprivileged children make somewhat better scores on standardized tests in reading when formal reading has been postponed a term than when they are initiated into such reading early in their first term in school. There was even a possibility that delaying their reading a longer time would have meant greater achievement a year or so

[13] Arthur I. Gates and Guy L. Bond, "Reading Readiness—A Study of Factors Determining Success and Failure in Beginning Reading," *Teachers College Record*, Vol. 37, p. 684, May, 1936.

[14] Helen P. Davidson, "An Experimental Study of Bright, Average, and Dull Children at the Four-Year Mental Level," *Genetic Psychology Monographs* 9, Nos. 3 and 4, 1931.

[15] Arthur I. Gates and David H. Russell, "The Effects of Delaying Beginning Reading a Half Year in the Case of Underprivileged Pupils with IQ's 75-95," *Journal of Educational Research*, Vol. 32, pp. 321-328, January, 1939.

later. The study demonstrated that it was better for these children to have a varied program of enrichment and adjustment activities without formal instruction in reading, writing, and arithmetic for the first term at least. Related to this finding is the discussion by Stock[16] based on observation in schools. He believed that "pupils capable of fast-learning are being moved too slowly and that slow-learning pupils are being moved too rapidly in their developmental reading programs."

There is also some evidence that early pressures for reading may have an unfavorable effect upon the child's later success. Gardner[17] showed that children in some English schools taught by early informal methods seemed to gain in later powers of persistence, intelligent application, and understanding over children in classes where formal reading was begun immediately in the first grade. If the teaching of reading to young children is postponed, some evidence reveals that early instruction in reading produces higher scores on reading tests at the end of the first grade, but that this advantage is lost within the next couple of years and that children who made the early good scores are even somewhat below comparable children who began reading later.[18]

The proper time to begin formal reading activities is a problem which has grown to huge proportions in many school systems. The lowering of age for admission to first grade to five and one-half years is common, a contrast to two or three generations ago, when children were often seven or eight years of age when they entered school. In an early article which is still pertinent today, Otto[19] pointed out that the chief criterion of promotion from kindergarten to the first grade is chronological age; but the basis shifts, and the chief criterion of promotion from first to second grade is usually reading ability. Otto doubted that the basis should shift so rapidly from the child to "the organized machinery of the school."

Another proposal of an administrative nature that has been made

16 Earl K. Stock, "Some Field Observations on Early-Grade Progress in Reading," *Elementary School Journal,* Vol. 55, pp. 517-521, May, 1955.

17 D. E. M. Gardner, *Testing Results in the Infant School,* 2nd ed. Methuen, London, 1948.

18 Eleanor G. Robison, "A Comparison of Three Beginning Reading Programs," unpublished master's thesis. University of California, Berkeley, 1948. Beatrice E. Bradley, "An Experimental Study of the Readiness Approach in Reading," *Elementary School Journal,* Vol. 56, pp. 262-267, February, 1956.

19 Henry J. Otto, "Implications for Administration and Teaching Growing out of Pupil Failures in First Grade," *Elementary School Journal,* Vol. 33, pp. 25-32, September, 1932.

from time to time is that boys enter school or start formal reading activities later than girls. For example, Pauly[20] proposed a higher legal entrance age for boys and, in other writing, the revision of educational norms to take account of sex differences. Because of the tremendous overlap in boys' and girls' abilities and because of inconvenience to parents, such proposals may be questioned. Prescott,[21] for example, found on the basis of nearly fifteen thousand cases that boys in first grade scored a little over two points less than girls on a readiness test, even when the boys were a little older. He concluded on the basis of over-age and under-age studies, however, that readiness norms by sex would have little practical value.

One administrative device to meet the needs of children not ready for reading from books is that of the "junior primary" or "junior first class." In one study of such provisions in California schools it was found that 43 per cent of the school systems replying to a questionnaire had, in addition to readiness programs in regular first grades, special classes given such names and stressing readiness activities.[22] A full description of such a plan in one city was given by Hagaman.[23] The program is characterized by an exceptionally large variety of worthwhile enterprises, many of which contribute to reading readiness. Most of the programs stress informal activities and flexibility in caring for the different needs of different children.

The role of kindergarten experiences in a reading readiness program is important and sometimes controversial. Some kindergartens are guided by the philosophy that the activities should be informal and concerned with general adjustment to school and group rather than directed specifically to reading or other school work. Some teachers and parents feel, on the other hand, that the most advanced and verbally competent in a group of five-year-olds are ready for somewhat more formal reading readiness or reading activities. They sometimes point to practices in such countries as Scotland and Australia where five-year-olds are commonly given formal instruction in reading.

[20] Frank R. Pauly, "Sex Differences and Legal School Entrance Age," *Journal of Educational Research,* Vol. 45, pp. 1-9, September, 1951.

[21] George A. Prescott, "Sex Differences in Metropolitan Readiness Test Results," *Journal of Educational Research,* Vol. 48, pp. 605-610, April, 1955.

[22] David H. Russell and Ruby L. Hill, "Provisions for Immature Five-and-Six-Year Olds in California Schools," *California Journal of Elementary Education,* Vol. 16, pp. 210-233, May, 1948.

[23] Neva C. Hagaman, "Transition First-Grade Classes and Their Values," *California Journal of Elementary Education,* Vol. 15, pp. 171-192, February, May, 1947.

The answer to the question can best be worked out by teachers and others for a particular school or school system in terms of a philosophy of desirable educational aims for young children and the research evidence available. Since definitive research is unavailable, the aims of parents and school people for young children's development must be given considerable weight. Should five-year-olds be developing large-muscle skills and abilities to get along with others or should they give considerable time to academic learnings? If the question is not "either–or," what place in the total program should specific readiness or general readiness activities be given?

Answers to such questions must be worked out partly in terms of the desires of parents for their children and partly in accordance with the knowledge of child development of teachers, the school psychologist, and other professional people.

The answers from research, although incomplete, indicate that both general and specific types of kindergarten programs have favorable effects on readiness and later reading success. For example, in an early study by Morrison[24] of the progress of 13,750 children showing non-promotion after Grade I, it was found that retardation was much more frequent for children who had not attended kindergarten. In a later study Fast[25] pointed out that many previous studies of the effects of kindergarten did not deal with comparable groups because of the factor of home influence in the voluntary nature of most kindergarten attendance. Furthermore, in some studies children did not attend the same schools. Fast controlled age, I.Q., home background, and school environment factors in three urban schools and found that children who had had kindergarten experience were superior to those who had not in tests of reading readiness at the beginning of the first grade, word recognition at the middle of the first year, and paragraph reading at the end of the year. Fast said that there were reading readiness activities in the kindergartens involved, but that reading was not formally taught, the major part of the program being "devoted to the more general development of social skills, the ability to work independently and in groups, and the acquisition of verbal and manual skills."[26]

[24] J. Cayce Morrison, "Influence of Kindergarten on the Age-Grade Progress of Children Entering School Under Six Years of Age: Abstract," *Role of Research in Educational Progress*, pp. 19-21. Official Report of American Educational Research Association, 1937.

[25] Irene Fast, "Kindergarten Training and Grade I Reading," *Journal of Educational Psychology*, Vol. 48, pp. 52-57, January, 1957.

[26] *Ibid.*, p. 56.

Based on experience rather than research is Cowin's[27] recommendation, "Although a formal type of readiness program has no place in the modern kindergarten, much can be done in an informal way." Cowin recommends such general experiences as free play, dramatic play, and planned excursions. She also advises using other activities somewhat more closely related to reading readiness, namely, storytelling, training in listening and carrying on a group discussion, learning one's own name, matching pictures and working puzzles, learning nursery rhymes, and engaging in oral expression activities.

In another type of study at the kindergarten level of factors related to readiness, Sutton[28] found as a result of tests given to 150 children and questionnaires given to parents and interviews with parents that the most significant correlation coefficients (some Pearson Product Moment and some bi-serial) with readiness scores were as follows: occupation of father .56, family trips .56, independent play .36, visits to regional library .31, interested in magazines .30, television set —.24 and mother working —.27. None of these corelations was high enough to give individual predictions of reading success or failure but they suggest some of the family factors which may affect the development of readiness at the kindergarten level. In a similar study of home factors related to first-grade reading achievement Almy[29] found that many children had had some variety of reading instruction in the home prior to first-grade attendance and that such experience in skills and attitudes related to beginning reading were important as they "fit into his whole life pattern." Positive relationships were found between reading success and such experiences as looking at books and magazines, being read to, and interest in words, letters and numbers.

In another study of children who learned to read before they entered first grade, Durkin[30] found about one per cent of children in this category in a large California city. At the beginning of the school year some fifty children had an average reading grade of 2.3 and at the end of one year the average was 3.7. Durkin believed the

[27] Shirley H. Cowin, "Reading Readiness Through Kindergarten Experience," *Elementary School Journal,* Vol. 52, pp. 96-99, October, 1951.

[28] Rachel S. Sutton, "A Study of Certain Factors Associated with Reading Readiness in the Kindergarten," *Journal of Educational Research,* Vol. 48, pp. 531-538, March, 1955.

[29] Millie C. Almy, *Children's Experiences Prior to First Grade and Success in Beginning Reading,* Contributions to Education, No. 954. Bureau of Publications, Teachers College, Columbia University, New York, 1949.

[30] Dolores Durkin, "The Precocious Reader: A Study of Pre-School Reading Ability," *California Journal for Instructional Improvement,* Vol. 2, pp. 24-28, December, 1959.

beginning reading ability could be attributed to (a) intelligence (b) personality characteristics and (c) family pressure. The mean I.Q. of the group was 122, they were "persistent" and "competitive," and the greatest pressure to read seemed to be their own curiosity plus a combination of the influence of parents and older siblings (usually mothers and sisters). The most frequent activities were being read to at home and parents' identifying words and helping the child with printing. In a follow-up study, Durkin has usually discovered superior progress where the school has made some special provisions for these good readers, but also has found that a few children do not continue to be superior readers.

Such studies of kindergarten and home influences suggest that children will vary widely in the factors in their backgrounds which are related to reading and that it is important for the first-grade teacher to know something of each child's previous experiences. Durkin's findings about special school arrangements for reading instruction and for ability grouping indicate that the problem of providing for differences among children begins early (see Chapter 15).

The question, then, of when an individual child shall begin rather formal reading from books is one which must be decided on an individual basis. Such factors as the relative values of different experiences, the available materials for the program, the maturity of the child, the nature of his background of experiences, and the question of his total social adjustment must be considered. In any case the transition from prereading activities to actual reading is a gradual one, and the best evidence the teacher can find of readiness for reading will come in the pupil's success with prereading activities closely related to the reading process. Such evidence may be collected on a form like the one on pages 177 to 179. School arrangements such as close relations between kindergarten and first-grade teachers and junior first or transition groups that give opportunity for study of individual children are valuable in determining when to begin more formal reading activities.

USE OF EXPERIENCE CHARTS

Experience charts are one of the best ways of making the gradual transition from prereading to actual reading. A complete description of how to make and use such charts was given by Lamoreaux and Lee.[31] They and other authorities suggested that charts can be used

[31] Lillian A. Lamoreaux and Doris M. Lee, *Learning to Read through Experience*. Appleton-Century, New York, 1943.

very early in the school career of almost any child. When the group have had an interesting experience, they probably want to talk about it. This desire to discuss the trip or the science experience in the classroom may not be apparent for a day or two after the actual happening. Following such discussion the teacher can suggest that she should write down one or two of the important parts of the story. After this has been done on the blackboard a few times, the teacher may wish to transfer the material to a more permanent tag-board chart. In the first work with charts the children are not required to know all the words or to read the chart exactly. Rather, the teacher is developing the idea that meanings can be recorded by a set of symbols. If charts are used, the children will become accustomed to the fact that certain symbols reappear; and eventually they may associate them more definitely with the words they represent. Finally they may be reading them rather exactly.

Certain mechanics for the making of charts are known to most teachers. The charts may be illustrated by pictures or the child's own drawing at the top or bottom. At first the charts should consist of only two or three simple sentences. Each of these should be on one line. Later they may be divided by phrases for a run-over line. Many teachers put the title about three inches from the top of the chart and the same distance from the first line. They plan the different lines to be about three inches apart and the different words about an inch apart. These may be written in manuscript writing with black ink and a lettering pen or with black crayon. (See illustration, page 193.) After the children have become used to chart-reading, most of the good charts should be made at least twice and the second one divided into sentences and later into phrases and word strips.

The following are the usual steps in constructing a chart:

1. The children have a common experience.
2. They discuss the experience and clarify their ideas about it.
3. The teacher notes the common concepts of the group.
4. The teacher records on the blackboard some of these common concepts.
5. The teacher prints the chart twice.
6. The children read the chart as a whole, then by parts, matching sentences or words and reassembling the parts. Finally they read it as a whole again.
7. The chart is filed with others for future reference and reviewed occasionally.

Father is big.
Mother is big.
Tom is not so big.
Betty is little.
Susan is little, too.

Go, go, go.
Up and down.
Up and down.
See Patrick's airplane.
Go, go, go.

Sample Charts Based on Experience and Leading to Basal Materials

With some direct guidance by the teacher most children find it easy to make the transition from charts to smaller books. The teacher may help the transition by having pupils refer occasionally to pictures in books to solve their problem. She may reproduce the chart exactly in a hectographed sheet, and a series of these may be combined in a booklet. As mentioned in Chapter 5, charts may be obtained commercially in the form of "big books" which reproduce exactly the first pages of a preprimer. During this transition time the teacher has been careful to restrict the vocabulary used in charts and to use words which will appear in the preprimer. At the same time she has encouraged the children to acquire some specific abilities in word recognition which they will develop further in the initial reading stage.

The use of charts should not be confined to the first grade or even the primary grades. They may be used in the intermediate and higher grades in such forms as these:

1. Planning for work in the social studies and related fields. "We need to know . . ."
2. Records of group experiences—the steps in an experiment in science, or the log of activities in social studies.
3. A summary of important information reorganized and simplified from certain texts—particularly useful for the poorer readers in the group.
4. Vocabulary lists—some common Spanish words, if the class is studying Latin America. "Words we know" in dictionary style.
5. Standards of performance or ways of working—what is a good citizen in the fifth grade, or qualities of a good oral report as worked out by the children over a period of time or independent activities. (See illustration on opposite page.)
6. Records of current events—weather charts, school news, special incidents in the community.

READING READINESS AT ALL SCHOOL LEVELS

Not only are charts useful at all elementary-school levels but the idea of reading readiness itself applies in all grades. It is important that teachers in the intermediate and upper grades be conscious of the problem and take definite steps to meet it. There are at least two reasons why readiness is an intrinsic part of the reading program in all grades.

First, pupils differ even more widely in the higher grades than they do in the first grade. As suggested above, children on entering school differ in almost every way we can measure them. Since wide differ-

Free Time

Assignment finished. All other work done?

Suggestions for free time.

1. Study spelling words for your next test.
2. Practice adding columns.
3. Read a library book.
4. Work on science report.
5. Find some poetry to read or learn.
6. Practice reading songs.
7. Draw pictures.
8. Write a story for class.

Perhaps you can think of something else you would like to do. Time is valuable--use it!

Chart of Suggestions for Independent Activities

ences exist in their ability to use language, their knowledge of stories, and their abilities in visual perception, for example, the first-grade teacher divides her classes into groups and plans a readiness program for the children who need it. But as children advance through the grades the differences between them tend to increase. The slow-learning child not only continues to learn more slowly, but his gains in achievement begin to taper off earlier. The bright child ordinarily learns more and continues such gains longer. Current systems of promotion where children are not retarded work out favorably for most children. In some schools, however, they may tend to increase differences in academic achievements in the upper grades. Present-day mobility of school children means that children in any one class may come from a large variety of different schools. All these factors tend to increase differences among children of any grade. Accordingly, as in the first grade, the teacher must plan readiness work for all the pupils and especially for the lower part of the group. A group of six-year-olds are not all ready to begin reading activities in a preprimer, and it is even more certain that a group of ten-year-olds are not all able to attack the materials of a fourth reader.

Second, the reading task becomes increasingly complex as the child or early adolescent moves through the different levels of the school program. What is accomplished reading in the third grade is not good reading in the sixth grade. Similarly, good reading at the sixth-grade level is not adequate at the ninth-grade level. The school curriculum is such that there are new demands at succeeding levels. Many pupils will not automatically acquire the ability to meet these reading tasks. They must be prepared for them. In the third grade a child may meet verbal problems in arithmetic or read simple biography for the first time. In the fourth grade he may be asked to use a wide variety of social-studies materials which demand such abilities as reading to understand the sequence of events or to interpret maps. In the ninth grade he may be called upon to read some rather abstract mathematical symbols or use new concepts of time, such as in geology or in ancient history. In general, then, a reading-readiness program stressing ways of attacking new materials is required.

Readiness at any level seems to depend upon previous achievements, general maturity, and orientation to the particular reading task at hand. In any grade the teacher is concerned with the background of related experiences possessed by the children, their interest in the material, and the clarity of their purposes in reading it. The steps a teacher may take to develop readiness at any level are not essentially different from the readiness program of the first grade. There are at least five ways in which the teacher of any grade may diagnose and develop readiness:

1. The teacher must make sure that basic reading skills have been developed earlier. An introduction to reading abilities is made in the primary grades, but not all pupils have acquired these abilities in sufficient amounts. Middle- and upper-grade teachers receive into their classes at least two groups, pupils who are adequately prepared for the work and those who are in various stages of incomplete preparation. Accordingly the teacher in the middle and upper grades must work to build up any deficiencies in earlier abilities, abilities which are sometimes assumed but not always present.

2. The teacher can stimulate interest in reading materials to be used. Setting the stage in terms of pupils' related experiences and indicating interesting items in the materials which will add to such experiences will be welcomed by most pupils. Such introductions suggest the importance of preparing the pupil for the reading task through introductory assignments, discussions, and audio-visual materials rather than mere checking on final results.

3. The teacher must be careful to build a background of concepts or ideas that are related to or occur in the reading materials. These concepts can be built best not by formal dictionary work but by providing experiences related to the ideas occurring in the selection to be read. Explanation, discussion, excursion, use of pictures, models, and maps may help in building related background. If the child is reading his first story of early California, he may need help with such concepts as *rancho, mission,* and *oxcart.* Meaning of words, phrases, and sentences must be developed before a whole selection can be read with profit by many of the children.

4. The teacher can provide a mental set for the material to be read. In literary materials there must be a matching of moods and purposes if pupils are to appreciate what they read. If pupils begin to read *Dr. Doolittle* or *Mary Poppins* in a mood of deadly seriousness, they will miss much of the purpose of the books. If the teacher will provide a little setting before the reading of *Hans Brinker* or of Abraham Lincoln's famous letter to Mrs. Bixby on the death of her five sons, the purposes of the reading will be related to the content of the material. Readiness for specific lessons must be created in this way.

5. Readiness in the middle and upper grades depends greatly upon making the pupil conscious of the method by which he may read a selection. As will be developed in later chapters, one of the important

lessons of the later school grades is that people read for a variety of purposes and suit their style of reading to the purpose. Good teachers now realize that there is no such thing as a single comprehension which covers all types of reading. Reading to get a general impression of the selection, for example, may be quite different from reading to note exact details in another selection. Pupils will learn that the approach to reading an adventure story for enjoyment may be quite different from that for tracing cause and effect in a socio-economic situation. It is important, then, that the pupil have a reason for his reading and that he understand how his method of reading may be adapted to it. One purpose may require only skimming; another may demand a careful organization of topics and subtopics. A consciousness of purpose plus suggestions for procedure is of value in most work-type reading or study situations. The teacher can provide specific readiness by helping the pupils to achieve this clear understanding of purpose and resulting method.

SUPPLEMENTARY READINGS

BETTS, E. A. *Foundations of Reading Instruction,* rev. ed. American Book, New York, 1957.

BOND, G. L., and WAGNER, EVA B. *Teaching the Child to Read,* 3rd ed. Macmillan, New York, 1960.

BRISTOW, W. H., and others. *Reading Readiness in the First Grade.* New York City Board of Education, Division of Curriculum Research, New York, 1942.

BROOM, M. E., and others. *Effective Reading Instruction in Elementary Schools,* 2nd ed. McGraw-Hill, New York, 1951.

COLE, L. *The Elementary School Subjects,* Chap. 6. Rinehart, New York, 1946.

DOLCH, E. W. *Teaching Primary Reading,* Chaps. 2, 3, 5, 6, 7. Garrard Press, New York, 1941.

GATES, A. I. "The Necessary Mental Age for Beginning Reading," *Elementary School Journal,* Vol. 37, pp. 497-508, March, 1937.

GATES, A. I.; BOND, G. L.; and RUSSELL, D. H. *Methods of Determining Reading Readiness.* Bureau of Publications, Teachers College, Columbia University, New York, 1939.

HARRIS, A. J. *How to Increase Reading Ability,* 3rd ed., Chap. 2. Longmans, Green, New York, 1956.

HARRISON, M. L. "Developing Readiness for Word Recognition," *Elementary English Review,* Vol. 23, pp. 122-131, March, 1946.

HARRISON, M. L. *Reading Readiness,* rev. ed. Houghton Mifflin, Boston, 1939.

HILDRETH, G. H. *Learning the 3 R's,* rev. ed., Chap. 7. Educational Publishers, St. Louis, Mo., 1947.

HILDRETH, G. H., comp. *Readiness for Learning.* Association for Childhood Education, Washington, D.C., 1941.

HILDRETH, G. H. *Readiness for School Beginners.* World Book, Yonkers, N.Y., 1950.

HUDSON, J. S. "Reading Readiness in the Intermediate Grades," *Elementary English Review,* Vol. 19, pp. 134-137, April, 1942.

HYMES, JAMES L. *Before the Child Reads.* Row, Peterson, Evanston, Ill., 1958.

LAMOREAUX, L., and LEE, D. M. *Learning to Read through Experience.* Appleton-Century, New York, 1943.

MONROE, MARION. *Growing Into Reading.* Scott, Foresman, Chicago, 1951.

RUSSELL, D. H. "Diagnosis of Reading Readiness at All School Levels," *The School,* Vol. 34, pp. 291-297, December, 1945.

SMITH, NILA B., chm. *Readiness for Reading and Related Language Arts.* Bulletin of National Conference on Research in English. National Council of Teachers of English, Champaign, Ill., 1950.

SULLIVAN, H. B., and McCARTHY, J. "Evaluation of Reading Readiness Materials," *Education,* Vol. 62, pp. 40-43, September, 1941.

WRIGHTSTONE, J. W. *Determining Readiness for Reading.* Educational Research Bulletin of Bureau of Reference, Research and Statistics. New York Board of Education, New York, 1943.

WULFING, G. "Maturation as a Factor in Learning," *California Journal of Elementary Education,* Vol. 4, pp. 72-84, 148-164, November, 1935, February, 1936.

Chapter 7

THE READING PROGRAM IN THE PRIMARY GRADES

In an elementary school, one of the greatest pleasures a visitor, parent, or professional educator can have is to observe a skilled teacher working with children in the primary grades who are learning to read. In successive classrooms the observer will note interested children, challenging materials, and teaching methods of a high order of efficiency. Research findings, publishers' ideas, and classroom experimentation by creative teachers have been combined over the years to produce excellent instruction in primary reading in most schools. The success of the usual program means that it may be regarded as a partial model for work in other curricular areas or at different levels of pupil development. Many different types of educational enterprise could be improved by similar clarity of aims, careful preparation of materials, and scientific studies of the advantages and disadvantages of various methods of teaching.

It is not the purpose of this chapter to give a complete list of suggestions for the efficient teaching of primary reading. Other chapters deal with specific parts of the program, such as the developing of meaning and recognition vocabularies (Chapters 9 and 10), providing for pupil differences (Chapter 15), and getting children to read critically and creatively (Chapter 14), for even young children are capable of this. In addition, good teachers' manuals which accompany readers give hundreds of specific suggestions for individual lessons, and many local courses of study contain other detailed suggestions for reading activities. It seems most important, then, to discuss the general nature of the primary program, the objectives of reading in this period, some controversial issues or vexing problems which primary teachers face, ways of planning a good primary program, and typical activities at various levels within the primary stage.

CHARACTERISTICS OF PRIMARY CHILDREN

One reason for the success of the primary reading program is its adaptation to the characteristics of the children involved. These characteristics are mentioned in Chapter 3, and the characteristics do not differ markedly from those of children beginning school, described in Chapter 6. Since growth is a continuous process, the less mature children in the second and even the third grade are somewhat like the most advanced beginners in school. Physical growth is still rapid, and there is a marked need for adequate food, rest, and sleep. The children have tremendous energy, but they still do not sense a need for rest. The group is capable of gradual growth in the fine motor co-ordinations, such as that involved in eye movements. Periods of concentration on one task are growing longer; but the teacher cannot ordinarily expect attention to one task, such as reading from a chart, for more than a few minutes. In the second and third grades concepts are becoming clearer, especially in social studies and science areas developed as part of the school program. This increases the children's comprehension abilities. The children's power to solve simple problems met in their reading and to make decisions for action based on it are increasing steadily if they have been given opportunities to do this. They are beginning to participate more in large group activities, such as audience reading. There is a wide range in the different abilities involved in reading, but most of the children will profit by the activities described below.

CHARACTERISTICS OF THE PRIMARY READING PROGRAM

In general, in the primary grades, children are going through four phases of their development in reading ability. These are: (1) the development of reading readiness described in Chapter 6; (2) initial success in the first skills in reading; (3) rapid progress in the learning of basic habits, skills, and attitudes connected with reading; and (4), on the part of some of the more advanced pupils, the transitional stage between primary reading and the relatively more mature and independent reading of the upper elementary grades.

Some of the characteristics of the initial period in learning to read may be listed as follows:

1. The initial period in learning to read is continuous with both the readiness period and the succeeding stage of rapid development.

There is no break between the different stages in these grades. For example, in working with the first experience charts toward the end of the readiness period the teacher will not demand that children recognize the words in the chart. This stage will gradually merge into the stage where children begin to recognize certain words which are repeated frequently or are of special interest to them. Similarly the child who at first can recognize only his own name will gradually acquire the ability to recognize the names of some of his friends or some of the characters in the books he will be reading. (See illustration on opposite page.)

2. Instruction emphasizes relationships between symbols and the ideas and things they represent. The teacher continually goes back to the meaning behind the abstract symbols. This is accomplished in such ways as the experience chart, which describes a common experience, fresh and vivid in children's minds, the use of pictures with easy first words and sentences, and the use of name tags and of labels on objects around the room.

3. The teacher gives the children opportunity to see many words, phrases, and sentences, not all of which they will learn to recognize automatically. After the wider experience, the teacher helps the children focus on a smaller group of useful words which they are expected to master eventually. These may be key words in classroom activities or in basal reading materials.

4. The teacher gives the child many opportunities to re-experience and restudy certain valuable words. Children meet these words on the chalkboard, on charts, on the bulletin board, in greetings or directions to the class, in a short letter, and in similar places. Mere repetition of a word, as in lists, is of little value as compared with repeated use in situations highly charged with the child's need to use the word.

5. The teacher relies on a combination of methods rather than single methods such as the "look-say" and "phonics" methods. In much of the work with charts and early work with books she proceeds from the whole to the parts and to the whole again. The group often goes from the short story or the sentence to phrases, then to words, then back to the whole sentence or story again. Some of the children will rely on memorization of the whole story at first. Then they will derive and use certain sentence clues in terms of position, size, and capital letters beginning the sentence. Eventually they will be able to pick out words that are the same, recognize them singly, and use them when they meet them in a slightly new context.

6. During the initial stages in using the combination of methods the teacher places considerable emphasis on building up a sight vocabulary. This includes words common in the environment and words used in the preprimers of the basic series the child will be read-

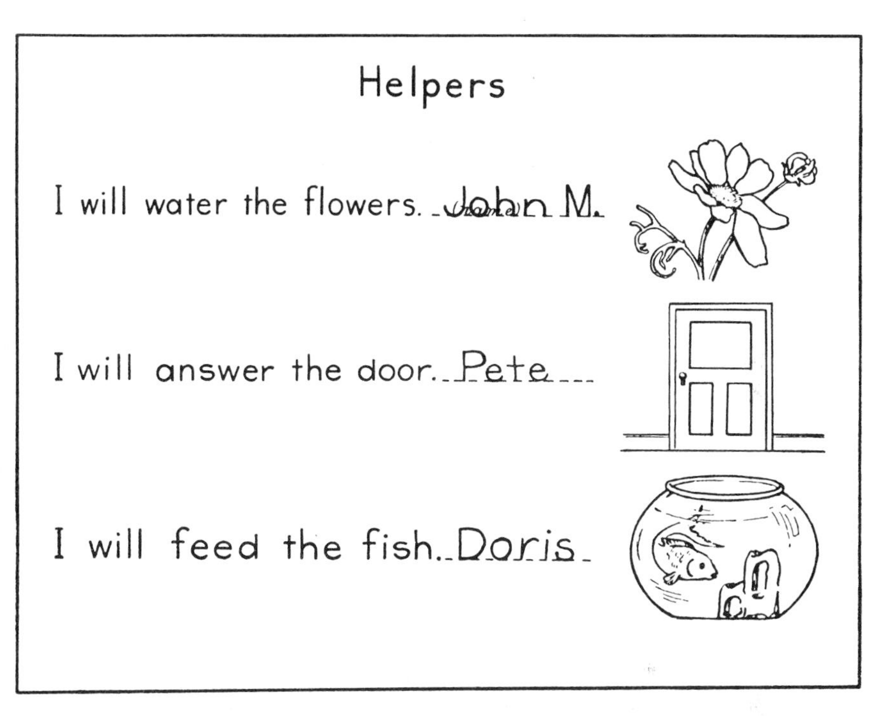

Early Use of Names (*Manual for Teaching the Pre-Primer Program,* rev. ed., p. 219. Ginn, Boston, 1957)

ing. Different writers disagree on the number of words a child should know before he begins directed work with books. It seems likely that this number will vary with individual children. Some writers used to suggest that the child should know at least fifty or seventy-five words at sight before he began reading preprimers. So large a number of sight words as this usually is no longer essential to early reading success, since many of the newer preprimers contain fewer different words than this. However, some first-grade teachers believe in teaching the words found in preprimers thoroughly and then using the book so that the child has an experience of reading a first preprimer easily in three or four sittings. This method gives the child a feeling of early success with books, but it often requires laborious word drill. The psychology of learning suggests that many words can be learned more easily in a meaningful setting in a sentence or sentences, often accompanied by pictures. The method here recommended, accordingly, is that of developing some of the preprimer vocabulary before the child uses the book, and of leaving other words to be studied in the meaningful context of the preprimer page.

7. Not only does the teacher aim to have the child recognize a group of important words automatically but she also plans to have each child acquire a variety of ways of working out new words for himself. This ability to unlock new words is one which grows after the initial learning period is completed, and which keeps on developing beyond the primary grades. There are at least seven different ways in which primary children recognize new or partly new words:

a. The general pattern of the word; for example, the word *dog* might look like

b. Special features of a word, such as a double *t* or the tail on the end of the word *monkey*.

c. Recognition of known parts in words—in compound words such as *mailman*, or seeing small words in large words, as *fast* in *faster*.

d. The use of context clues—an intelligent guess at the words from the meaning of the rest of the sentence.

e. The use of pictures as clues, somewhat similar to context or meaning clues.

f. Some phonetic analysis of the word—knowing sounds of letters or combinations of letters and blending them into a word.

g. Structural analysis of a word—recognizing the stem and affixes such as *re* and *ing*.

h. A combination of methods such as using the sounds of *m* and *j* and seeing the common phonogram for *ail* in going from the known word *mail* to the new word *jail*.

In the primary grades some children will recognize that words begin with the same sounds, or rhyme, or contain the same phonograms. The teacher may use this perception of similarities as a basis for word recognition; some teachers prefer to build up these habits in a more systematic way. The child who uses a combination of several of these methods has a great advantage over the child who uses one or none of them.

8. Although the primary teacher emphasizes accurate word recognition, this emphasis exists in the larger setting of accurate comprehension. The relating of symbol and experience is not confined to the initial reading stage. At every level of achievement the relation-

ships of words, sentences, and paragraphs to the realities back of them are stressed. In other words, even in the primary grades comprehension and use are part of any reading. In the early grades the teacher will help children to read for general understanding, for exact details, for grasping a sequence of ideas, and for following directions.

9. In emphasizing word recognition and comprehension the primary teacher is always aware of the attitudes and appreciations that accompany a successful reading program. The children's enjoyment of particular stories and of reading in general, and their desire to read other related materials, are among the best signs of the effectiveness of the primary reading program.

10. The reading program is connected with the whole primary program and gains strength from it in a large variety of activities. Some of these are discussed below in terms of the reading environment and curricular experiences related to reading.

11. Evaluation of the program in the primary stages of learning to read is concerned largely with (*a*) the child's growth in word-recognition abilities; (*b*) his comprehension of what he reads, chiefly main idea, details, or a sequence of ideas; (*c*) his attitude toward reading; and (*d*) his integration of reading with his thinking. If reading tests are used, in general they are simple tests of word recognition or of sentence or of short paragraph reading for different purposes. The teacher often relies upon observation of the child's behavior in determining attitudes of pleasure or dislike in reading.

These eleven characteristics describe procedures in the stages of beginning reading. Children develop abilities connected with this beginning level at different rates and then are ready to progress rapidly in some basic reading abilities.

READING ENVIRONMENT

One of the reasons for the general success of the primary reading program is that most teachers arrange a meaningful and challenging classroom setting conducive to learning to read. The most important aspect of the environment, of course, is the teacher herself. The modern primary teacher understands that the children of any one class are very different individuals, with different abilities and motivations for learning to read. If one child fails to learn to read easily, the teacher knows that the child requires not blame or scolding so much as understanding followed by attempts to change parts of the reading program so that failure will be prevented. The primary teacher is herself enthusiastic about books and stories and delights in sharing her pleasure in them with the children in her class. The understanding and enthusiasm of the teacher are an essential part of the stimulating environment.

Television Fun

We look at television at home.
Dianne likes to look at puppets.
Fred likes to see Play School.
Jimmy likes cowboys.
It is fun to look at television.

Chart Growing out of Pupil Discussion (*Manual for Teaching the Primer Program* to accompany *The Little White House,* rev. ed., p. 374. Ginn, Boston, 1957)

Skillful primary teachers do not rely only on their personal qualities for teaching children to read but provide, in addition, a physical setting which stimulates development. In one corner of a good primary classroom there is a library corner or book table with a variety of interesting and colorful books easily reached. The pupils usually take turns in caring for the book shelves or library corner. Scattered around the walls of the room are other guides to reading, often composed and written by the teacher and pupils. (See chart above.) Information is given on charts, notices and directions are given on the bulletin board, and class or individual scrapbooks and booklets are in evidence. On the chalkboard may be plans, lists of supplies, and directions. Signs and labels accompany pictures. Sometimes the room may exhibit children's work in the form of letters, explanations, greeting cards, and original stories. Children have ready access to many books, multigraphed materials, and possibly a typewriter with primer-size type. Everywhere is evidence of what the children are doing, the best stimulus to reading and further profitable work.

As suggested in Chapter 5, the environment contains a variety not only of story or library books but of basic readers. Since the children are at many levels of accomplishment, they are not all able to use a primer or a second reader, for example. The primary classroom accordingly contains books ranging in difficulty over at least four or five levels of both basic books and other supplementary readers. Such levels may be described as preprimer, primer, first-reader, easy second-reader, harder second-reader, easy third-reader, harder third-reader, and easy fourth-reader materials. The books on some of these eight levels, combined with the items mentioned above, provide a material basis for the great progress in reading characteristic of most primary classes.

OBJECTIVES

When a child has made a successful start in chart work and other initial reading experiences, as described in the previous chapter, he is ready to strengthen and consolidate his beginning reading abilities. From labels around the room, a bulletin board, experience charts, and other materials, he has made a start in recognizing and interpreting printed symbols. He has usually developed a liking for reading and some sense of accomplishment through knowing a few words. Now in the latter parts of the first grade and in the succeeding primary grades he has new reading worlds to conquer.

The objectives of the initial reading stage naturally vary with the maturation and achievement of the children involved. During the period the first-grade teacher will ordinarily hope for such accomplishments in each child as the following:

1. The ability to read one-line and two-line sentences with understanding and good oral expression.
2. Ready participation in the reading activities of the group, both as leader and as follower.
3. Increased ability to use picture clues, special features of words, context clues, and phonetic and structural components in word recognition.
4. The development of the ability to read, with ease and satisfaction, the preprimers, primer, and first reader of the basic-reading series.

5. Enjoyment and ease in reading the preprimers and primers of other series.

6. The ability to read without undue vocalization and without finger-pointing or a marker.

7. Increasing ability to make adjustments in reading method and rate for such purposes as recalling details, comprehending the main idea, and following an orderly sequence.

8. The development of skills in noting similarities and differences in known words.

9. The desire to read on many occasions when the class program permits freely chosen activities.

These general aims of the beginning reading period can, of course, be modified, expanded, or otherwise changed to meet the needs of a particular child or group of children.

When a child has progressed in most of the nine achievements set forth above, he ordinarily enters a period of rapid learning of specific reading attitudes and abilities. Of course his initial learnings in reading merge gradually into this period of rapid progress. The characteristics of the period are the same as those listed above for the initial period of learning to read, with a broadening of many activities. The objectives of this broader program may be summarized from the National Society for the Study of Education Thirty-sixth Yearbook, *The Teaching of Reading: A Second Report,* as follows:

1. *Attitudes*
   a. A lively interest in reading for pleasure and information as shown by voluntary borrowing of books, bringing books to school, etc.
   b. An attitude that will lead to a permanent interest in reading.
   c. A desire to share some special story with others.
   d. An understanding of the possibilities which reading affords in the solution of problems or the enrichment of experience.
   e. An appreciation of the author and his experiences involved in securing the material for the story. (For example, read animal stories—the necessary preparations and dangers encountered.)

2. *Habits*
   a. The habit of locating material by use of the table of contents.
   b. The habit of handling a book correctly.
   c. The habit of self-helpfulness in using materials to gain information on class interests.
   d. The habit of reading independently for information and pleasure.

e. The habit of reading silently without head, finger, or lip movements.
f. The habit of attacking new words through pictures, contexts, or knowledge of phonetic elements.
g. The habit of correct position of body and book, with attention to proper lighting.

3. *Skills*

a. The ability to read, with ease and understanding, an average (second) (third) reader.
b. The ability to recognize, accurately and independently, new words in such readers by context, by known parts, by more detailed analysis.
c. Ability to read aloud with rhythm and with expression, holding the attention of the audience.
d. Ability to read more rapidly silently than orally.
e. Ability to select and group ideas, answer questions, and follow directions.
f. Knowledge of correct posture and proper lighting for reading.
g. A beginning of ability to use reading as a means of obtaining information relating to various interests and problems.
h. In third grade, the ability to master a word phonetically.
i. In third grade, knowledge of physical make-up of a book: (1) title page, (2) table of contents, (3) list of illustrations, (4) index.
j. An increase in the rate and accurate span of recognition, with rhythmical eye progress along the lines and accurate return sweeps.

The objectives above indicate that pupils in the second and third grades often read for the sake of reading—for the pleasure of information or help they can get from it. They also begin to acquire some of the work-type skills associated with the use of books as distinct from the more specific mechanical skills such as eye movements or the physical care of books. In other words, pupils in these grades begin activities which they will continue, with greater emphasis, in the intermediate grades. At the same time many of them will still be developing skills associated with initial learning to read. By this level the teacher will be using all of the six main types of activities common to most reading programs listed on page 145.

The compressed list of attitudes, habits, and skills given above may be considered as objectives for the second stage of rapid progress in reading achievements. Actually they must be considered as beginning in the initial stage of learning to read, developing in a period of rapid growth, and extending into a transition period in which the child is becoming a relatively independent reader. Some writers and school systems prefer to state these growths in the form of as many as eight or ten stages. The value of using such stages may be in more accurate placement of children in small reading groups. On the other hand, the dangers of subdividing children into limited reading categories are many. There is no sharp break between reading achievement at consecutive stages, such as the preprimer and primer or the hard-second-reader and easy-third-reader levels, and such fine distinctions cannot be made scientifically. Furthermore, no child stays at one level of reading in all his work. Although he may ordinarily read best at first-reader level, if the story is very interesting or he is otherwise highly motivated he may read just as well at the second-reader level. The teacher and curriculum worker should beware, accordingly, of a multiplicity of reading stages or levels, with too narrow distinctions between them.

CONTROVERSIAL ISSUES IN PRIMARY READING

Although this chapter, the succeeding one, and others referred to above make many specific statements about children and their instruction in reading, all the problems are by no means settled. In some areas, research workers still do not give definitive answers. In many others, different teachers have tried out varying solutions to problems and tend to prefer a method which works for them and in which they feel comfortable. Furthermore, the complexity of childhood and of the reading process suggests that there is seldom one "right" answer or one "best" method of doing things. All these factors suggest that the teacher of primary reading should be aware that there are genuine disagreements and valid variations in points of view about her work. The answers are not ready-made. Instead of asking for a final solution from authority or keeping rigidly to one approach, the teacher can be aware of problems, know some proposed solutions, and herself experiment where the problems seem close to home. Some of the questions which are unsettled for some primary teachers are:

What About Readiness?

Some school systems advocate a readiness program of a certain pattern and length, such as six or eight weeks, for most children. Some teachers believe the readiness program should be more flexible in

	GROUP 1 (HIGH)	GROUP 2 (AVERAGE	GROUP 3 (LOW)
Monday	Reading in texts in social studies, science, health. Directed by questions on problems from planning period.	Assignment in basic readers directed by questions on blackboard. Teacher should check on above.	Reading from basic readers. *Direct teacher guidance.*
	Free reading: individual interests.	Reading from basic readers. *Direct teacher guidance.*	Work-type period, using mimeographed or hectographed exercises, games, devices. Teacher should check above.
Tuesday	Reading from basic or supplementary readers. *Direct teacher guidance.*	Independent work-type exercises: content based on unit of work.	Free reading: story and picture books.
	Combined groups: reading club, audience reading, library, choral reading, story hour, dramatization, etc.		
Wednesday	Reading in texts in social studies, health, etc. Directed by questions or planning.	Reading in texts in social studies, health, etc. Directed by questions or planning.	Work-type period. Reading from basic readers. *Direct teacher guidance.*
	Preparation for reading period next day and independent activities.	Work-type period or reading from basic readers. *Direct teacher guidance.*	Work-type period. Exercises based on **unit of work.**
Thursday	Reading from basic or supplementary readers or related texts. *Direct teacher guidance.*	Independent work-type exercises or questions for next period.	Free reading: story and picture books.
	Reading from readers or supplementary texts: free choice.	Work-type period or reading from basic readers. *Direct teacher guidance.*	Assignment in basic readers. Preparation for Friday morning.
Friday	Free reading: story and picture books.	Free reading: story and picture books. Preparation for next period.	Reading from basic readers. *Direct teacher guidance.*
	Combined groups: reading club, library period, choral reading, etc.		

A Suggested Week's Program in Reading for the Second Grade[1]

[1] Pasadena City Schools, *Some Questions and Answers about Reading in the Elementary School Program,* Reading Bulletin No. I. Pasadena City Schools, Pasadena, Calif., 1946.

length and in types of activity. Others may say that children today in *their* school need little readiness work in Grade I. Teachers, principals, and parents vary in their philosophy of the role of the kindergarten in reading readiness.

Here, then, is one area in which there are few fixed and final answers. This book suggests in several places a number of agreements in research and practice. (1) Children differ so widely in their experience and verbal abilities that five- and six-year-olds may profit by a program stretching approximately from no pre-reading activities to a six months' preparatory program. (2) Readiness is a complex of various factors, and therefore a readiness program should contain a variety of visual, auditory, and experiential activities, depending upon the needs of the children in the group. (3) Readiness is a factor at all grade levels. At second or sixth grades, it may be considered as (a) general, *i.e.,* depending upon the maturity of the child as reflected in his physical equipment, knowledge, interest, etc.; and (b) specific, *i.e.,* depending upon the special knowledge required for using new words and concepts met in the story. (4) Because of the specific nature of readiness, a teacher often does some of her best teaching in reading before the children open their books to a particular selection, especially in the case of slow-learning children who lack ideas to bring to the printed page.

What About Specific Methods?

For many years controversy has raged over methods of teaching, and methods have changed with the years (see Chapter 2). One of the sharpest of the current issues is that of the whole or look-say methods versus part or synthetic approaches, especially phonics methods. As suggested on page 309, this book takes the position that the question is not an "either—or" matter, and that both have their place in a combination of various methods for teaching reading. However, to explore the problem briefly, the teacher can be aware of the variety of activities or names of methods and devices which may be grouped in the two main categories. These are overlapping and varied types of description:

Whole Methods	*Part Methods*
Word lists (as in Webster and early McGuffey)	Alphabet (Pestalozzi; New England Primer)
Nursery rhymes	Special features of words
Configuration	Similarity to known parts

Whole Methods (Cont.)	*Part Methods (Cont.)*
Picture clues	Phonics
Association	Structural analysis
Look-say	Combining auditory and visual elements
Experience charts	Dictionary
Context clues	

The evidence on most of these methods is considered further in Chapters 4 and 10. Variations in the methods as used around the world have been described by Gray.[2] It seems fairly well agreed that (1) children learn somewhat different habits and skills when teachers stress different methods; (2) any one method is not "best" for all children or even for one child at different times; (3) some combination of methods is now used in most teaching programs, with somewhat different emphases by different teachers; (4) most of the above descriptions emphasize word identification and recognition and must be supplemented by other procedures to strengthen comprehension abilities and use of materials; and (5) skilled readers use a variety of techniques in word-attack and interpretation procedures. These facts suggest that the teacher employ varied teaching methods but that they be based on definite reasons and aims.

What About Oral Reading?

Until 1915, reading practice in elementary school was largely oral. After that time, research and practice emphasized the values of silent reading to such an extent that some schools gave oral reading little attention in their activities. Today many teachers believe that oral reading has some merit but are unsure of its use, and teachers vary considerably in the place they plan for it.

Primary grade teachers can teach children to learn to read by non-oral methods, but most prefer to use considerable oral reading, particularly when children are in the beginning stages of learning to use books, establishing left-to-right eye movements, dropping down to the next line, learning a few useful words, and acquiring other rudimentary techniques. At this stage, oral reading enables the teacher to detect an error immediately and to correct it by suitable practice. After children have learned some of the initial skills, it is probably unwise to have much "oral reading around the group," especially if skilled readers must silently follow halting oral readers.

[2] William S. Gray, *The Teaching of Reading and Writing,* Monographs on Fundamental Education, No. 10. UNESCO, Paris, 1956.

Furthermore, certain abilities in oral reading, such as phrasing and following punctuation guides, must be taught specifically. It is not enough simply to "hear" children read. Finally, oral reading is usually essential to the enjoyment of poetry, but since most poetry is somewhat difficult, children in the primary grades will begin by hearing the teacher or some other adult read it.[3] These suggestions indicate that problems of oral reading are not unlike those of phonics —it is not a case of "yes" or "no," so much as how oral reading can be used profitably.

What About Grouping Children?

This question is much less controversial in the primary grades than in later parts of the school, for surveys of practice show that 80 to 90 per cent of primary teachers do some grouping for reading instruction. As in other issues, the problem accordingly is one of *what, when,* and *how*. Most teachers prefer three groups; some use two and a few have four or five groups. Some teachers regard groups as fairly fixed, but others try to keep them flexible. Some teachers feel that children in the first two grades are rather young to act as group leaders; others give them certain responsibilities. Some teachers group only for basal reading instruction and some do it for other reading work. Some teachers group on the basis of children's achievement in reading, some try to use other data such as general ability and friendships.

As in the other controversies, there are not final answers to all these alternatives, and, within limits, each teacher should be encouraged to develop her own "style," her own ways of doing things. Research indicates that there is no fixed number of groups best for all classes; many abilities are efficiently acquired by individuals or in small group teaching, but some can be learned by whole classes. Most psychologists recommend that grouping be related to social factors as well as children's achievements. Good primary teachers form different groups for different purposes, so that in any one school day, a child may belong to four or five different groups. These and other aspects of grouping are considered further in Chapter 15, under the general topic of "Providing for Individual Differences in Reading Ability." This chapter and the paragraphs above suggest that not all questions are settled once and for all. The good primary teacher is

[3] Louise W. Worthington, *Oral Reading? Certainly!* Contributions to Education, No. 16. Ginn, Boston, 1957.

aware of the problems and works on adaptations of solutions to suit pupils' needs and her own interests and abilities.

PLANNING THE WEEKLY PRIMARY PROGRAM

The incorporation of the five activities involving basic readers, supplementary books, work-type periods, creative activities, and free reading in a program requires careful planning. Any week's activities in reading will vary with the nature of the other activities of the class and the maturation of the individuals involved, but tentative suggestions for such a program are given above. The week's program would never be exactly the same from week to week and would always be flexible in adapting to current needs of the group of children. The outline is at best suggestive of how a teacher may plan her week's work more directly related to reading. (See page 211.) It does not indicate the many, many possibilities for using reading in connection with social studies, science, language, and other activities.

CURRICULAR EXPERIENCES RELATED TO READING

Since there is a danger in some schools that the reading program may be confined to somewhat formal dealings with books, it seems important to re-emphasize that the above weekly program does not represent the whole of reading activities during the week. It is a vital part of the pupil's development, and of his parents' understanding of the school program that he realize that reading is an activity existing in many forms. Some primary-grade activities that involve reading or are closely related to it are as follows:

1. Teacher and pupils plan the room environment so that it contains:
   a) A science table with specimens or displays and books and pictures relative to the exhibit.
   b) A library corner with table and chairs arranged with thought for good lighting. Attractive materials on the table, including pictures and stereographs.
   c) Arrangements of pictures showing immediate interests (depending upon unit of work).
2. The teacher encourages children to bring materials from home to share with others: a story book, an interesting collection, pictures, toys that help to clarify concepts when studying a unit of work, construction tools, and science materials.
3. Group situations stimulate children to relate various home and out-of-school experiences that will be of interest to members of the class: a

television program, a new pet, a birthday present, a week-end vacation, chores done at home, an interesting hike, a home garden, etc.

4. Teacher and principal provide special occasions for the children to invite parents to the school. Opportunities for children to show their work and to explain it may be very valuable. Preparation for the event includes planning a program, dramatizing a story, learning new songs, assuming committee responsibility, displaying materials to advantage, and arranging flowers attractively.

5. After group planning the children invite community workers to talk to them: the mailman, the milkman, the fireman, the fire warden, a Scout leader. Children should always be encouraged to ask questions and to participate in the discussion. The teacher records findings on charts.

6. The school staff and pupils plan opportunities for sharing with another room and with the entire school. This may contribute to a good school spirit. Such activities as the following are worthwhile in relation to reading: presenting a play for another room, reading a story to the assembly, taking part in a school program, entertaining another class, participating in a school debate, assuming responsibility for open house, taking part in school organizations.

7. Service activities may increase social competence and add to reading abilities. These include writing a letter to a sick classmate, sending a book or flowers to one who is ill, making presents for holidays, inviting parents to special occasions, participating in Red Cross activities, etc.

8. The dramatization of nursery rhymes, poems, and stories is of value to the child personally and in relation to reading experiences.

9. The teacher and class must plan for a special time for telling or reading stories. Sometimes a child may read to the class and sometimes the teacher may do so. Pupils may recommend books to be read for enjoyment and tell something about them to stimulate interest.

10. Many primary children like to make scrapbooks with captions under the pictures.

11. At regular intervals a class should visit the public library if it is accessible and learn how to find materials. Making children feel at home in a library is an excellent objective at any grade level.

12. The skillful primary teacher provides situations in which problems will arise: how to arrange the flowers, the best way to put up the display, the appropriate size for the chart, the approximate length of the garden, and the right type of clothing or food. Some of these problems may be solved by consulting appropriate books.

13. The teacher introduces the children to the interpretation of charts and graphs. These may often be taken from newspapers and magazines, which the children will bring to school.

14. In the democratic classroom the group may appoint committees and have them assume responsibility for keeping the work table in good order, for caring for the reading table, for planning a class play, for providing entertainment for guests, for keeping library records, and for caring for science materials.

15. The teacher may stimulate play activities and help to provide vicarious experiences that give opportunities for expression: ordering the groceries over the telephone, introducing two friends, playing store, keeping the classroom bank account, listening to experiences of others, sharing experiences with the group, and recording and rereading experiences of particular interest.

These fifteen items suggest how the various aspects of the whole primary program are related to reading activities and how many enterprises may be enriched by reading.

READING IN RELATION TO SPELLING, HANDWRITING, AND LANGUAGE

In the primary grades the child not only begins to read but ordinarily also acquires some abilities in handwriting and spelling. Chapter 3 of this book emphasizes that reading is one of a tightly knit group of activities usually called the language arts. The closeness of this association is evidenced by the relationships between methods employed in beginning reading and methods in the early development of handwriting and spelling abilities. At the same time the child's language abilities, many of them developed in preschool years, contribute to development in reading, handwriting, and spelling. The problem of relating all these different kinds of growth and making them contribute to each other extends all through the school, but it is often especially acute at the second- and third-grade levels.

In terms of chronological development the child's use of oral language is the first activity to appear. Language abilities develop rapidly, and are quite complex by the time the child enters school. In most cases reading is the third major language ability to be acquired after speaking and listening, usually at about six or seven years of age. Before the child can read, he must be able to associate words with the things they represent. In turn, as he develops ability to recognize words somewhere in the first grade he often wants to write them too. This he first does by copying. Accordingly handwriting is usually well started before the necessity for spelling appears. Spelling ability enters the picture when the child needs to write words which are not in sight for copying. Spelling ordinarily should not be attempted as a regular "subject," then, until the child has well-developed abilities in oral language, reading, and handwriting.

There is now considerable research evidence to suggest that abilities in language, reading, handwriting, and spelling are closely related and contribute to one another, especially in the primary grades.[4] Betts[5] gave a general picture of the usual sequence in language development to suggest that reading and spelling are correlative growths. He pointed out that all children go through six stages in developing language abilities, as follows:

1. *Experience.* Through seeing, hearing, feeling, and other processes the child acquires a necessary basis for later language activities.
2. *Hearing comprehension.* The child develops the ability to associate speech sounds with other sensory experiences involving objects and situations.
3. *Speech production.* The child learns to use speech sounds to communicate with others. At four months he may babble, by twelve months he usually begins to use a word or two, after eighteen months his speaking vocabulary grows rapidly, in later preschool years he improves in sentence usage and has made considerable progress in learning to symbolize, that is, in substituting words, phrases, and sentences for the reality they represent.
4. *Reading.* The child learns to use symbols even more abstract than speech sounds, namely, visual symbols. At this stage, instead of earlier auditory perception, visual perception is essential to normal language development. Before the child reads, he usually goes through a "scribble stage," writing wiggly lines and other marks. These represent a certain readiness for writing and the fifth stage of development.
5. *Writing.* The child begins to use symbols for communicating with others instead of merely interpreting visual symbols. To communicate with others he needs control over writing. So that others may understand him easily he must put his writing into some sort of standard form in regard to spelling, sentence structure, paragraphing, grammar, and handwriting. The seven-year-old is confronted with a large group of social demands in relation to his writing which he ordinarily can acquire only over a number of years.
6. *Refinement of language control.* Improvement in oral and written language develops through maturation and a wide variety of experiences which stimulate the communication of ideas. The written language, including spelling, depends upon the oral language, which in turn depends upon experiences, including reading experiences. Speech, reading, writing, and spelling are all facets of growth in communication abilities necessary to personal adjustment, group interaction, and the health of a democracy.

[4] A. Sterl Artley, chm., *Interrelationships Among the Language Arts,* Bulletin of the National Conference on Research in English. National Council of Teachers of English, Champaign, Ill., 1954.

[5] Emmett A. Betts, "Inter-relationship of Reading and Spelling," *Elementary English Review,* Vol. 22, pp. 12-23, January, 1945.

This rough outline suggests that language abilities grow together and tend to contribute to one another. Specific research studies give further details of relatedness. Gates[6] showed that reading and spelling abilities are based on such common factors as visual perception, phonetic abilities, and habits of writing. Russell[7] found that, in the first and second grades, readiness for spelling activities depends upon other language abilities usually regarded as speaking or reading abilities. For example, abilities in word recognition, recognition of capital and lower-case letters, visual discrimination, such as recognizing small differences in words, and auditory perception abilities apply to both reading and spelling. The children who were studied had had some practice in seeing word parts and had developed habits of close attention to words in their reading; they seemed likely to be more successful than others in their subsequent work in spelling. There is some evidence, accordingly, that phonetic analysis of words may be useful in developing spelling competence as well as ability in attacking words.

Although similarities are great, the primary teacher must also be aware of differences in the various language arts. After a survey of research studies Eames[8] concluded that speech and reading difficulties may go together, especially if there are neurological lesions in the language centers of the brain, and that emotional reactions to speech difficulties may impair reading, but that the evidence is still not conclusive about these relationships. In regard to context reading and spelling, most primary teachers use different approaches. In the first, the children are encouraged to work in units of phrases, sentences, or even short paragraphs to get the meaning. In the second, they must study words closely to note the order of *e* and *i*, the silent letters or similar features—a detailed analysis which would destroy sentence or paragraph continuity.

Enough research evidence has been cited to suggest that primary teachers must think of their school program as a language-arts program rather than as a collection of separate activities in reading, writing, spelling, speech, and composition. Oral-language abilities are basic to any abilities developed later, so that most emphasis must be

[6] Arthur I. Gates, "Reading in Relation to Spelling," *Teachers' Service Bulletin in Reading*, Vol. 6, No. 2, Macmillan, October, 1944.

[7] David H. Russell, "A Diagnostic Study of Spelling Readiness," *Journal of Educational Research*, Vol. 37, pp. 276-283, December, 1943.

[8] Thomas H. Eames, "The Relationship of Reading and Speech Difficulties," *Journal of Educational Psychology*, Vol. 41, pp. 51-55, January, 1950.

given to conversation, discussion, oral reporting, storytelling, announcing, and activities that stimulate them. The association of meaning with symbols is a first requirement for any reading. Oral-language activities are one of the best ways of developing meaning and so are an essential part of a reading lesson. As the child matures he feels the need of written communication. His ability to write words, to spell them correctly, and to put them in clear sentence and paragraph patterns will depend upon abilities he has developed during reading activities. In a rare case a child may be retarded in reading and good in spelling or the reverse; but, in general, success in one language art contributes to desirable accomplishment in the other language arts. The teacher plans her work so that a variety of language activities are a background for reading and, in turn, are enriched by reading.

A SECOND-GRADE READING PROGRAM

There are as many second-grade reading programs as there are second grades. Since school systems differ greatly in their philosophy of how to teach reading, and since groups of children vary widely in all abilities related to reading, there is no prescription for all second-grade programs.

At the same time it is equally true that all children and teachers of the second grade face a number of similar problems relating to growth in reading abilities. Although there may be no such thing as an average second grade, the fact that all children go through similar stages in reading development and the fact that the reading process is somewhat the same for all printed materials in English make it possible to discuss one or two of the aims and practices of a good second-grade program.

Most children in the second grade have passed through at least part of the beginning-reading stage and have developed some abilities in word recognition and thought-getting. They usually need further help in getting the thought clearly rather than merely recognizing the words. They have had some experience in reading preprimers and primers outside a basic series and in browsing in library books, but their previous reading has been relatively limited. They have begun to enjoy reading on their own, but this feeling has begun only in a small way. The aims of the second-grade teacher, accordingly, are to increase the power to work out the recognition of unfamiliar or partly familiar words, to develop ability to extract meaning from the printed page, to extend reading experiences in a wider range of materials, and to increase independence in reading.

The second grade is ordinarily a time when the child enjoys his growing skill in reading and wants to read many things. Anything the teacher can do to foster this enjoyment of a new skill is worthwhile. Thus the provision of a variety of interesting materials is essential to the success of the reading program. Since independence is in its beginning stages, these materials must not contain many unrecognizable words or strange ideas. Difficult materials may be a cause of inaccurate skimming and other superficial techniques. Given materials which he can master and use with a reasonable amount of effort, the child continues to develop keen interests and enjoyment in reading.

A few sample accomplishments of a typical second-grader follow:

He participates enthusiastically in several types of reading situations.

He reads for pleasure and information in easy books when he has some spare time.

He has developed some skill in reading so that he can answer different types of questions dealing with, for example, the main idea or the sequence of events in a story.

He can make simple inferences about characters or happenings which go beyond the literal facts of a selection.

He is increasing his repertoire of phonetic skills in unlocking new words.

He uses structural analysis in recognizing variant forms of basic words.

He checks his word analysis by considering the meaning of the word in a sentence.

He likes to read orally and to listen to others.

He enjoys group reading activities such as choral reading of poetry or dramatization of a story.

The second grade is sometimes a critical period in the child's development of such accomplishments and attitudes, because so many of the basic abilities that go to make up the reading process are being established. The attitudes, habits, and skills given earlier in this chapter from *The Teaching of Reading: A Second Report* indicate the fundamental nature of growth in reading at this grade level. The period is a critical one, for good or bad techniques may be developed in a rather permanent way. If failure and frustration accompany the child's reading regularly, unfavorable attitudes may be set up for a lifetime. In most second grades, careful adjustment of materials and methods leads to sound progress in reading by the typical pupil. This happy outcome is not the result of chance or a developmental level but a proof of the teacher's energy and insight in meeting the reading needs of the individuals in the class.

IMPORTANCE OF READING AT THE THIRD-GRADE LEVEL

Some point near the end of the primary grades may be regarded as a crucial stage in any school's developmental reading program. In former years there was a "pile-up" here of many children who had not mastered the basic reading skills and habits deemed by school people in certain school systems as essential to future progress. Even for children who seemed to be making normal progress, the transition from primary materials to reading materials used in the high third and fourth grades was a difficult one. While the practice of "failing" or retarding pupils has diminished as its ineffectiveness has become evident, demands of current texts in the content subjects still make the third grade an important level in the child's growth in reading abilities.

Most basic readers in the primary grades are nicely graded in their vocabulary and other sources of reading difficulties. Not all readers, and fewer textbooks, however, continue this gradual growth into the fourth grade materials. The mere fact that the pupil has met a restricted vocabulary in his primary books will serve to make the fourth-grade books more difficult than they would otherwise be. The solution would seem to lie in adjusting fourth readers, and particularly other fourth-grade texts, to build upon the primary program rather than in making primary books more difficult. A number of fourth readers meet this requirement, but, in general, textbooks in social studies (or history and geography), in arithmetic, in health, in science, and in other content fields are still much too difficult.[9] Typically they are condensations of longer books which lack the illustrative material, the details, and the general interest of books which can take space to tell a story or develop a concept. Many books intended for the intermediate grades lack telling, vivid facts. They contain many difficult concepts and do not give sufficient detail to develop understanding of the concepts. One way to solve the problem is to give more space to important concepts and to

[9] Jeanne Chall, *Readability*. Ohio State University Press, Columbus, 1958.

control the introduction of concepts which are beyond the experience of the children using the book. At the same time the school program emphasizes the importance of children's reading better than they have before in content fields, a topic developed more fully in Chapters 8 and 11.

Since it takes time to change difficult textbooks and since, in the fourth grade, any child will face more reading demands, it seems important that the third-grade teacher sense the problem and take steps to provide for a smooth transition to the reading tasks of the intermediate grades for many of her pupils. It is still true, however, that the third-grade program must provide for children at different levels of achievement. By the end of the third year one group of children may be able to profit by the challenge of materials only on the primer level. Others at the upper end of the group may have reading abilities as high as those of the average seventh-grade pupil. Provisions for a wide range of abilities in any one class are described in Chapter 15. A teacher, then, through grouping, the use of materials on different levels of difficulty, and similar plans provides a variety of reading experiences; but within this variety she must help children to grow continuously in reading abilities involving somewhat more difficult materials. The program therefore will place emphasis upon achieving independence in reading—how to work out new words for oneself, how to use books and libraries to find information one wants, and how to record and organize such information so that it will be useful later. The third grade thus marks a definite level for the acquisition of work-type habits and skills valuable in using a wide variety of materials for different purposes.

In achieving some independence in reading which enables him to work with materials in the intermediate grades the child has acquired at least three abilities:

1. The ability to comprehend in different ways, to vary somewhat his style of reading to suit the materials and purposes he has for reading. This ability will develop further in the intermediate grades (see Chapter 8).
2. The ability to work out new words successfully by using, in most cases, some combination of the methods in recognizing a word which are listed on page 204, and especially the more advanced methods of phonetic analysis, structural analysis, and use of context. To these may be added some simple skills in using picture dictionaries, as readiness for more specific dictionary work in the fourth grade.[10]

[10] Margaret B. Parke, "Picture Dictionaries," *Elementary English*, Vol. 32, pp. 519-524, December, 1955.

3. The ability to use reading for various purposes. The reading process will not stop at mere understanding but will be used as a stimulus to further thinking, as a basis for related activity such as giving a report or answering a question, and as a guide to interpretation of other experiences in home, school, and community.

EVALUATION OF THE PRIMARY PROGRAM

As in any other evaluation, evaluation of the primary reading program must be expressed in terms of the children's behavior and in the light of the objectives of instruction during the period.

In terms of children's behavior the teacher, principal, and supervisor may evaluate by answering such questions as these:

1. Do the children approach the reading periods in their various groups with pleasurable anticipation and evident interest?
2. Do the attitudes of the children throughout the actual reading period give evidence of interest, enjoyment, and an attempt to improve standards of work?
3. Do the children work successfully in independent reading periods with books, workbooks, and teacher-made activities?
4. Do the children show about the range of achievement in reading on some standardized test usual for a group with their abilities and backgrounds?
5. Do the children use books frequently in the free-time periods of the school week?
6. Do the children make use of both school and public libraries where they are accessible?
7. Have the children acquired a basic sight vocabulary needed for success in working with their basal readers?
8. In addition to a basal reader vocabulary have the children acquired a sight vocabulary of other useful words, such as are needed in their social-studies activities, or the 220 listed by Dolch,[11] or the 663 listed by Kyte?[12]
9. Have the children acquired abilities in independent word recognition which will be useful to them in reading content materials containing new words?
10. Have the more mature pupils had the opportunity to explore and enjoy supplementary books and other texts at the intermediate-grade levels of difficulty?

[11] Edward W. Dolch, *Teaching Primary Reading*, p. 205. Garrard Press, Champaign, Ill., 1941.

[12] George C. Kyte, "A Core Vocabulary in the Language Arts," *Phi Delta Kappan*, Vol. 34, pp. 231-234, March, 1953.

The objectives of instruction during the primary period vary with the maturity of the children and with different school systems, so that methods of evaluation also vary. In many school systems the objectives are stated in terms of pupil behavior and may parallel the ten items listed above. Other schools list the total number of story books a child reads, determine his score on reading tests made locally, or rate his oral-reading and speech habits on some sort of check list. Still other schools emphasize the growth and adjustments of the whole child and how his reading activities fit into his personality pattern.

The specific devices that children and teachers use to appraise their growth in reading are so numerous that only a few samples can be mentioned here.

One kindergarten teacher believes that her objectives for the year include the development of reading readiness and abilities to keep related records. Accordingly she has her class check themselves daily on an illustrated chart which covers one week's activities. The children may check such items as "told about something at home," "colored with crayon," "said a poem," and "looked at a storybook." A collection of the weekly chart records is one measure of the different children's development.

One second-grade teacher attempts to evaluate her whole program, including reading, in terms of the needs of the children in the group. Sometimes in individual interviews, sometimes in group writing, she has them answer the question "If you had three wishes that would come true, what would you wish for?" The teacher cannot see that all these wishes are answered, because, for example, one boy wished for "a bag of money that would never grow empty" and a girl who had a stepmother wished for "my own mother back again." The method is of some value, however, because young children will often state wishes that are important to them. With this added insight into the child's needs the teacher can sometimes arrange the reading situation or select reading materials so that the needs are partly met.

A number of school systems have the teacher or children keep a record of all the books the children read. It is usually desirable for the teacher to be responsible for the record in the first and sometimes the second grade. The record may show where the child is reading in terms of stated level of books. For example, it can show levels rather exactly in basal and supplementary readers. (See page

	CO-BASAL SERIES		SUPPLEMENTARY SERIES			ADDITIONAL BOOKS READ
	Series 1 (Title)	Series 2 (Title)	Series 3 (Title)	Series 4 (Title)	Series 5 (Title)	(Titles)
Third Reader II						
Third Reader I						
Second Reader II						
Second Reader I						
First Reader						
Primer						
Preprimer III						
Preprimer II						
Preprimer I						
Readiness						

Name .... Date of Birth ....

Test Records	Date	R.G.	Date	R.G.	Date	R.G.

A Plan for Record of Books and Related Facts for a Pupil in One of the Primary Grades

226.) These may be somewhat higher in level than the texts or stories that are being read in free reading periods. Such a record helps to avoid overlapping and repetition from grade to grade and gives a rather clear picture of the effectiveness of a reading program in terms of actual reading accomplished by different children.

The few samples given here suggest that the modern school no longer relies only on standardized test results to evaluate the effectiveness of its reading program. Further suggestions for planning a complete appraisal of the program are given in Chapter 16. Varied, continuous evaluation of the child's growth, both in general adjustments and in more specific reading abilities, is a mark of a modern reading program.

SUPPLEMENTARY READINGS

ANDERSON, I. H., and DEARBORN, W. F. *The Psychology of Teaching Reading.* Ronald, New York, 1952.

BETTS, E. A. *Foundations of Reading Instruction,* rev. ed. American Book, New York, 1957.

BOND, G. L., and WAGNER, EVA. *Teaching the Child to Read,* 3rd ed. Macmillan, New York, 1960.

BONEY, C. D., and LYNCH, J. E. "A Study of Reading Growths in the Primary Grades," *Elementary English Review,* Vol. 19, pp. 115-121, April, 1942.

BROOM, M. E., and others. *Effective Reading Instruction in the Elementary School,* 2nd ed. McGraw-Hill, New York, 1942.

BROWNELL, W. A. "Current Practices with Respect to Phonetic Analysis in the Primary Grades," *Elementary School Journal,* Vol. 42, pp. 195-206, November, 1941.

DAWSON, MILDRED A., and BAMMAN, HENRY. *Fundamentals of Basic Reading Instruction.* Longmans, Green, New York, 1959.

DEBOER, JOHN, and DALLMAN, MARTHA. *The Teaching of Reading.* New York, Holt, 1960.

DOLCH, E. W. *Methods in Reading.* Garrard Press, Champaign, Ill., 1955.

DONELLY, H. E. "Growth of Word Recognition Skills in Grade One," *Education,* Vol. 56, pp. 40-43, September, 1935.

DURRELL, D. D. *Improving Reading Instruction.* World Book, Yonkers, N.Y., 1956.

GILBERT, L. C. "Effect on Silent Reading of Attempting to Follow Oral Reading," *Elementary School Journal,* Vol. 40, pp. 614-621, April, 1940.

GRAY, LILLIAN, and REESE, D. *Teaching Children to Read,* 2nd ed. Ronald, New York, 1957.

HILDRETH, G. *Learning the 3 R's,* 2nd ed., Chaps. 8, 9. Educational Publishers, St. Louis, Mo., 1947.

HILL, M. B. "A Study of the Process of Word Discrimination in Individuals Beginning to Read," *Journal of Educational Research,* Vol. 29, pp. 487-500, March, 1936.

LAMOREAUX, L. A., and LEE, D. M. *Learning to Read through Experience.* Appleton-Century, New York, 1943.

MCKEE, P. G. *Teaching of Reading in the Elementary School,* Chaps. 8, 9, 10. Houghton Mifflin, Boston, 1948.

MCKIM, MARGARET. *Guiding Growth in Reading.* Macmillan, New York, 1955.

RUSSELL, D. H. "Opinions of Experts about Primary-Grade Basic Reading Programs," *Elementary School Journal,* Vol. 44, pp. 602-609, June, 1944.

SPACHE, G. *Resources in Teaching Reading.* Reading Laboratory and Clinic, University of Florida, Gainesville, 1955.

WILSON, F. T. "Early Achievement in Reading," *Elementary School Journal,* Vol. 42, pp. 609-615, April, 1942.

WILSON, F. T., and FLEMING, C. W. W. "Grade Trends in Reading Progress in Kindergarten and Primary Grades," *Journal of Educational Psychology,* Vol. 31, pp. 1-13, January, 1940.

YOAKAM, G. A. *Basal Instruction in Reading.* McGraw-Hill, New York, 1955.

Chapter 8

THE READING PROGRAM IN THE INTERMEDIATE AND JUNIOR HIGH SCHOOL GRADES

OVERVIEW

A reading program in the post-primary grades of the elementary school and in junior-high-school classes must be built upon (1) the reading abilities the pupils have acquired in the primary grades, (2) the expanding interests of later childhood and early adolescence, (3) the need for continued development of skillful, fluent, and differentiated reading abilities, and (4) the reading demands of the total curriculum and of out-of-school activities. When children enter the fourth grade, many of them have acquired competence in word recognition and the ability to read for comprehension in three or four different ways such as, for example, finding the main idea of a selection. They have a positive attitude toward books. On these fundamental learnings, new competencies and interests must be built gradually and continuously. No longer do school people accept the belief of a generation or two ago that children "learn to read" in the primary grades. Instead teachers, school administrators, and many parents accept the fact that reading instruction must continue through the intermediate grades and, for many children, through the junior- and perhaps the senior-high-school years. At these levels pupils will become increasingly independent of teacher help but even the best readers in junior-high-school classes will profit from some planned teacher guidance in reading skills and activities. Even more, children of the intermediate grades need some help from the teacher in developing their "do-it-yourself" reading abilities, and in learning how to find, use, and enjoy the varied reading materials available today.

Later childhood is a period of expanding environment and widening horizons. It is a time of much learning in team games, in social relationships, in verbal skills, and in cognitive abilities. In keeping with the increasing maturity of the children, the school curriculum demands bigger vocabularies (Chapters 9, 10), more precise abilities in functional reading or study skills (Chapter 11), and a higher level of critical and creative activities growing out of reading (Chapter 14). Accordingly, reading moves out from the limited areas of the primary grades into a wider world of both content and technique. It becomes increasingly an activity performed independent of direct teacher help but also one which can be shared for greater enjoyment and understanding in many kinds of group and class activities.

CHARACTERISTICS OF NINE-TO-TWELVE-YEAR-OLDS AND THEIR IMPLICATIONS FOR READING

Children of approximately nine to twelve years are growing physically in a continuous sense, but at a relatively slow rate. They are usually sturdy and active—so active physically that they sometimes find physical activities requiring endurance, speed, and skill more satisfying than reading. However, more exact motor control and better general co-ordination mean that the finer control needed in reading does not place so much strain on the child's visual equipment as formerly. Physically he often prefers a wide range of activities, but he is also more ready for somewhat sustained reading than ever before.

The mental development of the intermediate-grade child proceeds at a rapid pace, with increasing need for ways of communicating ideas, including reading. The typical child is increasingly self-directive, and interests become more specialized; hence more initiative will be shown in choosing one's own reading materials. Interest in how things function and increased ability to distinguish between the real and unreal usually result in a rise of interest in reading factual, utilitarian materials. Accordingly, the modern classroom library cannot be composed only of stories. Since the children are developing a better sense of time and are beginning to distinguish historical periods, materials on people of other times and places may interest them. In general, broader intellectual horizons are reflected in a broader variety of reading activities.

In their social-emotional development the influence of adults on most of these children is waning, to be replaced by the opinions and pressures of the clique, the gang, or the peer group, particularly of the same sex. For this reason, children at this level will read what the others are reading. For example, they may be like one bright girl who read the comics so as to know what the others were talking about, although she really preferred other books. The tendency of some of the group to become hero-worshipers may start an interest in biography, in series repeating the same character, or even in screen magazines. Occasional apparent antagonism between the boys and the girls means that few boys will be found reading "sissy" girls' books, although the girls are usually allowed to read boys' stories without incurring the censure of their group. Boys' interests in competitive sports may lead them, toward the end of the period, to regular reading of the sports pages of the newspaper. Such social-emotional maturation and the increasing differentiation in reading purposes and materials offer many suggestions for the teaching of reading in the intermediate grades.

CHARACTERISTICS OF JUNIOR HIGH SCHOOL STUDENTS

Children of approximately twelve through fifteen years continue the growth patterns of their later childhood. A growth spurt and the onset of puberty may bring many physical changes easily observed, but other social, emotional, and intellectual developments may be equally important and more difficult to diagnose. One need only stand near the steps of a junior high school when the children leave for the day to realize some of the differences found in the early teens' group; there are the short and the tall, the "little" boy and the physically mature girl, the scholar with a pile of books, the athlete with some games' equipment, the solitary child and the chattering bevy, the girl with the drama book and the boy with the electronics magazine.

Although the individuals of the junior-high-school population differ in almost every way that can be measured, there are a few general characteristics of the period which have implications for the reading program. Both boys and girls increase in size and strength and are capable of more sustained physical and mental effort. If growth is very rapid for a period, the child may tire easily and apparently lose interest in a book or activity. His muscular co-ordination may apparently decline as he grows accustomed to new lengths of arm and leg, but fatigue in reading is more likely to result from loss of interest than from physical factors. As in later childhood, the influence of adults continues to wane and the mores of the group will be more likely to influence the kind and amount of reading. Social-emotional developments may influence choice of recreational reading materials with the girls reading more "adult" novels of romance and the women's magazines, while boys still stick with adventure stories or more specialized interests such as model plane building and space travel. In providing for this group, accordingly, a school must have a well-stocked library where the pupil has a chance to select not only from familiar series or writers but in an area such as science or biography where he may have developed specialized interests.

In their mental development children in the early teens are acquiring broader and deeper concepts, greater facility in problem solving, and increased experience in, and capacity for, critical and creative thinking.[1] As they increase in ability to abstract and generalize, the children are increasingly able to use printed materials as tools for intellectual work. As they increase in capacity for emotional response and intellectual understanding, they are better able to appreciate some literary qualities in writing and to judge the worth of the material read. In reader, anthology, text, or in newspaper or other fugitive material they can more subtly detect a point of view, judge relevancy to their purpose, and use the materials to produce a new or fresh or individual outcome. In so doing, they may increasingly read "between the lines" and more skillfully translate into enjoyment or practical use.

The standards reached in the junior-high-school reading program will differ with different children, but a school staff may differentiate roughly three groups in the school population. The reading achievements of these groups will not necessarily coincide with achievements in sports, mechanical skills, social leadership, or school citizenship, but they are usually related to other academic factors. The three groups of students in a typical junior high school are:

(1) A group slow in acquiring verbal skills which may be reading at the third or fourth grade levels. They will need help in basic skills, will do best with somewhat simplified material, and should be encouraged to develop life-time interest in parts of the newspaper, the less offensive pulps, and simple functional materials used in various occupations.

[1] David H. Russell, *Children's Thinking*. Ginn, Boston, 1956

(2) A group who read near grade level but need help in adjusting reading to purpose and in the thinking aspects of reading—associating, problem solving, following directions, and criticizing where necessary. This group can be encouraged to develop habits of recreational reading which will continue in later life in such "middle brow" magazines as *Time, Reader's Digest,* and the *Saturday Evening Post.* They must be helped to see and use good books, not too difficult, on hobbies, science, current events, travel, and other topics.

(3) A group who are already reading as well as the typical senior high school student or even the college freshman. This group must be encouraged in refining their reading skills and tastes. They may need a little guidance in developing library-research techniques to find answers to their specialized interests and needs. They can be guided toward genuine appreciation of some classics and the highly skilled reading of certain kinds of technical materials.

In junior high school, the modern student usually finds that many more demands are made on his time—school homework, social and special interest groups, sports, television—all these and others may subtract from reading time and the development of reading skill. But by the end of this period the reading habits of a lifetime may be fairly well established, and no school can do less than its best in developing in the junior-high-school years abilities in reading and a love of it.

DEVELOPMENTAL ASPECTS OF THE POST-PRIMARY PROGRAM

Modern authorities now conceive the reading program as a developmental program stretching all the way from readiness activities in kindergarten and first grade through the high school and perhaps even the junior college.[2] In some school systems this idea is still accepted in theory rather than practice. In others, a planned program of reading activities is a regular part of the post-primary curriculum.

Early studies by Buswell[3] and others indicated that the curve of learning showing some of the mechanical aspects of reading typically

[2] *Development In and Through Reading,* Sixtieth Yearbook, Part II, National Society for Study of Education, University of Chicago Press, Chicago, 1961.

[3] Guy T. Buswell, *An Experimental Study of the Eye-Voice Span in Reading,* Supplementary Educational Monographs, No. 17, 106 p. Department of Education, University of Chicago, Chicago, 1920.

rises rapidly in the first three grades and then, about the fourth or fifth grade, begins to level off, with little improvement after the fifth grade. This condition seems a result of the fact that many children are given little real help in reading after the fourth or fifth grades. Their teacher may call their activities a reading lesson, but actually they may be having a literature or discussion experience rather than direct guidance in their reading.

The idea of the developmental reading program is based on the fact that children can continue to improve their reading abilities beyond the fourth-grade level—indeed, that they must continue on higher levels of ability to cope with the reading tasks of the upper elementary school, the secondary school, and modern adult living. The developmental program assumes that what is good reading at the third-grade level is not good reading in the sixth grade, and, even more, what is good reading at the fifth-grade level is not sufficient for the reading demands of the tenth grade or adult life. It gives a place to increasing differentiation of reading purposes and abilities. The following facts are related to the concept of the developmental program:

1. Reading abilities develop gradually over the years.

2. Reading achievement is closely related to school success in both the upper elementary and secondary schools.

3. Reading abilities have significance in the personal and social adjustment of the individual and in his contribution to the group at all ages.

4. Reading abilities vary as much as two or three grades in primary classes and five or six grades in higher classes. Accordingly, many pupils need guidance in their reading activities at all school levels.

5. Reading is a complex process which requires quite different abilities in different situations. For example, a good reader of historical or literary materials may be a poor reader of scientific materials in the intermediate or upper grades. Accordingly reading may be profitably stressed in the different subject-matter fields.

6. Most children do not acquire new reading abilities automatically. As both good and poor students meet new materials and read for new purposes, some teacher help on a preventive rather than a remedial level is desirable.

The above six facts all suggest that a developmental program of reading instruction must be included in the curricular activities of intermediate and senior grades. Suggestions for such activities are given below.

ORGANIZATION OF READING PROGRAMS IN POST-PRIMARY GRADES

The type of reading program planned by a teacher or a curriculum committee for intermediate- and junior-high-school classes will depend upon certain external aspects of the school's organization. Reading activities will vary in such plans as the following:

The self-contained classroom
The departmentalized school
Ability grouping (three "streams," etc.)
Inter-class grouping for reading
The individualized program

Each of the above types of organization, with the possible exception of the individualized program, also allows for grouping within one class, with its virtues and problems (Chapter 15). Each of the plans has some advantages and some disadvantages. For example, the self-contained classroom allows more opportunities for reading abilities to be practiced in content fields, such as science or health, at the points of difficulty at which children can profit most from additional practice. On the other hand, it may result in a very wide range of reading ability in one classroom with consequent problems of materials and of methods of instruction. Similarly inter-class grouping, such as advocated in the "Joplin plan"[4] and carried out in San Francisco some fifteen years earlier,[5] may have some advantages in reducing range of reading ability in one class but some disadvantages in "labelling" children and in placing them with teachers who do not know them well.

Whatever the plan used in a school or school system, the classroom teacher in the intermediate and upper grades typically confronts three instructional problems: (a) What reading abilities are best

[4] Cecil Floyd, "Meeting Children's Reading Needs in the Intermediate Grades: A Preliminary Report," *Elementary School Journal,* Vol. 55, pp. 99-103, October, 1954.

[5] David H. Russell, "Inter-Class Grouping for Reading Instruction in the Intermediate Grades," *Journal of Educational Research,* Vol. 39, pp. 462-470, February, 1946.

learned as a class, in a small group, and individually? (b) What materials are available? and (c) How can a weekly program be planned as a whole, to include groups working with the teacher, and others not working directly under the teacher's guidance?

The division of activities into class, group, and individualized procedures will necessarily shift with the maturity of pupils and their specific needs, but the following general suggestions of possible activities for intermediate grades and junior high school may be made:

Whole Class	*Small Group*	*Individual*
1. Introducing a new work-type skill such as use of guide words in a dictionary.	1. Developing comprehension abilities from basal materials.	1. Recreational reading.
2. Reviewing a skill taught earlier but in need of improvement, such as alphabetizing or differences between a table of contents and an index.	2. Reading to prepare a committee report in a content area.	2. Getting help from teacher on a specific difficulty.
3. The teacher reads to the class something she herself enjoys.	3. Practicing some needed word recognition skills such as syllabication.	3. Practice exercises for reading skills.
4. Sharing an important selection which all the class must know or use in some way—newspaper, announcements, etc.	4. Choral reading of poetry.	4. Following directions for construction, hobby, etc.
5. Audience oral reading by pupils, etc.	5. Word and reading games, etc.	5. Building vocabulary as in keeping "My Word List," etc.

The important thing about any such division is that a teacher or school staff think through the advantages and disadvantages of allocating various types of reading activities to these three categories.

The second question of locating diverse and suitable materials will vary from school to school. In most primary grades, a school seems reasonably well stocked with materials if the classroom contains a variety of readers, of individual library books, and of workbooks, charts, labels, and reading "games." In the intermediate and upper grades, however, the list must be broadened to include:

A wide range of readers
A classroom collection of fiction and non-fiction
A library
Newspapers planned for children (such as *My Weekly Reader, Junior Scholastic, and Current Events*)
Dictionaries
Encyclopedias
Other reference series (such as *Our Wonderful World*)
Individual reference books (such as *Subject Index to Books for Intermediate Grades*[6] and *The Junior Book of Authors*[7])
Tape recorder
Recordings of verse and prose
Films
Film strips and slides
Teacher-prepared exercises
Booklets of pupils' own writings
Magazines

The materials available will depend upon the interests and abilities of the group and the other activities of the class in units of work and co-curricular activities. The above list suggests the range of present-day reading materials but is far from exhaustive. More suggestions about materials are made in Chapter 13.

TYPICAL WEEKLY PROGRAMS

The variety of reading experiences in the intermediate grades necessitates planning on more than a daily basis. Most teachers are not satisfied to restrict a reading program to direct teacher guidance from a basic reader. As suggested above, many other work-type and

[6] Eloise Rue, *Subject Index to Books for Intermediate Grades,* 2nd ed. American Library Association, Chicago, 1950.
[7] Stanley J. Kunitz and Howard Haycraft, *Junior Book of Authors,* 2nd ed. Wilson, New York, 1951.

recreational experiences are neded for a balanced program. Both individual and group reading experiences must be included. Accordingly, planning cannot be done on a day-to-day basis. A number of teachers achieve variety and balance in their reading program by planning a week's work at a time.

A Pasadena elementary-school bulletin[8] suggests a typical weekly program for a fifth-grade class which is divided into three groups for guidance in basic reading but recombined in various ways for other activities. (See page 239.) These activities would naturally vary with the needs of the group. The Pasadena plan provides for forty minutes devoted specifically to reading activities each day, but the actual preparation of materials involves considerably more time on the part of the teacher. The chart does not include, of course, the many reading activities of each group in connection with their daily work in social studies, arithmetic, and other curricular activities. In addition, the plans will change somewhat from week to week, again depending upon the needs of the group.

The program outlined is concerned with activities of the developmental reading program, the experiences designed to give children rather direct practice in fundamental reading habits and skills. As suggested in Chapter 5 and the section below entitled "Basic Reading Instruction in the Intermediate Grades," the use of basic readers with direct teacher guidance is only one part of the total reading program in the intermediate and upper grades. One way of summarizing the point of view in this chapter and of supplementing the suggestions given on page 237 is to restate the reading program at these levels. Teachers and other curriculum workers should consider the reading program over a weekly or monthly period as consisting of at least five main types of experiences:

1. *The developmental reading program.* Systematic group and individual instruction using the basic readers and their related materials and, for work-type reading, selected sections from textbook materials.

2. *The functional reading program.* The reading of textbooks to solve problems in social studies, mathematics, science, and other areas along with the reading of daily plans, announcements, reports, and resource materials found in the library.

[8] Pasadena City Schools, *Some Questions and Answers about Reading in the Elementary School Program,* Elementary Curriculum Department, Reading Bulletin No. 1, September, 1946, 29 p.

	GROUP 1 (HIGH)	GROUP 2 (AVERAGE)	GROUP 3 (LOW)
Monday	Silent reading to answer questions. Readers, texts, reference books.	Silent reading to answer questions on blackboard or on hectographed sheets. Reader, social-studies books. (Allow ten minutes to check answers.)	Reading practice from basic reader. *Direct teacher guidance*. (Allow ten minutes to check answers in Group 2.)
Tuesday	Free reading period, using individual library books.	Reading practice from readers and texts. *Direct teacher guidance*.	Independent work activities, games, exercises, workbooks, etc.
	Ten to fifteen minutes. All-group activity: audience reading, choral reading, reading of children's original stories, etc.		
Wednesday	Oral and silent reading practice from readers and texts. *Direct teacher guidance*. (Leave ten to fifteen minutes for Group 3.)	Free reading period with individual library books. Preparation for audience reading.	Reading from readers and texts to answer questions. *Direct teacher guidance* on questions and difficulties.
Thursday	Free reading period with individual library books. Preparation for audience reading.	Oral and silent reading practice from readers and texts. *Direct teacher guidance*.	Work-type study activities, games, exercises.
	All-group activity: audience reading, dictionary work, word study, etc.		
Friday	Work-type study activities as needed by individuals, games, devices.		Reading practice from basic readers. *Direct teacher guidance*. (Leave twenty minutes for all-group activity.)
	Twenty minutes. All-group activity: library, dramatization, story-telling, dictionary work, etc.		

A Suggested Week's Program in Developmental Reading Activities for the Fifth Grade[9]

[9] Pasadena City Schools, *Some Questions and Answers about Reading in the Elementary School Program*, Reading Bulletin No. I. Pasadena City Schools, Pasadena, Calif., 1946.

3. *The recreational program.* Reading for oneself and with others for enjoyment and information, to fulfill needs for relaxation and fun, and for satisfying curiosity.

4. *The enrichment program.* Using reading to enrich and extend one's experiences in relation to other language-arts activities, such as dramatization or conversation, and to provide other stimulating experiences which are enjoyed vicariously through reading in such areas as travel or nature.

5. *The remedial program.* Giving special help to a few children who are considerably retarded in reading abilities. This is usually done on an individual or small-group basis. In a case of extreme disability clinical help may be needed.

The well-balanced reading program in an intermediate or upper grade contains experiences of each of the first four types over a week's time. Any one child has, then, a considerable variety of reading experiences, both individually and in different groups, at different times. Another type of program which provides for the teacher's working with each group each day and for a variety of individual activities has been proposed by Doak.[10] It formulates a simple method for keying related activities to the reading of any one day. (See chart, page 241.)

TYPES OF ACTIVITIES

Children in the primary grades are concerned with acquiring some of the basic skills in reading such as the use of books, building up a small recognition vocabulary, and simple comprehension of relatively short passages. In the intermediate and senior grades these activities are typically broadened. The primary aim of reading instruction becomes the provision of rich and meaningful experiences through reading. To accomplish this aim the reading instructor will include development of abilities in

1. Free, independent reading of various materials on different levels of difficulty and with ample provision of rather easy materials.
2. Reference reading, learning to use the resources of the library, the encyclopedia, and other authoritative sources.

[10] Helen P. Doak, "Weekly Organization of the Class for Reading and Reading Activities—Middle and Upper Grades," Bulletin of Alhambra City Schools, Alhambra, Calif., no date.

3. Group reading for discussion and application to group enterprises, as in social studies.

4. Reading for the main idea, for more exact details, for an orderly sequence of events or outlining of the selection, and for using or doing something about the material in a creative way.[11]

WEEKLY ORGANIZATION OF THE CLASS FOR READING AND READING ACTIVITIES
MIDDLE AND UPPER GRADES

(Helen P. Deak, Supervisor, Alhambra City Schools)

Monday	Choice from III Work with Teacher Assignment	Assignment Choice from IV Work with Teacher	Work with Teacher Assignment Choice from I
Tuesday	Choice from I Work with Teacher Assignment	Assignment Choice from III Work with Teacher	Work with Teacher Assignment Choice from II
Wednesday	Choice from IV Work with Teacher Assignment	Assignment Choice from V Work with Teacher	Work with Teacher Assignment Choice from III
Thursday	Choice from II Work with Teacher Assignment	Assignment Choice from I Work with Teacher	Work with Teacher Assignment Choice from V
Friday	Choice from V Work with Teacher Assignment	Assignment Choice from II Work with Teacher	Work with Teacher Assignment Choice from IV

SUGGESTED AREAS FOR INDEPENDENT ACTIVITIES

Area I Arts, Music, Etc.	Area II Social Studies	Area III Indiv. or Group Interest	Area IV Games	Area V Preparation for Sharing Reading
Painting Clay Chalk Crayola Stenciling Block Printing Weaving Murals Music Flower Arranging	Map Making Graph Making Chart Making Time Lines Costumes Books or Booklets Bulletin Board Arrangement Scrap Books Arranging Displaying Cataloging Material	Interest Reading Looking at Magazines, Newspapers Hobbies	Teacher-prepared or Commercial	Bibliographies Scripts or Dramatizations Puppets Book Reports Book Reviews Annotations Class File Working on Individual Unfinished Work Spelling Arithmetic Language

As part of his approach to the problem Durrell[12] discussed the scope of the reading program in the intermediate grades with em-

[11] Constance M. McCullough, "Broadening Experiences through Reading in the Elementary School," *Elementary English Review*, Vol. 23, pp. 101-107, March, 1946.

[12] Donald D. Durrell, "Basic Abilities in Intermediate Grade Reading," *Education*, Vol. 59, pp. 45-50, September, 1938.

phasis upon the mechanical aspects of reading, by listing a variety of "exercises" which he regarded as "minimum essentials for a middle grade reading program." These are the following:

1. Vocabulary exercises in silent reading—both recognition and meaning vocabularies.
2. Exercises for increasing attention and simple comprehension.
3. Exercises for increasing speed.
4. Exercises for improving study skills.
5. Exercises for improving voluntary recall—oral and written.

Durrell's description of the fourth item in this list helps to reduce the somewhat mechanical nature of the proposals. He suggested that improving study skills involves thoroughness of comprehension, greater flexibility, and associational skills needed for thinking while reading. He gave the following specific suggestions for improving association or relating reading to other activities:

1. Reading to think of new illustrations of the author's point.
2. Finding exceptions to the author's point.
3. Drawing generalizations from reading.
4. Reading to discover activities to be carried out.
5. Reading to discover topics for further study.
6. Reading to criticize form and style.

These are study skills which can be begun rather than perfected in the intermediate grades. Since the whole reading program is regarded as a continuous, developmental program, specific reading activities such as the six listed can be begun when readiness for them is established and can be continued at various levels of difficulty as the child matures and acquires related learnings. The factor of readiness at all levels has been discussed in Chapter 6.

Stone[13] gave a somewhat more comprehensive list of activities that comprise the intermediate grade program. These are the following:

1. Preparatory exercises (on blackboard, in workbook, or in text)
2. Group interpretative reading (class-fashion procedure with same selection in hands of all the group)
3. Individual recreative reading and related activities
4. Work-type and practice reading (silent)
   a. Practice for speed in cursory reading
   b. Practice for skills in careful or study reading

[13] Clarence R. Stone, *Better Advanced Reading*, 282 p. Webster, St. Louis, Mo., 1937.

5. Systematic vocabulary lessons
   a. Exercises related to fluency, accuracy, and independence in word recognition
   b. Exercises related to word meanings
6. Practice in oral reading
   a. Group reading
      (1) Rereading prepared selections
      (2) Sight reading of new selections
      (3) Practice following silent reading
   b. Individual remedial practice
7. Audience reading
8. Reading in connection with other activities and subjects: incidental, correlated, integrated reading

This list of Stone's might serve as a check list for the teacher or principal in evaluating the variety of reading experiences provided in his intermediate-grade program. The check list can be used only in the light of the maturity and needs of the group involved, and equal weight cannot be given to each of the eight items for all groups. For example, in average or superior groups the eighth item, reading in connection with other activities and subjects, may be the most important part of the program.

In the suggestions made by McCullough, Durrell, and Stone and in the list of available materials given above there seems to be a basis of agreement that the intermediate program should include practice in basic reading procedures, guidance in reading the materials of various school subjects, and enjoyment of activities in literature. These are phases of the same thing rather than separate parts of the program, but some suggestions for each are made below.

BASIC READING INSTRUCTION IN THE INTERMEDIATE GRADES

Basic reading instruction is associated with the use of basal readers and other materials organized to encourage gradual growth in vocabulary and comprehension abilities and in work-type procedures. Actually many so-called basic readers are better adapted to literature experiences than to other types of reading. If a series is truly basic, it should provide some foundation for a variety of the most important types of reading activity in which most intermediate-grade children engage. It should, therefore, contain both fictional and factual materials, and the teacher's manual accompanying the book should indicate some of the different ways in which the selections may be studied. The reader, with its accompanying workbook and manual, should provide a well-rounded and balanced program of reading abilities which will be a firm foundation for the varied reading activities of the intermediate and upper grades. Such a program will not neglect textbooks in content fields but rather will incorporate them into the total program as a step beyond basic reading experiences.

There is some uncertainty among school people regarding the place of basic readers in the total reading program. Such a place for a particular class must be decided in terms of the children's needs and community demands on the school. Even gifted children need guidance at this level, and all children seem to profit from continued instruction in reading, as opposed to merely "hearing the children read."[14] With a large class and a wide variety of learning activities to be planned each week, many teachers are grateful for the carefully graded and richly varied reading experiences provided in a good basic series. The consensus of the whole school staff rather than the desires of one teacher should influence the extent to which basic readers are used. Most groups of children seem to profit by having considerable emphasis given to the direct learning involved in the use of a basic series.

Some of the advantages and disadvantages of basic series and some hints for their use have been given by Gates,[15] by Russell,[16] and by Herrick.[17] In general the value of any series depends upon the way it is used. Most modern series have been carefully prepared from the point of view of content and gradation. If the teacher follows the methods suggested in the accompanying manuals, varying them in the light of her own experience and the pupils' needs, she will be guiding pupils in a variety of basic learning experiences. As indicated above, these will include many phases of reading such as the following: increased skill in word recognition, development of a

[14] David H. Russell, "The Role in Pupil Development of a Sound Foundation in Reading," Supplementary Educational Monographs, No. 65. University of Chicago Press, Chicago, 1948.

[15] Arthur I. Gates, "Characteristics of Today's Basal Reading Materials," *Teachers' Service Bulletin in Reading,* Vol. 7, No. 5, Macmillan, January, 1946.

[16] David H. Russell, *The Basic Reading Program in the Modern School,* Contributions in Reading, No. 1. Ginn, Boston, 1954.

[17] Virgil E. Herrick, "Basal Instructional Materials in Reading," *Development In and Through Reading,* Sixtieth Yearbook, Part II, Chap. 10, National Society for Study of Education, University of Chicago Press, Chicago, 1961.

larger meaning vocabulary, improved oral reading, growth of various comprehension abilities, and increased skill in the use of books containing various types of subject matter. These and other results of the basic program are treated in Chapter 5 and other chapters of this book. Since the growth of recognition and meaning vocabularies is considered in Chapters 9 and 10 in detail, and the place and improvement of oral reading in Chapter 4, this chapter deals with the last two examples of outcomes of the basic program, growth in comprehension abilities and increased skill in the use of books in the content fields.

COMPREHENSION ABILITIES

Some writers define *comprehension* as the ability to get meaning from the printed page in the form in which the author presents it and *interpretation* as occurring when the reader goes beyond the stated meaning. The two often overlap. In the intermediate and upper grades it seems more exact to speak of many reading comprehensions rather than a single comprehension for all reading. As indicated above, pupils who are good readers for details may fail to grasp the significance of a whole section. In the primary grades the comprehension of many pupils is limited to individual words, to grasping sentence meaning, and to reading short paragraphs or stories for general impression or for some details. At some stage in the intermediate grades most children will be able to expand these abilities gradually so as to acquire a wider range of comprehension. Analysis of reading activities in intermediate and senior grades indicates that a least ten or twelve comprehension abilities should be practiced and maintained in the intermediate and senior grades. The chart on page 246 gives such a list as developed by a committee in the Detroit public schools.[18]

Each of these comprehensions suggests reading for something, or reading as a basis for action. The pupils of any intermediate or upper-grade class will, of course, vary widely in their readiness for these purposes in reading. Pupils will also differ in the comprehensions that they will acquire in the intermediate grades. As in other reading activities the teacher will study the pupils to determine their

[18] *A Guide to Instruction in the Language Arts Grades 4, 5, and 6.* The Board of Education of the City of Detroit, Detroit, 1959.

readiness, plan activities that help to develop readiness, and, through guidance in subgroups, develop the pupils' abilities at the level where they will profit most. In general, pupils at any level can be helped in putting their reading to work by use of pictures, films, and excursions centered around the same topic.

Skills in Comprehension and Interpretation

Skill	Grade 1	2	3	4	5	6	7	8
Discover a specific fact or facts	—	—	—	—	—	—	—	—
Follow a sequence of ideas or events								
Events of a story	—	—	—	—	—	—	—	—
Steps in a process			—	—	—	—	—	—
Cause-and-effect relationships						—	—	—
Note and recall significant details	—	—	—	—	—	—	—	—
Remember what is read								
Grasp the ideas as presented	—	—	—	—	—	—	—	—
Summarize and organize important ideas				—	—	—	—	—
Gather, assemble, and organize ideas on a problem					—	—	—	—
Follow directions given in reading material		—	—	—	—	—	—	—
Read critically and evaluate what is read								
Anticipate outcomes	—	—	—	—	—	—	—	—
React to the mood or tone of a selection	—	—	—	—	—	—	—	—
Recognize emotional reactions and motives of story characters	—	—	—	—	—	—	—	—
Consider ideas in the light of one's knowledge and experiences	—	—	—	—	—	—	—	—
Draw inferences from a passage	—	—	—	—	—	—	—	—
Distinguish between statements of fact and opinion				—	—	—	—	—
Examine the support of statements made					—	—	—	—
Reach broad generalizations and conclusions					—	—	—	—
Read for main ideas								
The general meaning or significance of the selection			—	—	—	—	—	—
The main idea of a passage				—	—	—	—	—
The main idea of a paragraph				—	—	—	—	—
Read to make comparisons								
Comparison of two or more versions of a story			—	—	—	—	—	—
Comparison of two or more printed sources of information					—	—	—	—
Grasp the organization of what is read								
The large thought divisions of a selection				—	—	—	—	—
The structure of paragraphs					—	—	—	—
The design of a writing						—	—	—

The intermediate grade teacher, too, must be aware of the difficulty of some of these comprehensions. Many of them typically are not perfected until high-school or college levels, even if then. For example, a study by Keneally[19] suggested just how difficult reading for the general idea and reading to organize can be. By controlling the factor of relative difficulty of selections she found that a group of sixth-grade pupils had only the following percentages correct:

	Percentage Correct
1. Supplying minor ideas in an outline which lists the major ideas	65
2. Selection of a statement which best summarizes a paragraph	50
3. Putting list of topics in the order in which they occur in the story	39
4. Matching headlines or topics with paragraphs	23
5. Supplying major topics in an outline in which minor ideas are given	16
6. Writing original headlines or topics for paragraphs	10

This list suggests procedures that teachers may use in increasing comprehension, but the percentages correct indicate that no teacher should expect a high degree of competence for most of an intermediate-grade class without specific guidance in reading for these purposes. Greater competence in work-type reading can be achieved if pupils and teacher work on the problem together.

Another comprehension listed in the chart, reading critically to appraise the value of the materials, was studied in part by Gans,[20] who determined the ability of intermediate-grade children to read different types of materials in order to select information pertinent to a specific problem. She found that critical reading in relation to acceptance or rejection is not measured closely in the usual standardized reading tests. Gans concluded that "the factors of authenticity of content and relevancy of content are not dealt with in the teaching of reading." Her study underlines the importance of a pupil's having his purpose clearly in mind while reading several selections.

[19] Katherine G. Keneally, *A Study of the Relative Order of Difficulty of Several Types of Study Skills*. Unpublished master's thesis, Boston University, Boston, 1939.

[20] Roma Gans, *Study of Critical Reading Comprehension in Intermediate Grades*, Teachers College Contributions to Education, No. 811. Bureau of Publications, Teachers College, Columbia University, New York, 1940.

GUIDANCE IN READING THE VARIOUS SCHOOL SUBJECTS

In addition to basic reading instruction stressing vocabulary growth and the development of various comprehension abilities, much of the reading done by an older child in the elementary school and in the junior high school is in particular subject-matter fields. In a typical day he reads some social-studies materials to solve some problem, to prepare a report, or to find help in drawing or in construction; he may read a story for enjoyment or to plan a dramatization; he probably reads some verbal arithmetic problems which he is asked to solve; he may read some science materials to get some specific information he needs; he may possibly be reading health materials to relate them to his own habits or community problems. In any one day, then, most intermediate-grade pupils read in a wide variety of subject-matter fields. Most of these subjects involve certain problems as far as reading is concerned. Not only do they often contain a specific type of material, such as specialized vocabulary, but they must each be read for some of the different purposes outlined above. In general, then, no one way of reading is adequate for the whole group. The teacher must help the children to develop *differentiated* ways of reading depending upon materials and purposes.[21]

The field of social studies offers many challenges to the teacher of reading. Bond and Wagner[22] summarized some of the difficulties met in reading this and other content subjects. For example, they listed and described the following main adjustments needed in reading social-studies materials:

1. Adjustment to vocabulary
2. Adjustment to complexity of ideas
3. Difficulties of locating supplementary material
4. Adjustment to organization
5. Difficulties of reading critically
6. Understanding the conditions and mores of a particular period
7. Using current materials

Such a list indicates that difficulties in reading social-studies materials exist in the background experiences of the child and in the

[21] Leo C. Fay, "The Relationship Between Specific Reading Skills and Selected Areas of Sixth Grade Achievement," *Journal of Educational Research,* Vol. 43, pp. 541-547, March, 1950.

[22] Guy L. Bond and Eva Wagner, *Teaching the Child to Read,* 3rd ed. Macmillan, New York, 1960.

type of materials included in the text. Children have difficulty with vocabulary because they lack experience in the area involved. They may recognize all the words in such a sentence as "The well produces three hundreds barrels a day" but have little concept of oil wells or petroleum production. They may quote "with liberty and justice for all" but they probably have little understanding of the hundreds of years of struggle in England and America for the idea of the rights of the individual. The solution to the problem lies in improving the children's background of ideas and in modifying the concepts included in the textbook. In many social-studies texts the ideas and examples lack reality for the child. The problems raised in the book are completely artificial to him. Research on children's concepts of time and space, for example, indicates that the teacher of the intermediate grades can take nothing for granted in the way of preliminary understanding of such words as *century,* B.C., or *width of the Atlantic.* These facts suggest that there should be more attention to the readability of social-studies texts and more emphasis by the teacher on readiness for reading a particular social-studies selection.

A description of a program in reading social-studies materials may be put more positively by suggesting actual activities to be attempted. McIntire,[23] for example, divided a group's possible activities into four sections: developing readiness, determining purpose for reading, actual reading, and follow-up procedures. In general, readiness may be achieved for certain social-studies printed materials by concrete activities in that area. Children may study and discuss the pictures accompanying the text and other pictures. They may use actual demonstration or experiment, such as taking the skin off an orange and laying it flat to demonstrate the Mercator projection, or picking the seeds from a cotton boll. During such activities they usually raise certain questions. These may be recorded by the teacher on the chalkboard, or in some other way, to round out the second stage of having specific purposes for reading. After the actual reading McIntire suggested such follow-up activities as organizing the information in tables or on maps, making notes for a report, or checking newspapers and magazines. These examples suggest that reading in the social studies is always closely tied in with other experiences the children are having.

[23] Alta McIntire, "Reading Social Studies Materials in the Middle Grades," *Elementary English Review,* Vol. 21, pp. 262-266, November, 1944.

As children go through the intermediate and upper grades they have increasing need of the ability to organize social studies and other materials they read. The ability to organize, like other phases of reading, develops slowly over the years from sentence comprehension to outlining and reworking complex passages. Goodykoontz,[24] in a valuable analysis of reading for organization, listed eighteen types of exercises which lead the child from simple location of answers to outlining and summarizing. Early analytical steps include such topics as matching titles or paragraph headings with paragraphs, improving paragraph headings, finding a keynote sentence in a paragraph, recognizing the climax of a story, and taking running notes. More advanced steps involving the relations of ideas include anticipating the content of a chapter, arranging ideas in order, classifying or grouping ideas, locating main points and subordinate points, and making an outline. Finally, the synthesis of ideas is involved in reproducing from an outline or from notes, securing material in answer to a problem, and summarizing. In addition, Goodykoontz suggested the types of exercise which will give practice in the different organizing activities.

Similarly, in other subject-matter fields there are purposes and content which require the development of special reading abilities. The child reading a mathematical problem must be able to read for details and to distinguish between what is given and what is required.[25] The child reading a long story for enjoyment must develop the ability to skim over the materials rather quickly while keeping in mind enough details for an understanding of plot or character. The child needing some facts in science must be able to consult the proper reference book and read rather exactly for the specific information he requires. These are all very different abilities, and no child develops them automatically. Consequently, every teacher at the upper-elementary and secondary-school level needs to provide specific help in reading materials in the various content fields.

Although different subject matter requires very different reading abilities, there are certain common capacities and achievements which are basic to most content reading. In a general way every inter-

24 Bess Goodykoontz, "Teaching Pupils to Organize What They Read," *Elementary English Review,* Vol. 7, pp. 87-90, 93, April, 1930.

25 David H. Russell, "Arithmetic Power Through Reading," *Instruction in Arithmetic,* Twenty-fifth Yearbook, Chap. 9, National Council of Teachers of Mathematics, Washington, D.C., 1960.

mediate or upper-grade teacher may give continuous guidance in helping boys and girls in the following ways:

1. Establishing the purpose for which the content is to be read.
2. Making a quick preliminary survey of all the material.
3. Checking from the dictionary or other sources the meanings of technical or specialized words occurring in the material.
4. Giving complete attention to the material in the light of the understood purpose.
5. Using related pictures, maps, charts, and tables to verify ideas in the verbal materials, particularly those dealing with locations, quantitative data, and time sequence.
6. Becoming accustomed to verbal clues which give ideas of size, a sense of the passage of time, and sequence of events or topics.
7. Checking the accuracy of the sources of information.
8. Reflecting on the ideas presented in the printed materials in the light of related past experiences.
9. Applying previous knowledge in order to make new generalizations and plans.
10. Where possible, subjecting these conclusions to the test of practical operation.

Most of these abilities are useful in reading arithmetic, science, social studies, health materials, and art materials. No teacher will ever be able to apply them all in any one reading of, for example, some supplementary texts; but the ten items provide a framework for reading in the content fields over a term or even the intermediate and upper grades.

LITERATURE EXPERIENCES

The above discussion of reading in the content fields has emphasized the work-type aspects of such reading. Even more than in the primary program of the previous chapter it is necessary to stress here that any reading program will be incomplete if it does not include, in addition to practice from basic books, and work-type activities, a considerable measure of recreational reading in which enjoyment is stressed. The intermediate-grades stage is peculiarly the time when such reading flourishes. Most children at this level have mastered the mechanical difficulties of reading, but they have not developed the social interests of early adolescence. Accordingly the years from approximately nine to twelve may be called the golden years for reading. For some children this period continues a year or two longer. Various interest studies, some of which are reported in Chapter 12, show that most children do more recreational reading during these years than at any other time in their lives.

As stated in Chapter 13 on the literature program, there is no final answer as to what children of any age want to read or should read. Many studies of children's interests, reviewed later in Chapter 12 of this book, indicate that these interests change not only with the increasing maturity of the child but also with the social conditions affecting his behavior. A new community enterprise, a movie, or a television program may mean a new reading interest. Further, there seems to be little guarantee that a selection will influence a child in a desirable way. Most children in intermediate grades will enjoy the humor of *Freddy the Detective* or *Homer Price,* and thrill to the adventure stories of Stephen Meader or Howard Pease in the upper grades, but reaction to the particular event or setting or idea cannot be predetermined for all boys and girls. An account of some part of life that has significance for a certain ten-year-old or thirteen-year-old is a very individual thing. Besides taking into account a child's level of reading ability when helping him to select a book for recreational reading, a teacher must know what kind of child he is, what books he has enjoyed before, and where his current activities are leading him.

The increase of reading ability characteristic of the intermediate and upper grades greatly enlarges book horizons. The typical child at these levels is mature enough to enlarge greatly his mental and emotional life through reading. This widening of horizon comes through the stimulating variety of content in modern children's books. Indians and helicopters, feudal castles and space travel, are as available as the nearest shelf. Increasingly, too, the child is able to project himself into the situation and share the triumph or disaster of the book friend or acquaintance. This enrichment of ideas and emotions will be partly on an individual basis, but it is equally true that social settings will enhance the emotional stimulus. In general, then, the teacher and class will plan regular opportunities for sharing with others in the audience situation or participating with others in dramatization and in choral reading or speaking. The literature program thus takes many forms in a variety of setting and content.

Chapters 12 and 13 of this book give intermediate-grade and junior-high-school teachers specific suggestions about purposes and procedures in literature activities and detailed information on book lists and other sources of material. Teachers can get help in planning for recreational reading from a librarian, a good bookstore, or from such standard book lists as *Adventuring With Books,*[26] *A Basic Book Collection for Junior High Schools,*[27] and *Children's Catalog.*[28] Helps in work-type reading are equally available, as in Cleary's[29] book on the use of libraries and Rue's[30] *Index to Books for Intermediate Grades,* which gives references in a wide variety of subject-matter areas. In addition, every teacher has a right to expect help from a teacher-librarian or a book committee on the flood of new, attractive books, both fiction and non-fiction, which are being printed every year. For example, one of the features of the book trade has been the large number of accurate and interesting books on science topics, suitable for young people, but incorporating some of the new ideas and findings of advanced science. Chapter 13 lists some series of books, often with twenty or thirty titles, which are useful for intermediate-grade and junior-high-school pupils and are connected by title, format, or content. Social studies units prepared as teachers' guides usually contain book lists. In other words, there are many sources of help to the teacher who wants to develop some avid and life-long readers in her classes. So great are the resources that some teachers develop specialized interests in literature depending upon the needs of their students. A list of booklists for retarded and for accelerated readers and a useful list of series were given by Peterson.[31] Books which are high in level of interest, and low in level of difficulty were listed by Spache[32] in various categories. Some specific titles which appear on a number of booklists of this sort and which are around the third- or fourth-grade level of difficulty but appeal to children as old as twelve and thirteen years are: Anderson's *Squanto and the Pilgrims;* Bendick's *First Book of Airplanes;* Botel's *Famous Moments in Sports;* Bulla's *A Dog Named Penny;* Cleary's *Henry*

[26] National Council of Teachers of English, 1956.

[27] American Library Association, 1956.

[28] Wilson, New York, 1956, and supplements.

[29] Florence D. Cleary, *Blueprints for Better Reading.* Wilson, New York, 1957.

[30] Eloise Rue, *op. cit.*

[31] Miriam E. Peterson, "Special Booklists Suggest Materials for the Exceptional Child," *The Reading Teacher,* Vol. 7, pp. 150-159, February, 1954.

[32] George D. Spache, *Good Reading for Poor Readers.* Garrard Press, Champaign, Ill., 1958.

Huggins and *Ellen Tebbets* books; the Epsteins' *Codes and Ciphers;* Gates' *River Ranch;* Huber, Salisbury, and Gates' *The Ranch Book;* Lent's *The Aviation Readers;* Meader's *Red Horse Hill;* Walker's *Cowboy Sam* Series; and Warner's *The Boxcar Children.*

Another teacher with a bright class gradually collected a short list of so-called "adult" books which were enjoyed by capable older boys and girls. Indicating that boys and girls who are good readers enjoy excursions into the adult world through fiction and adventure, the list included:

Bagnold, Enid, *National Velvet*
Forester, C. S., *Mr. Midshipman Hornblower*
Gypson, Fred, *Old Yeller*
Herzog, Maurice, *Annapurna*
Heyerdahl, Thor, *Kon-Tiki*
Knight, Eric, *Lassie Come Home*
London, Jack, *The Sea Wolf*
Mowat, Farley, *The Dog Who Wouldn't Be*
Nordhoff, Charles and James Hall, *Mutiny on the Bounty*
O'Hara, Mary, *My Friend Flicka*
Orczy, Baroness, *The Scarlet Pimpernel*
Sabatini, Rafael, *Captain Blood*
Schaefer, Jack, *Shane*
Steinbeck, John, *The Red Pony*
Stevenson, Robert L., *The Strange Case of Dr. Jekyll and Mr. Hyde*

Most of these books are published in several editions and are available in paperbacks. They may not represent top literary quality, but they usually represent a higher level of writing than the typical "juvenile" books or the book written expressly for adolescents. The upper grades of the elementary school and the junior-high school are not too early to develop, among the capable readers, some acquaintance with, and liking for, "adult" books. Children who have such experiences may be "constant readers" for the rest of their lives.

There are many other directions that encouragement of reading interests may take. The two lists above which are aimed at specialized interests and abilities are related to the old adage that teachers should start at a level at which children can enjoy the materials and go on from there to new ideas and fresh fields. They assume, moreover, that comprehension will depend upon interest or motivation for reading.[33] Finally, they are based on the hypothesis that different children get different ideas from the same materials. Studies by McKillop,[34] Groff,[35] and others have shown that interpretation of passages is related to the type of material read, to the general attitudes of the reader, and to the purposes for which he reads. There is not always one "right answer" for different children reading imaginative fiction which evokes emotional responses. But some of this ambiguity of meaning and response, this element of personal interpretation, may make the literature experience more vivid for both pupil and teacher. Because many children may miss the deeper meanings of a story, the teacher may sometimes encourage reading in depth to understand symbols or below-the-surface ideas, especially in imaginative fiction and in poetry, including that found in readers and anthologies.[36]

EVALUATION OF THE INTERMEDIATE- AND UPPER-GRADES PROGRAM

The evaluation of the reading program, discussed more fully in Chapter 16, depends upon the nature of the children and the instructional aims involved. This chapter has discussed some of the characteristics of children aged nine to fourteen years and given some of the possible aims and activities of reading programs for these children. It suggests, accordingly, a few questions that any group of teachers or curriculum committee may set up in evaluating their programs. A few questions that might be asked about the post-primary program are these:

1. Do our teachers recognize the contribution of reading to the wholesome development of boys and girls?
2. Do our teachers conceive reading as a developmental program, not stopping at about the fifth grade, but operating continuously from kindergarten at least through the high school?

33 Margery R. Bernstein, "Relationship between Interest and Reading Comprehension," *Journal of Educational Research,* Vol. 49, pp. 283-288, December, 1955.

34 Ann S. McKillop, *The Relationship between the Reader's Attitude and Certain Types of Reading Responses.* Bureau of Publications, Teachers College, Columbia University, New York, 1952.

35 Patrick J. Groff, *Children's Attitudes Toward Reading and Their Critical Reading Abilities in Four Content Type Materials.* Unpublished Ed.D. dissertation, University of California, Berkeley, 1955.

36 David H. Russell, "Personal Values in Reading," *The Reading Teacher,* Vol. 12, pp. 3-9, October, 1958.

3. Do our teachers achieve a balance in their reading programs between oral and silent reading and between individual and group skills in reading?

4. To achieve this balance do our teachers plan their programs at least on a weekly basis?

5. Have our teachers the ability to study individual children so that they can adapt reading activities, particularly in their literature aspects, to the needs of each child?

6. Do our pupils show continuous growth in fundamental reading habits, skills, and attitudes through these grades?

7. Do our pupils exhibit increasing independence in their reading habits and abilities during these years?

8. Do our pupils show increasing ability to differentiate their styles of reading in accordance with various purposes for reading?

9. Do our pupils display increasing ability to fulfill the reading demands made by the content subjects?

10. Do our pupils show greater maturity in applying what they read—in reorganizing, in summarizing, in comparing ideas received in reading with other sources of information, and in carrying such ideas into actual solutions of problems rather than mere discussion?

These are only a few questions that an evaluation committee or a single teacher may raise in appraising the success of a program. In such appraisal, teachers may use standardized reading tests, but the questions suggest that many other means of evaluation will be needed for accurate determination of the success of the program. Some of these techniques are discussed more fully in Chapter 16. Arriving at answers to the foregoing questions in teachers' meetings may be one method of evaluation. The individual teacher may observe the behavior of her pupils in the school library, she may check the children's records of books read during the year, she may investigate borrowings from the public library if one is available, and she will continuously diagnose pupils' successes and failures in individual and group reading situations. Like reading itself, the evaluation program becomes varied and a continuous developmental process.

SUPPLEMENTARY READINGS

ARTLEY, A. S. "The Appraisal of Reading Comprehension," *Journal of Educational Psychology,* Vol. 34, pp. 55-60, January, 1943.

BETTS, E. A. *Foundations of Reading Instruction,* rev. ed., Chaps. 6, 7, 22-25. American Book, New York, 1957.

BETTS, E. A. "Reading Problems at the Intermediate Grade Level," *Elementary School Journal,* Vol. 40, pp. 737-746, June, 1940.

BOND, G. L., and WAGNER, E. *Child Growth in Reading.* Lyons and Carnahan, Chicago, 1955.

BROOM, M. E., and others. *Effective Reading Instruction in the Elementary School,* 2nd ed. McGraw-Hill, New York, 1951.

BURROWS, ALVINA T. *Teaching Children in the Middle Grades.* Heath, Boston, 1952.

DALE, E. *How to Read a Newspaper.* Scott, Foresman, Chicago, 1941.

DAW, S. E. "The Persistence of Errors in Oral Reading in Grades Four and Five," *Journal of Educational Research,* Vol. 32, pp. 81-90, October, 1938.

DOLCH, E. W. "Goals in Intermediate Reading," *Elementary School Journal,* Vol. 35, pp. 682-690, May, 1935.

DURRELL, D. D. "Basic Abilities in Intermediate Grade Reading," *Education,* Vol. 59, pp. 45-50, September, 1938.

DURRELL, D. D. *Improving Reading Instruction.* World Book, Yonkers, N.Y., 1956.

EDGERTON, R. B. "How Difficult are Children's Encyclopedias? I and II," *Elementary School Journal,* Vol. 45, pp. 379-385, 455-464, March, April, 1945.

GRAY, LILLIAN, and REESE, D. *Teaching Children to Read,* 2nd ed. Ronald, New York, 1957.

HARRIS, A. J. *How to Increase Reading Ability,* 3rd ed. Longmans, Green, New York, 1956.

HILDRETH, GERTRUDE H. *Teaching Reading,* especially Chaps. 17, 19, 20. Holt, New York, 1958.

HUDSON, J. S. "Reading Readiness in the Intermediate Grades," *Elementary English,* Vol. 19, pp. 134-137, April, 1942.

KNAPP, J. V. "Improving Reading Skills in Content Areas," *Elementary English,* Vol. 24, pp. 542-550, December, 1947.

LAZAR, MAY, ed. *The Retarded Reader in the Junior High School.* Staff of the Reading Guidance Center, New York City Public Schools, September, 1952.

MCCULLOUGH, C. M. "Broadening Experiences through Reading in the Elementary School," *Elementary English Review,* Vol. 23. pp. 101-107, March, 1946.

MCINTIRE, A. "Reading Social Studies Materials in the Middle Grades," *Elementary English Review,* Vol. 21, pp. 262-266, November, 1944.

MCKEE, P. G. *Teaching of Reading in the Elementary School,* Chaps. 11, 12. Houghton, Mifflin, Boston, 1948.

MCKIM, MARGARET. *Guiding Growth in Reading.* Macmillan, New York, 1955.

National Conference on Research in English. *Reading in the Intermediate Grades.* Scott, Foresman, Chicago, 1941.

National Society for Study of Education. *Development In and Through Reading,* Sixtieth Yearbook, Part II, Chaps. 13, 16, and 17. University of Chicago Press, Chicago, 1961.

PARKER, B. M. "Reading in an Intermediate Grade Science Program," *Elementary School Journal,* Vol. 38, pp. 38-43, September, 1937.

RUSSELL, D. H., and ANDERSON, M. A. "Professional Opinions about Basic Reading Programs in the Middle and Upper Grades of the Elementary School," *Elementary School Journal,* Vol. 46, pp. 81-88, October, 1945.

RUSSELL, D. H. "A Reading Program for the Seventh and Eighth Grades," Contributions in Reading, No. 13. Ginn, Boston, 1958.

SHORES, J. H. "Skills Related to the Ability to Read History and Science," *Journal of Educational Research,* Vol. 36, pp. 584-593, April, 1943.

SPACHE, GEORGE D. "Types and Purposes of Reading in Various Curriculum Fields," *The Reading Teacher,* Vol. 11, pp. 158-164, February, 1958.

STEWART, L. JANE; HELLER, F.; and ALBERTY, E. *Improving Reading in the Junior High School.* Appleton-Century-Crofts, New York, 1957.

STONE, C. R. *Better Advanced Reading.* Webster, St. Louis, Mo., 1937.

STRANG, R. *Study Type of Reading Exercises,* rev. ed. Bureau of Publications, Teachers College, Columbia University, New York, 1956.

TREACY, J. P. "Relationship of Reading Skills to the Ability to Solve Arithmetic Problems," *Journal of Educational Research,* Vol. 38, pp. 86-96, October, 1944.

YOAKAM, GERALD A. *Basal Reading Instruction.* McGraw-Hill, New York, 1955.

YOUNG, W. E. "Recent Research on Reading in the Social Studies," *Education,* Vol. 62, pp. 18-26, September, 1941.

WITTY, P. A. "Reading of Social Studies Materials," *Elementary English,* Vol. 27, pp. 1-8, January, 1950.

Part III

DEVELOPMENTAL PHASES OF THE READING PROGRAM

Chapter 9

BUILDING MEANING VOCABULARIES

Part III of this book, devoted to various developmental phases of learning to read, properly opens with a chapter on the development of meaning vocabularies. Although meaning is closely tied to word recognition in the next chapter, the latter stresses identification and recognition techniques such as phonetic and structural analysis which may or may not include work on meaning. In contrast, the present chapter emphasizes understanding of verbal materials. Reading is not taught today as a simple recognition technique of "word calling" or "barking at words." Although not all linguistic scientists accept the point of view (see Chapter 2), most school people agree that reading is essentially a process of getting meanings from printed symbols. Accurate perception and recognition must always be accompanied by accurate and lively responses to the meanings of words, phrases, sentences, or passages. Lewis Mumford in describing Van Loon's *Story of Mankind* once said, "The words are for children and the meanings are for men."

Accurate word recognition and knowledge of word meaning have been shown in many research studies to be closely related to the reader's comprehension of a passage or story. For example, Piekarz[1] found that children classed as poor readers, with word recognition difficulties, could not make as many free associations to a passage as could the good readers who responded with many related ideas. In reply to questions, a sixth-grader with poor vocabulary did fairly well on literal surface meanings of a selection but less well on interpretations such as making inferences and evaluating relevancy. The high-level reader made a greater variety of responses, especially on an objective and general level; the child with vocabulary difficulties had trouble with emotional involvement, even in getting literal meanings. The good reader must be capable of accurate word recognition

[1] Josephine A. Piekarz, "Getting Meaning from Reading," *Elementary School Journal,* Vol. 56, pp. 303-309, March, 1956.

but even more he must know meanings of individual words and be able to work out relations among the meanings of words in groups. His knowledge of individual words, his store of meanings, thus become basic to his reading achievement.

The important role of understanding or comprehension has been mentioned in Chapter 2, discussed in Chapter 4, and runs through many other chapters of this book. Meanings are usually associated with morphemes or words rather than with phonemes, but they also depend upon longer contextual cues such as are found in a sentence or even a paragraph. A pupil does not know whether *magazine* refers to a publication, a part of a gun, or a storage place for powder in earlier days until he reads the whole sentence, "The powder magazine stood in the center of the fort." This and many other words complicate the process of understanding for the child because they are multi-meaning words. In addition, however, his interpretation is also affected by the occurrence of homonyms (bow and bough), by the writer's intention or purpose, and by the teacher's demand that he have some depth of understanding of important words or ideas. Furthermore for many words he will have not only denotative knowledge (a *municipality* is a town or city or other district having powers of local self-government) but also connotative meanings (attached to *municipality* may be ideas of good government, or a city manager plan or corruption or overlapping functions of local government or a favorable tax rate). The process of building understandings, therefore, is not a simple one and must be part of reading and language activities for many school years if the child is to master a suitable percentage of the more than 600,000 words in the English language.

How many words should the child know? Studies by Ernest Horn and by Rinsland indicated many years ago that a few words do most of the work in his speaking and writing. About one hundred common words such as *said, and,* and *home* make up nearly 60 per cent of the words he writes in elementary school, and approximately two thousand common words constitute about 95 per cent of the words he will need in reading and writing at all school levels. This well-established fact suggests the importance of the knowledge and ability to write this common store of words, but it does not limit vocabulary work to these words. Books and other reading materials sometimes seem hard in the intermediate grades just because they go beyond this fundamental list of two thousand basic meanings to related ideas. In a fifth reader (describing Johnny Appleseed) the pupil meets such a sentence as "Dressed in his coffee-sack shirt and his kettle hat, he planted his seeds wherever he went," and the pupil must interpret the words *coffee-sack shirt* and *kettle hat* if he is to read with understanding. In addition, a unit in social studies, a project in science, or a chapter on mediaeval times requires knowledge of other special words. Indeed, the child's or adolescent's own interests will take him far beyond the commonest words. If a girl is an avid reader of horse stories she will get to know words like *bridle, stirrup, stallion,* and *jockey*. If a boy reads Westerns he must know words like *tomahawk, moccasins, portage,* and *canyon*. An adolescent interested in cars or "hot-rods" needs words like *ignition, carburetor, chassis,* and *transmission*. Hildreth[2] estimates that ten thousand words are necessary for everyday reading at the average adult literacy level. Probably the typical educated American adult uses thirty or forty thousand words at some time and may know many more. In other words, in the post-primary grades children and youth must be encouraged to go beyond a "basic" list of approximately two thousand words to develop enriched, functional, and somewhat individualized vocabularies. They can all be helped to discover "the wonderful world of words."

RELATION OF VOCABULARY TO SCHOOL ACHIEVEMENT

Teachers have always recognized that knowing words is a great asset to children in their schoolwork and that it has values in out-of-school activities. In ordinary conversation or writing the ability to use not only the correct word but occasionally a vivid, meaningful word adds greatly to the charm and effectiveness of the idea presented. As Seegers[3] put it, "The child's ability to read, to speak, to write, and to think are inevitably conditioned by his vocabulary."

The close relationship between size of vocabulary and school achievement has been shown in different research studies. This is not surprising, because, in turn, both vocabulary and school achievement are closely related to general intelligence. For example, Spache[4]

[2] Gertrude H. Hildreth, *Teaching Reading*, p. 125. Holt, New York, 1958.

[3] J. Conrad Seegers, "Vocabulary Problems in the Elementary School," *Elementary English Review*, Vol. 16, pp. 199-204, May, 1939. Also published as a Bulletin of the National Conference on Research in English. Scott, Foresman, Chicago.

[4] George Spache, "The Vocabulary Tests of the Revised Stanford-Binet as Independent Measures of Intelligence," *Journal of Educational Research*, Vol. 36, pp. 512-516, March, 1943.

found that a rather good prediction of mental age on the entire test of the Revised Stanford-Binet Scale may be made from the vocabulary sections, and Thorndike[5] found that a fairly valid test of verbal intelligence could be administered to adults in the form of a twenty-word, multiple-choice vocabulary test. Even when the factor of intelligence is held constant, however, a close relationship between vocabulary and school achievement is evident. For example, Traxler[6] found that the partial correlations between vocabulary and total scores on the Stanford Achievement Test with intelligence quotients held constant range from .65 to .84 in grades IV to VIII, with a median of .73. In another study Wesman[7] discovered that the results of a test of verbal ability correlated more highly with academic achievement scores (average r = .48) than did test scores of number ability and spatial relationships. In a study of nearly six hundred ninth grade students Shaw[8] found that "verbal-meaning ability is highly related to every high-school achievement measure used in the present investigation" with correlations ranging from .58 to .78. This positive relationship indicates that size of vocabulary is closely related to the child's general success in school. This value of a good vocabulary is not surprising, because most teachers rely so much on words in presenting learning situations and because pupils use words to react to the situations.

If a good vocabulary is important in general school achievement, it would seem particularly necessary in spelling, reading, and the other language arts. Early in the scientific study of the curriculum Hollingworth[9] observed that knowledge of vocabulary was an important component of spelling ability. More recently, Townsend,[10] for example, found a median correlation of about .63 between spelling and meaning vocabulary. The correlations between the two increased

[5] Robert L. Thorndike, "Two Screening Tests of Verbal Intelligence," *Journal of Applied Psychology,* Vol. 26, pp. 128-135, 1942.

[6] Arthur E. Traxler, "The Relationship between Vocabulary and General Achievement in the Elementary School," *Elementary School Journal,* Vol. 45, pp. 331-333, February, 1945.

[7] A. G. Wesman, *A Study of Transfer of Training,* Teachers College Contributions to Education, No. 909. Bureau of Publications, Teachers College, Columbia University, New York, 1945.

[8] D. C. Shaw, "Study of Relationships between Thurstone Primary Mental Abilities and High School Achievement," *Journal of Educational Psychology,* Vol. 40, pp. 239-249, April, 1949.

[9] Leta S. Hollingworth, *The Psychology of Special Disability in Spelling,* Contributions to Education, No. 88. Teachers College, Columbia University, New York, 1918.

[10] Agatha Townsend, "An Investigation of Certain Relationships of Spelling with Reading and Academic Aptitude," *Journal of Educational Research,* Vol. 40, pp. 465-471, February, 1947.

slightly from the third through the twelfth grade. Townsend found the correlation between spelling and vocabulary higher than between spelling and reading comprehension (median r = .51). Although knowledge of words is closely related to spelling ability, it is logically even more closely correlated with most measures of reading ability. Indeed, recognition vocabulary and knowledge of word meanings are often considered as component parts of general reading ability. Such well-known standardized reading tests as the *Gates Reading Survey for Grades 3 to 10,* the *Iowa Tests of Basic Skills,* the *California Reading Test,* the *Reading Capacity and Achievement Test* (by Durrell and Sullivan), and the *Stanford Achievement Test* all contain tests of meaning vocabulary. Obviously a child's understanding and interpretation of sentences and paragraphs will depend considerably upon his knowledge of the individual words in the larger units.

There is some research evidence to indicate that vocabulary may not be so closely related to reading success as are intelligence and other factors for typical children in the first two grades. Typical children coming from English-speaking homes ordinarily have a speaking vocabulary of at least 2500 words about the time they enter the first grade.[11] Modern basic readers and supplementary books written for the primary grades usually have a controlled vocabulary of not more than a few hundred common words. For example, in preprimers, primers, and first readers planned for a basic reading program in the first grade the total number of new words is likely to be between 300 and 400 different words. By the end of the third grade the basic materials often contain only about 1400 or 1500 different words. Of course children read many other books in the primary grades; but in general a small vocabulary will not begin to affect their reading much until some time in the third grade, when they begin to branch out more widely in their reading. Then, and in later grades, as they begin to work with the extensive printed materials available today their vocabularies will be closely related to their reading and other school success. The facts in the primary grades are not, however, a justification for increasing vocabulary load in primary readers, as advocated by some proponents of the return to "hard" books such as the old McGuffey Readers. One reason for not equating reading and understanding vocabularies is given in the next section.

[11] Madorah E. Smith, "An Investigation of the Development of the Sentence and the Extent of Vocabulary in Young Children," *University of Iowa Studies in Child Welfare,* Vol. 3, No. 5, 1926.

TYPES OF VOCABULARY

Actually, children use not one vocabulary but several vocabularies. The discussion above has mentioned understanding vocabularies and recognition vocabularies. Some writers list the four different vocabularies as follows:

1. Hearing vocabulary—the words a child understands when he hears them
2. Reading vocabulary—the words a child can recognize in printed material
3. Speaking vocabulary—the words a child uses in different speech situations
4. Writing vocabulary—the words a child uses in letters, reports, and other writing activities

The relative sizes of these different vocabularies change with children's development. When most children come to school, their hearing (or understanding) vocabularies are relatively large. As mentioned by Smith above, their speaking vocabularies are ordinarily considerably less, and their reading and writing vocabularies probably are nonexistent or not more than a few words. Beginning in the first grade, often in the second half of it, their reading or word-recognition vocabularies begin to grow rapidly. In the first grade most children begin to write a few words. The reading and writing vocabularies continue to grow rapidly in the primary grades, and, somewhere about the fourth- or fifth-grade level, the reading vocabulary overtakes and passes the speaking vocabulary. That is, the child can recognize and interpret more printed words than he ordinarily uses in speech. The four vocabularies of most children and adolescents continue to grow through the upper elementary and secondary grades, but at a reduced rate. The writing vocabulary of most children usually remains the smallest of the four different vocabularies throughout the school years. A few sample studies of vocabulary growth are given below.

STUDIES OF GROWTH IN SIZE OF VOCABULARY

There have been many scientific studies of children's vocabularies at different age levels, especially in the preschool stages of development. Most of the studies seem to have been of children's speaking vocabulary; but estimates of reading vocabulary have been made in reading tests, of understanding vocabulary in such tests as the vocabulary subtest of the Stanford-Binet individual intelligence test, and of written vocabulary in various studies in the field of spelling. In general, these studies are not directly applicable to the teaching of reading in the elementary school, but they have some implications for teaching procedures. A few sample studies are given below.

Many studies of vocabulary growth have been summarized by McCarthy[12] in the *Manual of Child Psychology*. Perhaps the best-known of the studies of preschool vocabulary growth is that of Madorah E. Smith,[13] who attempted to get at children's total vocabulary by recording sentences spoken and by testing through the use of objects, pictures, and questions. Smith found the following sizes for total vocabularies: 1 year, 3 words; 1½ years, 22 words; 2 years, 272 words; 3 years, 896 words; 4 years, 1540 words; 5 years, 2072 words; and 6 years, 2562 words. In more recent use an improved form of the Smith test has increased these numbers somewhat. For example, Grigsby[14] reported an average vocabulary at 3 years of 1507 words, at 5 years of 2527 words, and at 6 years of 3054 words.

An early study by Cuff[15] suggested that growth is relatively rapid in the preschool years, that it slows down somewhat during the first two years of school, that it develops more rapidly in the third and fourth years, but that the rate of increase usually begins to drop somewhere about the fifth grade. Cuff estimated some average total vocabularies as follows: third grade, 7425 words; fifth grade, 12,460 words; eighth grade, 16,800 words; and twelfth grade, 21,840 words. These must be regarded as approximations, because other investigators obtained somewhat different results, and the range of vocabulary ability at any one grade level is enormous.

A different method of selecting samples of words to be included in vocabulary tests resulted in assigning much larger hearing vocabularies to children and adults than these earlier studies indicate. Mary K. Smith[16] in a more recent investigation found an average

[12] Dorothea McCarthy, "Language Development in Children," in, Leonard Carmichael, ed., *Manual of Child Psychology*, pp. 476-581. Wiley, New York, 1946.

[13] Madorah E. Smith, *op. cit.*

[14] Olive J. Grigsby, "An Experimental Study of the Development of Concepts of Relationship in Pre-School Children as Evidenced by Their Expressive Ability," *Journal of Experimental Education*, Vol. 1, pp. 144-162, December, 1932.

[15] Noel B. Cuff, "Vocabulary Tests," *Journal of Educational Psychology*, Vol. 21, pp. 212-220, March, 1930.

[16] Mary K. Smith, "Measurement of the Size of General English Vocabulary through the Elementary Grades and High School," *Genetic Psychology Monographs*, Vol. 24, pp. 311-345, 1941.

vocabulary of over 23,000 words in the first grade and of over 80,000 words in the twelfth grade. On the same test Seashore and Eckerson[17] estimated that the average vocabulary of college undergraduates is over 150,000 words. This result seems high to some investigators when they remember that Shakespeare used approximately 20,000 different words in his plays. The results by Smith, Seashore, and Eckerson give much larger and seemingly more accurate estimates of understanding vocabulary size than earlier studies. One reason for the higher estimates is that these investigators used a multiple-choice test of four possible answers which gives a higher score than a test that simply asks for a synonym of the single word or that calls for definition of the meaning of a word as it occurs in a sentence. Some corroboration of these findings is given in a study by Rinsland[18] of children's writing vocabularies. In an analysis of over 100,000 individual papers by children in grades one to eight, Rinsland found that first-graders use over 5000 different words, fifth-graders over 11,000 different words, and eighth-graders about 18,000 different words. These results were true of the combined grade group rather than of individuals; but, when it is recalled that writing vocabularies are much smaller than understanding vocabularies, they suggest that children's vocabularies may be larger than previous results indicate. It seems to be here, accordingly, that teachers and curriculum workers can revise upward the earlier estimates of children's vocabularies. As suggested in Chapter 6, the child who has watched many television programs may have at least a casual acquaintance with words unknown to a six-year-old of an earlier generation. As Dolch[19] put it, there is a "reservoir of word knowledge which is little touched by the recording of speech." Children who have a reasonably rich experience do seem to *know* more words in context than they ever *use* in their speaking or writing. This upward revision of vocabulary estimates should influence school procedures perhaps not so much in the reading materials of the first two grades as in the variety of language experiences the school may provide at all levels.

17 R. H. Seashore and L. D. Eckerson, "The Measurement of Individual Differences in General English Vocabularies," *Journal of Educational Psychology*, Vol. 31, pp. 14-38, January, 1940.

18 Henry D. Rinsland, *A Basic Vocabulary of Elementary School Children*. Macmillan, New York, 1945.

19 Edward W. Dolch, "How Much Word Knowledge Do Children Bring to Grade One?" *Elementary English Review*, Vol. 13, pp. 177-183, May, 1936.

QUALITATIVE DEVELOPMENT IN CHILDREN'S VOCABULARY

When an American politician defined *democracy* as "liberty plus groceries" there were many hidden meanings below an apparently simple statement. The factor of quality in the child's vocabulary and his ability to use his store of meanings are probably just as important as the total size of his vocabulary. The child with the large vocabulary may be capable of a more precise or exact use of words but may not always know the full range of meanings of some words or may rely on superficial recognition rather than complete understanding. Furthermore, a child's understanding or definition of words will change as he has more experiences to associate with the words. At five years he will typically define in terms of use or description and say, "A chair is to sit on." Later he will make more use of synonym, explanation, and demonstration.[20] To pass a Stanford-Binet test at twelve years he must know two of the four words *constant, courage, charity,* and *defend.* As he grows older he may generalize more about words and develop some understandings of more difficult abstract terms, such as *justice* or *virtue* or, in other words, may increase in his ability to use concepts, marked both by generalization and discrimination.[21] Thus his vocabulary powers are closely linked to more general thinking abilities.

Teachers must continually make decisions about how much time and effort are to be given to the meanings of individual words. If a fifth grade meets a word like *tournament* in a story of King Arthur, should the teacher and group be content with superficial recognition and general meaning of knights in combat or should it be discussed in application to a modern tennis tournament, to Olympic sports, and to chess? Certainly words like *justice* and *virtue* mentioned above are so important that the group may go on adding certain meanings to them throughout most of their lives. In making decisions, teacher and pupil can be guided by the frequency with which the word occurs in general speech and writing, the importance of the ideas to which it relates in terms of personal or social development (*jealousy* may be more important to some children than *Guatemala*), and the usefulness of the word in current class activities. (The knowl-

[20] H. Feifel and I. B. Lorge, "Qualitative Differences in the Vocabulary Responses of Children," *Journal of Educational Psychology,* Vol. 41, pp. 1-18, January, 1950.

[21] David H. Russell, *Children's Thinking,* Chap. 8. Ginn, Boston, 1956.

edge of meaning of a word may be lost if it is not "put to work" within a short time.) Such lists as the *Teacher's Word Book*[22] give a measure of the frequency of word usage. Other lists such as *Spelling Difficulties in 3,786 Words* give the grade level at which words are normally understood by a certain percentage of a class or age group.[23] But beyond the general guidance given by such lists are the individual needs of pupils in their speaking, writing, reading, and listening activities, and the question of how much to know about a word. For example, Cronbach[24] analyzed behavior called for in understanding a word into five categories:

1. Generalization—Can the child define the word?
2. Application—Can the child recognize when an illustration of the word is properly named by the word?
3. Breadth of meaning—Can the pupil recall different meanings of a word?
4. Precision—Can the pupil apply the term correctly in all possible situations?
5. Availability—Does the child actually use the word?

To these may be added a dimension of "depth of meaning" in terms of knowing a great deal about important words such as *liberty* or *patriotism*. One study[25] was successful in isolating a "breadth of meaning" factor somewhat separate from other vocabulary scores by such tests as having children fill in the same term in five different contexts. For example, in a series of 20 sentences the pupil was asked to use one of the five words *frost, net, pitch, powder,* and *scale* by filling in blanks in sentences. The sentences for which *net* was the correct word were:

3. Some fish are caught with a ________.
9. He tried to ________ the butterfly by creeping close to it.
15. The ________ price of apples is $3.00 a box.
19. Part of her dress was made of ________.

In this study the attempt to get at a separate factor of depth in comprehension by having children answer ten true-false questions of

[22] Edward L. Thorndike and Irving Lorge, *Teacher's Word Book of 30,000 Words*. Bureau of Publications, Teachers College, Columbia University, New York, 1944.

[23] Arthur I. Gates, *Spelling Difficulties in 3,786 Words*. Bureau of Publications, Teachers College, Columbia University, New York, 1937.

[24] Lee J. Cronbach, "Analysis of Techniques for Diagnostic Vocabulary Testing," *Journal of Educational Research*, Vol. 36, pp. 206-217, November, 1942.

[25] David H. Russell, *Dimensions of Children's Meaning Vocabularies in Grades Four through Twelve*, University of California Publications in Education, Vol. 11, No. 5, 1954.

increasing difficulty about any one concept such as *tribe* or *peace* did not isolate any ability very different from results on a general vocabulary test. One conclusion of the study was that "there is some evidence that children's vocabularies are not adequately tested by a general vocabulary test containing items from many subject-matter areas and requiring only a superficial recognition of a closest synonym."[26]

Other research concerned with qualitative factors in vocabulary was done by Osgood[27] and his colleagues. Osgood was interested in connotative meanings, not direct synonyms but the constellation of ideas which may relate to a particular word for some individual. By asking the subject to associate freely he obtained a cluster of words which surrounded the original word and then analyzed these associated responses. Osgood found that the collection of associations varied widely with individuals and believed that it may give clues to personality, attitude, and related factors. He identified patterns of responses and described them as showing an "evaluative factor," "strength factor," and "activity factor." In this approach a concept is a central core of meaning with many peripheral meanings attached. In another study of pupils in grades 3, 5, 7, and 8 and of college students, responses to different kinds of answers in multiple-choice items indicated that younger children used more repetition-illustration-inferior explanation, but older children made an increasing choice of synonyms (denotative meanings). No significant differences among answers which gave use or description occurred at the various levels.

This sampling of research gives no clear directive to the teacher beyond the fact that superficial recognition is not regarded as enough information about some important words. As suggested in Chapter 6, television may give children many partial meanings. For some words, pupils and teacher must be aware of the value of building meanings that are both broad and deep. Words are defined differently at various age levels; and meanings selected by the reader, especially in emotionally-toned passages, may be highly individual. Teachers may expect and work for some precision in denotative meanings, but it seems that connotative meanings will often be personal affairs. The psychological literature on concept development

[26] *Ibid.*, p. 372.

[27] Charles E. Osgood, G. J. Suci, and P. H. Tannenbaum, *The Measurement of Meaning*. University of Illinois Press, Urbana, 1958.

overlaps with some of the studies cited and may provide other hints regarding the management of classroom situations to provide better vocabularies.

DEVELOPMENT OF CHILDREN'S UNDERSTANDING OF CONCEPTS

Perhaps more important to teachers than the total number of words a child knows are the amount and kind of meaning he attaches to particular words. The child who, after an excursion, described firemen as "Men who slide down poles and have a red engine" knew something about *firemen,* but did not have a very complete understanding of the word. Children may be able to give a sentence or two about such words as *chair* and *river* or even *community* and *democracy;* but they may have very incomplete concepts in these areas, a very meager supply of ideas or generalizations they can associate with the word.

Teachers and children may be concerned with extensiveness of meaning because so many common English words have at least half a dozen different meanings. A three-year-old showed a typical difficulty when he said, "My foot is a bear" after he had heard someone talk of "bare feet." Writers on semantics have suggested the importance of extensiveness of meanings and how these meanings may shift in the words of a speaker or writer. In the early grades of school the children may come to realize that the word *strike* has at least as many meanings as the ones illustrated in the following sentences:

> Do not strike the glass.
> The umpire called one strike.
> As he started fishing he had a good strike.
> The men went out on strike.
> He will strike a match.
> They may strike oil if they dig here.
> The clock will soon strike ten.
> Strike out the last word.

In addition to recognizing a number of different meanings it is sometimes desirable that children attach depth of meaning so that they have a thorough rather than a superficial knowledge of certain valuable words. In the second sentence above, most fourth-grade boys might add to the meaning of *strike* by surrounding it with such concepts as "curve," "pitcher," "home plate," "cutting the corner of the plate." Probably not until they are adults will they have a reasonably complete understanding of *strike* as used in the fourth sentence, involving higher wages or closed shop or "escalator clauses" and other difficult concepts. The point of emphasis here is that many children may recognize a word but have little real understanding of it.

Children's knowledge may be classed as facts, such as the date, 1492, when Columbus discovered America, or as concepts which are responses applying to a whole group or class of phenomena such as *chair, treaty, patience,* or the *Stars and Stripes.* Children also make use of some generalizations such as definitions, rules, or laws in science usually stated as a series of interconnected concepts such as in the statement, "Green leaves produce chlorophyll in the presence of sunlight." Knowledge is of various sorts, but the important branch of concepts, then, refers to categories of events or ideas. A concept is a sort of shorthand representation of a group of facts such as are symbolized in the words *green leaves* or *pity.* It represents discrimination (a *car* is not a *truck*) and generalization (*apple* refers to many small, green, as well as large, round objects having certain characteristics) and employs symbolization (usually words but objects such as the flag or the plus sign are also included).

Having a store of concepts is of enormous value to the child. Every time he sees a new or strange *grocery store* or *helicopter* or reads the word *jungle* he does not need to stop and think through what the object or word means. Thus he can take advantage of his past experience by using known labels, can organize the present situation, and may be able to find out about grocery stores or jungles. In the process of learning concepts Bruner[28] identified such activities as: (1) "learning the properties of a class of functionally equivalent objects," (2) learning the redundancy of the environment," (3) learning formal schemata that "may be used to organize arrays of diverse information," and (4) "constructing a theory which enables one to go beyond present data." The possession of such information and abilities is of enormous advantage to a child in learning about his environment and himself.

Research findings give some clues about the way children and adults learn concepts and contain many results of studies of the kinds of concepts children tend to know at different age levels. They go

[28] Jerome S. Bruner, J. J. Goodnow, and G. A. Austin, *A Study of Thinking.* Wiley, New York, 1956.

back to the classic studies of G. Stanley Hall,[29] reported as early as 1891, and concerned with "the content of children's minds." Bruner's[30] work illustrated certain "strategies" in categorizing or developing understanding of concepts, such as looking for similarities in a group (*simultaneous-scanning*) and concentrating on one or two characteristics and excluding apparently irrelevant factors in the group (*conservative-focusing*). Since concepts may grow out of sensory experiences, it is of interest to know what individual factors dominate in determining concepts and how certain factors may be combined. As an example of the research available, Reichard[31] and others found that in manipulating twelve pieces of cardboard of four different colors and three different shapes, children up to five years used one or the other characteristic but not both, and that at about eight years 75 per cent or more could use both color and form groupings. Furthermore, they believed that as children became older in the four to fourteen age group they moved away from categorizing on the basis of nonessential, incidental features, to the basis of function or use, and finally to an abstract definition.

This notion of changes in the kinds of thinking children do at various age levels has as its chief proponent Jean Piaget, of the Universities of Paris and Geneva, and the most prolific writer on children's concepts. Between 1924 and 1937 Piaget published at least five books on the development of children's thought through such stages as autistic thinking (three to five years), egocentric thinking (six to eight years), and logical thinking (after eleven years). In the period since 1937 Piaget has carried out a long series of investigations of children's understanding of concepts of quantity, space, time, movement, velocity, and number. Piaget's methods and findings about children's concepts have been criticized widely, but the total volume and importance of his work is unparalleled in child study.[32]

In addition to the work of Piaget, many individual investigators in the United States and England have studied children's concept

[29] G. Stanley Hall, "The Content of Children's Minds on Entering School," *Pedagogical Seminary,* Vol. 1, pp. 139-173, No. 2, 1891. G. Stanley Hall and C. E. Brown, "Children's Ideas of Fire, Heat, Frost and Cold," *Pedagogical Seminary,* Vol. 10, pp. 27-85, March, 1903.

[30] J. S. Bruner, *op. cit.*

[31] S. Reichard, M. Schneider, and D. Rapaport, "The Development of Concept Formation in Children," *American Journal of Orthopsychiatry,* Vol. 14, pp. 156-162, January, 1944.

[32] David H. Russell, *Children's Thinking,* pp. 155-162. Evelyn Lawrence, T. R. Theakston, and N. Isaacs, *Some Aspects of Piaget's Work.* National Froebel Foundation, London, 1957.

growth. One summary[33] lists 162 references on concepts, many of which give specific information regarding what children know about mathematical concepts (number, quantity, space, and the number system), concepts of time, science concepts, concepts of the self, social concepts, moral-religious concepts and values, and a miscellaneous group which includes concepts of *death* and of *responsibility*. This range of researches illustrates the diversity of concepts needed in modern life and the tremendous task of teacher and children in developing understanding of a complex culture. They illustrate the growth in understanding of concepts from infancy through adolescence. "Concepts change from immediate to remote, concrete to abstract, simple to complex, egocentric to social, diffuse to focussed, vague to specific, and contradictory to consistent."[34]

The researches illustrate also the fact that children of any one age vary widely in the concepts they know and any one school child still has many "areas of ignorance." They show that ability to give a synonym or repeat a definition are not true measures of understanding. They indicate a close relationship between concept development and general vocabulary growth. Finally, they give many suggestions for developing understandings in subject-matter areas such as arithmetic or in cause-and-effect relationships as in history or science. Some of these implications are given in the last section of this chapter.

SOME VOCABULARY LISTS

In addition to knowing how many words children may be expected to recognize and understand at a particular grade level, teachers will find that studies of words in use, or word-frequency counts, have implications for the reading program. In general, such word lists have been made up on the basis of their frequency of use in different situations, such as their occurrence in well-known books or newspapers, or appearance in children's writing. Different lists give different results, depending upon the sources from which the words were counted and listed as of most frequent or of less frequent use. Since the early 1930's, too, a number of word lists have appeared which are composites of other lists. Thus teachers, curriculum workers, and textbook writers have some good guides as to the most useful words for children to know. A few of the most useful lists in the elementary school are as follows:

[33] David H. Russell, "Concepts," in C. W. Harris, ed., *Encyclopedia of Educational Research,* 3rd ed. Macmillan, New York, 1960.
[34] *Ibid.*, p. 328.

BUCKINGHAM, B. R., and DOLCH, E. W. *A Combined Word List.* Ginn, Boston, 1936. [One of the most useful of the combined lists of frequently used words. It is based on some ten different vocabulary studies and shows their overlapping and comparative ratings by giving after each word the studies in which it appears and the grade or frequency assigned by each study.]

DALE, EDGAR. "Dale 3000 Words," in *A Formula for Predicting Readability* by Edgar Dale and Jeanne S. Chall. Bureau of Educational Research, Ohio State University, 1948. [A list of 3,000 words (plus some derivatives) known by 80 per cent of fourth-graders from a list of 10,000 words, not on the basis of frequency but on understanding of meaning. Used in computing the Dale-Chall readability formula.]

DOLCH, E. W. "Sight Vocabulary," *Teaching Primary Reading,* Chap. 10. Garrard Press, Champaign, Ill., 1941. [This chapter contains two word lists (on pages 205, 207) of a basic sight vocabulary, omitting nouns, of 220 words, and of a second list of 95 nouns both of which are useful for remedial work or building primary-grade vocabularies. The list is based on three other lists, including the Gates list.]

DURRELL, D. D. *Improving Reading Instructions.* World Book, New York, 1956. [An appendix contains two lists (1) *Remedial Reading Vocabulary for Primary Grades* 754 words arranged alphabetically and according to seven frequency levels, (2) a list of words useful in grades four, five, and six derived from word counts of books frequently used in these grades and not contained in the Gates Primary list—roughly 600 to 800 words for each grade.]

FITZGERALD, J. A. "The Vocabulary of Children's Letters Written in Life Outside the School," *Elementary School Journal,* Vol. 34, pp. 358-370, January, 1934. [An example of a study of words most frequently used in children's writing, and accordingly a guide in the preparation of spelling lists.]

GATES, A. I. *A List of Spelling Difficulties in 3876 Words.* Bureau of Publications, Teachers College, Columbia University, New York, 1937. [As the title implies, primarily a list of hard spots in common words, but of value in reading because it gives the grade levels at which 40 per cent, 50 per cent, 60 per cent, 70 per cent, 80 per cent, and 90 per cent, respectively, of the pupils tested knew the meaning of each word on a multiple-choice test.]

GATES, A. I. *A Reading Vocabulary for the Primary Grades.* Bureau of Publications, Teachers College, Columbia University, New York, 1935. [A list of approximately 1500 words based on six previous studies. Probably the best single source for checking words that should ordinarily appear in the basic reading vocabulary of the primary grades.]

HORN, E. *A Basic Writing Vocabulary.* University of Iowa Monographs in Education, No. 4, 1926. [A pioneer combination list built up from early studies and the author's own researches. Contains 10,000 words most likely to be written by adults and therefore valuable for older children.]

LORGE, IRVING. *The Semantic Count of the 570 Commonest English Words.* Bureau of Publications, Teachers College, Columbia University, New York, 1949. [As its title implies, this volume gives not only the common words but it tells the frequency with which meanings of multi-meaning words are used. The *Oxford English Dictionary* must be consulted in using this volume.]

RINSLAND, HENRY D. *A Basic Vocabulary of Elementary School Children.* Macmillan, New York, 1945. [A list of over 25,000 words based on one of the most careful counts of children's writing vocabulary obtained from over 100,000 individual letters, stories, expositions, projects, etc. in grades one to eight. Gives frequency of occurrence of the words in children's writing by grades.]

STONE, CLARENCE R. *Stone's Graded Vocabulary for Primary Reading.* Webster, St. Louis, 1941. [A list of 2164 words selected from those appearing most frequently in twenty-one of each of preprimers, primers, first readers, second readers, and third readers published between 1931 and 1941. The words are graded into ten reading levels ranging from (1) preprimer, (2) preprimer or primer, (3) primer, (4) primer or first reader, to (10) third or fourth reader. See also Stone's revision of the Dale list of 769 easy words in Spache's *Good Reading for Poor Readers* (Garrard, 1958) as used in the Spache Readability Formula for primary grades.]

THORNDIKE, EDWARD L., and LORGE, IRVING. *Teacher's Word Book of 30,000 Words.* Bureau of Publications, Teachers College, Columbia University, New York, 1944. [This is a revision and extension of perhaps the best-known standard word lists—*The Teacher's Word Book,* published in 1921 and containing 10,000 words, and *The Teacher's Word Book of* 20,000 *Words,* published in 1932. These two counts were based on a wide sampling of adult writing including children's literature. The books indicate in which thousand each word falls as to frequency, with no reference to different meanings of the same word. The third volume (1944) lists words in terms of their frequency of appearance per 1,000,000 running words, per 4,000,000 running words, and in magazines, juvenile books, and semantic counts. Separate lists of the first 500 and the second 500 words occurring most frequently.]

In addition to these standard references on vocabulary the teacher may profit by the results of a number of other studies which have produced restricted word lists. For example, Reese[35] listed 150 words found in at least six out of seven current reading programs for first grade (preprimer through first reader). Such a list is useful where children read from a number of series. Berglund[36] compiled a list of

[35] Olive R. Reese, "Vocabulary of Seven Primary Reading Series," *Elementary English,* Vol. 35, pp. 337-339, April, 1958.

[36] A. O. Berglund, "A Reading Vocabulary for the Fourth Grade," *Journal of Educational Research,* Vol. 31, pp. 172-180, November, 1937.

words useful in the fourth grade which do not appear in Gates's *Reading Vocabulary for the Primary Grades.* Leavell and Marcum[37] presented a list of three hundred words which they believed could be used as diagnosis of word-recognition abilities at the primary level. Kyte[38] compiled an even more refined list of one hundred words which he believed could be a central core of words useful in all phases of school work involving words. They are related to different basic-reading plans and the nature of the difficulties involving them in writing and spelling are known. Kyte's one hundred words are:

I	go	all	that
a	went	name	girl
the	her	school	out
and	when	are	much
my	for	Santa Claus	party
to	you	said	am
is	has	then	going
we	very	father	sister
in	little	time	man
like	they	snowman	get
it	good	new	were
he	had	toys	make
have	snow	so	birthday
on	at	will	but
was	some	every	pet
me	day	saw	see
play	can	big	boys
with	got	home	not
dog	baby	our	brother
she	him	boy	cat
of	do	nice	them
too	house	up	ball
Christmas	there	fun	Saturday
doll	his	train	put
one	likes	balloon	children

Kyte[39] has also suggested a list of 663 words as a "core vocabulary" for language in the primary and intermediate grades. Another type of study made in Australia and, so far as the writer knows, not re-

[37] Ullin W. Leavell and Dixie M. Marcum, "Reading Recognition Vocabulary Test as Diagnostic Instrument," *Peabody Journal of Education,* Vol. 22, pp. 157-169, November, 1944.

[38] George C. Kyte, "A Core Vocabulary for the Primary Grades," *Elementary School Journal,* Vol. 44, pp. 157-166, November, 1943.

[39] George C. Kyte, "A Core Vocabulary for the Language Arts," *Phi Delta Kappan,* Vol. 34, pp. 231-234, March, 1953.

peated to date in the United States, Canada, or England was an analysis of the oral vocabulary of adult workers by Schonell[40] and others. In this study research assistants "went into homes and shops, into railway stations and tram depots—travelled on buses, trams and trains and listened in to workers' conversations—They visited factories, mills, wharves and warehouses and talked with road gangs, street workers and laborers on all kind of construction works." From over 512,000 words they compiled sub-lists of common idioms, the commonest 1,000 words, and other items. Then by comparing these sub-lists with other standard lists they got specific words common to an oral vocabulary such as *marvellous, Dad,* and *nerve,* words common to an Australian vocabulary such as *bloke, pub* and *quid,* and words common to semi-skilled and unskilled workers such as *boss, wages,* and *foreman.* Similar studies in the United States would be valuable, especially for schools in which most of the children come from homes of unskilled or semi-skilled laborers.

The many studies of children's vocabulary development, the careful records of most-frequently-used words, and smaller studies of more restricted vocabularies, samples of each of which have been given above, all place a large amount of information about children's vocabularies at the teacher's disposal. As suggested above, not all these studies have direct application to classroom procedures, but most of them do have implications for the teacher's work.

IMPLICATIONS OF VOCABULARY STUDIES FOR THE READING PROGRAM

1. The size and usefulness of a child's stock of words are one of the most important factors in his reading and general school success.

2. Vocabulary development is closely related to general maturation and a varied interaction with a stimulating environment. Teachers cannot expect adequate vocabularies in immature or underprivileged children.

3. A child has four overlapping but distinct vocabularies. In order of size after the fourth-grade level they are (*a*) listening or understanding vocabulary, (*b*) reading vocabulary, (*c*) speaking vocabulary, and (*d*) writing vocabulary. In reading the teacher may be trying to bring the second up to near the level of the first; in other

[40] Fred J. Schonell, I. G. Meddleton, and B. A. Shaw, *A Study of the Oral Vocabulary of Adults.* University of Queensland Press, Australia, 1956.

language-arts activities of an expressive nature she tries to bring the third and fourth up toward the level of the second and first.

4. As the teacher has time to study children she may find it profitable to discover what words a child *knows* in addition to the words he *uses* in speech or writing.

5. In any one class the range of vocabulary is tremendous, and the overlap with successive grades is considerable. Teachers may group for reading instruction partly on the basis of vocabulary abilities. Then certain groups will require more directed, detailed study of words than others.

6. The size of a child's listening or understanding vocabulary does not ordinarly affect his reading success until the third grade. Except in special cases such as a non-English-speaking home, children come to school with such a store of language experience that they do not have difficulty with the ideas they meet in printed material. Vocabulary growth for other purposes is important in these grades. After the second-grade level increasing importance attaches to clear concepts for an adequate comprehension of materials read.

7. The teacher is concerned not only with the apparent size of the child's vocabulary but with the extensiveness and the depth of meaning associated with certain words. There may be certain key concepts, or generalized ideas, such as *home, my country,* or *co-operation,* about which a child cannot know too much.

8. It is very normal and usual for children in the elementary school to have vague or incomplete concepts of some ideas basic to modern living. In general their knowledge of concrete terms such as *mountain* is more exact than it is for abstract terms such as *co-operation* or *laws.* Understanding of important ideas can be definitely increased by appropriate activities in the whole school program. For example, a one-room rural school understood *conservation* better after a trip to a forest ranger's lookout and a discussion of his work.

9. Teachers (and parents) will enjoy keeping a record of unusual words or phrases expressed by the child. Overstreet[41] told how one teacher of five-year-olds kept a record of the group's expressions during the year. One day, when the teacher said, "Let's be quiet," one girl said, "Let's be quiet as closing your eyes." Other similes were: quiet as a thermometer goes up; easy as spilling; hard as being careful not to have any drips when you paint; slow as a new tooth comes

[41] Bonaro W. Overstreet, "You Are as Young as Your Words," *National Parent-Teacher,* Vol. 39, pp. 14-16, November, 1944.

in; soft as mashed potatoes. Records of the child's vocabulary will often give an insight into what sort of person he is.

10. Standard word lists are available which give clearly the most useful words in reading and spelling. The frequency of use of a word does not necessarily indicate its ease or meaningfulness for a child. Some of the word lists described give approximate grade placements for words in terms of usefulness or current practice. Gates, Bond, and Russell[42] indicated the degree of understanding of some of Thorndike's 20,000 words at various grade levels; and the Thorndike-Lorge *Teacher's Word Book of 30,000 Words* gives approximate locations where words "should be taught for permanent knowledge."

11. If a particular word is valuable, according to a word list, and if a child or group need to use the word frequently in social studies or other activities, it probably merits careful study in terms of both recognition and meaning. Teachers can also utilize children's specialized knowledge related to their interests (model airplanes, dolls from foreign countries) or to their family backgrounds (*factory* or *stocks and bonds*).

12. A vocabulary building program is a service program, not so valuable for its own sake as for its contribution to other abilities and to personal development. Methods for building a meaning vocabulary are described below. Building a sight or recognition vocabulary is a somewhat different problem on which sufficient evidence exists for a discussion of it to be included in a separate chapter, Chapter 10.

METHODS IN VOCABULARY DEVELOPMENT

The close relationship of vocabulary development to many other phases of child development may encourage some teachers just to let vocabulary grow "naturally." One hears that "maturation will take care of it." Educators have still not resolved the problem, raised by Rousseau and others, of how much the child should be let alone in his development, including vocabulary development. The value of a rich background of experiences is accepted by all. Opinion is somewhat more divided about the value of a direct attack on vocabulary problems.

Practice and research in vocabulary-building today indicate con-

[42] Arthur I. Gates, Guy L. Bond, and David H. Russell, "Relative Meaning and Pronunciation Difficulties of the Thorndike 20,000 Words," *Journal of Educational Research,* Vol. 32, pp. 161-167, November, 1938.

siderable faith among school people in direct instruction in vocabulary. All teachers accept the necessity of some instruction in word recognition, as described in the next chapter; but nearly as many believe in direct instruction in building meaning or understanding vocabularies. For example, Addy[43] surveyed the opinions of teacher-training personnel, and supervisors and teachers of grades four, five, and six about methods of selecting, presenting, and developing understanding of words they thought should become a part of children's general meaning vocabulary. Addy found that there was a greater agreement among teachers as to the relative effectiveness of techniques of teaching word meanings than as to the relative effectiveness of types of lessons or sources of words for study. The results of 250 questionnaires showed that teachers use many techniques to teach the meanings of new words. More teachers use the dictionary than any other type of lesson. The highest number of sixth-grade teachers have the pupils note the use of the word in the sentence in which it appears; most fifth grades studied the context in which the word appears; and most fourth grades related new words to their previous experiences. These findings suggest the variety of meaningful experiences provided in a vocabulary-building program.

A number of research studies have supported the view that teachers should attempt direct instruction in meaning vocabulary. One of the best of these is by Gray and Holmes,[44] who summarized research up to 1937 and compiled suggestions and methods then in use. They concluded that many methods may be used in promoting vocabulary growth and that, to obtain different advantages, a broad program including several types of guidance was desirable.

In an attempt to resolve some of the conflicts regarding direct and indirect methods of vocabulary development, Gray and Holmes conducted a series of studies comparing direct and incidental methods of building vocabulary in the fourth grade. Their experimental groups had "specific guidance . . . in correcting and enlarging meanings and in acquiring a mastery of new words." In the directed study of words the teacher presented the words in a meaningful setting, illustrated their uses, sometimes with pictures, presented the form of the word on the chalkboard, and encouraged use of the new

43 Martha L. Addy, "Development of a Meaning Vocabulary in the Intermediate Grades," *Elementary English Review*, Vol. 18, pp. 22-26, 30, January, 1941.

44 William S. Gray and Eleanor Holmes, *The Development of Meaning Vocabularies in Reading*, Publications of the Laboratory Schools of the University of Chicago, No. 6. University of Chicago Press, Chicago, 1938.

words in class discussion. The control groups did not study words this way, but could ask the teacher individually about their pronunciation and meaning if they wished. Both experimental and control groups then used the words in "assimilative reading." The groups studied intensively were small, but Gray and Holmes believed that direct word study "promotes greater accuracy of word recognition in oral reading, more fluent and orderly habits of recognition in silent reading, more detailed and accurate comprehension of what is read, a clearer grasp of relationships between the various elements of meaning, and a more orderly organization of the ideas secured through reading." The authors warned, however, that "These statements should not be interpreted to mean that the direct method of vocabulary development should be used to the exclusion of wide independent reading in acquiring ideas and in enriching experience."[45]

Since the evidence of this and other studies demonstrates the value of direct teaching of the meaning of important words, any teacher must plan a variety of such activities, suited to the needs of her group and to individuals in it. A number of possible methods for such vocabulary development were summarized by Beery.[46] Some of the general activities to be included in such a program over the months are the following:

1. *The Provision of a Wide Background of First-hand Experiences*

Since, at best, words represent a second-hand, or vicarious, experience, the teacher will provide many opportunities for children, especially young children, to touch, taste, hear, see, or manipulate the thing for which the word stands. Additional background for understanding will be built through dramatic play, dramatization, games, excursions, construction, and science experiences. By such activities the teacher avoids mere verbalization in favor of true learning.

2. *Visual Aids*

Pictures and models in various forms offer a more direct experience than most words. Flat pictures, drawings, slides, film-strips,

[45] *Ibid.*, p. 77.

[46] Althea Beery, "Development of Reading Vocabulary and Word Recognition," *Reading in the Elementary School*, Forty-eighth Yearbook, Part II, Chap. 8, National Society for Study of Education, University of Chicago Press, Chicago, 1949.

movies, and charts all give children a chance to associate words with more or less concrete objects and activities, especially when there is liberal opportunity for talking about the visual aid. Recent improvements in the illustration of science books, for example, offer many avenues to new experiences.

3. Numerous Opportunities for Oral-Language Expression and Listening

Since the meaning of words can probably be learned best by using words, the teacher will plan many opportunities for discussing, storytelling, reporting, explaining, listening to stories, and other language-arts activities. A new word picked up in a television program may be worth some study by a group or class.

4. Explanation by the Teacher

This is the obvious form of building meanings attempted by most teachers. It is included here because there can be no substitute for an explanation by a teacher who knows the present level of thinking in the group and who can approach a new idea or concept in a variety of ways to build meaning. For example, after a second grade has kept a weather record for a month, the teacher may lead the children in thinking over some of the many things that go to make up our concept of "weather."

5. Oral Reading and Storytelling by the Teacher

In addition to oral reading and storytelling by the children themselves there may be some special values for the group in hearing the teacher. A number of these values are discussed in Chapter 13, on children's literature. The teacher who knows children's books can select stories which supplement and enrich ideas being developed. For example, after first- or second-grade children have read a simple story about airplanes, the teacher may enrich their information by oral reading of Bendick's *The First Book of Airplanes* or Lois Lenski's *The Little Airplane*. Because the teacher can read materials somewhat more advanced than the children read for themselves, the opportunities to extend understanding are many.

6. Use of Pupil-made Materials

Projects which children work out themselves usually have considerable meaning for them. The teacher may capitalize on interest in such activities as making charts, "My Word Book," or a picture dictionary. These may be alphabetical or they may be classified as to animals, art, food, people, travel, etc. In the lower grades stories which the teacher has recorded as the children told them to her are reread often and may contain ideas with which useful words can be associated. In the intermediate grades a committee report by three or four pupils may present and illustrate new concepts for a whole class.

7. Emphasis upon Concept-building in the Content Fields

The social studies, science, and children's literature offer many opportunities for the development of vocabulary; indeed, meanings must be clarified in these fields if the child is to profit by experiences in them. For example, in a fourth grade studying China the teacher must take definite steps to develop such concepts as *houseboat, chopsticks, rice field,* and *rickshaw.* Current events from *My Weekly Reader* or the daily newspaper[47] suggest new and interesting words.

8. Wide Reading

There is considerable experimental evidence that wide reading has a favorable effect on vocabulary development. As suggested above, this ordinarily becomes an effective method after the second or third grades. Some time ago Thorndike[48] suggested that pupils in the middle grades read far too little to develop adequate reading ability because materials are not available in the classroom or are not used when available. LaBrant and Heller[49] stated that "Under continuous exposure to the free-reading program a definite gain was made both in quantity of reading done and in ability to discriminate." As children have an opportunity to meet words in meaningful settings the words are incorporated in their vocabularies.

9. Use of the Dictionary

From the fourth grade on, the dictionary has many values in clarifying pronunciation and sharpening and extending meanings of words. Methods of dictionary study are given in the section below.

[47] F. B. Baxter, "Vocabulary Development Through the Reading of the Daily Newspaper," *English Journal,* Vol. 40, pp. 570-571, December, 1951.

[48] Edward L. Thorndike, *Improving the Ability to Read,* pp. 4-6. Bureau of Publications, Teachers College, Columbia University, New York, 1935.

[49] Lou L. LaBrant and Frieda M. Heller, *An Evaluation of Free Reading in Grades Seven to Twelve, Inclusive,* Ohio State University Studies, Contributions to Education, No. 4, p. 37. Ohio State University Press, Columbus, 1939.

10. Informal Word Study

From the early grades and throughout high school the teacher can do much to promote an interest in words. Having fun with words, through seeing how they change their meaning or how they have changed through the years, can grow into a fascinating hobby. Books such as Ernst's *Words. English Roots and How They Grow*[50] and *Picturesque Word Origins*[51] have bibliographies of books about words and may be placed in the hands of children. Many other books written for adults are useful references for teachers who wish to extend their own knowledge of words and who can adapt some of the vocabulary and activities in the books to the needs of younger people. These include books such as Gowers' *Plain Words: Their ABC,*[52] the Evans' *Dictionary of Contemporary American Usage,*[53] and Nicholson's *A Dictionary of American-English Usage,*[54] the latter being a paperback based on Fowler's famous *Modern English Usage.* Another source of ideas available to any teacher who has access to a good newsstand is the paperback books on vocabulary development. Some of these containing ideas which may be adapted to elementary school and junior high school are:

HORACE COON. *How to Spell and Increase Your Word Power,* Signet Key Book. New American Library, New York, 1959.

WILFRED FUNK and NORMAN LEWIS. *30 Days to a More Powerful Vocabulary,* 29th printing. Pocket Books, New York, 1958.

ROGER B. GOODMAN and DAVID LEWIN. *New Ways to Greater Word Power.* Dell, New York, 1955.

NORMAN LEWIS. *Word Power Made Easy,* 12th printing. Perma Books (Pocket Books), New York, May, 1959.

The Madison Public Schools issued a bulletin[55] which gives suggestions such as the following for informal word study:

a. Having pupils collect as many meanings as they can for words with multiple meanings, such as *run, deck,* and *base.*

[50] Margaret S. Ernst, *Words. English Roots and How They Grow,* 3rd ed. Knopf, New York, 1954.

[51] *Picturesque Word Origins.* G. & C. Merriam, Springfield, Mass., 1933.

[52] Sir Ernest Gowers, *Plain Words: Their ABC.* Knopf, New York, 1955.

[53] Bergen Evans and Cornelia Evans, *A Dictionary of Contemporary American Usage.* Random House, New York, 1957.

[54] Margaret Nicholson, *A Dictionary of American-English Usage.* Signet Books, New American Library, New York, 1958.

[55] Madison Public Schools, *Developing Word Meaning.* Curriculum Department, Madison Public Schools, 1943, Mimeog.

b. Finding words from other language; for example, *port* meaning to *carry* in *porter, portfolio, transport,* and *portage.*

c. Listing manufactured words such as *nylon* or *Kodak.*

d. Finding new word combinations or compounds such as *lunchroom, rattlesnake,* and *chalkboard.*

e. Collecting words suggestive of sounds, such as *buzz, crackle,* and *clang.*

f. In the upper grades, tracing classical or legendary words: *martial* (from Mars, the god of war), *cereal* (from Ceres), *herculean* (from Hercules).

g. Studying personal names—their literal meaning: *Peter,* a rock; *Florence,* a flower; *Arthur,* noble.

h. Tracing the origin of common idioms such as "take the bit in his teeth," "kick the bucket," and "a rolling stone."

i. Avoiding the overuse of such words as *bad, lovely, nice, awful,* and *cute.*

j. Substituting more colorful words for monotonous words, such as *said* and *went.* For example, for "The cat went across the lawn to catch the robin" the class might write, "The cat *sneaked, darted, crept, sprang, crawled,* etc."

k. Playing word games such as "Daffynitions" in which children attempt amusing definitions. Two examples are an *adult* is a person who has stopped growing at both ends and started growing in the middle and *Christmas* is the season when we get children something for their fathers to play with.

11. Direct Word Study

In addition to "fun with words" in the informal ways mentioned above, many teachers find that children profit by the direct study of words. The following are suggestions for such work:

a. Study of word parts. The word-analysis program described in the next chapter suggests that, beginning at about the third grade, children will profit from a knowledge of some common prefixes, suffixes, and stem words. With a little guidance a fifth grade might work out the meanings of such words as *pronunciation* or *illiterate,* if they needed to use them.

b. Exercises on synonyms and antonyms, such as the following.

In each line below find a word which means the opposite of the first word in the line.

short	loud	hard	tall
lost	raw	found	went

c. Classification game—such as adding a word to a group like *rose, iris,* and *pansy* or arranging a mixed group of words like *train, carrot, rabbit, ship, bear, wolf, cabbage, turnip,* and *airplane* under their proper headings.

d. Working on the relations of words in such analogies as *grass* is to *green* as *lily* is to *long, leaf, white,* or *sweet.*

e. Building word lists of things that go together, often in connection with the social-studies unit. For example, in a unit on Mexico:

Spanish Words	Transportation	Food
serape	airplane	tortillas
vaquero	donkey	enchiladas
fiesta	cart	chili

f. Practice in using the exact term, such as writing the plural of *horse, ox,* and *goose* or naming the young of the *bear,* the *deer,* the *frog,* the *horse,* and the *duck.*

g. Learning to use context to derive meanings. The use of context in word recognition is described in Chapter 10. In relation to meaning Deighton[56] has pointed out that context always *determines* the meaning of a word but does not necessarily *reveal* the meaning. It gives one meaning and sometimes a partial meaning rather than all meanings. Nevertheless, meaning is revealed in at least five ways: by definition, example, modifiers, restatement and inference. Deighton gives examples of these which seem most useful at secondary school levels but which can be adapted to younger children.

h. Books on words and vocabulary development for children provide activities and stimulate interest. The teacher might try the Epsteins' *The First Book of Words,* Watts, New York, 1954; C. W. Hardwick's *Words Are Important* series, Hammond, Maplewood, N.J., 1955; or Helen Randolph's and Irma Pixley's *The Words You Use,* Books I and II, Henry Regnery, Chicago, 1955.

i. Some manuals accompanying basic readers and many language books give further examples of the formal and informal study of words. The value of specific exercises such as those suggested above will vary considerably with different children. In general, such work can be conducted in the spirit of "fun with words" rather than meaningless repetition of useless vocabulary. The closer such activities are to the needs discovered in the reading program and the other school activities, the more value they will tend to have. Finally, such activities as those listed above must be combined with others stressing such goals as speed of reading, comprehension, and interpretation of what is read.

USE OF THE DICTIONARY IN THE MIDDLE GRADES

Learning to use the dictionary is one of the steps in building a meaning vocabulary, and it is also related to developing word-recognition abilities as discussed in the following chapter. In plan-

[56] Lee C. Deighton, *Vocabulary Development in the Classroom.* Bureau of Publications, Teachers College, Columbia University, New York, 1959.

ning a program of dictionary usage a teacher in the fourth, fifth, or sixth grade may ask such questions as the following:

1. What dictionary should my class use?
2. What are some objectives in teaching the use of the dictionary?
3. What is involved in readiness for the use of the dictionary?
4. What are some suitable first lessons in dictionary usage?
5. What are some more advanced abilities in dictionary usage that should be acquired by all boys and girls?

Children who have had readiness experiences with their own word lists or word files, with picture dictionaries and with glossaries (see Chapter 10) are often ready for more intensive word study with a dictionary planned by its authors for use by children in the upper elementary and junior high school grades. In answer to the first question teacher or school staff may consider a list including:

Elementary Dictionary for Boys and Girls. American Book Co.
Thorndike-Barnhart Beginning Dictionary. Scott, Foresman.
Thorndike-Barnhart Junior Dictionary. Scott, Foresman.
Webster's Elementary Dictionary. G. & C. Merriam.
Webster Junior Dictionary. G. & C. Merriam.
Winston Simplified Dictionary for Schools. Winston.

Murray[57] has given some hints for the selection of a dictionary for classroom use. Unfortunately, the dictionaries listed differ considerably in their pronunciation guides, and it is difficult for children to transfer from one to another or to an unabridged dictionary. Examples of differences are the use of the schwa (ə) and certain kinds of diacritical marks. Whatever dictionary is used, a number of specific skills must be practiced. In general, such dictionaries contain only the commonest words and the commonest meanings of these words. They are easier to use than unabridged dictionaries, because they have larger type and because they give more space to pronunciation aids and more examples in sentences, pictures, maps, and charts.

In answering the second problem regarding objectives the teacher realizes that the dictionary is not taught for its own sake but as a tool in securing knowledge. The final test of the program is the extent to which the child can use the dictionary to get the information he

[57] C. Merrill Murray, "Selecting an Elementary School Dictionary," *Elementary English,* Vol. 34, pp. 293-297, May, 1957.

wants. Accordingly, the teacher will aim to have the pupil able and willing (1) to locate words in the dictionary, (2) to obtain a meaning that fits into the total thought, and (3) to derive the correct pronunciation and the correct spelling of a word.

Before a teacher can profitably begin dictionary work in any one of the fourth, fifth, or sixth grades, she must know if the children have developed the preliminary abilities needed for such work. In the broadest sense these abilities began to develop at least as soon as the child began to talk. More specifically the child must be able to use (1) an alphabetical arrangement, (2) context clues to check meaning, (3) the sounds of letters singly and blended, and (4) some knowledge of syllables or other word parts. These may be called elements in dictionary readiness.

Since such language abilities vary widely at any level, the teacher will ordinarily have to review and develop some of these four types of abilities with part of her intermediate-grade class. When this has been at least partly accomplished, there will follow a discovery and examination period in which the children find that the dictionary is a book to help them to study words. After such orientation the teacher will plan lessons to develop such abilities as these:

1. Alphabetizing lists of words beginning with different letters.
2. Alphabetizing lists of words beginning with the same letter.
3. Alphabetizing lists of words beginning with two or more of the same letters, such as *pantaloon, pancake, panacea, panic, panther,* and *pancreas.*
4. Developing speed and accuracy in using the guide words at the top of each page.
5. Understanding the diacritical markings used in the dictionary.
6. Using the pronunciation key, accented syllables, and other aids to correct pronunciation.
7. Noting stems and affixes.
8. Selecting the best of alternative meanings.
9. Making use of homonyms, synonyms, and antonyms.
10. Knowing special parts of the dictionary, such as lists of abbreviations and the biographical dictionary.
11. Combining the foregoing skills in different speaking and writing activities.

Most of these abilities can be developed through direct use of school dictionaries in settings where the children need to acquire the information the dictionary contains. For their own reference some teachers may desire to obtain a workbook of dictionary exercises or bulletins and charts prepared by publishers to aid the use of a specific dictionary.

CONCLUSIONS

It should be evident that the elementary school has an important function to perform in helping children to equip themselves with good working vocabularies and with the means of adding to their vocabularies continuously. Probably these vocabularies should be both extensive and intensive. The influences of modern living on vocabulary, the key role of a good vocabulary in a child's school success, and considerable research on frequently used words all encourage special work in this area. There is no substitute for a rich variety of concrete, first-hand experiences in developing a meaningful vocabulary which is basic to reading, speaking, and writing vocabularies. At the same time many children seem to profit from and enjoy different work-type procedures with words. A variety of these activities have been suggested for adaptation to the vocabulary needs of individuals and groups of children. Problems and means of developing a reading or recognition vocabulary are amplified in the succeeding chapter.

SUPPLEMENTARY READINGS

APPLEGATE, MAUREE. "Words are New Worlds," *Helping Children Write,* Chap. 7. International Textbook, Scranton, Pa., 1949.

BETTS, EMMETT A. *Foundations of Reading Instruction.* American Book, New York, 1957.

BUCKINGHAM, B. R., and DOLCH, E. W. *A Combined Word List.* Ginn, Boston, 1936.

COLE, LUELLA. "General and Technical Vocabulary," *The Elementary School Subjects,* Chap. 2. Rinehart, New York, 1946.

DALE, EDGAR, and REICHERT, DONALD. *Bibliography of Vocabulary Studies,* rev. ed. Bureau of Educational Research, Ohio State University, Columbus, 1957.

DURRELL, DONALD D. "A Vocabulary for Corrective Reading," *Elementary English Review,* Vol. 11, pp. 106-109, April, 1934.

GATES, ARTHUR I. *A List of Spelling Difficulties in 3876 Words.* Bureau of Publications, Teachers College, Columbia University, New York, 1937.

GATES, ARTHUR I. *A Reading Vocabulary for the Primary Grades,* rev. and enlarged. Bureau of Publications, Teachers College, Columbia University, New York, 1937.

GRAY, W. S., and HOLMES, ELEANOR. *The Development of Meaning Vocabularies in Reading.* University of Chicago Press, Chicago, 1943.

HILDRETH, GERTRUDE H. *Teaching Reading,* Chaps. 8, 20. Holt, New York, 1958.

JERSILD, ARTHUR T. "Language Development," *Child Psychology,* 3rd ed., Chap. 9. Prentice-Hall, New York, 1947.

LAMBERT, ELOISE. *Our Language: The Story of the Words We Use.* Lothrop, Lee, and Shepard, New York, 1955.

MCCARTHY, DOROTHEA. "Language Development in Children," in Leonard Carmichael, ed., *Manual of Child Psychology,* 2nd ed., Chap. 10. Wiley, New York, 1954.

MCKEE, PAUL. "Vocabulary Development," *The Teaching of Reading: A Second Report,* Thirty-sixth Yearbook, Part I, Chap. 9, National Society for Study of Education. Public School Publishing Co., Bloomington, Ill., 1937.

MCKIM, MARGARET G. *Guiding Growth in Reading.* Macmillan, New York, 1955.

PIAGET, JEAN. *Language and Thought of the Child.* Harcourt, Brace, New York, 1926.

RINSLAND, HENRY D. *A Basic Vocabulary of Elementary School Children.* Macmillan, New York, 1945.

RUSSELL, DAVID H. *Dimensions of Children's Meaning Vocabularies in Grades 4 through 12.* University of California Publications in Education, Vol. 11, No. 5. University of California, Berkeley, 1954.

RUSSELL, DAVID H. "Concepts," in C. W. Harris, ed., *Encyclopedia of Educational Research,* 3rd ed., pp. 323-333. Macmillan, New York, 1960.

SEASHORE, ROBERT. "The Importance of Vocabulary in Learning Language Skills," *Elementary English,* Vol. 25, pp. 137-152, March, 1948.

STAUFFER, RUSSELL G. "A Study of Prefixes in the Thorndike List to Establish a List of Prefixes That Should Be Taught in the Elementary School," *Journal of Educational Research,* Vol. 35, pp. 453-458, February, 1942.

THORNDIKE, E. L., and LORGE, IRVING. *The Teacher's Word Book of 30,000 Words.* Bureau of Publications, Teachers College, Columbia University, New York, 1944.

WITTY, P. A. "Some Suggestions for Vocabulary Development in Public Schools," *Educational Administration and Supervision,* Vol. 31, pp. 271-282, May, 1945.

Chapter 10

A DEVELOPMENTAL WORD RECOGNITION PROGRAM

One of the chief aims of reading instruction in the primary grades is the development of abilities in identifying new words and recognizing familiar and partly-known words. In the intermediate grades most children have acquired some of these "do-it-yourself" techniques with words but need more skill in attacking a wide variety of new words. Thus the development of abilities in word recognition is an important part of the reading program in all elementary grades and may, indeed, be a persistent problem for some students at the secondary-school level.

Previous chapters have indicated that a child has four vocabularies that he uses in various communication activities. In order of size for the primary-grade child these are his

hearing or understanding vocabulary
speaking vocabulary
reading vocabulary
writing vocabulary

These are overlapping but are still somewhat separate. A child will usually not speak, read, or write a word which he does not understand, although young children may sometimes experiment with words for sheer fun. Similarly, a child learns to read more easily a word that he understands and that he uses in his own speech. Again, his writing vocabulary is smaller than the others but is ordinarily based on his reading, his speaking, and especially on his understanding vocabulary. Research also shows that in about the fifth or sixth grade a child's reading vocabulary becomes larger than his speaking vocabulary. As his reading abilities mature and he uses a wider variety of reading materials he recognizes from context or by other methods words which he does not ordinarily use in conversation.

Even though a child knows the meaning of a word it does not follow that he can identify it the first time he is asked to read it or recognize it even after he has met it a few times on chart or in book. In addition to understanding he must have some skills in "unlocking" new or partly known words. In other words, he must develop the ability to "attack" verbal symbols so that he can pronounce them correctly and clothe them with some meaning. He must develop abilities in word perception which lead to automatic recognition of words previously studied, and also in the ways of working out unfamiliar or partly known words.

According to Chapter 7, on the primary program, most children learn a half dozen ways of recognizing new or partly known words. By the end of the third grade they are able to use one suitable method of word attack or to combine two or three methods in working out a new word. These methods of attack may be summarized in three overlapping categories:

Predominantly Visual Clues	1. Picture aids
	2. Sight words
	3. General pattern or configuration
	4. Peculiarities in appearance
	5. Familiar parts
Emphasis on Meaning	6. Context clues
	7. Compounds of known parts
Mainly Analytical Clues	8. Phonetic analysis
	9. Structural analysis
	10. Dictionary aids to pronunciation

This list of ten methods suggests that word recognition abilities may be complex. It shows, moreover, that a skillful reader, even by the second or third grade, has several strings to his bow—he does not rely exclusively on one method of attack for all kinds of words. It implies further that advocates of any one method of word recognition tend to limit children's learnings. Not all of these skills are acquired by all elementary school children, but the successful reader is usually one who can use most of these procedures and who can combine two or more suitable methods in dealing with an unknown word.

RESEARCH BACKGROUNDS ON WORD PERCEPTION

Much of the early literature and some current writing on word recognition reveal a tendency for writers to be concerned with pedagogical aspects of the mechanical analysis of words rather than with basic psychological problems of word perception. Fortunately, more recent research on word perception and on children's development of language skills, such as summarized in Chapters 3 and 4, gives more authentic clues to teaching procedures. In addition, the history of reading instruction[1] provides perspective on various methods and especially on the controversy over "sight" or "look-say" methods, as contrasted to phonics and other analytical approaches. Many teachers are most interested in the applied research which deals directly with classroom procedures; a few conclusions, however, from psychological research may be stated succinctly. In the list below only one reference is given in support of a statement, but the other references and the summaries of research cited in the bibliography at the end of this chapter add more complete documentation for the statements.

1. Visual and auditory perceptual skills are important factors in readiness for learning to read.[2]

2. Skills in perception and recognition of words as tested at beginning stages of reading are more closely related to reading achievement than is general mental ability.[3]

3. Skills in word perception tend to be specific rather than general.[4]

4. Perceptual skills break down under stress. This may mean loss of power when a child is frustrated by material too difficult for him.[5]

5. Perception is influenced by personal factors such as the ex-

[1] Emmett A. Betts, "Phonics: Practical Considerations Based on Research," *Elementary English,* Vol. 33, pp. 357-371, October, 1956. Nila B. Smith, *American Reading Instruction.* Silver Burdett, New York, 1934.

[2] Arthur I. Gates, G. L. Bond, and D. H. Russell, *Methods of Determining Reading Readiness.* Bureau of Publications, Teachers College, Columbia University, New York, 1939.

[3] Muriel C. Potter, *Perceptions of Symbol Orientation and Early Reading Success,* Contributions to Education, No. 939. Bureau of Publications, Teachers College, Columbia University, New York, 1949.

[4] Arthur I. Gates, *The Psychology of Reading and Spelling,* Contributions to Education, No. 129. Teachers College, Columbia University, New York, 1922.

[5] Leo Postman and J. S. Bruner, "Perception Under Stress," *Psychological Review,* Vol. 55, pp. 314-323, November, 1948.

pectancies and needs of the learner. Emotionally toned words or situations may also affect his perception.[6]

6. The perception of words depends upon relationships surrounding the word. A meaningful setting may be a guide to more accurate perception.[7]

7. Frequency of word usage is related to ease of recognition. With increasing familiarity of a word or phrase the individual tends to use reduced cues (some letters, not the whole word) in word recognition.[8]

8. Tendencies toward reversals and inversions of letters or words are common at five and six years of age, and may persist until seven or eight years.[9]

9. Children may use single letter-sound combinations, two-letter sound combinations, or letter-group-sound combinations in auditory methods of attacking new words. These are often accompanied by visual techniques, especially in longer words which can be divided into stems and affixes.[10]

10. Most modern programs of teaching word recognition in primary grades start with whole words and break them into parts (an analytic method) rather than starting with parts and building them into words (a synthetic method). In general, a combination of methods is used.[11]

11. Most basic reading programs contain a thorough approach to phonics skills, and most teachers believe in studying consonant and vowel sounds, digraphs and blends, phonograms and syllables, and other phonics materials involving auditory perception as part of a total reading program.[12]

12. Activities in reading referred to as "phonics" or sometimes "phonetics" are not closely related to the findings of modern, scientific linguistics. On the other hand, the modern field of linguistics

[6] Magdalen D. Vernon, *Backwardness in Reading: A Study of Its Nature and Origin.* Cambridge University Press, New York, 1957.

[7] Magdalen D. Vernon, *A Further Study of Visual Perception.* Cambridge University Press, New York, 1952.

[8] Leo Postman and Mark R. Rosenzweig, "Perceptual Recognition of Words," *Journal of Speech and Hearing Disorders,* Vol. 22, pp. 245-253, June, 1957.

[9] Frances L. Ilg and Louise Ames, "Developmental Trends in Reading Behavior," *Journal of Genetic Psychology,* Vol. 76, pp. 291-312, June, 1950.

[10] Edward W. Dolch, "How a Child Sounds Out a Word," *Elementary English Review,* Vol. 22, pp. 275-280, November, 1945.

[11] Barbara A. Purcell, "Methods of Teaching Reading: A Report of a Tri-State Survey," *Elementary School Journal,* Vol. 58; pp. 449-453, May, 1958.

[12] David H. Russell, "Teachers' Views on Phonics," *Elementary English,* Vol. 32, pp. 371-375, October, 1955.

tends to be concerned with the sounds but not the meanings of words and may therefore require adaptations before being useful to the teacher of reading.[13]

13. More precise research on children's auditory and visual perception abilities is needed, especially at the primary grade levels. For example, the statements of some followers of Gestalt psychology that words are seen as "wholes" may be criticized because the early findings of this school of psychology were based not on the perception of words but usually on space relationships in optical illusions.[14]

14. Visual and auditory perceptions are complex, and the process of improving perception of words is one which involves continuous reorganization and new patterning. Some children may be satisfied with a low level of attack and need considerable help in going beyond it.[15]

DEVELOPING WORD-PERCEPTION ABILITIES

Most children have had considerable experience in hearing words and in seeing some of them during early childhood and in a reading-readiness program. To the first grade they typically bring certain abilities in auditory and visual discrimination, and it becomes the task of the primary teacher to sharpen and direct these potential reading abilities. Partly as a result of the teacher's planned guidance, most high-first-grade children can recognize gross similarities and differences in the appearance of objects, pictures, and word forms. They have also partly developed habits of listening to words and some sensitivity to rhyming words and other similarities in word sounds.

Most authorities agree that children rely on auditory cues for words before they use visual ones. During the readiness and preprimer periods, accordingly, teachers give considerable place to listening activities. The teacher holds up pictures of a pin, a pear, and a pencil and asks how the words are alike. Children gradually begin to recognize rhyming words and words beginning with the same consonant sound. Gradually, however, they are exposed also to the

[13] John B. Carroll, *The Study of Language.* Harvard University Press, Cambridge, 1953.

[14] Joyce N. Morris, "The Relative Effectiveness of Different Methods of Teaching Reading," *Educational Research,* Vol. 1, pp. 61-74, London, February, 1959.

[15] Arthur I. Gates, "Implications of the Psychology of Perception for Word Study," *Education,* Vol. 75, pp. 589-595, May, 1955.

appearance of words. Some recognize their own names on the blackboard or chart; others recognize a few labels around the room, even when the labels are removed from the corresponding objects and mixed up together. Some of the group begin to recognize certain words, phrases, or sentences on the experience charts which the teacher has written with the help of the group. In other words, auditory and visual perception abilities develop gradually under the teacher's guidance.

Each of the ten word-recognition abilities listed above applies best to different words and is used differently by individual pupils. *Picture aids* are useful in early stages for introducing concrete nouns. *Sight words* may be high frequency words and words with a pleasant emotional tone such as one's name or *ice cream*. The *general pattern* of a word is a rough form of perception which may not apply to certain words. For example, *man* and *was* may look much alike in general shape. On the other hand, a good visual cue is provided when words have a special shape such as *apple* 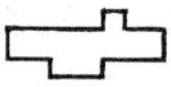 or when no other cues to the word are recognized. *Peculiarities in appearance* of a word might be the double *t* in *butter* or the two wheels (*c's*) in *bicycle*. Both teacher and pupils may call attention to *familiar parts*. For example, if the children know *boat*, they may make a good guess at *goat*. The *recognition of familiar parts* may also occur in compound words, such as *fireman*, or in the case of "small words in large words." This last recognition technique should be used sparingly, since it does not apply in many words. There is no *hen* in *Stephen* or *but* in *butcher*. On the other hand, there is, for example, a *lion* in *dandelion* and a *wind* in *window*. The teacher or pupil may apply it occasionally, to make a more intelligent attempt at recognition.

In addition to these methods with a heavy weighting of skill in visual perception, the teacher from the first emphasizes that reading involves meaningful associations. The simplest context clue is probably the label on the picture or concrete object in the room which aids association between a word and its referent. The experience "story" is also recorded on chalkboard and chart as a direct result of an excursion or a classroom event. If a second grader is reading a sentence in which he knows all the words except the last one he is encouraged to think of a suitable word to fill the gap in such a sentence as "Betty gave her cat some milk in a *saucer*." Similarly *compounds of known parts* encourage children to look for meanings in such words as *grandmother* and *bathtub*.

When a child has had some experience with words, their sounds, and their parts, he is usually ready for more specific analytical procedures and may be helped to generalize about their sounds or structure. Thus, at some time in the first grade the teacher begins *phonics* by working for recognition of rhymes, of initial consonants, ending consonants, and later, of some consonant digraphs (ch, sh, th, wh) and of consonant blends (such as bl, st, and fr). A group of children will vary widely in their readiness for such analytical procedures, and the teacher must work to keep their generalizations about sounds and letters as meaningful as possible. At much the same time as a child is becoming conscious of "word families" he is ready for more specific work in *structural analysis* involving stem words and their affixes. Both the phonetic and structural approaches help him become more competent in syllabication, for example, as a means of attacking new words.

Finally, simple pictures with their labels attached may be arranged in order, the letters named and learned as an alphabet, and the child may begin using a picture dictionary, usually in the second or third grade. These activities will help him in first work with a more formal school dictionary, usually begun in the fourth grade. With this reference the child has several types of help in unlocking new words for himself and is usually on the way to considerable independence in word recognition.

It is important that the teacher be alert to the application of these four methods in terms of the words a group of children already recognize and in terms of what sort of perception will work in the particular case of the new word. Always the teacher will direct attention from any mechanical aspects of recognition over into the meaning of the word which the children were originally seeking.

DEVELOPING RECOGNITION THROUGH MEANINGFUL ASSOCIATION

The phonetic and structural methods of word recognition described briefly above become more valuable as they are checked against the meaning of the sentence or paragraph. Similarly, if a difficult word is encountered, the child may make an intelligent guess at it by glancing at an accompanying picture, by using *picture clues,* or by thinking through what the word might be from the meaning of the selection, by using *context clues.* The first technique is provided for by good illustrations of readers and elementary-school texts in the content subjects. The second needs definite development under teacher guidance, and it is valuable because it places continued emphasis upon reading for meaning.

McCullough[16] suggested that there are seven different types of context clues. She described these as follows:

1. *Definition.* Where the descriptive context defines the unknown word. For example: Tom and Dick *lived next door.* They were _____.
2. *Experience.* Children may rely on their past concrete experiences. For example: Jack gave his dog a _____ to chew.
3. *Comparison with known idea.* The unknown word is compared to something known. For example: You do not have to run, you can _____.
4. *Synonym.* For example: When the captain gave up, the crew had to _____, too.
5. *Familiar expression.* This requires an acquaintance with familiar language patterns. For example: As they sat on the bank, Bill expected the fish to _____.
6. *Summary.* The unknown word summarizes the several ideas that have preceded it. For example: Down the street they came. First there were the elephants, then the clowns, then the lions in cages, and then the performers. It was a circus _____.
7. *Reflection of a mood or situation.* For example: The clouds were black. Scarcely any light came in through the windows. The whole house was dark and _____.

The experience of some teachers seems to indicate that these types are not always distinct in a particular selection and that there may be overlapping between them, particularly in more difficult reading material. In the lower elementary grades they can be used as an active attack on words in response to the teacher's suggestion rather than with emphasis on the seven technical names.

Artley[17] suggested other aids in context which include the following: (1) typographical aids, such as quotation marks, italics, boldface type, parenthesis, and footnotes; (2) structural aids, such as the appositive phrase or clause and the interpolated phrase or clause; (3) word elements—stems, prefixes, and suffixes (usually called aids to structural analysis); and (4) figures of speech—similes and metaphors. Again, these are often too technical for systematic use in the ele-

[16] Constance M. McCullough, "Recognition of Context Clues in Reading," *Elementary English Review,* Vol. 22, pp. 1-5, January, 1945.

[17] A. Sterl Artley, "Teaching Word Meaning through Context," *Elementary English Review,* Vol. 20, pp. 68-74, February, 1943.

mentary school, but occasional reference to them may aid pupils in deriving a word. The use of context has the great advantage of reliance upon meaning. When combined with some word-analysis activities, as described below, it does much to ensure recognition of unknown and partly known words.

CHANGES IN WORD-ANALYSIS PROGRAMS

The use of analytical methods in word recognition has always been a highly controversial topic whenever teachers and other school people meet to discuss their problems. The previous discussion has suggested that phonetic analysis and structural analysis are only two of a number of methods of developing word-recognition abilities. However, because of some uncertainty and even controversy about the values and uses of word analysis, the topic is significant enough to be discussed at some length in this chapter. It is important that beginning and experienced teachers of reading have clearly in mind the place of phonics and structural analysis in the total reading program.

The uncertainty and disagreements over phonics arise partly from the history of its use in schools. The alphabet spelling method probably goes back as far as ancient times, and the look-and-say or whole-word method was devised by Comenius in the 17th century. That great teacher of children, Pestalozzi, devised an extreme form of word analysis and applied it to beginning reading in his schools from about 1800 to 1825. For example, his *Leonard and Gertrude* describes what would now be called a reading-readiness program, followed by the use of ABC books and the memorizing of letters and syllables, not words. Later the system was adopted in United States programs and flourished particularly in the 1900's and 1910's. Different authors and publishers produced highly organized systems of "sounding out" words and of large charts grouping words according to phonetic similarities in which teachers "drilled" their pupils. These systems led to such absurdities as children's basic reading being confined to sentences like "The fat cat Pat sat on the mat." Most of the systems required children, because they needed the word *jump,* also to learn the words *bump, pump, lump,* and *dump. Sap* might be a good and useful word for, say, the average third-grade pupil, but obviously *sop, sup,* or *sip* might be neither understood nor used. Because the methods were rigidly organized and the content was unrelated to children's actual experiences, phonetic systems of learning to read became highly artificial.

In the late 1920's a natural reaction against such artificial methods set in. Capable teachers discovered that many children do not learn initially by word parts but by larger units of words, phrases, or sentences. Learning to read through nursery rhymes, phrase cards, sentences-with-pictures, and similar devices replaced a wholly analytical or phonetic approach. The movement may have been hastened by a study by Gates setting forth rather clearly the values of the "intrinsic" method rather than phonics methods. Gates described the materials of the "intrinsic method" as "a number of exercises arranged wholly to stimulate reading to secure the thought and a number arranged not only to emphasize comprehension but also to demand accurate discrimination of words and phrases."[18] The exercises were of true-false, completion selection, directions, and matching types. Many teachers and supervisors took the study as a complete indictment of the phonics method—which it was not. However, with an increasing emphasis upon silent reading in the 1920's the phonics method of word recognition languished and was forgotten in some schools.

The latter half of the 1940's and the 1950's saw part of a swing of the pendulum back to a middle position for phonetic analysis in word-recognition programs. Most basal reading programs continued to advocate use of phonetics as part of the word-recognition skills systematically introduced in their programs, but they pointed out more clearly in teachers' manuals and other sources the steps to be taken in developing skills in phonetic analysis. Greater emphasis was given to phonics in certain series of workbooks for developing reading skills.[19] Even greater prominence was given to the place of phonics in reading by authors of individual books, at least one of which by Flesch[20] enjoyed circulation of a "best-seller" variety. Another book[21] had less spectacular sales than the Flesch volume but contained fewer errors of fact than the one written by a specialist in

[18]Arthur I. Gates, *New Methods in Primary Reading.* Teachers College, Columbia University, New York, 1928.

[19] Julie Hay and Charles E. Wing, *Reading with Phonics.* Lippincott, Philadelphia. Eleanor Johnson, *Phonics Skill Texts.* Merrill, Columbus. Mary Meighen and others, *Phonics We Use.* Lyons and Carnahan, Chicago.

[20] Rudolf Flesch, *Why Johnny Can't Read and What You Can Do About It.* Harper, New York, 1955. Also *Teaching Johnny to Read.* Grossett, Dunlap, New York, 1956.

[21] Sibyl Terman and C. C. Wolcutt, *Reading: Chaos and Cure.* McGraw-Hill, New York, 1958.

readability of adult materials rather than the instruction of children. A number of Flesch's errors and false assumptions were pointed out by various writers in professional sources.[22] The final effect of the Flesch book, however, may have been that of encouraging teachers and other school people to think more carefully about the place and objectives of phonics in a total reading program. By 1960 there was a trend in many school systems toward variable amounts of phonetic-analysis activities as part of a basic-reading program or as a valuable section of a remedial program used with many retarded readers.

In determining what part phonetic-analysis activities should play in the reading program a teacher will usually be guided by the suggestions for such activities made in the manuals of the basic-reading program she is using. In addition to these specific activities, she may profit by knowing some of the usual arguments for and against phonics, some of the research findings from careful studies of phonics in use, and the principles which should guide any program of phonics.

ARGUMENTS FOR AND AGAINST PHONICS

In a study which gives general support to the teaching of phonics Agnew[23] stated such reasons for teaching a method of phonetic analysis as these:

1. It increases independence in recognizing words previously learned.
2. It aids in "unlocking" new words by giving the pupil a method of sound analysis.
3. It encourages correct pronunciation.
4. It improves the quality of oral reading.

There is also some evidence[24] to suggest that:

5. It develops habits of close attention to words and word parts which may have a favorable influence on later spelling achievement.

[22] Arthur I. Gates, "Why Mr. Flesch is Wrong," *N. E. A. Journal,* Vol. 44, pp. 332-334, September, 1955. *Johnny Can Read,* Field Service Leaflet, No. 5. Department of Education, University of California, Berkeley, 1955. Paul A. Witty, "Public is Misled on Meaning of Reading," *Nations Schools,* Vol. 56, pp. 35-40, July, 1955. School Publishing Company, Bloomington, Ill., 1925.

[23] D. C. Agnew, *Effect of Varied Amounts of Phonetic Training on Primary Reading.* Duke University Press, Durham, N.C., 1939.

[24] David H. Russell, "Diagnostic Study of Spelling Readiness," *Journal of Educational Research,* Vol. 37, pp. 276-283, December, 1943.

On the other hand, many writers such as Spache[25] indicated some of the arguments against programs of phonetic analysis. Spache mentioned such reasons as the following:

1. The English language is complex and irregular in its phonetic aspects. A teacher cannot generalize completely about a basic vocabulary, since, for example, the thirteen vowel sounds of language may be represented in one hundred and four ways. Furthermore, the same groups of letters may have very different sounds, as in the eight words *dough, bough, bought, cough, rough, through, thorough,* and *hiccough.* However, Spache pointed out that 86 per cent of English monosyllables are regularly phonetic.

2. Teaching phonics may set up undesirable habits of detailed word analysis to the neglect of understanding of rapid reading when it should be used.

3. Extensive use of phonetic analysis produces painstakingly slow and unenthusiastic reading. Interest is sacrificed, because attention is directed to form rather than meaning.

4. Research results show that there is no advantage in the phonetic method of teaching over other methods. In the study by Gates mentioned above, pupils who used the phonics method were superior in attention to smaller details of words, but inferior in comprehension and in study of total words, syllables, and the longer phonograms. In an evaluation of a Chicago program Buswell[26] has shown that children learn to read at least as well by a non-oral method as by a method emphasizing some sounding and auditory techniques.

The advantages and disadvantages of the phonics method may be summarized by saying that there is no superiority in the phonics method, when used as the sole or principal method of teaching, over other methods. However, it may have values in combination with other methods, particularly for certain pupils who seem to respond readily to auditory clues. For teachers the important point is not phonics versus no phonics but the extent to which it should be used and the methods and materials employed by the pupils in phonetic-analysis activities. The question is not how phonics can be crammed into early reading, but how it can be used by varied learners in different reading situations. Accordingly, some contrasts in timing and

[25] George Spache, "Phonics Manual for Primary and Remedial Teachers," *Elementary English Review,* Vol. 16, pp. 147-150, 191-198, April, May, 1939.

[26] Guy T. Buswell, *Non-Oral Reading A Study of Its Use in Chicago Public Schools.* University of Chicago Press, Chicago, 1945.

procedures and some principles for the use of phonetic analysis in the reading program are important in teacher and curriculum planning.

PROCEDURES AND PRINCIPLES IN PHONICS PROGRAMS

Sometimes the ideas behind differences in current theory and practice can be sharpened by presenting contrasting positions. The comparisons below reflect the thinking of active proponents of two sets of ideas:

Phonics Methods	*Combination of Methods*
1. The pupil is introduced to phonetic training as soon as he enters Grade I.	1. Phonetic activities follow some work in developing readiness for sounding and blending.
2. Early emphasis is given to the sounds of single vowels and then consonants, or vice versa.	2. Specific phonics work begins after rhyming and the establishment of a small sight vocabulary.
3. The first work is on isolated letters, followed by blends, digraphs, and phonograms.	3. The first phonics work is on the analysis of known words.
4. The general method is synthetic—the building up of whole words from letters and parts.	4. The general method is from the whole to parts to the whole again—an analytic-synthetic process.
5. Intensive training is given in the use of phonetic rules and principles. The treatment is usually deductive.	5. A few rules and principles are derived as the result of examples met in reading for comprehension. The procedure is partly inductive.
6. The emphasis is on auditory methods of attacking words.	6. Auditory procedures are combined with visual methods and contextual clues to words.

As stated above, teachers in few school systems make such sharp distinctions between phonics methods and combination methods. Rather, teachers and curriculum guides range somewhere between the two columns. The current interest in individualized reading suggests that some schools base the use of phonics more on an assessment of the pupil's individual needs than on the two types of systematic programs described above.

SOME RESEARCH ON PHONICS INSTRUCTION

The research studies on phonics may be divided into three categories: (a) studies comparing the results of instruction in phonics with those produced by other methods; (b) analysis of primary and intermediate reading materials to see what kinds of phonics skills they require and; (c) correlational studies between tests of phonics abilities and more general reading achievements. Controversy on the place of phonics instruction has stimulated a number of writers such as Betts, Burrows, Smith, and Witty to make comprehensive summaries of available research. These summaries are listed in a special section in the bibliography at the end of this chapter. The present section mentions only a few representative studies.

Careful studies comparing the results of phonics instruction to those of other methods go back at least to one made by Gill[27] in England in 1911 in which a sentence-method group of children exceeded two phonics groups on a somewhat artificial test of reading speed. In a later English study Winch[28] gave results of the alphabetic, the look-and-say, and two variations of phonics methods on small groups of children in a poor district of London. Winch's individual tests produced results favorable to the phonics methods. He also concluded that there was a need to adapt reading instruction to the socio-economic environment of the children involved; he was one of the first to make this statement. Since the 1920's many comparative studies have also been made in the United States and are summarized in the sources indicated.

One of the most careful comparative studies was the one by Agnew[29] quoted above. In a 1928 study Sexton and Herron[30] found little value in phonics instruction given in the first five months in school, some value in work given in the second five months, and still better results from instruction given in second grade. Garrison and Heard[31] also came to the conclusion that specific phonics training may be useful at second- and third-grade levels; Dolch and Bloom-

27 Edmund J. Gill, "Methods of Teaching Reading," *Journal of Experimental Pedagogy,* Vol. 1, pp. 243-248, 1911-1912.

28 W. H. Winch, "Teaching Beginners to Read in England: Its Methods, Results and Psychological Bases," *Journal of Educational Research Monographs,* No. 8. Public School Publishing Co., Bloomington, Ill., 1925.

29 D. C. Agnew, *op. cit.*

30 K. Sexton and J. S. Herron, "The Newark Phonics Experiment," *Elementary School Journal,* Vol. 28, pp. 690-701, May, 1928.

31 Sidney C. Garrison and N. T. Heard, "An Experimental Study of the Value of Phonetics," *Peabody Journal of Education,* Vol. 9, pp. 9-14, July, 1931.

ster[32] gave a mental age of seven years as a prerequisite to success in phonics skills under ordinary conditions of instruction. It is doubtful if a specific mental age can be stated as a baseline for all children, and the above findings do not provide evidence against informal activities with words leading to readiness for phonetic analysis activities. The work of Agnew and other comparative studies such as one by Gates and Russell[33] gave support to "moderate" amounts of phonics in first grade rather than little or large amounts; Agnew found results most promising at the third-grade level. These and other studies also suggested that children learn different things when they use different methods. Tate[34] warned against "unbalanced development" of the abilities to comprehend words, sentences, and paragraphs, and a later study by McDowell[35] found that children with a heavy phonics program excelled in alphabetizing and spelling but were below other pupils in speed, and in understanding words and paragraphs. In another study Mills[36] compared the effects of four lessons in each of visual, phonics, kinaesthetic and combination methods of word recognition. Although his sample of pupils and lessons was small, he declared, "The study showed conclusively that different children learn to recognize words more efficiently by different teaching methods and that no one method is best for all children." In another study Sparks and Fay[37] were able to compare results on eight hundred pupils in the first four grades, one group of whom used reading materials which introduced phonics at the beginning of Grade I and the other a basal reading program which stressed the use of sight words at first, followed by phonetic work on names and sounds of initial consonants and other phonetic elements. At the end of Grade I the first phonics group was somewhat superior to the second group in vocabulary and in reading comprehension. The authors pointed out that the difference may be due to

[32] Edward W. Dolch and M. Bloomster, "Phonic Readiness," *Elementary School Journal,* Vol. 38, pp. 201-205, November, 1937.

[33] Arthur I. Gates and D. H. Russell, "Types of Material, Vocabulary Burden, Word Analysis and other Factors in Beginning Reading," *Elementary School Journal,* Vol. 39, pp. 27-35, 119-128, September, October, 1938.

[34] Harry L. Tate, "The Influence of Phonics on Silent Reading in Grade I," *Elementary School Journal,* Vol. 37, pp. 752-763, June, 1937.

[35] John B. McDowell, "A Report on the Phonetic Method of Teaching Children to Read," *Catholic Educational Review,* Vol. 51, pp. 506-519, October, 1953.

[36] Robert E. Mills, "An Evaluation of Techniques for Teaching Word Recognition," *Elementary School Journal,* Vol. 56, pp. 221-225, January, 1956.

[37] Paul E. Sparks and Leo C. Fay, "An Evaluation of Two Methods of Teaching Reading," *Elementary School Journal,* Vol. 57, pp. 386-390, April, 1957.

the tests used, one of which had three sections out of six on phonetic skills. In the second and third grades there were no reliable differences between the two groups, and in the fourth grade the basal reading group were more accurate readers. The authors concluded that the two approaches produced much the same results with the exception of the accuracy finding at the fourth grade. Other studies favor emphasis on phonics instruction for some learnings and emphasis on a combination of methods when other phases of reading ability are involved. The overall impressions from many studies may be summarized as in certain generalizations below.

A second category of studies pertinent to the phonics program analyzes sounds, phonograms, and other units found in primary vocabulary lists and readers. Such materials are also available for the structural analysis program described in a later section. Teachers' manuals often give such information for a specific basic vocabulary. The range of materials available may be illustrated by Templin's[38] test of children's articulation abilities, Osburn's[39] analysis of the commonest syllables in children's written vocabularies, and Oaks'[40] compilation of the frequency of vowels, their sounds, and their combinations in basal readers planned for primary grades. For example, Oaks noted that one-third of the vowel situations appear as early as the primer, that short vowels should probably be taught before long vowels, and that "silent" vowels, as in digraphs, appear infrequently at the lower levels. A sequence for the teaching of phonics "principles" suggests that only one treatment of single, short vowels followed by a consonant in a stressed syllable need be introduced in the second- and third-reader levels. Such standards give rather specific guides to what may ordinarily be attempted in phonics programs.

The third type of research is a group of correlational studies relating ability in phonetic analysis to other reading abilities. The amount of relationship between tests of auditory and visual perception abilities and measures of reading such as comprehension questions seems to vary considerably with the tests used. For example, Templin's[41] five tests of sound-symbol association and sound discrim-

[38] Mildred C. Templin, "A Note on a Screening Test of Articulation of Speech," *Journal of Pediatrics,* Vol. 45, pp. 443-445, October, 1954.

[39] Worth J. Osburn, "Teaching Spelling by Teaching Syllables and Root Words," *Elementary School Journal,* Vol. 55, pp. 32-41, September, 1954.

[40] Ruth E. Oaks, "A Study of the Vowel Situation in a Primary Vocabulary," *Education,* Vol. 72, pp. 604-617, May, 1952.

[41] Mildred C. Templin, "Phonic Knowledge and Its Relation to the Spelling and Reading Achievements of Fourth Grade Pupils," *Journal of Educational Research,* Vol. 47, pp. 441-454, February, 1954.

ination correlated more highly with spelling than with reading. Correlations with measures of reading achievement ranged from .25 to .47, the highest being a test of identifying, from four choices, the word which contained a stimulus sound. Mulder and Curtin[42] found that the correlation of a test of synthesizing or "blending" ability with silent reading test scores was .44 at the fourth-grade level. Rudisill[43] reported results for 315 children in third grade and reviewed pertinent research. She found a correlation of .71 between reading and phonic knowledge which was reduced to .42 when the effects of spelling were partialled out. Rudisill believes that "functional" phonic knowledge makes a substantial contribution to achievement in reading. She defines functional as "the sounds of letters and combinations of letters" used not in isolation but "heard and used in normal word pronunciation."

The samples of research given here in comparing teaching methods, in the results of analysis of primary words, and in correlational studies suggest that the question of the place of phonics can be settled on a research basis and need not be determined by opinion or emotion. They also indicate a few generalizations which can be safely made about instructions in phonics.

As a result of this historical development and the many research studies in the field, the principles guiding a phonics program may be stated positively:

1. Phonetic Analysis Is Only One of Several Good Methods of Word Recognition

Teachers must never consider phonics a total reading program. It is one part of one part of the total program: word-recognition activities. Word recognition is but one element in the total reading program, which emphasizes development of sentence and paragraph comprehension and enjoyment and interpretation of the content read (see Chapter 5). Phonetic analysis does not constitute the whole of the word-recognition program, since, as described above, children learn to recognize words by general pattern, by similarity to known words, by context clues, and by dictionary aids. However, for most children it is one of the methods by which they can learn to recognize new or partly known words.

[42] Robert L. Mulder and James Curtin, "Vocal Phonic Ability and Silent-Reading Achievement: A First Report," *Elementary School Journal*, Vol. 56, pp. 121-123, November, 1955.

[43] Mabel Rudisill, "Interrelations of Functional Phonic Knowledge, Reading, Spelling and Mental Age," *Elementary School Journal*, Vol. 57, pp. 264-267, February, 1957.

2. *A Program of Phonetic Analysis Must Be Intrinsic*

The memorizing of isolated sounds or of word lists just because the words are similar phonetically is a sterile, unprofitable practice. In modern programs the first practice in phonetic analysis is conducted with known words, and later practice is carried on with words important in the child's basic vocabulary. Phonics is essentially a system of generalizing about the sounds of words; and before the child can generalize, he must know a number of word samples which illustrate the generalization. As with sounds and analysis techniques, he may apply his skill to new words; but ability to do so successfully is a culmination, not a beginning part of the program.

3. *Readiness for Phonetic Analysis Must Be Established as for Other Reading Activities*

Children need background experiences, an adequate speaking vocabulary and sight vocabulary, and many chances to hear rhymes and other word sounds before they are ready for the more advanced, systematic analysis of words. This means considerable maturity on the part of the child before instruction in word analysis is likely to be successful. For example, Tronsberg[44] suggested a list of eleven achievements needed in readiness for phonics. Some of the clues to check whether a child is ready are: "(a) If he can recognize similarities and differences in words he hears, (b) If he can distinguish likenesses and differences in written words, (e) If he has mastered a sight vocabulary large enough to give him a basis for generalizing about sounds, (h) If he can read to answer questions, (i) If he has formed the habit of reading silently before reading orally, (j) If he has developed a desire to read." Of course, not all these steps will be complete or mastered before a child can begin with profit some phonics activities. Accordingly, successful primary teachers plan programs of so-called "ear training": listening to rhymes, similarities in beginnings of names such as *Tom* and *Tina,* judging sounds for pitch and distance, and enjoying books such as Margaret Wise Brown's *Noisy Books.*[45]

4. *Since Phonics Is a Series of Generalizations about Words, the Teacher Will Teach Inductively*

The inductive approach means that teachers and children will collect a number of examples of the same fact or rule before they try

[44] Josephine Tronsberg, "The Place of Phonics in Basal Reading Instruction," *Reading Teacher,* Vol. 8, pp. 18-20, 38, October, 1954.

[45] William R. Scott, North Bennington, Vermont.

to generalize about it. Most of the high first grade must recognize the first names of three of their class, *Jim, Jean,* and *Jerry,* before they can suggest the initial *j* sound. Children will need to know a number of words at sight, such as *can* and *cane, man* and *mane,* before they can generalize about the effect of the silent *e* ending on the medial *a.* Similarly, they should know other words involving the other medial vowels, such as *pin* and *pine,* before they can generalize completely about the effect of the silent *e* ending in one-syllable words.

5. Teachers Must Plan Carefully When They Will Introduce Word-Analysis Techniques into a lesson

Since the first work with young children is to establish readiness and to strengthen all language abilities, phonics activities will be part of other reading activities, based on known words, with the teacher directing attention as opportunities arise. For example, if one child comments that *hat* and *cat* sound alike, the teacher may write them together on the blackboard so that the children may also see the likeness. As the children develop, phonetic analysis will be separate from many types of reading experience. Later practice in phonetic and structural analysis will be included in a work-type lesson or part of a lesson rather than in the audience-reading or recreational-reading situation. Again, some pupils will profit much more than others from laboratory work-type situations for work with words, and so the teacher will vary the use of word-analysis techniques with the different groups in her class. Both in timing and in amount, the work in word analysis must be planned in relation to other reading activities and not just in terms of the words which are to be studied.

6. Lessons Should Be Designed So that Children Have a Chance to Practice and Synthesize Various Methods of Recognizing New Words

The suggestions above have indicated that phonetic analysis is best used not alone but in combination with visual and context clues. Sometimes a child may make a good guess at a word from context and then verify by some phonetic clue, such as the initial consonant sound. The aim is to have each child establish a method of attack on words which seems easy and natural to him and which gives him a sense of security and word power necessary for smooth reading.

7. Teachers Should Have a Systematic Approach in Teaching the Use of Phonetic Analysis

Teachers will find such a systematic approach in the teachers' guides of the better basic-reading series. Different series may contain some minor discrepancies in the phonics work suggested and in their grade-placement of these activities. Since the programs must be intrinsic (Principle 2), the activities suggested at any one level will be dependent upon the basic vocabulary used up to that level. However, there is general agreement on how such a program should be developed (see page 315). The teacher and curriculum worker should note the recommendation for a sequence of preparatory learnings, concentrated practice, and follow-up maintenance of various skills. In referring to this outline, teachers, supervisors, and curriculum workers are also reminded that different boys and girls may profit from different amounts of work in phonetic analysis and that any program must be considered as a continuous development rather than a rigid placement of certain activities at any one stage or grade level.

STRUCTURAL ANALYSIS IN WORD RECOGNITION

A number of writers believe it is helpful to distinguish between phonetic analysis and structural analysis of words. As indicated above, phonetic analysis relates in general to the use of sounds or auditory characteristics of words in improving word perception and independence in word recognition. Structural analysis relates to the recognition and use of word parts or the visual characteristics of words. Children may see two known words in *mailman* by "looking hard" at the word or they may recognize that *jumping* is made up of the known word *jump* and the common *ing* ending. Betts,[46] for example, described structural analysis as "limited to these considerations: compound words, prefixes, suffixes, roots, inflections, and the general problem of syllabication and accent." He believed that more attention should be given to structural analysis after facility in phonetic analysis is achieved.

Research studies have not given clear evidence of the values of structural analysis when taught by itself as a technique of word recognition. In a study in which the structure of 250 words was taught in

[46] Emmett A. Betts, *Foundations of Reading Instruction,* p. 645. American Book, New York, 1946.

ten seventh-grade classes Otterman[47] found a significant gain only for the superior children on a test of interpretation of new words. Apparently little transfer of training was obtained. The experimental group was significantly higher than the control group on a test of spelling but not on other tests of general vocabulary or reading comprehension. On the other hand, Hunt[48] found positive relationships between ability in structural analysis and scores on vocabulary and on reading comprehension of a group of university students. For example, tests of word-elements, and word-meaning construction and word-derivation ranged in correlations from .30 to .44 with vocabulary scores. Hunt's tests and procedures should be adapted to a study of elementary and secondary students. Correlations of vocabulary and level of comprehension ability with ability to use context were somewhat higher than with abilities in structural analysis.

One example of an aid to structural analysis is a study by Stauffer[49] of the prefixes in Thorndike's *Teacher's Word Book of 20,000 Words*. He found that 24 per cent of the words have prefixes and that fifteen prefixes account for 82 per cent of the total number of prefixes. These are:

ab (from)	com (with)	en (in)	in (not)	re (back)
ad (to)	de (from)	ex (out)	pre (before)	sub (under)
be (by)	dis (apart)	in (into)	pro (in front of)	un (not)

It would seem that a knowledge of these common prefixes can help pupils in their word-analysis activities in the middle and upper elementary grades. Further guidance for the teacher may be found in a study by Thorndike[50] of the commonest suffixes in useful English words. An analysis by Osburn[51] of the commonest syllables in the Rinsland word list is also helpful. The most frequently appearing

[47] Lois M. Otterman, "The Value of Teaching Prefixes and Word-Roots," *Journal of Educational Research,* Vol. 48, pp. 611-616, April, 1955.

[48] Jacob T. Hunt, *The Relationship of Structural Ability in Word Analysis and Ability to Use Context Clues to Vocabulary and Reading*. Doctoral dissertation, University of California, Berkeley, 1951.

[49] Russell G. Stauffer, "Study of Prefixes in the Thorndike List to Establish a List of Prefixes That Should Be Taught in Elementary Schools," *Journal of Educational Research,* Vol. 35, pp. 453-458, February, 1942.

[50] Edward L. Thorndike, *Teaching of English Suffixes,* Contributions to Education, No. 847. Bureau of Publications, Teachers College, Columbia University, New York, 1941.

[51] Worth J. Osburn, *op. cit.*

affixes are the suffixes *ing, ed, er, ly,* and also *es, tion,* and *y.*

Although the commonest stems and affixes are known from such studies as these, the gains from teaching structure and the best way of doing so have not been clearly indicated by research. Many young children are unable to transfer their knowledge of word parts to new situations involving new words. For example, in her study of teaching prefixes and "word-roots" to children as old as seventh-graders Otterman[52] found that after thirty lessons, only the brightest students made significant gains in the ability to interpret new words. There was no significant difference favoring the experimental group in perception, general vocabulary, reading comprehension, and reading speed. It may be that other methods and materials would give better results, although it is doubtful if young children can generalize as well as seventh graders.

The value of making a sharp distinction between phonetic analysis and structural analysis in the word-recognition programs of the lower grades may be questioned. The most useful clues for recognition of words vary from word to word. Most teachers will want to use both rather than one of them. In the early stages of learning to read, where a large number of the words are monosyllables, ability in translating individual letters, blends or digraphs (such as *br* or *ch*) into sounds usually ensures success in recognizing an unfamiliar or partly familiar word. In the high second or low third grades, where polysyllabic words begin to constitute more of the basic vocabulary, ability to detect known parts, phonograms such as *ight* and *ound,* and the syllables of words becomes more valuable. For example, sounding out the individual letters of *automobile* or *unlikely* is not a profitable procedure at this stage.

Furthermore, particularly beyond the second grade, when children have had considerable experience with words, it is difficult to know whether a child is relying upon visual or auditory clues to "unlock" a new word. The best guess seems to be that he will rely upon both, particularly if he has had some help from the teacher in combining them. Indeed, one of the teacher's chief aims in teaching word-analysis abilities is to have pupils gain skill in combining several approaches in word study. In a practical situation, accordingly, the problem is not one of phonetic analysis *versus* structural analysis but the best combined method of word attack. The outline below indi-

52 Lois M. Otterman, *op. cit.*

cates how phonetic and structural analysis are gradually combined in a word-analysis program.

OUTLINE OF A DEVELOPMENTAL PROGRAM OF WORD-ANALYSIS ACTIVITIES[53]

The suggestions for a developmental program below assume that at any level after the first, children will continue work as needed on the skills of the preceding levels. The outline must be considered as a general statement rather than a definite prescription for any one level or group of children.

1. *Readiness level.* Readiness activities for later phonetic analysis: listening to sounds—near and far, high and low, individual voices; listening to and saying nursery rhymes and other rhyming words; careful enunciation in conversation; noting and imitating sounds of animals and common objects; noting and reproducing sounds made by the teacher.
2. *Preprimer level.* Further readiness activities and the beginning of some attention to sounds of letters and word parts: associating auditory and visual symbols with specific objects and pictures; developing a sight vocabulary of fifty or sixty words; reproducing rhymes and rhythms; auditory perception of words with the same initial consonant sounds; supplying other words with the same initial consonant sound; introduction to noting known words in compounds, such as *father* in *grandfather;* selecting rhyming words.
3. *Primer level.* Emphasis upon similarities and differences in words and word parts: recognizing sound and appearance of words beginning with same or different consonants; identifying *s, d, ed,* and *ing* forms of known words; identifying stems in variant words ending in *s, d, ed,* and *ing;* beginning practice in blending initial consonant with known parts of words; analyzing compound words composed of two known words; completing and composing rhymes.
4. *First-reader level.* The use of simple analogy and generalization in recognizing words: applying knowledge of consonant sounds in working out new words; strengthening ability to analyze compound words with known parts; identifying little words in big words in specific examples where the technique applies; adding to knowledge of consonant sounds; discovering consonant sounds in medial and final, as well as initial, positions; developing the idea of the alphabet; distinguishing between similar words often confused, such as *there, then* and *something, sometime.*
5. *Second-reader level.* Developing some independence in use of word-recognition techniques: attacking new words by blending with initial consonants; using ending and medial consonants in blending; using con-

53 Developed with the assistance of Verna L. Wadleigh.

sonant digraphs; observing variant forms, including *ies, er,* and *ly* endings; learning some contractions, such as *I'll, don't,* and *can't;* short and long vowel sounds; vowels lengthened by final *e;* vowel digraphs such as *ai* and *ea;* recognition of some of the commonest phonograms, such as *ell* and *ick;* activities leading to the generalization that one letter may have several sounds and that different letters may represent the same sound (such as *f* and *ph*); making a start in combining structural and phonetic analysis in attack upon words; combining analysis techniques with context clues, similarities, and other clues in word recognition.

6. *Third-reader level.* Applying word-analysis techniques to words of more than one syllable: further recognition and use of phonograms; study of derivatives formed by adding prefixes and suffixes; further practice in combining phonetic, structural, context, and other clues in word attack; strengthening the generalization that vowels have different sounds—affected by *r,* second one silent in digraphs such as *ai,* etc.; compound and hyphenated words; possessives and contractions that drop more than one letter; readiness for dictionary usage by alphabet study, recognizing variant meanings of words, etc.; readiness for syllabication by mention that syllables contain one vowel sound, by seeing words with first syllable or known word, such as *beside,* by beginning work on accent, etc.

7. *Fourth-reader level.* Achieving independence in using a wide variety of word-recognition techniques: further practice in combining visual, auditory, and context clues in recognizing words; reviewing work on consonant and vowel sounds and digraphs which pupils cannot use easily; extension of knowledge and use of commonest phonograms; use of the glossary and dictionary and its various guides in determining pronunciation and meaning; further study of synonyms, antonyms, homonyms, and multiple meanings of words; applying word-analysis techniques in spelling situations.

8. *Higher grades.* Continuation of program of earlier grades as needed: review of phonograms; structural analysis of more difficult words; skills and habit of dictionary usage established. Amount and type of instruction determined even more by the child's individual needs.

The outline above suggests what may be taught in a developmental program of word-analysis activities. It is included here not because it must be developed fully with all children, but so that teachers can see the activities that are usually recommended at different levels of development. The outline when used as a guide may discourage certain teachers from placing too much faith in any one method of improving the child's word-recognition abilities. In addition, it may encourage other teachers to adopt a systematic developmental approach to word-analysis activities with children who seem to profit by such procedures.

THE ALPHABET

Many children come to school saying they "know" the alphabet, and many parents believe that learning the alphabet is the first step in learning to read. Unfortunately, "knowing" the alphabet usually means that the child can rhyme off the letters in sequence from A to Z but that he cannot use the alphabet in a functional way to help his reading. A few authorities, including Durrell, have stressed the value of the first grader knowing his A, B, C's. However, the positive relationship between knowing the alphabet and success in first-grade reading is not necessarily a causal one; it may reflect the influence of a good home or superior mental ability. As Betts[54] put it, the substantial relationship between letter-making ability and achievement in beginning reading "cannot be interpreted as an endorsement of the rote memorizing of the alphabet."

Instead of early rote learning the teacher can present to parents or others the following facts:

1. Schools do teach the alphabet.
2. In beginning reading, ability to name a letter is probably not so valuable as ability to sound it, and to combine this with adjacent sounds.
3. Children often learn the names of their first letters not in sequence but in terms of initial consonants of words they know.
4. After children have learned to identify many single letters by name as they appear in words there is some advantage in learning their sequence from A to Z.
5. Knowledge of letter names is useful when children begin to write and spell, often in the second half of grade one.
6. Just knowing the sequence of letters is not so useful as knowing in which part of the alphabet *l* comes, the letter before *n*, which letter comes first of *j* and *l*, and similar facts. In other words, knowledge of the alphabet must function in building up one's own vocabulary list, using the picture dictionary, and then in spelling and dictionary work.

Such a list suggests that the alphabet is best learned, not as a rote chart, but as a series of skills which can be applied in many ways.

[54] Emmett A. Betts, *op. cit.*

LEARNING TO USE THE DICTIONARY

One of the most useful products of knowing the alphabet is found in dictionary usage. As suggested in Chapter 7, this activity usually begins with a pupil's own word list or box of word cards and with a picture dictionary. There are at least fifteen different picture dictonaries that have been published, with prices ranging from twenty-five cents to five dollars. The titles tend to change rapidly in the small corner bookstores and the supermarkets, but the following are fairly standard volumes:

MOORE, LILLIAN. *A Child's First Picture Dictionary*. Wonder Books.
PARKE, MARGARET. *Young Reader's Dictionary*. Wonder Books.
PARKE, MARGARET. *Young Reader's Color-Picture Dictionary*. Grosset and Dunlap.
REED, MARY, and OSSWALD, EDITH. *My Little Golden Dictionary*. Simon and Schuster.
SCOTT, ALICE, and CENTER, STELLA. *A Picture Dictionary for Boys and Girls*. Doubleday.
WALPOLE, ELLEN W. *The Golden Dictionary*. Simon and Schuster.
WATTERS, GARNETTE, and COURTIS, S. A. *Picture Dictionary for Children*, 3rd ed. Grossett and Dunlap.
WRIGHT, W. W. *The Rainbow Dictionary*. World Publishing Co.

Such volumes make possible some "do-it-yourself" in getting to know new words as well as providing readiness work for the use of a regular school dictionary beginning around the fourth-grade level. Parke[55] and other writers have described procedures to use with picture dictionaries and believe they are an aid to reading, spelling, and writing at the second- and third-grade levels. Some classes or groups enjoy making their own picture dictionaries.

One other approach to dictionary usage is through the use of a glossary such as found in the back of some basal readers. Because a glossary is a "little dictionary" usually restricted to the hard words of the one book, it is usually easier for a child to locate a word in it. Having located the word, he may check for (1) number of syllables and accent, (2) preferred pronunciation, and (3) suitable meaning of multi-meaning words. The glossary may also help skills in structural analysis by indicating stem and affixes or possible derivatives

[55] Margaret Parke, "Picture Dictionaries," *Elementary English*, Vol. 32, pp. 519-524, December, 1955.

of a word. Sometimes pairs of pupils may test one another on a selected sample of glossary words. A short teacher-made test of ability to get information from a glossary may indicate strengths and weaknesses in a group and whether or not more help is needed before the pupils begin regular dictionary work as outlined in the previous chapter.

HINTS ON METHODS OF GUIDING WORD-ANALYSIS ACTIVITIES

Some general methods of guiding word-analysis activities are presented under "Guiding Principles for Phonics Programs" above. These suggest that the newer program differs from the older practices of the 1910's. In general, the newer approach is to utilize a variety of techniques in word perception and to build up word analysis abilities in a more psychological and coherent fashion. Some specific hints regarding newer methods may be summarized as follows:

1. After a word has been discovered in a meaningful context, the teacher may or may not decide to present it for deliberate study. Some words are not sufficiently useful to be studied carefully or are not adapted to phonetic or structural analysis. Not all new words must be analyzed.
2. Not only should early phonics activities be based on whole words, but there may be some advantages in starting on short, simple words of regular phonetic structure, such as *cat, bit,* and *hot,* and avoiding words like *bear* and *know.* One series of books[56] published in England is based on this approach, but further research is needed to evaluate the advantages and disadvantages.
3. If a word is to be studied analytically, the teacher will usually ask the group to point out what seem to them the most useful parts or characteristics of the word. Different children recognize different things in words, and it may be necessary for the teacher to point out the best clue for determining the word.
4. Most new words can be compared to known words with some similar feature, such as the same initial consonant or the same *y* ending.

[56] J. C. Daniels and H. Diack, "The Phonic Word Method," *The Reading Teacher,* Vol. 13, pp. 14-21, October, 1959.

5. After analysis activities, the teacher will always direct the group to the meaning in the larger context. She will also give many exercises in analysis which relate to comprehension of the whole. An example of such an exercise is

I am little and white. I like milk.

	mitten
I am a	kitchen
	kitten

6. The teacher should be alert to words frequently confused by members of the group. Exercises somewhat like the above may be used to require pupils to analyze carefully such pairs as *walk* and *talk* or *what* and *which*.

7. Writers differ on the order of presentation but in the first grade easy sounds, like those of *s* and *m*, should probably be introduced before more difficult ones, like those of *b* and *p*.

8. The teacher should always present the whole word as the meaningful unit first, and then by underlining, covering, or boxing between two fingers or hands she may direct attention to a certain part of the word.

9. Word-analysis techniques should probably be discontinued for a time with a child or group of children who are extremely slow, word-by-word readers.

10. The need for individual help is as great in phonics as in other phases of reading or even greater. The word-analysis techniques used will correspond to the general reading ability of the pupil rather than to his actual grade position.

11. Complete mastery of one phonetic element is not essential before another is introduced, because this element will be met from time to time in the child's reading. An adequate working knowledge of phonics, such as needed for fluent context reading, will normally require some three or four years' work.

12. The development of sensitivity to phonetic and structural elements in words and an attitude of positive attack on unknown words are more important than the study of all the common phonetic elements in the language.

13. Since work on sounds tends to be divorced from meaning, especially for young children, many phonics activities should be treated as games to play or "word fun" with such names as "Word Detective," "What Word Am I?" "Syllable Bingo," etc. Such small-

group activities may often be supplemented by individual, work-type exercises prepared by the teacher or suggested by manuals and booklets of reading activities.

14. Success in learning word-analysis abilities, as in other areas, depends upon the ability of the teacher to adjust her methods to the needs of the group, to discover the ways in which individual children succeed most readily, and to help each child to develop the word-recognition techniques that are most helpful to him.

15. Particularly at the third- and fourth-grade levels the teacher may recall frequently that skilled readers and adults use syllabification, other structural cues, and the dictionary in discovering pronunciation and meaning of many new words.

SUMMARIES OF RESEARCH ON PHONICS

BETTS, E. A. "Phonics: Practical Considerations Based on Research," *Elementary English,* Vol. 33, pp. 357-371, October, 1956.

BURROWS, ALVINA T. *What About Phonics.* Bulletin No. 57, Association for Childhood Education International, Washington, D.C., 1951.

GATES, ARTHUR I. *A Review of Rudolf Flesch, Why Johnny Can't Read,* Macmillan, New York, 1955. 18 p.

GRAY, W. S. "Reading: IV The Teaching of Reading," in C. W. Harris, ed., *Encyclopedia of Educational Research,* 3rd ed. Macmillan, New York, 1960.

HILDRETH, GERTRUDE H. "The Role of Pronouncing and Sounding in Learning to Read," *Elementary School Journal,* Vol. 55, pp. 141-147, November, 1954.

MORRIS, JOYCE M. "The Relative Effectiveness of Different Methods of Teaching," *Educational Research,* Vol. 1, pp. 38-49, 61-75, London, November, 1958, February, 1959.

"Phonics in Reading Instruction," *The Reading Teacher,* Vol. 9, pp. 67-117, December, 1955. Whole issue.

SMITH, NILA B. "What Research Says About Phonics Instruction," *Journal of Educational Research,* Vol. 51, pp. 1-9, September, 1957.

SMITH, NILA B. "What Research Tells Us About Word Recognition," *Elementary School Journal,* Vol. 55, pp. 440-446, April, 1955.

SPACHE, GEORGE D. "A Phonics Manual for Primary and Remedial Teachers," *Elementary English Review,* Vol. 16, pp. 147-150, 191-198, April, May, 1939.

WITTY, P. A. "Phonics Study and Word Analysis," *Elementary English,* Vol. 30, pp. 296-305, 373-379, May, October, 1953.

WITTY, P. A., and SIZEMORE, R. A. "Phonics in the Reading Program: A Review and an Evaluation," *Elementary English,* Vol. 32, pp. 355-371, October, 1955.

SUPPLEMENTARY READINGS

AGNEW, DONALD C. *Effect of Varied Amounts of Phonetic Training on Primary Reading.* Duke University Press, Durham, N.C., 1939.

ARTLEY, A. S. "Teaching Word-Meaning through Context," *Elementary English Review,* Vol. 20, pp. 68-74, February, 1943.

BENNETT, A. "Analysis of Errors in Word Recognition Made by Retarded Readers," *Journal of Educational Psychology,* Vol. 33, pp. 25-38, January, 1942.

BETTS, EMMETT A. *Foundations of Reading Instruction,* rev. ed. American Book, New York, 1957.

BOND, G. L., and WAGNER, EVA. *Teaching the Child to Read,* 3rd ed. Macmillan, New York, 1960.

BROWNELL, WILLIAM A. "Current Practices with Respect to Phonetic Analysis in the Primary Grades," *Elementary School Journal,* Vol. 42, pp. 195-206, November, 1941.

CHALL, JEANNE, and ROSWELL, FLORENCE. "Helping Poor Readers with Word Recognition Skills," *The Reading Teacher,* Vol. 10, pp. 200-204, April, 1957.

DOLCH, EDWARD W. "How a Child Sounds Out a Word," *Elementary English Review,* Vol. 22, pp. 275-280, November, 1945.

DOLCH, EDWARD W., and BLOOMSTER, M. "Phonic Readiness," *Elementary School Journal,* Vol. 38, pp. 201-205, November, 1937.

DURRELL, DONALD, D. *Improving Reading Instruction.* World Book, Yonkers, N.Y., 1956.

DURRELL, DONALD D., and others. *Building Word Power in Primary Reading,* rev. ed. World Book, Yonkers, N.Y., 1945.

GATES, ARTHUR I. *The Improvement of Reading,* 3rd ed., Chaps. 7, 8, 9. Macmillan, New York, 1947.

GRAY, WILLIAM S. *On Their Own in Reading: How to Give Children Independence in Attacking New Words.* Scott, Foresman, Chicago, 1948.

GRAY, WILLIAM S. *The Teaching of Reading and Writing, An International Survey.* Monographs on Fundamental Education. No. 10. UNESCO Report. Scott, Foresman, Chicago, 1956.

HARRIS, ALBERT J. *How to Increase Reading Ability,* 3rd ed., Chaps. 12, 13, 14. Longmans, Green, New York, 1956.

HARRISON, M. LUCILE. "Developing Readiness for Word Recognition," *Elementary English Review,* Vol. 23, pp. 122-131, March, 1946.

HILDRETH, GERTRUDE. "Reading in the Primary Grades—Part II," *Learning the 3 R's,* rev. ed., Chap. 9. Educational Publishers, Minneapolis, 1947.

HILL, M. B. "A Study of the Process of Word Discrimination in Individuals Beginning to Read," *Journal of Educational Research,* Vol. 29, pp. 487-500, 1936.

KOTTMEYER, WILLIAM. "Appraisal of Current Methods of Promoting Growth in Word Perception in the Elementary Grades," in William S. Gray, comp. and ed., *Appraisal of Current Practices in Reading,* pp. 181-187. University of Chicago Press, Chicago, 1945.

MCCULLOUGH, C. M. "Recognition of Context Clues in Reading," *Elementary English Review,* Vol. 22, pp. 1-5, January, 1945.

SELKE, E. "Word-Recognition Difficulties of Second-Grade Pupils," *Elementary English Review,* Vol. 20, pp. 155-156, April, 1943.

TATE, H. L. "The Influence of Phonics on Silent Reading in Grade I," *Elementary School Journal,* Vol. 37, pp. 752-763, June, 1937.

TRABUE, M. R. "Special Tools that Facilitate Expression: Use of the Dictionary," Forty-third Yearbook, Part II, pp. 187-193, National Society for Study of Education. University of Chicago Press, Chicago, 1944.

Chapter 11

THE PROGRAM IN WORK-TYPE READING AND STUDY SKILLS

TYPES OF READING

The Government Printing Office in Washington has printed reference volumes which range from *A Bibliography of Early American Secular Music* to a two-volume census report on occupations and industries in the United States. A public library in a small city catalogued over 675 how-to-do-it books with titles all beginning "How to" and ranging from "How to Abandon Ship" to "How to Write Songs That Sell." Thus reading can be part of a workaday world.

The day is long since gone when teachers regarded reading only as something to do with reading textbooks. In the days of Noah Webster's *Blue-back Speller* or even the McGuffey Readers the reading text was the only book for reading and indeed may have been the only text in the child's hands. Such factors as modern production of inexpensive books and other printed materials and increasing scientific knowledge of how children learn have changed any single-reading-text system. In contrast the modern emphasis is upon reading for different purposes in a wide variety of materials. This chapter is concerned with reading to solve some problem or to achieve some practical purpose. It discusses instrumental values of reading and how reading can be used as a tool to accomplish many things the child wants to do.

This work-type phase of reading may be seen most clearly in relation to the total reading program. As suggested in Chapter 5, the activities of the total reading program may be divided into four main divisions, as follows: (1) developmental reading, (2) functional reading, (3) recreational reading, and (4) personal reading for enrichment. The developmental reading part of the program is concerned with the growth of reading habits, skills, and attitudes needed for living in modern society. It is stressed throughout this book, especially in Parts II and III. Recreational reading includes reading the various kinds of children's literature as described in Chapter 4 and Chapters 12 and 13. Reading for personal enrichment involves the same children's literature but goes beyond reading for fun to deeper meanings and clearer insights. It is described in Chapter 4 in the section on the effects of reading and in Chapter 13. Functional reading, as described in this chapter, is the utilization of work-type and study skills to get something done, to fulfill some need, to put reading to work.

Functional reading may be considered in at least three ways. Reading is put to work in terms of (1) purposes or outcomes of reading, as in noting exact details, getting a general impression of an author's point of view, criticizing arguments or predicting what will happen next; (2) content areas, with different tasks in reading arithmetic problems, a history chapter, directions for a science experiment, or a piece of fiction; and (3) the tools used, such as an encyclopedia or an atlas, or a library card catalogue. With all the easy attractive books available today, children may start such functional reading in the first grade and may use many brands of it in other primary years as well as in the wider-ranging materials of the post-primary grades. The research evidence is fairly clear that these varied kinds of reading demand somewhat different abilities and that there are specific skills which go with reading in different curricular areas and for different purposes.

FUNCTIONAL READING

Although the modern reading program is necessarily concerned with the development of reading abilities, habits, and tastes, it stresses throughout the importance of the child's *using* reading to accomplish his purposes. If this view is accepted, the nature of the work-type program will depend upon the needs and interests of the pupils and the sort of activities in which they engage during other parts of the school day and at home. This means that work-type and study activities must be planned in relation to the reading activities of the pupil as a person and the pupil as a member of a group.

In order to satisfy group and individual needs, children need to use other printed materials in addition to reading textbooks. Not all pupils in the first two grades develop the habit of using a variety of materials. Most readers contain considerable information and a variety of types of material, but even at these levels a series of basic books cannot contain all a child may wish to know. By the second grade he may wish to check a word in a picture dictionary or find illustrations and facts about stones or butterflies or dairy products. This is even more true of the child in the third grade or above. If he is after information, he may wish to consult an encyclopedia. If he wants to become familiar with current affairs, he may use the newspaper or magazine. In solving certain problems he may consult a booklet of instructions, a weather report, a train schedule, a map, or a blueprint. Also, the ordinary school program requires that the pupils of the middle and upper elementary grades read in several different content fields. A fifth-grade pupil, for example, may have to follow a chain of events in history, check wool production figures on a graph in a social-studies textbook, follow directions for performing an experiment in a science book, or note details in a verbal-arithmetic problem. Accordingly, work-type reading both in and out of school requires children to read varied kinds of materials in different ways.

In general the need for reading different types of printed material for different purposes arises naturally in a stimulating school situation. The child's own interests and his need to solve school problems ensure purposeful reading in different settings. For example, a San Francisco bulletin[1] on reading suggests how functional reading operates during the day:

> Whenever the pupil is aware that he is reading to solve an actual life or school problem, to meet a life or school need, he is reading functionally. The teacher in planning with her pupils has helped them to sense these problems and needs. Functional reading is, therefore, an all-inclusive term. The pupil on his way to school reads traffic signals, a theater marquee, the newspaper headlines, the price listing of a toy he'd like to buy. He is reading functionally. Upon his arrival in class he remembers that his committee members are planning a play centered around the building of Mission Dolores. He re-reads the plans made the day before. He selects books from the class library shelf that will provide the necessary historical data. He finds that he needs to use the alphabetized picture file to study the costumes of the Franciscan Fathers and of the Spanish settlers. In meeting all of these needs, the pupil is reading functionally.

Although the pupil's purpose in reading certain materials is to find the answer to some specific problem or to carry out some project, the teacher is aware that functional reading also contributes to

[1] San Francisco Public Schools, *Teaching Guide: Reading. Kindergarten-Grade 12,* p. 31. Curriculum Bulletin, No. 201. San Francisco Public Schools, San Francisco, 1946.

developmental reading. As a pupil works with certain materials with the motivation of strong personal interest or group needs, he is acquiring, probably in the most efficient way, some reading habits, skills, and attitudes which are goals of the developmental program. As suggested earlier, these are acquired best not in isolated reading drills but in situations where strong purposes direct the reading activity.

IMPORTANCE OF PURPOSE IN WORK-TYPE READING

In some curriculum bulletins and books on reading, too much emphasis has been placed on differences between materials that are read for recreation and materials which are "studied." Some school systems list books for pleasure reading and others for work-type reading, but a book on trains or airplanes listed as "informational reading" may be pleasure reading for certain boys. Similarly, a book listed for pleasure reading, such as Swift's *Little Blacknose* or Kipling's *Jungle Book,* may give a child considerable organized information about trains or animals. In making a distinction between functional reading and recreational reading, accordingly, the purpose as well as the type of material should be emphasized.

Since purpose is the most important guide to much reading, the teacher must take definite steps to have children clarify their purposes in reading any one selection and must plan to give practice in reading for a variety of purposes over the school term or year. To accomplish the first, she stresses the readiness activities which introduce every reading lesson (see page 153) and gives careful direction to reading assignments in social studies and other content fields. Only as the child has a purpose clearly in mind or has a definite problem to solve is he able to turn to suitable materials or employ proper procedures. To accomplish the second, the teacher must have in mind the purposes children usually have when they read and must plan occasions for using these purposes over a term of years. These may be stated in a logical sequence of abilities dependent upon purpose, as follows:[2]

1. Ability to define a specific purpose for reading
2. Skill in locating information
    a. Skill in using the table of contents

[2] The author is indebted to Marion A. Anderson and Constance M. McCullough for this sequential organization of purposes in reading.

   b. Skill in using the index
   c. Skill in using the dictionary or glossary
   d. Skill in using an encyclopedia
   e. Skill in using a card file and other library tools
   f. Skill in using maps, graphs, charts, and tables
   g. Skill in using pictures
   h. Skill in skimming
   i. Skill in using headings and other typographical aids
3. Ability to comprehend and organize what is read
   a. Ability to find the main idea
   b. Ability to see the consequence of ideas
   c. Ability to find details
   d. Ability to draw conclusions, see relationships, and make inferences
4. Ability to select and evaluate information
   a. Ability to select suitable sources of information
   b. Ability to distinguish between relevant and irrelevant, important and unimportant information
   c. Ability to recognize the difference between fact and opinion
   d. Ability to judge the validity of one's information
   e. Ability to use several sources to solve a problem
   f. Ability to judge the adequacy of one's information
5. Ability to adjust the method and rate of reading to one's purpose and to the nature of the material
6. Skill in using information
   a. Skill in following directions
   b. Skill in taking notes
   c. Skill in classification
   d. Skill in outlining
   e. Skill in summarizing
7. Ability to remember what is read
   a. Ability to use the aids to retention
   b. Ability to select facts to be remembered

Good basic reading programs, through factual selections in the reader and through workbook and manual suggestions, give a careful place to the development of the abilities listed above. None of these is mastered at any one grade level, but most of them develop continuously throughout the elementary school years. For example, a first-grade child learns to use a very simple table of contents, to find the main idea in a sentence, and to follow easy directions in marking a word or picture. Older children learn more complex ways of locating information and following directions for construction activities, playing games, and performing experiments. In general, the abilities and skills listed will be begun in the primary grades, sometimes in the form of readiness activities. Included under numbers 2 through

6 are somewhat more advanced abilities which may not be practiced directly in average groups until about the fourth or fifth grade. These include the ability to recognize the difference between fact and opinion, to judge the validity of one's information, and to do creative reading in its wider sense. It is still true, however, that activities leading to these must be planned in the lower grades. One example of judging validity at the first-grade level is an exercise like the following. After a simple story involving a child's lunch box, the group reading in a first reader might be given the following exercises with teacher direction and explanation followed by individual work.

Draw a line under each phrase that tells something you can put in Mary's lunch box. Then below draw a picture of two of the things.

A toy duck	A big boat
An apple	Seven toy trains
Seven candles	A piece of carrot
Father's hat	Some birthday cake
Something to eat	A green book

While the same materials may be used for quite different reading purposes, teachers must recognize that certain types of materials ordinarily lend themselves to work-type procedures better than others. Snedaker and Horn[3] stated that factual materials are superior to the usual children's fiction for the purpose of illustrating study procedures. In discussing work-type reading they said, "The materials should be largely informational in character (science, history,

[3] Mabel Snedaker and Ernest Horn, "Reading in the Various Fields of the Curriculum," *The Teaching of Reading: A Second Report,* Thirty-sixth Yearbook, Part I, Chap. 5, pp. 133-182, National Society for Study of Education. Public School Publishing Company, Bloomington, Ill., 1937.

geography, arithmetic, biography and similar factual materials)."[4] McKee[5] gave a complete description of work-type procedures, in at least five chapters of the 1948 edition of his book. The exercises and references in these chapters offer many illustrations of work-type procedures and materials from different content fields. Durrell[6] suggested three main purposes in work-type reading: (1) thorough or analytical reading, (2) skimming or speeded reading, and (3) elaborative thinking in relation to reading. He gave many specific examples of there for classroom practice. The thirty skills and abilities listed above, like those described by McKee and Durrell, can be developed by children who are ready to profit by direct instruction. Some readers contain specific work-type exercises for children to use directly. Most manuals for basal reading series give many suggestions for developing skill in reading for different purposes, and some have indexes which provide a comprehensive listing of related practice activities.[7]

BOOKLETS AND MANUALS FOR WORK-TYPE AND STUDY SKILLS

In addition to reading textbooks and consumable workbooks, there are many booklets of nonconsumable materials which are excellent sources of work-type activities. Some of those available at the elementary- and junior-high school level are these:

DENISON, CAROL. *Passwords to People.* Dodd, Mead, New York, 1956. [Profusely illustrated books on words and their origins. Reading level appropriate for grade four.]

ELFERT, WM., and WEINSTEIN, ALFRED. *Achieving Reading Skills.* Globe, New York, 1958. [Fifty short stories at levels of difficulty from grade three to grade seven, with a variety of comprehension and vocabulary questions after each story. The final thirty pages include groups of superficial "remedial drills."]

FREDERICK, ROBERT W. *How to Study Handbook.* Appleton-Century, New York, 1938. [One of the few how-to-study books which are adapted to the use of elementary-school pupils. May be used in the upper grades in developing such study skills as how to read by skimming, how to use

4 *Ibid.*, p. 158.

5 Paul G. McKee, *Teaching of Reading in the Elementary School.* Houghton Mifflin, Boston, 1948.

6 Donald D. Durrell, *Improving Reading Instruction,* Chaps. 13, 14. World Book, Yonkers, N.Y., 1956.

7 Aileen J. Birch, *An Analysis of Study Skills as Taught by Primary Basal Readers.* Unpublished master's thesis, San Diego State College, San Diego, 1953.

table of contents, how to read tables, how to read maps, how to use the library, how to prepare talks, and how to solve problems. The suggestions are practical and clear, but some may be used best when adapted by the teacher to the group using them.]

GAINSBURG, J. C., and SPECTOR, S. I. *Better Reading.* Globe, New York. [Provides exercises in skimming, main ideas, making inferences, outlining, careful reading, and study skills for junior-high-school level.]

GATES, A. I., and PEARDON, C. C. *Practice Exercises in Reading,* rev. Bureau of Publications, Teachers College, Columbia University, New York. [Sixteen booklets at levels of difficulty marked III, IV, V, and VI. At each level are four booklets with paragraphs followed by directions of the following types: (a) Reading for general significance; (b) Reading to predict outcomes; (c) Reading to follow directions; and (d) Reading to note details.]

GERKEN, C. D'A, and KEMP, ALICE. *Make Your Study Hours Count.* Science Research Associates, Chicago, 1956. [A booklet for junior high-school pupils. Simple, practical suggestions for more efficient use of time and study habits.]

GRAY, WILLIAM S.; MONROE, MARION; and ARTLEY, A. STERL. *Basic Reading Skills for Junior High School Use.* Scott, Foresman, Chicago. [Offers exercises on word analysis and comprehension based on workbooks of the Curriculum Foundation basal reading series. Includes two survey tests and an annotated reading list.]

HOVIOUS, CAROL, and SHEARER, ELGA M. *Wings for Reading.* Heath, Boston. [Grade six, level. Offers groups of short stories and exercises to give practice in skills of self-inventory, main ideas, details, and word study; also additional tests and exercises in word study.]

KINCHELOE, ISABEL M., and ANDERSON, HAROLD A. *Advanced Reading Skill Builder.* Books I, II, III, Reader's Digest Educational Department, Pleasantville, N.Y., 1958. [Based on articles in the journal with a variety of comprehension and other exercises.]

MCCALL, W. A.; COOK, L. B.; and NORVELL, G. W. *Experiments in Reading.* Harcourt, Brace, New York. [Books marked I, II, and III for grades seven, eight, and nine. A variety of types of comprehension exercises for senior pupils.]

MCCALL, W. A., and CRABBS, L. M. *Standard Test Lessons in Reading.* Bureau of Publications, Teachers College, Columbia University, New York. [Each booklet contains one-page exercises consisting of a short selection followed by a variety of types of question. Time limit and approximate equivalence in grade norms give an interesting way for pupils to check their own progress.]

MURPHY, GEORGE; MILLER, HELEN RAND; and MILLER, NELL APPY. *Let's Read.* Holt, New York, 1953, 1955. [Series of four books offered for pupils of grades seven to ten with reading ability of grades five to eight. Includes reading selections followed by exercises on comprehension or vocabulary. Teacher's manual and key available.]

PARKER, DON H., and others. *SRA Elementary Reading Laboratory.* Science Research Associates, Chicago, 1958. [One hundred and fifty carefully graded selections at reading levels 2 to 9. Each selection accompanied by exercises in comprehension and vocabulary. Pupil record books and teacher's handbook. Attractively printed and boxed. The same publishers have an *SRA Reading Laboratory, Grades 7 to 12.*]

SPENCER, PAUL R., and others. *Finding New Trails. Exploring New Trails. Traveling New Trails.* Lyons and Carnahan, New York. [Work-type reading materials for grade four stressing comprehension, rate, reading, arithmetic problems, and use of the dictionary; fifth grade, reading maps, tables and graphs, using reference materials; sixth grade, use of library in addition to these other topics.]

STONE, C. R., and GROVER, C. C. *Practice Readers.* [Books I to IV, starting at about third-grade level. The selections are of one page, followed by a page of questions on main ideas, details, implied ideas, or vocabulary. Types of comprehension are spaced throughout the book.]

STRANG, RUTH. *Study Type of Reading Exercises.* Bureau of Publications, Teachers College, Columbia University, New York, 1956. [One-thousand-word articles on the improvement of reading skills. Intended for high school, but useful for good readers at lower levels.]

STROUD, JAMES J.; AMMONS, ROBERT B.; and BAMMAN, HENRY A. *Improving Reading Ability,* 2nd ed. Appleton-Century-Crofts, New York. [Exercises in speeded reading of various types and critical reading.]

WAGNER, GUY L., and others. *Readers Digest Reading Skill Builder.* Readers Digest Educational Service, Inc., New York. [Selections adapted from the *Readers Digest* form the basis for exercises in rate, vocabulary, and comprehension. Two separate booklets for each of grades four, five, and six.]

WILKINSON, H. S., and BROWN, B. D. *Improving Your Reading.* Noble, New York, 1953. [A book rather than a booklet or manual, with one of the largest available collections of exercises on comprehension, recall, locating information, etc. Mostly for fourth grade and beyond.]

WITTY, PAUL. *How to Become A Better Reader.* Science Research Associates, Chicago, 1953. [Offers twenty brief lessons on self-improvement in reading followed by short exercises stressing varied skills, plus twenty general reading exercises of greater length. For junior high school.]

Spache[8] has published a comprehensive list of consumable workbooks, nonconsumable materials, and reading games and devices which include most of the above books and suggest the wide range of materials available for helping comprehension and other reading abilities. The list is planned for use by teachers of poor readers but is equally helpful in suggesting materials for the development of comprehension in regular classes.

[8] George D. Spache, *Good Reading for Poor Readers.* Garrard, Champaign, Ill., 1958.

Any one of these books may be adapted to use in grades other than the one indicated in them or in the teacher's manual accompanying them. They give hundreds of suggestions for work-type reading and supply some materials for it. If a child or group needs special help in work-type reading procedures, the teacher will find in these books some activities related to the specific needs of the individual or group.

The suggestions in the general books on the teaching of reading, in the workbooks accompanying the basic series used, in other workbooks, in special manuals of exercises to promote comprehension, and in work-type reading textbooks all combine to make a wide variety of work-type activities available to most teachers. Any teacher who is planning special work in reading with her class has the right to expect that her school system will supply at least enough of some of these materials for a group in her class to have the special practice they need. These should be supplemented by teacher-prepared exercises, hectographed or mimeographed for the class, which can be based directly on the content and type of reading activity on which the group is working. It is equally true, however, that work-type reading must be considered not as something for special exercises but as a proceeding necessary in solving many daily problems. The good teacher, therefore, is alert to opportunities that arise every day for pupils to read to accomplish their practical purposes. The San Francisco bulletin on reading suggests, accordingly, that pupils in grades four to eight should use, and should be guided in using, the materials listed on the next page.[9]

While there may be doubt among some teachers about the extent to which a child actually reads some of the following, the list nevertheless suggests the many kinds of work-type functional reading that are possible for the elementary-school child. As suggested above, many of these are somewhat specialized reading activities in which most children will profit by some direct help from the teacher, especially when they meet the reading situation for the first time as they work on various problems. In the materials mentioned and listed above, and in the following list, a clear realization of purpose will help the child function efficiently in his reading. Purposes which go beyond the literal meaning of sentence or page are also discussed in Chapter 14.

[9] San Francisco Public Schools, *Teaching Guide: Reading. Kindergarten-Grade* 12, Curriculum Bulletin, No. 201, pp. 176-177. San Francisco Public Schools, San Francisco, 1946.

READING MATERIALS FOR INDIVIDUAL GROWTH

trade marks
clock faces
advertisements
signs and sign boards
picture books
books
money coins and bills
recipes
labels
captions
titles
letters and postcards
comic books
speedometers
compasses
scales
radio dials
instructions for hand work
magazines
weather reports
telephone dial
bus transfers
tickets
coupons for premiums
hymn book
prayer cards
directions for care and repair of radio, camera, typewriter, etc.
Book of Knowledge
printed mottoes, maxims
music rests, time signatures
instructions for using preparations
standardized tests
newspaper headlines
telephone book
manufacturers' guarantees
bank checks
schedules and timetables for train, steamship, bus, airline
business forms
want-ad columns
gas, electric, water meters
family budgets
weather charts
encyclopedias
standard dictionary
job applications
applications for licenses, permits, etc.
receipts
thermometers
music key signatures, other music notations
descriptions of scientific processes
pamphlets issued by manufacturers
scores on sports, such as baseball, football, tennis
card catalogue
newspaper
charts and posters
calendar
maps
graphs and tables
questionnaires
games
election pamphlets, sample ballots
reports, minutes, summaries of club groups
constitutions of clubs, etc.
government bulletins
census statistics
latitude and longitude
pamphlets of civic regulations
codes

DEVELOPING FUNCTIONAL READING ABILITIES IN THE CONTENT FIELDS

In addition to the need for special help in work-type reading, such as workbooks and teacher-prepared exercises, and for considerable emphasis on daily reading needs of a practical sort, most boys and girls profit from some direct help in their reading or study in the different content fields. For better or for worse, our schools are still largely reading schools. In the more traditional curriculum much stress is put on the use of textbooks; in the newer activity programs even greater demands for wide reading are placed upon the pupils. In fact, no type of curriculum design can be genuinely successful unless there is available to pupils a large store of books which supplement their concrete first-hand experiences. Books and pupils' abilities to read in various fields, therefore, are the allies of all kinds of teaching.[10]

Teachers have always recognized that the various areas of a curriculum are very different. In the more conservatively organized curriculum, literature is different from geography or general science or health. In the newer curricula the language arts are somewhat different from the social studies or the sciences or the industrial arts. But, although teachers recognize these differences in subjects, in the past they have not always provided for them in their reading instruction. Too often reading instruction has been confined to the rather literary type of material, largely fiction, found in many basic readers and anthologies. Actually, the children of the middle and upper grades of the average school need more positive help in reading scientific or mathematical or social-studies material than they do in reading literary material. Fictional material is most common in out-of-school situations, and therefore children have more practice in reading it. What they often need most in school, then, is guidance in how to read in content areas of the curriculum.

In general, there are at least three main problems which pupils encounter in reading any type of specific content such as history or science or arithmetic. These are (1) the technical vocabulary; (2) the different types of organization or patterns of thought; and (3) specialized devices for conveying ideas, such as maps, graphs, tables, and thermometers. In addition to these general problems in all content fields, most of the fields present certain specific reading problems to the middle- or upper-grade pupil.

Technical Vocabulary

Every school subject has a vocabulary of its own that must be learned. Chapter 10, on vocabulary development, has pointed out that it is a difficult and often slow process for children to acquire gen-

[10] Gordon N. Mackenzie, "The Role of Reading in Different Curriculum Designs," in W. S. Gray, ed., *Improving Reading in All Curriculum Areas*, Supplementary Educational Monographs, No. 76. University of Chicago Press, Chicago, 1952.

eralized ideas, or concepts. However, they must learn what an *isthmus* or *industry* is in social studies, they must recognize a *dividend* or *discount* in arithmetic, they must know a *barometer* or *chlorophyll* in science, and similar words in other subjects. Many school textbooks are written by subject-matter specialists, and one may contain literally hundreds of words a group of children have not met before. The extent of the special vocabularies was recorded by Cole in her *Handbook of Technical Vocabulary*,[11] a book which gave teachers and other curriculum workers a list of some of the most valuable words in arithmetic, history, geography, English, and other fields and which should be supplemented by recent additions to the language. A complete listing of vocabulary studies up through 1955 compiled by Dale and Reichert[12] lists sources which contain many suggestions for developing vocabularies.

Opportunities to familiarize pupils with valuable words of a technical sort arise in a number of ways. Often an event in the neighborhood or a current happening recorded in the newspapers or magazines read by the class involves useful social studies or science concepts. As the teacher or parent stimulates discussion of the event, he helps to introduce new vocabulary or enriches partly known words. Direct study of words listed by pupils as causing them difficulty may be valuable, particularly in the beginning stages of a unit of work. Some of the devices listed in Chapter 9, on vocabulary-building, apply to this work. Perhaps the most valuable approach to the growth of technical vocabulary is that discussed under the heading of readiness. The teacher who is conscious of and diagnoses specific factors which determine whether or not a child is ready to read a selection will inevitably give some place to developing the meaning of technical words peculiar to the particular area studied. As suggested in the discussion of readiness, pictures, conversation about related experiences, concrete first-hand experiences, and other audiovisual aids may all help to build accurate knowledge of technical terms to be met in reading materials.

Different Thought Patterns

Because the different disciplines are areas of quite different knowledge, they are organized in contrasting ways, new facts or conclusions

[11] Luella Cole, *Handbook of Technical Vocabulary*. Public School Publishing Company, Bloomington, Ill., 1945.

[12] Edgar Dale and Donald Reichert, *Bibliography of Vocabulary Studies*, rev. ed. Bureau of Educational Research, Ohio State University, Columbus, 1957.

are discovered in different ways, and different types of thinking are required of persons working in those areas. Scientific materials are often organized around some principle or law; historical materials may be organized in chronological sequence. In arithmetic a child must be critical of the size of his answer to a problem, but in social studies he must be critical of his sources of information. In science he may be concerned with discovery, but in health he is usually making applications of known facts. For example, Beauchamp[13] listed eleven types of content and organization which apply directly to science, but not much to other subject-matter areas. These are the following:

1. Principles and laws of science
2. Concepts of class—machines, industries, etc.
3. Experiments
4. Theories and hypotheses
5. Processes—evaporation, growth, etc.
6. Natural phenomena—seasons, weather, etc.
7. Descriptions of specific things—oxygen, grasshopper, etc.
8. Applications to industry and agriculture
9. Scientific method and scientific attitude
10. Devices and materials in common use
11. Social implications of science

These items tend to be peculiar to the field of science and compose patterns of thinking and writing found in science materials.

Other subject-matter areas have been developed and are developing in quite different ways and therefore contain patterns of organization which contrast with the science content above. History involves concepts of time. Geography often uses a pattern of space relationships and cause-and-effect relationships. Literature may present the subtleties of human character. Teachers are particularly concerned with these very different patterns of thinking because they often affect the purpose for which the child reads and, accordingly, his method of reading.

7

Specialized Devices

Finally, every subject has special forms and devices for recording or conveying ideas. The graph on page 337 is typical of a social-

[13] Wilbur L. Beauchamp, "Promoting Growth in Reading and Studying in Science," in W. S. Gray, ed. and comp., *Recent Trends in Reading*, pp. 288-294. Supplementary Educational Monographs, No. 49. University of Chicago Press, Chicago, 1939.

EDUCATION AND THE AMERICAN WORKER

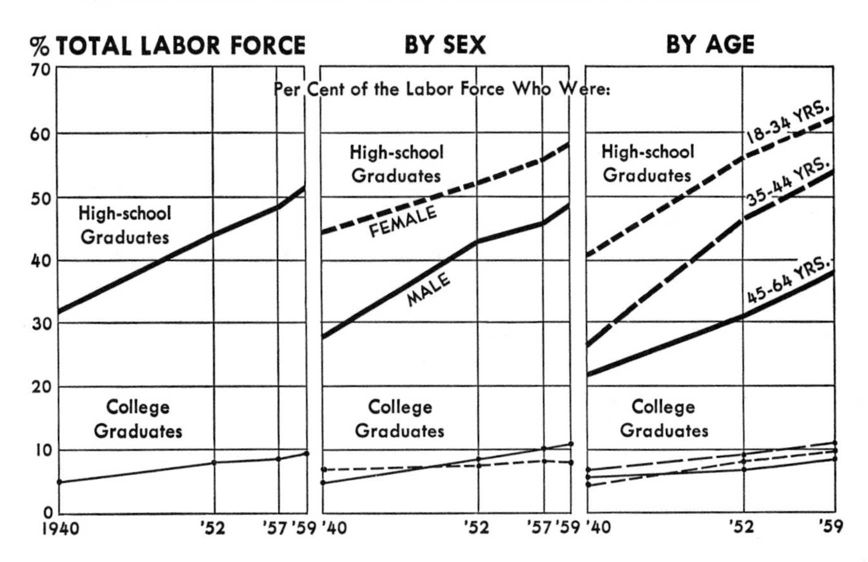

EDUCATION AND OCCUPATION

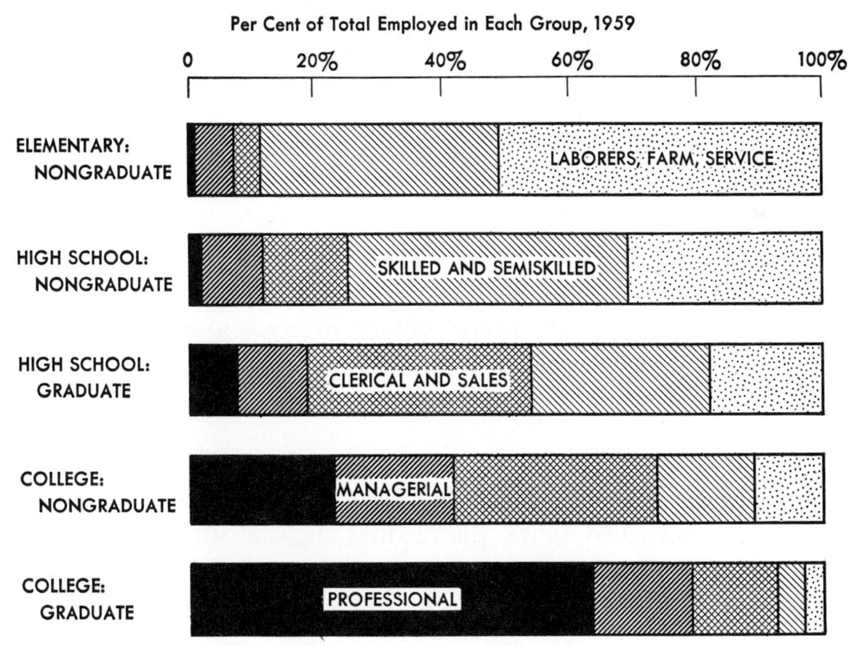

Adapted from *Road Maps of Industry,* No. 1268, by permission of the National Industrial Conference Board.

studies record of information. Children need help in reading such a graph, to get accurate facts and to make comparisons. Research indicates that pictographs and circle graphs are easier to read than bar graphs, which in turn are easier than line graphs.[14] Direct teacher guidance in interpreting a graph is needed when pupils meet a particular type of graph for the first time, and further help may be required in studying other examples of this form of information. After preliminary study, practice in constructing a particular type of graph may help a child to read more accurately the next example he meets of such a graph. Similarly, other curricular areas have specialized devices for presenting information. Arithmetical materials contain symbols such as = and %, peculiar to this area, and more difficult formulas and equations such as the one for the area of a circle ($A = \pi r^2$), which demand considerable background for the accurate reading that involves interpretation. In the modern school many curricular activities involve the use of maps, beginning perhaps with simple pictorial maps. Even more technical sources of information in special maps, such as geodetic maps or weather maps, form important reference material for reading in geography or science. Indeed, every subject-matter area involves rather specialized devices for conveying information. Some ability in reading these special devices is needed for competent reading in the second half of the elementary school.

SAMPLE SUGGESTIONS

In addition to the three general problems described above, which run through most reading in all content fields, there are special problems associated with each specific field. These are so numerous that only a few of them can be illustrated here, as guides to the teacher in studying the needs of her own class.

Social Studies

In addition to problems of vocabulary, organization, and specialized devices described above, the reading of social studies presents a wide variety of reading purposes and materials in a well-equipped school. Some purposes especially important in this area include read-

[14] C. O. Mathews, *Grade Placement of Curriculum Materials in Social Studies,* Teachers College Contributions to Education, No. 241. Bureau of Publications, Teachers College, Columbia University, New York, 1926.

ing for a sequence of events, reading to explore cause and effect relationships, ability to read maps and charts, and ability to read critically to determine an author's point of view or relevance to a topic. Michaelis[15] has suggested the wide range of materials used in a well-balanced social studies program. These include:

Textbooks in social studies, history, geography and government.

Reference materials, including almanacs, atlases, encyclopedias, and yearbooks.

Fugitive materials, such as pamphlets, bulletins, folders, and other free and inexpensive items.

Current materials, including children's and adults' newspapers and magazines and special news reviews.

Literary materials, as in fiction, folklore, biography and travel books.

Source materials, as found in original letters, logs of activities, diaries, minutes, directions, ballots and maps.

Reading charts, dealing with group plans, standards, vocabulary, questions, and directions for work.

One other way to note reading requirements in social studies and science is to analyze textbooks and reference materials, such as the 18-volume set *Our Wonderful World*[16] or a children's encyclopedia.

A number of research studies have shown the close relationships among certain reading abilities and achievement in the social studies. For example, Rudolf[17] found at the eighth-grade level that a group which was given special reading instruction over a five-month period made better test scores of social-studies information than a similar group which had no extra practice in reading but used the same total time for social studies. The instruction given included (1) comprehension, interpretation, and application of social studies materials, (2) reference work, and (3) note-taking, outlining, and summarizing. Rudolf gives a tabular list of twenty-six specific skills and activities in social studies. In another study Arnold[18] found that children in the fifth and sixth grades who had practice in the problem-

[15] John U. Michaelis, *Social Studies for Children in a Democracy,* rev. ed., Chap. 12. Prentice-Hall, Englewood Cliffs, N.J., 1956.

[16] Herbert S. Zim, ed. in chief, *Our Wonderful World,* 18 vols. Spencer Press, Chicago, 1957.

[17] Kathleen B. Rudolf, *The Effect of Reading Instruction on Achievement in 8th Grade Social Studies,* Teachers College Contributions to Education, No. 945. Bureau of Publications, Teachers College, Columbia University, New York, 1949.

[18] Dwight L. Arnold, "Testing Ability to use Data in the Fifth and Sixth Grades," *Educational Research Bulletin,* Vol. 27, pp. 255-259, December, 1938.

discussion technique improved in critical thinking abilities involving the recognition of relevance, bias in source, and adequacy of data. In a study of 380 pupils in the low ninth grade Shores[19] found that abilities needed in reading history were quite different from those needed in reading science. History required abilities in the location of information and comprehension of the general meaning of a passage more than vocabulary knowledge and an exact type of reading. Quick location of information sometimes may be achieved by accurate skimming. In a summary of research studies Seegers[20] concluded that skimming ability could be taught by definite practice. It may be of value, of course, in fields other than social studies.

In working out a program of reading instruction in the social studies a teacher may have three guides in mind:

1. Reading materials should be related to the other activities of the class. If the class is doing a unit on pioneers in this country, they should be provided with reading material on how to dip candles, how to make soap, the wild game that pioneers used, and similar topics. In addition to the regular sources of information, Bailey's *Children of the Handcrafts* or Wilder's *Little House in the Big Woods* gives a picture of different types of pioneer life. Some of Ernest Thompson Seton's books, such as *Wild Animals I Have Known,* describe the animals important to some pioneers. Brink's *Caddie Woodlawn* gives a picture of pioneer Wisconsin life in Civil War days, and Hubbard's *Vinnie Ream and Mr. Lincoln* shifts the scene to Washington about the same time. These are only samples of possible reading materials in one unit which are related to the other activities involved. In planning units in the modern school system the teacher or curriculum committee includes a complete list of reading references.

2. Reading a rich variety of materials is a partial substitute for and the best supplement to first-hand experiences. Not all children can sail on Hudson Bay or the Atlantic Ocean; not all can watch the teeming life of a great city; not all can stand on the Lincoln Memorial steps in Washington; but all children can read about these things. The meager backgrounds of some pupils demand enrichment by these reading materials. The teacher then supplements the text and the basic set of readers with as much social-studies material

[19] J. Harlan Shores, "Skills Related to the Ability to Read History and Science," *Journal of Educational Research,* Vol. 36, pp. 584-593, April, 1943.

[20] J. Conrad Seegers, "Reading for Meaning," *Elementary English Review,* Vol. 23, pp. 247-250, October, 1946.

as she and her pupils can find. The rule may be, "Provide more, and then more, material."

3. Pupils in elementary and secondary schools need special help in reading social-studies materials. Most teachers realize now that an intermediate or senior pupil does not possess a general skill of reading; actually he possesses a number of different skills, and as he reaches higher grades he needs more and more of these specialized skills. Some of the special types of reading in the social studies which require specific guidance by the teacher are these:

a. Ability to locate information—in reference books and other social-studies sources
b. Ability to read several kinds of maps
c. Ability to select the main topic and supporting details of a selection
d. Ability to take notes from one's reading
e. Ability to summarize
f. Ability to see connections between a series of related events
g. Ability to discriminate between relevant and irrelevant material
h. Ability to recognize the difference between facts and opinion
i. Ability to help plan a report to a larger group

4. Pupils of the intermediate and senior grades need guidance in reading newspapers and magazines. Many social-studies problems are essentially modern ones, and the best textbooks lag several years behind current happenings. Vital work in the social studies, therefore, can be ensured only by use of current newspapers and magazines. For the primary and intermediate grades, travel and geographic magazines are probably the best sources for pictures of other, simpler civilizations, such as the Eskimos, African tribes, or American Indians. In the senior grades the teacher makes more direct use of current publications.

In regard to newspapers many pupils need to be helped in developing the idea that an item is not necessarily correct just because it is in print. The sacredness of print is a tradition not easily broken down in communities where printed materials are rare. One way of developing a critical attitude is by analyzing extravagant claims of advertisements or by comparing advertisements of similar products, each claiming to be the best of its kind. From advertising, a transition may be made to newspaper accounts of speeches given by persons with an obvious bias, such as those of opposed political parties.[21]

[21] Edgar Dale, *How to Read a Newspaper*. Scott, Foresman, Chicago, 1941. Geraldine Saltzberg, *Knowing Your Newspaper*. World Book, Yonkers, N.Y., 1953.

The next stage might be an examination of conflicting news stories in different newspapers or from different sources regarding the same event. Developing habits of critical reading is an important aim of the social studies. This topic is discussed more fully in Chapter 14. The suggestions above must be regarded as only a few examples of possible reading activities in the social studies. A more detailed discussion of possibilities is given by Horn,[22] by Michaelis,[23] by Tiegs and Adams,[24] and by Wesley and Adams.[25]

Mathematics

Reading arithmetical and other mathematical materials involves perception, understanding, and use of mathematical symbols and verbal problems. It may include knowledge of $\div$ and π, the ability to read explanations and directions, and the ability to analyze such verbal statements as, "If a store buys ball-point pens at $3 a dozen and sells them at 39¢ a piece, what is its profit on each pen?" Reading may also relate to the understanding of our number system and to the appreciation of the role of mathematics in man's development such as given in Bendick's *How Much and How Many,*[26] or in *The Wonderful World of Mathematics.*[27] Similarly, it may involve reading such materials as found in the reference set, *Our Wonderful World,*[28] which combines mathematics, science, and social-studies materials. Accordingly, the reading of mathematics usually involves detailed, exact comprehension, but it may also develop attitudes of interest and appreciation.

A summary of some forty references[29] indicates that the role of reading in arithmetic achievement has been studied by research methods. The close relationships between certain kinds of reading abilities and arithmetic scores suggest that the teacher can help many children to higher arithmetical achievement by helping them be-

22 Ernest Horn, *Methods of Instruction in the Social Studies.* American Historical Association, Committee on the Social Studies, Vol. 15. Scribner, New York, 1937.

23 John U. Michaelis, *op. cit.,* Chap. 12.

24 Ernest W. Tiegs and Fay Adams, *Teaching Social Studies A Guide to Better Citizenship,* Chap. 13. Ginn, Boston, 1959.

25 Edgar B. Wesley and Mary Adams, *Teaching Social Studies in Elementary Schools,* rev. ed., Chaps. 17, 19. Heath, Boston, 1952.

26 Jeanne Bendick, *How Much and How Many?* Whittlesey House, New York, 1947.

27 Lancelot Hogben, *The Wonderful World of Mathematics.* Garden City, New York, 1955.

28 Herbert S. Zim, *op. cit.*

29 David H. Russell, "Arithmetic Power Through Reading," *Instruction in Arithmetic,* Twenty-fifth Yearbook, Chap. 9, National Council of Teachers of Mathematics, Washington, D.C., 1960.

come more accurate and analytical readers. The research on reading mathematical symbols is meager. The Wheelers[30] discovered some of the difficulties of first- and second-graders in learning to read numbers and found certain games and devices of value in developing accurate perceptions. In 1925 Lessenger[31] stated that "the desirability of specific training in the reading of signs which show the operation—is clearly indicated."

Research on the role of reading in solving verbal problems has been more detailed. As early as 1918 Monroe[32] demonstrated that the same problem, involving identical quantitative relationships, could be put in words in twenty-eight different ways. Obviously, reading skill is demanded in working with such varied presentations. Later studies showed that the solving of verbal problems is not close to general reading ability as usually tested but correlates highly with certain specific reading abilities. For example, Treacy[33] found that good and poor achievers in solving verbal problems differed significantly on a test of "Retention of Clearly Stated Details." Equally or more useful in distinguishing between the two groups were four tests of arithmetical vocabulary and three of association of related elements, as in seeing relationships or drawing inferences from content. He believed that in arithmetic, reading "should be regarded as a composite of specific skills rather than as a generalized ability."[34] In another study Hansen[35] established that solving verbal problems in sixth-grade arithmetic depended partly upon the ability to read graphs, charts, and tables. From these and similar studies the teacher can derive certain suggestions for improving work-type reading. For example, the teacher might jot down in her plan book such reading needs as the following in arithmetic:

The ability to note details
The ability to know what is given in a problem

[30] Lester R. Wheeler and Viola D. Wheeler, "Experimental Study in Learning to Read Numerals," *Mathematics Teacher,* Vol. 33, pp. 25-31, January, 1940.

[31] W. E. Lessenger, "Reading Difficulties in Arithmetic Computation," *Journal of Educational Research,* Vol. 11, pp. 287-291, April, 1925.

[32] Walter S. Monroe, "The Derivation of Reasoning Tests in Arithmetic," *School and Society,* Vol. 8, pp. 295-299, 324-329, September 7, 14, 1918.

[33] John P. Treacy, "Relationship of Reading Skills to Ability to Solve Arithmetic Problems," *Journal of Educational Research,* Vol. 38, pp. 86-96, October, 1944.

[34] *Ibid.,* p. 92.

[35] Carl W. Hansen, "Factors Associated with Successful Achievement in Problem Solving in Sixth-Grade Arithmetic," *Journal of Educational Research,* Vol. 38, pp. 111-118, October, 1944.

The ability to know what is required in a problem
The ability to plan a solution
The ability to check the reasonableness of an answer
Increasing knowledge of arithmetical concepts

Having determined the needs of her pupils in each of these factors in reading mathematics, she can devise practice exercises which will contribute to these skills. The busy teacher may feel that she has little time to make up and hectograph such exercises. The only answer to such a doubt is to consider whether or not the other activities of the classroom are as worth while. Help in devising such exercises may be obtained in the books on reading, the workbooks, and the manuals mentioned above. A few sample exercises (which should be increased to six or eight for any one lesson) based on the aims stated above are given in the two sections below.

The summary of some forty researches mentioned above[36] concludes with the following suggestions for the teacher's work in improving the reading of verbal problems:

"(1) Help children to use the first reading to visualize the problem-situation as a whole.

(2) Direct attention to the question usually stated near the end of the whole problem.

(3) Have pupils reread the problem to analyze it into a series of steps necessary for a solution.

(4) Give practice in estimating reasonable answers after a second or third reading.

(5) Have pupils select the first process and write their first statement only after two or more readings of the problem.

(6) Give help in spotting irrelevant sentences.

(7) Give specific help in building understanding of quantitative terms like *numerator* and *acre* and of processes such as obtaining a *batting average* or calculating a *percentage profit*. Vocabulary games may help.

(8) Without giving numbers, have children state how they would solve problems such as, "Tom is a boy who got three separate birthday gifts of money. He wants to know if he has enough money to buy a basketball. What should he do?"

(9) Have children rewrite problems in simpler terms and try out on other members of their group.

(10) Have pupils list some of the purposes for which they read (main idea, details, directions, fun, etc.) and decide which are most useful in solving verbal problems.

(11) Encourage the reading of stories involving quantitative situations such as *Five Puppies for Sale, The Five Chinese Brothers* and *Millions of*

[36] David H. Russell, *op. cit.*, p. 219.

Cats in the primary grades. Such books as Bendick's *How Much and How Many* may challenge fifth and sixth graders and science fiction may appeal around the seventh to ninth grade levels.

(12) Have children bring stories clipped from magazines and newspapers which involve mathematical data. These may involve the flying log of a prominent world traveller or the calculation of the speed and orbit of an artificial earth satellite. Here the procedure is understanding plus criticism plus use where possible."[37]

Reading Science Materials

The teaching of science in the elementary school, largely unknown a half-century ago and stimulated especially by world events in the 1950's, has assumed an increasing importance in the curriculum.[38] Such expansion has brought many new demands for reading scientific materials not only in textbooks but in a wide range of trade books and articles on specific scientific topics. *The First Book* series (Watts) and the *All about Series* (Random House), for example, contain such titles as *The First Book of Stones, All About the Atom* and *All about the Arctic and Antarctic.* The illustration below shows a typical page from a third-grade science textbook, a page demanding the ability to understand terms like *pumice, sponge,* and *float* and to interpret the fact that even some rocks float.

These and other science materials are often compactly written with a high concept load and are, therefore, a contrast to basal reader materials of the first two grades which are usually story materials enlivened by characterization, conversation, description, and action. Children must, therefore, learn some new reading techniques as they begin to read more science materials in the third and fourth grades and as they use the wide variety of scientific reference materials available at later grade levels.

A number of research studies have shown that, in reading science materials, children need both a strong foundation in basic reading habits and skills plus special abilities and patterns related to reading purposes in science. At the eighth-grade level Swenson[39] found con-

[37] *Instruction in Arithmetic,* Twenty-fifth Yearbook, Chap. 13, National Council of Teachers of Mathematics, Washington, D.C., 1960. By permission of National Council of Teachers of Mathematics.

[38] Gerald S. Craig, "Elementary School Science in the Past Century," *Science Teacher,* Vol. 24, pp. 11-14, 37, February, 1957.

[39] Esther J. Swenson, "A Study of the Relationships among Various Types of Reading Scores on General and Science Materials," *Journal of Educational Research,* Vol. 36, pp. 81-90, October, 1942.

Air Makes Things Float

There is enough air in some rocks to make them float. The air in a piece of pumice will make it float.

A sponge has air in it. Put a sponge in a dish of water. Will it float? How long?

As long as air fills the spaces in a sponge, it will float. As some of the air comes out and the water goes into the spaces, the sponge sinks lower in the water. Will the sponge sink to the bottom of the dish? Can you tell why?

Place a balloon in a dish of water as the boy in the picture is doing. Does the balloon float?

Now blow up the balloon and close the opening. Then put the blown-up balloon in the water again. Will it float? Tell why.

The air which is in some things makes them float.

Page from *Science Everywhere*
(Gerald S. Craig and Marguerite W. Lembach, p. 91. Ginn, Boston, 1958)

siderable overlap in abilities to read general and science materials and verified earlier statements that speed is not an important factor in reading science materials. Instead, pupils should be encouraged to do exact, detailed reading of most scientific matter. Similarly, Shores[40] demonstrated that ability in reading science was related to general power of reading comprehension, to vocabulary knowledge, and to a type of exact reading but not to ability to locate information or to comprehend the general meaning of a passage. In a later study Shores and Saupe[41] found that a "Test of Reading for Problem Solving in Science" gave results different from a measure of general reading ability and concluded that the test involved specific abilities to read different kinds of materials for different purposes. In a related study, Fay[42] used tests of skills in (1) reading to predict outcomes of given events, (2) reading to understand precise directions, (3) general reading comprehension, (4) reading of maps, graphs, charts, and tables, and (5) use of index, reference, and dictionary. He found that the second and third of these abilities were positively related to achievement in science but that the other three were not. The first, second, and fourth abilities, in contrast, were positively related to achievement in the social studies at the sixth-grade level.

Such studies indicate that the task of the teacher, especially in the intermediate and upper grades, is to develop pupils as strong as possible in fundamental reading abilities but also to give them practice in specific types of reading relating to purposes and scientific materials. Some of these unique abilities have been described by Beauchamp (see page 336) and others, and some appear frequently as a class works with a variety of materials in science on day-by-day projects. Such daily activities may include study of new science words such as *telemetering* or *Mach 3* but must go beyond word study to longer bodies of organized information as in a chapter or a newspaper story of a current discovery.

Many teachers and scientists would maintain that science activities in the elementary school should stress appreciation of science and understanding of the scientific method, even at some sacrifice of factual content. Accordingly, science books must be read, not as

40 J. Harlan Shores, *op. cit.*

41 J. Harlan Shores and J. L. Saupe, "Reading for Problem Solving in Science," *Journal of Educational Psychology*, Vol. 44, pp. 149-159, March, 1953.

42 Leo C. Fay, "The Relationship between Specific Reading Skills and Selected Areas of Sixth Grade Achievement," *Journal of Educational Research*, Vol. 43, pp. 541-547, March, 1950.

accumulations of facts and principles, but as examples of the scientific method of solving problems. Pupils should be asked not to absorb a mass of scientific facts so much as to understand the scientific method and its applications to many personal problems. Louis Agassiz, the famous scientist and teacher, who began the American half of his work about the middle of the nineteenth century, once remarked of the texts of his day, "If you study nature in books, when you go outdoors you cannot find her." Although the books have greatly improved, especially for the young, teachers must help many children to go beyond the facts of the book to understand the methods of science. Sharpe[43] illustrated this point about the scientific method by showing that it should not be memorized in five or six steps but that its meaning should gradually be built over the years by reading and by direct experiences. He described three stages in understanding the scientific method as follows:

1. *State problems clearly*

(Look for information so we can get an answer. This stage, identified by Aristotle and Bacon, involves problems of direct observation such as in answering "How many legs has a spider?" and "How do weeds scatter their seeds?" This approach seems reasonable to us, but Galileo was denounced by men who refused to look through his telescope.)

2. *Guess and Test*

(This stage includes the first step of isolating the problem and looking for data, but goes beyond it to forming and testing a hypothesis. It was used by Galileo and other early scientists. It may be applied by children's combining books and direct observation to answer questions such as "Does handling toads cause warts?" and "What is the matter with my swimming?")

3. *The Above, Plus Verifying, Experimenting and Predicting*

(This stage, perhaps first fully used by Newton, may be involved in such questions as "Is air matter?" and "Why are most plants green?" which may include not only questions but experimentation and prediction beyond a limited number of cases.)

This outline suggests that books are only one aid in the process of building understanding of the scientific method. They are not merely records of facts and generalizations but, properly written and used, may contribute to scientific thinking abilities.

[43] Philip B. Sharpe, "Elementary Science Teaching," *School Science and Mathematics*, Vol. 38, pp. 120-125, February, 1938.

Finally, the process of reading science materials today is nearly as broad as the reading process itself. Such lists as *Growing Up with Science Books*[44] and other bibliographies[45] illustrate the wide variety of science materials available today, even to young children. Reading such books may range from casual inspection for recreational purposes, through attentive reading to get some main ideas and supporting facts, to detailed reading of highly technical material for intricate experimentation or creative prediction. As stated above, the value of most of this reading will be enhanced as it accompanies other direct experience. Children need help in reading inductively to discover for themselves, not just to borrow facts or principles secondhand. As Blough[46] put it, "It is important to get into the book when we need it and get out of it when we don't." Teachers can help children in this way not only to acquire scientific knowledge but also to use reading to help solve science problems which challenge them.

SAMPLE PRACTICE EXERCISES

Because the previous sections emphasize the importance of reading as a regular part of other curricular activities it may be justifiable to add a few specific suggestions for practice in various kinds of work-type reading. Three dangers found in some current reading programs, especially in the post-primary grades, are: (1) they are restricted to a limited set of reading materials; (2) they emphasize isolated drill on stereotyped reading activities such as selecting main ideas, finding details, or giving outcomes; or (3) they use oral reading to promote comprehension on the assumption that following someone else's reading adds to one's understanding. Despite these dangers, the research on diagnostic and remedial work and the experience of capable teachers suggest that specific practice focussed on concrete and particular skills may help many children achieve more in their reading. A few samples of such practice exercises are given below.

44 Library Journal, *Growing Up with Science Books.* Distributed by R. R. Bowker, New York, no date.

45 Paul E. Kambly, "The Elementary School Science Library for 1958," *School Science and Mathematics,* Vol. 59, pp. 294-303, April, 1959.

46 Glenn O. Blough, "Using Books in an Active Elementary Science Program," Wesleyan University Department of School Services and Publications Curriculum Letter, No. 12, January, 1955.

Reading to Note Details

Read the following paragraph as quickly as you can; but read it carefully, so you may be able to answer questions on all parts of it:

There were over three hundred excited people at the meeting that night. The question of what kind of school the town should have and when it should be built had been talked over many times since the old school burned down. When a motion was made that a five-roomed brick school costing $82,000 be built, over two hundred and twenty people voted for it. The question of the location of the school was not so easily settled, and finally this problem was left to a committee of five members, three to be appointed by the meeting and two by the school board.

Now underline the correct word at the first of each statement.

True False 1. More than half the people at the meeting voted for a new brick school.
True False 2. The commitee to determine the location of the new school had two members.
True False 3. The old school had blown down.
True False 4. There were just three hundred people at the meeting.
True False 5. The people at the meeting were excited.

Reading to See the Parts of a Problem

1. John bought a book for 45¢ and two exercise books at 10¢ each. How much money must he pay the storekeeper?

( ) *A.* Which of the following facts are you asked to find out?
1. The number of books John bought
2. How much money John had
3. How much they cost him altogether
4. The change John should receive

( ) *B.* Which of the following facts is given?
1. The price of each book
2. How much money John had
3. The kind of exercise books he bought
4. How much he gave the storekeeper

( ) *C.* Which of the following is the most reasonable answer?
1. $1.25 2. 60¢ 3. 40¢ 4. $4.00

The following are some possible objectives in reading scientific material which a teacher might record in her plan book as a guide to future lessons. The objectives she will stress will depend, of course, on the specific needs of her pupils.

1. The ability to note details
2. The ability to increase one's vocabulary (develop concepts)

3. The ability to recognize the steps in an experiment
4. The ability to see cause-and-effect relationships

Examples of an exercise in noting details, much like the one suggested above, may also be used in science. Sample exercises for each of the other three needs are given below.

Reading to Increase One's Vocabulary

Read the following paragraph carefully enough so that you can answer questions about the words in it:

In Sweden most of the forests consist of conifers, or cone-bearing trees, such as spruce and pine. These furnish the raw material for ordinary sawed timber, as well as for cellulose and paper. A steadily increasing quantity of cellulose is being used for making artificial silk, and it is used also in other manufacturing processes. The smaller numbers of hardwood trees, such as the birch and beech, form the basis for a large furniture industry. The forests also yield a supply of fuel, used partly for household purposes and partly for the charcoal needed in manufacturing iron and steel.

1. *Fill the blanks in the following:*

a. Trees such as spruce and pine are called ____.

b. Artificial silk is made from a part of wood called ____.

c. Trees such as birch and beech are called ____.

2. *Underline the best one of the three answers:*

a. Furniture in Sweden is made from (spruce, cellulose, hardwood).

b. The manufacture of iron and steel requires (conifers, charcoal, cellulose).

c. Swedish households use wood as (fuel, forest, industry).

Reading to Recognize the Steps of an Experiment

Benjamin Franklin wanted to know more about lightning; so he planned an experiment. He fastened a key to the end of a very long kite string and flew the kite during a storm of thunder and lightning. When the storm was raging, he held his knuckle near the key, and an electric spark flashed from the key to his knuckle. This proved to Franklin that lightning is caused by electric charges. As a result of this experiment Franklin invented lightning rods to protect homes and farm buildings by carrying the electricity to the ground from the clouds as his kite had done.

Answer these questions on the experiment described above.

1. What was the problem of the experiment?
2. What did Franklin observe?
3. What did he prove?
4. Why do lightning rods protect buildings?

Reading to See Cause-and-Effect Relationships

Below you are given a fact, followed by a number of statements. If a statement is a *cause* of the fact, write C beside it; if it is a *result* of the fact, write R beside it; if it is not related to the fact, write N beside it.

C: Cause R: Result N: Not Related

FACT: *Light rays ordinarily do not shine around an object*

1. The shadow of a tree falls on the ground. 1. ____
2. The street light does not shine in the window when we draw the dark shade. 2. ____
3. The reading glass enables us to read fine print. 3. ____
4. Light travels in straight lines. 4. ____
5. A cloudy day is a dark day. 5. ____
6. A recent eclipse of the moon lasted over an hour. 6. ____
7. A plant must grow in the presence of light rays if it is to have green leaves. 7. ____

The foregoing exercises are only a few samples of the type of practice that can be given in reading mathematical and scientific materials. Exercises similar to these may be hectographed and given to pupils, six or eight exercises to a lesson. Similarly, a teacher may record the reading needs of her pupils in social studies or other areas, and plan to give them definite practice on those needs. The ability to read intelligently in the various school subjects, using the different types of reading that different subjects demand, can be achieved only by wide reading and by directed practice. Such practice will make pupils more efficient in the necessary skills of reading and study.

USING THE TOOLS

As noted in the introduction to this chapter, work-type reading may be considered not only in terms of purposes and of content fields, but also in relation to the tools employed. What are some of the things to be learned about using textbooks, reference materials and libraries, if one is to achieve growing independence in using reading to aid a variety of functional activities? The mechanical aids available within books and in any school building or public library vary widely from book to book and from school to school, and most of these ways of utilizing reading can be mastered only through actual practice and use. There is little point, for example, in teaching the devices of a library card catalogue to a pupil who lives twenty miles from such a catalogue and never sees one. The library catalogue, like the other aids mentioned here, is best mastered not for some hypothetical future date but in daily use. As Leary[47] has suggested, study aids come into use when children ask questions like the following. A first-grader says, "We are getting an incubator in our room. Can you help us find books about raising chickens?" Or a class studying the Western Movement asks, "Where can we find some folk songs and cowboy songs as we wrap up in blankets beside the fire along a trail?" Or a sixth-grader inquires, "Our parents are worried about crime pictures on television. Where can we find out how many there are and if they influence children?" The better the whole school program, the more the requests for help in finding sources of material that come to teacher and librarian.

The variety of materials in a well-stocked school precludes a complete discussion of the use of each type of resource. The following list contains a *sample* only of possible materials and activities.

1. *Charts.* Charts are desirably the child's first contact with work-type reading. Although stories in readers and trade books have advantages of ease and action in maintaining interest, charts may have an immediacy and concreteness in relation to the activities of the week. Some different kinds of charts for the primary grades are:

Experience chart based on first-hand experiences such as a pet in the classroom, a trip or construction.

Standards chart with rules for work periods, discussions, reports, and committee work.

Directions chart with specific guides for making and doing.

Vocabulary chart with new and useful words recorded for reference or further practice.

Creative expression chart to record stories, poems, or songs that have been devised by members of the group.

In addition to these charts used in the primary grades many intermediate-grade pupils will profit from use of the following:

Information chart, which may simplify some complex material from text or other reference so it is readily available for retarded readers as well as average or superior readers.

Sequence chart, which gives clear steps in a process or a record of events; especially useful in relation to social studies as in time-lines, calendars of events, logs, and records of progress.

47 Bernice E. Leary, "Nature of Materials Needed to Facilitate Progress," in W. S. Gray, ed., *Improving Reading in All Curriculum Areas,* Supplementary Educational Monographs, No. 76, pp. 22-26. University of Chicago Press, Chicago, 1952.

Organization chart used in two senses—as organization of work in committees, etc. (also used in primary grades), and as organization of ideas into main headings, sub-headings, and related details. Useful as a summary of several days' work and as an aid to development of ability to organize complex materials for reports, booklets, and other pupil writing.

Several of these eight types of chart lead rather directly to textbook materials.

2. *Textbooks.* The easiest textbooks in the primary grades can give a good start in using a table of contents, predicting from titles, and getting information from pictures. By the third and fourth grades, and in later years, most of the following aids to work-type reading can be put to work:

Glossary—as an introduction to more detailed dictionary work.

Index—including how to find a topic and how to use cross references.

Maps, graphs, and *diagrams*—as more detailed sources of information than pictures.

Headings and typographical aids—such as titles and sub-titles, guide words, and italic and bold-face type.

Such aids can be used in a first quick survey of material to determine its relevance to the topic in hand. This will involve a critical reading of title, examining pictures and other graphic materials, noting headings and sub-headings, and reading an introductory paragraph and a summary, if available. Such a survey will help determine whether the passage is to be ignored, skimmed, read at a moderate rate, or studied in detail.

3. *Trade books.* Trade books as distinguished from textbooks are usually aimed at a more general audience and may deal with only one topic, elaborated in considerable detail, or in the case of fiction, with one long plot rather than the short selections of a reader. Authentic fiction, of course, may contain many facts about persons and places far away in time or location. Not all trade books, however, need be read as a whole; some of the modern books dealing with topics in science, for example, are almost reference books. Trade books differ so widely that it is difficult to give many suggestions for their use. The following ideas often apply:

Trade books may be used for recreation or for many specific

purposes. Accordingly, they must be approached as problems to be attacked individually, with some juvenile books used for their illustrations, some for their facts, some for enrichment of ideas stated in summary form in a textbook.

Encourage membership in a public library.

Teach library aids, as suggested below, and especially the use of topics in the card catalog.

In terms of topic and difficulty, provide a wide range of books in the classroom and in the school library. Use the "unfinished story" technique to encourage independent reading.

In the intermediate and upper grades help children get acquainted with the "types" of literature available in short stories, novels, plays, poetry, biography, and essay and develop a few ways of approaching these different kinds of material.

In the upper grades pupils can benefit from the author's guides within a passage, as, for example, the topic sentence, or the use of connecting words and phrases such as *the next, still another, let us now turn to, however, while, accordingly,* and *in conclusion.*[48]

4. *Reference Materials.* Today's reference materials include dictionaries, encyclopedias, almanacs, yearbooks, atlases, bibliographies and government bulletins. As in the case of trade books, the range is wide. Dictionaries are described briefly in Chapter 9 and the following sample suggestions will be limited to encyclopedias. Some simple one-volume "encyclopedias" such as *The Golden Encyclopedia*[49] may help develop readiness for the more complete reference materials. The three comprehensive sets usually recommended for the intermediate- and the junior-high-school grades are *Britannica Junior Encyclopedia, Compton's Pictured Encyclopedia,* and *World Book Encyclopedia* which follow the alphabetical arrangement typical of adult sets. Organized topically rather than alphabetically, but with complete indexes, are the *Book of Knowledge* and *Our Wonderful World.* An article[50] prepared by the staff of the *Library Journal* gives some of the advantages and disadvantages of the various sets and arrangements. Studies by Edgerton[51] suggest that most of the

48 Phillip Shaw, "Rhetorical Guides to Reading Comprehension," *The Reading Teacher,* Vol. 11, pp. 239-243, April, 1958.

49 Dorothy A. Bennett, *The Golden Encyclopedia.* Simon and Schuster, New York, 1946.

50 "Recommended Reference Sets for Home Libraries," *Junior Libraries,* Vol. 4, pp. 9-12, April, 1958.

51 Ronald B. Edgerton, "How Difficult Are Children's Encyclopedias? A Second Report," *Elementary School Journal,* Vol. 55, pp. 219-225, December, 1954.

articles in the junior encyclopedias, with their high concept loads, are at least of eighth-grade level of difficulty and are therefore hard for a typical elementary school pupil unless he is highly motivated toward the reading of the particular article. The publishers of a newer, smaller encyclopedia in eight volumes, *The Golden Book Encyclopedia,*[52] claim a reading level suitable for grades three to six. Many companies publishing encyclopedias produce material to show how their books may be used profitably.[53] The bulletins may include suggestions on using reference features such as index and bibliographies and how to incorporate materials into the classwork in science, social studies and the language arts. Some of the specific skills required for using an encyclopedia successfully are:

Locating and using alphabetically arranged information.
Using guide words.
Using the index, including cross references.
Locating information from several different topics.
Selecting needed information from a comprehensive article.
Learning to outline.
Interpreting map legends, symbols and scale of miles.

Other needs arise in the use of an encyclopedia in terms of the demands of a particular project.

5. *Library.* Most reference books are found in libraries, and the use of encyclopedias and other reference volumes may be taught as part of regularly scheduled library periods. In the elementary school, the use of a small classroom library may be an introduction to the wider range of a school library, and a school library, in turn, may help establish readiness for use of a public library. First learnings include (1) the general location of materials, (2) rules for checking out books, and (3) the use of the card catalogue.

Some of the specific guides that children may find useful, in addition to the dictionaries, encyclopedias, and card catalogue mentioned above, are: city directories, *World Almanac, Information Please Almanac, Junior Book of Authors, Readers' Guide to Periodical Literature,* Rue's *Subject Index to Books for Primary Grades* (and

[52] Bertha N. Parker, ed., *The Golden Book Encyclopedia,* 8 vols. Golden Press, Educational Division, New York, 1959.

[53] For example, *Compton's At Work in the Classroom.* F. E. Compton, Chicago, 1956.

supplement) and *Subject Index to Books for Intermediate Grades,* publishers' catalogues, and booklists, such as *Children's Catalog, Adventuring with Books,* and *Bibliography of Books for Children.* (See also Chapter 13). The use of such books should be taught as they are available and as children find clear needs for consulting them. Chapter 13 contains more examples of using libraries in connection with the enjoyment of children's literature. Especially in the social studies and in science, using the library may also mean locating and utilizing film strips, pictures, models, and recordings.

6. *Current Materials.* As suggested in Chapter 1, millions of adult Americans depend upon newspapers and magazines as almost their sole source of contact with printed ideas. Although such reading is common, more detailed study of the kinds of popular magazines and of the most frequently read parts of newspapers gives cause for concern. In one study the only part of the newspaper read by more than half the people was the comic-strip section. The "pulps" outsell the "slicks," and stories about war, disaster, human mishaps, and weather are widely read, in contrast to serious and challenging topics such as government, international relations, education, and religion. If governmental discussions and actions are to rely on an informed public, children must begin early to develop interest in the significant issues of the day. Reading about current events and problems can have a vitality that fiction or history may not have for many pupils.

Because young children are not ready for the typical adult newspaper, teachers may have them subscribe to magazines or newspapers written for the young, such as *My Weekly Reader, Current Events, Current Science and Aviation,* and *Read Magazine* (all published by American Education Publications, Columbus 16, Ohio), and *Explorer, Newstime,* and *Junior Scholastic* (all published by Scholastic Magazines, 334 W. 42nd St., New York 36, N.Y.) The teachers' guides that accompany these materials give many ideas for using the materials to develop vocabulary, to improve comprehension, and for working on problems in social studies and science. A number of the suggestions help teacher and pupil go below the surface to see some of the deeper meanings in current news.

Work with the newspapers prepared for school use helps create readiness for using the daily newspaper, the news magazines, *Time, Newsweek,* or *U.S. News and World Report,* and other periodicals. As suggested in Chapter 1, the mass magazines, including women's magazines, often run articles which are provocative and timely, especially for teen agers. Similarly, the daily newspaper records events important to children and to all citizens, sometimes local, sometimes national, sometimes international. Many of Dale's suggestions on *How to Read a Newspaper*[54] are still good ones, and superior readers in junior high school will be helped to read critically by employing Saltzberg's[55] suggestions. Children need help in scanning headlines, relating headlines to the stories they introduce, picking out the main points in a journalistic account, reading with an awareness of the newspaper's or writer's point of view, and putting one day's isolated news story into a context of previous and subsequent happenings. Some newspapers, perhaps in Sunday editions, and some columnists present interpretations of the news which attempt a larger context, and the news magazines regularly run "feature stories" or "cover stories" which may encompass considerable time or scientific progress or one person's life-time. These longer stories must be read with some attempt to outline main and subordinate ideas if they are being used in any detail. Some of the skills in critical reading, as discussed in Chapter 14, are best developed with newspaper and news magazine materials.

SUMMARY AND IMPLICATIONS FOR THE TEACHER

1. Children learn to read so that they can translate purpose into action. Reading is a tool whereby all sorts of printed materials are made available in solving problems in the curriculum fields and in out-of-school activities. Early in their school careers boys and girls transfer from developmental procedures under direct teacher guidance to functional and recreational reading of personal and social value.

2. In the primary grades reading does not vary greatly in different situations, but from the third or fourth grade upward it must be considered as a complex process composed of a number of very different activities. There is probably no such thing as a single reading ability, but there are different reading abilities which apply to different situations.

3. In learning to read in a number of different ways, teachers and

[54] Edgar Dale, *op. cit.*
[55] Geraldine Saltzberg, *op. cit.*

children can be guided best by the purposes for which the reading is being done. Reading to find one or two specific facts is quite different from reading to discover an all-over sequence of events. In all reading, then, the purpose must be clear to the pupils. For example, "Group I, read pages 34 to 42" is not an efficient beginning of reading activities.

4. Purposes for reading develop best out of the school, home, and community activities of boys and girls. When they meet problems in schoolwork, hobbies, or group activities that can be solved, or partly solved, by reading and know how to begin the solution through reading, the stage is set for an excellent work-type reading or study situation.

5. Since most boys and girls do not develop these abilities automatically, in readiness activities and as the need arises the teacher guides them in adjusting their method and rate of reading to the problem in hand. Probably more children need practice in adjusting their reading than in simply speeding it up.

6. In addition to basic reading abilities of recognition and comprehension practiced in the developmental reading program there are certain abilities which are a part of all work-type reading. These may be named in different ways and are mentioned here as follows: skill in locating information; ability to select and evaluate information; ability to adjust the method and rate of reading to one's purpose and the nature of the material; ability to comprehend and organize what is read; skill in using information; and ability to remember what is read. Such abilities and skills are best developed in a rich curricular program, where a child has many uses for reading. In addition, many books, workbooks, and manuals give sample exercises as specific practice material for developing these abilities.

7. No child has been taught to read effectively until he can read in the various content fields, such as health, arithmetic, and social studies. In all content fields there are certain common reading problems, such as a technical vocabulary, a unique type of organization or pattern of thought, and specialized devices such as maps or barometric pressures for conveying ideas. In addition, each content field presents some specific reading problems of its own.

8. The specific reading problems that a particular group or class has in one of the content fields will vary with the maturity of the group, the reading achievements of the group, and the nature of the reading materials and curriculum in that content field. Thus it is

impossible to say what reading problems a particular fifth grade will have in science or a certain group within a sixth grade will have in geography. The teacher has the vital task of studying her pupils' reading needs in a certain field and planning some specific helps, such as the samples given above.

9. Because different content areas have problems peculiar to each area, the elementary teacher may do some teaching of reading in a science period, and a junior-high-school teacher of mathematics, for example, has some responsibility for teaching pupils the special reading techniques required in arithmetic or other mathematics. The English teacher may be concerned with basic reading skills, but the teacher of any one subject, such as history or physics, is responsible for developing particular skills needed in reading in these areas.

10. In addition to the teacher's responsibility in planning to meet the work-type needs of her class, the principal and the school system have a responsibility for over-all planning. The best teacher in the fourth grade or the seventh grade or the tenth grade cannot guide pupils to complete mastery of work-type or study skills. Rather, the program must be conceived as a developmental one stretching at least from the first to the twelfth grade. At any one level in elementary or secondary school the teacher will work with pupils where they are, help them to achieve better study skills and habits, and attempt to solve their reading problems by direct attack on the materials with which the children are working anyway, in and out of school.

SUPPLEMENTARY READINGS

Broom, M. E., and others. *Effective Reading Instruction,* rev. ed., Chap. 9. McGraw-Hill, New York, 1951.

Burton, William H. "The Development of Independence in Study," *The Guidance of Learning Activities,* Chap. 12. Appleton-Century, New York, 1944.

Cole, Luella. "Comprehension, Especially in the Social Sciences," *The Elementary School Subjects,* Chap. 3. Rinehart, New York, 1946.

Dale, Edgar. *How to Read a Newspaper*. Scott, Foresman, Chicago, 1941.

Edgerton, Ronald B. "How Difficult are Children's Encyclopedias? A Second Report," *Elementary School Journal,* Vol. 55, pp. 219-225, December, 1954.

Frederick, Robert W. *How to Study Handbook*. Appleton-Century, New York, 1938.

Gates, Arthur I. *The Improvement of Reading,* 3rd ed., Chaps. 11-15. Macmillan, New York, 1947.

Gray, William S., comp. and ed. *Improving Reading In All Curriculum Areas.* Supplementary Educational Monographs, No. 76. University of Chicago Press, Chicago, 1952.

GRAY, WILLIAM S. "Reading Readiness in Content Subjects," *Elementary School Journal,* Vol. 42 pp. 645-646, May, 1942.

HARRIS, ALBERT J. *How to Increase Reading Ability,* rev. ed., Chaps. 15, 16. Longmans, Green, New York, 1956.

HUTCHESON, RUTH, and others. "The Elementary School Mathematics Library," *The Arithmetic Teacher,* Vol. 3, pp. 8-15, February, 1956.

KNAPP, J. V. "Improving Reading Skills in Content Areas," *Elementary English,* Vol. 24, pp. 542-550, December, 1947.

LAYCOCK, SAMUEL R., and RUSSELL, DAVID H. "An Analysis of Thirty-eight How-to Study Manuals," *School Review,* Vol. 49, pp. 370-379, May, 1941.

LODGE, WILLIAM J. *Reading and the Content Subjects.* Contributions In Reading, No. 17. Ginn, Boston, 1957.

MCINTIRE, ALTA. "Reading Social Studies Materials in the Middle Grades," *Elementary English Review,* Vol. 21, pp. 262-266, November, 1944.

MICHAELIS, JOHN U. *Social Studies for Children in a Democracy,* 2nd ed., Chap. 12. Prentice-Hall, Englewood Cliffs, N.J., 1956.

NATIONAL ELEMENTARY PRINCIPALS' ASSOCIATION. *Elementary School Libraries Today.* The Association, National Education Association, Washington, D.C., 1954.

NATIONAL SOCIETY FOR STUDY OF EDUCATION. *The Measurement of Understanding,* Forty-fifth Yearbook, Part I, especially Chaps. 2, 3, 4. University of Chicago Press, Chicago, 1946.

NATIONAL SOCIETY FOR STUDY OF EDUCATION. *Reading in High School and College,* Forty-seventh Yearbook, Part II, Chaps. 6, 7, 8. University of Chicago Press, Chicago, 1948.

NATIONAL SOCIETY FOR THE STUDY OF EDUCATION. *Social Studies in the Elementary School.* Fifty-sixth Yearbook, Part II, especially chapters 5, 8. University of Chicago Press, Chicago, 1957.

PARKER, B. M. "Reading in the Intermediate Grade Science Program," *Elementary School Journal,* Vol. 38, pp. 38-43, September, 1947.

ROBINSON, F. P. *Effective Study.* Harper, New York, 1946.

SHORES, J. HARLAN. "Skills Related to the Abilities to Read History and Science," *Journal of Educational Research,* Vol. 36, pp. 584-593, April, 1943.

SNEDAKER, MABEL, and HORN, ERNEST. "Reading the Various Fields of the Curriculum," *The Teaching of Reading: A Second Report,* Thirty-sixth Yearbook, Part I, Chap. 5, National Society for Study of Education. Public School Publishing Company, Bloomington, Ill., 1937.

SPACHE, GEORGE D. "Types and Purposes of Reading in Various Curriculum Fields," *Reading Teacher,* Vol. 11, pp. 158-164, February, 1958.

STRANG, R. *Study Type of Reading Exercises,* rev. ed. Bureau of Publications, Teachers College, Columbia University, New York, 1956.

STRANG, RUTH M.; MCCULLOUGH, CONSTANCE M.; and TRAXLER, ARTHUR E. *Problems in the Improvement of Reading,* rev. ed., Chaps. 3, 7. McGraw-Hill, New York, 1955.

TIEGS, ERNEST W., and ADAMS, FAY. *Teaching Social Studies: A Guide to Better Citizenship,* Chap. 13. Ginn, Boston, 1959.

WESLEY, EDGAR B., and ADAMS, MARY. *Teaching Social Studies in Elementary Schools,* rev. ed., Chaps. 17, 19. Heath, Boston, 1952.

WITTY, PAUL A. "Reading of Social Studies Materials," *Elementary English,* Vol. 27, pp. 1-8, January, 1950.

YOAKAM, GERALD A. "Essential Relationships between Reading and the Subject Fields or Areas of the Curriculum," *Journal of Educational Research,* Vol. 38, pp. 462-469, February, 1945.

Chapter 12

THE DEVELOPMENT OF READING PREFERENCES AND TASTES

READING HABITS

A typical child actually reads a maximum of about five hundred books between seven and fourteen years. If he averages more than a book a week in what is the "best" period of his life for recreational reading this is all he can manage. Under such circumstances he simply cannot afford the commonplace. Parents, teachers, and the child himself must see that he has access to the best books in these years when his reading habits and tastes are taking shape.

The acid test of any reading program is whether or not the children in it or graduated from it read for themselves. There is little value in developing competent reading ability unless it is voluntarily put to use. One of the aims of any modern program, as suggested in Chapter 5, is the development not only of skills but of habits of reading and positive attitudes toward it. The best means of evaluation of the success of a school program is not a score on a standardized test but rather the amount and quality of the materials children read. The development of worth-while interests and tastes may be regarded as the crowning achievement of any reading program. A good program creates the desire to read and develops habits of reading not only for recreation but as a means of personal development.

The development of a permanent interest in reading seems to have a number of social and personal values. As suggested in Chapter 1, the health of a democracy is dependent upon a citizenry equipped with some knowledge of the problems faced by the total group. Unless these problems are known to all, and unless possible solutions are communicated through the printed word, without this unifying influence the democracy may become an oligarchy, an anarchy, or a fascist state. One of the personal values in the habit of wide reading during the school years is the favorable effect on reading ability itself. One of the best ways of becoming a competent reader, as measured by a standardized test or any other instrument, is to do much reading of different kinds of materials. Probably more important, the habit of reading can contribute to the child's knowledge of himself, his acquaintances, and his world in a way few other activities can.

Although interest in reading and the habit of reading may have such social and personal values, surveys of the reading habits of children and adults indicate that these values are being realized by comparatively few people. Chapter 1 summarizes some of the discouraging evidence about reading habits. Some years ago Leary[1] put some of the less agreeable facts about people's reading in a way that is still largely true. She said:

1. That in "an ordinary good library town," card holders, of whom half are school children, comprise only 25 to 30 per cent of the population.
2. That the typical borrower is a young woman who reads in the course of a month four novels of no particular worth, one better novel, one popular biography or autobiography, and one entertaining travel account, usually written by an indifferent author, whose name will never "be cut in marble on the face of library buildings."
3. That, in New York City, 10 per cent of the readers account for 67 per cent of the books withdrawn.
4. That, whereas increases in American expenditures tend to parallel increases in income, they do so in the following order, recreation, contributions, personal taxes, education, tobacco, and finally reading.
5. That the actual amount spent for reading materials varies only from about $10 per year for families at the $500-income level, to $40 for families at the $6000-income level, with a steady decline beyond the $7500-income level.
6. That elementary pupils show a discouraging lack of familiarity with good current books despite the fact that over 650,000 teachers are daily engaged in teaching them how to read.

Chapter 1 of this book indicates that although the picture is dark, there has been some progress in increasing the amount of reading done in the United States and in improving the quality of materials read. Leary pointed out that high-school pupils read "a wholesome mixture of front-page news, sports, humor, romantic fiction, real people doing real things, speed and adventure." School programs

[1] Bernice E. Leary, "What Does Research Say about Reading?" *Journal of Educational Research,* Vol. 39, pp. 434-444, February, 1946.

may be requiring some pupils to read books they do not enjoy, but at least they do stimulate reading. For example, Waples[2] found that half the books circulating from public libraries are withdrawn by teachers or by students for use in connection with schoolwork. Many current studies of adult reading interests deplore the low level of popular taste, but the long-term trends are more encouraging. Children and adults are reading more than they have ever read before, and the level of the material in books, magazines, and newspapers is, with occasional lapses, improving slowly but perceptibly.[3] This slow but general improvement is associated with better education throughout the country. In the improvement of such reading habits and tastes the school plays the most important role. As Smith put it, "The reading interests with which pupils come to school are our opportunity, but the reading interests with which they leave school are our responsibility."[4]

NATURE OF INTERESTS

As Smith indicated, interests may be regarded as initial springboards of behavior and as final products of activity. Dewey, in his classic *Democracy and Education,*[5] suggested this twofold nature when he said,

> Interest and aims, concern and purpose are necessarily connected. Such words as aim, intent, end, emphasize the *results* which are wanted and striven for. . . . Such words as interest, affection, concern, motivation, emphasize [the individual's] active desire to act to secure a possible result.

Psychologists agree that there are only a few natural interests closely connected with children's wants or needs. Most interests, including reading interests, may have some natural basis, but they are largely the result of the content of the child's environment. Thus interests which are a product of the child's interaction with his environment become, in turn, a source of motivation for further activity.

There seems to be no question of the dynamic qualities of reading

[2] Douglas Waples, *People and Print.* University of Chicago Press, Chicago, 1938.

[3] *Adult Reading,* Fifty-fifth Yearbook, Part II, National Society for Study of Education, University of Chicago Press, Chicago, 1956.

[4] Dora V. Smith, "Current Issues Relating to Development of Reading Interests and Tastes," in W. S. Gray, ed., *Recent Trends in Reading,* Supplementary Educational Monograph, No. 49. University of Chicago Press, Chicago, 1939.

[5] John Dewey, *Democracy and Education,* p. 147. Macmillan, New York, 1933.

interests and attitudes. Thorndike[6] suggested that interests "have great potency in directing the course of ideas and acts. Thought and action occur largely in the service of wants, interests, and attitudes and are stimulated and guided by them." Teachers know of pupils who are interested in topics such as trains or radios who will read about them happily and carefully, using materials which may be two or three grade levels above their usual reading fare. Thorndike suggested too that interests may be classed conveniently as potential and as active. Because of his general developmental level a boy may be ready to be interested in reading about model airplane construction or buried treasure, but an actual absorbing interest in these can grow only as he has contacts with materials on these subjects. The teacher's own enthusiasm and interest in these topics or the example of his peers may serve to transfer the interest from a potential to an active one, initiating and directing reading activities.

Harris[7] has given one explanation of children's motives, interests, and attitudes. He believed that interests and attitudes are expressions of more basic motives. In turn, interests may be regarded as enduring attitudes concerned with a group or class of objects rather than a single object. Harris pointed out that interest arises only in situations involving freedom of choice plus some elements of spontaneity in choosing. He found a reciprocal relationship between interest and ability. He believed that interests and attitudes can be modified but that true changes were rare and slow. In changing interests, the group approach and the didactic approach are often unsuccessful; change is affected by emotional appeal and personal relationship. Cumulative use may reinforce both attitude and interest over a period of time.

Perhaps enough has been said about interests to suggest their importance in any reading program. A truly educated person is characterized by breadth of interests and probably by depth of interest in two or three worth-while areas. Children have a few natural interests, arising largely from biological needs, but they early acquire social and cultural interests which may relate to reading. In school the teacher has a dual task: to capitalize upon children's present interests as motivation for reading and other learning and

[6] Edward L. Thorndike, *The Psychology of Wants, Interests and Abilities*. Appleton-Century, New York, 1935.

[7] Dale B. Harris, "How Children Learn Interest, Motives, and Attitudes," Forty-ninth Yearbook, Part I, pp. 129-155, National Society for Study of Education, University of Chicago Press, Chicago, 1950.

to redirect old interests and stimulate new and productive ones. The reading program is one of the best ways of changing many potential interests to active ones and of developing new and broader interests.

STUDIES OF CHILDREN'S INTERESTS

No teacher can give successful leadership in reading activities unless she knows the interests of the individual boys and girls in the group. When the teacher meets a new class at the beginning of the school year, she is meeting ten or twenty or forty individuals with different interests directing their activities along different lines. Some of these interests may be shared by most of the group and thus form an excellent starting point for reading, social studies, and other group-learning experiences. Some children may have specialized interests which set them apart from the rest of the group, but through which the teacher can effectively direct their learning. One of the first tasks of the teacher, accordingly, is to get to know the common interests and the individual interests of the pupils in her class.

Teachers can become acquainted with their pupils' interests by:

1. Knowing what research says about the content of children's interests at different age levels.
2. Understanding what research studies tell about factors affecting children's interests.
3. Studying the interests of the individuals in the class by means of conversation, observation, interest questionnaires, and other devices.

This section summarizes findings about children's interests in general, the following section gives some research results regarding children's reading interests, and a later section describes how a teacher may study the reading interests of children in her class.

Several hundred studies and descriptions of children's interests have been published within recent years. Super[8] has noted that in such studies interests have been measured in the following ways:

(1) *expressions* of interest, as in verbal statements about an object or activity, which have often proved unstable in school-age children.

[8] Donald Super, "Interests," in C. W. Harris, ed., *Encyclopedia of Educational Research,* 3rd ed., pp. 728-733. Macmillan, New York, 1960.

(2) *manifestations* of interest found in examples of observable behavior such as library borrowings.
(3) *tests* of interest, so far not widely used.
(4) *inventories* of interest, which have been most successful, as in studies of occupational interests by Strong and by Kuder.

Davis and Taylor,[9] for example, summarized approximately 150 such studies published in the ten-year period up to 1943. They believed that interests can be classified into seven groups: play, motion pictures, radio, hobbies (including collecting), academic, vocational, and reading. Vocational interests are usually not very consistent or practical at the elementary-school level.[10] If a teacher has some idea of the findings of research in these other areas, she will know roughly what to expect of a group of, say, seven-year-olds or twelve-year-olds. Then, by studying the group and individuals, she can discover how much the interest patterns conform to or deviate from the usual interest patterns of children. The whole pattern of group interests rather than reading interests alone is the teacher's concern.

1. Play Interests

Any parent or teacher recognizes that play interests differ markedly with age. A baby will play with his hands and feet at the age of four months and manipulate blocks by one year. By the age of three years the nursery school child is ready to climb a jungle gym, hammer a nail, or ride a tricycle; but ordinarily these activities would not appeal to him at the sixth-grade level. One of the most complete studies of play interests was made by Lehman and Witty,[11] by means of over 26,000 reports on play activities of pupils from the primary grades to college level. The table on page 368, adapted from their report, indicates the most popular play interests at three age levels. This report was published in 1927, and probably certain changes, such as watching television, would appear in a more modern study. The data were gathered largely in Kansas, and boys of fifteen years in other parts of the country might not exhibit the same interest in hunting. However, the table illustrates clearly the changes from rather individual play at five years, through the active sports and team games of the middle years, to the more passive and social inter-

[9] Robert A. Davis and Hazel E. Taylor, "Significance of Research on Interests for the Classroom Teacher," *Educational Administration and Supervision*, Vol. 29, pp. 357-369, September, 1943.

[10] Douglas Fryer, *The Measurement of Interests*. Holt, New York, 1931.

[11] H. C. Lehman and P. A. Witty, *The Psychology of Play Activities*. Barnes, New York, 1927.

ests of adolescence. It shows, too, that boys and girls have largely the same interests at five years, but that girls' activities are less active and competitive in the middle years and that sex-social interests appear earlier and more prominently in their later activities. Lehman and Witty also found that the number of different play activities engaged in during a week's time was high for the intermediate-grade child and gradually dropped as he grew older. For example, the median number of different activites at age eight was about forty and at age fifteen about twenty-three. Wide differences in breadth of activities existed in each group.

THE TEN MOST POPULAR PLAY ACTIVITIES AT AGES 5, 10, AND 15
(ADAPTED FROM LEHMAN AND WITTY)

Boys	*Girls*
5 YEARS	
Playing with a ball	Playing house
Playing with blocks	Playing with dolls
Playing with a wagon	Playing with a ball
Playing house	Playing school
Playing horse	Drawing
Hide-and-seek	Mulberry bush
Playing tag	Playing with blocks
Drawing	Skipping
Playing school	Making things
Playing in a sand pile	Jumping rope
10 YEARS	
Football	Playing the piano
Baseball	Going to the movies
Boxing	Looking at the "funny" paper
Just playing catch	Playing with dolls
Riding a bicycle	Roller skating
Basketball	Riding in an automobile
Wrestling	Reading books
Playing cowboy	Playing school
Roller skating	Jacks
Marbles	Listening to the victrola
15 YEARS	
Basketball	Reading books
Football	Going to the movies
Baseball	Social dancing
Driving an automobile	Playing the piano
Tennis	Riding in an automobile

Watching athletic sports	Having "dates"
Hunting	Watching athletic sports
Going to the movies	Going to parties and picnics
Boxing	Basketball
Reading books	Doing gymnasium work

Witty[12] has compared his earlier studies with more recent findings about interests in free-time activities. He found that there was a modern trend toward more participation in sedentary activities, because of the influence of the mass media, especially television. He found that boys still play baseball and football, swim, and ride bicycles, but there is less playing marbles, fishing, hunting, hiking, flying kites, and picnicking than in earlier years. Perhaps most important are the wide ranges of activities of different children and variations with location and with season. So great are these individual differences that Witty believes it is important for each teacher to study the interests of his own class.

Seeds[13] gave a graphic account of the wide variety of activities of 109 children aged nine to twelve years during one Saturday. Ninety-six of the children engaged in strenuous physical activities, such as climbing garages and trees, riding bicycles, digging trenches, swimming, cleaning house, gardening, and riding horseback. Eighty of the children on this one day engaged in dramatic play, much of it of a momentary nature, such as a circus, cowboys and Indians, fireman, midget racers, and school. Large numbers of the group worked at some form of construction, usually in connection with dramatic play, and satisfied their curiosity by direct experimentation and by reading. The whole picture was one of strenuous activity, often in groups, with more social interests in the play of a few of the girls.

In a related, later study McCullough[14] had 391 fifth-graders in "waterfront," "central," and "hill" districts of three social-economic areas of a California city keep "logs" of their out-of-school activities for one week. She found the group engaged in a total of twenty-six recreational and fourteen work activities. Televiewing was much

12 Paul A. Witty, "Role of Interests," *Development In and Through Reading,* Sixtieth Yearbook, Chap. 8, National Society for Study of Education, University of Chicago Press, Chicago, 1961.

13 Corinne A. Seeds, "What Learning Experiences Are Likely to Prove Developmental during Later Childhood," *California Journal of Elementary Education,* Vol. 10, pp. 41-55, August, 1941.

14 Constance M. McCullough, "A Log of Children's Out-of-School Activities," *Elementary School Journal,* Vol. 58, pp. 157-165, December, 1957.

the most popular pursuit of both boys and girls. Next most frequent for boys were sports, caring for pets, games, homework, caring for one's room, and visiting friends. For girls, the next most frequent activities were preparing meals, looking after one's room, washing dishes, and sports. Book reading was low for all children except in the "hill" or upper-level district where about half the children reported recreational reading.

2. Motion Pictures

The movies are a major interest of older children in all places where theaters are accessible. The advent of television in the 1950's drastically affected attendance at movie theaters, but toward the end of the decade adolescents began increasing their movie-going again, perhaps because many of the films were geared to their interests. Younger children who watch television over twenty hours a week may not go to a movie as often as once a week. Older children watch television less and see movies oftener than younger children do. Different studies have found different choices of favorite motion pictures, depending upon current films being exhibited, but some general age trends are evident. Children in the middle and upper elementary grades choose books, movies, and television programs that are roughly parallel in content, since in each they like action and adventure, comedy, and mystery. With age increase there is a declining interest in Western movies and melodrama and an increasing interest, especially by the girls, in romantic pictures with more conversation and less action.

The actual effects of movies on children have been debated widely. They may have certain physical effects, such as inducing more restless sleep,[15] and they obviously affect children's dramatic play. There seems little doubt that, especially among older girls in the elementary school, they constitute standards for clothes, social behavior, and a somewhat insidious emphasis upon luxury and affectation. The Institute for Propaganda Analysis[16] listed the following five examples of conscious or unconscious propaganda in the commercial movies:

a. The successful culmination of a romance will solve most of the dilemmas of the hero and the heroine.

[15] Samuel Renshaw, V. L. Miller, and D. P. Marquis, *Children's Sleep*. Macmillan, New York, 1933.

[16] *Propaganda Analysis,* Publications of Institute for Propaganda Analysis, Vol. I, p. 29. The Institute, New York, 1938.

b. Catch the criminal and you solve the crime problem.

c. War and preparation for war are thrilling, heroic, and glamorous.

d. The good life is the acquisitive life, with its emphasis on luxury, fine homes, and automobiles, evening dress, swank, and suavity.

e. Certain races, nationalities, or minority groups are comical, dull-witted, or possess traits that mark them as greatly different from and inferior to native white Americans.

There are, of course, individual motion pictures which do not contain these stereotypes, and it has never been shown how much some of them affect the relatively immature elementary-school child. However, where such ideas are presented to children week after week, often in subtle or indirect ways, teachers and parents must be alert to possible harmful effects on personality and on other leisure-time behavior. At the same time they must be ready to capitalize the favorable effects a good movie may have in stimulating imagination, enriching concepts, and directing attention to a certain book or story.

3. Television and Radio Interests

Nearly every home in the United States has at least one radio set and, except in scattered areas, the great majority have television sets. Studies of children's choices in radio and television programs vary somewhat from year to year and from locality to locality, depending upon what programs are available. In general, movie, radio, and television choices of content parallel reading interests. Children tend to favor melodrama and variety, mystery, and crime programs largely designed for adults. "Juvenile" programs like "juvenile" books are often viewed by children who are somewhat younger than the age-group at which the program is aimed. The annual studies of Witty[17] have shown that elementary-school children in the Chicago area, on the average, spend over twenty hours per week viewing television but that for high-school youth this average drops to about twelve hours per week. Elementary-school children greatly prefer television over radio, but adolescents are about equally divided in their liking for the two. Various writers have commented that televiewing is the favorite leisure-time activity of both elementary-school children and adults. Witty states that parental and teacher attitudes toward TV have been "varied and intense from the start." Although unfavorable criticisms decreased during the 1950's in terms of effects on children's

[17] Paul A. Witty, "A Tenth Yearly Study and Comments on a Decade of Televiewing," *Elementary English*, Vol. 36, pp. 581-586, December, 1959.

sleep, recreation and reading, criticisms of the quality of programs increased toward the end of the decade, perhaps because of the heavy programming of westerns and crime pictures.

Surveys made in the early 1950's brought out that the advent of television meant a reduction in movie-going, radio listening and, to a lesser extent, reading. Studies by Seagoe,[18] Witty,[19] and others demonstrated that television was preferred over radio and that there was a reduction in movie and sports attendance and in reading. Seagoe and others found a positive relationship between amount of televiewing and low socio-economic status. Later studies gave evidence that whenever a new TV area was opened up, there was a drop in reading, but after a short time, the opposite effect occurred. One possibility is that families with new television sets get used to staying home, but after a year or so, when interest in many television programs wanes or not all the family want to see a program, the amount of reading again increases. Wells and Lynch[20] discovered that the amount of recreational reading of pupils in the fifth and sixth grades averaged only about four or five hours a week and that there was a small positive correlation between the amount of reading and amount of televiewing. A study of the habits of 4,500 children in England by Himmelweit[21] showed a decline in reading but a rise in book reading, compared to the reading of comics, after television was well established. Television stimulated interest in reading through its serial dramatizations of books and aroused interest in a wider range of books, particularly non-fiction. However, the authors warned that "Television stimulates interest, but only fleetingly. It is up to the adults around the child to maintain these interests and turn them into action." It may be noted that English children averaged only about twelve or thirteen hours a week of televiewing and, like American children, they watched the so-called "adult" programs from at least the age of ten onwards.

Although television tended to dominate other media in its early years, by the end of the 1950's radio was still a strong interest. Witty[22]

[18] May V. Seagoe, "Children's Television Habits and Preferences," *Quarterly of Film, Radio and Television,* Vol. 6, pp.143-152, Spring, 1952.

[19] Paul A. Witty, "Children's Interests in Comics, Radio, Motion Pictures and TV," *Educational Administration and Supervision,* Vol. 38, pp. 138-147, 1952.

[20] Charles A. Wells and Timothy J. Lynch, "The Amount of Free Reading Engaged in by Intermediate Grade Pupils Who Have Viewed Television for One Year or More," *Journal of Educational Research,* Vol. 47, pp. 473-477, February, 1954.

[21] Hilda Himmelweit and others, *Television and the Child.* Oxford University Press, New York, 1958.

[22] Witty, *op. cit.*

found that children in grades three to six spent an average of eight hours per week in radio listening, just about the amount spent in recreational reading. The older children spent more time listening to radio than the children in grades three to six, perhaps because some local radio stations aim many of their musical programs at the teen-age audience.

In an important study of children's televiewing habits in a Boston suburb Bailyn[23] studied in some depth the correlates of televiewing of over six hundred boys and girls in the fifth and sixth grades. She found that indices of the frequency of exposure to various media, from most to least frequent, gave the following order: television, comic strips, books, comic books, radio, and movies. Correlations among the amounts of time spent led Bailyn to the conclusion that there are two "clusters of media" which may influence children. One consists of the pictorial media, television, movies, and comics; the other consists of radio and books. "Children who listen to radio and read books tend not to be highly exposed to the pictorial media and, conversely, those heavily exposed to the pictorial media do not spend much time listening to the radio or reading books. Girls are more often radio and book fans; boys concentrate more on the pictorial media" (p. 31). She also found that factors associated with high exposure to the pictorial media are lack of parental restriction, low I.Q., fathers with worker or service occupations, and type of religious affiliation. Boys with high exposure tend to classify people in a stereotyped way (black-and-white-categories), show little concern for the motivation of characters, have a passive attitude toward the socio-economic situation of the father, and gain a bit of their self-image in the aggressive-hero types. Girls do not show these correlates. The Bailyn study is an example of growing concern with the effects of various kinds of children's literature as discussed in Chapters 4 and 13.

As is the case with the movies, radio and television programs may have favorable or unfavorable effects upon children's development. Radio undoubtedly gives children pleasure, often in a relaxed sort of situation desirable after a stimulating day in school. Radio and television programs extend experience and enrich concepts far beyond the narrow limits of the immediate environment. The values

[23] Lotte Bailyn, "Mass Media and Children: A Study of Exposure Habits and Cognitive Effects," *Psychological Monographs*, 73, No. 1, 48 p., 1959.

to all members of the family having a child confined to bed may be considerable. Sharing certain programs, moreover, may contribute to family unity. One study by Scott[24] found at the sixth- and seventh-grade levels that pupils' school achievements were unfavorably related to excessive televiewing, but that the latter did not seem to affect their personal adjustments, social adjustments, or other leisure-time interests. On the negative side, radio and television, like movies, may overstimulate children, producing fears and nightmares. Indoor programs may take children away from active outdoor pursuits which they seem to need for good physical development through much of their elementary-school careers. As in the movies, emphasis in radio and television programs upon violence and crime may lead to undesirable social attitudes. As with the motion pictures, some guidance by the teacher and critical appraisal by the group may aid in producing more desirable television and radio interests.

4. Hobby Interests

Hobbies are transitional forms of activity combining play and work. Like play they are based on the interests and free choice of the child. Like work they become systematized into stamp collections or various airplane models and are directed toward certain definite goals. Research shows that hobby interests change with the years and are affected by the mental ability of the child involved. In regard to collecting activities Durost[25] believed that "Only children of better than normal intelligence make systematic collections of things requiring a high degree of classification." In a study involving 45,000 children in grades four to eight Lewis and McGehee[26] found that bright children are more interested in music, reading, dramatics, religious activities, Scouting and campfire activities, and collecting than dull children of the same chronological age. Dull girls expressed more interest in housework than bright girls, and dull boys more interest in working, in stores or on the farm, for example, than

[24] Lloyd F. Scott, "Television and School Achievement," *Phi Delta Kappan,* Vol. 38, pp. 25-28, October, 1956.

[25] Walter N. Durost, *Children's Collecting Activity Related to Social Factors.* Bureau of Publications, Teachers College, Columbia University, New York, 1932.

[26] W. Drayton Lewis and William McGehee, "A Comparison of Interests of Mentally Superior and Retarded Children," *School and Society,* Vol. 52, pp. 597-600, December 7, 1940.

bright boys. Over twelve times as many mentally retarded as gifted children are shown to have no hobby.

There are a few indications from research that certain hobbies are associated with desirable personality traits. Boynton's study[27] of 4779 children in the sixth grade found the following hobbies in use: reading; active games and sports; quiet games; playing musical instruments; listening to the radio; sewing, knitting, etc.; housework; going to shows; dramatics; dramatic play; religious activity; construction; traveling; studying; working; clubs; Scouting; and collecting. Boynton observed that "There does not seem to be any significant tendency for boys or girls who possess any given hobby to have either more or fewer extremely undesirable (personality) traits . . . than is the case with boys or girls who have any other hobby."[28] However, he believed that absence of a hobby appears to be associated with less desirable types of personality adjustment than is found in any hobby group. He found that sex differences in hobbies, and the significance attached to them, are pronounced. For boys at this level, good emotional traits seem to be associated with studying, traveling, collecting, and playing musical instruments. For girls good adjustments are associated with working, social dancing, studying, and Scouting. Boynton suggested, however, that there is not necessarily any causal relation between hobbies and good personality adjustments.

5. *Academic Interests*

Interests in school activities vary tremendously with the type of child, the teacher, and the school. There is evidence that interest in different school subjects shifts from year to year, but that elementary-school pupils mention academic subjects oftener than junior- or senior-high-school pupils, who are more likely to mention sports, industrial and mechanical arts, vocational preparation, and relations with others of their own age. In a study reported by Jersild[29] about 80 per cent of the pupils liked academic work best in the first six grades, but only about 50 per cent liked it best in grades nine to twelve. School games and sports, on the other hand, were

[27] Paul L. Boynton, "Relationship of Hobbies to Personality Characteristics of School Children," *Journal of Experimental Education,* Vol. 8, pp. 363-367, June, 1940.

[28] *Ibid.,* p. 365.

[29] Arthur T. Jersild, *Child Psychology,* 4th ed. Prentice-Hall, Englewood Cliffs, N.J., 1954.

liked best by only about 5 per cent of the children in grades one to six, and by about 30 per cent of the pupils in grades seven to twelve. In her group of nine- to twelve-year-olds Seeds[30] noted that, in descending order, the boys preferred arithmetic, reading, spelling, drawing, history, and geography; the girls, reading, art, arithmetic, spelling, French, and music.

Jersild and Tasch[31] reported the results of a study of two groups of children totalling over three thousand individuals. Children were asked eleven questions about their in-school and out-of-school likes and dislikes, their wishes, and related matters. In one group, children in the fourth through sixth grades named games, play, sports, and the like as their favorite out-of-school activity. This preference was particularly strong in the lower socioeconomic populations. At these grade levels, only 2.5 per cent named reading as their favorite activity outside of school. The best-liked activities in school were arithmetic and the language arts of reading and writing. Only 11 per cent mentioned activities outside the academic curriculum as best-liked. In general, Jersild and Tasch noted a decline with age in educational morale.

In another study of children's preferences for in-school and out-of-school activities in a California community, Miles[32] found that sixth-graders differed considerably in various socio-economic groups. Sports activities were most popular with boys of both groups. The children from lower status homes ranked games and play and motion picture attendance higher than the other group. Children from higher status homes were more frequently collectors, players of musical instruments, and participants in Boy or Girl Scout activities. Comic books and newspaper funnies were frequent reading materials in both groups; the higher status group rated reading a little higher than did the lower status children. A significantly greater number of lower status children named reading as a most valuable school subject. A child's interest in various school activities is largely an individual matter, closely related in most cases to the child's success in a particular area. However, the child's academic interests, like his play, movie, television, and hobby interests, may be significant for teacher-pupil planning of reading experiences.

[30] Corinne A. Seeds, *op. cit.*

[31] Arthur T. Jersild and R. J. Tasch, *Children's Interests.* Bureau of Publications, Teachers College, Columbia University, New York, 1949.

[32] Logan Miles, *Children's Preferences for School and Out-of-School Activities.* Doctoral dissertation, University of California, Berkeley, 1954.

CHILDREN'S READING INTERESTS

A child's reading interests are only one part of his total pattern of interests. In many cases they are closely related to his other interests, because he is the kind of child he is and because often reading can contribute to his other interests. For example, the somewhat isolated or introverted child who may prefer quiet games and who has several hobbies, such as collecting stamps, probably uses reading because he is not too social and because he can gain further knowledge of stamps and the countries from which they come. There are children who are absorbed in one interest or hobby to the exclusion of all others, but in general the teacher may expect a child to possess a group of related interests in which reading may play a major or minor role.

There are at least two hundred careful studies of children's reading interests reported in professional literature, so that it is possible here to mention only a few representative ones which are "classics" or which are recently published. Summaries of interest studies have been made by Anderson,[33] Gray,[34] Jordan,[35] Kramer,[36] Norvell,[37] Rankin,[38] Traxler,[39] and others.

One of the earliest studies giving developmental changes in reading interests is that of Terman and Lima.[40] Their findings about principal interests at various levels may be summarized as follows:

Before five years: Mother Goose rhymes, other jingles, simple fairy tales, and little nature stories

Six and seven years: Animal talking stories, Mother Goose, some of shorter fairy tales

33 Harold A. Anderson, "Reading Interests and Tastes," in W. S. Gray, ed., *Reading in General Education,* Chap. 7, pp. 217-271. American Council on Education, Washington, D.C., 1940.

34 William S. Gray, "Reading Interests," in C. W. Harris, ed., *Encyclopedia of Educational Research,* 3rd ed., pp. 1105-1108. Macmillan, New York, 1960.

35 Arthur M. Jordan, "Children's Interests in Reading," *The High School Journal,* Vol. 25, pp. 323-330, November-December, 1942.

36 Sister M. Immaculata Kramer, "Reading Preferences of Elementary and High School Pupils," *Catholic Education Review,* Vol. 37, pp. 310-325, 440-453, May, September, 1939.

37 George W. Norvell, *The Reading Interests of Young People,* Chap. 12. Heath, Boston, 1950.

38 Marie Rankin, "Children's Interests in Library Books of Fiction," Teachers College Contributions to Education, No. 906. Bureau of Publications, Teachers College, Columbia University, New York, 1944.

39 Arthur E. Traxler and Ann Jungeblut. *Research in Reading During Another Four Years.* Educational Records Bureau, New York, 1960.

40 Lewis M. Terman and Margaret Lima, *Children's Reading. A Guide for Parents and Teachers,* 2nd ed., Chap. 5. Appleton-Century, New York, 1935.

Eight years: Fairy tales, beginning interest in stories of real life

Nine years: Realistic stories, continued but less interest in fairy tales, reading used to satisfy curiosity

Ten years: Adventure, stories of other lands, travel, beginning of interest in biography, boys beginning to read books on mechanics and invention, some myths and legends

Eleven years: Series repeating same characters in adventure and mystery, boys' increasing interest in science, interest in animal and nature stories declining

Twelve years: Reading interest at its highest, biography, stories of home and school life, boys' interest in more sensational adventure, girls beginning to read so-called adult fiction

Thirteen, fourteen years: New reading interests of more specialized type, often related to hobbies, boys' mechanical and scientific interests intensified, girls reading more romantic fiction and perhaps reading boys' adventure stories

Fifteen years: Noticeable decline in amount of reading, continued specialization of interests

The Terman and Lima study was first published in 1925, and although it has since been revised, its findings may not give an entirely accurate picture of children's reading interests today. This is particularly true since both writers and publishers have made many changes in children's books since 1930. For example, with a wider variety of books available, not all teachers or parents may find the chief interest in fairy stories at about the age of eight years, as mentioned above. The summary above may not give sufficient place to children's interest in animal stories. Because of the more recent development of children's books with factual backgrounds it does not mention as early as it might children's interests in books about trains, airplanes, steam shovels, and other signs of a mechanized world. Certainly, too, older children are reading considerably in magazines and newspapers not mentioned in this study. The outline of the findings is included here because the study takes a developmental point of view and attempts to interpret changes in children's interests as they mature.

Witty and others[41] listed the favorite books of 7879 children from kindergarten through grade eight in the spring of 1945. Approximately the first twelve of the favorite books at different levels were as follows:

[41] Paul A. Witty, Anne Coomer, and Dilla McBean, "Children's Choices of Favorite Books: A Study Conducted in Ten Elementary Schools," *Journal of Educational Psychology,* Vol. 37, pp. 266-278, May, 1946.

KINDERGARTEN

Little Golden Book of Fairy Tales; FLACK, *Angus and the Ducks;* BANNERMAN, *Little Black Sambo;* GRUELLE, *Raggedy Ann;* LINDMAN, *Snipp, Snurr* books; POTTER, *Tale of Peter Rabbit;* FLACK, *Ask Mr. Bear;* FLACK, *Story about Ping;* FRISKEY, *Seven Diving Ducks;* HUBER, *I Know a Story;* LOWREY, *Poky Little Puppy;* WEHR animated edition of *Hansel and Gretel;* BISHOP, *Five Chinese Brothers;* FLACK, *Restless Robin*

GRADES ONE TO THREE

DISNEY version of *Bambi;* BANNERMAN, *Little Black Sambo;* MCCLOSKEY, *Make Way for Ducklings;* LANG, *Cinderella;* DISNEY version of *Pinocchio;* ANDERSON, *Billy and Blaze;* AUSTIN, *Peter Churchmouse;* GAG, *Snippy and Snappy;* PIPER, *The Little Engine That Could;* BARNETT, *They Hunted High and Low;* DISNEY, *Donald Duck and His Nephews;* HUBER, *It Happened One Day;* GRIMM, *Fairy Tales*

GRADES FOUR TO SIX

KNIGHT, *Lassie Come Home;* ATWATER, *Mr. Popper's Penquins;* SEWELL, *Black Beauty;* CLEMENS, *Adventures of Tom Sawyer;* Fairy Stories (no edition given); RAINS, *Lazy Liza Lizard;* MCCLOSKEY, *Homer Price;* GRIMM, *Fairy Tales;* ESTES, The *Moffat* books; BROOKS, *Freddy the Detective;* GEISEL, *The Five Hundred Hats of Bartholomew Cubbins;* O'BRIEN, *Silver Chief*

GRADES SEVEN TO EIGHT

KNIGHT, *Lassie Come Home;* ESTES, The *Moffat* books; BOYLSTON, *Sue Barton* books; TUNIS, *Keystone Kids;* O'BRIEN, *Silver Chief;* TERHUNE, *Lad;* TUNIS, *All American;* BRINK, *Caddie Woodlawn;* SPERRY, *Call It Courage;* STEVENSON, *Treasure Island;* SEWELL, *Black Beauty;* TUNIS, *Kid from Tomkinsville;* FORBES, *Johnny Tremain;* CLEMENS, *Adventures of Tom Sawyer;* SEREDY, *The Good Master*

The authors of the report believed that in general the children chose desirable books. Most of them appear on approved lists, and a good proportion of the books awarded the Newbery and Caldecott medals appear on these lists. Not all these prize books, however, are popular with children, and children do not always read as desirable books as those listed above.

Another study showing developmental trends is that of Colby.[42] As a result of her experience with a group of children, known as the Junior Reviewers, who appraise materials from the standpoint of the publisher, Colby gives the following guides to reading materials:

[42] Jean P. Colby, *The Children's Book Field.* Pellegrini and Cudahy, New York, 1952.

First Real Book Age, three to five: An idea which appeals to the emotions is essential. Text must be simple and reassuring. Material should be based on the child's small world. Main interests are family, other children, nature, weather, and mechanical objects. Stories must be short; forty-eight pages is a good average. Illustrations must be true-to-life. Bindings must be sturdy; type, large.

Beginning to Read to Themselves Age, six to nine years: There must be appeal in both text and illustrations. Situations must be convincing and understandable. Suspense and action are essential to a story; there must be characterization. If fiction, 150 pages is a good length; if non-fiction, 100 pages. Durable bindings, short sentences, limited vocabulary, and large-sized type are other important factors.

Major Reading Age, nine to twelve: Clarity and appeal in both text and illustrations are essentials. Subject matter is limitless, but there must be plenty of action, characterization, and atmosphere. If non-fiction, it must be presented in an interesting and lucid manner. Children in the story should carry out the plot themselves and not be pushed around for plot purposes. There should be no writing down and there must be proper slant for the sex concerned. The page size, type, and general book make-up must complement the story; color is not essential.

Many other studies of reading interests show typical choices in books, newspapers, and magazines at different age levels. Many of the studies, like those above, emphasize the change in reading interests with age, but a partial exception to this point of view is made in a study by Thorndike.[43] His findings were based on the reactions of 2891 children in grades four to twelve (largely four to nine) to fictitious titles and annotations such as the following:

Friends among the Stars. How to know the stars. How to learn their names and where to find them.

Cabin Boy for Columbus. The adventures of Angelo, who sailed with Columbus on his great voyage of discovery.

Although Thorndike found some differences in interest level for different age and ability groups, for many of the titles a consistent interest or dislike was shown at all levels. He concluded, "There is a consistent pattern of boy interests . . . and, to a somewhat lesser extent, a pattern of girl interests cutting across all age and intelligence differences" in the group of children nine years and older. Some ficti-

[43] Robert L. Thorndike, *Children's Reading Interests,* Based on a Fictitious Annotated Titles Questionnaire. Bureau of Publications, Teachers College, Columbia University, New York, 1941.

tious titles which showed a definite decline in interest were these: *When the Circus Comes to Town; Little Tony's Pony; The Wolf Pack Hunts Again;* and *Magic Wishing Ring.* The larger group in which there was consistent interest throughout included *Call in the G-Men; Men from Mars; Queen of the Silver Screen;* and *Murder in the Green House.* From his findings Thorndike concluded that "the ten-year-old boy and the fifteen-year-old boy are more alike than different in their interests" and that there are distinct sex differences in book choices except for the mystery stories, animal stories, and mild adventure stories.

Although Thorndike stressed the similarity of interests at different levels, it should be noted that he might have obtained somewhat different results with a wider range of titles, and that his study eliminated reading difficulty as a factor. When children choose actual books, they are almost forced to pick ones they can read; therefore the results in terms of books read will differ considerably at different levels. Thorndike showed similarities in potential interests rather than actual interests. For example, in reporting a study of books actually read by children Kramer[44] stated that "the books most often read by pupils in grades V, VI make a list quite different from the list of books most popular in Grades IX to XI." She found, for example, no mystery books in the ten most popular in grades five and six, but several of these in the higher-grade list. The Thorndike and other studies illustrate the fact that children of a given age or grade level may be potentially interested in topics usually thought to be above them and that the problem is one of providing materials sufficiently mature in interest, but easy enough in terms of readability for the children to be able to use them.

A number of later studies of children's reading interests should also be mentioned, partly because of the rapidly changing nature of the juvenile book field. One of the most comprehensive of these was the investigation by Rudman[45] reporting returns from over six thousand pupils in grades four through eight, along with over four thousand parents of these pupils, over two hundred teachers, and somewhat fewer librarians. Rudman distinguished between children's "read-about" and their "ask-about" interests. He found that literature, animals, sports, and science were top topics in interests and that

[44] Sister M. Immaculata Kramer, *op. cit.*

[45] Herbert C. Rudman, "Informational Needs and Reading Interests of Children in Grades IV through VIII," *Elementary School Journal,* Vol. 55, pp. 502-512, May, 1955.

as children progressed through grades four to eight, they showed less interest in cowboy and fairy stories and more interest in mystery stories. Interest in animal stories was continuous in the elementary grades, but interest in sports and recreational activities went up at these ages. Parents wanted children to read more reference books, and librarians wished them to read more biographies of famous people than the children apparently chose for themselves. In their "ask-about" lists children showed strong interest in questions relating to ethics, values, and religion, and greater concern with personal problems and peer groups as they approached puberty. In general, children read about and ask about topics adults approve, but parents would like them to ask more about vocations, and teachers are more concerned than are the children with social skills.

A more recent study[46] of children's free reading gave evidence of the competition of television. It found that the amount of book reading outside school increases from first grade through sixth grade, but changes only slightly thereafter. Girls read more than boys at all ages. The survey estimated that the average pupil in the elementary grades reads between one half and one book per month during the school year. This estimate is lower than that of other studies and showed also a decline in comic book reading at about two comic books per month. Although the California children read some of the old favorites, such as *Black Beauty* and *Little Women,* the chief finding was the spread in titles read, rather than concentration, in any of the elementary-school years.

The modern tendency is to probe more deeply into children's interests than is possible by compiling a listing of favorite titles. This trend is illustrated by a study by Lynch,[47] who obtained typical patterns of reading interests for groups of children in grades four, five, and six and then interviewed individuals who typified these accepted patterns. Lynch found that children read more than indicated in the Terman and Lima study twenty-five years earlier and that boys read somewhat more widely than girls, especially in non-fiction. Popular girls read more than the average, but the omnivorous reader among the boys was sometimes not the best liked. He may be a "lonesome reader." For some reason Lynch could not fathom, girls at these ages

[46] Stanford Institute for Communication Research, "The San Francisco Study of Children and Communication," Preliminary Report, No. 2, Mimeog. The Institute, Palo Alto, Cal., 1959.

[47] Margaret Lynch, *Children's Ideas About Their Favorite Books.* Master's Thesis, University of California, Berkeley, 1958.

read horse stories, and boys read dog stories. She pointed out that lists of popular books at these age levels sometimes disregarded popular authors. For example, the popularity of *Tom Sawyer* put Mark Twain on the list, but other authors not included in a most popular list, such as Willie Ley and Beverly Cleary, should be included when the readership of their books is totalled from a listing of popular titles.

In another deviation from the usual interest study Vandament and Thalman[48] investigated reactions of over one thousand children to types of fantasy. The sixth and tenth grades involved preferred story books, comic books, and magazines—in that order. The achievement type of fantasy was associated with story books and magazines, and the social and aggressive types with comic books. Girls showed more interest than boys in social types of reading. No differences in aggression were found in the preferences of the various socio-economic groups.

Two other studies of a more conventional sort are those of Norvell,[49] one involving students in high school, the other children in grades three through six. Large numbers of children responded to selections frequently taught in school. In the older group, Norvell found few grade-level or age differences but found sex was a "highly significant factor" in responses to the selections. He believed that schools should provide separate materials for boys and girls, with more changes in present materials needed for the boys. In his sample of younger children (24,000 in New York State in grades three to six), Norvell observed that many books increased in appeal to a high point and declined thereafter. Aesop's fables and fairy tales were popular in grades three to five; and myths, legends, and hero and folk tales were popular in grades five and six and above. Elements in stories favored by boys were adventurous action, physical struggle, human characters, animals, humor, courage, and patriotism. Preferred by girls were stories of adventure, home and school life, human characters, pets, romantic love, sentiment, and mystery.

In still another type of study Droney[50] recorded pupil preferences

[48] William E. Vandament and W. A. Thalman, "An Investigation into the Reading Interests of Children," *Journal of Educational Research,* Vol. 49, pp. 467-470, February, 1956.

[49] George W. Norvell, *The Reading Interests of Young People.* Heath, Boston, 1950. *What Boys and Girls Like to Read.* Silver Burdett, New York, 1958.

[50] Margaret L. Droney and others, "Pupil Preferences for Titles and Stories in Basal Readers for the Intermediate Grades," *Journal of Educational Research,* Vol. 47, pp. 271-277, December, 1953.

for materials in basal readers for the intermediate grades. In the first part of the investigation some 1,400 children in grades four to six rated titles of reader stories for interest, and in the second part 744 children rated the titles and actual stories. Titles which contained unfamiliar words were unpopular, those which employed familiar vocabulary most popular. The stories in the readers were better liked than some of the titles. Boys tended to reject titles suggesting stories about girls, such as "The Princess Who Could not Cry," and expressed interest in titles suggesting animals, out-of-doors, adventure, exploration, and heroes.

Another variety of interest study related to specific materials is that concerned with children's reactions to poetry. A large number of investigations put interest in poetry low as compared with other literary materials, and in many cases boys and girls expressed active dislike of poetry. In one study of children's reactions to poetry, Kyte[51] found strong preferences for poems which tell a story. The most favored narrative poems are those including humor and dramatic action along with pleasant experiences. In a study of children in grades four, five, and six, Avegno[52] compared choices of some poems published prior to 1900 with others published since 1932. Teachers read five poems to their classes each day, making a total of 250 poems in ten weeks. The children were given the opportunity for two weeks to read for themselves poems heard the previous week. After listening to the teacher read a poem, the children rated it on a five-point, qualitative scale. The poems most preferred by all groups were recent poems, "Kindness to Animals" and "So Many Monkeys." In the fourth and fifth grades, girls rated the poems higher than the boys. Frequency of liking was much the same for both "old" and "new" poems. Principal reasons for liking poetry were rhyme, musical effect, emotional tone, vocabulary, story, and descriptions. The chief reason for disliking a poem was failure to understand it.

One correlate of children's reading may be the reading done by their teachers. While responsibility in developing reading habits and tastes is a shared concern of parents and teachers (see Chapter 17), there can be little question that for many children, a love of reading can be "caught" only if the teacher enjoys books and shares that

[51] George C. Kyte, "Children's Reactions to Fifty Selected Poems," *Elementary School Journal,* Vol. 47, pp. 331-339, February, 1947.

[52] T. Sylvia Avegno, "Intermediate-Grade Children's Choices of Poetry," *Elementary English,* Vol. 33, pp. 428-432, November, 1956.

enjoyment. Burrows[53] has made an exploratory study by interview and questionnaire of the reading habits of ninety-two teachers in a typical county of New York State. She investigated book reading, borrowing, purchasing, and the reading of professional books. Burrows found that teachers read about as much in books and newspapers as other persons of the same educational background. They used a library more than do people the country over, but about 15 per cent never borrowed books from library or friends. Book purchasing showed typical patterns of "consumption" common to many adults, with a few very active buyers. Both active and less active readers (about half the group were classed as "active") read more general than professional literature. The more active readers also tended to give more place to reading in classroom activities.

PLACE OF THE COMICS

The fact that maturity and interest of content and some ease of reading material have been combined in the comics may account for their continued popularity. Teachers, parents, and writers are divided in their opinions of the comics, with expressions ranging from "vicious" and "immoral" on one side to "emotional outlets" and "aids to good reading ability" on the other. With the enormous hold they have on the reading habits of children and adults, it is not very realistic for teachers or parents to condemn the comics outright and ban them from classroom or home. The probable effect of such a ban will be to produce undercover activity. Rather, the task of parent and teacher seems to be to assay the advantages and disadvantages of the comics, to arrange situations which will give most weight to the possible advantages, and to use the comics in developing more desirable reading habits and tastes.

The popularity of the comics increased through the 1940's but began to wane somewhat in the 1950's, at least partly because of the rise of television. In the 1940's comic books were the most widely purchased materials in military posts, and there was some evidence that both civilian and military adults read them even more than children. In this period, for example, Marston[54] estimated that one hundred million Americans read comic books or comic strips. In a group of

[53] Alvina T. Burrows, *Teachers Reading Values: An Exploratory Investigation,* 42 p. School of Education, New York University, New York, 1957.

[54] William M. Marston, "Why 100,000,000 Americans Read Comics," *The American Scholar,* Vol. 13, pp. 35-44, January, 1944.

children in the fourth, fifth, and sixth grades, Witty[55] found an average reading of thirteen comic books or magazines and twenty-five comic strips, as they appeared, but DeBoer and others suggested that many adults read more of this material than children did. Even at this time, however, there was evidence of some decline of interest in comics after approximately thirteen years of age, and this decline may have been projected later into the adult population. Although the evidence is ambiguous, one of the chief factors in the reduction in comic book publication and reading in the decade of the 1950's would seem to be the rise of television. Because most television programs of this era were of the "entertainment" variety (the light comedy, variety show, or crime or Western film), televiewing cut most strongly into the light "escape" reading of the comics rather than other types of reading. As suggested in Chapter 1, the serious reading of Americans, with the increase of quality paperbacks and other factors, continued to expand during the period, but television, increased economic prosperity resulting in travel, and other conditions operated to reduce the reading of comic books. Since comic strips appear in newspapers and newspaper reading increased slowly, the decline in the comics field seemed to be largely in comic books or magazines.

Although the reading of comics has declined, Frank[56] has suggested that they are still "Big Business." In the 1950's, some three hundred different comic books were bought by over fifty million purchasers, and they were probably one of the basic media of barter or exchange over the world. In evaluating their influence, it is important that parent and teacher distinguish between comic strips and comic magazines, and that the comic magazines themselves be divided into such categories as adventure, fantasy, crime and detective, westerns, humor, anthropomorphized animals, teen-age activities, biographies, and current events. Unfortunately, most comic books are displayed on the same rack, the vicious along with the wholesome. By the end of the 1950's, however, parents and teachers were as much concerned with sadism, murder, and violence in television programs as in comic books. The comics, then, should be studied as one of a group of communication media which may influence children and adolescents.

[55] Paul A. Witty, "Children's Interest in Reading the Comics," *Journal of Experimental Education,* Vol. 10, pp. 100-104, December, 1941.

[56] Josette Frank, *Comics, TV, Radio, Movies—What Do They Offer Children?* Public Affairs Pamphlet, No. 148. 1955.

Because of their place as one of the influences on youth, it is important to evaluate their effects on children. Are they demoralizing or are they educational? Are they responsible for excluding a certain boy or girl from more desirable activities or do they enrich the experience and provide a sort of catharsis for the child? In weighing the advantages of the comics, teachers should perhaps recall that picture stories have a long history. They were used by the Egyptians and Assyrians, for example, to record military triumphs and domestic discords. Their development in modern times has depended largely on the ability to reproduce simple line drawings that told a story with humor or dramatic power. In the United States the first comic cartoons which appeared in sequence in the newspapers were published in the 1890's. Popular early strips were *Buster Brown,* the *Katzenjammer Kids,* and *Happy Hooligan.*

Marston[57] divided the modern development of the comics into three stages. In the first, from 1900 to 1920, the comics were largely supposed to be humorous. The second period began about 1920, with the hesitant introduction of pathos and "human interest" into the continuities, and reached full fruition about 1930, when leading comics openly stopped trying to be funny and became adventure strips. The first comic books appeared in 1933. Marston believed that the third period in the development of comics began definitely in 1938 with the advent of *Superman.* This marked a shift from dramatic adventure to the emotional appeal of wish fulfillment. Children wish to be strong, to be brave, to be right, and to have a chance to identify themselves with such virtues in the comics. While such appeal is characteristic of certain comics, humor and adventure are still found in certain strips and even books, so that Marston's three stages cannot be regarded entirely as distinct stages.

In evaluating the influence of the comics on an individual or group the teacher should be aware, too, of some of the supposed advantages and disadvantages of the comics. Their dangers have been stressed by Landsdowne,[58] McCarthy and Smith,[59] Strang,[60] Wer-

[57] William M. Marston, *op. cit.*

[58] James D. Landsdowne, "The Viciousness of the Comic Book," *Journal of Education,* Vol. 127, pp. 14-15, January, 1944.

[59] Sister M. Katherine McCarthy and Marion W. Smith, "Much Discussed Comics," *Elementary School Journal,* Vol. 44, pp. 97-101, October, 1943.

[60] Ruth M. Strang, "Why Children Read the Comics," *Elementary School Journal,* Vol. 43, pp. 336-342, February, 1943.

tham,[61] and others. In appraising both the good and the bad points of the comic Strang offered the following objections:

1. The comics tend to crowd out reading of a more desirable type.
2. Many poor readers merely get the story from the pictures without making an effort to read the text.
3. The adventures portrayed in the comics are so far removed from reality that children do not acquire an understanding of the world as it is, such as they can obtain from their reading of material that is closer to real life.
4. There is little or no progression of reading experience within the area of the comics.
5. The art of most of the comic strips is of inferior quality.

Other objections are the poor qualities of color, type, and paper used; the incorrect grammar spoken; the presentation of crime as sensational and the solution of crime by one person, acting extralegally; and the effects on character of pornographic, unethical, and anti-democratic materials.

Similarly, the comics or certain features of them have been defended by Emery,[62] Frank,[63] Sones,[64] Strang,[65] Thorndike,[66] and others. Strang summarized some of the favorable arguments as follows:

1. The comics constitute a kind of modern folklore corresponding to the Greek and Norse myths.
2. They meet children's needs for overcoming, in imagination, some of the limitations of their age and ability and for obtaining a sense of adventure denied them in real life.
3. To normal children the comics offer the mental catharsis which Aristotle claimed for the drama. Thus the readers are released from feelings of inadequacy and insecurity and from fear of aggression toward or from others.
4. The comics supply to children of limited reading ability a form of reading experience which is thoroughly enjoyable.
5. If the children actually read the text of the comics, they will profit

[61] Frederic Wertham, *The Seduction of the Innocent.* Rinehart, New York, 1954.

[62] James N. Emery, "Those Vicious Comics," *Journal of Education,* Vol. 127, pp. 90-91, March, 1944.

[63] Josette Frank, *op. cit.*

[64] Warren W. D. Sones, "Comics in the Classroom," *School Executive,* Vol. 63, pp. 31-32, October, 1943.

[65] Ruth M. Strang, *op. cit.*

[66] Robert L. Thorndike, "Words and the Comics," *Journal of Experimental Education,* Vol. 10, pp. 110-113, December, 1941.

by extensive supplementary reading and will be introduced to a wide range of vocabulary, using many words which they repeatedly encounter in other reading.

Other advantages of comics have been stated as follows: learning to like reading, improving sense of humor, gaining factual information, and contributing to hobbies.

In evaluating the influence of the comics, teachers must be aware that, like television and the movies, they carry certain propaganda. This may not be deliberately planned by artist or writer, but certain ideas and stereotypes may be repeated so often that children and adults may accept them automatically. Kessel[67] found what he believed to be the following assumptions in comic strips in a series of Chicago newspapers over about four months' time:

Race and nationality: The white race was considered superior, although American Indians were also given certain admirable qualities. Strange and foreign customs were inferior to our own. Orientals were an especially sinister and sadistic race. The English were most honorable of the European peoples. The United States is the greatest country in the world.

Morality and ethics: 1. It is right and natural for those who have been wronged to seek revenge.

2. Criminals can be recognized by characteristic physical stigmata.
3. We should obey the laws, because if we do not we shall be punished.
4. All people are either good or bad.

Government and politics: 1. Such terms as "democracy," "liberty," "American way," "Americanism" and "un-American" have definite meanings that are self-evident. Many times their use seemed forced, the main purpose being to get them into the lines regardless of context.

2. America is a land of equal opportunity for all people.
3. American government is today unqualifiedly and completely democratic.
4. In our society today the law provides the best method of settling disputes.
5. The Second World War was caused by the ambitions of a few power-mad dictators.

Education: 1. Education is worthwhile because those who have it reap greater financial returns. Education helps one to "get ahead." Higher education outside of professional training is interesting but useless.

2. Culture is a personal quality which can be acquired through certain activities.

[67] Lawrence Kessel, "Some Assumptions in Newspaper Comics," *Childhood Education,* Vol. 19, pp. 349-353, April, 1943.

3. Serious literature and the great books are dull reading material.
4. Works of art are an expensive, impractical extravagance.
5. Scientists are sinister people. In science they are usually evil and abnormal persons often physically imperfect.

Socioeconomic: 1. If one does his work faithfully and well, he is sure to be successful.
2. If a man really wants to work, he can find a job.
3. If a man has money, he is worth considering in matrimony.
4. Social and economic status are fixed, and one should not step out of his class.
5. Simple things in life are best, and happiness is independent of material comfort.
6. Industrial leaders of the nation are altruistic in their war efforts.
7. Financial independence develops along with chronological maturity.
8. Rich people are snobbish, lazy, and have bad habits and manners.
9. The employer has no responsibility for his employee's security.

Such analyses of the content of comics do not prove that they affect children in the designated ways. Many careful studies of comic strips and magazines, such as some fifty summarized by Witty and Sizemore,[68] do not establish a one-to-one relationship between comic book reading and maladjustment or school failure or delinquency. For example, in one study, 235 girls and boys, ages ten to seventeen, who had been arrested for juvenile delinquency, were compared with a group of non-delinquents. Hoult[69] found delinquents read more comics categorized as harmful and questionable, but he did not establish causal connection between the two. In another investigation, Blakely[70] found no relationship between type and frequency of comic books read and such factors as reading ability, general school achievement, intelligence, or behavior problem status as related by teachers. Blakely also found that seventh-grade children who read comics also read more library books than children who read no comic books, thus giving a little more evidence of the existence of a group of active consumers of various media in contrast to a group who make little use of various communcation media. These and other studies rule out the possibility of comics as a single cause of difficulty, except in isolated cases, but they do not negate multiple causation or the neces-

68 Paul A. Witty and Robert A. Sizemore, "Reading the Comics: A Summary of Studies and an Evaluation," *Elementary English,* Vols. 31 and 32, pp. 501-506, 43-49, 109-114, December, 1954, January, February, 1955.

69 T. F. Hoult, "Comic Books and Juvenile Delinquency," *Sociological and Social Research,* Vol. 33, pp. 279-284, 1949.

70 W. Paul Blakely, "Study of Seventh Grade Children's Reading of Comic Books," *Journal of Genetic Psychology,* Vol. 93, pp. 291-301, December, 1958.

sity of parental and teacher supervision. Teachers and parents should be aware that discussions of the comics and other mass media need not stay at the opinion level but can have a factual basis. Sources such as the Witty and Sizemore summary and the careful analyses of Schramm[71] and of Spiegelman[72] are examples of research evidence bearing on the problem.

As the teacher studies the influences of the comics on the reading and the lives of her class she may decide to ban all comics, to ignore them, or use them for promoting the best reading and personality development of the pupils. The last approach seems the most fruitful, positive one. Some of the positive ways of using the comics are summarized below:

1. *Help the Class to Appraise Comics*

A study of the content of the comics may reveal their interesting points but also their essential monotony. One fifth grade[73] studied comic books and found that the books divided themselves into three main classes:

- *a. Informational:* relatively wholesome
  - (1) True Comics
  - (2) Classic Comics
  - (3) Real Life Comics
  - (4) True Aviation
  - (5) Bible Stories
- *b. Harmless:* amusing stories
  - (1) Walt Disney
  - (2) Looney Tunes
  - (3) Ace Comics
  - (4) Jolly Jingles
  - (5) Terry Toons
- *c. Unwholesome:* dealing with crime, murder, hatred, revenge
  - (1) Human Torch
  - (2) Bad Man
  - (3) Whiz
  - (4) Action Comics
  - (5) Prize Comics

71 Wilbur Schramm, "The Effects of Mass Communication: A Review," *Journalism Quarterly*, Vol. 26, pp. 397-409, 1949.

72 Marvin Spiegelman and others, "The Content of Comic Strips: A Study of a Mass Medium of Communication," *Journal of Social Psychology*, Vol. 35, pp. 37-57, February, 1952.

73 Lena Denecke, "Fifth-Graders Study the Comic Books," *Elementary English Review*, Vol. 22, pp. 6-8, January, 1945.

Comparison of comic books and comic strips may reveal a somewhat more uniform level in the latter because of the standards of "family" newspapers.

2. Use Comics to Initiate Reading Habits

If one or two children of the class read nothing voluntarily, the comics may be a first step in establishing the habit of reading for enjoyment.

3. Transfer Interest from Poorer to Better Comics

As suggested above, like any other class of publication, comic strips and particularly comic books vary greatly in the desirability of their content. The Parents' Institute Press publishes three high-grade books, *True Comics, Real Heroes,* and *Calling All Girls.* Some picture-script booklets published by several different companies give science and social-studies material in form similar to the comics. Some teachers in Protestant church schools like *Picture Stories from the Bible.* Many teachers find it easy to transfer interest from undesirable comic books to better comic books and strips.

4. Use Materials from the Comics in Related Lessons

Instead of confiscating all copies the teacher may use a group interest in comics as a basis for much language work. Discussion, development of word meaning, individual and class appraisal, locating parallel stories in literature or current events, and dramatization of the story may all grow out of reading the comics. Occasionally, material in history and geography can be submitted and appraised. Identification of scientific absurdities can often be made in the science class. In such cases the comics act as motivation leading to better authorities.

5. Relate Materials in Comics to Desirable Books

Since there are few real plots and many variations of one plot, the alert teacher can often refer the child who is reading the comic book to a short story or book containing the same kind of plot, characters, or setting. If the comic book deals with pirates, the teacher can ask, "Have you ever read *Treasure Island?*" If it concerns buried treasure, she may mention McSwigan's *Snow Treasure,* the story of the Norwegian children who took gold out of their country under the very noses of their enemy. From *Tarzan* to Kipling's *The Jungle*

Books may not be a long step for a mature child. The Disney comics may form a basis for reading a well-illustrated animal story, like some of the dozens listed under "Animals" in *Bibliography of Books for Children.*[74]

These five main types of activity suggest that the teacher can make use of current reading of the comics and that she can direct it toward reading tastes on a higher level. In planning such an attack on the problem it seems unwise to condemn comics wholesale, first, because both comic strips and comic books vary widely in content, and second, because most boys and girls in the upper half of elementary school, including the good readers, read them part of the time anyway. The teacher will aim not for elimination of the comics but for a balanced reading fare. General maturation and acquaintance with the richer stores of books and magazines will usually provide for the gradual disappearance of the comics reading habit. In the fourth to seventh grades such reading may today be regarded as a typical developmental pattern, offering a number of opportunities to the teacher.

FACTORS AFFECTING READING INTERESTS

From the studies above and other related ones a clear picture emerges of factors affecting children's reading interests. These may be summarized under (1) factors inherent in the child, (2) factors in the reading material, and (3) environmental factors.

1. Factors Inherent in the Child

a. Sex. Boys and girls have similar interests when young children, but these diverge as they mature. For example, Terman and Lima found that at about eleven years boys were more interested than girls in realistic stories and were becoming interested in science and mechanics, while girls were beginning to read romantic "adult" fiction. Thorndike found clear sex differences, except that girls will read some boys' stories, and that only mystery, animal, and mild adventure stories are enjoyed by both sexes. Lazar's study[75] of over two thousand children, aged ten to twelve years, in New York City

[74] Association for Childhood Education, *Bibliography of Books for Children,* Bulletin, No. 37. The Association, Washington, D.C., 1954.

[75] May Lazar, *Reading Interests, Activities and Opportunities of Bright, Average, and Dull Children,* Contributions to Education, No. 707. Bureau of Publications, Teachers College, Columbia University, New York, 1937.

schools, also found both sexes enjoying mystery, adventure, and history, but disagreeing on such items as novels, poetry, stories of home and school, fairy tales, and detective stories. Most studies reveal that older boys do more magazine and newspaper reading and girls more book reading. Thorndike's[76] study of children's reactions to fictitious titles and annotations showed the clearest differences in the choices of the sexes. In general, girls read more than boys at every age.

b. Age. The studies reported above noted changes in interests as boys and girls mature. The Thorndike study indicated less change in interest from ten to fifteen years, especially among boys, when it is a case of selecting titles rather than reading the book. Many other studies show similar differences. For example, Hockett and Forry[77] in a study of pupils from grades three to seven found the younger children expressing interest in a great variety of topics and the older children showing more discrimination in choosing certain topics. In these grades boys' interest in the topic "How a poor girl found a prince" dropped rapidly. By nine or ten years sex differences begin to appear. Girls read boys' books more than boys read girls' books. Some sort of peak in free reading activities is reached around twelve or thirteen years, but the amount of such reading usually begins to decline around thirteen or fourteen years.

c. Mental Ability. In general, mental ability is associated with chronological age; but where there are deviations toward acceleration or retardation, there are deviations in reading interests. A number of studies report that dull children like books only a little more mature in theme than younger children of the same mental age. Thorndike[78] reported, for example, that bright children's interests are most like those of a group of mentally slower children who are two or three years older than they are. Lazar[79] found that the actual titles "most enjoyed" did not vary much for her bright, average, and dull groups except that the bright knew a wider range of titles. Average and dull girls read more than average and dull boys, and, for boys, there was a close association between intelligence and the num-

[76] Robert L. Thorndike, *Children's Reading Interests*. Bureau of Publications, Teachers College, Columbia University, New York, 1941.

[77] John A. Hockett and Kenneth M. Forry, "Reading Interests," *Children's Interests*, Twelfth Yearbook, Part IV, pp. 89-100, California Elementary Principals' Association, 1940.

[78] Robert L. Thorndike, "Words and the Comics," *Journal of Experimental Education*, Vol. 10, pp. 110-113, December, 1941.

[79] Lazar, *op. cit.*

ber of books read. Terman and Lima reported that bright children read three or four times as many books as average children and do not taper off in reading activities after thirteen years as much as the average child does. Despite these three main influences, Wollner[80] has shown that patterns of reading activities are highly individual.

2. Factors in the Reading Material

Most children will leaf through a book to get some impression of its content (and perhaps difficulty) before they borrow it from a school or public library. Rankin[81] found that children twelve to fourteen years old reported they were most influenced by the theme of the book, the format of the book, a sampling of the text, the recommendation of other persons, previous knowledge of book or author, and the style of writing—in that order. This list does not mention the difficulty of the book, undoubtedly a potent factor in determining whether or not a particular child will enjoy the book. Efforts to control the vocabulary and sentence structure of primary-children's books,[82] and research on readability,[83] have helped to develop plans for some control of the difficulty of a book or shorter selection. Trends toward greater use of pictures and of color have increased the attractiveness of most children's books. Improvements in the attractiveness of school texts in reading, science, social studies, and other fields enable texts to compete successfully with many children's "library books." Rudisill,[84] Whipple,[85] and others have studied the interest appeal of various types of illustrations in children's books.

Especially at the age of from ten to twelve years children read series such as the *Hardy Boys, Sue Barton, Nancy Drew,* and *Freddy the Pig* books. Undoubtedly, similarity in author, title, or character

80 Mary H. B. Wollner, *Children's Voluntary Reading as an Expression of Individuality,* Contributions to Education, No. 944. Bureau of Publications, Teachers College, Columbia University, New York, 1949.

81 Marie Rankin, *Children's Interests in Library Books of Fiction,* Contributions to Education, No. 906. Bureau of Publications, Teachers College, Columbia University, New York, 1944.

82 For example: (a) George Spache, "New Trends in Primary Grade Readers," *Elementary School Journal,* Vol. 42, pp. 283-290, December, 1941. (b) Nolen Kearney, "Sentence Length in 121 Representative First-Grade Readers," *Journal of Educational Research,* Vol. 38, pp. 447-461, February, 1945.

83 For example, Jeanne Chall, *Readability.* Ohio State University, Columbus, 1957.

84 Mabel Rudisill, "Children's Preferences for Color versus Other Qualities in Illustrations," *Elementary School Journal,* Vol. 52, pp. 444-445, April, 1952.

85 Gertrude Whipple, "Appraisal of the Interest Appeal of Illustrations," *Elementary School Journal,* Vol. 53, pp. 262-269, January, 1953.

will influence choice of book. Rankin[86] found that 39 per cent of the children studied mentioned knowledge of the author's name as a reason for selecting certain books.

Most of the studies mentioned above give examples of the qualities in stories that children like. Most lists include such concepts as surprise, action, animalness, humor, conversation, and plot. In a study of four thousand junior-high-school pupils Zeller[87] found the factors of "humor" and "action" exerting the greatest influence, the former positively, the latter positively for boys and negatively for girls. The rise of non-fiction for children in the last decade suggests that children can be just as interested in factual materials attractively presented as they are in fiction. Many writers have attempted to state "what is a good story for children." Most agree that it must be about a definite idea or theme, that something must happen, and that there must be some revelation about character or life itself. Irvine[88] summarized that children like a story with (1) a quick beginning, (2) a definite ending, (3) plenty of action in between, (4) at least one situation with which they are familiar, (5) a character their own age or a little older so that they can identify with him, and (6) an ethical, sympathetic, and realistic treatment of subject matter which is meaningful because of situation or character. Such a list can be interpreted in light of the individual, even idiosyncratic nature of children's reading interests.

3. *Environmental Factors*

a. Accessibility. Most studies reveal that children's free reading is influenced by the school curriculum and that children will read what is accessible to them. In a summary of studies of reading interests Betzner and Lyman[89] concluded, "Probably the most significant single factor in the development of wholesome reading habits and tastes is the informal exposure of children to an abundance of good books

[86] Marie Rankin, *op. cit.*

[87] Dale Zeller, *The Relative Importance of Factors of Interest in Reading Material for Junior High School Pupils,* Contributions to Education No. 841. Bureau of Publications, Teachers College, Columbia University, New York, 1941.

[88] Emily G. Irvine, "The Content, Selection and Use of Children's Literature," *Proceedings of Eighth Annual Conference on Reading.* University of Pittsburgh, Pittsburgh, 1952.

[89] Jean Betzner and R. L. Lyman, "The Development of Reading Interests and Tastes," *The Teaching of Reading: A Second Report,* Thirty-sixth Yearbook, Part I, Chap. 6, pp. 185-205, National Society for Study of Education, Public School Publishing Company, Bloomington, Ill., 1937.

and magazines in the home, school and public library." The moral for teachers, principals, and school boards seems clear. Lazar[90] found that more books, magazines, and newspapers are available in the homes of higher socioeconomic status and that, naturally enough, children read more widely and at a more mature level of interest in such an environment. Hockett[91] and Rudman[92] have shown that children of the same age, ability, and sex do not vary much in their reading interests in different parts of the country or in rural, urban, and metropolitan centers.

b. Recommendations of Others. Rankin[93] found that 41 per cent of the children of twelve to fourteen years in her study relied on the recommendations of others, especially their friends. A number of studies indicate that the teacher's recommendations are not usually regarded with favor. The newness of the book and printed book reviews do not seem to affect the pupils' choices. These results were true also of a different type of study of children's and adults' reading made by Johnson[94] in Duluth. Johnson also found that about 80 per cent of the boys and girls studied in grades eight to eleven used the public library. There was a tendency for the younger pupils to use the school library more than the older group and for the older pupils to use the public library more than the younger group.

The influence of the home situation has been regarded by most writers as a major influence on reading habits and tastes. Children whose parents are college-educated and of good socioeconomic level usually have access to more books, magazines, and newspapers and tend to read more of them. However, parents' and children's specific preferences do not always coincide. Rudman,[95] for example, found that parents wanted children to read more about vocational choices than the children themselves were interested in doing. In a careful exploration of relationships, Jefferson[96] compared preferences of 305 children in grades three to six with the ideas of their parents about

90 May Lazar, *op. cit.*

91 John A. Hockett and Kenneth Forry, *op. cit.*

92 Herbert C. Rudman, *op. cit.*

93 Marie Rankin, *op. cit.*

94 B. Lamar Johnson, "Children's Reading Interests as Related to Sex and Grade in School," *School Review,* Vol. 40, pp. 257-272, April, 1932.

95 Herbert C. Rudman, *op. cit.*

96 Benjamin F. Jefferson, "Some Relationships between Parents' and Children's Preferences in Juvenile Literature," Doctoral dissertation, University of California, Berkeley, 1956. Also *Elementary School Journal,* Vol. 58, pp. 212-218, January, 1958.

children's books, using a fictitious, annotated questionnaire and actual copies of books. The total group of children's and parents' choices showed high agreement, with correlations clustered around .72. However, the children showed more interest in such types of stories as "mystery and detective" and "humor and whimsy" and less interest in "travel stories" than their parents expected them to have. Parents of girls underestimated their interest in stories of the "love and romance" type. Parents of boys voted differently from parents of girls, indicating that parents were well aware of sex differences in reading interests. Parents, however, varied greatly in their understanding of their own children's choices, with correlations ranging from .7 to —.3 and centering about .4. Ratings of specific books by parents and their own children were approximately in the same range. Jefferson's results suggest that homes influence reading interest not so much in terms of specific titles or types of material but in terms of a general climate of interest in books.

The wide variety of influences affecting children's choices of reading material gives one clue to the great individual differences found in reading interests. Some implications of these interests and the way they develop are summarized below.

SUMMARY AND IMPLICATIONS OF INTEREST STUDIES

Studies of children's interests, including those reported above, give the following guide lines to the teacher of reading:

1. Children's interests vary widely from person to person and may shift rapidly for any one person, but they do constitute an important source of motivation for much school learning.
2. Although one of the chief results of interest studies is the tremendous variety of interests found in any one group of children, it is true also that there are common developmental patterns for interests in the lives of most children.
3. In general, interests develop from the simple and individual ones of early childhood, through the vigorous, complex, and social ones of middle childhood, to the more individual, less active, and more restricted interests of later adolescence and adulthood.
4. A teacher can understand a group of children better if she knows the research results about the usual interests at their age level

and if she studies individual and group deviations from the usual patterns.

5. A child's interests develop within limitations set by his physical and economic environment, his own physical and mental capabilities, and the attitudes and customs of the groups in which he lives.

6. A teacher or parent may use interests as an initial motivation for desirable learning activities or work toward them as end products of such activities.

7. Reading interests possess the characteristics summarized above and show considerable development parallel to movie, radio, television, hobby, and other interests.

8. Like other interests, reading interests are affected by the cultural environment, and, accordingly, the results of published studies reflect the influence of home environment and the usual school curriculum instead of depicting fully what children might be interested in.

9. Specific studies of reading interests reveal a list of books or types of material which are common to many other studies, and therefore may be regarded as a good nucleus for an elementary (or secondary) school's book collection.

10. Children's book choices seem to be related to the content of the books, to their difficulty, and to their format as it gives clues to these two items.

11. The newer investigations of reading interests go beyond a mere listing of titles and themes to attempt studies in depth of reasons for reading, reactions to specific materials, and personality and environmental factors that may affect reading interests.

12. The chief environmental factors influencing choices of books are accessibility or availability, curricular demands, the recommendation of friends, and the habit of reading in the family.

13. Children in the upper elementary grades, especially boys, regularly read such sections of the newspaper as the comic strips, the sport page, and news. Boys begin to read the picture magazines, the semiscientific magazines, and general magazines popular with adults; girls begin to read the picture magazines, general magazines, and movie magazines. From the third or fourth grade through the seventh grade, comic strips and comic books are frequently read. All these represent for the teacher not reading tastes to be condemned but opportunities for introducing many learning situations and moving toward higher standards in reading materials.

14. As children mature they tend to change from use of a class-

room library to use of a school library and a public library. Such a sequence is an incentive to reading and one of the best assurances of permanent reading habits. Chapter 1 shows that many children, especially in rural areas, do not have access to public libraries. There the importance of classroom and school libraries is intensified. Where public libraries are accessible the close co-operation of school and public library is the best foundation for desirable reading tastes.

15. Research gives evidence that improved reading interests and habits result from a careful study of children's present interests and a varied school program for developing more desirable reading habits and tastes. Suggestions for these two phases of a complete reading program are given in the succeeding sections.

STUDYING CHILDREN'S READING INTERESTS

The foregoing descriptions of children's interests and their implications are of value to the teacher and labrarian only as they put them to use in understanding pupils' interests and guiding their reading in voluntary and schoolwork situations. Some of the ways a teacher may study the potential and actual reading interests of her class are as follows:

1. Observation

One of the easiest and most effective ways of discovering a child's interests is to watch his daily activities in school, on the playground, and, if possible, in the community. In school situations where children have opportunities to express themselves in conversation, dramatic play, drawing, construction, and other activities, the teacher will often note an interest which she can jot down in the form of an anecdotal note for the pupil's file and her later reference. The boy who is always drawing horses may obviously be interested in reading about them. Such notes as "Florence told the class about her visit to the hospital, with special admiration of the work of nurses" may remind the teacher to recommend *Sue Barton: Student Nurse* to the active eleven-year-old girl who hasn't been reading much. If the teacher notes of a fourth-grade boy that "Frank enjoyed being part of the train in the rhythms period," she may feel that Frank is ready to read Lent's *Clear Track Ahead* or Henry's excellently illustrated *Trains.*

2. *Interview*

Every wise teacher arranges a time when she can have a quiet talk with a pupil. During the interview the teacher encourages the child to talk about what he does out of school, what he likes in school, his favorite games, movies, and radio programs. Some teachers plan a semistandardized interview by using a mimeographed form to record such information for the child's file and for her own and the principal's future use. Interviewing is very time-consuming, but it does not take long to jot down such items as favorite books, favorite television programs, favorite movies, out-of-school activities, and possible suggestions for future reading.

3. *Questionnaires*

Older children can save the teacher's time and give rather complete information about their interests on a questionnaire blank if there is an atmosphere of confidence and no pressure for good results in the classroom. Suggestions for such interest blanks have been made by Harris,[97] Witty and Kopel,[98] and others. In general these are check lists of leisure-time activities or play activities, questions about recent activities, lists of magazines read, type of story enjoyed, and related information. Some school staffs and groups of teachers have enjoyed preparing such a questionnaire co-operatively and sharing results with one another.

A suggestion for recording reading interests which shows rough patterns of interest was made by Simpson in the form of *My Reading Design*.[99] By means of grouping books read into such categories as animals, other lands, aviation, workers, travel, mystery, and poetry the *Design* shows actual and potential interests and possible gaps in the child's reading.

4. *Hobby Club*

Some teachers in the middle and upper elementary grades plan their weekly schedule so that an occasional period is freed for chil-

[97] Albert J. Harris, *How to Increase Reading Ability,* 3rd ed., pp. 482, 483. Longmans, Green, New York, 1956.

[98] Paul A. Witty and David Kopel, "Diagnostic Child Study Record," *Reading and the Educative Process,* pp. 311-334. Ginn, Boston, 1939.

[99] G. O. Simpson, *My Reading Design,* Form A Grades 1 to 3, Form B Grades 4 to 6, Form C Grades 7 to 9, and Form D Grades 10-12. The News-Journal, North Manchester, Ind., 1945.

dren to work singly or in groups on their hobbies. If there is a class Reading Club, children share with others some selections they themselves have enjoyed. Through stamp, model airplane, and nature collections, and similar hobbies the teacher can come to know a child's interests and possibly to suggest some materials which will enrich these or lead to new, worth-while interests.

5. Library Borrowings

Encouraging children to keep a record of the books they borrow from the school or public library gives teachers a source of information about reading interests and also is a stimulus to reading. Keeping records of books read by means of wall charts and other classroom devices also gives clues to interests and is one of the methods of improving interests and habits discussed in the following section.

PROCEDURES FOR STIMULATING DESIRABLE READING INTERESTS AND TASTES

A large number of articles report methods that teachers and librarians have used to stimulate desirable reading habits and tastes. In general, they do not report scientifically controlled experiments, but they do give interesting accounts of changes in pupils' reading. Lazar[100] summarized a number of the methods and devices to encourage more and better reading. Humphrey[101] showed that such definite guidance is needed by intermediate-grade pupils even after available materials have been increased and some help in selection has been given.

Some of the methods a teacher may use to increase the amount and quality of voluntary reading among her pupils are as follows:

1. Wall Charts

As mentioned above, these may record and stimulate free reading. One teacher printed the heading "There is no frigate like a book to take us lands away," and then the children added beside their

100 May Lazar, *Guiding the Growth of Reading Interests,* Educational Research Bulletin of Bureau of Reference, Research and Statistics. Board of Education of City of New York, May, 1945.

101 Phila Humphreys, "The Reading Interests and Habits of Six Hundred Children in the Intermediate Grades," *Language Arts in the Elementary School,* Twentieth Yearbook, pp. 421-428. Department of Elementary School Principals, National Education Association, Washington, D.C., 1941.

names paper boats bearing the titles of books read when they completed them. Easier books for the poorer readers of the group were given as much credit as books on the high-school level. Some classes use pocket charts and add a slip bearing author and title or short book reports to their individual pockets when they finish reading the books.

2. Book Reports

As mentioned in Chapter 4, short book reports are one method of stimulating desirable reading habits and tastes. There is a considerable danger that book reports may become a bore and a tedious duty. They must be short and must be used only occasionally. Written reports must be of a simple form, giving space only to items such as (*a*) author, (*b*) title, (*c*) publisher and date, (*d*) type of content, and (*e*) why I liked or disliked the book. Oral book reports also must be short. They may be given under these five headings and should never reveal all the plot of a story. Through reports a teacher may encourage self-evaluation of a pupil's reading. As a result of an experimental program in improving voluntary habits Fox[102] concluded that "Intermediate grade children can intelligently evaluate their own reading accomplishments and deficiencies if they are made aware that they should be critical of their own performances."

3. A Reading Corner

Every classroom should have a quiet corner where books and other materials are attractively displayed and a few chairs invite free reading. Some teachers use a few rows of bookcases partly to screen off the space from the rest of the room.

4. Display of Book Jackets and Advertisements

A few colorful jackets or advertisements displayed in the book corner and elsewhere in the room will stimulate interest in the books represented, particularly if teacher or pupils give a few hints about a book's contents.

5. Reading Stories to the Class

Most teachers know a few sure-fire children's stories which never fail to interest a group of children of a certain age level. If the teach-

[102] Maude G. Fox, "Experiment in Promoting Interest in Reading," *Elementary School Journal,* Vol. 47, pp. 451-460, April, 1947.

ers, and possibly some of the good readers, read these stories to the class, part of one every day, they rarely fail to interest the children in these and related stories. For any group of children there are some humorous stories and adventure stories which can be enjoyed by all.

6. Definitely Scheduled Free Reading Periods

Time in the week's program must be scheduled when children can enjoy books or magazines of their own choice from the school or public library. This necessarily involves mastering the use of the library facilities and may include sharing one's joys in a book with others in the group. Teachers will soon know which pupils need their judicious guidance in selecting a book suitable in theme and in difficulty. In this situation a knowledge of the child's general interests is invaluable. It is still true, however, that the period should be a *free* reading perod. Most good readers in an elementary school read a certain amount of trash and may read it in this period as well as at any other time.

7. A Book Club

A book club with pupil officers who change month by month may be one of a number of hobby clubs or may be given a regular spot on the week's program. The book club often takes over the class after a free reading period. Thus a class which has been working individually is united in an audience reading situation. Lazar[103] suggested the following activities for book clubs: (*a*) corresponding with authors or illustrators of children's books, (*b*) helping to arrange a class story hour for younger children, (*c*) conducting a book column in the class or school newspaper, (*d*) inviting appropriate guests to speak at the school, (*e*) organizing contests such as "Best Biography of an Author," (*f*) keeping a library of published reviews of children's books, and (*g*) making posters for special book occasions.

8. Exhibits

Book exhibits in a corridor case or some other prominent place may stimulate interest in certain books and certain topics. If a town is looking forward to a fair, the children may be encouraged to read stories about fairs or books about horses or cattle or other exhibits at the fair. Special days such as birthdays of historical figures, news-

[103] Lazar, *op. cit.*

paper headlines, or a campaign to collect reading material for less fortunate children may lend themselves to a book exhibit.

9. Programs

Programs for Book Week, assemblies, and class meetings may include games such as charades involving titles or authors, pantomimes of situations in stories to be identified, radio skits and plays based on well-liked stories, as well as readings from poetry and other material with strong emotional or dramatic appeal.

Perhaps the best way the teacher can stimulate interest in reading is by continual reference to possible sources in all her teaching and by showing her own interest and enthusiasm for reading. Developing reading interests and tastes is a complex task which cannot be confined to the nine methods and devices above but must be based on the spirit of the whole instructional program. The companionship of books can permeate much of the day's teaching. The methods listed above have emphasized creating intial interest in books, but follow-up of reading activities may be equally important. Broening[104] listed the commonest practices of Baltimore teachers in initiating interest as follows: discussing the background, displaying books, letting children simply select from the collection, recalling books by the same author, and setting up activities that call for books. Then she went on to suggest that certain follow-up activities may be equally important. Those used frequently in Baltimore were these: book programs, informal discussion, telling interesting parts, reading interesting parts, and contributing relevant information to school subjects. Her list illustrates the point that opportunities for encouragement and guidance of reading interests and tastes come in all parts of the school's program. A teacher can plan and work for the development of reading interests and tastes as definitely as she can give a place to the development of the more mechanical reading skills and abilities.

The nine main activities listed above can be subdivided into hundreds of activities for an enthusiastic teacher and class. The next chapter, Chapter 13, is concerned with the content of children's literature, with the materials used to stimulate interests and make them into permanent, life-time habits. An important point of both

104 Angela M. Broening, "Factors Influencing Pupils' Reading of Library Books," *Elementary English Review,* Vol. 11, pp. 155-158, June, 1934.

chapters is that children, especially young children, develop reading interests not in passive listening situations but in active participation in literature. Storytelling, dramatization, choral reading, and book games are only a few of the main possibilities. Jensen,[105] for example, has described no less than fifty means of active participation in literature and of developing permanent interests in all sorts of writing. Her article is a mine of practical suggestions which teachers can adapt to their own classes.

The opening sentence of this book gave two main purposes for the reading program, that children shall learn to read skilfully and that they shall love to read. This chapter has been concerned with the second main aim. It indicates what reading interests are, how they grow, and some ways by which a teacher can help boys and girls weave reading experiences into the pattern of their lives. It emphasizes an active approach to children's literature, rather than passive listening, as a way of building permanent interests. It suggests that the teacher has the responsibility for taking most children beyond the *Bobbsey Twins, Nancy Drew,* and *The Hardy Boys* to some of the great books, old and new, of juvenile literature. It declares that the creation of a strong love for reading and of permanent interests in reading is the crowning achievement of a modern reading program.

SUPPLEMENTARY READINGS

Bailyn, Lotte. "Mass Media and Children: A Study of Exposure Habits and Cognitive Effects," *Psychological Monographs,* No. 471.

Bauchard, Philippe. *The Child Audience.* UNESCO, Paris, 1954.

Betzner, J., and Lyman, R. L. "The Development of Reading Interests and Tastes," Chap. VI of *Teaching of Reading,* Thirty-sixth Yearbook of National Society for Study of Education. Public School Publishing Company, Ill., 1937.

Bond, G. L. and Wagner, Eva. *Teaching the Child to Read,* Chap. XII, "Reading Interests and Tastes." Macmillan, New York, 1960.

Cole, Luella. *The Elementary School Subjects,* Chap. IV, "Interest, Taste and Dynamics." Rinehart, New York, 1946.

Fox, M. G. "An Experiment in Promoting Interest in Reading," *Elementary School Journal,* Vol. 47, pp. 451-460, April, 1947.

Frank, Josette. *Comics, TV, Radio, Movies—What Do They Offer Children?* Public Affairs Pamphlets, No. 148. Washington, 1955.

Gramks, Jean D. *The Development of Lifetime Reading Habits.* American Book Publishers Council, New York, 1954.

[105] Amy E. Jensen, "Attracting Children to Books," *Elementary English,* Vol. 33, pp. 332-339, October, 1956.

HARRIS, ALBERT J. *How to Increase Reading Ability,* 3rd ed., "Developing Reading Interests." Longmans Green, New York, 1956.

HARRIS, DALE B. "How Children Learn Interests, Motives and Attitudes," Forty-ninth Yearbook, Part I, National Society for Study of Education. University of Chicago Press, Chicago, 1950.

HEISLER, F. "A Comparison of Comic Book and Non-Comic Book Readers of the Elementary School," *Journal of Educational Research,* Vol. 40, pp. 458-464, February, 1947.

JENKINSON, A. J. *What Do Boys and Girls Read?* Methuen, London, 1940.

JENSEN, AMY E. "Attracting Children to Books," *Elementary English,* Vol. 33, pp. 332-339, October, 1956.

JERSILD, ARTHUR T., and TASCH, RUTH J. *Children's Interests.* Bureau of Publications, Teachers College, Columbia University, New York, 1949.

JORDAN, A. M. "Children's Interests in Reading: A Review of Research Articles from 1935 through 1939," *High School Journal,* Vol. 25, pp. 323-330, November, 1942.

KRAMER, SISTER M. I. "Children's Interests in Magazines and Newspapers," *Catholic Educational Review,* Vol. 39, pp. 284-290, 348-358, May-June, 1941.

LAZAR, MAY. *Guiding the Growth of Reading Interests,* Bulletin of Bureau of Reference, Research and Statistics. New York Board of Education, New York, 1945.

MALCHOW, E. C. "Reading Interests of Junior High School Pupils," *School Review,* Vol. 45, pp. 175-185, March, 1937.

NORVELL, G. W. *What Boys and Girls Like to Read.* Silver Burdett, New York, 1958.

RANKIN, M. *Children's Interests in Library Books of Fiction.* Contributions to Education, No. 906. Bureau of Publications, Teachers College, Columbia University, New York, 1944.

ROBINSON, HELEN, comp. and ed. *Developing Permanent Interest in Reading.* Supplementary Educational Monographs, No. 85. University of Chicago Press, Chicago, 1956.

SIMPSON, G. O. *My Reading Design,* Forms A, B, C, D. The News-Journal, North Manchester, Ind., 1945.

STERNER, ALICE P. *Radio, Motion Picture and Reading Interests: A Study of* High School Pupils. Contributions to Education, No. 932. Bureau of Publications, Teachers College, Columbia University, New York, 1947.

STRANG, R. M. *Exploration in Reading Patterns.* University of Chicago Press, Chicago, 1942. Summary, *Teachers College Record,* Vol. 45, pp. 281, January, 1944.

STRANG, R. M. "Why Children Read the Comics," *Elementary School Journal,* Vol. 43, pp. 336-342, February, 1943.

TERMAN, L. M., and LIMA, M. *Children's Reading.* Appleton-Century, New York, 1935.

THORNDIKE, R. L. *Children's Reading Interests.* Bureau of Publications, Teachers College, Columbia University, New York, 1941.

VON QUALEN, V. D., and KAMBLY, P. E. "Children's Interests in Science as Indicated by Choices of Reading Materials," *School Science and Mathematics,* Vol. 45, pp. 798-806, December, 1945.

WAPLES, DOUGLAS, and TYLER, RALPH W. *What People Want to Read About.* University of Chicago Press, Chicago, 1931.

WAUGH, COULTON, *The Comics.* Macmillan, New York, 1947.

WILSON, F. T. "Reading Interests of Young Children," *Pedagogical Seminary,* Vol. 58, pp. 363-389, June, 1941.

WITTY, PAUL A., and COOMER, A. "Fostering a Balanced Reading Program: The Role of Parent, Teacher and Librarian," *Elementary English Review,* Vol. 23, pp. 241-246, October, 1946.

WITTY, PAUL A., and others. "Children's Choices of Favorite Books: A Study Conducted in Ten Elementary Schools," *Journal of Educational Psychology,* Vol. 37, pp. 266-278, May, 1946.

WITTY, PAUL A., and SIZEMORE, ROBERT A. "Reading the Comics: A Summary of Studies and An Evaluation," *Elementary English,* Vol. 31, 32, pp. 501-506, 43-49, 109-114, December 1954, January, February, 1955.

Chapter 13

PERSONAL GROWTH THROUGH READING AND LITERATURE

Literature for young people is today "big business" from the points of view both of publishers and of teachers and children using the books. Books for children and adolescents are being published in quantities unknown previously. As described briefly in Chapter 1, the "paperback revolution" has changed modern book-buying and book-reading habits. This revolution has extended to books for children, but to it must be added the increase in quantity of hard-back books in a wide price range aimed at the juvenile market. For example, a news-note in *The Saturday Review* stated that one "line" of books of one publisher, the Little Golden Books, between 1942 and 1959 sold 600,000,000 copies. In the year 1959 alone, 80,000,000 "juveniles" were sold to a population of 30,000,000 children and over 125 Little Golden Books had sales of over one million copies each. Another publisher reported about the same time that over a five-year period, about six million Landmark Books had been sold and a million and a quarter copies, exclusive of book club sales, of the Farley *Black Stallion* series had gone to young readers. Similarly, in school, most teachers and children have available, in classroom and library, many more books than a previous generation could obtain. The opportunities of reading for information, for enjoyment, and for personal enrichment are greater than ever before. The quantities of books now available mean that more than ever, teachers and librarians must be able to select and to recognize quality in writing which will have the most beneficial effects on young people.

In the past, many teachers and parents viewed reading as a sort of mechanical ability made up of specific skills to be learned in order. The aim of much instruction was to build up a collection of reading abilities as soon as possible, without any thought to other effects of the teaching on the child as a person. More recently, emphasis has shifted from specific reading skills to larger patterns of development.

Teachers are becoming increasingly concerned with the effects of reading on the child. They still give large place to reading competences, but they include other aims as well. The modern teacher does not ask, "What is Johnny doing in reading?" so often as she asks, "What is reading doing to Johnny?"

The interrelationships of reading and child development are discussed briefly in Chapters 3 and 4 of this book. In much of the book there has been consideration of the influence of children's characteristics and needs on types of reading activities. In this chapter the emphasis is upon materials available and upon the effects of reading. It discusses the influences reading and literature may have upon wholesome child development and then gives specific examples of how activities in reading and literature can be carried out with this aim in mind.

Not only the increase in books, but the growth of other communication media, such as television, makes many forms of literature available to children. Their total influence on the life of the nation has been enormous. Teachers, then, must know modern children's books because of the large part they play in modern living. Even more, they must know books, stories, television programs, radio, and recordings, and how to use them so that they can influence effectively the lives of individual children. The rich potentialties of literature for stimulating the wholesome development and healthy adjustment of boys and girls are just beginning to be realized by many teachers.

EFFECTS OF READING ON CHILDREN

Teachers in all times have used literature to influence children's growth. For example, literature was a large part of the curriculum of the boys of ancient Greece, where the aim was the development of good citizens and loyalty to the city-state. In schools today children laugh or weep with the hero of the book read aloud by the teacher or thrill to the triumphs and disasters of a favorite character in story book, movie, or television program. Some teachers share literature a bit like Jack Horner, occasionally getting a plum for children in the group. The present chapter suggests how the teacher can take experiences in literature off a hit-or-miss basis and plan a program to affect the ideas and adjustments of most children in the class.

In planning a consecutive program of experiences in literature with the class, a teacher will ordinarily stress a variety of activities, because research gives no definite information about the effects of particular types of stories or activities on individual children. The negative relationships between reading and personality have been studied more thoroughly by research workers. There seems no doubt that reading difficulties are often the causes, concomitants, or results of personality maladjustments.[1] Sometimes undue pressure from the teacher or a parent may be interrelated with feelings of insecurity and low reading achievement.[2] Occasionally personality difficulties may be associated with superior achievement in reading;[3] but when it is a question of the positive, upbuilding effects of reading and literature, research results give very few leads to classroom activities. Since the teacher can never hope to affect positively every child in a class through one type of material or literature experience, she must attempt a varied program in the hope of influencing children with wide individual differences in interests, abilities, and adjustments. Some leads as to possible effects on children can, however, be given to guide such a program of varied activities.

As an example of possible effects of reading and literature upon children's development the suggestions of Smith[4] should be noted:

1. Reading can help young people gauge themselves accurately, to understand the motives of human conduct in general and their own in particular.
2. Books can furnish young people the information that they need to do the things life challenges them to do and to understand its ever widening and deepening problems.
3. Reading is a necessary adjunct to understanding firsthand experiences and an inevitable substitute for experience in all our knowledge of the distant in time and space.
4. Young people come, through reading, to a clearer definition of their own basic philosophy and of their own conviction as to what values are of most worth.

[1] Arthur I. Gates, "Role of Personality Maladjustment in Reading Disability," *Pedagogical Seminary*, Vol. 59, pp. 77-83, September, 1941. David H. Russell, "Reading Disabilities and Mental Health: A Review of Research," *Understanding the Child*, Vol. 16, pp. 24-32, January, 1947.

[2] Mary I. Preston, "Reading Failure and the Child's Security," *American Journal of Orthopsychiatry*, Vol. 10, pp. 239-252, April, 1940.

[3] Robert S. Stewart, *Personality Maladjustment and Reading Achievement*. Unpublished doctoral dissertation, University of California, Berkeley, 1947.

[4] Dora V. Smith, "Nature of the Reading Program to Meet Personal and Social Needs" in W. S. Gray, ed., *Promoting Personal and Social Development through Reading*, Supplementary Educational Monographs, No. 64, pp. 11-16. University of Chicago Press, Chicago, 1947.

5. A final service of reading is to offer escape from the difficult or strained conditions of life in modern times.

In an article emphasizing the place of child development in the reading program from another point of view McCullough[5] said that many of the real values of reading "wither and fade in the classroom of the teacher who sits up nights making flash cards and spends her days listening to oral-reading-around-the-room. Here are some of them: the ability to get along with others, the ability to read fluently and efficiently, the ability to think and feel as a reader, the ability to solve problems alone, the ability to express oneself." The evidence suggests that children learn what they practice rather directly, in reading as in other activities. Accordingly, if they are to interpret what they read, to apply their reading to their own problems or self-concepts or social insights, they must be encouraged in such thinking by their teacher.

The meager research about the effects of reading on young people's lives suggests that this impact depends upon at least three factors: (1) the needs, attitudes, and "set" of the reader himself; (2) the content of the materials read; and (3) the circumstances or setting in which the reading takes place.[6] In much of the reading that goes on in school, the pupil works at the level of literal comprehension, to get the main idea, sequence, or conclusion as stated. In such circumstances the responses are fairly objective and can probably be classed as right, partly right, or wrong. But when the child or adolescent in his free reading or in a literature lesson moves over into the realm of imaginative literature to some of the areas mentioned by Smith above, the reader's interpretation may vary much more widely, and, therefore, the effects of the reading on an individual are much less predictable. For example, when one group of students read the poem "Richard Cory," by Edward Arlington Robinson, different individuals stated the main theme in very different ways.[7] One said it concerns "The personal problems of Richard Cory." Another, "Money is not everything;" still another, "All that looks perfect may not be so; the deceptiveness of appearances." Still

[5] Constance M. McCullough, "Recognizing Child Development in the Reading Program," *Elemenary English,* Vol. 25, pp. 1-11, January, 1948.

[6] David H. Russell, "Some Research on the Impact of Reading," *English Journal,* Vol. 47, pp. 398-413, October, 1958.

[7] Marion Scribner, "Responses of Older Adolescents, Teachers and Literary Critics to the Content of Selected Poetry," Doctoral dissertation, University of California, Berkeley, 1960.

others said, "Contrast between rich and poor." Such a poem may be a bit of a "shocker" to young people used to the happy endings of Hollywood or television fiction. For these students, one cannot say that one response was more "correct" than the others because each was giving his thoughtful, honest reaction to the material. We may, indeed, go further and say that good literature is marked by the power to evoke different kinds of responses in different people or, as Virginia Woolf put it, "There is an ambiguity which is the work of the highest poetry; we cannot know exactly what it means." It seems apparent, accordingly, that a character, a story, a poem, or a play may be interpreted in varied ways, and may, therefore, have quite different effects on different persons. Thus there is probably no such thing as "a good book" for everybody. About the best that a teacher or librarian can estimate is that here is a book likely to be good for a particular person at a particular time. The situation in which "boy meets book" must be arranged on a small-group or individual basis of reading to affect underlying attitudes, deeper layers of personality, or the values an individual holds dear.

Despite the individual nature of the response to literature, some beginning research gives clues to possible effects of good books and other communication media. In one group of studies Smith,[8] Weingarten,[9] and Russell[10] had elementary pupils, adolescents, and elementary teachers each write about the effects of reading on their lives. Smith found that 60 per cent of the elementary pupils reported changes in their attitudes and 30 per cent changes in their concepts and ideas as a result of reading, but that only 9 per cent of the group indicated changes in behavior. Weingarten's survey of the responses of over twelve hundred adolescents demonstrated that in reading these young people could attain understanding of themselves, a worthy concept of self, recognition of an ideal person to emulate, understanding of other persons' motivations, and awareness of others' solutions to their problems. Elementary teachers indicated that in their childhood reading, the most frequent effects were identification with character(s), enjoyment of humor and adventure,

[8] Nila B. Smith, "Some Effects of Reading on Children," *Elementary English,* Vol. 25, pp. 271-278, May, 1948.

[9] Samuel Weingarten, "Developmental Values in Voluntary Reading," *School Review,* Vol. 62, pp. 222-230, April, 1954.

[10] David H. Russell, "Teachers' Memories and Opinions of Children's Literature," *Elementary English,* Vol. 26, pp. 475-482, December, 1949.

enrichment of everyday experiences, enjoyment of fantasy, stimulus to dramatic play, and added knowledge. While the results of these studies may have been influenced by the respondents' desires to give favorable replies to direct questions, the findings show that the effects of reading may be widespread and profound. When the second-grade teacher reads a good story to her class, or the seventh-grade teacher encourages responses to a play or poem, they may be affecting fundamental values and young people's lives. The responsibility is enormous. The teacher must realize that there is no guarantee that profound effects will take place but must do her best to match children and relevant literature.

In addition, there is no final evidence that any one literature experience will help to satisfy some of the needs of a particular child. At best the teacher can hope to recognize the predominance of one or more of these needs in the child and then, from her larger knowledge of available literature, attempt to supply materials which will help to satisfy the need. If an older boy is lonely and needs the satisfaction of achieving group status, he may be helped through reading a group of books such as Cronin's *Green Years,* French's *Lance of Kanana,* Gates's *North Fork,* or Tunis's *All-American.* A rather spoiled little girl from a home in a favored social-economic position may need to know the trials of poverty depicted in Estes's *The Moffats* or the insecurity of the child of an itinerant worker in Gates's *Blue Willow.* There is no guarantee that any one of the books mentioned will affect the child's personality in the way desired, but with wise guidance by the teacher and reinforcement of ideas through other experiences, these stories may help to fulfil the child's needs.

AIMS OF LITERATURE

The ideas of Smith and the research quoted above suggest that the aims of literature teaching are not the same as the aims of all reading instruction. This is because they are concerned with effects on the child rather than abilities to be acquired. Another way of stating the difference is to say that the teaching of literature is concerned more with attitudes and appreciations than with knowledge or skill. It is not a matter of weekly reports or regular tests so much as it is of shared enjoyment and inner meanings. It is not an occasion for drill and work-type procedures so much as it is one for individual enjoyment and creative participation in group activities.

One has only to realize the modern reading needs of children or adults to know that reading for enjoyment of literary or aesthetic characteristics is only one type of reading done today. A glance through almost any basic reader or at any newsstand or bookshop will confirm the variety of materials a person must be able to read intelligently. The reading of literary materials is associated with pleasure or recreational activities; in addition there are many work-type purposes in reading. As indicated in Chapter 11, one reads to skim latest events from a newspaper, to discover specific facts in a science article, to follow directions in a book for some construction, or to organize a sequence of events from historical materials. By the time they reach the fourth or fifth grade, nearly all children read for at least ten or twelve different purposes, and many of these aims do not involve literature in its usual sense. The reading of literature is only one type of reading. Just as reading geographical or arithmetical materials is an example of restricted reading so the reading of literary materials is only a part of the whole.

However, although it is only one of many types of reading in which a child engages, the reading of literary materials and participation in other language-arts activities have a number of values not often realized by other school activities. As suggested in the previous chapter, a teacher of reading is concerned not only with how a child reads but with what he reads. In addition, the teacher is concerned with attitudes toward reading and the establishment of habits of reading which will help the child to grow in understanding other people better or will make him feel the positive effects of achievement connected with successful reading.

The teaching of literature, accordingly, is directed toward such goals as the following:

1. The Extension and Enrichment of the Child's Experience of the Complex Ways of Man's Living

The child who cannot set down Howard Pyle's *Men of Iron* until he has finished it gains insight into ways of living around an English castle in the days of chivalry. For a younger child, Lattimore's *Little Pear* not only presents life in China but suggests how children everywhere are much alike. Properly used, books can extend experience as Emily Dickinson has suggested:

> There is no frigate like a book
> To take us lands away.

2. Giving Opportunity to Relive and Re-experience the Adventures and Ideas of Others

Children who read *On the Banks of Plum Creek, Little House in the Big Woods,* and other books in Wilder's series will have a feeling for the adventures and life of pioneer times which they can never hope to achieve directly. Books are doors to the faraway and long ago and one of the best ways of acquainting children with their cultural heritage.

3. Gaining Insight into One's Own Personality and Problems

The boy who plays tricks to avoid his responsibilities may gain self-insight as well as enjoyment from Henry's *Auno and Tauno.* A little girl who is timid about losing her way in the city may gain courage from the way Betsy was helped to find her school in Haywood's *"B" is for Betsy.* Children identify themselves rather easily with the problems and solutions to problems of likable characters in the stories they read.

4. Providing Materials Which Help to Create an Appreciation and Understanding of the Problems of Others

Children develop rather slowly, particularly in the primary grades, in their feelings toward groups. Minority groups, for example, appear in many modern children's books. Davis's stories in *Americans Every One,* the Beims's *Two Is a Team,* and Eberle's *Very Good Neighbors* are children's books depicting how different groups can work together. Such stories as *And Now Miguel,* and *Rabbit Hill* and its sequel *Tough Winter* show human warmth and kindliness toward others. At all ages different groups can work together. At all ages children can be helped in feelings of sympathy and empathy for other children.

5. The Development of Love of Country and Democratic Ideals

Good books about early Americans, such as the d'Aulaires's *George Washington,* Daugherty's *Daniel Boone* or *Lincoln,* or Forbes's *Johnny Tremain,* help to develop an understanding of the earlier development of one's own country. Current stories laid in different parts of the United States, such as Lenski's continuing series about *Bayou Suzette, Strawberry Girl, Blue Ridge Billy, Judy's Journey,* and others, give an appreciation of the variety and color of life here today. Through such books children develop a love and understanding of their own country which they never would get in formal attempts to teach patriotism.

6. The Discovery of Ethical Values Which Are Common to Different Creeds and Which Form a Foundation of Good Character in the Modern World

Kircher's *Character Education through Books*[11] lists many books with the qualities of character, such as bravery and friendliness, that they illustrate. In many good children's books, such as Edmonds's *Two Logs Crossing* or Enright's *Kintu,* a character is faced with a decision to be made, a decision which exemplifies, positively or negatively, an application of ethical values. In identifying themselves with such decisions children can be helped in achieving higher values.

7. Providing Opportunities for Fun and for Escape

No one who knows children would deny them the opportunity to laugh at Atwater's *Mr. Popper's Penguins,* share in the excitement provided by Cleary's *Henry Huggins and Ribsy,* adventure with the ducks in McCloskey's *Make Way for the Ducklings,* or revel in the humorous magic of Travers's *Mary Poppins.* Most teachers and parents enjoy sharing collections of humorous stories, such as those of Fenner[12] of Scoggin,[13] and of Cole.[14] All teachers and children have their own favorites, but "just for fun" must always be high on the list of reasons for literature experiences.

8. The Development of Worth-While Tastes and Permanent Interests in Good Literature

No teacher will ever confess such an aim to a class, but over the months she will note how the boys and girls in the group are growing in their reading attitudes and habits. If one boy stays with the comics in his leisure reading, he may need a different kind of guidance. If another reads only dog stories, he too may need help. This aim does not mean that all children must end by reading the classics.

[11] Clara J. Kircher, comp., *Character Formation through Books: A Bibliography.* Catholic University of America Press, Washington, D.C., 1945.

[12] Phyllis R. Fenner, ed., *Time to Laugh.* Knopf, New York, 1942.

[13] Margaret C. Scoggin, *Chucklebait.* Knopf, New York, 1945.

[14] William Cole, *Humorous Poetry for Children.* World Publishing, Cleveland, Ohio, 1955.

Mark Twain suggested that "a classic is something that everybody wants to have read and nobody wants to read," and what is good literature to one child may be trash to another. The meaning of literature to a child is explored further after the next section, which considers the eight aims from another point of view.

IMPORTANCE OF ATTITUDES

The eight aims discussed above emphasize the development of attitudes rather than the gaining of information or acquiring of skill. Accordingly, literature is taught to create an emotional response as a subtle contagion of spirit rather than as drill on specific facts. To accomplish this, it is important that the teacher enjoy the selection herself. In general, too, extensive reading to get important whole impressions and the author's purpose is more important than dissection into minute details. After a short introduction the competent oral reading of a worth-while selection with no particular pressure to remember details usually will help to create the attitudes desired. Sometimes such attitudes can be sharpened or clarified in discussion or other use of the material.

An attitude is usually defined as a readiness to respond. Allport called it a "state of readiness, organized through experiences, which exacts a directive or dynamic response to all objects and situations to which it is related."[15] Because a child has an attitude toward *Buck Rogers* or *danger* or *Chinese* or *wealth,* he will react to these ideas in a certain way. The way he responds will gradually be built up or organized through his experiences, some of which may be experiences in literature. In acquiring attitudes, learning often is subtle. Enthusiasms and, unfortunately, prejudices are contagious. Attitudes are acquired when a series of experiences tend to reinforce, indirectly perhaps, the same responses. They often are connected with emotional experiences which also can be provided in literature. They are not separate learnings but often are related to skills or abilities; this is one reason why reading ability as such is an essential for enjoyment of literature. Since attitudes are learned in such ways, the teacher who is attempting to affect children's attitudes will plan and carry out experiences in literature and other reading through activities

[15] Gordon W. Allport, "Attitudes," in C. Murchison, ed., *Handbook of Social Psychology,* Chap. 17, p. 810. Clark University Press, Worcester, Mass., 1935.

which are not of sledge-hammer directness, which are organized to reinforce one another, which give a place to emotion, and which are related to other activities.

There is considerable evidence to suggest that reading done in childhood builds attitudes that persist throughout a lifetime, often because they are unconscious attitudes. Reactions to names, to places, to occupations, are predetermined, in part at least, by one's early reading. In the field of international attitudes T. S. Eliot, the English poet and critic, suggested that American attitudes toward Britain have been affected by the fact that many United States citizens as children read *Little Lord Fauntleroy*. Similarly, British attitudes toward America are determined by the fact that many British children used to read *The Last of the Mohicans*. Paul Hazard,[16] in his delightful *Books, Children and Men*, said, "We can disregard the literature for childhood only if we consider unimportant the way in which a national soul is formed and sustained." And later: "But we must not stop at this point. For children's books repudiate instinctively antagonisms and hatred, mixing indissolubly with a sense of patriotism a sense of humanity."

Of course attitudes other than international ones may be built partly through reading. Articles with such titles as "America in Story: A Regional Bibliography"[17] "Children's Books on the Negro: To Help Build a Better World,"[18] and "Biography for Young Readers"[19] indicate other possibilities in developing attitudes.

TRENDS IN CHILDREN'S LITERATURE

To teachers who remember literature as something made up of items like *Ivanhoe, The Daffodils,* and *The Great Stone Face,* the newer concept of children's literature should be mentioned. Modern invention and the wide variety of purposes for teaching literature combine to make available to the schools many modern forms of children's literature. In general this literature may be described as records of man's experience which have value for the child or adult

[16] Paul Hazard, *Books, Children and Men,* pp. 111, 144. Horn Book Co., Boston, 1944.

[17] Pearl W. Lyons, "America in Story: A Regional Bibliography," *Elementary English Review,* Vol. 18, pp. 216-224, 270-272, 306-309, October, November, December, 1941.

[18] C. Rollins, "Children's Books on the Negro: To Help Build a Better World," *Elementary English Review,* Vol. 20, pp. 219-223, October, 1943.

[19] Lillian Hollowell, "Biography for Young Readers," *Elemenary English Review,* Vol. 23, pp. 262-266, October, 1946.

using them. Experience has usually been recorded in words, but modern developments have widened the scope of our records. As Betzner put it,

> The concept of literature presented in this monograph, therefore, is that of a body of preserved writings having significance for the persons using them. Since recorded experience is not confined to writing, it is necessary to include in any consideration of children's literature pictures not only in books but wherever found, phonograph records, and the records made over the radio. Moreover, because it is impossible to deal with these materials apart from the forms used for preserving them, books, magazines, newspapers, signboards, children's own writings, the story hour, motion pictures, radio programs, phonograph records, and the theater will be included as appropriate considerations in any program of literature.[20]

The history of children's books in the United States goes back to the *New England Primer* published about 1690, famous for its Puritanical, theological content and for its alphabet rhymes. One of these may be just as true today as then:

> My book and heart
> Must never part

Later literature was influenced by English books and especially by John Newbery who began publishing in London books especially planned for children, beginning with the *Pretty Little Pocket Book* of 1744. The wide sources and rich materials of children's literature have been described in detail by Arbuthnot,[21] by Meigs,[22] and others. Besides consulting these sources teachers may be aware of current trends in the field of juvenile literature. The following are trends in a rapidly growing field:

1. There are many more books for very young children.
2. A larger number of books present social studies, science and other factual material in attractive form.
3. Fairy tale and folk and hero literature is being recommended for somewhat older children than before, the former around eight and nine years, the latter around eleven to thirteen years.

20 Jean Betzner, *Exploring Literature with Children,* Practical Suggestions for Teaching, No. 7, p. 2. Bureau of Publications, Teachers College, Columbia University, New York, 1943.

21 May H. Arbuthnot, *Children and Books,* rev. ed., Scott-Foresman, Chicago, 1957.

22 Cornelia Meigs and others, *A Critical History of Children's Literature,* Macmillan, New York, 1953.

4. The series is flourishing once again, for both fact and fiction, with considerable variation in desirability, both between series and within the volumes of any one series.

5. Teachers and librarians have moved somewhat in evaluating the worth of a book from literary value to function in the life of a child as a main criterion.

6. Many stories for children have changed from strongly plotted accounts of opposing forces and struggle to simple incident and exposition.

7. Poetry is being more carefully selected, with emphasis upon its relation to the chid's or adolescent's experience.

8. A wider variety of types of literature is available than ever before, especially in the form of recordings and television.

9. Children are increasingly using materials aimed somewhat above their actual age level, with earlier exposure to "adult" magazines, books, and television programs.

10. School programs place more emphasis on children's producing more of their own literature in varied kinds of writing.

With this increasing amount of children's literature, teachers need help in selecting and in finding needed materials. The sources given at the end of this chapter are aids in finding good books. The best way of finding out about current children's books is, of course, to borrow, beg, or buy them and read them for oneself. There is no substitute for the direct experience, and some teachers read three or four children's books in a night at the hobby-enjoyment level. In addition one may (1) know and use some of the best anthologies of child literature which are bulky but which compress much material between two covers (these have been compiled by Arbuthnot, by Hollowell, by Huber, and others); (2) skim current children's magazines and newspapers; (3) know some of the books about children's books such as those of Duff, Eaton, Larrick, and Smith (see Appendix D); (4) use current general book lists such as those given at the end of this chapter (many of these indicate difficulty and hint at content); (5) know some special book lists adapted to different purposes which are a current concern or need of a class or group, such as easy books for the retarded and reluctant reader,[23]

[23] "The Bookshelf: For the Reluctant Reader," *N.E.A. Journal*, Vol. 47, pp. 644, 652, December, 1958.

books about foreign countries,[24] or science books;[25] (6) read current reviews of children's books such as found in *Elementary English, The Horn Book, Junior Libraries, Library Journal, Parents' Magazine, Saturday Review,* and book-review sections in newspapers; and (7) consult school and public librarians and work with a committee buying for the school library.

This wide range of activities and the even wider assortment of children's books available today mean that teacher and parent alike must develop some criteria in determining what is a good book for children. The funds for school and classroom libraries are often limited, and they must be spent on the best books possible. The preceding sections have indicated that a good book to one child may leave another bored or repelled, but individual teachers or purchasing committees can develop a set of criteria for evaluating books which may include the following:

Are the theme and content suitable to the age level for which the book is planned?

Is the theme or main idea developed with unity?

In fiction, is the plot developed logically and realistically, with action leading to a satisfying conclusion?

Does the book illustrate ethical values or contain important truths?

Is the physical format (type, illustrations, etc.) well done and in keeping with the theme of the book?

These are general questions, but they may be applied more specifically to particular books. The criteria may vary but the central concern is still the impact of the book on the young person. Elizabeth Yates, author of *Amos Fortune, Prudence Crandall,* and other books for children, put it this way:

> To the query "What is a good book?" I suggest it is any book that enriches experience and helps us to live more understandingly, deeply, joyously. Such a book has life because it gives life. It brings the reader forward to a new frontier with wider eyes, keener ears, and a more responsive heart. A writer only begins a book, it is the reader who completes it; for the reader takes up where the writer left off as new thoughts stir within him. Whether that reader be child or man, the book is as good as its effect on him.

[24] Marjorie Scherwitzsky, "Children's Literature about Foreign Countries," *Wilson Library Bulletin,* Vol. 32, pp. 142-148, October, 1957.

[25] Paul E. Kambly, "Science Books for the Elementary School Library," *School Science and Mathematics,* Vol. 159, pp. 294-303, April, 1959.

The core of the literature program in most classrooms will be certain selections in the basic readers and individual copies of children's stories in the classroom and school library. Teachers should be careful to distinguish the literary selections for enjoyment and appreciation from the more factual selections for work-type reading in basic-reading series. Some teachers actually look over a whole book and mark the selections in terms of these two approaches. However, certain selections may contain both elements or may be used in different ways at different times. Betzner's statement above (page 420) indicates, however, that teachers must be aware of chances for increasing the "literature environment." A primary room may be full of suggestions on bulletin board and wall for pictures, movies, books, and the children's own writing. A class studying the westward movement may enjoy singing "Oh, Susanna," listening to other songs of the period, or dancing the quadrilles, reels, and other dances of the times. The teacher may recommend a movie or television program which will provide a significant experience for the child. Modern juvenile literature exists in many forms.

ACTIVITIES IN THE LITERATURE PROGRAM

The wide variety of materials mentioned above indicates that there can be no one best method of teaching literature from basic readers or any other source. The aims given suggest that such practices as expecting a large group of children to enjoy reading the same story within the same time limit or limiting story books to a strict test-score level in reading or making literature a sort of rarefied experience separate from the rest of the school day will help to destroy any love of literature a child has. On the other hand, desirable literature activities are many and varied. Some of the ways literature may be enjoyed are these:

1. Oral and silent reading by the class.
2. Oral reading by the teacher.
3. Audience reading by competent pupils.
4. Listening to the radio and the phonograph; seeing and hearing movies.
5. Free periods of silent reading—using materials of the individual's own selection.
6. Book or reading reports.
7. Dramatization.

8. Choral speaking and reading.
9. Dramatic play.
10. Creative writing—making one's own literature.
11. Memorization.
12. Literary programs—book riddles, showing pictures, maps and cartoons, homemade movies, music, etc.

In using all these methods to provide experiences in literature the wise teacher will not follow set guides. A summary of research on teaching literature says that "much more quantitative research is available in reading skills than in the teaching of literature."[26] Since literature exists in so many forms, since literary experiences may be so varied, and since response to literature is highly individual and personal, it is fortunate that literature lessons are not formalized or fixed by research.

Although literature experiences are informal and varied, a few hints about each of the above activities, particularly as they relate to reading, may be suggested briefly.

1. Oral and Silent Reading by Class

This is of course the commonest means of entering the realm of literature. Both these activities mean that the teacher ordinarily will help to set the stage by the introduction of interesting ideas related to the materials read. She may do this by calling for pupils' experiences in the areas involved, and by encouraging discussion of the selection to be read through such means as guessing from the title and from pictures. Silent reading ordinarily will be used for prose materials; but when these are particularly rhythmical and euphonious, they may be read orally. Poetry ordinarily will be read aloud. However, all oral reading should be preceded by silent reading of the selection or the part of it used. The teacher should avoid having one pupil read orally while the rest follow silently with their books. The audience situation should be encouraged rather than the examination climate, in which other pupils are ready to pounce upon errors made by the pupil reading orally. Much oral reading should be in the form of audience reading mentioned below.

2. Oral Reading by the Teacher

The teacher who plans story hours and other reading for her pupils is contributing to their development in a way which can

[26] Robert Pooley, "English—Literature" in C. W. Harris, ed., *Encyclopedia of Educational Research,* 3rd ed., p. 470. Macmillan, New York, 1960.

scarcely be equaled by other methods. Each teacher will develop her own method of reading or storytelling. Suggestions for storytelling are developed more fully in a book by Tooze.[27] Children often enjoy a bit of dramatization as a selection is being read. Variations in tone and volume help to create the spell of good literature. In order to select materials to give true appreciation experiences, every teacher must be acquainted with a considerable volume of children's literature. (This knowledge will include the classics of children's literature and current books and stories as they appear.) Suggestions at the end of this chapter introduce the teacher to a knowledge of materials, such as children's anthologies, and methods, such as hints for storytelling, which will enable her to provide a wide variety of listening and participating experiences for her pupils. It is a safe rule to say that every elementary teacher should read orally to her class at least once every day.

3. Audience Reading by Competent Pupils

Many pupils are still compelled to listen to familiar materials read by other pupils in an unsatisfactory way. Audience reading implies an enjoyable situation in which the class listens to new stories which are read with fluency and skill. Ordinarily, any one child will read to an audience once every three or four weeks. He will then share with the rest of the class something which he himself has enjoyed and which he may have practiced for several weeks so that he can read it well. This material will often be fresh to the rest of the class, such as a story from a newspaper or a new book or a poem from a little-known collection. A child may do functional oral reading of a paragraph or a committee report upon numerous occasions. But oral reading of carefully prepared materials once every three or four weeks will do more to benefit a child's oral reading than continual practice on poorly prepared materials. In addition the well-prepared reader will give to other members of his class a true literary experience in which they enjoy a selection read well by one of themselves.

4. Experiences Involving Audio-Visual Materials

Experiences involving the radio, the phonograph, films, film-strips, the tape-recorder, and other audio-visual aids, must be prepared for and followed up. If children are to listen to the recording of Vachel Lindsay's "The Congo" read by himself or to Robert Frost saying one of his poems, some background about the author and the selec-

[27] Ruth Tooze, *Storytelling*. Prentice-Hall, Englewood Cliffs, N.J., 1959.

tion will be needed if the pupils are to enjoy the selection fully. Similarly, pupils may need a little help in interpreting a recorded ballad, such as the *Skye Boat Song,* because of differences in language. The teacher will avoid dissection of the selection, but can always point out with the pupils a few of the main ideas and a few things to look for. The advantage of most recordings is that they can be used many times. If a radio program has not been recorded, it is particularly important that the teacher guide the pupils' discussion of the program heard while it is still fresh in their minds. Some radio programs and materials prepared by the children themselves may be put on tape for later use.

The emotional impact of many movies is great, and few of the commercial films are prepared for children, particularly young children. The teacher, accordingly, has a responsibility for encouraging children to see only the best of commercial films and for gradually developing certain standards for good movies. Since most children see movies regularly outside school anyway, guidance in choices and gradual development of critical judgment is important. Of the so-called "educational films" the teacher's introduction and approach to a story for enjoyment will vary considerably, from preparation for an informational film to be viewed for specific facts, to preparation for enjoyment and appreciation of ideas without reference to details. Experiments such as that reported by Witty[28] using Encyclopaedia Britannica films are not closely related to reading as such, but they are useful in stimulating other language arts activities.

5. *Television*

Television programs belong with the audio-visual experiences described above but are so important a part of many children's lives that they deserve a separate statement. As noted in the previous chapter, most families have television sets, and elementary-school children may spend an average of about three hours a day looking at programs. The rise of the non-commercial, educational television station has meant that there are now more programs adapted to children's needs than commercial stations, with their obligation to draw a large viewing audience, have felt they could offer. Although a few of these are concerned with children's literature, such programs are not the

[28] Paul A. Witty, "The Use of Films in Stimulating Creative Expression and in Identifying Talented Pupils," *Elementary English,* Vol. 33, pp. 340-344, October, 1956.

concern of this section. Despite the excellence of some "educational" programs, the great mass of children still view commercial television with the attendant dangers of unlimited exposure to portrayals of violence and crime, stereotyping, and other television "sins."

Because so much of the fare is questionable, and because children are exposed to it so thoroughly, no teacher can escape the responsibility to help children select the best programs and to develop critical standards of judgment about what they do see and hear. Programs change constantly, but a number of good series in past years such as *Robin Hood, Lassie,* some of the Disney productions, and a few of the better Westerns may perhaps be classed as desirable children's literature. Programs of quality, single or in series, may be discussed ahead of time and television schedules marked for events related to class interests or activities. In addition, standards of judging programs may gradually be built. One manual on listening activities[29] suggests the following standards to be developed in intermediate-grade classes:

1. *Purpose.* Is the program planned to accomplish something worthwhile (give information, recount adventure, provide genuine fun, etc)?
2. *Consistency.* Is the program always good or does it have "ups and downs?"
3. *Presentation.* If fictional, is the story told well? If informational, are the facts clear?
4. *Personnel.* Do announcers, actors, and others speak well and seem genuine?
5. *Advertising.* Are the advertisements clever? Do they intrude too much on the program?
6. *Effects.* Does the program leave you with the feeling you have gained something from it? Do you remember the ideas, the situations, or the humor?

By gradually developing simple standards in the primary grades and moving toward questions such as these in the intermediate grades the teachers can help children become more selective in their televiewing.

6. Using Magazines and Newspapers

Magazines and newspapers are usually classed with the mass media mentioned above. Much of the material contained in them cannot be classed as children's literature, for their purpose is usually to inform

[29] David H. Russell and Elizabeth F. Russell, *Listening Aids Through the Grades.* Bureau of Publications, Teachers College, Columbia University, New York, 1959.

about current events, and their contents are directed to adults except for a few juvenile magazines described below. Nevertheless, both newspapers and magazines may provide materials important to the child's life and illuminating human relationships. For example, the "human interest" story run occasionally in most newspapers (*e.g.*, the familiar tale of a boy and his lost dog) may be read and enjoyed by a class. Magazines are useful in developing bulletin board displays and in providing materials for pupils' scrapbooks. Teachers may read or summarize articles that are difficult, especially in the lower grades. Magazines are also stimuli to independent reading for the more able pupil.

One survey[30] found that the most frequently used magazines in elementary and secondary classrooms were *Life, National Geographic, Newsweek, Time, Reader's Digest, Look, Saturday Evening Post, U. S. News and World Report,* and *Holiday.* The content of many of these suggests an emphasis upon current events and social studies rather than upon literature as such, and yet they all contain materials which may stimulate children's writing—and therefore his reading. Although not as useful in primary grades as materials especially written for children, they can sometimes provide a challenge to the reader who is tired of "baby stuff" and who feels that he is ready to explore some of the adult world.

7. *Free Periods of Silent Reading*

Such periods are possible in schools which provide a variety of reading materials at different grade levels for any one class. In this period, monitors may distribute individual copies of books to children who have their names on a slip of paper in them, or children may go to the library shelves to select their own books. For the period each child reads something he wants to read in the library or in his own classroom. During this period the teacher may aid some individual pupils who need special help with their reading or offer some guidance to children who are unable to select books adapted to their reading abilities and interests. Such periods not only provide for enjoyment of literature in the way the teacher hopes it will operate throughout the pupil's liftetime but give an opportunity for individual activities in which the teacher can affect the developing per-

[30] "Teachers in All Fields Use Magazines in the Classroom," *N.E.A. Research Bulletin,* Vol. 38, pp. 27-31, February, 1960.

BOOK REPORT

Author ....
Title ....
Publisher .... Date ....
Theme ....
....
What I liked about the book ....
....
What I disliked about the book ....
....
(Put other comments on the back.)

....
Name of reporter

A form for a brief report

sonalities of her pupils. The individualized reading program as described by Miel,[31] by Veatch,[32] and others, and as evaluated by Witty,[33] may produce favorable attitudes to reading and promote personal growth through reading. (See also Chapter 15.)

8. Book or Reading Reports

In the free reading situation described above, the teacher may wish to have some check on materials covered by each pupil. One way of doing this is to have a brief report on the materials read by the boys and girls. Small mimeographed sheets like the illustration often may be used (see above). These reports must never become long or burdensome to the child or teacher. In addition, oral reports on books are often helpful in the class, particularly after a new group of books has been placed in the classroom or school library. In such reports the pupils may show the books or book jackets and tell a little about the author and the setting for the story. In previous discussion the teacher and pupils will have brought up the point that a good book report should not tell the whole story, but rather should leave much of the information or plot to be discovered by the individual reader.

[31] Alice Miel, ed., *Individualized Reading Practices.* Bureau of Publications, Teachers College, Columbia University, New York, 1958.

[32] Jeannette Veatch, comp., *Individualizing Your Reading Program.* Putnam, New York, 1959.

[33] Paul A. Witty, "Individualized Reading: A Summary and Evaluation," *Elementary English,* Vol. 36, pp. 401-412, 450, October, 1959.

9. Dramatization

Some selections in a basic reader and other books lend themselves to dramatization by the pupils. This may range from very informal to rather fixed activities. In any case, considerable knowledge of the story is required. In informal dramatization the pupils may suggest very roughly what happened through action and may supply words which they think are appropriate but which are not closely related to the original story. In a slightly more planned situation pupils may work out a number of scenes which make up the story and then read from their books the actual speeches of the characters. In a more elaborate situation pupils may spend a number of periods planning the scenes, the costumes, the action, and the dialogue. Some teachers find it valuable to have different groups do different scenes. Often two or more committees may work on the same scene, and the best of the dialogue and action from each committee's plan may be combined for the finished production. The final production may involve the memorization of the parts, and fairly elaborate presentation, often to other groups. The teacher will plan the procedure so that all members of the class, if possible, have some share in the dramatic production.

A play worked out by the children themselves for formal presentation is usually a much more valuable experience than a memorized play from some book, but it must be used infrequently because of time and other factors. Much oftener the children can engage in informal creative dramatizations. Pre-school and primary children often derive most benefit from dramatic play, growing out of an incident or story, rather than a dramatization performed for others. As suggested above, the teacher and children build the play from a story they have enjoyed, and no lines or specific actions are memorized. Characters are discussed, different children enact their version of the scene, and there is evaluation of the efforts. Such sources as books by Lease and Siks,[34] and by Ward[35] suggest ways of using children's stories which lead to development of understanding, avoidance of imitation, the importance of involvement, and emphasis upon the creative process rather than a finished product.

[34] Ruth G. Lease and Geraldine Siks, *Creative Dramatics in Home, School, and Community*. Harper, New York, 1952.

[35] Winifred Ward, *Playmaking with Children*. Appleton-Century, New York, 1947.

10. Choral Speaking or Reading

While some special work in speech is desirable, teachers should not feel that it is necessary to have such background before they attempt choral speaking or reading with their pupils. Choral reading especially may be of an informal sort of activity for enjoyment. Poetry is ordinarily better material than prose for these activities, and with a little practice teachers can discover what sort of selection helps to bring good results. With a little practice, also, the teacher may group low and high or dark and light voices. Suggestions made in books on choral speaking by Abney,[36] Gullan,[37] Keppie,[38] and others apply in many cases to the choral reading situation. One advantage of choral reading is that it may help the unrhythmical word-by-word oral reader. Perhaps even more important, it gives children a security in the group, a sense of social participation, and an enjoyment of sound and rhythm which is not always possible in individual reading.

Different writers[39] have given practical suggestions for relating ordinary reading and choral reading experiences. These practical hints often include the following advice:

Well-liked poetry is the best material for first attempts.

Six to eight children are best for informal work (as compared to a larger verse chorus).

Choral reading is primarily for enjoyment and for practice in oral interpretation.

In beginning the activity, the first requirement is that the group understand the meaning and mood of the poem. The rhythm of the poem must be felt and sing-song must be avoided.

The first choral reading should be done softly.

Lines may be spoken in solo, duet, quartet, a line a child, alternat-

36 Louise Abney and Grace Rowe, *Choral Speaking Arrangements for the Lower Grades* and *Choral Speaking Arrangements for the Upper Grades.* Expression Company, Magnolia, Mass., 1944.

37 Marjorie Gullan, *Choral Speaking,* 2nd ed. Expression Company, Magnolia, Mass., 1933. Marjorie Gullan, *Speech Choir.* Harper, New York, 1937.

38 Elizabeth E. Keppie, *Choral Verse Speaking.* Expression Company, Magnolia, Mass., 1939. Elizabeth E. Keppie, Conrad F. Wedberg, and Miriam Keslar, *Speech Improvement through Choral Speaking.* Expression Company, Magnolia, Mass., 1942.

39 For example, Philena Cox and Rosalind Hughes, *Effective Choral Speaking and Reading,* Contributions in Reading, No. 9. Ginn, Boston, 1957. See also Gullan and Keppie, *op. cit.*

ing boys and girls, and in unison, depending upon meaning and sound effect.

Choral readers should use their voices to express varied meanings as is done in natural conversation—variations in speed, tone, and volume add to effectiveness.

Some children, especially in the pre-school and primary years, enjoy combining choral speaking or reading with bodily rhythms, as in such poems as "Rope Skipping" or A. A. Milne's "Shoes and Stockings."

Children may take turns as audience and readers.

Every teacher and many children will have their favorites, but if the group is inexperienced, it is better to begin with relatively simple poems such as some nursery rhymes. The solo-refrain type of poem, often with question and answer, is easier than a chorus for a whole poem. After some try-outs, a teacher may divide the children into low, medium, and high voices and use the different groups for contrast and for characterization. Some collections of poems, such as that of Brown and Heltman,[40] and of Abney and Rowe,[41] have been arranged for different voices and effects, but many teachers, and children who have had some practice in choral reading, will want to read a poem carefully and then decide themselves how it may be presented. Some teachers keep card files of poems they have found useful for choral reading, in terms of enjoyment and of relevance to other curricular activities.

11. Creative Writing

In addition to the creative activities mentioned above, another literature experience occurs in creative writing itself. Children who have had interesting and vivid experiences want to talk about them in some way. With teacher guidance they may wish to make more permanent records of the experience. In preparing these records they may do some writing which can be classed as literary; but whether or not a sample reaches the highest standards, for the child himself it may be a direct creative experience. Such creative writing may be done on an individual or a group basis. It is not accomplished by teachers' forcing pupils to write on a particular topic or by everyone's

[40] Helen A. Brown and Harry Heltman, *Let's Read Together Poems,* 4 books. Row-Peterson, Evanston, Ill., 1949, 1950.

[41] Louise Abney and Grace Rowe, *Choral Speaking Arrangements for the Lower Grades,* rev. ed. Expression Co., Magnolia, Mass., 1953.

helping to grind out a group poem. Rather it comes as a bit of "inspiration," when a child expresses something particularly well and when others in the group respond to that child's enthusiasm and the teacher's respect for what he is saying or writing. This is the time for the teacher to say, "Let's write down what Marie said," or "Wouldn't that be a good first line for a poem? Who could add a line to it?" Since inspiration is not enough, the teacher may help the individual or the group to improve the writing, but such correction often is most effective two or three days after the first creative effort. Suggestions for encouraging children's writing are given in such books as Burrows's *They All Want to Write,*[42] Applegate's *Helping Children Write,*[43] and other books on the language arts.[44]

12. Memorization

Memorization, like creative writing, is not something that can be forced. Rather it grows out of great interest and intense desire to have some permanent record. A well-loved poem will be repeated so often by children in different circumstances that many of them will soon acquire it as their own. With a little guidance and help from the teacher the actual memorization will be accomplished very easily. The teacher may suggest from time to time the value of having this permanent use of the poem or selection. Occasionally, children may recite some poems they know in a situation much like the audience-reading situation. Sometimes favorite poems may be incorporated in a child's or a class book. Experience seems to indicate that the poems learned in childhood are retained rather easily, to add enjoyment not only in later school years but in adulthood. The ability to quote bits of great literature is often useful to many adults. Memorization on an informal and individual basis is therefore an important part of the literature program.

13. Literary Programs

Literary programs may consist of children's reciting of poems, as mentioned above, but ordinarily they have a wider scope. Activities

[42] Alvina T. Burrows and others, *They All Want to Write.* Prentice-Hall, Englewood Cliffs, N.J., 1952.

[43] Mauree Applegate, *Helping Children Write.* International Textbook, Scranton, Pa., 1949.

[44] Commission on the English Curriculum, *Language Arts for Today's Children,* Chap. 7. Appleton-Century-Crofts, New York, 1954. Ruth G. Strickland, *The Language Arts in the Elementary School,* 2nd ed., Chaps. 12, 13. Heath, Boston, 1957.

mentioned, such as book riddles, picture maps and stories, cartoons, and dramatizations, may all be used in the program. Some children enjoy quizzes they themselves make up about authors or quotations. In general, all these activities should be a natural development of the day-by-day work of the class instead of an entirely extracurricular activity which must be practiced at odd intervals. Good suggestions for such programs are made in Murray and Bathurst's *Creative Ways for Children's Programs* and other books.[45]

14. Using the Paperbacks

Boutwell[46] has called the inexpensive paperback book "the best invention since the sandwich." Most of the paperbacks are prepared for the adult reader, but some are being used in the book clubs for teenagers, and many of the inexpensive books on the super-market shelves, such as the Little Golden Books mentioned at the first of this chapter, fall into the same category of a mass-produced, cheaply-bound, and relatively inexpensive source of reading material. Because the books are made inexpensively, they cannot be expected to last long in the hard use they get in a primary classroom; thus librarians and book committees usually purchase more durable books. Teachers in junior- and senior-high schools, however, have had considerable success in using such books with groups of eight or ten students, or even whole classes, and the advantages of such sources in the elementary classroom are many.

Because of the rapid production of new titles teachers face two problems: (1) knowing what books are available, and (2) finding books suitable for young readers. Some fifteen publishers, such as Bantam, Dell, New American Library (Signet and Mentor), Pocket, and TAB Books offer a wide variety of materials; and another group of publishers present "quality" materials for adults, usually somewhat higher priced. Teachers who wish to check on available titles will find in their library or bookstore the semi-annual volume *Paperbound Books in Print* (R. R. Bowker). Different publishers will send lists of books suitable for school use. The selection of books from drugstores, newsstands, or catalogues is difficult for the publishers

[45] Josephine Murray and Effie G. Bathurst, *Creative Ways for Children's Programs,* 396 p. Silver-Burdett, New York, 1938.

[46] William D. Boutwell, "Paper-Backs; The Best Invention Since the Sandwich," *N. E. A. Journal,* Vol. 48, pp. 55-56, October, 1959.

mentioned, but is even more hazardous in books prepared for the juvenile mass market. These books vary widely in quality and cannot be acquired in a blanket order; an adult reader or a book committee must evaluate individual titles before purchasing.

Elementary schools have not yet realized the possibilities in the use of the paperback and the mass-produced juvenile book. As suggested above, most volumes are planned for adults, but recent publishers' lists have included many books suitable for older elementary and junior-high-school pupils, such as Jack London's *Call of the Wild,* Mark Twain's *Connecticut Yankee in King Arthur's Court, Tom Sawyer,* and *Huckleberry Finn,* Arthur C. Clarke's science fiction stories, the Hornblower books and other stories by C. S. Forester, and such writers as Henry G. Felsen, Jim Kjelgaard, Rutherford Montgomery, Howard Pease, and Armstrong Sperry. Sections such as "Humor," "Juveniles," and "Sports" in *Paperbound Books in Print* offer many possibilities for individual recreational reading and group sharing reactions to stories.

Successful teachers include in their programs certain activities involving literature not included in the fourteen above. Various writers have assembled a wide variety of activities which involve children's active participation in literature experiences. As suggested above, Jensen[47] listed no less than fifty "things to do" in a literature program. Martin[48] described a wide range of enrichment activities that can be used in the reading programs of superior children, from phonics and vocabulary work, through library activites, to mythology, "literary charades," and book fairs. Similarly, Dawson[49] has listed activities to stimulate interest in literature in classroom, in school or within a total school system. She suggested such items as:

1. *Bulletin board displays*
   a. Jackets of newly purchased books
   b. Posters about reading or special books
   c. Children's original illustrations for favorite stories
   d. Picture strips to show the steps in a plot
   e. Simple book reports

47 Amy E. Jensen, *op. cit.*

48 Ruth Martin, *Enrichment Activities for the Superior Child in the Reading Program,* Contributions in Reading, No. 22. Ginn, Boston, 1958.

49 Mildred A. Dawson, "Making Friends of Books," *Language Arts Notes,* No. 4. World Book, Yonkers, N.Y., 1949.

2. *Exhibits on shelves or tables*
   - *a.* Clay modelling of story characters and settings
   - *b.* Peep shows of scenes from favorite books
   - *c.* Sand table picture of a dramatic incident from a book
   - *d.* Dolls dressed as book characters
   - *e.* Favorite books brought from home

3. *Activities*
   - *a.* Listening to recordings of stories
   - *b.* Storytelling period by teacher, guest, or capable pupil
   - *c.* Dramatization of scenes from a new or favorite story
   - *d.* Telling original riddles about book characters or plots
   - *e.* Assembly programs—talk by an author or illustrator, dramatization and shadow plays, movie of a literary classic, etc.
   - *f.* Making literary maps or friezes

Probably the basic necessities are providing a reading table or "center" with shelves and chairs in a corner of the classroom and allowing time each week on the class schedule for free, recreational reading. Some pupils enjoy keeping reading lists or cards in a reading file, which is categorized into pets, horse stories, foreign lands, etc. Television programs may stimulate interest in specific kinds of books. Teachers, librarians, and children can unite in some special events celebrating Children's Book Week. A wide variety of activities will help turn some casual readers into constant readers. Then more children as they grow older will feel like Phyllis McGinley:

> But every now and then
> I want
> A plot that thickens—
> Something like Christie,
> Something like Dickens,
> Something like Trollope at his most methodical,
> Something like something
> From a ladies' periodical.
> If the style's not gloomy
> And no symbols clash,
> A classic will do me—
> Even classic trash.[50]

The way the fourteen items included above and the specific suggestions listed here should be used will vary with the maturity and interests of the group of children. The brief notes made above sug-

[50] Reprinted, by permission, from a poem in *The New Yorker* © 1958. The New Yorker Magazine, Inc.

gest that these activities can contribute to children's wholesome growth, that children develop *through* reading and related literature activities.

WHAT ABOUT POETRY?

Many children enjoy nursery and folk rhymes in their pre-school years but develop an indifference to or dislike of poetry by the time they are in the intermediate grades. Some boys, especially, regard it as "wishy-washy" or "sissy," and some teachers themselves do not enjoy reading or speaking poetry. Some basal readers for elementary grades contain poetry; others do not. The reasons for the failure to develop some appreciation of poetry undoubtedly are complex, but probably one of them has been the choice of poetry offered to children in the schools of the past. After the bouncy rhythm and humor of Mother Goose and folk rhymes of the preschool years children were expected, often rather suddenly, to enjoy the work of "good" or recognized poets or of poetry judged suitable by adult standards. The modern point of view, now applied in many schools, is that taste is established gradually and that children, especially in the lower elementary grades, will react favorably to verse which is not great literature but which contains action, humor, or other recognizable characteristics. One of the trends in children's literature noted above is the increasing use of poetry which is child-like, or closely related to some experience of childhood. The eight-year old living in a city apartment may not be ready to enjoy the work of a "nature poet" of an earlier, rural day, but he may appreciate the clatter and speed of Rachel Field's *Taxis* or Dorothy Baruch's *Stop-Go.* Probably the most influential factors in determining a child's attitude to verse are his background of experience and the theme of the poem.

The stages through which children develop in their appreciation of poetry have not been isolated in research. Poetry can be judged not only in terms of a child's understanding of it, but in the sensory reactions, imagination, and emotion it arouses. One teachers' bulletin[51] suggests five developmental stages:

1. Enjoyment of
   a. sound in poetry
   b. story element
2. Appreciation of
   a. rhyme and rhythm
   b. literature as related to one's own experiences

51 Oakland Public Schools, *Language Arts Unit: Suggestions for Developing Growth in Appreciation of Literature.* Mimeograph, June 30, 1959.

3. Projection of the reader into a world other than that in which he lives.
4. Understanding of symbolism and hidden meaning through interpretive reading.
5. Sensitivity to literary style and patterns of writing.

Most children in elementary school do not get beyond the first three stages and many adults have difficulty with the fourth and fifth levels. Illustrations of poems at the first level are nursery rhymes, jingles, ballads, simple narrative poems, such as *Casey Jones* and *Casey at The Bat,* and some easy poems about people, as in the Benets' *Book of Americans.* Some Ogden Nash and Robert Service may belong here. The second stage of focus on rhyme and rhythm may include limericks, ballads, and long narrative poems with marked rhythms, such as *Paul Revere, Lochinvar,* and Kipling's *Ballad of East and West.* The third may include poems about animals, other days, various occupations, and other lands and cultures, such as Robert Frost's *The Runaway,* John Masefield's *Sea Fever* and *Cargoes,* Carl Sandburg's Chicago poems, Edwin Markham's *The Man With the Hoe,* and Robert Louis Stevenson's *Travel.* In the upper grades of the elementary school a start can be made on interpretation and understanding symbolism through beginning with Aesop's fables, some of Thurber's fables, some of the shorter Frost poems such as "Mending Wall" and "The Road Not Taken," and some simpler Millay verse such as "Afternoon on a Hill" or "Trains." All of these specific examples will change with the knowledge and taste of the teacher and the needs of the group, but they illustrate general stages which help the teacher in deciding what level of material to try with the group. As the teacher is able to illustrate that poetry can be robust, humorous, well-plotted, and stimulating to the imagination, she prepares some pupils for the later, serious study of literary work. Some talented children will be ready for this, in individual or small group projects, before they enter the junior-high school.

As suggested for choral reading, some teachers keep card-files of poems they and their pupils have enjoyed. Books by Arnstein[52] and by Wrinn[53] give many suggestions for the reading and writing of poetry in the classroom. In looking for poetry related to special days,

[52] Flora J. Arnstein, *Adventure Into Poetry.* Stanford University Press, Stanford, Calif., 1951.
[53] Mary J. J. Wrinn, *The Hollow Reed.* Harper, New York, 1935.

other class activities, and curriculum content, some teachers and librarians are able to use the indexes compiled by the Brewtons. All teachers should be acquainted with attractive sets of literary books of poetry and prose, such as:

LELAND JACOBS and ELEANOR JOHNSON. *Treasury of Literature,* 4 vols. Merrill, Columbus, Ohio, 1954.

MARJORIE BARROWS, ed. *The Children's Hour,* 16 vols. Spencer Press, New York, 1953, 1954.

JEANNE HALE, ed. in chief. *Through Golden Windows,* 10 vols. Hale, Eau Claire, Wis., 1958.

Other attractive anthologies of poetry such as those of Arbuthnot, Bennett, Cole, Ferris, Hubbard, Sechrist, Stevenson, and Untermeyer are given in Appendix C at the end of this chapter. In all these different teachers and children have different favorites, as is only right.

EVALUATION OF THE PROGRAM IN LITERATURE

As indicated in Chapter 16 evaluation of children's development is no longer confined to a written test given before some report-card period. This is particularly true of the activities discussed in this chapter. The usual teacher-made or standardized tests have always been particularly unsuited to studying children's development in appreciation and enjoyment or their personality changes through literature. Rather, modern evaluation grows out of the purposes and nature of such procedures as those outlined above. The teacher will measure the success of her work and her pupils' development through such items as:

1. The kind and number of books read
2. The use made of magazines, newspapers, and pamphlets
3. The desire of pupils to read to others selections they have enjoyed
4. The desire to tell stories that have appealed to them
5. The participation in dramatization of stories read
6. The quality of children's expressive activities, such as original stories or paintings developing from stories
7. The extent to which children bring available books from home to share with others
8. The number of books borrowed for home reading

9. The use of books in free periods
10. The ease and enjoyment with which children memorize poetry or other selections
11. The quality of choices in radio and television programs, recordings, and films
12. The form and maturity of pupils' comments about their tastes and preferences

As suggested above, no experience in literature can probably change children's personalities and values unless it is supported by related experiences in the home, school, and community. The effects of a book or recording may be so subtle as to defy the usual measurement. Occasionally the teacher can rely only on the posture, the glances, the requests for more or less, the more intangible effects of a literature experience. The dozen items in the evaluation suggested above cannot stand alone; but, put together in combinations of four or six items, they may indicate to the teacher, supervisor, or principal some of the results of a literature program.

BECOMING ACQUAINTED WITH CHILDREN'S LITERATURE

Most teachers and parents have had some experience with children's literature. They have usually suffered with *Black Beauty,* enjoyed life with *Little Women,* entered Wonderland with *Alice,* or gone adventuring with *Tom Sawyer.* However, knowledge of a few children's classics, read many years before, is not sufficient background for the modern teacher. As well as certain classics, she must know some of the splendid children's stories published in recent years, and she must be able to use such stories and other factual books in enriching the social studies and other activities of the class. The storytelling hour, the individual reading period, and the class problem requiring reading for its solution all demand a wide knowledge of children's literature. Most teachers will greatly enlarge their understanding and appreciation of such literature by a study of the appendixes accompanying this chapter and by following the five suggestions given below.

1. The best way, of course, for any teacher to improve her acquaintance with children's literature is to read children's books and, if possible, share them with others. Until one has read about the

disappearance of Wanda Gág's *Millions of Cats,* or seen Rojankovsky's illustrations for *The Tall Book of Mother Goose,* or investigated barnyard crime with *Freddy the Detective* all for oneself, one is not ready to share these experiences with children. The first step for teachers, then, is to borrow from school or public libraries and to visit bookshops when they are accessible. Rural teachers may have to depend more upon recordings, selected radio and television programs, book catalogues, and occasional visits to libraries.

Over the years many teachers develop lists of their favorite books. One such list is presented in Appendix A at the end of this chapter. Other groups of teachers may enjoy developing their own basic lists.

2. In addition to the enjoyment of individual books most teachers will profit by a reading of some good anthologies of children's literature. Some of these anthologies include a great variety of materials at a very reasonable price. They are among the best bargains in children's books. They are therefore particularly valuable for rural teachers or for small school libraries, where other sources of literature are limited. Some of the best anthologies of poems, both traditional and modern, are listed in Appendix C.

3. Many teachers and parents enjoy children's literature through current children's magazines. Librarians are not agreed as to the most suitable magazines for children, and older children read many so-called adult magazines, such as *Life, Reader's Digest, National Geographic,* and *Popular Mechanics.* Juvenile magazines are not popular with advertisers and have a hard time surviving on subscriptions alone. Most children's magazines are of a specialized nature, such as those published by the Junior Red Cross, the Boy Scouts, and various religious organizations. A few of the most popular children's magazines and newspapers (excluding comic books), which many teachers will wish to examine at their leisure, are listed in Appendix B.

4. In addition to the actual contact with children's books and magazines, most teachers will increase their understanding of children's literature by reading books about it. Such books give the author's personal and often delightful interpretations of materials written for children. Teachers will enjoy different books in different ways. One teacher who has a family of her own may enjoy Duff's *Bequest of Wings.* Another wanting lots of information about types of literature may prefer Arbuthnot's *Children and Books.* Both parents and teachers find much help in Larrick's *A Parent's Guide to Children's Read-*

ing, published in both library and paperback editions, and in her companion volume *A Teacher's Guide to Children's Literature*. Information about the history of children's literature adds to one's enjoyment of modern writings. The teacher who realizes the place of fables and folklore in our literature, who shares John Newbery's early struggles for attractive children's books in his London shop, and who traces the change from the theological to the childlike emphasis in American juvenile literature brings much to the literature activities of her class. Some of the books which will add to a teacher's understanding and appreciation of children's literature are listed in Appendix D.

5. Finally, a teacher or parent may grow in knowledge of children's literature by using book lists and consulting reviews and announcements of current books. These appear in daily newspapers (sometimes a weekend edition) and in selected magazines. Most book lists give brief annotations describing the content of the book and sometimes its approximate level of difficulty. Perhaps the most complete record of children's books is in the *Children's Catalog* (H. W. Wilson Co.); but other lists are most valuable, particularly since they often place the books under topics which are related to other parts of the school program. Unlike the materials in Appendixes A, B, and C, the sources and book lists in Appendixes D, E, and F contain suggestions for adults rather than actual material to be placed in the hands of children. However, they are excellent sources for teachers who want to know about materials available by any topic or author, or who want to be informed about the new children's books as they are published. Some current reviews are fascinating reading for their own sake.

SUPPLEMENTARY READINGS

ARBUTHNOT, MAY H. "Some Criteria for Judging Stories for Children," *Childhood Education,* Vol. 12, pp. 65-72, November, 1935.

BALDWIN, HELEN B. "Library Activities for an Elementary School," *Wilson Library Bulletin,* Vol. 23, pp. 142-145, October, 1958.

BLAIR, VIRGINIA B. "Recognizing Problems Thru' Fiction," *Childhood Education,* Vol. 28, pp. 169-172, December, 1951.

BREWTON, JOHN E. "Glimpses of Glory in Children's Books," *Elementary English Review,* Vol. 19, pp. 154-162, May, 1942.

BROWN, R. A., and BROWN, M. R. "Biography in the Social Studies: The Middle Grades," *Social Education,* Vol. 18, pp. 171-174, April, 1954.

BURTON, DWIGHT L. *Literature Study in the High Schools.* Holt, New York, 1959.

CAPPA, DANTE. *Reactions of Kindergarten Children to Story Books Read by Teachers*. Doctoral dissertation. University of California, Berkeley, 1953. 185 p.
CHILDREN'S BOOK COUNCIL. *The World of Children's Books*. The Council, New York, 1952.
COLLIER, MARY J., and GAIER, EUGENE L. "Adult Reactions to Preferred Childhood Stories," *Child Development,* Vol. 29, pp. 97-103, March, 1958.
DUFF, ANNIS. "Literary Heritage of Childhood," *Wilson Library Bulletin,* Vol. 33, pp. 563-570, April, 1959.
EAKIN, MARY K. "Trends in Children's Literature," *Library Quarterly,* Vol. 25, pp. 47-57, January, 1955.
FOSTER, JEANNETTE H. "An Approach to Fiction through the Characteristics of Its Readers," *Library Quarterly,* Vol. 6, pp. 124-174, April, 1936.
GRAY, WILLIAM S., ed. *Promoting Personal and Social Development through Reading*. Supplementary Educational Monographs, No. 64. University of Chicago Press, Chicago, 1947. 236 p.
GREEN, IVAH. "Improving the School Library," *Elementary English,* Vol. 24, pp. 367-371, October, 1947.
HANLON, M. "Needed: Science Stories for Younger Readers," *School Science and Mathematics,* Vol. 58, pp. 677-689, December, 1958.
HANNA, GENEVA R., and MCALLISTER, M. *Books, Young People, and Reading Guidance*. Harper, New York, 1960. 219 p.
JENNINGS, F. G. "Literature for Adolescents: Pap or Protein?" *English Journal,* Vol. 45, pp. 526-531, December, 1956.
KIRCHER, CLARA J., comp. *Character Formation through Books,* 2nd ed. Catholic University of America Press, Washington, D.C., 1945.
LEARY, BERNICE E. "Literature in School Instruction," *Review of Educational Research,* Vol. 13, pp. 88-102, April, 1943.
LEARY, BERNICE E. *Milestones in Children's Books*. Monograph on Reading, No. 23. Row, Peterson, Evanston, Ill., 1940.
LOBAN, WALTER. "Teaching Literature: A Multiple Approach," *English Journal,* Vol. 45, pp. 75-78, February, 1956.
LOBAN, WALTER. *Literature and Social Sensitivity*. National Council of Teachers of English, Champaign, Ill., 1954.
MCCONNELL, GAITHER A. *An Analysis of Biographical Literature for Children*. Doctoral dissertation. University of California, Berkeley, 1952.
MAIB, FRANCES. "Improving Children's Literary Tastes," *Elementary English,* Vol. 36, pp. 180-184, March, 1959.
MOOD, R. G. "Let 'em Read Trash," *Elementary English,* Vol. 34, pp. 444-450, November, 1957.
RUSSELL, D. H. "Reading Success and Personality Development," *Elementary English,* Vol. 25, pp. 73-82, February, 1948.
RUSSELL, D. H. "Identification through Literature," *Childhood Education,* Vol. 25, pp. 397-401, May, 1949.
SAUCIER, E. N. "Some Significant Firsts in Children's Literature," *Peabody Journal of Education,* Vol. 19, pp. 141-147, November, 1941.
SAWYER, RUTH. *The Way of the Story Teller*. Viking, New York, 1942.
SAYERS, FRANCES C. "Books that Enchant: What Makes a Classic," *NEA Journal,* Vol. 46, pp. 9-11, January, 1957.
SMITH, DORA V. "How Literature is Taught," *NEA Journal,* Vol. 40, pp. 295-297, 1951.
SQUIRE, JAMES R. *The Responses of Adolescents to Literature Involving Selected*

Experiences of Personal Development. Doctoral dissertation. University of California, Berkeley, 1956.
SULLENGER, T. EARL, and others. "The Leisure-Time Activities of Elementary School Children," *Journal of Educational Research,* Vol. 46, pp. 552-554, March, 1953.
TOOZE, RUTH. *Storytelling.* Prentice-Hall, Englewood Cliffs, N.J., 1959.
TOOZE, RUTH. *Your Children Want to Read.* Prentice-Hall, Englewood Cliffs, N.J., 1957.
TREZEVANT, BLANCHE. "Function of Literature in the Elementary School," *Elementary English Review,* Vol. 22, pp. 100-105, March, 1945.
WHITEHEAD, FRANK. "The Attitudes of Grammar School Pupils Towards some Novels Commonly Read in School," *British Journal of Educational Psychology,* Vol. 26, pp. 104-111, June, 1956.
WEINGARTEN, SAMUEL. "Developmental Values in Voluntary Reading," *School Review,* Vol. 62, pp. 222-230, April, 1954.
WOLLNER, MARY H. B. *Children's Voluntary Reading as an Expression of Individuality.* Bureau of Publications, Teachers College, Columbia University, New York, 1949. 117 p.

APPENDIX A. ONE HUNDRED BEST BOOKS FOR CHILDREN[54]

First Rhymes and Pictures

BROOKE, L. LESLIE. *Johnny Crow's Garden.* Warne, 1904.
CALDECOTT, RANDOLPH. *Picture Books.* Warne.
ETS, MARIE HALL. *Play With Me.* Viking, 1955.
GAG, WANDA. *A B C Bunny.* Coward, 1933.
Lavender's Blue (*Mother Goose*), compiled by Kathleen Lines. Illustrated by Harold Jones. Watts, 1954.
ROSSETTI, CHRISTINA G. *Sing-Song: A Nursery Rhyme Book and Other Poems for Children.* Macmillan (New Little Library), 1924.

Picture and Picture-Story Books

BEMELMANS, LUDWIG. *Madeline.* Simon and Schuster, 1939.
BROOKE, L. LESLIE. *Golden Goose Book,* Warne, 1906.
BRUNHOFF, JEAN DE. *The Story of Babar, The Little Elephant.* Translated from the French by Merle S. Haas. Random, 1933.
BURTON, VIRGINIA LEE. *The Little House.* Houghton, 1942.
DAUGHERTY, JAMES. *Andy and The Lion.* Viking, 1938.
FISCHER, HANS. *Pitschi.* Harcourt, 1953.
GAG, WANDA. *Millions of Cats.* Coward, 1928.
GEISEL, THEODOR SEUSS. *And To Think That I Saw It On Mulberry Street.* Vanguard, 1937.
MCCLOSKEY, ROBERT. *Make Way for Ducklings.* Viking, 1941.
PETERSHAM, MAUD and MISKA. *The Christ Child As Told By Matthew and Luke.* Doubleday, 1931.

[54] "One Hundred Best Books for Children," selected by Virginia Haviland, Ruth Gagliando, and Elizabeth Nesbitt, *McCall's,* Vol. 84, pp. 42-44, November, 1956. Reprinted by permission from McCall's.

POTTER, BEATRIX. *Peter Rabbit* Series. Warne, 1903-14.
WARD, LYND. *The Biggest Bear*. Houghton, 1952.

First Fantasy—For Reading Aloud

BAILEY, CAROLYN S. *Miss Hickory*. Illustrated by Ruth Gannett. Viking, 1946.
DICKENS, CHARLES. *The Magic Fishbone*. Illustrated by Louis Slobodkin. Vanguard, 1953.
GODDEN, RUMER. *The Dolls' House*. Illustrated by Dana Saintsbury. Viking, 1947.
KIPLING, RUDYARD. *Just So Stories*. Illustrated by Nicholas Mordvinoff. Garden City, 1952.
LAWSON, ROBERT. *Rabbit Hill*. Viking, 1944.
LOFTING, HUGH. *The Story of Doctor Dolittle*. Lippincott, 1920.
LORENZINI, CARLO (pseud., C. COLLODI). *Adventures of Pinocchio*. With illustrations after Attilio Mussino. Macmillan (New Children's Classics), 1951.
MACDONALD, GEORGE. *The Princess and the Goblin*. Illustrated by Nora S. Unwin. Macmillan (New Children's Classics), 1951.
MILNE, A. A. *Winnie-the-Pooh*. Illustrated by Ernest H. Shepard. Dutton, 1950.
PARRISH, ANN. *Floating Island*. Harper, 1930.
TRAVERS, PAMELA L. *Mary Poppins*. Illustrated by Mary Shepard. Harcourt, 1934.
WHITE, E. B. *Charlotte's Web*. Illustrated by Garth Williams. Harper, 1922.

More Fantasy—Beauty, Wisdom and Humor

BARRIE, SIR JAMES M. *Peter Pan*. Illustrated by Nora S. Unwin. Scribner, 1950.
CARROLL, LEWIS. *Alice's Adventures in Wonderland* and *Through The Looking-Glass*. Illustrated by John Tenniel. Macmillan (New Children's Classics), 1946.
DICKENS, CHARLES. *A Christmas Carol*. Illustrated by Robert Ball. Macmillan (New Children's Classics), 1950.
EAGER, EDWARD. *Half Magic*. Illustrated by N. M. Bodecker. Harcourt, 1954.
GRAHAME, KENNETH. *The Wind in The Willows*. Illustrated by Ernest H. Shepard. Scribner, New ed., 1953.
KIPLING, RUDYARD. *Jungle Book*. Illustrated by Kurt Wiese. Doubleday, 1932.
LAGERLOF, SELMA. *The Wonderful Adventures of Nils*. Translated by Velma Swanston Howard. Illustrated by Hans Baumhauer. Pantheon, 1947.
LEWIS, C. S. *The Lion, The Witch, and The Wardrobe*. Illustrated by Pauline Baynes. Macmillan, 1950.
NORTON, MARY. *The Borrowers*. Illustrated by Beth and Joe Krush. Harcourt, 1953.
PYLE, HOWARD. *Pepper and Salt: Or, Seasoning for Young Folk*. Harper, 1887.
TOLKIEN, JOHN R. R. *The Hobbit: Or, There and Back Again*. Houghton, 1938.

Tales from America

HARRIS, JOEL CHANDLER. *The Favorite Uncle Remus*. Illustrated by A. B. Frost. Houghton, 1948.
MALCOLMSON, ANNE. *Yankee Doodle's Cousins*. Illustrated by Robert McCloskey. Houghton, 1941.
SANDBERG, CARL. *The Rootabaga Stories*. Illustrated by Maud and Miska Petersham. Harcourt, 1922-23.

The World's Great Imaginative Literature

AESOP. *The Fables of Aesop*. Selected by Joseph Jacobs. Illustrated by Kurt Wiese. Macmillan (New Children's Classics), 1950.

ANDERSEN, HANS CHRISTIAN. *It's Perfectly True, and Other Stories.* Translated from the Danish by Paul Leyssac. Illustrated by Richard Bennett. Harcourt, 1938.

Arabian Nights: Their Best-Known Tales. Edited by Kate Douglas Wiggin and Nora A. Smith. Illustrated by Maxfield Parrish. Scribner, 1909.

COLUM, PADRAIC. *The Children's Homer: The Adventures of Odysseus and The Tale of Troy.* Illustrated by Willy Pogany. Macmillan, 1918.

GRIMM, JACOB LUDWIG KARL and WILHELM KARL. *Tales From Grimm.* Translated and illustrated by Wanda Gag. Coward.

HAWTHORNE, NATHANIEL. *A Wonder-Book and Tanglewood Tales.* Illustrated by Gustaf Tenggren. Houghton (Riverside Bookshelf), 1923.

JACOBS, JOSEPH. *English Fairy Tales.* Illustrated by John D. Batten. Putnam, 1892.

LAMB, CHARLES and MARY. *Tales From Shakespeare.* Illustrated by John C. Wonsetler. Macmillan (New Children's Classics), 1950.

LANG, ANDREW, editor. *The Blue Fairy Book.* Illustrated by Ben Kutcher. Longmans, new ed., 1948.

PYLE, HOWARD. *The Merry Adventures of Robin Hood.* Scribner, 1946.

PYLE, HOWARD. *The Story of King Arthur and His Knights.* Scribner, 1933.

Children and Families

ALCOTT, LOUISA M. *Little Women.* Illustrated by Barbara Cooney. Crowell, 1955.

BLAND, EDITH (NESBIT). *The Story of the Treasure Seekers.* Illustrated by C. Walter Hodges. Coward, 1928.

BRINK, CAROL RYRIE. *Caddie Woodlawn.* Illustrated by Kate Seredy. Macmillan, 1935.

COATSWORTH, ELIZABETH. *Away Goes Sally.* Pictures by Helen Sewell. Macmillan, 1934.

DALGLIESH, ALICE. *The Courage of Sarah Noble.* Illustrated by Leonard Weisgard. Scribner, 1954.

DEJONG, MEINDERT. *The Wheel on the School.* Illustrated by Maurice Sendak. Harper, 1954.

DODGE, MARY MAPES. *Hans Brinker: Or, The Silver Skates.* Illustrated by George W. Edwards. Scribner (Illustrated Classics), 1915.

ESTES, ELEANOR. *The Moffats.* Illustrated by Louis Slobodkin. Harcourt, 1941.

RANSOME, ARTHUR. *Swallows and Amazons.* Illustrated by Helene Carter. Lippincott, 1931.

SEREDY, KATE. *The Good Master.* Viking, 1935.

SPYRI, JOHANNA. *Heidi.* Illustrated by Leonard Weisgard. World (Rainbow Classics), 1946.

WILDER, LAURA INGALLS. *Little House in the Big Woods.* Illustrated by Garth Williams. Harper, New ed., 1953.

Adventures in Strange Lands

DEFOE, DANIEL. *The Adventures of Robinson Crusoe.* Illustrated by Roger Duvoisin. World (Rainbow Classics), 1950.

FIELD, RACHEL. *Hitty: Her First Hundred Years.* Illustrated by Dorothy P. Lathrop. Macmillan, 1929.

MUHLENWEG, FRITZ. *Big Tiger and Christian.* Translated by Isabel and Florence McHugh. Illustrated by Rafaello Busoni. Pantheon, 1952.

RANKIN, LOUISE. *Daughter of the Mountains.* Illustrated by Kurt Wiese. Viking, 1948.

SPERRY, ARMSTRONG. *Call It Courage.* Macmillan, 1940.
SWIFT, JONATHAN. *Gulliver's Travels.* Illustrated by Fritz Eichenberg. Heritage, 1947.

"Funny" Books

ATWATER, RICHARD and FLORENCE. *Mr. Popper's Penguins.* Illustrated by Robert Lawson. Little, 1938.
HALE, LUCRETIA. *The Peterkin Papers.* With illustrations by Harold M. Brett. Houghton (Riverside Bookshelf), 1924.
LAWSON, ROBERT. *Ben and Me.* Little, 1939.
MCCLOSKEY, ROBERT. *Homer Price.* Viking, 1943.

Fiction for Older Boys and Girls

BENNETT, JOHN. *Master Skylark: A Story of Shakespeare's Time.* Illustrated by Reginald B. Birch. Grosset (Thrushwood Books), 1947.
CLEMENS, SAMUEL L. *The Adventures of Huckleberry Finn.* Illustrated by Baldwin Hawes. World (Rainbow Classics), 1947.
CLEMENS, SAMUEL L. *The Adventures of Tom Sawyer.* Illustrated by Louis Slobodkin. World (Rainbow Classics), 1950.
COOPER, JAMES FENIMORE. *The Last of the Mohicans: A Narrative of 1757.* Scribner (Illustrated Classics), 1919.
DUBOIS, WILLIAM PENE. *The Twenty-One Balloons.* Viking, 1947.
FORBES, ESTHER. *Johnny Tremain, A Novel for Old and Young.* Illustrated by Lynd Ward. Houghton, 1943.
MEIGS, CORNELIA. *Master Simon's Garden.* Illustrated by John Rae. Macmillan, 1929.
PYLE, HOWARD. *Men of Iron.* Harper, 1891.
RAWLINGS, MARJORIE KINNAN. *The Yearling.* Illustrated by N. C. Wyeth. Scribner, 1947.
SCOTT, SIR WALTER. *Ivanhoe: A Romance.* Illustrated by E. Boyd Smith. Houghton (Riverside Bookshelf), 1913.
STEVENSON, ROBERT LOUIS. *Treasure Island.* Illustrated in color by N. C. Wyeth. Scribner (Illustrated Classics), 1924.
VERNE, JULES. *Twenty Thousand Leagues Under the Sea.* Illustrated by W. J. Aylward. Scribner (Illustrated Classics), 1925.

Great Religious Writings

SMITH, RUTH, Editor. *The Tree of Life.* Illustrated by Boris Artzybasheff. Viking, 1942.

Great Lives and Great Events

DAUGHERTY, JAMES H. *Daniel Boone.* Viking, 1939.
EATON, JEANETTE. *Narcissi Whitman, Pioneer of Oregon.* Illustrated by Woodi Ishmael. Harcourt, 1941.
FOSTER, GENEVIEVE. *George Washington's World.* Scribner, 1941.
GRAY, ELIZABETH JANET. *Penn.* Illustrated by George Gillett Whitney. Viking, 1938.
SANDBURG, CARL. *Abe Lincoln Grows Up.* Illustrated by James Daugherty. Harcourt, 1938.

"An Inheritance of Poetry"

ADSHEAD, GLADYS L., and DUFF, ANNIS, compilers. *An Inheritance of Poetry.* Decorations by Nora S. Unwin. Houghton, 1948.

De la Mare, Walter. *Rhymes and Verses: Collected Poems for Children.* Illustrated by Elinore Blaisdell. Holt, 1947.

Lear, Edward. *Complete Nonsense Book.* Edited by Lady Strachey. Dodd, 1943.

Milne, A. A. *When We Were Very Young* and *Now We Are Six.* Illustrated by Ernest H. Shepard. Dutton, 1950.

Stevenson, Robert Louis. *A Child's Garden of Verses.* Illustrated by Jessie Wilcox Smith. Scribner (Illustrated Classics), 1905.

APPENDIX B. CHILDREN'S MAGAZINES AND PAPERS

American Girl, The. Published monthly by Girl Scouts of the U.S.A., 830 Third Avenue, New York 22, N.Y. $3. Girls, ages 10 to 15.

Boys' Life. Published monthly by the Boy Scouts of America, New Brunswick, N.J. $3. Boys, ages 10 to 16.

Calling All Girls. Published monthly except June to August by Parents' Institute, Inc., 52 Vanderbilt Avenue, New York 17, N.Y. $3.50. Girls, ages 7 to 14.

Child Life. Published monthly at 30 Federal Street, Boston 10, Mass. $4. Ages 3 to 9.

Children's Digest. Published monthly except July and August by Parents' Magazine Press, Inc., 52 Vanderbilt Avenue, New York 17, N.Y. $3.50. Ages 6 to 12.

Humpty Dumpty's Magazine. Published monthly except June to August by the Parents' Magazine Press, Inc., 52 Vanderbilt Avenue, New York 17, N.Y. $3.50. Ages 3 to 7.

Jack and Jill. Published monthly by Curtis Publishing Co., Independence Square, Philadelphia 5, Pa. $3.50. Ages 3 to 10.

Junior Natural History. Published ten times a year by American Museum of Natural History, Central Park West at 79th Street, New York 24, N.Y. $1.50. Ages 8 to 12.

Junior Scholastic. Published weekly except June to August by Scholastic Magazines, 33 West 42nd Street, New York 36, N.Y. Published five times during the summer months. In lots of five or more, 80 cents per year, single subscriptions, $1.50. Grades 6, 7, and 8.

My Weekly Reader. Published weekly except June to September by American Education Publications, Education Center, Columbus 16, Ohio. In quantities of five or more, 50 cents. *Surprise News Pilot,* Kindergarten, Grade 1; *News Ranger,* Grade 2; *News Trail,* Grade 3; *Explorer,* Grade 4; *Newstime,* Grades 5 and 6.

Natural History, incorporating *Nature.* Published ten times a year by American Museum of Natural History, Central Park West at 79th Street, New York 24, N.Y. $5.

Popular Mechanics. Published monthly by Popular Mechanics Co., 200 East Ontario Street, Chicago 11, Ill. $3.50.

Read Magazine. Published semi-monthly except June to August by American Education Publications, Education Center, Columbus 16, Ohio. 50 cents. Junior high ages.

Science World. Published bi-weekly except June to August with the official cooperation of the National Science Teachers Association by Scholastic Magazines, 33 West 42nd Street, New York 36, N.Y. $1.50.

Young Americans. Published monthly except July and August by Strong Publications Inc., Box 1399, Grand Central P.O., New York 17, N.Y. $4. Ages 10 to 14.

Young Catholic Messenger. Published monthly except June to August by George A. Pflum, Publisher, 38 West Fifth Street, Dayton 2, Ohio. $1.60. Junior high ages.

APPENDIX C. POETRY ANTHOLOGIES

ARBUTHNOT, MAY HILL, comp. *Time for Poetry.* Scott, Foresman, Chicago, 1952.
ADSHEAD, GLADYS L., and DUFF, ANNIS. *An Inheritance of Poetry.* Riverside Press, Houghton Mifflin, Boston, 1948.
AUSLANDER, JOSEPH, and HILL, FRANK ERNEST. *The Winged Horse.* (The story of the poets and their poetry.) Doubleday, Doran, Garden City, N.Y., 1929.
BENNET, ROWENA. *Story-Teller Poems.* Winston, Philadelphia, 1948.
BREWTON, JOHN E., comp. *Gaily We Parade.* Macmillan, New York, 1940.
BREWTON, JOHN E., comp. *Under the Tent of the Sky.* Macmillan, New York, 1937.
BREWTON, SARA and JOHN E. *Bridled with Rainbows.* Macmillan, New York, 1949.
COLE, WILLIAM. *Humorous Poetry for Children.* World Publishing, Cleveland, Ohio, 1955.
DE LA MARE, WALTER. *Come Hither.* Knopf, New York, 1923.
FERRIS, HELEN, comp. *Favorite Poems, Old and New.* Doubleday, New York, 1957.
HUBBARD, ALICE L., and BABBITT, ADELINE, comps. *The Golden Flute.* John Day, New York, 1932.
HUFFARD, GRADE T.; CARLISLE, LAURA MAE; and FERRIS, HELEN J., comps. *My Poetry Book,* rev. ed. Winston, Philadelphia, 1956.
HUGHES, ROSLAND, arr. *Let's Enjoy Poetry.* Houghton Mifflin, Boston, 1958.
MCDONALD, GERALD D. *A Way of Knowing.* Crowell, New York, 1959.
MCGINLEY, PHYLLIS. *All Around the Town.* Lippincott, Philadelphia, 1948.
OPIE, IONA, and OPIE, PETER, eds. *The Oxford Dictionary of Nursery Rhymes.* Oxford, New York, 1951.
SECHRIST, ELIZABETH H., comp. *One Thousand Poems for Children.* Macrae-Smith, Philadelphia, 1946.
STEVENSON, BURTON EGBERT, ed. *The Home Book of Verse for Young Folks,* rev. ed. Holt, New York, 1929.
UNTERMEYER, LOUIS. *This Singing World.* Harcourt Brace, New York, 1926.

APPENDIX D. BOOKS AND BULLETINS ABOUT CHILDREN'S LITERATURE

ADAMS, BESS PORTER. *About Books and Children.* Holt, New York, 1953.
ARBUTHNOT, MAY H. *Children and Books,* 2nd ed. Scott, Foresman, Chicago, 1957.
THE ASSOCIATION FOR CHILDHOOD EDUCATION INTERNATIONAL. *Adventuring in Literature with Children.* Association for Childhood Education International, Washington, D.C., 1946.
BECKER, MAY LAMBERTON. *Adventures in Reading,* new ed. Lippincott, Philadelphia, 1946.
BETZNER, JEAN. *Exploring Literature with Children in the Elementary School.* Bureau of Publications, Teachers College, Columbia University, New York, 1943.
BETZNER, JEAN, and MOORE, A. E. *Every Child and Books.* Bobbs-Merrill, Indianapolis, Ind., 1940.
DALGLEISH, A. *First Experiences with Literature.* Scribner, New York, 1937.
DUFF, ANNIS. *Bequest of Wings: A Family's Pleasure with Books.* Viking, New York, 1944. Book and Record Lists revised, 1954.
DUFF, ANNIS. *Longer Flight: A Family Grows up With Books.* Viking, New York, 1955.
EATON, ANNE THAXTER. *Treasure for the Taking,* rev. ed. Viking, New York, 1957.

EATON, ANNE THAXTER. *Reading with Children.* Viking, New York, 1940.

FENNER, PHYLLIS. *The Proof of the Pudding: What Children Read.* John Day, New York, 1957.

FENNER, PHYLLIS. *Something Shared: Children and Books.* John Day, New York, 1959.

GATES, DORIS. *Helping Children Discover Books.* Science Research Associates, Chicago, 1956.

HAZARD, PAUL. *Books, Children and Men.* Horn Book, Boston, 1948.

LARRICK, NANCY. *A Parent's Guide to Children's Reading.* Doubleday, New York, 1958. Also Cardinal Edition, C-314. Pocket Books, New York, 1958.

LARRICK, NANCY. *A Teacher's Guide to Children's Literature.* Merrill, Columbus, Ohio, 1960.

LEWIS, CLAUDIA. *Writing for Young Children.* Simon and Schuster, New York, 1954.

MAHONEY, BERTHA E., and others. *Illustrators of Children's Books, 1944-1945.* Horn Book, Boston, 1947. *Supplement,* Vigners, Ruth Hill. *Illustrators of Children's Books, 1946-1956.* Horn Book, Boston, 1958.

MAHONEY, BERTHA E., and FIELD, ELINOR W. *Caldecott Medal Books: 1938-1957.* Horn Book, Boston, 1957.

MARTIGNONI, MARGARET E., ed. *The Illustrated Treasury of Children's Literature.* Grosset & Dunlap, New York, 1955.

MARTIN, LAURA K. *Magazines for School Libraries,* rev. ed. Wilson, New York, 1950.

MEIGS, CORNELIA, and others. *A Critical History of Children's Literature.* Macmillan, New York, 1953.

MOORE, A. E. *My Roads to Childhood.* Doubleday, Garden City, N.Y., 1939.

ROSENBACH, A. S. W. *Early American Children's Books.* Southworth Press, Portland, Me., 1933.

SAWYER, RUTH. *The Way of the Story Teller.* Viking, New York, 1942.

SHEDLOCK, MARIE L. *The Art of the Story-Teller.* Dover Publications, New York, 1951.

SMITH, E. S. *History of Children's Literature.* American Library Association, Chicago, 1937.

SMITH, IRENE. *History of the Newbery and Caldecott Medal.* Viking, New York, 1957.

SMITH, LILLIAN H. *The Unreluctant Years: A Critical Approach to Children's Literature.* American Library Association, Chicago, 1953.

TERMAN, L. M., and LIMA, M. *Children's Reading.* Century, New York, 1935.

TOOZE, RUTH. *Storytelling.* Prentice-Hall, Englewood Cliffs, N.J., 1959.

TOOZE, RUTH. *Your Children Want to Read, A Guide for Teachers and Parents.* Prentice-Hall, Englewood Cliffs, N.J., 1957.

TUER, ANDREW W., ed. *Pages and Pictures from Forgotten Children's Books.* Leadenhall Press, London, 1898-1899.

APPENDIX E. SOURCES OF CURRENT REVIEWS OF CHILDREN'S BOOKS

The Booklists and Subscription Books Bulletin. American Library Association, 50 East Huron Street, Chicago, Ill. Published twice monthly except in August, when only one issue. $6.

Bulletin of the Center for Children's Books. University of Chicago Press, Graduate Library School, Chicago, Ill. Monthly reviewing service. Nine hundred to one thousand books are evaluated yearly.

Childhood Education. Journal of the Association for Childhood Education, 1200 15th Street, N.W., Washington 5, D.C. Monthly, September through May. Reviews. $4.50.

Elementary English. National Council of Teachers of English, 704 South 6th Street, Champaign, Ill. Monthly, October through May. Reviews. $4.

The Horn Book Magazine. 585 Boylston Street, Boston 16, Mass. "Books and Reading for Young People." Bi-Monthly. $4.50.

Junior Libraries. R. R. Bowker Co., 62 West 45th Street, New York 36, N.Y. Monthly, September through May. $3.50.

New York Herald-Tribune Book Review. New York Herald-Tribune, 230 West 41st Street, New York, 36, N.Y. A weekly book section containing a department devoted to children's books.

New York Times Book Review. New York Times, 299 West 43rd Street, New York 36, N.Y. A weekly book section containing a department reviewing children's books.

Publisher's Weekly. R. R. Bowker Co., 62 West 45th Street, New York 36, N.Y. Weekly. Current listings for the book trade; includes children's books. $11.

Saturday Review. Saturday Review, Inc., 25 West 45th Street, New York 36, N.Y. Weekly. Articles and Reviews. $7.

Catalogues and announcements of children's books will be mailed by all publishers.

APPENDIX F. CHILDREN'S BOOK CLUBS

Arrow Book Club. Scholastic Book Services, 33 West 42nd St., New York 36, N.Y. For grades 4, 5, and 6. A book club offering paperbound books at $.25 and $.35 for middle-graders. Five book offers are made during the school year, each offer consisting of eighteen books. Books are reviewed by an Editorial Advisory Board and each offer includes books for slow, average, and accelerated readers. Books include adventure, animals, children's classics, historical fiction, sports, humor, mystery, and how-to-do. *Memo: to Teachers* is sent to each teacher sponsor of club.

Catholic Children's Book Club. 260 Summit Ave., St. Paul 2, Minn. A book club for five age levels ranging from 6 to 16. Monthly (or every other month) offerings September through June. Selections show preference for Catholic background or theme; emphasis on building character, moral values, and family relationships.

Catholic Youth Book Club. Garden City, N.Y. Monthly offerings for ages 9-15 at $1.49 each plus shipping costs. Biographical books on great Catholic figures in history.

Junior Literary Guild. Garden City, N.Y. Monthly offerings for five age groups from 5 to 16 at $1.75.

Parents' Magazine's Book Club for Children. Bergenfield, N.J. Monthly offerings for age levels 7 to 12 at $1.47 each plus postage.

Teen Age Book Club. Scholastic Book Services, 33 West 42nd Street, New York 36, N.Y. Paperbound books, at $.25 and $.35. For grades 7, 8, 9 and 10. Eight monthly offerings are made during school year; each offer consisting of eighteen books. Selections include fiction, adventure, horse and dog stories, personal growth, biography, sports, mystery, classics, and science. *Memo: to Teachers* is supplied to teacher sponsor.

The Weekly Reader Children's Book Club. Education Center, Columbus 16, Ohio. Two levels: 1) Books for ages 5 to 8; 2) Books for ages 8 to 12. Members get six books a year, including a free bonus book. Books include animal tales, folklore, fairy tales, science, fantasy, humor, adventure, biography, other lands, and other times.

Young Readers of America (Division of Book-of-the-Month Club). 345 Hudson St., New York 14, N.Y. Monthly offerings for ages 9 to 14 at $1.75 each plus shipping costs. History, science, and nature.

APPENDIX G. SELECTED BOOK LISTS

American Association for the Advancement of Science. *The Elementary School Science Library.* The Association, Washington, D.C., 1959.

American Library Association. *Annual List of Children's Literature.* American Library Association Publishing Department, Chicago, Ill. Obtainable at any public library.

American Library Association. *Basic Book Collection for Elementary Grades,* 6th ed. American Library Association Publishing Department, Chicago, Ill., 1956. 133 p. Contains 1020 books and 24 magazines, catalogued and annotated. Developed primarily for use of schools.

American Library Association. *Basic Book Collection for Junior High Schools,* 2nd ed. American Library Association Publishing Department, Chicago, Ill., 1956. 127 p. Selected list of 1004 books and 24 magazines developed for schools.

Arbuthnot, May Hill. *Children's Books too Good to Miss.* Western Reserve University, Cleveland, Ohio, 1953.

Association for Childhood Education. *Bibliography of Books for Children.* The Association, Washington, D.C., 1956. 130 p. Designed as a "list for extensive supplementary reading for elementary school children and covers a wide range of interests and reading abilities."

Association for Childhood Education. *Children's Books for $1.25 or Less,* rev. ed. The Association, Washington, D.C., 1959.

Brewton, J. E., and Brewton, S. W. *Index to Children's Poetry.* H. W. Wilson, New York, 1942. First Supplement. Wilson, New York, 1952. A title, subject, author, and first-line index to poetry in collections for children and youth.

Child Study Association of America. *Books of the Year for Children.* The Association, New York. A pamphlet published annually by the Children's Book Committee of the Child Study Association. Graded, annotated list with subject headings to meet the varied interests and reading abilities of boys and girls.

Condit, Martha Olson. *Trade Books for Beginning Readers.* Wilson, New York, 1960. Reprinted from the December, 1959, *Wilson Library Bulletin.* A list of 151 books for independent reading for children in grades one, two, and three, selected through a study made by the Graduate School of Library Service at Rutgers University. A supplementary list selected by the author, but not tested, is included. Each book is carefully annotated with a synopsis and a technical analysis.

Dawson, Mildred A., and Pfeiffer, Louise. *A Treasury of Books for the Primary Grades.* Howard Chandler, San Francisco, 1959. "An annotated bibliography of 300 choice books recommended for use as a basic library for children in the kindergarten and primary grades." The criteria for selection are given: Books divided into eight categories: books of verse, picture books, fanciful stories, animal stories, stories for fun, stories of other lands, American history, and miscellaneous titles.

Eakin, Mary K. *Good Books for Children.* University of Chicago Press, Chicago, 1960. Based on bulletins of the Center for Children's Books over a ten-year period.

EATON, ANNE THAXTER. *Treasure for the Taking.* Viking, New York, 1946. Annotated list from picture books through high school. Designed for personal libraries. Books are arranged according to subjects, with seventy headings.

EATON, ANNE THAXTER. *Reading with Children.* Viking, New York, 1940.

FENNER, PHYLLIS. *Proof of the Pudding: What Children Read.* John Day, New York, 1957. 246 p. A guide to the books children like with annotated lists grouped by types of books and by children's ages.

Growing Up with Books. An annotated list. Bowker, New York.

LARRICK, NANCY. *A Parents Guide to Children's Reading.* Cardinal ed., Pocket Books, New York, 1958. A handbook initiated by the National Book Committee, Inc., New York, and compiled with the advice of eighteen national organizations representing children, parents, librarians, and teachers. Includes annotated lists for 1) Pre-school, 2) Children aged six to eight, 3) Children aged nine to twelve, 4) For family fun. See also *A Teacher's Guide to Children's Books,* Merrill, Columbus, Ohio, 1960.

MARKEY, LOIS R. *Books are Vacations!* Horn Book, Boston, 1956. A Horn Book annotated reading list for children eight to twelve years of age.

McCall's List of 100 Best Books for Children. Selected by Virginia Haviland, Ruth Gagliardo, and Elizabeth Nesbitt. McCall's Modern Homemaker, P.O. Box 1390, Grand Central Station, New York 17, N.Y. 1956. In addition to the carefully selected list of 100 books there are personal selections made by each of the compilers. List is thoroughly annotated and publisher and price are listed. See Appendix A.

MCCONNELL, MARION L., and WEST, DOROTHY HERBERT, comps. *Children's Catalogue,* 9th ed. Wilson, New York, 1956. *Children's Catalogue 1957-1959,* Supplement to 9th ed. Edited by Dorothy Herbert West and Rachel Shor. Sold on a service basis. Includes annotated classified catalogue; author, title, subject, and analytical entries are arranged in one alphabet; graded list; and publishers' directory.

MOORE, ANNE CARROLL. *Seven Stories High.* Compton, Chicago, 1958. Single copies free to librarians and teachers. A list of books chosen by Anne Carroll Moore for children's own libraries. Reprinted from Compton's Pictured Encyclopedia. Basic book list arranged in age spans. Includes "fiction, poetry, folk, and fairy lore, nonsense, history, adventure and biography."

NATIONAL COUNCIL OF TEACHERS OF ENGLISH. *Adventuring with Books.* The Council, Champaign, Ill., 1960. Prepared by the Elementary Reading List Committee.

NATIONAL COUNCIL OF TEACHERS OF ENGLISH. *Your Reading.* The Council, Champaign, Ill., 1954. Annotated list of books for Junior High School. Symbols indicate easy or challenging books.

SELL, VIOLET, and others. *Subject Index to Poetry for Children and Young People.* American Library Association, Chicago, 1957. The list of books indexed (pages 1-7) includes many of the best poems for children.

SPACHE, GEORGE D. *Good Reading for Poor Readers.* Garrard, Champaign, Ill., 1958. Annotated list of trade books, textbooks, and other materials arranged topically and graded in reading and interest levels.

STRANG, RUTH, and others. *Gateways to Readable Books,* 2nd ed. Wilson, New York, 1952. An annotated, graded list of books in many fields for adolescents who find reading difficult.

THOMPSON, JEAN. *Books for Boys and Girls,* rev. ed. Ryerson Press, Toronto, 1959. Books are arranged in "broad informal subjects" that follow children's reading interests. Earlier editions edited by Lillian Smith.

Chapter 14

THE DEVELOPMENT OF CREATIVE READING ABILITIES

FOUR LEVELS OF READING

A fourth-grader once remarked, "I like stories that mean more than they mean." The boy was well on his way to being a mature reader. He was learning to look below the surface, to read between the lines, to think as he read. Because this boy was putting something of his experience and his thinking ability into his reading, the process was not only more meaningful and satisfying to him, but it was helping him to become a more useful citizen and a person of greater potential. No fourth-grader is an Einstein or Toscanini, but the roots of creativity probably begin in the early years; and reading can be one of those roots.

The importance of such thinking in the life of the individual and the nation cannot be overestimated. Somehow, in contemporary life, many people find themselves too busy to look back, too busy to look ahead, too busy to read, too busy to think. As Norman Cousins[1] put it, "We have bigger homes, bigger television sets, bigger cars, bigger theatres, bigger schools. We have everything we need, in fact, except the most important thing of all—time to think and the habit of thought. We lack time for the one indispensable." The habit of thought and thinking ability begin early in life and develop gradually. Although every individual must think about many things in varied circumstances, such as personal relationships and vocational problems, the act of reading is one of the most valuable resources for developing habits and abilities of thinking.

The point of view throughout this book is that much reading is a high-grade mental activity. It assumes that both children and adults need to develop the habit of reacting actively to what they see and

[1] Norman Cousins, "Does Anyone Have Time to Think?" *Saturday Review,* Vol. 38, p. 22, March 26, 1955.

hear. For example, the discussions on comprehension (Chapter 4), study skills (Chapter 11), and the effects of literature (Chapter 13) are only three main divisions of a large group of activities involving thinking while reading. Some of these ideas in the various chapters may be summarized by suggesting that children, adolescents, and adults typically read at four overlapping levels. In ascending order these are:

1. Word identification
2. Casual skimming
3. Reading for exact, literal meanings
4. Creative reading for
   a. implied and inferred meanings
   b. appreciative reactions
   c. critical evaluations

At the first level, the reader is concerned with getting the word or phrase correct. Sometimes he may be merely word-calling in a vocabulary drill, but often genuine effort involving phonetic and structural analysis, context clues, and other aids may be employed in an earnest attempt to read accurately. At the second level the child or adult is often snatching at meanings or getting a vague impression. He may be reading a comic book with considerable attention to pictures as well as sentences. He may be racing through the story to discover how the hero was rescued from the cliff or scanning a newspaper before dashing to work. The other two levels are more demanding. In the third, there is a conscious effort to get the main idea, the exact date, or the causes of the social phenomenon. Much of the textbook study required in schools is at this level, and the suburbanite following "how to do it yourself" directions for a weekend project must read literally and accurately. It is at the fourth level, however, that reflective or interpretive or creative reading occurs. All four levels are important, but at this one, the reader must use his past experience and his thinking abilities for some sort of active response to the materials which goes beyond the literal ideas in the passage. As Emerson has put it," 'Tis the good reader that makes the good book," or as the novelist Proust wrote, "Every reader reads himself." The written materials are only a stimulus by which the reader feels excitement, enjoys beauty, or gains insight into his own or others' problems.

The three types of creative reading listed above overlap in some details but can be distinguished from one another. They are described and suggestions for teaching them are given in the sections below. They are all called creative because each involves the production of fresh, original ideas not explicitly stated in the story, poem, passage, or chapter. Each type brings into existence or invests with new characteristics ideas, images, concepts, or generalizations which are products of the reader's thought. The third-grader or ninth-grader who is reading creatively keeps adding to what the author has written. He becomes a sort of co-author as he visualizes, recalls his own related experiences, guesses ahead, or occasionally catches the author in some bias or blunder.

Reading for implied and inferred meanings involves using given facts to derive fresh meanings or relationships. The new meaning may be implied in the written materials by the author or inferred freshly by the reader. Accurate reading of the given facts is the first essential. Then the child may predict what will happen next or put together speech and action in the story to deduce character or to judge behavior. The author may not say "The man was angry" but he does write, "Ben clenched his fist." Even the kindergarten child can do this interpretive kind of thinking. What does it mean when the three bears come back from their walk, find the food eaten and the chair broken? What has been happening? When some fifth-graders find in their reader story about Johnny Appleseed, "In time he became a sort of living newspaper and postman for the people in the wilderness," they can deduce some of Johnny's activities. In many areas, and particularly in imaginative literature, the child or adolescent adds his own interpretations.

Like reading for implied or inferred meanings, *reading for appreciative reactions* involves literal understanding and going beyond the stated facts. But where the first relies heavily on intellectual understanding, the second has more of an emotional component. In reading for appreciative reactions the child may employ imagery—he may hear the sound of the bells or the whining voice of the coward. He may picture the beauty of the Swiss village or the spring garden. He may react personally and emotionally to a story character's changing fortunes or increase his sympathy for the character as he gradually understands the person's motivations. Imagery, identification, and projection all have emotional components. The girl who weeps over *Black Beauty* or *Little Women,* the boy who chuckles over *Homer Price* or *Henry Huggins,* the reader who finds a bit of himself or his family in *The Moffats* or *Blue Willow* are responding emotionally to the printed materials. Such interpretive reading with emotional overtones comprises appreciative reading.

In the third type of creative reading the reader must suppress emotion to become more objective and analytical. In *critical* reading he must judge. He must compare what the book, newspaper, or magazine says with what he knows from his previous experience or what is stated in another source. The term critical thinking is used in many ways in educational writing, but the essential factors seem to be: (1) an attitude of suspending judgment until the evidence is considered, and (2) skills in clarifying and attacking a specific problem presented in the materials. In some cases, the problem lies outside the materials, as in determining the author's purpose or bias. Sometimes it is stated explicitly with arguments on two sides of the question and an invitation to the reader to make up his own mind. Sometimes it is implied in printed message, as in a story about a rancher's use of pasture land which raises questions about general principles of land conservation. Second-graders, for example, can distinguish between the true and the false, discriminate between the relevant and irrelevant, and judge the worth of a conclusion made from given facts, if they are encouraged by the teacher to have a critical attitude and if the content lies, at least in part, within their experience. Specific examples of these or related skills are given in some teachers' manuals accompanying readers and in the succeeding sections of this chapter.

The concept that even primary children can read creatively for implications, for appreciations, and for evaluation of the materials adds to the complexity of the reading program and to the task of a pupil and teacher sometimes already burdened. Not all of the reading in schools, elementary or secondary, is creative. There are many mechanical skills and abilities in literal comprehension to be learned and used all through school, and even in college. Most reading from texts in spelling, arithmetics, science, and other areas is work-type reading (Chapter 11), not creative reading. Children and youth must acquire basic reading abilities, but they should not stop there. Sometimes they need to appreciate the devotion and methods of a scientist as they read of his life. Sometimes they need to be able to detect bias or propaganda in novels, newspapers or news magazines. Sometimes they will live more fully if they can enter imaginatively into the work of the literary artist—see the beauties, appreciate the wit, savor the wisdom. The other levels of reading are essential to adequate functioning as pupil, parent, or citizen, but the three types of creative reading make for the enrichment of the individual life and the vitality of a whole culture. The roots of such creative reading are found in early childhood and in the school's reading program.

Since creative reading emphasizes the thinking phases of the reading process, some description of children's thinking should clarify the meaning of creative reading and its place in the whole program. This description follows in two sections: (1) the nature of thinking and (2) the development of thinking abilities in childhood.

NATURE OF THINKING AND ITS RELATION TO READING

Different writers have described the process of thinking in different ways. All agree that thinking may take place in a number of different ways. It may be mere guessing, as when the child says, "I am wondering how I can earn a dime." It may be a sort of daydream or reverie, in which somewhat unconnected ideas come to mind. It may be attempting to remember, as when the child says, "What is the name of that book on South Africa?" It may mean appreciation of the rhythm in a musical recording or in the gaiety of a children's poem. It may mean combining scattered experiences to understand more fully concepts like *isthmus, transportation,* or *justice.* It may mean organizing ideas to come to some sort of decision or to make up one's mind, as when the chairman of the committee asks, "In the light of these facts what is our next step?" It may mean solving a definite problem, as when the child asks, "How can an airplane fly?" In creative reading as defined above, the emphasis is upon the three types of thinking—organizing materials to arrive at some conclusion about them, responding emotionally and intellectually to ideas on form, and being critically aware of some problem and taking steps to solve it. Creative readers add some of the products of their other experiences to synthesize them with their reading experience or to solve some problem through their reading.

One of the most influential and fruitful descriptions of thinking is that of Dewey,[2] who described it in some five or six steps, as follows: (1) the awareness of a problem, (2) the collection and classification of data related to the problem, (3) the formulation of a tentative hypothesis, (4) the judging of the worth of the hypothesis by mental

[2] John Dewey, *How We Think.* Heath, Boston, 1933.

tryout, accepting or rejecting, (5) actual test of the hypothesis, and (6) possibly some conclusion or some solution of the problem.

Obviously, children do not always use all these six steps in solving their problems. They may proceed in one step from awareness of the problem to some conclusion or solution of it, perhaps on an emotional or habitual basis. Some types of thinking required in school, home, and community may not be of this problem-solving sort. For example, some reading may involve a process of reflection or of association, such as adding to the meaning of a concept. A child reading McDonald's *The Little Island* may add to his concepts of *island* and of *weather* without solving a specific problem.

In the period after Dewey's formulation, the study of the whole process of thinking was neglected in British and American psychology in favor of the investigation of more specific aspects of human behavior. In the attempt to get objective, scientific measurements, psychologists studied bits of observable behavior such as eyeblinks or paper-and-pencil responses rather than the larger processes. Within recent years, however, there has been a revival of work in the thinking processes from the varied points of view of different research workers.[3] In England, Bartlett[4] and Burt[5] have developed theories influenced respectively by a neo-behaviorist point of view and studies in factor analysis of mental test results. In Switzerland, Piaget produced in the 1920's and 1930's a long series of studies of children's language, concepts, and reasoning abilities followed by more general studies of intelligence and mental life.[6] In the United States the research has been wide-ranging, sometimes contradictory and isolated. Thurstone at Chicago, and Guilford and his co-workers at the University of Southern California each applied factor-analytic

[3] David H. Russell, "Concepts" and "Higher Mental Processes" in C. W. Harris, ed., *Encyclopedia of Educational Research*, 3rd ed., pp. 323-333, 645-661. Macmillan, New York, 1960.

[4] Sir Frederick Bartlett, *Thinking: An Experimental and Social Study*. Allen and Unwin, London, 1958.

[5] Cyril Burt, "The Differentiation of Intellectual Ability," *British Journal of Educational Psychology*, Vol. 24, pp. 76-90, 1954.

[6] Examples of concept studies are:

Jean Piaget and others, *The Moral Judgment of the Child*. Harcourt, New York, 1932.

Jean Piaget, *The Child's Conception of Number*. Routledge, London, 1952.

More general studies include:

Jean Piaget, *The Psychology of Intelligence*. Harcourt, New York, 1950.

Barbel Inhelder and Jean Piaget, *The Growth of Logical Thinking from Childhood to Adolescence*. Basic Books, New York, 1958.

techniques in a series of studies of different types of intellectual functioning. Guilford, for example, has given a long list of factors which contribute to problem-solving abilities and to creative abilities and has attempted to organize all thinking into about fifty primary intellectual abilities which he has described in terms of contents, operations, and products.[7] Such research workers as Heidbreder, Welch, and Bruner and co-workers have made series of studies of concept formation. Books which organize the wide range of research materials in an eclectic fashion have been written by Johnson,[8] by Russell,[9] and by Vinacke.[10] Attempts to apply what we know about the psychology of thinking to reading instruction have not been very intensive or fruitful in the past, but the current interest in the area promises many new developments.

Teachers who are interested in exploring the relationships of reading and thinking may start by study of one or more of the three summaries by Johnson, by Russell, and by Vinacke. In these books, there is some agreement that the teacher may distinguish between the child's materials of thinking (the percepts, concepts, images, and memories) which are myriad, even for small children, and his processes of thinking, which are very few. The processes have been identified by various labels by different writers but may be called perceptual thinking, associative thinking, convergent thinking (leading to concepts and generalizations), problem solving, critical thinking or judgment, and creative thinking. The child uses perceptual and associative processes as he first learns to recognize words and word parts. In convergent thinking he may use reading as a set of various experiences which help him understand in some depth words like *neighbor* or rules like, "Do as you would be done by." Here various reading experiences, perhaps widely separated, may converge in one product. He may use reading to help solve problems such as, "Why did cities grow where they now are?" He may be critical of what he reads and he may achieve some fresh original outcome through reading. Reading enters into many of the materials and all of the seven processes of thinking, but it is with the three main divisions of creative reading that this chapter is especially concerned.

[7] J. P. Guilford, "The Structure of Intellect," *Psychological Bulletin,* Vol. 53, pp. 267-293, 1956.

[8] Donald M. Johnson, *The Psychology of Thought and Judgment.* Harper, New York, 1955.

[9] David H. Russell, *Children's Thinking.* Ginn, Boston, 1956.

[10] W. Edgar Vinacke, *The Psychology of Thinking.* McGraw-Hill, New York, 1952.

As suggested above, beginning work in critical thinking and creative reading is within the grasp of even primary children. Most competent teachers employ the above ideas in their daily direction of reading and other activities, even if they have not studied a psychology of thinking. Most teachers ask for word or sound association only with meaningful materials. If a fourth-grade child in a group studying California raises a question about the age of the redwood trees, the teacher emphasizes the importance of related experience by asking, "What must we know before we can answer this question?" If a social-studies group finds in a particular book an attitude of condescension toward the people of Mexico, the teacher encourages a questioning attitude and suspended judgment about the statements until further evidence is produced. If a seventh-grade class becomes concerned when reading about the treatment of minority groups, the teacher may raise the question of actually doing something about the problem in the group's immediate community. All these activities imply that creative reading may involve seeing implications and developing appreciations. They imply, too, that elementary-school children have considerable ability to think critically and act on their judgments. The next section summarizes some of the evidence on this point.

CHILD DEVELOPMENT IN THINKING ABILITIES

Established facts in child development lend support to creative reading activities in the total program. Many scientific studies have been made of children's ability to think. These include investigation of the child's perception, his memory, his ability to concentrate, and his reasoning ability. Chapter 9 reviews some studies of his knowledge of concepts. Studies of reasoning and of concept formation are the most pertinent in a discussion of creative reading, but only a few samples can be mentioned here. Valuable summaries of scientific investigation in these areas have been made by Curti,[11] Hurlock,[12] Jersild,[13] Munn,[14] and others.

[11] Margaret W. Curti, *Child Psychology*, 2nd ed. Longmans, Green, New York, 1938.

[12] Elizabeth B. Hurlock, "The Development of Understanding," *Child Development*, rev. ed., Chap. 11. McGraw-Hill, New York, 1956.

[13] Arthur T. Jersild, "The Growth of Understanding," *Child Psychology*, 4th ed., Chaps. 13, 14. Prentice-Hall, Englewood Cliffs, N.J., 1954.

[14] Norman L. Munn, "Investigations of Basic Symbolic Processes in Children," *Psychological Development*, Chap. 11. Houghton Mifflin, Boston, 1938.

Most child psychologists agree that the infant and young child first learn to perceive accurately and to judge in terms of the immediate physical environment. During the first three years a child makes rapid strides in discriminating different sizes and shapes, in judging distances, and in associating meaning with his sensory impressions. There is no direct evidence in research that a child is capable of reasoning about problems during these years. Some of his ideas and solutions may seem entirely usual and logical to the adult, others entirely illogical. The lines between fancy and fact have not yet been drawn.

There seems considerable evidence that reasoning ability does not appear suddenly at three or six or twelve years but is a gradual growth, with irregular advances in different areas. For example, Heidbreder[15] gave children of varying ages and adults the problem of determining the location of an object in a box through use of spatial and geometric figure cues and concluded that "The total reaction involved in solving problems is recognizably present in four-year-old children." Moore[16] found children capable of syllogistic reasoning at six years, the youngest age tested. Haupt[17] found that children in the first grade had some ability to generalize about scientific experiments they witnessed, and Deutsche[18] found that although children's ideas of true causes developed year by year, their explanations of such things as lighted candles going out developed gradually from year to year. Many teachers note samples of thinking and reasoning in social play at about five years of age. Webb[19] believed that by eight years most children have the ability to see a problem through to its conclusion and to note its contexts and implications, whereas earlier they tend to see only parts of the whole process. She gave samples to show that children are capable of self-appraisal in the group situation at this age, an important point in relation to critical reading. Webb stated that elementary-school pupils are "not often capable of work-

[15] Edna F. Heidbreder, "Problem Solving in Children and Adults," *Journal of Genetic Psychology*, Vol. 35, pp. 522-545, December, 1928.

[16] Thomas V. Moore, *The Reasoning Ability of Children in the First Years of School Life*. Williams and Wilkins, Baltimore, Md., 1929.

[17] George W. Haupt, *An Experimental Application of a Philosophy of Science Teaching in an Elementary School,* Contributions to Education, No. 633. Bureau of Publications, Teachers College, Columbia University, New York, 1935.

[18] Jean M. Deutsche, *The Development of Children's Concepts of Causal Relations.* University of Minnesota Press, Minneapolis, 1937.

[19] Ruth K. Webb, "All Children Think and Plan," *Childhood Education,* Vol. 23, pp. 315-321, March, 1947.

ing with abstract principles" but reason, solve problems, and evaluate correctly in more specific situations.

A number of other researches give supporting evidence that productive, appreciative, and critical thinking occur in the activities of pre-school and elementary-school children. Some writers indicate that most children's learning can be termed *creative* as a fresh synthesis or grasp of relationship for the individual himself; it seems desirable, however, to restrict the term to the production of new ideas or objects. In the pre-school years, the child may be creative in his play (as in building a bridge across a river with blocks) and in his early efforts in drawing, music, and language. The spontaneity and freshness of young children's ideas have been discovered by many teachers, as in a slow-learning first grade where pupils created such "poetry" as "fog is like stepping on tiptoes," "fog is quiet, like somebody daydreaming," and "fog makes you feel cold inside."[20] Jersild[21] and Updegraff[22] have studied children's responses to music in the ages two to five and found specific examples of appreciative response to rhythm and pitch. Mursell[23] has given ten steps in the development of music abilities beginning with undifferentiated emotional responses and going on to more specific response and performance.

Before they enter school many children learn to manipulate paints and crayons in "scribble" and beginnings of "schematic" stages. Freyberger[24] continued earlier studies of maturity in children's drawings and found greater differences due to age and grade than to socioeconomic or ethnic background.

There is some evidence that creativity in language may lie somewhere between creativity in the fine arts which contains large elements of emotional, imaginative response, and the creativity needed in scientific and mathematical situations, which demands large amounts of logical, problem-solving types of behavior. Studies such

20 Pupils of Kathryn Breslauer, Berkeley Public Schools, Calif.

21 Arthur T. Jersild and others, "Training and Growth in the Development of Children," *Child Development Monographs,* No. 10, 1932.

22 Ruth Updegraff and others, "The Effect of Training upon Singing Ability and Musical Interest of Three-, Four-, and Five-Year-Old Children," *University of Iowa Studies in Child Welfare,* Vol. 14, No. 346, 1938.

23 James L. Mursell, *The Psychology of Music.* Norton, New York, 1937.

24 Ruth M. Freyberger, "Differences in the Creative Drawings of Children of Varying Ethnic and Socio-Economic Backgrounds in Pennsylvania Based on Samplings in Grades One through Six," *Research in Art Education,* Seventh Yearbook, pp. 15-25, National Art Education Association, Washington, D.C., 1956.

as those of Bear[25] and others summarized by McCarthy[26] indicate typical length of sentence, length of composition, and other characteristics of children's writing at various age levels. One study by Carlson[27] reliably identified the following five characteristics in children's creative writing: structure, novelty, emotion, individuality, and style. Each of these elements was described by some specific components such as "unusual beginning," "ingenuity in solving situations," and "unusual perceptive sensitivity."

Scientific evidence of critical thinking in young children is sparse, but if the considerable data indicating problem-solving and creative thinking abilities are accepted, by analogy, the ability to do critical thinking about problems within one's experience is also a part of childhood. Some of this evidence up to 1955 has been summarized by Russell,[28] and later studies such as that of Hendrickson[29] have obtained evidence of critical thinking abilities at the elementary school level. The work of Guilford and his associates[30] with adults may have implications for testing the critical abilities of younger people. This brief sampling illustrates possibilities in research as well as direct evidence that elementary school children are capable of, and participate in various kinds of creative and critical thinking.

The gradual development of the ability to think creatively and critically has not been wholly accepted in American education. Some schools still are based on the idea that elementary schools are concerned only with the three R's, not with thinking or reasoning, partly, at least, because of the writings of Piaget.[31] From his studies of children in Geneva, Switzerland, Piaget concluded that there are definite stages in children's language and thinking. Up to seven or eight years children make decisions and conclusions to suit their

25 Mata V. Bear, "Children's Growth in the Use of Written Language," *Elementary English Review*, Vol. 16, pp. 312-319, December, 1939.

26 Dorothea McCarthy, "Language Development in Children," in Leonard Carmichael, ed., *Manual of Child Psychology*, 2nd ed., pp. 492-630. Wiley, New York, 1954.

27 Ruth K. Carlson, *Stimulating Children in Grades Four, Five and Six to Write Original Stories*. Doctoral dissertation, University of California, Berkeley, 1959.

28 David H. Russell, *op. cit.*

29 Dale Hendrickson, *Correlates of the Critical Thinking Abilities of Fifth-Grade Children*. Doctoral dissertation, University of California, Berkeley, 1960.

30 J. P. Guilford and others, "A Factor-Analytic Study of Evaluative Abilities: I. Hypotheses and Descriptions of Tests; II. Administration of Tests and Analysis of Results," *Reports from the Psychological Laboratory*, Nos. 7 and 9. University of Southern California, Los Angeles, 1952, 1953.

31 Jean Piaget, *Judgment and Reasoning in the Child*. Harcourt, Brace, New York, 1928. Jean Piaget, *The Language and Thought of the Child*. Harcourt, Brace, New York, 1926.

whims and desires. He maintained that they reason only in terms of particular cases, feel no need for verification, and have difficulty in making generalizations or deductions. After seven or eight, children grow in their control of words and in their awareness of their own mental processes; but it is not until eleven or twelve years that they are capable of verbal problem-solving or reasoning in the adult sense of the term.

Much of the experimental work with children in America has failed to verify Piaget's conclusions. Rather the studies by Heidbreder and others, quoted above, and others presenting similar conclusions, tend to verify the presence of some elementary reasoning abilities about the age of three years and the gradual development of these as the child gains wider experience. Criticisms of Piaget's findings have been summarized by Brownell,[32] by McCarthy,[33] by Russell,[34] and others. They believed that in confining reasoning ability to tasks which can be accomplished only at the age of eleven or twelve years, Piaget failed to note the prejudicial character of the problems he set for children. Further, he restricted his definition of reasoning to a highly formal type of thinking involved in verifying hypotheses of a verbal nature and neglected the behavior of children in solving other problems involving physical features of their environment. They also believed that Piaget's contrast between children's thinking and the logical reasoning of adults seems to give too much credit to adults, who betray in their thinking the logical weaknesses and egocentricity that Piaget ascribed only to children. Finally, the doctrine of definite stages in thinking ability is contrary to thousands of verified facts about child development which represent it in general as a gradual, continuous process, proceeding unevenly in different areas, and not as a series of separate and distinct developmental patterns.

In general, then, scientific studies of children's thinking support the view that critical, creative reading is possible at all levels of the elementary school. Reasoning ability seems to begin at about three years of age and to develop gradually with experience and language. It develops continuously rather than appearing at fixed stages. There seems to be little difference in the way adults and children think, except that adults have a wider experience against which they may

[32] William A. Brownell, "Problem Solving," *The Psychology of Learning*, Forty-first Yearbook, Part II, Chap. 12, pp. 415-443, National Society for the Study of Education, Public School Publishing Co., Bloomington, Ill., 1942.

[33] Dorothea McCarthy, *op. cit.*

[34] David Russell, *op. cit.*, pp. 155-162.

check their hypotheses and conclusions. Accordingly, the influence of the teacher in developing reasoning and problem-solving abilities is paramount. The encouragement of creative activities in reading may be a large part of such influence.

The conclusion above may be used to stimulate teachers in the attempt to develop creative reading abilities but never to discourage them for lack of progress in a particular group. A teacher must always remember that ability to recognize what a selection really means comes only after ease in word recognition or ability to tell what the words "say." She must always recall that the different content fields demand a wide variety of reading abilities, even on a fairly mechanical level. There is probably no such thing as perfect comprehension and interpretation of all types of material among adults of wide background, much less among immature children. For example, primary children have little or no concept of time in the historical sense. Fifth-grade children know only about one half of indefinite time words such as *present, recent, century, eternal,* and *B.C.*[35] In the seventh and eighth grades the percentages of one group having some knowledge of the following terms were as follows: taxation, 72 per cent; banking, 63 per cent; insurance, 56 per cent; and merchandising, 48 per cent.[36] Even at the end of the elementary-school period this result is not surprising, because of children's lack of experience in these areas. It is not until about eleven years, according to the Stanford-Binet tests, that a child can tell how three things such as a *snake, cow,* and *sparrow* are all alike. These sample results of research simply indicate that it is overly optimistic to expect formal and verbalized problem-solving, creative thinking, and judgment to flourish in elementary-school children. Rather, the elementary teacher plans a rich program of varied activities which will give concrete experiences in important phases of modern living and thus equip children with some of the information and skill in attacking problems prerequisite to all good thinking.

In the field of reading, the extent to which children develop creative abilities depends largely upon their teachers. Attitudes can be both caught and taught, including the attitude of critical appraisal. Many facets of modern life tend to make children accepting conform-

[35] Kopple C. Friedman, "Time Concepts of Elementary School Children," *Elementary School Journal,* Vol. 44, pp. 337-342, February, 1944.

[36] Foster E. Grossnickle, "Concepts in Social Arithmetic for Eighth-Grade Level," *Journal of Educational Research,* Vol. 30, pp. 475-488, March, 1937.

ists rather than questioning individualists. They wear the same kinds of clothes, submit to necessary school routines in large groups, go to the same shops, and see the same television programs. The whole effect of the various mass media may be standardization of taste and judgment. It is in reading, as one child reacts to one book, that individual response is still possible. It is in the way the teacher motivates reading or questions about material read that creative abilities can be developed.

For example, the following selection and the questions succeeding it illustrate the four levels at which pupils and teacher may work. The selection is from a fifth grade test.[37]

"Abandon ship!" the captain roared.
Ned flung himself out of his bunk and reached for his trousers.
"I'll be a hero," he thought to himself. "I'll rescue all the passengers."
"Don't be frightened!" he yelled. "I'm coming."
At that moment he opened his eyes to find his brother shaking his shoulder.
"Be quiet!" his brother grumbled.
Grinning foolishly, Ned snuggled down into his warm blankets.

Literal Interpretation—Main Idea	a. A good name for this story is ____ The Rescue ____ Abandon Ship ____ Ned is a Hero ____ Ned's Dream
Literal Interpretation—Specific Fact	b. Ned was really with ____ the captain. ____ his brother. ____ his father. ____ his mother.
Creative Reading for Sequence Implied in Paragraph	c. The first thing Ned said was ____ "Abandon ship!" ____ "I'll rescue all the passengers." ____ "Don't be frightened." ____ "Be quiet!"
Creative Reading in Which The Reader Makes an Original Inference (4 possible answers may be omitted in favor of a blank space)	d. What do you think Ned will do next? ____ Go to sleep. ____ Put on his trousers. ____ Find the captain. ____ Rescue the passengers.

[37] Constance M. McCullough and David H. Russell, *Fifth Reader Readiness Test*, experimental ed. Ginn, Boston, 1951.

Similarly, almost any paragraph or story can be treated by skimming it casually, reading for certain types of literal comprehension, and reading which goes beyond the stated materials to the author's assumptions or the reader's own conclusions. Young children will acquire these abilities, especially the last two, only after much specific practice encouraged by the teacher.

Although one of the chief aims of the elementary-school program is to build a background of information and understanding, it is the thesis of this chapter that reading and related activities must go one step further. Bearing in mind the limitations of immaturity and inexperience, the teacher must still encourage the development of creative and critical thinking abilities. All modern teachers subscribe to the task of teaching children not what to think but how to think. Information, particularly in the form of unrelated facts, is forgotten at an alarming rate. In contrast, questioning attitudes and habits of objective judgment involved in good thinking are rather permanent learnings. An emphasis in the past upon names, dates, locations, rules, and definitions in the elementary school has been shifted to children's use of facts and concepts in situations demanding clear thinking.

This section has given some of the limitations on the development of creative thinking, but has also included evidence that even young children are capable of careful thinking in reading and related activities. The elementary program, therefore, must include specific activities leading toward good habits of thought and providing for the gradual development of thinking ability at all stages of development. Only as the powers of creative and critical thinking are developed at all stages can the schools help to produce the inventive, clear-thinking citizenry which is the bulwark of any democracy.

ASPECTS OF CREATIVE READING

In planning greater emphasis upon creative reading the teacher or curriculum consultant must have specific suggestions to make to pupils or teachers. An individual teacher or school staff may attack the problem in different ways, such as: studying the psychology of thinking, hearing different speakers on the meaning of such topics as concept formation, problem-solving, or creative thinking; checking teachers' manuals for specific suggestions for activities; and attempting some "action" or "operations" research which stresses thinking processes involved in reading. Such general labels as "creative reading" can be made more specific in terms of possible sequences in group activities or in terms of the characteristics of the individual reader. Research on the problem is not sufficiently advanced to indicate a series of clear-cut stages in creative reading or a group of discrete characteristics of a creative reader, and it may be that overlapping and intermixing of abilities and of procedures will always be true of the process or the person. At our present stage of knowledge, we can use the results of observation in classrooms and logical analysis of task, rather than scientifically determined facts. With this limitation, it is possible to propose a sequence of the usual events in creative reading and to describe the creative reader.

The introduction to this chapter suggested the importance of accuracy in the more mechanical aspects of reading and then going beyond these. The sequence looks something like this:

Accurate perception of words and thought-units
↓
Understanding literal meanings
↓
Integration of ideas with past experience
↓
Seeing implied relationships, hidden meanings, reacting to symbols
↓
Developing new ideas either appreciative or critical
↓
Using these new ideas in other activities

When the child has read accurately and with understanding of literal meanings in a story, the teacher may ask the general question, "What do you think about the story?" In many cases, however, this free-response type of question may be followed by a more specific question concerning plot or character, "From what you know about (farm boys or shy girls or wheat farmers, etc.) do you think the individuals would act this way (character) or things would happen this way (plot)?" Having established authenticity or relevance or the reverse, the group, or individual, may be ready for the next type of question, such as, "Do you think of anything that ever happened to you like this?" or "What were the events in order that made the family decide to move to a new location?" Having checked on some of the exact literal meanings of the passage, the group, or individual, then goes one of two ways, depending upon the nature of the selection or the purpose of teacher and children. If they have been reading part of Gates' *Blue Willow,* the teacher may say "What does the blue willow plate stand for in Janey's life?" (appreciation of symbol), or "Why was Bounce Reyburn, the ranch employee, a person to be despised?" (criticism of character or ethical values). Finally, after discussion of these or related types of questions, the teacher may ask, "What should we do about it?" or "What are other stories with related ideas?" (using other activities) Thus children are encouraged to incorporate the materials of a story into their own thinking and to apply ideas in the solution of some immediate or practical problem. The final stage of use may occur sooner or later. For example, as a boy enjoys Edwards' *The Matchlock Gun* and a girl reacts to some of Rachel Field's poems, they enrich their concepts of other times and places, produce ideas of courage or beauty, but may not actually use these until some later time.

The sequence of possible events in creative reading may also be considered from the point of view of the reader himself. Different writers give the characteristics in somewhat different terms, and vary the emphasis on what can be expected at various age levels, but the creative reader can be described under the three main divisions of creative reading given in the introduction to this chapter:

1. *The creative reader sees relationships and draws inferences.*
   a. He relates his reading to previous experiences.
   b. He gives illustrations of his own.
   c. He integrates facts and ideas from various sources.
   d. He discovers relationships in such terms as
      association
      time
      place
      sequence of ideas
      general-specific
      main and subordinate ideas
      cause and effect
      analogy

e. He uses discovered relationships to infer and predict
f. He uses reading in solving problems by
   finding the facts
   organizing the facts
   suggesting hypotheses
   evaluating each hypothesis
   coming to a conclusion
g. He applies ideas in materials read to his other activities.

2. *The creative reader develops appreciations.*
   a. He forms and reacts to sensory images.
   b. He recognizes emotions and motives of characters.
   c. He identifies with situation or character.
   d. He recognizes humor, exaggeration, and incongruity.
   e. He develops sensitivity to ethical values such as unselfishness, truthfulness, and courage.
3. *The creative reader makes critical evaluations.*
   a. He judges the validity of statements, distinguishing fact and opinion.
   b. He checks an author's conclusions against his facts.
   c. He determines relevancy of materials to his own purposes.
   d. He compares with his previous experience or with related statements.
   e. He assesses the author's purpose and special point of view.
   f. He attempts to get at all sides of a controversial issue.
   g. He detects the use of emotional appeals and of propaganda devices.
   h. In the above activities he attempts an objective, problem-solving approach to issues.

These general statements about the creative and critical reader can be divided into many sub-groups or into a wide variety of specific classroom activities. The teacher's guidance of individual or group purposes is usually needed if children are to read at these levels. The teacher is aware that certain material should be read literally, not creatively, as in getting the facts about the size of New York City. In other reading, interpretation, appreciation, or judgment may be the important factor. Specific examples of such activities are many—organizing the facts in a new way, interpreting character, predicting outcomes, checking agreement between headlines or titles and facts, detecting propaganda devices, enjoying figurative language—these are only a few of the purposes of creative and critical reading.

The two terms *critical reading* and *creative reading* are sometimes confusing. As used in this chapter, critical reading is one kind of creative reading, but the two are not identical. The word *creative* implies production of something new; in creative reading, the reader adds his experience to the printed page to arrive at some original outcomes. *Critical* reading does not imply that the reader is faultfinding or only looking for defects. Rather, in the words of *Webster's New Collegiate Dictionary critical* implies "an effort to see a thing clearly and truly in order to judge it fairly." Critical reading is a part of creative reading, because criticism may be a creative act. In reacting to a paragraph, the critical reader may achieve a fresh insight, a unique synthesis, which makes his reading creative. On the other hand, creative reading may or may not include critical elements. In appreciative responses to the beauty of a poem, the lucidity of the argument, or the excitement of the plot, the reader may have an appreciative, emotional response without the element of criticism in it. The extent to which criticism enters into a creative product is a matter of degree. Similarities and differences in the two activities become clearer in the summaries of research below.

The two analyses of creative reading activities given above are based on observation of classroom practices and logical listing of component parts rather than complete research findings. However, enough research evidence exists in the two areas to permit brief summaries of it in the next two sections.

RESEARCH ON CREATIVE READING

The act of creative reading can be understood in terms of the research on the creative process and specific applications of creativity in the reading act. For many years in English and American psychology, the higher mental processes were disregarded in the laboratory research in favor of less complex processes. Recent years have seen a tremendous growth of interest in concept formation, problem solving, creativity, and other complex processes. The classic statement in the field, based on introspection rather than experiment, is that of Wallas,[38] who stated that the process of thinking can be described in four overlapping stages:

1. *Preparation*—defining and organizing the problem, relating needed facts and experiences.

[38] Graham Wallas, *The Art of Thought*. Harcourt, Brace, New York, 1926.

2. *Incubation*—a period of conscious and unconscious organizing over almost any period of time.
3. *Illumination*—developing insight; may involve imagination and less conscious, "fringe" thoughts.
4. *Verification*—reasoning about the proposed solution in (3); critical thinking often involved.

This statement has received some verification in the work of Patrick[39] but is criticized by Vinacke[40] and others as being oversimplified since artists, writers, and inventors have widely different work habits, and many other processes such as search, integration of isolated phenomena, whole-part relationships, and motivational factors may be involved. The complexity of the process has been illustrated by Wilson, Guilford, and associates,[41] who believed that creativity could be measured by tests of ability in giving clever plot titles, uncommonness of responses to words and drawings, giving unusual uses for common objects such as a newspaper or a brick, and a remoteness-of-association test requiring the subject to give one word relating to both words of a pair such as Indian—money and tree—dog. Other analyses of the creative process have been given by Russell[42] and in the volume edited by Anderson.[43]

An exploratory study of creativity in school situations was made by Ferris,[44] who used interviews with teachers to identify creative behavior. He made such conclusions from interviews and the literature as:

Creativity may be a generalized ability or occur in specific areas.

There is not a direct positive relationship between high intelligence and creativity.

Facility in some medium of expression is necessary for the communication of creative ideas.

School activities that allow time for the child to develop his own ideas encourage creativity.

Self-confidence seems related to children's creative expression.

39 Catherine Patrick, *What is Creative Thinking?* Philosophical Library, New York, 1955.

40 W. Edgar Vinacke, *op. cit.*

41 R. C. Wilson, J. P. Guilford, and P. R. Christensen, "The Measurement of Individual Differences in Originality," *Psychological Bulletin,* Vol. 50, pp. 362-370, September, 1953.

42 David H. Russell, *op. cit.*

43 Harold H. Anderson, ed., *Creativity and Its Cultivation.* Harper, New York, 1959.

44 Donald R. Ferris, *Creative Behavior in Fifth and Sixth Grade Elementary School Pupils.* Ed.D. dissertation, University of Illinois, Urbana, 1959.

The creative child has many ideas when faced by a problem—not all of them good.

The creative child is likely to be flexible in finding solutions.

Some of these general statements have been studied in reading or test situations. For example, Tyler[45] found that the ability to select the most reasonable inference from a given list is not the same as the ability to propose an original inference. Bedell[46] had eighth- and ninth-grade students read paragraphs containing science information and concluded that their ability to infer from such facts is different from the ability to recall the facts. Similarly, Cobb[47] found that ability of sixth-grade pupils in certain types of literal comprehension was not closely related to ability in problem solving from printed materials. On the other hand, McCullough[48] found positive correlations (median $r = .47$) between tests of literal comprehension and of creative reading (seeing relationships, drawing conclusions, and passing judgments). She concluded that the two types of reading may involve a common factor of fact-getting ability but that the relationships between the tests do not justify testing children on only one type of ability.

Other studies support the evidence for low but positive relationships among the different types of reading abilities. Shores and Saupe[49] found that this was true of science materials, and Artley[50] obtained similar results using social-studies materials. His measures included literal comprehension such as knowledge of vocabulary, ability to obtain facts and ability to organize. He labelled other tests, "ability to interpret," "ability to apply generalizations," "ability to perceive logical relationships," and "ability to evaluate arguments." Of twenty-eight intercorrelations among the tests, Artley found the median correlation to be .48. He also found that vocabulary cor-

45 Ralph W. Tyler, "Measuring the Ability to Infer," *Educational Research Bulletin*, Vol. 9, pp. 475-480, 1930.

46 Ralph C. Bedell, "The Relationship between the Ability to Recall and the Ability to Infer in Special Learning Situations," *Science Education*, Vol. 18, pp. 158-162, 1934.

47 Jacob E. Cobb, *A Study of Functional Reading*, Contributions to Education, No. 388. George Peabody College for Teachers, Nashville, Tenn., 1947.

48 Constance M. McCullough, "Responses of Elementary School Children to Common Types of Reading Comprehension Questions," *Journal of Educational Research*, Vol. 51, pp. 65-70, September, 1957.

49 J. Harlan Shores and J. L. Saupe, "Reading for Problem-Solving in Science," *Journal of Educational Psychology*, Vol. 44, pp. 149-158, March, 1953.

50 A. Sterl Artley, "A Study of Certain Relationships Existing between General Reading Comprehension and Reading Comprehension in a Specific Subject-Matter Area," *Journal of Educational Research*, Vol. 38, pp. 464-473, February, 1944.

related more highly with other tests than did the tests of creative reading ability. The question of the possible difficulty of various comprehension abilities was explored by Bell.[51] In a group of Scottish students he found that good readers made their fewest errors on questions of detail and on grasp of the main plot. In order of difficulty from easy to hard he classified questions as follows:

1. *Direct reference*—answer found in text in same words as the questions.
2. *Indirect reference*—answer found in text but with slightly different wording.
3. *Easy inference*—answer not directly in text but inferred without difficulty.
4. *Inference related to qualifying phrases*—answer dependent on words such as *largely, alone, chief, only* or *full.*
5. *Difficult inferences*—obscure relationships.

Bell's third and fifth categories require more specific analysis to include some of the types of reading mentioned above, but his statement gives leads to a hierarchy of difficulty in interpreting.

Because creative reading involves seeing relationships in what may be scattered materials, the suggestions of McCullough about seven types of context clues (see page 300) may aid creative reading. In addition, Artley[52] has identified ten aids in identifying meanings:

1. Typographical aids—quotation marks, italics, bold-face type, etc.
2. Structural aids—appositive phrases or clauses.
3. Substituted words—synonyms or antonyms.
4. Word parts—roots, affixes.
5. Figures of speech—simile and metaphor.
6. Inference—using words to infer meanings.
7. Pictorial representation—graphs and charts.
8. Definition in context.
9. Experience.
10. Subjective clues—tone, mood and intent of writer.

Both McCullough's and Artley's clues would seem to differ in kind and in difficulty and should be explored in further research studies.

Clark[53] exemplified such a study in another area of creative read-

[51] Harold Bell, "Comprehension in Silent Reading," *British Journal of Educational Psychology,* Vol. 12, pp. 47-55, February, 1942.

[52] A. Sterl Artley, *op. cit.*

[53] Charles M. Clark, *Teaching Sixth Grade Students to Make Predictions from Reading Materials.* Doctoral dissertation, University of California, Berkeley, 1959.

ing, that of teaching pupils to predict from printed materials. An experimental group of six classes studied twenty-three lessons on prediction of the self-help variety over an eight-week period. Teachers of the control group taught the making of predictions as they would usually do it, except that the teaching was concentrated in an eight-week period instead of being spread over the year. Clark found that his experimental group gained rapidly on an experimental test, on the Gates Reading Test, Type B (Reading to Predict Outcomes of Given Events), and that the experimental group gained significantly more than the control group on the Gates test. The experimental test and the type B of the Gates battery correlated .29, and the two tests were somewhat independent of the ordinary measures of vocabulary and comprehension. One of the contributions of the Clark study was the careful analysis of abilities needed to predict as given in the self-administering lessons and their accompanying teacher's manual. The abilities were divided into the general categories of (1) the collection or selection of information and (2) the synthesis of the information to make a prediction. Specific lesson topics included: facts on which to base a prediction, using the main topic and supporting facts in making a prediction, selection of information, gathering information, using past experience to help make a prediction, using the sequence of ideas to make a prediction, predicting by noting the trend, selecting information from more than one source, finding the true causes for events, and using generalizations to make predictions.

Research on creative reading as appreciation included early attempts to measure appreciation of literary materials by paper and pencil tests. Some of these were reviewed by Harris,[54] who developed other tests and found a general factor of appreciation running through them. Some of the subsequent findings about appreciation were summarized in the following statements:

1. Most children do not seem to respond to literary devices such as metaphor or personification before they are in their teens.
2. Children's appreciations are influenced by their attitudes toward the reading situation.
3. Responses of adolescents to literature may be classed as interpretive reactions, narration, association, self-involvement, literary judgment, and prescriptive judgment.
4. Responses to literature are largely individual. Members of the same group may see a story or poem in very different ways.

[54] Chester W. Harris, "Measurement of Comprehension of Literature," *School Review,* Vol. 56, pp. 280-289, 332-343, May, June, 1948.

5. Literary judgment and emotional involvement vary inversely.
6. Young people show a powerful desire for a happy ending.[55]

Related to the fifth finding, Fennema[56] found that a response involving much imagery may cut down on accuracy of literal comprehension of a story or passage in the third and fourth grades. This suggests that teacher and pupils must decide whether their main purpose is to note accurate details or to "see the author's pictures." Durrell[57] gave suggestions for encouraging responses involving imagery.

The above studies suggest that reading is often a complex act but that the high-level abilities involved in it can be taught. Accurate recognition and literal comprehension are needed before children can draw fresh conclusions, infer and predict. However, ability to find the facts or select the main idea in a passage does not guarantee ability to do more creative reading. Such reading seems to involve certain types of relational thinking, usually involving past experience, based rather directly on the passage as in placing events in order, or departing from known facts to original conclusions as in describing character or predicting future events. Many of these are difficult skills. For example, with a group of sixth graders Nardelli[58] found that, in a six-week period of instruction, it was harder to teach the creative skills of interpreting authors' suggestions and interpreting feelings than it was to teach critical reading for the recognition of propaganda devices. Additional research on critical reading does not suggest, however, that the process is an easy one.

RESEARCH ON CRITICAL READING

Research on critical reading has been summarized in the monograph prepared by Sochor[59] and her committee. The publication is concerned with the meanings of the term critical reading, its use in the content areas and in basal reading series, and factors affecting the

[55] David H. Russell, "Contributions of Reading to Personal Development," *Teachers College Record,* Vol. 61, pp. 435-442, May, 1960.

[56] Elizabeth H. Fennema, "Mental Imagery and the Reading Process," *Elementary School Journal,* Vol. 59, pp. 286-289, February, 1959.

[57] Donald D. Durrell, *Improving Reading Instruction,* Chap. 14. World Book, Yonkers, N.Y., 1956.

[58] Robert R. Nardelli, *A Study of Some Aspects of Creative Reading.* Doctoral dissertation, University of California, Berkeley, 1954.

[59] E. Elona Sochor, chm., *Critical Reading: An Introduction,* Bulletin of the National Conference on Research in English. National Council of Teachers of English, Champaign, Ill., 1959.

reader's critical abilities. Sochor points out that the term *critical reading* is used in many different ways by different writers, perhaps partly because the phrase *critical thinking* has been given a wide variety of usages. In an earlier article Pingry[60] identified at least five emphases:

"1. Critical thinking as collecting data, organizing data, and formulating hypotheses from data.
2. Critical thinking as one of correct principles of logic and understanding the nature of proof.
3. Critical thinking as criticism of thinking.
4. Critical thinking as related to understanding of the psychology of propaganda and advertising techniques.
5. Critical thinking as synonymous with problem solving."

Each of these emphases have also appeared in discussions of critical reading. In addition, there is the emphasis which describes critical reading essentially as a process of making judgments, behavior described in some detail by Johnson.[61] He says that good judgment seems to require such abilities as: "(1) Abstracting the pertinent data from the complex situation, (2) adopting and maintaining a set for these pertinent data, (3) attending to several data simultaneously, (4) weighing each appropriately, and (5) integrating all this information somehow so that it is related to one of the response alternatives rather than others. Presumably such judgment requires (6) delaying or inhibiting response, i.e., carefulness, caution, or deliberateness" (page 422).

As suggested above, creative reading occurs when the reader draws his own conclusion from a passage—when he envisages, predicts, infers, or evaluates. In the point of view of this book, the critical reading may overlap with the other activities, but it is centered in the evaluative response.

Evidence from studies in child development suggests that children are capable of thinking critically about problems within their experience by the time they enter school. The range and safeguards for such thinking will have increased greatly by the junior- and senior-high-school years, but there seems to be no valid reason for post-

[60] R. E. Pingry, "Critical Thinking: What Is It?" *Mathematics Teacher,* Vol. 44, pp. 466-470, November, 1951.

[61] Donald M. Johnson, *The Psychology of Thought and Judgment,* esp. Chaps. 6-11. Harper, New York, 1955.

poning practice in critical reading and thinking until that time. Research shows that the child's sense organs and receptors are relatively highly developed by three years so that it would seem natural for him to base much of his thinking on perception of the environment. Such perceptual response is incorporated into the child's first concepts, as illustrated in the rapid growth of vocabulary between two and five years. As the child grows older, his increasing store of concepts and understandings enables him to deal with more complex problems, including criticism of proposed solutions. Patterns of problem-solving thinking may appear as early as three years,[62] if the problem is related to the child's experience and the goals are valuable to him. Johnson[63] has suggested that "Readiness for critical reading should and can be developed even before actual reading is being done" (page 392); and Petty[64] has shown some uses of critical thinking in the primary grades.

Curriculum bulletins, especially in reading and in social studies, and basal reading programs attest to the importance of critical reading in the intermediate and upper grades. The research summarized by Eller and Dykstra[65] suggests that the reader's attitude may affect his ability to read critically, and that this attitude may be based on "individual considerations" and "social and cultural considerations." Other studies such as that of Sochor[66] suggest that the correlation between ability to read critically and with literal comprehension is positive but low ($r = .23$) with social-studies materials. Maney[67] also found that "critical reading in science is a complex of skills or abilities, each of which is relatively independent of the ability to read literally" (page 62). Such results suggest that critical reading abilities will not develop as part of general comprehension but must be practiced specifically.

[62] David H. Russell, *Children's Thinking,* Chap. 9. Ginn, Boston, 1956.

[63] Marjorie S. Johnson, "Readiness for Critical Reading," *Education,* Vol. 73, pp. 391-396, February, 1953.

[64] Walter T. Petty, "Critical Reading in the Primary Grades," *Elementary English,* Vol. 33, pp. 298-302, May, 1956.

[65] William Eller and Robert Dykstra, "Persuasion and Personality: Readers' Predisposition as a Factor in Critical Reading," in E. Sochor, chm., *Critical Reading,* Bulletin of the National Conference on Research in English. National Council of Teachers of English, Champaign, Ill., 1959.

[66] Elona E. Sochor, "Literal and Critical Reading in the Social Studies," *Journal of Experimental Education,* Vol. 27, pp. 49-56, September, 1958.

[67] Ethel S. Maney, "Literal and Critical Reading in Science," *Journal of Experimental Education,* Vol. 27, pp. 57-64, September, 1958.

Although his work was not based directly on research, Gainsburg[68] has given a useful list of situations in which critical reading may be practiced:

"*Finding inferences about*

character
appearance
setting
motives of the characters
their actions
their feelings
anticipations
the meaning of figurative language

Recognizing clues from which inferences may be drawn

conversation by, to, and about a character
his actions, gross and subtle
few but suggestive details
emotional words and connotative expressions
figurative language, especially irony and exaggeration
unusual language style (choppy sentences or telescoping of events to show haste; sentence inversion for word emphasis)"

Other specific suggestions for teaching critical thinking at the elementary-school level have been made by various writers. For example, Kottmeyer[69] reported three successful units used in the upper elementary grades on propaganda analysis, reading of newspaper editorials, and interpretation of cartoons. Nardelli[70] reported success in the sixth grade. Other suggestions for teaching critical thinking have been made by Dale[71] and by Russell.[72] Most of these writers warn against the idea that critical reading can be taught in six lessons or in six months. Rather it must permeate reading and other curriculum activities over the years. The thinking cannot be done by the teacher or the textbook. Children can be both critical and creative in social studies, in arithmetic, and in health education—they can discover for themselves, and they can evaluate facts, character, action,

[68] Joseph C. Gainsburg, *op. cit.*, p. 25.
[69] William Kottmeyer, "Classroom Activities in Critical Reading," *School Review*, Vol. 52, pp. 557-564, November, 1944.
[70] Robert R. Nardelli, *op. cit.*
[71] Edgar Dale, "Teaching Critical Thinking," *The Newsletter*, Ohio State University, Vol. 24, pp. 1-4, January, 1959.
[72] David H. Russell, *op. cit.*, Chaps. 10, 13.

author's intention, and simple controversial issues. Few elementary children have any background for thinking critically about foreign policy, but they all can judge classroom procedures of direct concern to them.[73] Since children are only learning to interpret and to evaluate, the teacher must guide them in recognizing places where the author has left things unsaid. Questions such as "Could this be true?" "Would a real boy have acted this way?" or "Which did he value more, the truth or his own safety?" all demand reading beyond the printed words and ability to evaluate what is said or left unsaid.

SPECIFIC SUGGESTIONS FOR CREATIVE READING

Curriculum bulletins and teachers' manuals for reading programs contain many practical devices for increasing ability to do creative and critical reading. In an analysis of eighty reading textbooks Williams[74] found 186 creative and critical skills taught. For example, the most frequently suggested critical skills were "making judgements," "distinguishing fact and opinion," and "identifying and evaluating character traits." A few other examples illustrate the range of possibilities in creative and critical reading. One curriculum guide[75] recommended the following activities for determining the genuineness of character or ideas: deciding whether a story is true or imaginary; deciding whether or not a real boy would act like the boy in the story; comparing the story about an airplane with what the group saw at the airport; remembering people who are like the characters in the story; choosing a person in the story whom some members of the group would hope to be like; discussing the ideas in one book in comparison to related ideas in another book.

As suggested above, the teacher can never predict just how a particular child will react to beauty of expression or inspiration or emotional appeal; but the San Francisco bulletin mentions such activities as the following for integrating reading with other experiences: picking out words of a poem or song that make one see pictures, hear sounds, or feel things; appreciating the way a classmate

[73] Fred E. Harris, "Do Children Think Critically About Classroom Procedures?" *Journal of Educational Psychology*, Vol. 39, pp. 52-59, January, 1948.

[74] Gertrude Williams, "Provisions for Critical Reading in Basic Readers," in E. Sochor, chm., *Critical Reading*, Bulletin of National Conference on Research in English. National Council of Teachers of English, Champaign, Ill., 1959.

[75] San Francisco Public Schools, *Teaching Guide: Reading*, Curriculum Bulletin No. 201. San Francisco Public Schools, San Francisco, Calif., 1946.

expresses an idea; responding to a poster for the Community Chest or a movie for the Red Cross; listening to stories of friendliness, neighborliness, winning and losing, and good manners; choosing favorite stanzas to memorize; making a collection of favorite poems; dramatizing scenes from a hero's life; recognizing such sources as the Declaration of Independence, Lincoln's Gettysburg Address, and parts of the Bible as great literature; appreciating such devices as simple figures of speech, variations in rhythm, and repetitions of theme as contributing to beauty or power of expression.

Critical reading is considered in a little book entitled *Reading and Reasoning*. In it Musson[76] pointed out the dangers in the emotional appeal of certain words and the necessity of analyzing metaphors, pseudoscientific terms, and meaningless words and phrases. He gave exercises on these which he used successfully with twelve-year-old boys in England and which encourage one to think about the material read. The following are samples somewhat similar to Musson's:

1. Using experience to be critical of words used loosely:
   a. Substitute for the words underlined more exact words or phrases.
      (1) I love <u>France.</u>
      (2) Let us enjoy <u>nature.</u>
      (3) <u>Life</u> is a great adventure.
   b. Translate the following into honest English:
      (1) Elderly lady has vacancies for a few gentlewomen as paying guests.
      (2) Our present government has given the nation peace and prosperity unequaled in our history.
      (3) For rent: charming, livable summer cottage near beach and trees. A perfect spot for rest and relaxation.
2. Using experience to be critical of metaphors:
   a. Rewrite the following passages in such a way that the appeal is to reason, not emotion.
      (1) I solemnly declare before this vast audience here assembled . . .
      (2) This organization is a giant bestriding the nation.
      (3) The members of this political party are the slaves of Wall Street.
3. Using experience to be critical of pseudoscientific terms:
   a. Try to find the real meaning of the terms used in the following. Put a circle around doubtful words or phrases.

[76] J. Windsor Musson, *Reading and Reasoning*. John Crowther, Sussex, England, no date.

(1) To put young and old on their feet again after illness, you must feed their nerves and blood with organic phosphorus and protein. Healthogen supplies this organic phosphorus and protein, and supplies it in a form we can all assimilate.
(2) We invite all women interested in scientific beauty treatments to try our new, perfected system of permanent waving.

The exercises mentioned will be most valuable in the upper elementary grades when they are used as a basis for group discussion. At this level, children enjoy reading followed by a pooling of results. They are often most efficient, too, in organizing committees or similar groups to get different parts of desired information. The teacher will find that most children from eight to eleven years of age are better in gathering facts than in reflecting on them. An evaluation of information or ideas in printed materials is more mature in the group situation under direct teacher guidance. DeBoer[77] suggested that in such situations the teacher has four responsibilities:

1. To help the reader identify his own assumptions.
2. To help the reader analyze the assumptions and issues in the printed material.
3. To help the child to broaden his background of knowledge out of which adequate standards of judgment emerge.
4. To provide a wide variety of materials used as a basis for discussion and evaluation, varied in level of difficulty and in point of view.

These examples and some of the activities listed above not only suggest ways of stimulating thought about material read and relating it to past experience but also indicate that integration with past experience may involve selection and judgment which merge into critical reading.

Other specific suggestions for various types of creative reading activities are given below. All these can be expanded, and all must be adapted to the needs of the particular child or group of children working on that ability. These are questions which may be raised by pupils or teacher. In attempting to answer them an individual or group is getting practice in creative reading activities.

[77] John J. DeBoer, "Teaching Critical Reading," *Elementary English Review,* Vol. 23, pp. 251-254, October, 1946.

1. *Seeing Relationship.* Why did the boy say ......? Which happened first? Could this happen here where we live? What took place before our story opens? After it closes?

2. *Organization of a Selection, Chapter, or Book.* How much space does the author give to each part? In a biography what parts of the subject's life are emphasized? What mechanical features such as headings or size of type are used to indicate divisions? Are the parts arranged chronologically, logically, or parallel? What should be included in an outline of the selection?

3. *Evaluation of the Logic of an Argument or Article.* In a controversial topic, what are signs of an emotional appeal? What are the steps the author takes to prove his point? Are there unproved statements? Is there a generalization based on a single instance, selected cases, or a wide variety of data? Does the author recognize both sides of the question? Does the author use high-pressure appeals, including the various propaganda devices?

4. *Agreement of the Headlines with the Facts.* Does the headline or the title reveal prejudice? How many people read newspaper headlines but not the stories under them? How do different publications headline the same event? In a controversial article underline the words with favorable and with unfavorable emotional tones. Have you seen Dale's *How to Read a Newspaper*?[78]

5. *Make a Comparison.* How can we compare life in the United States with life in other countries? What are some contrasts between conditions now and conditions one hundred years ago? What are some differences in the ways two authors handle the same material? Do authors offering the same facts come to the same conclusions? How do your knowledge and the author's ideas compare?

6. *Predict Outcomes.* From what you know of a character, what is he likely to do in a given situation? What are some hints in a character's conversation about what he will do? Considering the total setting of the events, what is likely to happen next?

7. *Propaganda.* What is meant by each of the propaganda devices known as card-stacking, glittering generalities, name-calling, transfer, plain folks, band wagon, boring from within, trial balloon? Can you find examples of each of these in advertising and in political speeches? What is meant by "A democracy is a place of conflicting propaganda, not one propaganda"? Compare what you know with what a piece of propaganda says.

[78] Edgar Dale, *How to Read a Newspaper.* Scott, Foresman, Chicago, 1941.

8. *Advertising.* Do you agree with the statement that advertisers urge us to buy things we do not need with money we do not have? Does some advertising appeal to social fears, such as fear of being different or left out or being criticized? What is the appeal in words like luxurious . . . elegant . . . exclusive? Contrast some useful, informative ads with others which are misleading or in bad taste.

9. *Figures of Speech.* What is meant by a simile, a metaphor, and an analogy? Can you find some good and some poor examples of descriptions by simile and by metaphor? (See page 482.) What are dangers of "reasoning by analogy"? Compare the figures of speech employed by a poet and by a politician.

10. *Significance of a Conclusion.* How important is the conclusion from a scientific experiment, from a period in history, or from conditions in geography? Does the author establish a relationship between cause and effects? Can you list the conditions which led to a certain conclusion and those which might lead to a different conclusion? In a story was the ending an accident or the result of previous conditions?

Many of the questions above may arise in social studies or in language activities, as well as in reading. They are given as a miscellaneous list, partly because that is the way such questions often arise. The teacher, in third grade or eighth grade, who has a critical attitude toward printed materials is probably most alert to the opportunities for having children consider such questions as those listed.

CONCLUSIONS

This chapter takes reading out of the rote response, association type of behavior to make it a cognitive process. The higher levels of reading involve hard thinking. In the past the chief goal of many reading programs has been to help children to recognize words and understand what they mean in a literal sense. The chapter supports a definition of reading, first given in Chapter 5, which suggests that the complete reading act goes beyond recognition and understanding to interpretation and use. When a child begins to interpret and judge the ideas presented and goes on to use them in some way that is new or fresh for him, then he is doing creative reading. There are times, such as in scanning an airline's timetable or using a recipe to bake a cake, when little creative reading is needed. The facts may be enough. But in many other types of reading in modern life literal understanding is not enough, and the school has a duty to perform.

This chapter has analyzed, in what may be an oversimplified way, the nature of thinking and some of the scientific facts about children's development of thinking abilities to show that creative reading activities are possible at all school levels. They can exist at any stage, but only if the teacher is willing and able to encourage them. In creative reading there are at least four ways an individual or group may proceed. The basis for creative reading is accurate comprehension of literal meaning. When this is attained the child may: (1) note relationships in the materials, indicated but not stated specifically, such as main and subordinate ideas or sequence of events; (2) from such relationships implied in the materials he may make fresh, personal inferences as in generalizing or predicting. In other circumstances the materials may lead to either (3) appreciative reactions or to (4) critical evaluations. These four phases of creative reading are not so complex as they may sound; good teachers have long been using them. For example, it does not take the second-grade child long to see the relationships in a simple sentence. Therefore he marks *No* opposite such a statement as "Trains go faster than airplanes." However, it may be some time before a sixth-grade group reaches a consensus on the ideas contained in a selection describing the treatment of Indians in the United States today. Both in marking the answer and in reaching some conclusion on this controversial topic the children involved draw upon their past experience to interpret the ideas presented in print. They contrast and compare, they organize, to come to some sort of conclusion about the materials read. In doing so they may be critical of the ideas presented. Since the conclusion is at least partly new for them, we may say that creative reading is taking place. Appreciative reactions are more likely in responding to a poem such as Robert Frost's "Stopping by Woods" or a story such as *Charlotte's Web*.

In addition to giving examples of ways of putting the three main phases of creative reading into action, the chapter makes some suggestions for miscellaneous creative activities in reading. These usually involve past experience and may be directed toward a definite problem, but they are stated as specific activities likely to arise in many classroom situations or as opportunities for the teacher to encourage critical thinking and creative reading. Most of these activities assume rather mature behavior on the part of the child. The attitude taken in this chapter, as in other phases of the reading program, is that mature behavior in creative reading can be developed only in mature children who have had many opportunities to practice thinking at all stages of their reading development.

SUPPLEMENTARY READINGS

ANDERSON, HAROLD H., ed. *Creativity and Its Cultivation.* Harper, New York, 1959.

BETTS, EMMETT A. "Reading as a Thinking Process," *National Elementary Principal,* Vol. 35, pp. 88-96, 1955.

BLOOM, BENJAMIN S. *The Taxonomy of Educational Objective.* Longmans, Green, New York, 1956.

BROWNELL, WILLIAM A. "Problem Solving," *The Psychology of Learning,* Forty-first Yearbook, National Society for the Study of Education. Public School Publishing Co., Bloomington, Ill., 1942.

DEBOER, JOHN J. "Teaching Critical Reading," *Elementary English Review,* Vol. 23, pp. 251-254, October, 1946.

GANS, ROMA. *Critical Reading Comprehension in the Intermediate Grades.* Contributions to Education, No. 811. Teachers College, Columbia University, New York, 1940.

GLASER, E. M. *An Experiment in the Development of Critical Thinking.* Contributions to Education, No. 843. Teachers College, Columbia University, New York, 1941.

GUILFORD, J. P. "Three Faces of Intellect," *American Psychologist,* Vol. 14, pp. 469-479, August, 1959.

HYRUM, G. H. "An Experiment in Developing Critical Thinking in Children," *Journal of Experimental Education,* Vol. 26, pp. 125-132, 1957.

JOHNSON, DONALD M. *The Psychology of Thought and Judgment.* Harper, New York, 1955.

KOTTMEYER, W. "Classroom Activities in Critical Reading," *School Review,* Vol. 52, pp. 557-564, November, 1944.

LANCELOT, W. H. *Permanent Learning.* Wiley, New York, 1944. See sections on "Developing Ability to Think Well," "Developing Exact Reasoning Abilities," and "Development of Judgment Abilities."

MCCULLOUGH, CONSTANCE M. *Creative Reading.* Contributions in Reading, No. 15. Ginn, Boston, 1959.

NARDELLI, R. R. "Some Aspects of Creative Reading," *Journal of Educational Research,* Vol. 50, pp. 495-508, 1957.

NATIONAL COUNCIL FOR THE SOCIAL STUDIES. *Teaching Critical Thinking in the Social Studies,* Thirteenth Yearbook, National Education Association. National Council for the Social Studies, Washington, D.C., 1942.

PATRICK, CATHERINE. *What is Creative Thinking?* Philosophical Library, New York, 1955.

RUSSELL, DAVID H. *Children's Thinking.* Ginn, Boston, 1956.

RUSSELL, DAVID H. "Higher Mental Processes," in C. W. Harris, ed., *Encyclopedia of Educational Research,* 3rd ed., pp. 645-661. Macmillan, New York, 1960.

RUSSELL, DAVID H. "Reading for Critical Thinking," *California Journal of Elementary Education,* Vol. 14, pp. 79-86, November, 1945.

Russell, David H. "The Child's Reading and Thinking," *Chicago Schools Journal,* Vol. 36, pp. 105-108, January-February, 1955.

Smith, Dora V. "Language and Thinking," *Teaching Language in the Elementary School,* Forty-third Yearbook, Part II, Chap. 4, pp. 59-71, National Society for the Study of Education. University of Chicago Press, Chicago, 1944.

Strickland, Ruth G. "Children, Reading and Creativity," *Elementary English,* Vol. 34, pp. 234-241, April, 1957.

Thomson, Robert. *The Psychology of Thinking.* Pelican Books A453. Penguin, Baltimore, Md., 1959.

Vinacke, W. Edgar. *The Psychology of Thinking.* McGraw-Hill, New York, 1952.

Wilson, R. C.; Guilford, J. P.; and others. "A Factor-Analytic Study of Creative Thinking Abilities," *Psychometrika,* Vol. 19, pp. 297-311, 1954.

Chapter 15

PROVIDING FOR INDIVIDUAL DIFFERENCES IN READING ABILITIES

THE PROBLEM OF DIFFERENCES

From the very first day a teacher meets a class she is aware of the wide differences among the pupils. They are short and tall, shy and anxious for the lime-light, attentive and restless, egocentric and social, eager to read and bored with books. In fact, they differ in every way that can be measured or observed. But not only do the children differ among themselves, they differ within themselves. In recent years, child psychology has been paying more attention to intra-individual differences, to the fact that a child may have wide differences in his verbal and mathematical abilities, in his relations with peers as compared to adults, in his knowledge of science in comparison with language, or in many other clusters of abilities.

If a first-grade class or a fourth-grade class all had the same reading abilities, or if any one child were equally adept at all kinds of reading such as enjoying a story and getting specific facts in science, the problem of the teacher would be greatly simplified. Unfortunately for the advocates of one book or one method for a whole class, such a teacher's Utopia never exists. Literally hundreds of careful studies of childhood suggest that in any one age or class group there will always be a wide range of differences among individuals and within certain individuals. Many studies show that, no matter how hard or skillfully the teacher tries to reduce the range, the children will always be different in reading or other abilities. In fact, there is some evidence that the better the teaching, the farther the children will be spread apart, especially if the most able children are challenged effectively. Some parents and commentators on education still expect the thirty pupils in a second grade or a fifth grade to be all alike in arithmetic or spelling or reading achievements. Every experienced teacher knows this will never happen and takes steps to meet the problem of individual differences in ability. Many teachers have gone beyond the point of trying to eradicate differences to believing that, in a democratic society, differences should be encouraged, that variety in individuals will do much to add to personal happiness and to the creativity of a culture. Such teachers believe that differences should be cherished. In reading as in other activities a wide range of individual differences is a fact of life. The success of any teacher of reading depends upon the encouragement of some of these differences and the ability to adapt materials and methods to the very different reading needs and abilities of pupils.

Down through the years the attitudes of most school people to differences among pupils have gradually changed. Responses to the problem of differences may be summarized historically into five main periods:

(1) In earlier days, teachers were largely unaware of individual differences and taught classes as a unit. This attitude persists today, especially in some high schools.

(2) Through the study of child and adolescent development, teachers became aware of differences in developmental status in a class group, but were not always successful in translating such knowledge into classroom practice.

(3) School people were aware of differences and made some efforts to provide for them by groupings, by promotion policies, by special classes, and by other *administrative* devices.

(4) Most teachers were aware of differences and attempted to provide for them by two or three *curricular* devices, such as subgrouping within the class and varied assignments and materials, but these teachers worked without the help of a well-planned program involving all parts of a school system.

(5) School people have become aware that individual differences not only exist and must be provided for, but that they should be cherished in the work of any one class and in a total school-system program.

THE NATURE OF DIFFERENCES

Most teachers do not find it sufficient to be aware of differences; they attempt to understand them, at least in part. In their preservice work, they took courses in educational psychology which had at least one or two sections devoted to the facts and problems of differences. As parts of their in-service work they may have explored the problem more carefully in a course on individual differences or in their professional reading of such books as those of Tyler[1] and of Anastasi.[2] These activities tend to broaden the concept of individual differences to include not only variations in reading or other achievements but also differences in relation to the influences of heredity and training, and associated with such factors as physique, age, sex, family, social class, intellect, and personality. Anastasi, for example, discussed traits as patterns of relationships within the individual's behavior and distinguished between common traits and individual traits. She defined common traits as general descriptions of relationships shared by a group of persons and found these much more in the intellectual than in the emotional and motivational spheres. Perhaps because there is more uniformity of experience, intellectual development shows common characteristics, but these change into increasing differentiation of abilities with age and education. Anastasi emphasizes the findings of anthropologists in attributing many differences in behavior to the culture or the sub-culture in which one lives.

Teachers who have consulted such sources or observed their own pupils closely are therefore not surprised to find wide differences among their students. They can accept, for example, Triggs's[3] statement that "Approximately 20 per cent of the young people entering our colleges and universities read less efficiently than does the average eighth grade pupil." At an earlier level, they will agree with Clymer's[4] statement that the usual range of differences in a heterogeneously grouped classroom is approximately two-thirds of the chronological age of the typical child in that classroom. They will also reinforce his statement that "The difference between the average reading scores of the top quarter and bottom quarter of an intermediate class is two to four times as great as the difference between the average scores of two successive grades." Experienced kindergarten and first-grade teachers know that children differ in every way on the first day they enter school, and other teachers know that these

[1] Leona E. Tyler, *The Psychology of Human Differences,* 2nd ed. Appleton-Century-Crofts, New York, 1956.

[2] Anne Anastasi, *Differential Psychology: Individual and Group Differences in Behavior,* 3rd ed. Macmillan, New York, 1958.

[3] Frances Triggs, *Remedial Reading: The Diagnosis and Correction of Reading Difficulties at the College Level.* University of Minnesota Press, Minneapolis, 1943.

[4] Theodore Clymer, "Criteria for Grouping for Reading Instruction," Supplementary Educational Monographs. University of Chicago Press, Chicago, 1959.

differences tend to increase with age and schooling. For example, vocabulary scores on reading tests given in the intermediate and upper grades of one large California city are illustrated in the graph which is shown on page 493. Two points may be made from the graph. One is the importance of getting a test which challenges the upper levels of the ability of the group; otherwise the mean score of the total number tested will be somewhat below the true abilities of the children of the city. The second point is the increasing spread in the scores between the fourth and ninth grades, a spread which would be even greater if individual scores rather than the top and bottom ten per cents were taken. At the fourth-grade level the range of reading abilities was over four years, at the ninth-grade level this range was actually six years with the ceiling, and theoretically could be estimated at least eight years' span. These scores are determined in part by the nature of the test items which have been included by their authors because they give a range and normal distribution of scores, but the fact remains that the tests illustrate increasing differences in reading ability in any class or group as children move through school. As suggested above, this fact should be regarded neither as unfortunate nor troublesome, since it may be part of the function of the school to increase differences among individuals. As one person put it, "The better you teach them, the farther you spread them apart." It may be that the best measure of success of a reading program in a school system is not the number of children who achieve some sort of national norm on the test, but the range of differences in the results for any one grade-level or other group.

PROVIDING FOR DIFFERENCES

Even before scientific facts about individual differences were thoroughly established, teachers attempted to provide for differences. Early European education was often individual. The concept of large-group teaching, borrowed in part from Prussia, produced problems of differences in common, public schools as developed in America. About forty years ago Frederic Burk of the San Francisco Normal School wrote about "The Lockstep in Education" and, with his teachers, devised methods of individual instruction. The Dalton plan also stressed individual goals and blocks of work in the form of "contracts." In the 1920's the officials and teachers of the Winnetka schools developed materials and methods stressing individual prog-

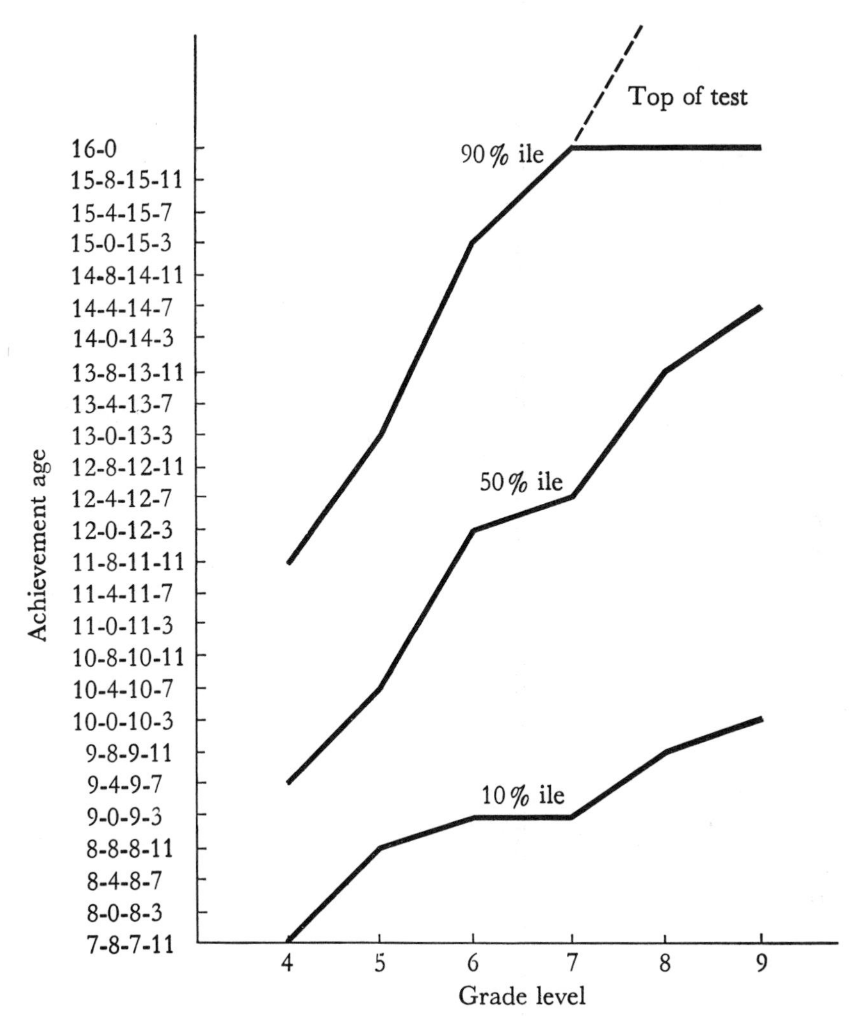

Vocabulary Scores in the Intermediate and Upper Grades of a California City on the Stanford Reading Achievement Tests, 1959 survey

ress in reading which became known all over the world. Unfortunately, the professional "know how" and the cost of producing these materials became more than any one school system could afford, but some similar principles of self-teaching are again being tested in experimental situations today. Since approximately 1900, then, school systems and individual teachers have attempted to provide for the wide range of differences found among their pupils. Some of these attempts have been at the administrative, system-wide level and others have operated on a single classroom basis.[5] Some twelve of these overlapping methods of providing for differences may be summarized as follows:

Whole-School or System-Wide Activities

1. Promotion policy—retardation and acceleration.
2. Streaming or ability grouping—assignment of pupils to slow, average or fast learning groups in successive years.
3. Flexible scheduling—easier at junior and senior high school but used in elementary schools for special interest or ability groups, workshops, etc.
4. Provision of remedial help—in special classes, clinics, workshops.
5. Flexibility in use of school personnel—making use of individual differences among faculty to work in special programs related to interest and competency.

Single-Class Provisions

6. Sub-grouping within a class in relation to achievement, interest, specific problem, etc.
7. Using a variety of instructional materials at different levels of difficulty and with a range of content.
8. Utilizing a range of teaching methods and pupil experiences.
9. Flexibility in requirements, assignments, and standards of work.
10. Readiness activities—both general and specific.
11. "Free" periods.
12. Individual teaching and self-help materials. Each of these dozen ways of providing for differences has many sub-divisions, some of which are developed in more detail below.

NATURE OF DIFFERENCES IN READING ABILITIES

On that milestone in their lives, the day they enter kindergarten or the first grade, children differ in every way that can be measured. They differ in height, weight, strength of grip, emotional control, and ways of working or playing with other children. More directly related to reading, they differ in their visual perception skills, their ability to follow directions, and their language powers. From the first day in school the teacher is faced by the problem of a wide range of abilities related to reading.

[5] J. Cecil Parker and David H. Russell, "Ways of Providing for Individual Differences," *Educational Leadership*, Vol. 11, pp. 168-174, December, 1953.

The problems faced by the kindergarten or first-grade teacher in providing for differences tend to increase as children mature. The effect of schooling and other experience is in general to increase differences among children rather than decrease them. No matter how hard teachers, principals, or supervisors try, they can never bring all pupils up to a single standard of reading achievement. They can only go ahead to provide for pupil variations in ability as adequately as possible. In doing so they will avoid undue pressures on certain pupils to reach norms and will encourage other pupils to achieve far beyond the norms, or usual achievement, for their grade. This is the basic principle of remedial work in reading which has engaged the attention of many teachers and which is discussed more fully below. Remedial work is not getting all pupils "up to grade" but providing adequate instruction for pupils who, for some reason or other, cannot benefit by the regular methods and materials used by most of the class. Remedial work is simply providing for individual pupils, each according to his need. During such special instruction the child may gain enough in reading power so that he can once again benefit by the regular teaching and materials used in one of the reading groups in his class. Even in this subgroup, however, the differences will continue to exist, and in the whole class they will be greater. Some pupils will always need special instruction in the form of careful presentation of new steps in reading or supplementary materials for extra practice in certain types of reading situations.

The teacher can provide for a wide range of abilities in the class only if she knows what the differences are. In the first week she will discover that not all children in the third grade can read in the basic third reader recommended for the class and that others in the class are enjoying materials of at least fourth- or fifth-grade difficulty. These general differences, in turn, are based upon more specific differences which naturally will vary somewhat with the general maturity of the group.

In the low first grade the teacher will find that children differ in abilities related to initial reading success, such as these:

1. Ability to make a contribution to a group experience, such as discussion of an excursion
2. Background of experience for understanding pictures and printed materials
3. Speaking and understanding vocabularies
4. Facility in the use of sentences

5. Auditory perception
6. Visual discrimination
7. Interest in learning to read

As they move through the primary grades these differences may persist, and some others may appear. A few differences which the primary teacher will study in her group include the following:

1. The seven items listed above
2. Ability to read orally from primary readers after a first silent reading
3. Ability to associate ideas with printed materials in books and charts
4. Ability to read for two or three different purposes, such as general impression, specific details, and following a sequence of ideas
5. Ability to move the eyes from left to right and make an accurate return sweep
6. Ability to care for books
7. Ability to work independently with books, workbooks, and word games

In the intermediate and upper grades, similarly, there will be a gradual shift from the differences listed above to those representing more mature habits of reading. In studying pupils in these grades the teacher will note differences in the following:

1. Basic skills and habits making for ease and efficiency in reading
2. Knowledge of stories, books, and authors
3. Knowledge of sources of information
4. Ability to use a varied approach in reading for different purposes
5. Work-type and study skills
6. Knowledge and appreciation of various forms of juvenile literature
7. Related resources in the other language arts

As the teacher is conscious of such differences as the ones listed, she can plan and help to execute activities in reading which will take account of these differences. Some of the practical ways of providing for wide ranges of reading ability are described below. These are the commonest methods of meeting the problem, but their applicability to different classrooms and school systems will vary.

PROVIDING FOR INDIVIDUAL DIFFERENCES IN READING ABILITY

Good teachers have always adapted teaching procedures to the needs of individual children in their classes. Sometimes the procedures have been concerned largely with organization; at other times they have involved changes in teaching methods and materials. Such teachers have made use of some of the chief ways of providing for differences in ability and achievement which are described below.

Grouping

In an effort to reduce the range of differences found in the children of a whole class many teachers divide the class, for purposes of reading instruction, into two or more groups. Probably three groups are the most usual number. The weekly plans for reading activities given on pages 226 and 239 indicate how the teacher may plan instruction to three reading groups within a class. Most teachers believe that with three groups they can plan work which will more nearly fit the present reading achievements, the interests, and the potential reading growth of individual pupils than with one or two groups.

There is no final answer to the question, often raised by teachers, "What is the best method of grouping pupils for reading instruction?" Usually reading achievement must be considered. If an intermediate or senior grade has the usual wide range of reading achievements, this factor should form one of the bases for grouping. For example, if a fifth grade contains pupils ranging from the second to the eighth grade in reading ability, the children who are capable of reading second- and third-grade materials will profit from the teacher's instruction in a group away from the children reading at the sixth-grade level and above. This method has been labelled *achievement grouping.*

In another type of situation a sixth-grade teacher gave a reading test and found that all her pupils scored at or near the sixth-grade level in reading ability. As she examined the tests more closely and worked with the class over several weeks, however, she discovered that a number of pupils scored what they did on the tests because they were slow but accurate readers. Several other children got quite a few items wrong on the test, but were able to make an average score because they read quickly and attempted a large number of items. A number of other children read well to obtain specific facts, but seemed to have little ability in organizing the larger ideas of a selection. Accordingly, although the pupils at first glance seemed to be a class who could work together, the teacher found it profitable to divide the class into three groups stressing speed of reading, slower and more accurate reading, and reading in social studies and science which especially required organization of the materials for other uses. Another teacher grouped pupils on the basis of different specific needs, such as special attention to word-recognition skills, or emphasis upon certain work-type, study skills, or encouragement of wide reading for recreational purposes. These plans show that the system of grouping should be closely related to the needs of the children involved. Such grouping has been labelled *special needs grouping*.

Work in social studies, science, and other curricular areas often includes special projects or reports from individuals or committees. This may involve finding and describing pictures, checking an encyclopedia, consulting several sources including newspapers and magazines and, finally, the presentation of unified findings to the rest of a group or class. Such reading may involve *research grouping*.

Close to this method may be individual or small-group work based on reading interests. A group of girls may report on horse stories, a group of boys on space-travel books, each series ranging from easy to difficult, depending on the skills of the readers, but with materials relating to the preferences of the individual or group. Such grouping is sometimes labelled *interest grouping*.

Teachers from the primary grades through the junior-high-school grades have discovered that many children work well with a congenial partner or in a small group under a pupil leader. Sometimes a pair can work on a common problem such as the vocabulary of a new story, sometimes a skillful pupil (who is going to grow up to be a teacher, perhaps) can help others with word-attack skills or reading for story sequence. Durrell[6] has shown how reading may be taught in small groups led by pupils or through partners working together. McHugh[7] reported superiority for the method in the sixth grade, but

[6] Donald D. Durrell, *Improving Reading Instruction*, pp. 125-130. World Book, Yonkers, N.Y., 1956.

[7] Walter J. McHugh, "Team Learning in Skill Subjects in Intermediate Grades," *Journal of Education*, Vol. 142, pp. 22-51, December, 1959.

not the fourth and fifth grades, during a year's try-out of team and partner procedures, using basal and differentiated materials in thirty-five classrooms. Such grouping is usually labelled *partner-grouping* or *pupil-leader grouping*.

These four or five labels suggest that in a busy classroom occupied with varied materials and procedures a teacher may group in several different ways, for different purposes, for different lengths of time, and that any one pupil may belong to several groups in a typical school day.

Any teacher who has ever tried grouping knows that it is a difficult situation demanding the teacher's best resources. Accordingly, beginning teachers and others who have not used it usually are advised to begin with two groups rather than three or four. An article by Wilson,[8] an experienced teacher and supervisor, described her difficulties in running a three-group situation in a typical third-grade class and gave a valuable list of factors, such as limited time and accessibility of materials, to be considered in planning group work.

Flexibility is a keynote of grouping. Flexibility of methods, materials, and pupil placement must be observed at all times. Whenever a pupil's reading behavior indicates clearly that he would make better progress in another group, he should be transferred to it.

A number of school systems have attempted grouping not within any one class but between classes in the fourth, fifth, and sixth grades. An evaluation[9] of such a procedure, involving 519 pupils in one city, indicates that interclassroom grouping for reading instruction does not give better results on reading-achievement tests. Some teachers believe that interclassroom groupings give better chances of enrichment for superior pupils and make possible reading materials better adapted to different levels, but they have the equally important disadvantages of making reading too isolated from the rest of the school program, of placing with teachers pupils they do not know well, and of wasting time in transferring pupils. A preliminary study[10] of a similar system in Joplin, Missouri, showed that ranges of reading achievement were reduced in the classes and that reading achievement was higher than expected over a four-month period.

[8] Mary C. Wilson, "The Teacher's Problems in a Differentiated Reading Program," *Elementary English*, Vol. 24, pp. 77-85, 118, February, 1947.

[9] David H. Russell, "Inter-Class Grouping for Reading Instruction in the Intermediate Grades," *Journal of Educational Research*, Vol. 39, pp. 462-470, February, 1946.

[10] Cecil Floyd, "Meeting Children's Reading Needs in the Intermediate Grades: A Preliminary Report," *Elementary School Journal*, Vol. 55, pp. 99-103, October, 1954.

Although various kinds of grouping for reading instruction are in wide-spread use, especially in the primary grades, research studies do not always illustrate superior results under the system. This seems to be especially true of grouping by bright, average, and dull "streams" or classrooms. Some of the research on grouping in general has been summarized by Cook,[11] by Goodlad,[12] and by Wrightstone.[13] In a summary of some twenty-five studies involving grouping for reading instruction, Figurel[14] concluded that heterogeneous grouping gave slightly superior results but that teachers tended to prefer a form of grouping that reduced the total range of reading abilities in any one group. For example, in England where the system of "streaming" has been in use for many years, Rudd[15] found that over a year's time, "streamed" groups did not achieve any more than heterogeneous groups. In an American study of first-grade achievement, Bremer[16] found no differences between achievement of low and average groups placed in separate classrooms or grouped heterogeneously, but that the group scoring high on readiness tests, heterogeneously grouped, scored reliably higher in reading achievement than the high group in a classroom by themselves. Because of the difficulty of controlling variables, clear-cut research results are difficult to obtain. Petty[17] has summarized some of the advantages and disadvantages of grouping within the class, and a California publication[18] summarizes current practice and ideas in such statements as the following:

1. Some form or forms of grouping are necessary in setting up classroom experiences.
2. Grouping is one of the basic ways of providing for individual differences.

[11] Walter W. Cook, *Grouping and Promotion in the Elementary School.* University of Minnesota Press, Minneapolis, 1941.

[12] John I. Goodlad, "Classroom Organization," in C. W. Harris. ed., *Encyclopedia of Educational Research,* 3rd ed., pp. 221-226. Macmillan, New York, 1960.

[13] J. Wayne Wrightstone, *Class Organization for Instruction.* What Research Says to the Teacher, No. 13. American Educational Research Association and Department of Classroom Teachers, Washington, D.C., 1957.

[14] J. Allen Figurel, "What Recent Research Tells us About Differentiated Instruction in Reading," *The Reading Teacher,* Vol. 6, pp. 27-33, September, 1952.

[15] W. G. A. Rudd, "Psychological Effects of Streaming by Attainment," *British Journal of Educational Psychology,* Vol. 28, pp. 47-60, February, 1958.

[16] Neville Bremer, "First-Grade Achievement Under Different Plans of Grouping," *Elementary English,* Vol. 35, pp. 324-326, May, 1958.

[17] Mary C. Petty, *Intraclass Grouping in the Elementary School,* University of Texas Publication, 5313. University of Texas Press, Austin, July, 1953.

[18] *California Journal of Elementary Education,* Vol. 27, pp. 65-128, November, 1958.

3. No one right or wrong way of grouping has been established by research.
4. Groups should change in composition and purpose as children and situations change.
5. Group size needs to be varied to suit purpose.
6. Children can and should learn techniques of forming and working in groups.
7. Grouping helps children learn from each other.
8. Children need to learn to identify with increasingly larger groups—the class, the school, the community.

To these may be added such ideas as:

9. Grouping should be done on the basis of multiple criteria, including reading achievement, specific purpose, and social structure of the group.
10. Small group research[19] emphasizes the importance of leadership and the need for considerable initial competence for the group to deal successfully with its problems.
11. Group solutions to problems are often superior to the sum of individual contributions to a problem; this fact would seem to be especially important in creative and critical reading.
12. The dynamics of the group may increase the individual's interest and emotional response.

Providing for Pupils Not Working under Direct Teacher Guidance

When a teacher has two or more reading groups, there are naturally times when part of the class cannot work directly with her in a smaller group. Many teachers find that providing for these pupils taxes their resources as they try to avoid the meaningless "seatwork" or "busywork" exercises of a generation or two ago. The problem of keeping one or more other groups occupied profitably can be solved only in the light of knowledge of the children involved. Obviously, they must be engaged in quiet activities, so as not to disturb the group reading with the teacher. It seems desirable that such quiet activities be related to reading at least part of the time.

The following are some suggestions for activities which may be adapted by the teacher to meet the needs of children who are not working directly with her in a reading group:

1. Silent reading to answer questions placed on the chalkboard

[19] For example, Harold H. Kelley and John W. Thibaut, "Experimental Studies of Group Problem Solving and Process," in Gardner Lindzey, ed., *Handbook of Social Psychology*, Vol. II, pp. 735-785. Addison-Wesley, Reading, Mass., 1954.

2. Silent reading to answer mimeographed or hectographed exercises at the children's desks or tables

3. Workbooks which can be checked soon by the teacher

4. Selecting and preparing a short story or poem for audience reading

5. Reading to prepare for some future activity, such as applications in drawing, maps, construction, dramatization, brief book reports, and storytelling

6. Reading library books or supplementary books

7. Drawing to illustrate some point in the materials read by the group

8. Reading under guidance of a pupil leader—usually not in classes below the third grade, and only after the teacher has helped the leaders in worth-while procedures

9. Using teacher-made and pupil-made games and exercises. These may involve word recognition, sentence or paragraph comprehension, classification, and self-check from mounted stories. (See also the following section on materials.)

10. Suggestions for free-time activities may be posted around the

Things To Do While We Wait

1. Write numbers.
2. Copy words.
3. Draw pictures.
4. Practice writing.
5. Read books.
6. Write ABC's.
7. Write in diary.

Second-grade chart to guide activities of pupils not working directly with teacher

room. For example, one second-grade teacher had the chart illustrated on page 502 to guide the pupils' activities.

In discussion or workshop it is often desirable for a group of teachers to exchange ideas of profitable activities for children not working directly with the teacher. Some further suggestions for independent pupil activities are given in the references listed in the following section.

Varied Reading Materials

There is no point in grouping pupils unless materials and methods are varied to meet the needs of the individuals in each group. In one fourth-grade class the teacher had been instructed by the principal to have three reading groups. The teacher had three groups; but when observed, each group was reading, or attempting to read, at practically the same page in the same fourth reader, and the teacher was doing the same sort of teaching with each group. Obviously the extra time given to the two additional groups was largely wasted. Changes in materials and methods naturally accompany the formation of two or more reading groups within a class.

Most successful teachers build a supply of interesting and varied reading materials, some of which can be used from year to year. Some of the materials that may be provided on different levels of difficulty and to meet the different interests of individual children are suggested below in check-list form for the teacher to use in evaluating the adequacy of materials in her class:

Yes *No*
( ) ( ) For developmental skills and habits—basic readers and supplementary readers on three or four levels of difficulty
( ) ( ) For information-getting—books on social studies, health, science, etc. on different levels of difficulty; encyclopedias, reference books, and dictionary for intermediate and senior grades
( ) ( ) For recording and guiding other curricular activities—charts, bulletin board, recipes, arithmetic books, science manuals, pupil-prepared materials
( ) ( ) For fun and appreciation—readers, single copies of library books or juvenile literature, magazines, clippings from magazines and newspapers
( ) ( ) For extra practice in certain phases of reading—workbooks, practice-exercise books, *My Weekly Reader*,[20] pupil-prepared word games, and reading games

20 Wesleyan University Press, Middletown, Conn.

The suggestions above underline the necessity for the teacher's doing much more than ordering basic readers at three different grade levels if she is to attempt seriously to meet the need of the pupils in her class for a wide range of reading materials. Other materials that may be used include a class newspaper, the building of a booklet entitled *My Word List,* a recognition-vocabulary list for each pupil, and word, sentence, or phrase cards to be used in small groups.

Every classroom should have, in addition to its library books, a few reading and word games on a certain shelf, to be used by one or more children in their free time. The games should be changed occasionally before children tire of them. As a new game is placed on the shelf its purpose and rules should be explained by the teacher so children may use it independently. Adaptations of games like *Bingo, Snap,* and *Old Maid* may be used. Puzzles involving words, word-matching, and classification exercises are useful. The games available should be related to the reading needs of the children in the room. Many teachers keep the games from year to year. They take time and effort to make, but the exchange of ideas and the actual construction of the games have been enjoyed by many teachers in workshop sessions. The following books contain descriptions of games and exercises which may be constructed by teachers:

Broom, M. E., and others. *Effective Reading Instruction,* rev. ed. McGraw-Hill, New York, 1951. 482 p.

Cole, Luella. *The Improvement of Reading with Special Reference to Remedial Instruction.* Farrar & Rinehart, New York, 1938. 388 p.

Dawson, M. A., and Bamman, H. A. *Fundamentals of Basic Reading Instruction.* Longmans, Green, New York, 1959.

Dolch, E. W. *A Manual for Remedial Reading,* 2nd ed. Garrard, Champaign, Ill., 1945. 460 p.

Durrell, D. D. *Improving Reading Instruction.* World Book, Yonkers, N.Y., 1956. 402 p.

Eckgren, B. L., and Fishel, V. *Five Hundred Live Ideas for the Grade Teacher.* Row, Peterson, Evanston, Ill., 1952.

Fernald, Grace. *Remedial Techniques in Basic School Subjects.* McGraw-Hill, New York, 1943. 349 p.

Gillingham, A., and Stillman, B. *Remedial Training for Children with Specific Disability in Reading, Spelling, and Penmanship.* Sackett and Wilhelms, New York, 1946.

Hildreth, G. H. *Learning the Three R's,* especially Chap. 11. Educational Publishers, Minneapolis, 1947. 824 p.

Hildreth, G. H. *Teaching Reading.* Holt, New York, 1958.

HILDRETH, G. H., and WRIGHT, J. *Helping Children to Read.* Teachers College, Columbia University, New York, 1940. 90 p.
KINGSLY, BERNARD. *Reading Skills: Simple Games, Aids and Devices to Stimulate Reading Skill in the Classroom.* Fearon, San Francisco, 1958.
LAZAR, MARY, ed. *The Retarded Reader in the Junior High School.* Bureau of Educational Research, Pub. No. 31. Board of Education, New York City, September, 1952.
Let's Play a Game. Ginn, Boston, 1954. 30 p.
MONROE, MARION. *Children Who Cannot Read.* University of Chicago Press, Chicago, 1932. 205 p.
MULAC, MARGARET. *Fun and Games,* Chaps. 13, 18. Harper, New York, 1956.
100 Good Ways to Strengthen Reading Skills. Scott, Foresman, Chicago, 1956. 24 p.
RUSSELL, D. H., and KARP, E. E. *Reading Aids through the Grades,* rev. ed. Bureau of Publications, Teachers College, Columbia University, New York, 1951.
RUSSELL, D. H., and RUSSELL, E. F. *Listening Aids Through the Grades.* Bureau of Publications, Teachers College, Columbia University, New York, 1959.
SCOTT, L. B., and THOMPSON, J. J. *Talking Time.* Webster, St. Louis, Mo., 1951. Speech and auditory development.
SMITH, N. B. *One Hundred Ways of Teaching Silent Reading.* World Book, Yonkers, N.Y., 1926, 149 p.
STANGER, M. A., and DONOHUE, E. K. *Prediction and Prevention of Reading Difficulties.* Oxford University Press, New York, 1937. 191 p.
STORM, G. E., and SMITH, N. B. *Reading Activities in the Primary Grades.* Ginn, Boston, 1930. 372 p.
WILKINSON, H. S., and BROWN, B. D. *Improving Your Reading.* Noble and Noble, New York, 1938.

The books and booklets listed above give specific descriptions of reading exercises, word games, and practice materials which may be adapted by teachers to the needs of their pupils and used as independent reading activities. Many of these can be constructed from cardboard and similar materials. More general books on diagnostic and remedial procedures in reading are given at the end of this chapter.

Free Reading Periods

When children have the opportunity to read an individual library book for their own enjoyment during the school week, an adaptation has been made to provide for differences in reading ability and interest. This free, or personal, reading period may be one of the most valuable parts of the whole weekly program in reading.

A typical individual reading period presents a scene of active participation by all. The period begins when monitors distribute the books according to bookmarkers giving the different children's names. As the pupils read and encounter difficulties they may raise their hands. If the teacher is free, she will walk to the pupil and quietly give the help needed. If the teacher is occupied, the child will record his difficulty in a notebook for later consultation with the teacher. When the group is well started, the teacher will ask individual pupils, or at most two or three children, to come to her desk for special help. For ten or fifteen minutes she can work individually with a number of children, and do this with different children on successive days.

If a child finishes a book during the period, he may write a short book report on it (two or three sentences should suffice) or answer a short objective test on it which the teacher uses from time to time for books read frequently by this particular class. When he has completed this work, he may add the book to his list on the class chart of books read. The reading period may close with an audience-reading situation, where several pupils share with the rest of the class some enjoyable parts of books or other materials they have been reading individually.

The free reading period has many values. It tends to be a purposeful, pleasant reading situation which may be contrasted with older practices of much drill on isolated words and oral reading without previous practice. The period often can be used for tying in reading with social studies and other class activities. It may strengthen both recognition and meaning vocabulary,[21] but its chief purpose is to develop greater interest in reading and a wider acquaintance with good children's literature.

If the free reading program of periods like the one described is to be a success, several conditions must obtain:

1. Individual books of considerable variety, both in content and in level of difficulty, must be available to the pupils.

2. The teacher or librarian must guide the children's choices of books in the light of their past reading and present needs.

3. The program should be given a definite place in the week's schedule.

[21] Ray B. Dean, "A Plan for Individual Reading in the Intermediate Grades," *National Elementary Principal,* Vol. 17, pp. 557-563, July, 1938.

4. The free reading period may occasionally be used as one possibility in a "choice of activity" period.

5. The free reading period does not constitute a balanced reading program in the elementary school (see Chapter 5) and must be supplemented by other work-type procedures in reading. These may come during direct teacher guidance in reading basic books; in practicing word attack through context clues, phonetic analysis, and other approaches; and in relatively independent activities with workbooks, mimeographed exercises, and similar devices.

6. The free reading period must be accompanied by some individual diagnosis and guidance. The teacher must be aware of the child's interests, the level of books suitable for him, and his particular difficulties in reading. Some of this diagnosis may be accomplished as the child comes to the teacher's desk during the free reading period. Particularly with retarded readers, more of it must be done at other times. Special provisions for such individualization are discussed in the section below.

Individualized Reading

The free reading period allows for development of interest and taste. It may also be extended to direct teaching and practice in basic reading skills.

As suggested above, the teacher often can help individual pupils for a few minutes while the rest of the class is engaged in free reading. Even in a large class the skillful teacher occasionally uses a few other moments throughout the day for individual reading guidance in social studies, science, or other periods. For the retarded child with serious difficulties in reading, such help is often not sufficient, and a definite remedial program must be set up if he is in the intermediate or senior grades. Usually special help by his own teacher will help the child most, particularly if the teacher has insight into possible causes of his reading difficulty. In some school systems the time factor makes it impossible for the regular classroom teacher to do much of this work.

To give special help to retarded pupils three main systems are currently in use. In the first of these every teacher is regarded as a remedial teacher and takes some responsibility for special cases in her class, perhaps with the help of the school psychologist, supervisor, or principal. In the second system certain teachers who show aptitude for remedial work are released part of the school day for work with individuals or small groups of retarded readers. In the third system full-time remedial teachers are members of the school staff. They spend all their time working with retarded pupils and may work in more than one school.

Whatever plan is in use, certain guiding principles for such work should influence teachers' practices. Perhaps the first important point to make is that individual or small-group remedial work differs only in degree from good developmental teaching. Instead of more reading practice of the kind on which the pupil has been failing, it offers specific help directed toward particular needs. This is simply a case of careful adjustment of materials to children's abilities. Similarly, when a pupil has been failing in one situation, it is better to change the materials and even the place where he has been working. For this reason special reading teachers often fit up an old office or similar space as a reading clubroom. In this room the pupil finds reading charts on the walls, a collection of reading games, and a profusion of new and interesting books, some of which are easier than the ones he has been trying. Gates[22] suggested a list of twenty-two guides regarding materials and practices in remedial work which should be studied thoughtfully by all teachers attempting remedial reading of an individualized nature. He suggested, for example, that remedial work should never cause the child to miss other cherished activities in the school program or be continued beyond the point where it is a pleasant, relaxed situation for child and teacher.

Hildreth[23] reported methods used by twenty-two experienced teachers in attempting to individualize reading instruction. In the primary grades the methods most commonly used were these: subgrouping, individual coaching for the slowest pupils, differentiated materials, the development of school and classroom libraries, reading-club activities, and various games and drills. In the intermediate and senior grades the methods most frequently employed were these: studying the individual's needs, subgrouping, individual coaching for the most seriously retarded pupils, differentiated materials, organization of classroom libraries, use of school and city libraries, and unit projects around which individualized reading is centered.

In addition to the concept of individual help for the pupil in difficulties, the idea of individualized reading may be extended to

22 Arthur I. Gates, *The Improvement of Reading*, 3rd ed., pp. 120-138. Macmillan, New York, 1947.

23 Gertrude H. Hildreth, "Individualizing Reading Instruction," *Teachers College Record*, Vol. 42, pp. 123-137, November, 1940.

readers of normal and superior achievement and to many parts of the weekly or monthly reading program. During the second half of the decade of the 1950's many teachers and writers emphasized the values of an individualized reading program and described how it was conducted in particular school systems. Articles by such writers as Lazar[24] and Jenkins,[25] issues of *The Reading Teacher, Elementary English,* the *California Journal of Elementary Education,* and other journals, and books such as those compiled by Miel[26] and by Veatch[27] all contributed to interest in the topic. As in the case of other educational movements, emphasis on individualized reading arose partly as a revolt against existing practices, including the more extreme forms of forcing all children into conformity to one method of instruction and one set of reading materials. Because no method can exist only as a protest, many positive values of individualized teaching were suggested in the above sources and other articles in the late 1950's and early 1960's. Some of the advantages attributed to individualized reading were:

1. The children actually do more reading.
2. There is no stigma of attachment to groups.
3. Provision is made for varying rates of progress.
4. Children develop greater interest in reading.
5. Individualized teaching does not eliminate the possibility of forming groups as needed.
6. Specific methods of word attack are not changed.
7. Teachers develop greater skill and flexibility as they move away from formal methods of instruction.

On the other hand, some of the weaknesses in individualized programs as usually conducted, have been pointed out by various writers. Examples were:

1. Children, and especially young children, profit from direct guidance more than from a laissez-faire situation.

24 May Lazar, "Individualized Reading: A Dynamic Approach," *Reading Teacher,* Vol. 11, pp. 75-83, December, 1957.

25 Marian Jenkins, "Self-selection in Reading," *Reading Teacher,* Vol. 11, pp. 84-90, December, 1957.

26 Alice Miel, ed., *Individualized Reading Practices.* Bureau of Publication, Teachers College, Columbia University, New York, 1958.

27 Jeannette Veatch, comp., *Individualizing Your Reading Program.* Putnam, New York, 1959.

2. Under incidental teaching, reading skills tend to be developed in haphazard fashion, if at all.

3. The individualized program demands unusual teacher ability in planning and conducting a complex program of activity for thirty or more individuals.

4. To be successful, individualized reading requires a complicated system of records of pupil activity which impose a heavy burden of clerical work on the teacher.

5. Children often make unwise selections in the things they want to read.

6. The individualized approach is not a "method" of teaching reading but simply one of a group of desirable ways of providing for individual differences.

7. Individualized reading makes little provision for readiness activities, such as the avoidance of difficulties in hard words and difficult concepts met in the reading materials.

These sample statements, pro and con, are partly at the opinion level and need to be checked by further research. A summary of the research up to 1959 has been prepared by Witty,[28] and criticized in a controversial manner by Veatch.[29] Witty concludes, "It seems that a defensible program in reading will combine the best features of both individualized and group instruction in reading . . . some basal materials . . . appear to be too highly repetitious and unrealistic, particularly for the primary grades. It is necessary, therefore, for teachers to select "basal materials" with care and to use them judiciously to meet individual and group needs. Beyond doubt there is need also for more diverse materials in any worthwhile reading program. . . . It is clear that today we have an unusual opportunity to cultivate independence in reading through the use of the many excellent children's books now available."

Veatch describes somewhat more fully some actual classroom practices in individualized reading, gives what she considers eleven "irreconcilable" issues between basal and individualized procedures, and adds a few researches to Witty's list.

[28] Paul A. Witty, "Individualized Reading—A Summary and Evaluation," *Elementary English,* Vol. 36, pp. 401-412, 450, October, 1959.

[29] Jeannette Veatch, "In Defense of Individualized Reading," *Elementary English,* Vol. 37, pp. 227-234, April, 1960.

Most proponents of the individualized reading program do not accept Witty's suggestion that it be considered a part of the total reading program. If it is to be regarded as a separate method, historical evidence is at least against its being called a new method. Stauffer[30] has pointed out that recommendations for individualizing reading instruction go back to the 1880's and were prominent in some yearbooks of the National Society for the Study of Education in the 1920's. The Hildreth article mentioned above listed practices in individualization used prior to 1940, and the Kaar[31] study, distinguished by careful planning of individualized techniques, was conducted in 1949-1950, for example, before the controversy about the procedures developed.

At the present stage of knowledge and experimentation there seems little reason why a black-and-white, either-or position should be taken in regard to individualized versus group procedures. Rather, a range of programs should be tested in longitudinal studies involving children's elementary school (and perhaps secondary school) careers. Teachers and school systems should be encouraged in action research on a wide variety of activities and materials. The question may be considered not as "Which method is better?" but "What do different methods and materials contribute to pupil development in reading?" Studies dating back to the 1920's indicate clearly that children in programs stressing individual and recreational reading learn somewhat different things than they do in programs of group instruction. As suggested about phonics (Chapter 10) they learn rather specifically what they practice, whether it is favorable attitudes to reading or a sequence of word-attack skills. Accordingly, our present stage of knowledge suggests that many types of reading materials and activities are essential in developing independent, versatile readers.

One group of teachers accepted the fact of different learnings under different conditions and listed what they thought were suitable activities for each of three types of classroom organization. Their suggestions may be found on the following page.

30 Russell G. Stauffer, "Individualizing Reading Instruction—A Backward Look," *Elementary English*, Vol. 36, pp. 335-341, May, 1959.

31 Harold W. Kaar, *An Evaluation of An Individualized Method of Teaching Reading in the Third Grade*. Doctoral dissertation, University of California, Berkeley, 1951.

Individual Activities

1. Teacher estimation of pupil's reading level.
2. Teacher diagnosis of specific difficulties.
3. Recreational reading.
4. Supplementary reading in curricular areas.
5. Practice in word-attack skills.
6. Library activities.

Small-Group Activities

1. Teacher-guided practice on specific skills.
2. Reading games and devices.
3. Adapting a story for dramatization.
4. Group study of stories at a challenging level of difficulty.
5. Oral interpretation by individuals or in choral reading.
6. Use of audio-visual instructional materials.

Whole-Class Activities

1. Audience reading of practiced materials.
2. News reports.
3. Introduction of new kinds of materials.
4. Introduction of skills generally needed, e.g., guide words in dictionary.
5. The teacher reads to the class.
6. Audio-visual appreciation—movies, records, etc.

Each of the above lists may be extended by a group of teachers to meet the special needs of children or a school situation. This process may itself be one in which certain group dynamics contribute to more proposed solutions about methods and materials than an individual teacher would ordinarily develop. At the present stage of knowledge it is important that an individual teacher or school staff consider as carefully as it can the learning possibilities in each of individual, small-group, and whole-class situations.

Teaching Methods

The best methods of teaching reading to slow-learning pupils are not necessarily most effective with the fast-learning group in the same class. Typical methods and materials for typical children have been described in Chapters 5 to 8. These are basic to any reading program, as are the methods suggested in a good teacher's manual accompanying a modern basic-reading series; but variations in these methods are necessary to meet the needs of exceptional children. Some of these variations may come in individualized help, some in small group instruction.

The adjustments in methods of teaching reading with a slow-learning group will depend, of course, upon the extent of the mental retardation of the group. In general, the methods used will not differ radically from those used with average children; they may vary in timing, amount of experience involved, and materials used. Some of the adjustments which may be profitable are as follows:

1. Beginning reading activities should be postponed beyond the usual age and should be introduced much more gradually than with an average group.[32]

2. The teacher should base her instruction on the fact that the pupils will stay in each stage of reading development (see page 128) longer than average-learning pupils. For example, a child with 75 I.Q. may be expected in general to make about three fourths of a year's progress in reading in one year and will be slower in reaching certain mature patterns of reading behavior.

3. The slow-learning child will often profit from more repetitions of material as long as these are meaningful and somewhat varied. This does not mean that children should have larger amounts of work-type and drill-type exercises at the expense of their recreational reading.[33] It does mean that material should be relatively easy—familiar words should be repeated frequently and new techniques, such as thinking about the best title for a paragraph, should have much practice in a variety of situations.

4. Much use of reading materials with a light recognition and meaning vocabulary burden. This is another way of saying that the children should understand the concepts presented in the reading material. Accordingly, instead of phonetic and other complicated drills on a limited word list, the slow-learning pupils need readiness work to develop meanings and the backing up of abstract symbols with related concrete materials, such as found in excursions, in audio-visual materials, in construction, and in dramatic play.

5. As with other children, a variety of methods seems to produce the best results. In one experiment in New York City with pupils having I.Q.'s largely from 70 to 90, a program of varied activities involving basal readers and accompanying materials, free reading periods, and much use of reading in planning and carrying out a variety of projects gave much better results than any rigid or formal system of reading.[34]

Other suggestions for teaching reading to this group of children

[32] Arthur I. Gates and David H. Russell, "The Effects of Delaying Beginning Reading a Half Year in the Case of Underprivileged Pupils with I.Q.'s 75-95," *Journal of Educational Research,* Vol. 32, pp. 321-328, January, 1939.

[33] Arthur I. Gates and David H. Russell, "Types of Materials, Vocabulary Burden, Word Analysis and Other Factors in Beginning Reading," *Elementary School Journal,* Vol. 39, pp. 27-35, 119-128, September, October, 1938.

[34] Arthur I. Gates and Miriam C. Pritchard, *Teaching Reading to Slow-Learning Pupils.* Teachers College, Columbia University, New York, 1942.

are given in books by Kirk,[35] by Ingram,[36] and by Kirk and Johnson.[37]

Although the needs of pupils retarded in reading are likely to loom larger in the teacher's or principal's mind, the fast-learning or bright pupil also needs special attention and help in reading. The democratic injunction of providing for each child according to his need and the social and economic loss consequent to neglecting the bright child make some special provisions imperative. In general, bright children are better readers than average or dull children, although individual exceptions may occur.[38] If the bright child is compelled to follow an average pattern, he may become bored with easy reading and a content which is too juvenile for him. In an extreme case he may waste many precious hours in "busy work" and grow to dislike school, books, and scholarship in general. In another situation he may resent the unpopularity with his peers which sometimes grows out of superior academic achievement and deliberately set low standards for his work.

Some of the adjustments in reading instruction which may be made in an effort to avoid such undesirable results and produce above-average achievement are as follows:

1. The gifted pupil must first be identified. In many cases he is reading at grade level or above grade but he is still a retarded reader. Although the correlation between reading ability and general mental ability is typically in the .50's or .60's, it seems fair to say that the fourth-grader, with average seventh-grade ability but reading at the fifth-grade level, is still a retarded reader. He causes no trouble because he reads better than the average of his class, but he is not living up to his potentialities. Such pupils must be discovered by testing and teacher observation before they can be helped.

2. Fast-learning children should be exempted from unnecessary routine drills and repetition of materials already known. For example, a bright child in the third grade may have such a large

[35] Samuel A. Kirk, *Teaching Reading to Slow-Learning Children,* 225 p. Houghton, Boston, 1940.

[36] Christine P. Ingram, *Education of the Slow-Learning Child.* Ronald, New York, 1953.

[37] Samuel A. Kirk and Orville G. Johnson, *Educating the Retarded Child.* Houghton Mifflin, Boston, 1951.

[38] Gertrude H. Hildreth, "The Educational Achievement of Gifted Children," *Child Development,* Vol. 9, pp. 365-371, 1938.

recognition vocabulary that special attention to word-analysis techniques is not needed.

3. Bright children usually profit from opportunities to use reading in creative ways. Some of them, through reading, bring large stores of information to social-studies activities; others use reading as background for writing, drawing, rhythms, and dramatizations. In the upper elementary grades fewer textbook assignments and more independent reading and study are usually in order.

4. The individual reading program is an important part of the bright child's total reading. The dull child needs this opportunity, too, as suggested above, and the teacher cannot single out the bright child for special freedom denied to others. On the other hand, the individual reading period makes it possible for the bright child to select books commensurate with his reading abilities and mature interests. A wide selection of books is undoubtedly one of the best means of enrichment for such children. They can easily learn to use the *Reader's Guide to Periodical Literature, Books in Print,* and other references to find materials for personal enjoyment and for sharing.

5. The bright child should be encouraged especially to use reading as an aid to reflective, critical thinking and, through it, to develop responsibility for translating ideas into desirable social action. Chapter 14 outlines creative reading activities which lie particularly within the reach of the bright child. In a survey of enrichment practices in high schools throughout the United States it was found that "The only modifications of instructional practice reported by as many as three quarters of the high schools are that superior students are expected to do more reading and more abstract and critical thinking."[39] A bright child should be encouraged and helped to use reference books, encyclopedias, the dictionary, and government bulletins even more than average children. These will often give him the raw data he needs in order to think critically about important problems and attempts at their solution.

6. The bright child should have as much individual guidance as the average or dull child. In general, such guidance will not be on specific reading difficulties so often as on problems like compiling a bibliography or organizing materials read. However, fast-learning children occasionally need specific help in reading skills. For example, some of them who read many storybooks at home and school

[39] National Education Association, "High School Methods with Superior Students," *Research Bulletin,* Vol. 19, p. 182, September, 1941.

develop the ability to read rapidly for a general impression of materials, but fail to adapt speed and method to the requirements of detailed reading. Often a few hints from the teacher in a face-to-face situation will clear up the difficulty. More frequently the teacher will have the problem of recommending enough books and other materials at a suitable level of maturity. In either case the individual guidance of the teacher is desirable and rewarding in terms of results. Scores of suggestions for specific enrichment activities for the superior child have been made by Martin.[40]

Teaching methods and materials will naturally vary for children who have extreme physical disabilities, such as loss of hearing or poor vision, which are serious enough to affect reading ability and development. Special techniques in teaching reading have been worked out for the hard-of-hearing child and the child in sight-saving classes. These techniques are somewhat specialized and are beyond the scope of this book. They are discussed in some of the books listed at the end of this chapter and in books dealing with instruction of exceptional children, such as those of Baker,[41] Frampton,[42] and Heck.[43]

The six methods of providing for differences in reading ability here discussed apply in different measure to different classes and children. In general, the good modern teacher is using a combination of two or more of these to help to meet one of her most difficult problems. Many variations of these methods are possible. One teacher may find that writing and reading a simple class newspaper provide reading and related activities in which children may share at their own level of ability. Another teacher discovers that practice on word, phrase, and sentence cards with a pupil leader benefits two or three children. A third teacher provides workbooks for some of her class who seem to profit by the activities contained in them. Another teacher works hard to give assignments and reports which vary according to reading ability. Still another teacher encourages her pupils to bring jokes, poems, and short human-interest newspaper stories from home which they have practiced there and which they

40 Ruth Martin, "Enrichment Activities for the Superior Child in the Reading Program," Contributions to Reading, No. 22. Ginn, Boston, 1958.

41 Harry J. Baker, *Introduction to Exceptional Children,* rev. ed. Macmillan, New York, 1953.

42 Merle E. Frampton and E. D. Gall, eds., *Special Education for the Exceptional,* 3 vols. Sargent, Boston, 1955-56.

43 Arch O. Heck, *The Education of Exceptional Children,* 2nd ed. McGraw-Hill, New York, 1953.

read to the rest of the class in an audience situation. These and many other activities are possible variations of the six main ways of providing for individual differences in reading ability.

THE DIAGNOSTIC POINT OF VIEW

The foregoing discussion of individual differences implies that a teacher must know how children in a class differ. This suggests in turn that the successful teacher studies the individuals in her class, discovers their strengths and weaknesses, their backgrounds and current problems, their interests and their motives. No teacher could possibly find time to study completely all the children in a class in any one year. She can, however, come to know some important facts about all her pupils, and to a few of them she can give enough time to know them thoroughly as persons. Fortunately, a number of good books, such as those by Driscoll,[44] Prescott,[45] Almy,[46] and Mitchell[47] are available to help teachers to understand children. In developing greater emphasis upon the study of children some school staffs find it profitable first to make a co-operative study of one pupil. One of the chief findings of such a study and of subsequent work with individuals is that behind any type of behavior lies some definite cause or causes. There are reasons, for example, why one child excels, why another makes normal progress, and why another has many difficulties in reading.

The diagnostic point of view indicates that behavior is caused and that the teacher attempt to understand, rather than blame, poor behavior or inadequate performance. If a child is a poor reader, the thoughtful teacher does not describe his behavior as "lazy" or label him as "dumb." Rather she seeks to understand the causes behind the inadequate reading. The modern teacher's point of view is not unlike that of a good physician diagnosing a patient who is physically ill. Two or three generations ago the general practitioner would merely look at the patient, take his pulse, perhaps thump him on the chest or raise his eyelids, and then prescribe a remedy. If the modern

[44] Gertrude Driscoll, *How to Study the Behavior of Children.* Bureau of Publications, Teachers College, Columbia University, New York, 1941.

[45] Commission on Teacher Education, *Helping Teachers Understand Children.* American Council on Education, Washington, D.C., 1945.

[46] Millie C. Almy, *Ways of Studying Children: A Manual for Teachers.* Bureau of Publications, Teachers College, Columbia University, New York, 1959.

[47] Lucy S. Mitchell, *Know Your Children in School.* Macmillan, New York, 1954.

physician suspects serious difficulties, on the other hand, he may order a long series of scientific tests, such as blood counts, X rays, and metabolism tests. He may put together the results of ten or fifteen tests before he makes final recommendations for treatment. Some teachers are still in the chest-thumping, eyelid-lifting stage of diagnosis. More and more are adopting the diagnostic point of view and getting as much information as they can about a child so that they can help him effectively.

A child's difficulties in reading can be discovered precisely only by an accurate diagnosis. In former times physicians and others studying children with reading disabilities were inclined to assume that a single cause, such as a brain lesion or mixed dominance or an extreme emotional maladjustment, was the cause of reading difficulties. Later, students with educational backgrounds believed that most reading disabilities were due to improper instruction and materials badly graded in terms of the child's needs and abilities. More recently writers and research workers have come to believe that not one but a group or constellation of related causes produces most reading disabilities. For example, poor hearing alone will not cause much retardation in reading, but poor hearing plus teaching methods that emphasize oral procedures plus placement near the back of a noisy classroom plus, perhaps, a non-English speaking home, would be almost sure to cause reading disabilities.

The modern point of view, therefore, is that a teacher cannot ensure reading success by removing any one cause of difficulty or hope to improve reading by any one gadget or teaching device. Rather, obtaining all the help she can, she must study the child as completely as possible in some sort of case-study procedure. Many children with minor reading difficulties may respond to the teacher's friendly interest. Other children with serious difficulties can be helped only after careful study of their cases.

Causes of reading difficulties, case studies of retarded readers, and appropriate remedial activities are too long and complicated for consideration in this book. They deserve a large book by themselves and are given this space in many of the books listed at the end of this chapter. Experienced teachers who are particularly interested in this phase of their work can usually take special courses in summer sessions or extension work on diagnostic and remedial work in reading. The section below is merely an introduction and overview of this phase of reading instruction.

STEPS IN DIAGNOSIS AND REMEDY OF READING DIFFICULTIES

Although this book cannot outline diagnostic and remedial work in sufficient detail to make a teacher specially competent in the field, every classroom teacher should be aware of what a school psychologist or remedial teacher is trying to do when he works with a pupil who is very retarded in reading. A summary outline of the usual procedures is given below to help the classroom teacher to understand the usual practices in remedial work and to give a few hints for her own procedures with one or more retarded pupils.

The following nine steps are essential to an adequate program of help to children with reading disabilities:

1. Classroom Observations

The teacher, psychologist, or case worker observes the child in typical classroom situations for symptoms which may be connected with the reading difficulty. Sometimes a check sheet may be used. The observer always looks for specific behaviors. For example, if he suspects visual difficulties, he may look for signs of eyes blinking or watering, frowning, moving up to see the blackboard, and confusing words that look alike. The observer may note also how well the child participates in group projects, his emotional control in difficult situations, his reactions to arithmetic and other school activities. Careful records of behavior are useful in gaining insight into a child's difficulties.

2. Use of Survey Tests

A good group test of reading will usually give the teacher some hints about the child's general status in reading, his relative abilities in phases of reading, such as isolated vocabulary versus comprehension in context, his speed and accuracy. This is not always final evidence, but it suggests leads for further study of the child's abilities. For example, if Tom in the third grade makes a reading grade score of 4.1 on the word-recognition test of the *Gates Primary Reading Tests* (Advanced)[48] and a score of 2.2 on the paragraph-reading test of the same series, the teacher can be reasonably sure that he needs less drill on isolated words and more chance to read in con-

[48] Published by Bureau of Publications, Teachers College, Columbia University, New York, 1958.

text, with emphasis upon meaning rather than mere word recognition. Similarly, other survey tests will give clues to pupils' strengths and weaknesses.

3. Use of Informal Classroom Tests

As well as administering a standardized test to a group, the teacher of reading is continually evaluating development in informal ways. In one sense, every time a child reads to the teacher or group, he is being tested. His ability to work independently in workbooks or work-type exercises is easily checked almost every day. His ability to organize materials into some sort of report is another check on reading abilities. One of the most valuable ways for the teacher to collect such information is by anecdotal records, quick notes on slips of paper, later inserted into a child's file. Over a period of time the informal classroom testing situation gives the observant teacher more information than she can gain in almost any other way.

4. Collection of Pertinent Information

The three procedures indicated above occur more or less simultaneously. The following steps appear in definite sequence. As suggested in 3 above, some sort of file is useful for putting together the results of classroom observations, survey tests, and informal teacher-made tests. Some teachers keep such information in a loose-leaf notebook; others prefer to keep a folder for each child. After the teacher or psychologist has been studying the child for some time, this information should be organized into such divisions as (*a*) difficulties inherent in the child—physical, personality, etc., (*b*) environmental factors—home and community opportunities for reading, (*c*) school history and related academic achievements—school progress, ability in spelling, language, etc., (*d*) limitations of school program—ways in which the school has been failing to meet the child's individual needs.

5. Tryout of Tentative Remedial Measures

When the teacher or psychologist has collected the information as suggested above, he will often have a number of leads or suggestions for remedial work. The person studying the child may make suggestions to the classroom teacher; or if the classroom teacher herself is making the study, certain changes in the child's reading activities and materials may be indicated. If arrangements can be made such as giving the child individual or small-group help based on the information, an improvement in his reading will often result after a period of consistent, insightful teaching. If the child has an extreme reading disability or is a particularly difficult case, the following steps will be taken.

6. *Administering a Series of Diagnostic Reading Tests*

These tests differ from the reading-survey tests in that they provide for a much more searching study of reading strengths and weaknesses. For example, the *Gates Reading Diagnostic Tests*[49] provide for some thirty-five different subtests of various phases of reading ability. The *Durrell-Sullivan Reading Capacity Test*[50] is a measure of a child's listening comprehension abilities which may indicate possible reading achievement. The *Durrell Analysis of Reading Difficulty*[51] is designed for pupils from nonreaders to the sixth grade, and the *Diagnostic Reading Tests*[52] are useful with older children. In general, these tests are given to the child individually, and the skilled examiner gets more information out of the testing situation than is revealed in the test scores alone. A comprehensive group of tests in a diagnostic series, plus a more complete case study of all possible factors affecting reading, will provide the information necessary for the seventh step.

7. *Individual or Small-Group Remedial Work*

As a result of the information collected above, the remedial teacher is ready to try a rather complete program of activities adapted to the strengths and weaknesses of the particular child receiving the help. This program usually will continue for some months or even years. After the teacher and child have given one method or type of material a reasonable try, it may be necessary to shift to other procedures and materials. Some children will respond quickly to such detailed help by a teacher; others, fortunately the minority, may have factors in their home or other environment which mean that little or no progress is made in six months or a year. Usually at this stage the child is getting the most skillful guidance that he will ever have in reading activities.

[49] Published by Bureau of Publications, Teachers College, Columbia University, New York, 1945.

[50] Donald D. Durrell and Helen B. Sullivan. World Book, Yonkers, N.Y., 1937.

[51] Donald D. Durrell. World Book, Yonkers, N.Y., 1955.

[52] Committee on Diagnostic Reading Tests, Frances Triggs, chm., New York.

8. Evaluation of Remedial Work

As the remedial teacher works with a child, she will note each day apparent successes and failures and adjust the program accordingly. Progress or lack of it may be measured in part by the level of difficulty of the books read or the amount of voluntary reading. In addition, it is well for the teacher to repeat a different form of the same test that was given in the second step above. Repeating different forms of the same test at intervals will give some objective evidence about change in general reading status. Other hints for evaluation are given in Chapter 16.

9. Possible Changes in Regular Classroom Procedures

Too often remedial teachers develop some excellent teaching methods and materials in reading, but these are unknown to the school system in which they work. If the diagnostician discovers that retarded children in one school have rather consistent weaknesses in some phase of reading, the teachers of the school should know this fact and should plan to correct it. If remedial teachers develop charts, booklets, games, and related activities which are particularly suited to a certain school system, these should be shared with all the teachers. Principals and other administrators, as well as remedial and classroom teachers, have a responsibility for seeing that diagnostic and remedial findings influence the whole school program.

The nine steps set forth above outline procedures in an adequate program of diagnostic and remedial work in reading. Such a program will have many local variations. Every teacher can profit by the ideas inherent in such a program in working with individuals or groups. As suggested above, no teacher has the time to make a complete case study of all the pupils in a class. However, she can study two or three rather thoroughly and use the principles suggested above in working with the total group. For example, Harry[53] taught reading in four seventh grades organized in a departmentalized plan. In two experimental classes she attempted some limited case studies, emphasized pupil planning and execution of work, and the relating of reading activities to other classroom activities. In the two control

[53] Gertrude Cady Harry, *A Comparison of the Effects of a Mental Hygiene Approach and a Formal Approach to Remedial Reading in Four Normal Classroom Situations.* Unpublished master's thesis, University of California, Berkeley, 1947.

classes more traditional procedures of teacher planning and somewhat isolated remedial exercises were used. The results of a three months' experiment showed somewhat higher reading gains and also improved adjustment scores on the California Test of Personality in the experiment group. Similarly, Seeman[54] and Fisher[55] have shown that a therapeutic approach and emphasis on group therapy produce favorable gains with retarded readers. These studies suggest that diagnostic and remedial work need not always include the nine steps above, and that the study of individual needs on even a limited basis may show favorable results. Some sort of diagnostic and remedial program in which the classroom teacher participates and is concerned with emotional problems is a fundamental part of any plan for providing for individual differences in reading ability.

SUPPLEMENTARY READINGS

A. General

BARBE, WALTER B. "Problems in Reading Encountered by Gifted Children," *Elementary English,* Vol. 33, pp. 274-278, May, 1956.

BOHNHORST, BEN A., and SELLARS, SOPHIA W. "Individual Reading Instruction vs Basal Textbook Instruction: Some Tentative Explorations," *Elementary English,* Vol. 36, pp. 185-190, March, 1959.

BOND, GUY L., and WAGNER, EVA B. *Teaching the Child to Read,* 3rd ed., Chap. 17. Macmillan, New York, 1960.

BURT, CYRIL, and LEWIS, R. B. "Teaching Backward Readers," *British Journal of Educational Psychology,* Vol. 16, pp. 116-132, November, 1946.

California Journal of Elementary Education, Vol. 29, pp. 65-128, November, 1958. Whole issue: Grouping for Instruction.

California Journal of Elementary Education, Vol. 27, pp. 129-192, February, 1959. Whole issue on reading with emphasis on the individual program.

CUTTS, NORMA E., and MOSELEY, NICHOLAS, eds. *Providing for Individual Differences in the Elementary School.* Prentice-Hall, Englewood Cliffs. N.J., 1960.

DOLCH, E. W. *Teaching Primary Reading,* 3rd ed. Garrard, Champaign, Ill., 1960.

DUNN, LLOYD M., and COPOBIANCO, RUDOLPH J. *Studies in Reading and Arithmetic in Mentally Retarded Boys.* Monographs of Society for Research in Child Development 19, No. 1. Child Development Publications, Champaign, Ill., 1954.

DURRELL, D. D. *Improving Reading Instruction,* Chaps. 15, 16. World Book, Yonkers, N.Y., 1956.

[54] Julius Seeman and Benner Edward, "A Therapeutic Approach to Reading Difficulties," *Journal of Consulting Psychology,* Vol. 18, pp. 451-453, December, 1954.

[55] Bernard Fisher, "Group Therapy with Retarded Readers," *Journal of Educational Psychology,* Vol. 44, pp. 354-360, October, 1953.

DURRELL, D. D. "Individual Differences and Their Implications with Respect to Instruction in Reading," *The Teaching of Reading: A Second Report,* Thirty-sixth Yearbook, Part I, Chap. 11, pp. 325-356, National Society for the Study of Education. Public School Publishing Co., Bloomington, Ill., 1937.

EPHRON, BEULAH K. *Emotional Difficulties in Reading: A Psychological Approach to Study Problems.* Julian Press, New York, 1953.

EVANS, N. DEAN. "An Individualized Reading Program for the Elementary School," *Elementary School Journal,* Vol. 54, pp. 157-162, November, 1953.

GRAY, W. S., ed. and comp. *Adjusting Reading Programs to Individuals.* University of Chicago Press, Chicago, 1941. 344 p.

HARRIS, ALBERT J., and ROSWELL, FLORENCE G. "Clinical Diagnosis of Reading Disability," *Journal of Psychology,* Vol. 36, pp. 323-340, 1953.

HILDRETH, GERTRUDE H. *Teaching Reading,* Chaps. 5, 23, 24. Holt, New York, 1958.

LAYCOCK, SAMUEL R. *Gifted Children: A Handbook for the Classroom Teacher.* Copp Clark, Toronto, 1957.

LAZAR, MAY. "Individualized Reading: A Dynamic Approach," *The Reading Teacher,* Vol. 11, pp. 75-85, December, 1957.

McCULLOUGH, CONSTANCE M. *Meeting Individual Needs by Grouping in Reading.* Contributions to Reading, No. 19. Ginn, Boston, 1957.

MIEL, ALICE, ed. *Individualized Reading Practices.* Practical Aids in Teaching, No. 14. Bureau of Publications, Teachers College, Columbia University, New York, 1958.

NATIONAL EDUCATION ASSOCIATION, Department of Elementary School Principals. "Meeting Special Needs of the Individual Child," *National Elementary Principal,* Vol. 19, pp. 229-736, July, 1940.

NATIONAL SOCIETY FOR THE STUDY OF EDUCATION. *Education for the Gifted,* in Jeannette Veatch, comp., Fifty-seventh Yearbook, Pt. II. University of Chicago Press, Chicago, 1958.

NEW YORK BOARD OF EDUCATION. *Effective Classroom Practices in Individualized Reading.* Bureau of Educational Research, New York City Board of Education, New York, 1958.

PARKER, J. CECIL, and RUSSELL, DAVID H. "Ways of Providing for Individual Differences," *Educational Leadership,* Vol. 11, pp. 168-174, December, 1953.

PETTY, MARY C. *Intraclass Grouping in the Elementary School.* University of Texas Press, Austin, 1953.

ROBINSON, HELEN M. "Factors Which Affect Success in Reading," *Elementary School Journal,* Vol. 55, pp. 263-269, January, 1955.

SPACHE, GEORGE D. "Integrating Diagnosis with Remediation in Reading," *Elementary School Journal,* Vol. 56, p. 26, September, 1955.

The Reading Teacher, Vol. 9, pp. 195-254, April, 1956. Whole Issue: Reading and the Gifted Child and Youth.

VAN ALLEN, R. "Initiating Reading Through Creative Writing," Twenty-second Yearbook, Claremont Reading Conference. Claremont College Curriculum Laboratory, Claremont, Calif., 1957.

VERNON, MAGDALEN M. *Backwardness in Reading: A Study of Its Nature and Origin.* Cambridge University Press, London, 1957.

WHEELER, LESTER R. "Dealing with Emotional Problems in the Classroom," *Education,* Vol. 74, pp. 566-571, May, 1954.

YOAKAM, GERALD A. "Providing for the Individual Reading Needs of Children," *Education Digest,* Vol. 20, pp. 47-50, October, 1954.

B. Books on Diagnostic and Remedial Methods

BOND, GUY L., and HANDLAN, BERTHA. *Adapting Instruction in Reading to Individual Differences.* University of Minnesota Press, Minneapolis, 1947.

BOND, G. L., and TINKER, M. H. *Reading Difficulties: Their Diagnosis and Correction.* Appleton-Century-Crofts, New York, 1957.

COLE, LUELLA. *The Improvement of Reading with Special Reference to Remedial Instruction.* Farrar & Rinehart, New York, 1938. 338 p.

DOLCH, E. W. *A Manual for Remedial Reading,* 2nd ed. Garrard, Champaign, Ill., 1945. 460 p.

FERNALD, GRACE. *Remedial Techniques in Basic School Subjects.* McGraw-Hill, New York, 1943. 349 p.

GATES, ARTHUR I. *The Improvement of Reading,* 3rd ed. Macmillan, New York, 1947. 657 p.

GILLINGHAM, A., and STILLMAN, B. *Remedial Training for Children with Specific Disability in Reading, Spelling, and Penmanship.* Sackett & Wilhelms, New York, 1940.

HARRIS, A. J. *How to Increase Reading Ability,* 3rd ed. Longmans, Green, New York, 1956.

HILDRETH, G., and WRIGHT, J. *Helping Children to Read.* Bureau of Publications, Teachers College, Columbia University, New York, 1940. 90 p.

KIRK, S. A. *Teaching Reading to Slow Learning Children.* Houghton Mifflin, Boston, 1940. 225 p.

MCCALLISTER, J. M. *Remedial and Corrective Instruction in Reading.* Appleton-Century, New York, 1936. 300 p.

MONROE, MARION. *Children Who Cannot Read.* University of Chicago Press, Chicago, 1932. 205 p.

RUSSELL, D. H.; KARP, E. E.; and KELLY, E. I. *Reading Aids through the Grades.* Bureau of Publications, Teachers College, Columbia University, New York, 1951.

SCHONELL, F. J. *Backwardness in the Basic Subjects.* Clarke, Irwin, Toronto, 1945.

STANGER, M. A., and Donohue, E. K. *Prediction and Prevention of Reading Difficulties.* Oxford University Press, New York, 1937. 191 p.

STRANG, R.; MCCULLOUGH, C. M.; and TRAXLER, A. E. *Problems in the Improvement of Reading,* rev. ed. McGraw-Hill, New York, 1955.

WITTY, P., and KOPEL, D. *Reading and the Educative Process.* Ginn, Boston, 1939. 374 p.

Chapter **16**

EVALUATION OF GROWTH IN AND THROUGH READING

DEVELOPMENT OF THE MODERN EVALUATION PROGRAM

Decisions about children's reading should be based on evidence—the best evidence possible. Such data may include scores on tests of general mental ability and of reading achievement, questionnaires on reading habits, sociograms showing interaction with a group, and other paper-and-pencil techniques. But using these tools to accumulate test scores is not performing an evaluation. The evaluation comes when a judgment about the child is made on the basis of the evidence. Most teachers make the decisions not only on the basis of certain scores but also from the clues to children's status and needs gleaned from the day-to-day work in the classroom. For example, ten children are in a reading group with Miss Brown, their fourth-grade teacher. After a discussion of the setting of the story and consideration of four or five difficult but key words in it Miss Brown has the group read the story to themselves to answer two questions she has written on the blackboard. The story is about a boy's heroism on a mountain-climbing expedition. In answering the first question Miss Brown notices that three girls misinterpret the boy's actions by calling them foolish and foolhardy. She therefore asks other members of the group to read a few sentences that give more correct clues to his character. Then she asks, "Read a paragraph that describes the mountains in autumn." After two children have read descriptions, she asks, "Who will find and read a paragraph that tells about the storm?" After two or three more children have read parts of the story orally, Miss Brown has the group refer to the chart they have made previously, entitled "Standards for Good Oral Reading." The children discuss how the oral reading met and did not meet these standards. They agree that each of the children read loud enough for all to hear, but that they might change their voices more, to show a change in meaning in the story. After some more silent and oral reading and discussion of the story Miss Brown gives the children hectographed sheets asking questions on the sequence of ideas in the story. They return to their own desks. Miss Brown makes notes about the reading of two children and then turns to another group.

This simplified account of the activities of a reading group suggests that modern evaluation techniques are part of all good teaching. As children made errors in general interpretation of character the teacher observed these and directed the group back to a rereading for more exact clues. Miss Brown noted children's ability to find specific descriptions, and the group practiced self-evaluation in using their chart. The test items on the story are another evaluative measure of reading ability, and Miss Brown's anecdotal record about the two pupils made a fourth example of evaluation techniques in use.

The variety of techniques used in this one lesson illustrates the fact that the modern evaluation program replaces older practices of testing pupils by means of teacher-made essay examinations administered at periodic intervals. As the goals of elementary- and secondary-school programs have been expanded and clarified, means of determining whether these goals are being reached have necessarily become both broader and more exact. Today evaluation is concerned with many possible outcomes of school instruction and therefore involves a wide variety of appraisal activities. It has become the process of collecting and interpreting data on the extent to which a school program is reaching desired goals, so that next steps in the program may be planned and undertaken effectively.

In reading, as in other school activities, the evaluation program is being enlarged, and at the same time is becoming more precise in its measurement. It is attempting to discover how well the aims of the program, such as those listed in Chapter 5, are being reached. In any one class it tries to discover how well the more specific objectives of the teacher and pupils are being reached, so that if necessary, changes in the program can be made. Since the aims of the modern program go beyond mere acquisition of reading skills, it follows that the evaluation program is concerned not only with specific reading techniques but with more general abilities; it includes, for example, the attempt to measure what reading interests and attitudes the child is developing. Finally, since good teachers are concerned with the effects of reading on the child, the modern evaluation program deals with the changes in pupil behavior and personality related to reading, *e.g.*, the program is one of evaluation of pupil growth both *in* and *through* reading.

Recent writing on evaluation indicates that many schools are just beginning to develop a modern, comprehensive program of appraisal. As early as 1940, in an article listing 129 references on evaluation, Orata[1] pointed out that there had been a shift in measurement from skill and information-getting to attitudes and appreciation, interests, personality adjustments, functional information, thinking abilities, study skills, and creativeness. He listed twelve changes in boys and girls, such as facility in the use of dependable sources of information and the habit of collecting and considering appropriate evidence and information before making decisions, "for which evaluation has been attempted with some degree of success." Orata's list may be a somewhat optimistic one, still, in the light of ordinary practice. For example, in a survey about the same time of evaluation practices in thirty communities of New York State, Hamalainen[2] found only four or five techniques in action. In a later study, Michaelis[3] found that some fifteen devices were used for evaluation in city school systems. Most popular were educational and psychological tests. Other devices included interviews, case studies, anecdotal records, observations, files of student materials, questionnaires, inventories, diaries, and sociograms. Such a list indicates a broadening basis in appraising children's development. Most of the above devices can be applied to the reading program or to a child's development in reading.

As school systems work on their evaluation programs in reading, they tend to expand their methods of appraising development in it. As suggested in this book, reading is a complex, many-sided type of behavior; therefore, if the evaluation is to be at all adequate, it must be varied and must sample many aspects of reading behavior. Groups of teachers often become convinced, too, that the evaluation program in reading should not only measure growth but produce growth. In

[1] Pedro T. Orata, "Evaluating Evaluation," *Journal of Educational Research,* Vol. 33, pp. 641-661, May, 1940.

[2] Arthur E. Hamalainen, "Existing Practices in the Evaluation of Pupil Growth in the Elementary School," *Elementary School Journal,* Vol. 42, pp. 175-183, November, 1941.

[3] John U. Michaelis, "Current Practices of Evaluation in City School Systems," *Educational and Psychological Measurement,* Vol. 9, pp. 15-22, Spring, 1949.

other words, the devices that are used in evaluation should be learning and teaching devices, as well as measuring devices. If the child has some sort of test in reading, or fills in an inventory of reading interests, the experience itself, and activities which may be used as a follow-up to the experience, should encourage learning, whether of some specific technique missed in the test or in some area of interest hitherto untouched. Some of the possibilities for broadening appraisal and for improving its possibilities of learning are suggested in the discussion of general steps in evaluation below.

Steps in Evaluation

The usual steps in an evaluation program have been pointed out by Tyler,[4] Wrightstone,[5] and others. These may be stated as follows:

1. The determination and acceptance of major objectives, stated in terms of children's behaviors.
2. The identification of a wide variety of situations in which children may be expected to show these behavior patterns.
3. The selection and trial of instruments or methods for the appraisal of each objective.
4. The use of the most promising instruments or methods to collect data about desirable behaviors.
5. The making of decisions, from the evidence collected, about the degree of present success of the program.
6. The drawing of inferences from the results for possible changes in school practices.

The first two of these steps may be described as preliminary evaluation steps, the second two as executive or conative steps, the last two as interpretive steps.

The two preliminary steps in the process of evaluation are philosophical and psychological. They are concerned with the aims of the school and how these aims may be realized in terms of children's conduct. Obviously, the aims in the reading program will differ with the community and the children involved. In addition to the broader aims of Chapter 5 which may influence reading instruction

[4] Ralph W. Tyler, "Evaluation as a Function of Supervision," *Elementary School Journal,* Vol. 44, pp. 264-273, January, 1944.

[5] J. Wayne Wrightstone, Joseph Justman, and Irving Robbins, *Evaluation in Modern Education.* American Book, New York, 1956.

in general, one school may have the specific aim for a year of guiding children away from reliance on television for recreation to the use of desirable children's books. Thus one type of behavior which the teachers will wish to observe will be the reading done in free periods in school or in terms of borrowings from school or public library. In another school a specific aim for a term may be to make reading more functional in the intermediate and upper grades, to make it of more value to pupils in social studies, health, science, and other activities. In this school the evaluation will not be concerned so much with recreational reading as with the effectiveness of reading as an aid to learning. Consequently, the evaluation staff will be concerned with activities in which children use textbooks, consult reference books, explore library resources, and utilize sources of information contained in pictures, graphs, maps, films, and related materials. In each case the evaluation staff has decided on a special aim or purpose or made a nontechnical use of educational philosophy. Then each staff has suggested behavioral or psychological situations in which children may be expected to exhibit conduct related to the aim.

In the third and fourth steps of the process of evaluation, the persons responsible for the program actually experiment with possible measures and decide upon a few devices that seem to get at the behaviors to be studied, that are comprehensive enough to give a fair sample of such behaviors, but yet are practical in terms of time, cost, and other considerations. For example, the first school mentioned above may find that it cannot get records of borrowings at the public library, but it can ask pupils to keep records of everything they read for three separate weeks in the school year. In the second school mentioned, the evaluation staff may decide that it cannot record all the textbooks children use throughout the term, but it can administer a test of ability to get information from encyclopedias and other reference books, the test to be given in two forms near the beginning and end of the semester. Probably both evaluation staffs will add other measures to the one mentioned here for each objective. The third and fourth steps of the process of evaluation will consist partly, in the first case, of having the children make the records of their reading and then the study of these records by the staff. In the second school the giving, scoring, and interpreting of the tests of ability to get information from useful sources will be a part of the third and fourth steps.

As the two evaluation staffs gather the information they want, they become ready for the final interpretive steps. On scanning the results they will undoubtedly consult with teachers, supervisors, and principals concerned. Even if one teacher has been conducting the experiment in evaluation in her own class, at this stage the help of others is desirable. In the first school a discussion of the results of the children's diaries of reading activities will be necessary, because the time of year may have affected them. Some children may have done more reading but included with it more viewing of television. In the second school the accessibility of the encylopedias and films may have varied with different classes. Even with rather objective scores interpretation may be intricate. Before the final step of making recommendations for another term or year, then, careful discussion of the results is the rule. This study and discussion of findings may be the most valuable part of the enterprise in terms of helping teachers to improve their reading programs in the near future.

Implications of These Steps

There are at least four implications for practice from the above descriptions:

(1) In each of the six steps above, it is important that all the teachers of any one school or school system have a chance to participate. Aims are of value as they are common aims. (More specific objectives may vary from class to class.) Plans for new procedures and recommendations for new methods of teaching are of value only as they are understood by all the school staff. One simple procedure for obtaining some sort of consensus is to have a staff go through a list of objectives in reading, check the ones with which they agree, and indicate after each one specific situations which may be provided to implement such purposes. The check list used by one group of teachers is given on page 532. The procedures listed by the group may then be used as a basis for determining possible instruments or measures of the reading program and, accordingly, of suggesting ways the program may need to be changed.

(2) It is important to suggest also that much evaluation of the school program does not proceed in formal steps involving group work over a period of weeks or months. An analysis of the above steps in the classroom situation suggests that all individual teachers use some or all of the six steps every day they teach. Their evaluation is a continuous process closely connected with all phases of their teach-

To the teacher:

Below are some specific objectives of a reading program which might be incorporated in a teacher's guide at various levels. Please rate these objectives as indicated. If you feel an objective is good, please list under "Procedures" any worth-while activities you have used to realize this objective. These activities will be listed later for other teachers.

Objective, or Purpose	General	Specific	Poor	Good	Procedures
1. To improve oral reading					
2. To review an interesting story, "We Go Away"					
3. To establish the meaning of the pronouns "you" and "I"					
4. To present new words and recall familiar words					
5. To drill on words					
6. To recall related ideas					
7. To reread the story in a dramatic situation					
8. To read for enjoyment					
9. To correct workbooks					
10. To improve comprehension					
11. To raise the standard of reading					
12. To read riddles they made up					
13. To encourage rapid reading, scanning					
14. To give practice in following directions					
15. To develop auditory recognition of initial consonant *w*					
16. To develop self-confidence in reading					
17. To help nonreaders through the use of phonics					

Sample rating sheet for determining teachers' opinions of suitable objectives and procedures in a reading program

ing. A second-grade teacher observes that nearly every member of the reading group is confusing the words *which* and *what;* so she either puts on the chalkboard an exercise which demands accurate perception of the two words, or she makes a note to prepare some materials involving the two words for the next work-type reading the group will do. A fourth-grade teacher observes that two members of a group have a good reading vocabulary, but that their voices become strained and high-pitched as they read orally. Accordingly, she works for conversational tones or helps the other members of the group to form an easy, relaxed social situation for reading. A seventh-grade teacher, observing that a half-dozen girls in the class read quickly but inaccurately, plans some work to give practice in reading for exact details. In each case the teacher is evaluating the reading as part of the teaching process. The three teachers mentioned have certain aims, or objectives, which they hope the group will reach; all attempt some sort of observation of pupils' behavior; and all make rather immediate changes in material or method in an attempt to improve the situation. The teacher may not be consciously using the six steps of the evaluative process; but actually she is using some sort of goal, appraisal situation, and interpretation to improve children's behavior in reading situations.

In addition to the inferences that evaluation is a common concern and is both periodic and continuous, two other implications of the six steps are important: (3) The third inference concerns the importance of self-evaluation to the pupil. If evaluation is conceived as part of the learning process, the effect on the child is crucial. Evaluation of his reading which makes him resentful or self-conscious or eager for the limelight is obviously undesirable. On the other hand, the psychology of learning suggests that knowledge of the goal is one of the best ways of making learning more efficient.[6] Self-evaluation may be the first step in independent learning. In democratic classroom situations pupils profit from helping to plan the next steps in their work. Pupil evaluation may be a personal or a group activity. The eight-year-old child may be helped to decide for himself that he should read books other than second readers that are easy for him. The reading group in the fifth grade may decide upon six standards for good oral reading, record these on a chalkboard or chart, and help one another to reach the standards. Pupil participation in the six steps of the process of evaluation is dependent upon a classroom or school climate of democratic participation, but it is essential to the success of the program in any school interested in the total growth of the child through reading.

(4) A fourth inference from the six steps in evaluation is that it is a changing, experimental sort of program. The great scientist Charles Darwin once said: "I love fools' experiments. I am always making them." Some of the same attitude may permeate an evaluation pro-

[6] Guy T. Buswell, "Helping Children Learn How to Learn," *Learning and the Teacher,* 1959 Yearbook of Association for Supervision and Curriculum Development, Chap. 8, National Education Association, Washington, D.C., 1959.

gram. Since evaluation of growth in reading involves many different objectives, it follows that many measuring methods and devices may be attempted. In addition to the usual teacher-made or standardized tests, observations, anecdotal records, stenographic reports, reports to parents, self-rating scales, and other records may be attempted. Some examples of these are given in succeeding sections. The feeling that they are trying something new is usually a stimulus to better teaching and evaluation for any school staff. Thus the six steps in the evaluation program should not become crystallized into hard-and-fast procedures but should be a constant and fresh stimulus to good teaching.

EVALUATION OF THE READING PROGRAM

The above description of steps suggests that evaluation may be conceived as a large-scale enterprise involving much of the life of a school or that it may relate itself to the more personal development of individuals. This section is concerned with the evaluation of a reading program as a program, that is, with methods, objectives, materials, provisions for individual differences, relative emphases which may be given to different activities, and similar problems. The succeeding sections deal with evaluation more directly in relation to individuals, and are concerned, therefore, with growth in reading interests and in reading abilities and the effects of reading on children. The sections thus suggest that evaluation may be in general and in personal terms.

Examples of criteria based upon the whole reading program have been so well expressed by others that only a few samples need be given here. In a discussion of the wider purposes of a reading program Herrick,[7] developed four main criteria for appraising the total program, as follows:

1. The criterion of defined goals: Do you have clearly defined goals which indicate the scope and direction of the reading program and which will form the basis for any appraisal of instructional practices and materials?
2. The criterion of continuity: Do your instructional procedures and materials contribute to the essential continuity of the child's present and future development?

[7] Virgil E. Herrick, "Criteria for Appraising Procedures Used to Promote Reading Development," *Elementary School Journal,* Vol. 46, pp. 191-199, 258-265, December, 1945, January, 1946.

3. The criterion of interrelationship: Do your instructional procedures and materials recognize and utilize the interrelationships which exist between reading and other functions of language and between language and other developmental areas?

4. The criterion of two-dimensional evaluation: Do you evaluate the adequacy of instructional procedures and materials used to contribute to reading development on the basis of (*a*) the goals to be achieved, and (*b*) the nature of the child's present reading development?

A somewhat more detailed list of criteria for a whole reading program was presented by Gray[8] as follows:

1. Is the reading program directed by two closely interrelated purposes, namely, (*a*) the purpose to contribute as largely as possible through reading to the all-round development of pupils, and (*b*) the purpose to aid the pupils in acquiring sufficient competence in reading to enable them to achieve readily the broader ends sought?

2. Does the program recognize that reading is only one of many aids to learning, and does it co-ordinate the use of reading with that of other forms of experience in attaining the broader ends which the school seeks to achieve?

3. Does the reading program recognize that reading, language, and thinking are closely interrelated processes?

4. Is the reading program continuous throughout the elementary and secondary school, and are the successive units closely and effectively coordinated?

5. Does the reading program move forward progressively in harmony with the dominant characteristics and interests of pupils at successive levels of advancement, promoting progress in those aspects of reading dictated by their developmental needs?

6. Is the reading program flexible, so that it can be readily adjusted at each level of advancement to wide variations in the characteristics and the needs of the pupils taught?

7. Does the reading program provide all the types of experience and guidance in reading needed at each level of advancement, and sufficient differentiation in emphasis among the various curricular fields to ensure maximum development?

8. Does the reading program make adequate provision for retarded and seriously deficient readers?

9. Does the reading program provide carefully planned activities and guidance in promoting essential types of development in and through reading?

10. Is the effectiveness of the reading program determined at frequent

[8] William S. Gray, "Criteria for Appraising the Scope and Organization of Reading Programs in Elementary and Secondary Schools," in W. S. Gray, ed. and comp., *The Appraisal of Current Practices in Reading,* Supplementary Educational Monographs, No. 61, pp. 15-22. University of Chicago Press, Chicago, 1945.

intervals through the use of various techniques of appraisal, and are needed improvements identified and planned co-operatively by the entire staff?

In this list the first criterion is a key statement, since many of the succeeding statements relate to either the all-round development of children or the growth of a certain competence in reading.

In applying such criteria as these to their own reading program, teachers, supervisors, and principals will want to change certain criteria or to emphasize some of the items on the list. The practical solution of school problems demands that, no matter how well criteria are developed, they must be used. This requires the co-operation of all persons concerned, including the pupils. If the appraisal is to be truly co-operative, certain conditions must exist in the school system and in the group working together. Broadly speaking, these include the following:

A democratic atmosphere in administration, supervision, and teaching

Some familiarity with the steps of critical or scientific thinking in solving problems

The reaching of agreements through group understanding rather than the imposition of the will of the majority

A favorable attitude among individuals toward contributing ideas or work time to the group effort

The ability of the teacher, curriculum co-ordinator, or other leader to use the special creativeness of group action

Just as psychologists suggest that "the whole is more than the sum of the parts," so the product of group thinking and action is often more than the sum of the individual contributions to the project. In evaluating the whole reading program according to certain criteria such as those above, the co-operative effort of a group working together is usually more acceptable and more creative than the best contribution of an individual expert. In the process, the in-service education of the total school staff proceeds more rapidly than in most other undertakings.

Evaluation of Experimental Programs

As well as appraising a typical, or traditional program, many school staffs or curriculum committees are faced with the problem of evaluating "experiments." They are concerned with fresh procedures and materials, and especially with new programs tried in a demonstration group of classroooms. As more schools and school systems attempt action research on reading programs, the need for skill in evaluating experimental or semi-experimental procedures increases. Attempts to evaluate some curriculum procedure may range all the way from personal opinion through group consensus to rigorous experimental testing. These methods of appraisal may be expressed in a continuum as follows:

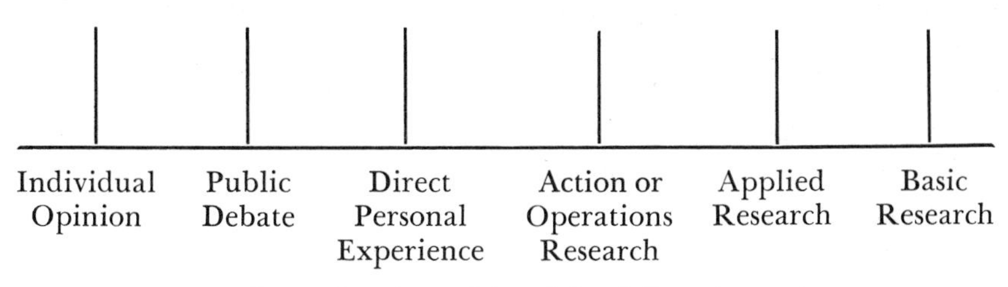

Bases for Appraising School Practices

In addition to being aware of the level at which an evaluation of a reading procedure is being made, a teacher or curriculum staff must be aware of possible limitations of new activities not fully evaluated in scientific research. When a teacher or school has tried out, with apparent success, some innovation such as emphasis upon phonics, greater use of individualized reading, a handwriting approach to reading, the use of machines, an enlarged testing program, or a heavy investment in children's literature, some of the evidence of children's development must be assessed. This evaluation may be extensive or limited, depending upon the purpose and scope of the tryout. It may involve interviews of individual children by principal, supervisor, or school psychologist. It may include reports from classroom teachers or the results of a city-wide or county-wide testing program. It may involve collecting evidence from self-report inventories, teacher-made tests, or records of activities such as book borrowings. Usually a number of related attempts to evaluate pupil progress are better than a single index.

Furthermore, the applicability of the findings is limited to the type of experimental group used and to the level at which the evaluation was made. Sometimes a teacher or supervisor feels that a method which works well for her should be adopted generally. Most books on educational research[9] warn of the dangers of over-generalization from the data of one small study. For example, what one principal finds as a result of new procedures in his school's reading program may be limited in application if the school has many bright children, or a considerable group of children from non-English speaking backgrounds, or if the teachers are specially motivated in their work, or if considerable enthusiasm is generated in pupils and teachers by visitors and newspaper publicity, or if parents participate in the school activities. All these facts may be typical and desirable for a particular school, and the participants in the experiment will deserve much credit, but the findings may "hold up" for only this school at this time. Many children, teachers, and schools profit greatly from the stimulus of new activities, and there is no question about the value of the program for the individuals involved. However, in such action research, it is desirable to distinguish clearly between something that is good for a particular individual, class, or school at a specific time and a program of activities that is widely applicable in most school situations.

Starting with Teachers' Problems

In enlisting the help of pupils and teachers as well as administrative staff in an evaluation of the whole reading program it is usually unwise to start with the results of a testing program in reading.[10] These may place teachers or pupils on the defensive. Insecure children or teachers are not likely to make voluntary, creative efforts in the solution of a group problem in the reading curriculum. Rather it will be profitable to discuss the possible objectives in the reading program with teachers or with pupils. A group of teachers may feel that much time spent on "useless aims" is wasted and may prefer to attack some of the immediate problems which they are facing. These problems will naturally differ with each school or school system, but teachers are usually ready to get help and exchange possible solutions on such problems as the following:

1. How should I select and provide for the different reading groups in my class? (See Chapter 15.)

[9] Carter V. Good, *Introduction to Educational Research*. Appleton-Century-Crofts, New York, 1959. Robert W. M. Travers, *An Introduction to Educational Research*. Macmillan, New York, 1958.

[10] Virgil E. Herrick, "The Nature of, and Techniques Involved in, Co-operative Effort to Improve Reading," in W. S. Gray, ed. and comp., *Co-operative Effort in Schools to Improve Reading*, Supplementary Educational Monographs, No. 56, pp. 41-46. University of Chicago Press, Chicago, 1942.

2. What place shall I give individualized reading and the language arts approach in my total reading program? (See Chapter 15.)

3. What special provisions should I make for the three or four gifted readers in my class? (See Chapter 15.)

4. Which of the recommended basic series should I use for continuity in developing word-attack skills, abilities in comprehension, and favorable attitude to a wide variety of content? (See Chapter 5.)

5. What are the children's stories and other books which will probably appeal most to the children in my class? (See Chapters 12 and 13.)

6. What are the occasions when a whole class may profitably read together? (See Chapter 15.)

7. How much phonics should I use in my word-recognition program? (See Chapter 10.)

8. How can I tell that a child has readiness to read at my particular grade level? (See Chapter 6.)

9. How can I relate the reading program to spelling, composition, and other language activities? (See Chapter 7.)

10. How can I use reading as a part of my character-education program? (See present chapter.)

These ten miscellaneous questions are typical of the specific problems which may be bothering a school staff and which may lead to an evaluation of current teaching procedures. They are usually better springboards to evaluation than test results or more general questions. When practical attempts to meet some of these needs have been evaluated, most groups are ready to turn to some of the more general problems involved in evaluation of the whole reading program.

In addition to evaluation of the total reading program as a program, it may be evaluated more personally in terms of desirable growths of boys and girls. Criteria and methods for such evaluation are given in the three sections below.

APPRAISING PUPIL GROWTH

A reading program may be evaluated in personal terms in relation to (1) its development of interests and tastes, (2) its development of reading abilities and competences, and (3) its effects on children. Each of these categories obviously overlaps and affects the other two.

A child's interest in reading certain materials will affect his skill in working with them. His reading abilities, in turn, will affect the emotional reactions he undergoes while reading. For convenience, however, the results of reading programs have been divided into these three categories, and examples of evaluation techniques are given under each category. Many of the following methods or devices of evaluation can be applied in one or both of the other categories.

Interests and Tastes

Some of the criteria for developing worth-while interests and tastes have been discussed in Chapters 12 and 13. An interest in reading generally, and attitudes and habits associated with the use of books, tend to be permanent learnings. Since they may persist through a lifetime, they have an important place in the evaluation program. Some of the questions about children which might be studied in this area of reading are these:

1. Are the children reading more than they did last year?
2. Are the children developing interests in varied types of reading materials?
3. Do the children have opportunities for simple enjoyment of reading without emphasis upon improving reading abilities?
4. Are the children developing thoughtful, inquiring attitudes as one result of their reading of nonfiction?
5. Is reading used as one basis for enjoyable expressive activities such as dramatization, choral reading, and music?
6. Are the pupils becoming better acquainted with the uses of books and libraries?

Some questions to be asked which concern the teachers as such are these:

1. Has the school staff reached any agreement on the place and use of basal programs, audio-visual aids in reading, and provisions for differences?
2. Are teachers able to give individual children guidance in their personal or recreational reading?
3. Have pupils, teachers, or curriculum workers developed some "reading ladders" to encourage gradual maturing of reading tastes along specific lines?
4. Have any teachers attempted to use "reading ladders" as a form of therapy, to help children to solve personal or social problems?

In discussing pupils' status or staff participation in the growth of reading interests and tastes, the usual tests of reading vocabulary and comprehension will be of little value. Rather, the teacher or curriculum consultant interested in evaluation will discover current habits and tastes through observing children's activities, talking about current reading in an informal group, or examining records of voluntary reading. A few specific examples of devices for evaluation in this area are as follows:

1. *An Inventory of Interests.* In each pair below put an X beside the one activity which you like better than the other:

_____ playing ball	_____ reading	_____ skating
_____ going to movies	_____ skating	_____ looking at television
_____ playing ball	_____ going to movies	_____ listening to radio
_____ reading	_____ listening to radio	_____ reading

2. *A Questionnaire about Reading.* List in order, starting with the best, the five best books or stories you have ever read.

3. *A Check List.* Check with an R the parts of a daily newspaper that you read regularly. If there are some parts that you read occasionally (1 out of 4 or 5 times), check them with an O.

_____ international news	_____ social events	_____ comics section
_____ local news	_____ editorial page	_____ advertising
_____ sport		

4. *A Record of Activities.* You are asked to record below the time you spent on everything you did yesterday. Show the length of time you spent in sleeping, working, listening to the radio, reading, playing, and other activities. One boy began his record this way:

9 to 7.30 Sleep	8.10 to 8.40 Homework
7.30 to 7.45 Dress	8.40 to 8.55 Going to school
7.45 to 8.05 Breakfast	9 to 12 School
8.05 to 8.10 Read newspaper	

As well as you can, put down exactly how you spent the time yesterday.

Other records, such as books borrowed from the library and observation of pupils' activities during a free period in school, will give some indication of pupils' reading interests and tastes. An indirect measure, such as that indicated in No. 4 above, may be particularly valuable. If asked directly about their reading, many children will try to oblige their teacher with a congenial answer. The record of all activities, taken for a number of different days, conceals the purpose of the questionnaire and may give a fair picture of the amount of reading done in relation to other leisure-time activities. By using some of these devices at the beginning of a term and repeating them near the end of the term the teacher will have some indication of any progress made during the period between the two collections of data. The way books are chosen, used, and discussed in class will always give clues for the evaluation of the success of a program in terms of reading interests and habits.

Reading Abilities and Competences

As in other school subjects, evaluation in reading has probably been most successful in relation to specific skills and abilities. Evaluation of certain reading achievements is certainly the commonest form of evaluation in reading. Every teacher listens for children's errors in recognition or pronunciation while they read orally. If the teacher is unable to give a standardized reading test to the group, she makes up exercises which require the children to recognize certain words or to read a paragraph with some particular type of comprehension. Some teachers regard interests or attitudes as intangibles, but feel they are on firm ground in checking vocabulary or phonics abilities or understanding of directions. Evaluation should never be limited to such reading skills and abilities, but an appraisal of them forms part of most evaluation programs.

It is almost impossible to list all the skills and abilities which may be aims of reading programs. Sample questions which a school may wish to include in planning its evaluation in this area are as follows:

1. Are children developing the ability to read various types of material in readers and in the content fields?
2. Are children learning to read in different ways for a half dozen or so different purposes, such as understanding the main idea, following directions, and noting specific details?
3. Are children developing the ability to adapt their rate of reading to the nature of the material and their purpose in reading it?
4. Are children increasing their independence and ability to recognize new words?
5. Are children learning the proper physical care of books?
6. Have children developed the ability to use an index, a table of contents, and other parts of a book as needed?

7. Are the pupils improving in their use of the library to obtain the information or recreation they desire?

8. Can upper-grade pupils organize an article into its main headings with a few subsections under each?

Standardized Tests

There are many more reading abilities which might be included in this list of questions. The list of reading habits, skills, and attitudes given in the National Society for Study of Education Thirty-sixth Yearbook and reproduced on pages 208 and 209 suggests other abilities which may be evaluated. These items should not be tested in isolation but in the situations in which children ordinarily use them. Standardized reading tests are beginning to include such situations among their test items and to include a wider variety of items in their subtests.

Even the better of the older tests did not provide for complete diagnosis of all reading abilities. The modern trend has been to make the standardized test more comprehensive and to supplement it with additional evaluative measures. A few examples of standardized reading tests which attempt to cover a number of reading skills or abilities are listed below, with the subtests indicating the breadth or scope of the test.

California Reading Tests

Primary, grades 1-3; Elementary, grades 4-6; Intermediate, grades 7-9; Advanced, grades 9-14. Each test has two main parts, vocabulary and comprehension, with several subtests in each part. California Test Bureau.

Durrell-Sullivan Reading Capacity and Achievement Tests

Primary, grades 2.5-4.5; Intermediate, grades 3-6. The *Capacity* test is a non-reading group test of ability to understand spoken language as a measure of potential reading ability; the *Achievement* test is a test of reading comprehension with two parts, paragraph meaning and vocabulary. World Book.

Gates Reading Survey

Grades 3-10. Provides separate measures of vocabulary, level of comprehension, rate of reading, and accuracy of comprehension. Bureau of Publications, Teachers College, Columbia University.

Gates Silent Reading Tests, Revised

Primary, grades 1 and 2. Three types in separate booklets: Type 1, word recognition; Type 2, sentence reading; Type 3, paragraph reading. Advanced Primary, grades 2 and 3. Type 1, word recognition, and Type 2, paragraph reading in separate booklets. Bureau of Publications, Teachers College, Columbia University.

Gates Basic Reading Tests

Grades 3-8. Four types, each in separate booklet: Type A, general significance; Type B, predict outcomes; Type C, follow directions; Type D, reading details. Bureau of Publications, Teachers College, Columbia University.

Metropolitan Achievement Tests

Primary I Battery, end of grade 1; Primary II Battery, grade 2; Elementary Reading Test, grades 3 and 4; Intermediate Reading Test, grades 5 and 6; Advanced Reading Test, grades 7, 8, first half of 9. World Book.

Roswell-Chall Diagnostic Reading Test of Word Analysis Skills

A short series of five tests for analyzing word recognition and word analysis skills. Primary grades and remedial pupils. Single consonants, consonant combinations, digraphs and diphthongs, syllabication, etc. No norms. Essay.

Sequential Tests of Educational Progress: Reading

Level 4, grades 4-6; Level 3, grades 7-9. (2 forms each.) Comprehension score on varied materials and questions. Educational Test Service.

Stanford Achievement Tests

Primary Battery, grades 1.9-3.5. Includes paragraph meaning, word meaning, spelling, arithmetic reasoning, and arithmetic computation. Elementary Reading Test, grades 3.0-4.9, paragraph meaning and word meaning; Intermediate Reading Test, grades 5, 6, paragraph meaning and word meaning; Advanced Reading Test, grades 7-9, paragraph meaning and word meaning. World Book.

These tests have not been listed as the best tests for every school system but as reading tests in common use which illustrate a trend toward more comprehensive testing of reading abilities.

Bond and Wagner[11] and Harris[12] give more complete lists of available reading tests. A school system planning a testing program should buy sample sets of certain tests to examine their suitability before purchasing in quantity for a testing program. In determining what reading test to use, a school staff should be guided also by discussions of the characteristics of good achievement tests given in books on tests and measurements such as those of Greene,[13] of Remmers,[14] and of Cronbach.[15] Testing should involve (1) repeated appraisals, (2) varied kinds of evidence, and (3) attempts to get at motivation and interests which powerfully influence reading achievement. The staff or committee on tests will be concerned with such factors as cost, time required for administration and scoring, and relation of the test items to the current curriculum. The value of the tests in relation to other evaluative measures and to the guidance program and as bases for research studies for the improvement of instruction should also be considered. The *Mental Measurements Yearbook*[16] gives critical reviews of published reading tests and Traxler[17] has given some of the advantages and disadvantages of standardized tests.

Most teachers and administrators are aware of the dangers of relying on the results of one standardized test in reading. Camp[18] pointed out that tests must be correctly administered, that their results must be interpreted with care, that clearly defined policies of reporting results are needed, and that tests results should be used along with background and educational information such as included in a cumulative record. Two criticisms of many tests of reading are that (1) they do not show pupil progress in the specific materials studied and (2) they do not measure development in aspects of critical and crea-

[11] Guy L. Bond and Eva B. Wagner, *Teaching the Child to Read,* 3rd ed. Macmillan, New York, 1960.

[12] Albert J. Harris, *How to Increase Reading Ability,* 3rd ed., Appendix A, pp. 577-591. Longmans, Green, New York, 1956.

[13] Harry A. Greene, Albert N. Jorgensen, and J. Raymond Gerberich, *Measurement and Evaluation in the Elementary School,* rev. ed. Longmans, Green, New York, 1953.

[14] H. H. Remmers, N. L. Gage, and J. F. Rummel, *A Practical Introduction to Measurement and Evaluation.* Harper, New York, 1955.

[15] Lee J. Cronbach, *Essentials of Psychological Testing,* rev. ed. Harper, New York, 1959.

[16] Oscar K. Buros, ed., *Fifth Mental Measurements Yearbook.* Gryphon Press, Highland Park, N.J., 1959.

[17] Arthur E. Traxler, "Values and Limitations of Standardized Reading Tests," in H. M. Robinson, ed., *Evaluation of Reading,* Supplementary Educational Monographs, No. 88. University of Chicago Press, Chicago, 1958.

[18] Dolph Camp, "Uses of Tests," in K. F. McLaughlin, ed., *Understanding Testing: Purposes and Interpretation for Pupil Development,* pp. 12, 13. U. S. Office of Education, Department of Health, Education and Welfare, Washington, D.C., 1960.

tive reading as described in Chapter 14. Some tests which have been devised to accompany certain basal reading programs are attempts to meet these criticisms of the more general standardized test.

Teacher-Made Tests

Since most standardized tests are not directly related to the work done in a particular reading group, many teachers also attempt to evaluate growth by means of tests they make themselves. They usually mimeograph or hectograph the test items, basing the materials on the books or other printed matter the children have been using in the preceding days or weeks. In the intermediate and upper grades some groups enjoy making up test items to be used by other groups or children. Suggestions for constructing such test items may be obtained from workbooks accompanying different readers, but items should never be borrowed directly. Other suggestions are given in the twenty-four books listed in Chapter 15 (pages 504-5), for exercises suggest a form for test items, and remedial activities are phases of certain developmental reading activities. Teachers will profit from studying a collection of test materials assembled by Snedaker and Horn.[19] A later collection by Gray[20] includes sample exercises or tests on "essential knowledge, attitudes, skills and procedures" in reading. Under perception he included measures of such abilities as accurate perception of word forms, of both word forms and meaning, and of words in context. Under comprehension he included test situations, such as recognition of importance and relationship of ideas, interpreting meaning in the light of a broader context, supplementing the specific meanings apprehended, reacting critically to what is read, and adjusting reading attitudes and procedures to different purposes. A few sample items will indicate here the sort of thing a teacher may prepare in quantity.

1. A sample perception exercise at the high-first-grade level might be in the following form:

[19] Mabel Snedaker and Ernest Horn, "Reading in the Various Fields of the Curriculum," *The Teaching of Reading: A Second Report,* Thirty-sixth Yearbook, Part I, Chap. 5, pp. 164-182, National Society for Study of Education, Public School Publishing Co., Bloomington, Ill., 1937.

[20] William S. Gray, "The Measurement of Understanding in the Language Arts: The Receptive Language Arts," *The Measurement of Understanding,* Forty-fifth Yearbook, Part I, pp. 189-200, National Society for Study of Education, University of Chicago Press, Chicago, 1946.

Tell the children that on the left of each sentence there is a small word, and ask them to find in the sentence a larger word that contains the small word and draw a line under it.

it	Let's sit down here.
and	Children play in the sand.
old	Mother told Ben a story.
eat	Uncle Harry plants wheat on his farm.
	Etc.

2. A perception exercise which requires association of meaning may be in the following form:

Ask the group to mark out the word that does not belong in each sentence:

1. We think
thank him for the toy.
2. The noise
nose came from the tractor.
3. Their faster
father is a painter.

Etc.

3. A comprehension exercise which goes beyond specific facts and tests ability to draw conclusions may be in the following form:

Father has three long poles. One little one is for Mary. Another little one is for Jack. The biggest pole is for Father. When they are all ready, they will go to the brook.	What will they do there? _____ get wet _____ get fish _____ get sand
The farmer started his tractor. He drove it up and down. He put corn in the warm, wet ground. The sun and rain helped the farmer.	What will grow in the field? _____ nothing at all _____ green apples _____ little corn plants

4. A comprehension exercise which requires both grasp of the main idea and reading for details may be in the following form:

Read the following paragraphs as quickly and carefully as you can and answer the questions after each. When you have finished one set of questions, go right on to the next paragraph.

Africa is the only continent in which the wild ostrich, producer of beautiful plumes, still flourishes. Here, in solitary waste lands, they often live in companies of four or five. Several ostrich hens lay their eggs in one and the same nest, a shallow pit scraped out by their feet, with the earth heaped round to form a kind of wall against which the outermost circle of eggs rests. After ten or a dozen eggs are laid, the ostriches take turns sitting on them; but this is to protect them from small animals rather than to hatch them, for that is sometimes left wholly to the sun. Some thirty eggs are laid in the nest, and around it are scattered perhaps as many more. These last are broken by the old birds for the newly hatched chicks whose stomachs cannot bear the hard food on which their parents thrive. The older birds are watchful of their young. The greatest care is taken to place the nest where it may not be discovered and the birds avoid being seen when going to or from it.

1. The best title for this paragraph is
   a. The value of the ostrich.
   b. How ostriches hatch their chicks.
   c. The cunning of the ostrich.
2. Ostriches sit on the eggs
   a. To keep them warm.
   b. To hatch the eggs.
   c. To guard them from small animals.
3. The ostrich chicks eat
   a. The same food as the old birds.
   b. Ostrich eggs that have been broken.
   c. The worms and bugs the old birds bring them.

5. Comprehension exercises which require critical reading abilities may be in several different forms:

a. "I am going to write a sentence about our story on the chalkboard but one idea in it is wrong. Find the word or words that are wrong and tell why they are wrong."
e.g. "The forest seemed dark, cheerful and gloomy to Ted. He began to feel afraid."

b. "Bill always liked to go to Blue Pond with his father and mother. They would have a ride in the car. They would stop at the side of the pond. Father and Bill liked to fish. They would all have lunch on the grass. It was a party for everyone.

(1) The party was most probably
   _____ in the city
   _____ out in the country
   _____ in an old house
   _____ in their back yard (correct and incorrect inferences)

(2) To go to the Blue Pond father had to
   _____ drive a car
   _____ bring a lunch
   _____ own a fishing pole
   _____ sit on the grass (related and unrelated facts)

(3) We know for sure that
_____ there are fish in Blue Pond
_____ Bill rode in a boat on Blue Pond
_____ Bill sometimes took a friend to the party
_____ Bill ate lunch in the grass (distinguishing facts and opinions)

6. Skills and competences in obtaining information and using the library may be measured as in the following exercises given a fifth grade.[21]

FIFTH-GRADE TEST ON THE USE OF A CARD CATALOGUE IN ONE SCHOOL

PART ONE. In what drawer should you find the following titles, authors, or subjects?

1. Westward movement ....
2. South America ....
3. Pirates ....
4. Louisa M. Alcott ....
5. Dr. Doolittle ....
6. The Prince and the Pauper ....
7. A Book of Americans ....

A–B	H–K	R
C–D	L–M	S
E–G	N–P	T–Z

PART TWO. Supply the missing parts in the following list:

AUTHORS	TITLES	SUBJECTS	CALL NUMBER
1. Gág, Wanda	....	....	....
2.	Davy Crockett	....	....
3. McGuire, Edna	....	....	930 M
4.	Children in Other Lands	....	....
5.	New Nations	....	....
6. Chadwick, George	....	....	784 C
7.	Stop, Look, Listen	....	....
8. Carpenter, Frances	....	....	....
9. Wright, Anna Marie	....	Horses	....
10. Beals, Frank L.	....	....	....
11.	....	Cities and Towns	....
12. Anderson, C. W.	....	....	....

PART THREE. Find an author and book title from the following number hints. You will want to find the books on the shelf by looking for the call number.

1. 973
M
2. 629.1
F
3. 910.2.
B
4. 822
M

[21] Developed by Mary Louise White, student teacher in Glenview School, Oakland, Calif.

FIFTH-GRADE TEST ON THE USE OF A SCHOOL LIBRARY

Library Test

Answer all the parts of the test. If you don't know one answer, go on to the next question.

PART ONE. Mark the following questions either true or false.

1. Nonfiction books do not have a call number. _____
2. Fiction books do not have a call number. _____
3. This number (780) is a call number. _____
4. This number $\begin{pmatrix} 620 \\ \text{A} \end{pmatrix}$ is a call number. _____
5. Fiction books are arranged on the shelves by the authors' names. ___
6. Nonfiction books are arranged on the shelves by the call numbers. _____

PART TWO

1. What will be on the first line of an author card in the card catalogue? _____
2. Title cards will have what on the first line? _____
3. What will subject cards have on the first line? _____
4. Where will the index cards have the call number? In what corner of the card will it be? _____
5. What system of classification do we use in the library to help us to arrange the books? _____
6. What are the outside guides of the card catalogue? _____
7. What are the inside guides of the card catalogue? _____
8. What letter of the alphabet should you find the book *A Child's History of Art* listed under in the card catalogue? _____ What would *The Prince and the Pauper* be under? _____
9. Do we use the author's first name or last name when we look it up in the card catalogue? _____
10. Can you check a book out of the library if you haven't a library card? _____

PART THREE. Write down the two cards that these inside guides will be between. Find the card just in front, and the one just behind these:

1. .... Animal Life ....
2. .... Storytelling ....

These examples of teacher-made perception, comprehension, and work-type tests are only limited samples in an almost unlimited area. Ordinarily, they can be used as teaching devices and as measures to supplement an evaluation made by a standardized test.

In the use of both teacher-made and standardized reading tests the important thing is not a total score or test result but the way the information from the tests is used. To say that a pupil had fourteen items out of twenty items correct on the teacher-made tests for one week, or that he had a reading grade of 4.2 on a standardized test, does not give much information about the child's reading. Actually, the teacher is concerned about the type of reading the child does easily and the tasks he misses. She wants to know how a word-recognition score compares with a score on understanding the general idea of a paragraph. She wants to know how ability to use library resources compares with ability to read for details. In other words, the diagnostic value of a test is usually its chief value. Most manuals accompanying standardized reading tests give considerable help to the teacher in using the test for a diagnosis of the individual's or the group's reading abilities. These should be studied carefully by the teacher, because they give hints not only for the use of the standardized test but for teacher-made tests. The topic is also considered carefully in the general books on tests and measurements mentioned above (see page 545).

Informal Inventories

As suggested above, standardized tests and teacher-made tests may be considered in evaluating pupil growth in reading. In actual practice teachers who can give time to individual pulpits, and especially to those in difficulty, combine test results with other data obtained in an informal inventory of reading habits, skills and attitudes. These data may be obtained in such steps as those outlined for the remedial case in Chapter 15 or as described in Robinson's[22] account of clinical procedures, with regard for limitations of time and staff. Such an inventory may include: (1) Reading in a group of basal readers or other graded materials, (2) check on sight vocabulary using lists such as Dolch's 220 words, (3) appraisal of abilities to use phonetic and structural analysis, (4) special interests including reading. Some teachers try to make informal estimates of a pupil's reading needs throughout the school year, not just at testing time. This may occur when a child enters a class midway in the school year or when the teacher is puzzled by an individual's lack of progress. Betts[23] and

[22] Helen M. Robinson, "Clinical Procedures in Diagnosing Seriously Retarded Readers," in W. S. Gray and Nancy Larrick, eds., *Better Readers for Our Times*, pp. 152-156. Scholastic Magazines, New York, 1956.

[23] Emmett A. Betts, *Informal Inventory Form B1*. Betts Reading Clinic, Haverford, Pa.

others have given suggestions for practical study of an individual pupil. For example, the chart below suggests an outline for a teacher to follow in an individual interview using materials at hand in most classrooms.

Most teachers analyse and correct errors every day as different children read orally. To make a record of errors, so that gains may be

Informal Reading Inventory

Name________________ Age____ Grade____ Date____________

A. Preliminary questions (subjects liked best and least; current reading; pupil description of reading problems, etc.)

B. Word Recognition:

Test used________________ Score timed____ Score untimed____

Difficult words:

Typical errors:

Analysis techniques:

C. Comprehension:

Reading Series____________. Level achieved: Independent:

________________(pre-primer, primer, third reader, etc.

Level achieved: Instructional:________________

1. Main idea:

2. Sequence:

3. Details:

4. Critical thinking:

5. Drawing conclusions:

noted at some later time, a teacher may use a mimeographed paragraph or selection and actually record errors as the pupil makes them. These should be recorded directly on the sheet, as follows:

1. Underline any whole word mispronounced and write in the attempt above, as

trick
tip

2. Underline part of a word mispronounced and write in above to show the wrong part, as

small
smile

3. Draw a circle around an omitted word or words, as

(was)

4. Draw a circle around part of a word omitted, as

play(ing)

5. Write in R in front of the first word repeated and continue it under any more repeated words, as

R Once again we

6. Draw a caret and note any word inserted, as

the
I like ^ meat

With very little practice a teacher can develop a system of marking such errors quickly, as a pupil reads. In marking such errors she will find that mispronunciations and omissions are normally much more frequent than repetitions or insertions. By asking the pupil to read the same mimeographed selection after a period of time, the teacher can note whether errors have been reduced, and has one evaluative measure of progress in oral reading.

Reports to Parents

Reports to parents are an example of periodic evaluation rather than the day-by-day evaluation included in teaching. Ideally the periodic evaluation should sum up the teacher's continuous evaluations over the preceding weeks or months. For that reason most teachers can make a more accurate estimate of a child's progress if they keep some sort of record of it, perhaps with the assistance of the child himself. Too much record-keeping may become burdensome for any teacher, but a few simple measures are indispensable to accurate evaluation for a report card or similar occasion. Some teachers keep a short check list of items for each pupil, such as the lists illustrated in earlier chapters for reading readiness and for speech characteristics of a child. Others use a system of anecdotal records and every day drop into the files of two or three pupils notes of a sentence or two about changes in their behavior. Such a note may read: "Jack seemed bored today with the stories in the second reader. Is he ready to read more difficult material?" Other teachers have children keep their own records of books read and their reactions to them and consult these records occasionally. Out of such sources of information the teacher is ready to give a more comprehensive evaluation of a child's reading than she would be able to do on the basis of a single test result.

Probably the best report to a parent can be made in a personal interview. Certainly the teacher should occasionally meet with parents of children who are making good progress, as well as parents of children who are having difficulties. Suggestions for parent-teacher conferences are given in Chapter 17. Since such interviews are time-consuming, most schools also use some sort of report to parents of the child's progress. The older type of report, which gave a letter or percentage grade for reading, did not convey much meaning to either parent or child. To say that a child gets *C* or *Satisfactory* on reading gives the parent and child no hint for possible improvement. Where teachers can get some stenographic help, evaluation is more accurate and comprehensive in the form of a short paragraph to the parent, built up from a number of evaluations in preceding weeks or months. A note reporting to parents about a fourth-grade boy may read as follows:

> James shows progress in his reading since the last report. He is beginning to read more quickly and can work out many of the new words he meets, so that he is in the stage of becoming an independent reader. He still feels insecure about his oral reading and does not like to read to the rest of his group. A few opportunities to read orally at home from books he knows well might increase his confidence in oral reading. His progress toward independent reading is shown in his increasing competence in work-type reading exercises practiced in school.

Such a report includes more than basic reading abilities, but concentrates somewhat on that area. Combined with standardized and teacher-made tests, observation of functional reading in the content fields, an occasional measure of speed of reading in the upper grades, and study of independence and differentiation in reading abilities, reports may be a part of a modern program of evaluation of reading skills and abilities.

Results or Effects of Reading

As suggested in Chapter 13, the modern teacher of reading asks not only, "What is Johnny doing in reading?" but also, "What is reading doing to Johnny?" The program of evaluation in reading, accordingly, is concerned not only with a child's growth in reading interests and abilities but also with the results or effects of reading on his total personality development. The eminent conductor, Bruno Walter, has said, "I am certain there is a fierce strength to be derived from music." Can similar strengths result from reading?

Attempts to measure the influence of reading on personality are of recent origin. As long as there have been schools, good teachers have attempted to influence youth's ideas and conduct through the literature they read; but only in recent years have teachers and other curriculum workers regularly included this aim in statements of reading objectives. The general objectives of modern reading programs give in Chapter 5 include such goals as developing attitudes associated with good citizenship and worthy character and extending and enriching children's experiences of living in the modern world. Wise teachers make these general aims more specific by attempting to give the child emotional outlets in reading, by giving him opportunities to identify himself with certain characters in stories he reads, and by providing experiences in which he may study the ethical ideas and values contained in good literature. The study of possible changes in the child along these lines is still in its beginning stages. Nevertheless, there is a trend today toward what Smith[24] called "the measurement of more dynamic outcomes in terms of human behavior and the development of personality."

In her summary of evaluation procedures in English, Smith listed nine bases of evaluation, at least six of which are concerned with the effects of English programs on pupils. These are equally applicable as bases for an evaluation program concerned with the results or effects of reading:

1. Ways of thinking demonstrated in the pupils' approach to everyday problems

[24] Dora V. Smith, "Recent Procedures in the Evaluation of Programs in English," *Journal of Educational Research,* Vol. 38, pp. 262-275, December, 1944.

2. Understandings and insights in regard to themselves and to society, demonstrated in the pupils' social behavior
3. The amount and nature of the knowledge gained and used by pupils in an attack upon personal and social problems
4. The degree of personal initiative and creative power revealed in pupil behavior
5. The character and intensity of the personal and social attitudes and beliefs with which the pupils leave school
6. The quality of the pupils' social behavior through which they demonstrate the sincerity and potency of their attitudes and beliefs

These bases may be translated into criteria whereby a teacher or committee can evaluate a certain reading program. Some progress has been made in devising methods and techniques for such evaluation, but the objective evaluation of these outcomes is today a major challenge to teachers and other curriculum workers. There is a tremendous need for better measures of adjustment, attitudes, values, and creative abilities. Such evaluative measures as have been used successfully are generally observation techniques of social behavior and the various personality measures. A short list follows, indicating how some of these measures of personality adjustment may be used in relation to the reading program.

1. *Observation.* Since other instruments for evaluation of children's adjustments and attitudes are not fully developed, a teacher must rely upon her observations of children's behavior to a considerable extent. This procedure, particularly if the teacher is checking some specific behaviors, has the advantage of direct study of the child. Some teachers gain insight into a child's interests and personality by observing the kinds of books he habitually chooses in voluntary reading periods. Teachers can note too the extent to which a child relies on his reading for his information or as a guide to action. Many teachers, in their leadership of a discussion group, encourage children to make ideas from books or other sources a part of their own thinking.

Some teachers go further and plan reading for the group or the individual in terms of certain expressed needs. As the teacher evaluates the social development and organization of her class, she may note a few children who seem out of place or who are not accepted by the rest of the group.[25] Such social difficulties may be deep-rooted,

[25] N. E. Gronkind, *Sociometry in the Classroom.* Harper, New York, 1959.

but many teachers can get a group to accept a stranger or to appreciate differences by reading to or with them a story in which such acceptance takes place. For example, in Lavinia Davis's *Americans Every One* the group may read of how another class accepted a foreign-born child, with different clothes and abilities, as an important member of their group. Lois Lenski's *Judy's Journey,* in her regional America series, may help some children in settled, comfortable homes to accept the children of itinerant workers who may come to their school or community. In using books to influence children's social attitudes and adjustments, the teacher will have to rely considerably on her observation of behavior in the classroom and on the playground.

2. *Personality Tests.* Many so-called personality tests measure only a few phases of adjustment, and it is doubtful if any simple paper-and-pencil test can be considered an adequate test of a child's total personality. The use of a personality test to measure effects or results of reading is accordingly considered at best an experimental undertaking. The range of personality tests is so great that teachers or curriculum workers need to study them carefully before using them with a group.[26] The typical paper-and-pencil test asks the pupil to answer questions concerning how he feels about himself or others; for example, "Do you like to meet new people?" or "Do your friends and classmates often want to help you?" Teachers going over these items not only get some general measures, such as "self-adjustment" and "social adjustment"[27] but, with their other knowledge of the child, gain considerable insight from answers to specific questions. After an initial test reveals a child's difficulties along certain lines, the teacher may plan reading experiences calculated to help the child in these areas. Reading experiences reinforced by other activities in home, school, or community may have greater effects than isolated reading. At a later date a second use of the test will help in evaluating the success of these reading experiences in influencing the child's adjustment scores. If the teacher can call upon psychological services, she may occasionally be able to study the relationships of reading to the results of other tests of personality.[28]

[26] Oscar K. Buros, *op. cit.*

[27] L. P. Thorpe, E. W. Tiegs, and W. W. Clark, *California Test of Personality—Elementary*. California Test Bureau, Los Angeles, 1953.

[28] H. H. Renemers and R. H. Bauernfeind, *SRA Junior Inventory*. Science Research Associates, Chicago, 1955. Harold H. Anderson, and G. L. Anderson, *An Introduction to Projective Techniques*. Prentice-Hall, Englewood Cliffs, N.J., 1951.

3. *Case Studies.* Case studies are more comprehensive investigations of the child's personality than observation or personality tests and, indeed, may include these as part of the attempt to make the broader study. Usually a number of persons, such as the parents, the child himself, a physician, a psychologist, and a social worker or visitor to the home, can contribute information to the teacher or evaluation committee making the case study. These persons or a group of teachers who know the child may pool their findings in a case conference. Troyer and Horrocks[29] prepared materials which help to evaluate ability to make diagnoses and select appropriate remedial activities when presented with data in case-study form.

Teachers and others who have ability and experience in making case studies will find in them a means of intensive evaluation not possible in any other single method. Case studies involve considerable time and effort for the teacher to attempt alone but may vary in completeness. When the data of the study are collected, they may be interpreted to apply to other phases of the child's behavior in addition to his reading activities. In connection with reading they are used most frequently in work with a severely retarded reader (see Chapter 15), but a school staff may find it valuable to combine efforts in a case study of an average reader or gifted reader as well. The rather intensive study of one child will give evidence of the effectiveness of the usual reading program or changes in it only for that one child. Within these limits it is the most comprehensive of the methods of evaluation discussed in this chapter.

4. *Anecdotal Records.* As suggested in the opening example of this chapter, a series of informal notes about a pupil's behavior, particularly in reading situations, will often throw light on his personality in relation to reading. Suggestions for using anecdotal records have been made by Randall,[30] Brown and Martin,[31] Ellingson,[32] and others. In general, such notes describe a specific happening in which a child is involved rather than give the teacher's opinion about his attitudes or behavior. For example, one teacher's note said, "John

29 Maurice E. Troyer and John Horrocks, *Evaluating Knowledge and Understanding of Human Growth and Development.* Syracuse University Press, Syracuse, 1947.

30 John A. Randall, "The Anecdotal Behavior Journal," *Progressive Education,* Vol. 13, pp. 21-26, January, 1936.

31 Marion A. Brown and Vibella Martin, "Anecdotal Records of Pupil Behavior," *California Journal of Secondary Education,* Vol. 13, pp. 205-208, April, 1938.

32 Mark Ellingson and Lawrence L. Jarvis, *A Handbook on the Anecdotal Behavior Journal.* University of Chicago Press, Chicago, 1940.

volunteered to read to his group for the first time today." Another teacher noted: "Shirley did well in getting a general impression of the story, but had some details wrong. She would not try to work out any of the new words in the story by herself. More help in word recognition techniques?" A series of notes on concrete situations such as these will build up, over a period of time, some data which often give considerable insight into a pupil's adjustments, particularly in relation to the different reading situations.

5. *Cumulative Records.* The above four methods of studying personality are usually more effective if their results are collected and accumulated in usable form. Suggestions for the use of such records have been made in a number of books on guidance, such as those of Strang[33] and in various other articles and handbooks.[34] The folders or files used should accumulate for each child not only records of physical and mental development but notes on special interests, aptitudes, and needs. They should include copies of reports to parents and notes on conferences with them. Also valuable are summaries of development by teachers, and possibly parents and children themselves, added year by year. Including such data as these, the cumulative record gives a long-term picture of behavior and personality which cannot be obtained in other ways. As such, it is much more valuable than measures applied at one specific testing period and then discontinued. The time spent on compiling adequate records is considerable. Teachers, principals, and other school people need to achieve an appropriate balance between time spent in keeping records and time spent in using them to help the child.

The test of adequate use applies equally to all the five measures of personality described above. In other words, there is no value in studying the personality and adjustments of children unless the facts obtained are used to overcome difficulties and bring about more wholesome development. The reading program is one area in which such aid can be given, but general prescriptions are impossible be-

33 Ruth M. Strang, *An Introduction to Child Study,* 4th ed. Macmillan, New York, 1959. Ruth M. Strang, *The Role of the Teacher in Personnel Work,* 4th ed. Bureau of Publications, Teachers College, Columbia University, New York, 1953.

34 *California Cumulative Guidance Record for Elementary Schools.* A Carlisle & Co., San Francisco, no date. See also Alvin E. Rhodes, "The California Cumulative Guidance Record for Elementary Schools," *Educational Leadership,* Vol. 2, pp. 300-302, April, 1945. Mildred L. Fisher, "The Cumulative Record as a Factor in Guidance," *Journal of Educational Sociology,* Vol. 5, pp. 344-358, February, 1932. National Committee on Cumulative Records, *Handbook of Cumulative Records,* Bulletin 1944, No. 5. United States Government Printing Office, Washington, D.C., 1944.

cause individual children react to reading situations in very different ways.

In a negative sense, the close relationship between reading and personality has been established in a number of studies which show that reading disabilities and personality difficulties are usually closely associated. Summaries of such studies have been made by Gates,[35] Russell,[36] Wilking,[37] and others. Gates came to such conclusions as the following:

1. There is no single personality pattern among pupils of adequate intelligence which is characteristic of reading failure.
2. Personality maladjustments do not always lead to reading maladjustment. In certain cases a given cause may produce directly opposite effects. For example, sibling rivalry may help to produce a poor or a good reader.
3. Symptoms such as nervousness, withdrawal, aggression, or chronic worry may appear when the maladjustment is the cause, the concomitant, or the result of reading disability.

On the more positive side the evidence is not so clear in regard to the relationships between good personality adjustments and reading habits and competences. In one summary it is pointed out that some emotional difficulties can be prevented.

Since many case studies of retarded readers reveal crucial points in the child's school history at which difficulties seem to multiply, teachers are increasingly aware of the importance of continuous evaluation of the child's progress and the desirability of preventive measures in the form of careful adjustment of instruction to each child's abilities and needs. Some emotional difficulties can be prevented by thorough knowledge of a child and adapting methods and materials in reading to his current developmental status.[38]

Even more positively the constructive effects of reading have been used by some teachers. The following quotation indicates that only a beginning has been made in this field.

Teachers and research workers are just beginning to study seriously the positive upbuilding effects of certain reading and language experi-

[35] Arthur I. Gates, "The Role of Personality Maladjustment in Reading Disability," *Pedagogical Seminary*, Vol. 59, pp. 77-83, September, 1941.

[36] David H. Russell, "Reading Disabilities and Mental Health: A Review of Research," *Understanding the Child*, Vol. 16, pp. 24-32, January, 1947.

[37] S. Vincent Wilking, "Personality Maladjustment as a Causative Factor in Reading Disability," *Elementary School Journal*, Vol. 42, pp. 268-279, December, 1941.

[38] David H. Russell, *op. cit.*

ences on children. Although research has just been started in the field of bibliotherapy, many teachers have accumulated a collection of books and stories which not only are enjoyed by their pupils but seem to make positive contributions to their personality development and mental health.[39]

Mention has already been made in previous chapters of pioneer attempts to group books according to the themes they illustrate for boys and girls. In helping an individual child or adolescent it may be hypothesized that reading a collection of books or series of stories illustrating such themes as courage or desirable family relationships may be more effective than a single exposure. Thus teachers use "ladders" or thematic units to influence groups or individuals. Sometimes these may be most effectively used in groups, because group dynamics may develop more solutions to problems and heighten emotional or appreciative response.[40] Furthermore, an individual child, reading for recreation, may stop at the surface level of literal comprehension and may need the support of teacher and group in going below the surface to the level of interpretive reading. Certainly there is a place for pure enjoyment, and not all reading must have a "moral," but the experienced and mature teacher is the one who can help the child or adolescent look for more fundamental ideas and human values.

Examples of reading at different levels, or depths, may be given from well-known books. *Tom Sawyer* may be read as a story of a boy growing up on the Mississippi years ago, or it may illustrate a more universal theme, experienced by all of us, of conflict between rectitude (illustrated by Aunt Polly) and the disreputable (symbolized by Huck Finn). *Little Women* may be read at one level as a story of a family, at a deeper level of problems of growing up, and at a still deeper level of respect for individual differences. Esther Forbes' *Johnny Tremain* may be read by the junior high school pupil as an exciting story of Revolutionary times, as the efforts of one boy to overcome some physical and personality difficulties, or as a study of growth from a self-centered boy to a mature person accepting himself, concerned with others, and helping build a world in which anyone could "stand up" in human dignity. A simple story in the

[39] *Ibid.*

[40] Harold H. Kelley and John W. Thibaut, "Experimental Studies of Group Problem Solving and Process," in G. Lindzey, ed., *Handbook of Social Psychology*, Vol. 2. Addison-Wesley, Reading, Mass., 1954.

primer may be an account of a trip to the airport, or it may go into the feelings of a family as they return to their own home. A third-reader poem may be a child-like experience, or it may touch on one or two human values such as friendship, love, or accepting differences. There is little doubt that stories and books will illustrate these and other themes for most adults and some children. It is very doubtful, however, if they will mean the same thing to all children. As suggested in the discussion of children's literature in Chapter 13, reaction to a piece of literature is a very individual thing. Undoubtedly, children bring their own particular experiences and personality to the interpretation of a story or other selection. No one selection or book can mean the same thing to all children.

On the other hand, if a teacher knows a child's background and personality, she is better equipped to estimate the effect of a particular book on him. In her class she has probably discovered a number of different personality patterns in relation to reading. In a typical fifth grade she will discover an active, sports-loving boy who just hasn't time to read very much. Only a few seats from him will be a more introverted boy, perhaps small for his age, who uses reading as an escape from some of the rigors of the playground. In the same class is a timid, insecure girl who reads a great many stories of home and school life on a rather immature level. Not far from her is a somewhat average girl for the class, already developing adolescent interests in boys, and reading, when she does read, so-called adult novels of romance. Only as she knows about these diverse personalities and can refer to a wide range of children's books can a teacher use reading as a positive upbuilding force in personality and character development.

CO-OPERATIVE EVALUATION PROGRAMS IN ACTION

This chapter has already referred to a number of actual programs which evaluate growth in reading. Smith's[41] comprehensive summary of methods of evaluating development in English applies equally to reading in evaluation of mastery of basic skills, ways of thinking, personal and social attitudes and beliefs, interests, and knowledge

[41] Dora V. Smith, "Recent Procedures in the Evaluation of Programs in English," *Journal of Educational Research,* Vol. 38, pp. 262-275, December, 1944.

acquired. Wrightstone's pioneer study,[42] applying new methods of evaluation to experimental and conventional schools, included both the usual standardized tests of reading and tests of obtaining facts, drawing conclusions, and applying generalizations. He followed this investigation with further reports of progress in developing evaluative measures, including the program used in a large-scale experiment comparing traditional and activity schools in New York City.[43] This book emphasizes evaluation of differing needs of individual pupils and their educational guidance, but evaluation may also be considered as appraisal of a total school program.

Programs of overall evaluation of school systems usually include some study of the reading program. From the system-wide point of view, the evaluation program desired by pupils, parents, teachers, and administrators has at least four characteristics:

(1) It is comprehensive from the point of view of both the learner and the curriculum.

(2) It is continuous and well-articulated from kindergarten through junior college.

(3) It is functional and practical for the persons engaging in it.

(4) It utilizes an integrated group of scientific and informal measuring instruments.

Suggestions for such programs which emphasize the role of the teacher have been made by Baron and Bernard,[44] by Rothney[45] and by Wrightstone.[46] A useful summary of twelve characteristics of a good evaluation program has been offered by Boykin.[47] These and other sources suggest that many factors operate to affect children's achievement in reading and other areas. The point that an evaluation program must be comprehensive is illustrated in the chart on page

[42] J. Wayne Wrightstone, *Appraisal of Newer Elementary School Practices,* Bureau of Publications, Teachers College, Columbia University, New York, 1938.

[43] J. Wayne Wrightstone, "Evaluation of the Experiment with the Activity Program in the New York City Elementary Schools," *Journal of Educational Research,* Vol. 38, pp. 252-257, December, 1944.

[44] D. Baron and H. W. Bernard, *Evaluation Techniques for Classroom Teachers.* McGraw-Hill, New York, 1958.

[45] J. W. M. Rothney, *Evaluating and Reporting Pupil Progress,* What Research Says to the Teacher, No. 7. National Education Association, Washington, D.C., 1955.

[46] J. W. Wrightstone, *op. cit.*

[47] L. L. Boykin, "What Is Evaluation?" *Journal of Educational Research,* Vol. 51, pp. 529-534, March, 1958.

565. The wide variety of factors affecting reading achievement makes it imperative that much more than a standardized reading test be used in evaluating strengths and weaknesses, failures and successes in the reading program.

More specific helps for evaluation procedures in elementary schools have been recorded in various articles such as those of Kottmeyer,[48] McIntire,[49] and Herrick.[50] Rasschaert[51] described a curriculum improvement project in the language arts at the junior-high-school level, which utilized action research and a work-group-conference approach. Kottmeyer gave an example of a testing program in a large city system followed by better adjustment of teaching to individual reading abilities. McIntire stressed the need for evaluation of readiness, for developing purpose, and for using follow-up materials in the social studies. She gave a list of questions by means of which pupils may be encouraged to evaluate their own reading in the social studies.

1. Can I pick out the most important ideas from what I read?
2. Can I tell why they are important?
3. Can I find information about these ideas in other books and materials?
4. Can I use an index to help me to find the information quickly?
5. Can I help myself in learning how to pronounce new words and in learning what they mean?
6. Do I understand better when I reread?
7. Can I get information from maps and globes?
8. Do I try to read the stories the pictures tell?
9. Do I read different kinds of materials in different ways?
10. Am I improving my ability to state understandings?

Herrick suggested six factors in developing an adequate program of evaluation:

1. "The essential focus . . . is on the reading behavior of the learner."
2. The broad range of objectives of a reading program necessitates a broad-gauge evaluation program.

[48] William Kottmeyer, "Improving Reading Instruction in the St. Louis Schools," *Elementary School Journal,* Vol. 45, pp. 33-38, September, 1944.

[49] Alta McIntire, "Reading Social Studies Materials in the Middle Grades," *Elementary English Review,* Vol. 21, pp. 262-266, November, 1944.

[50] Virgil E. Herrick, "Purposes and Needs for an Evaluation Program in Reading," in H. M. Robinson, ed., *Evaluation of Reading,* Supplementary Educational Monographs, No. 88. University of Chicago Press, Chicago, 1958.

[51] William M. Rasschaert, "A Descriptive Analysis of a Departmental Curriculum Improvement Project in an Urban Junior High School," *Journal of Experimental Education,* Vol. 27, pp. 36-48, September, 1958.

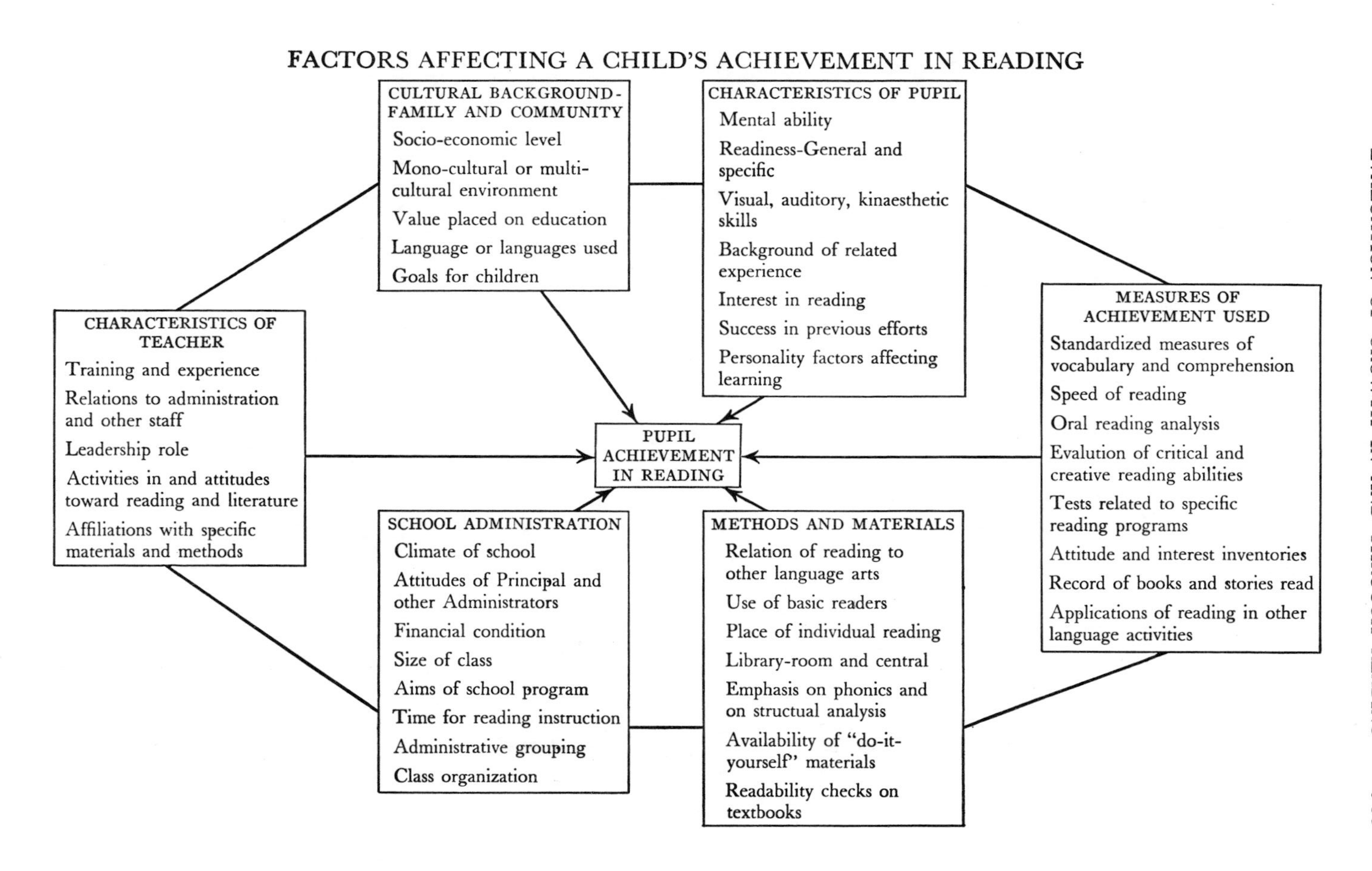

FACTORS AFFECTING A CHILD'S ACHIEVEMENT IN READING

3. An evaluation program is made more valid and accessible by "careful selection of what to observe, more consistent and dependable observations, better records of observations, the use of a broader range of observational situations and devices, and better analysis and interpretations of observations."
4. Evaluation is more meaningful if it is recognized that the *same* reading behavior can be evaluated on different bases involving different values.
5. The role of the learner as the evaluator should be strengthened—he puts the results of evaluation into action.
6. "Evaluation is an integral part of all school learning and a necessary part of teaching."

Evaluation programs such as the samples mentioned are one of the most useful means of in-service education. The teacher who wishes to improve her professional competence, or the school administrator who desires to raise the general level of educational service in a school system will find that participation in an evaluation program can do much to realize these aims. An in-service program should include a number of other activities, such as orientation workshops, demonstration teaching, use of professional library, studying community resources, and conferences with specialists,[52] but experience suggests that an evaluation program is one of the best single methods of obtaining higher teacher morale and competence. Evaluation of the reading program may increase teachers' objectivity in studying their own methods. Evaluation offers opportunity for making new ideas in the teaching of reading available through co-operative sharing of experience. It lays the groundwork for a better course of study or curriculum guide by clarifying objectives and the means by which these are reached in reading instruction. It focuses attention on the study of children and ways in which their individual needs in reading can be met. It provides a ready route for the co-ordination of the work of the different personnel in a school system. Thus it improves the reading abilities of boys and girls and makes them better members of a democratic society and an interdependent world.

SUPPLEMENTARY READINGS

Adkins, D. C. "Measurement in Relation to the Educational Process," *Educational and Psychological Measurement,* Vol. 18, pp. 221-240, 1958.

[52] *In-Service Education,* Fifty-sixth Yearbook, Part I, National Society for Study of Education, University of Chicago Press, Chicago, 1957.

AHMANN, J. S., and GLOCK, M. D. *Evaluating Pupil Growth.* Allyn and Bacon, Englewood Cliffs, N.J., 1959.

BOND, GUY L., and WAGNER, EVA B. *Teaching the Child to Read,* 3rd ed., Chap. 16. Macmillan, New York, 1960.

BUREAU OF CURRICULUM RESEARCH. *Evaluation: A Memorandum for Curriculum Workers.* Board of Education, New York City, Curriculum Center, April, 1959.

BUREAU OF EDUCATION RESEARCH. *Evaluating Pupil Progress: 1960 Edition.* California State Department of Education, Sacramento, 1960.

COOK, W. W. "Evaluation in the Language Arts Program," *Teaching Language in the Elementary School,* Forty-third Yearbook, Part II, pp. 194-214, National Society for Study of Education. University of Chicago Press, Chicago, 1944.

GATES, ARTHUR I. *The Improvement of Reading,* 3rd ed. Macmillan, New York, 1947.

GATES, ARTHUR I. "The Measurement and Evaluation of Achievement in Reading," *The Teaching of Reading: A Second Report,* Thirty-sixth Yearbook, Chap. 12, National Society for Study of Education. Public School Publishing Co., Bloomington, Ill., 1937.

GRAY, W. S., comp. and ed. *The Appraisal of Current Practices in Reading.* Supplementary Educational Monographs, No. 61. University of Chicago Press, Chicago, 1945.

GREENE, H. A.; JORGENSON, A. N.; and GERBERICH, J. R. *Measurement and Evaluation in the Elementary School.* Longmans, Green, New York, 1953.

HAMALAINEN, A. E. "Existing Practices in the Evaluation of Pupil Growth in the Elementary School," *Elementary School Journal,* Vol. 42, pp. 175-183, November, 1941.

HARRIS, ALBERT J. *How to Increase Reading Ability,* 3rd ed. Longmans, Green, New York, 1956.

HERRICK, V. E. "Criteria for Appraising Procedures Used to Promote Reading Development," *Elementary School Journal,* Vol. 46, pp. 191-199, 258-265, December, 1945, January, 1946.

KIRKENDALL, L. A. "Problems of an Evaluation Program," *Educational Administration and Supervision,* Vol. 29, pp. 377-382, September, 1943.

MCKIM, MARGARET G. *Guiding Growth in Reading,* Chap. 13. Macmillan, New York, 1955.

NATIONAL SOCIETY FOR STUDY OF EDUCATION. *The Measurement of Understanding,* Forty-fifth Yearbook, Part I, especially Chap. 9. University of Chicago Press, Chicago, 1946.

OLSON, H. F. "Evaluating Growth in Language Ability," *Journal of Educational Research,* Vol. 39, pp. 241-253, December, 1945.

OLSON, WILLARD C. "Reading as a Function of the Total Growth of the Child," *Reading and Pupil Development,* pp. 233-237. Supplementary Educational Monographs, No. 51. University of Chicago Press, Chicago, 1940.

REMMERS, H. H.; GAGE, N. L.; and RUMMELL, J. F. *A Practical Introduction to Measurement and Evaluation.* Harper, New York, 1960.

RUSSELL, DAVID H. "Evaluation of the Elementary School Program," *California Journal of Elementary Education,* Vol. 13, pp. 183-192, February, 1945.

RUSSELL, DAVID H. "Evaluation of Pupil Growth in and through Reading," *Reading in the Elementary School,* Forty-eighth Yearbook, Part II, Chap. 14, National Society for the Study of Education. University of Chicago Press, Chicago, 1949.

RUSSELL, DAVID H. "Personal Values in Reading," *The Reading Teacher,* Vol. 12, pp. 3-9, October, 1958.

STRANG, RUTH. "Evaluation of Growth In and Through Reading," *Development In and Through Reading,* Sixtieth Yearbook, Chap. 21, National Society for Study of Education. University of Chicago Press, Chicago, 1961.

TABA, HILDA. "Current Evaluation Techniques," *Childhood Education,* Vol. 18, pp. 14-20, September, 1941.

THOMAS, R. MURRAY. *Judging Student Progress,* 2nd ed. Longmans, Green, New York, 1960.

TYLER, R. W. "General Statement on Evaluation," *Journal of Educational Research,* Vol. 35, pp. 492-501, March, 1942.

WRIGHTSTONE, J. W. "Techniques for Measuring Newer Values in Education," *Journal of Educational Research,* Vol. 35, pp. 517-524, March, 1942.

WRIGHTSTONE, J. W.; JUSTMAN, J.; and ROBBINS, I. *Evaluation in Modern Education.* American Book, New York, 1956.

Chapter 17

PARENTS, TEACHERS, AND READING

Parents and teachers are partners in the work of aiding the child's educational development. The day has long since gone when the teacher regarded parents' interest in education as something which interfered with school work, or when the teacher merely ignored the parent. In contrast, the modern teacher knows that much of the child's development comes in his early years and, accordingly, that the influence of the home can be crucial. The teacher knows also that if school and home are pulling the child in opposite directions the school can scarcely ever hope to dominate. Consequently, teachers and school staffs have become more and more interested in what parents want for their children and increasingly concerned in the study of ways teachers and parents can work together to produce the best environments for children's learning.

When this learning is concerned with "academic" matters, such as learning to read, the professionally trained teacher should usually be the senior member in the partnership. The teacher's influence becomes significant only after four or five important years in the child's life, but it is usually the direct stimulus and guide in learning to read. Home, church, playground, and community will have contributed to much other learning, but the unique function of the school is the development of certain intellectual tools and abilities, such as reading. Thus after a child is five or six years old, a teacher or a school staff should usually take the initiative in getting home and school to work together. The day has also gone by when most parents are timid about visiting the school or teacher, but it is still usually necessary for a school person to initiate steps in bringing the two agencies together for the improvement of reading readiness and reading achievements.

Some of the usual ways of communication between school and

home which involve not only reading but all parts of the school's work are as follows:

Parent-teacher conferences
Parent-teacher-pupil conferences
Report cards—with space for home and school comments
Informal reports, with notes on individual progress
Letters or booklets on class activities (see illustration, page 571).
Examples of children's completed work sent home, including books read
Open house for parents' visit to whole school
Demonstrations and visits in one child's room
Parent Teacher Association meetings which help explain the school program
School or class newsletter or newspaper, sent home
Attractive bulletins about reading program sent to parents
Mothers helping as school librarians

The purpose of such communication is not only to inform parents about a child's individual progress or the more general reading program in which he is participating but to give parents a chance to send their ideas to teacher or school. Communication is a two-way process. Parents can often help teachers in understanding a child's present status and current interests, and this information may be useful in planning for his reading level and content. Parents may also submit more general ideas about such topics as reference materials or the school library. Free communication between home and school will ordinarily mean more useful reading activities for the individual child and a better reading program for the whole school.

WHAT PARENTS WANT

Because school people have worked with reading programs for many years they are usually clear in their ideas about the aims of the reading program, especially in the primary grades. Parents, on the other hand, may be often unsure of their role and the school program, particularly if the first child in the family is involved. It is therefore the teacher's job to take the initiative in finding out parents' ideas about their child's reading and other school activities.

Dear Parents:

We hope you will enjoy reading over our little diary with your child. It tells about some of the happenings in Room 7 during the year.

We had many many activities and really enjoyed "learning together."

We hope you have a very happy summer.

Sincerely,

Second Grade

Juanita Poppe

Teacher

FEBRUARY

We made valentines and had a party.

We read stories about Abraham Lincoln and George Washington.

We walked to the pet shop and got two turtles. We took care of the turtles and when they started to hibernate, Mrs. Poppe took them home.

We learned about our "shadows." We measured them at different times during the day and found out our shadows change size.

We learned many new songs.

We started writing more of our own stories.

We got new spelling books and started learning how to study spelling.

Two pages of a second-grade diary booklet sent from school to parents (Mrs. Juanita Poppe, teacher, Whittier School, Berkeley, Calif.)

One or two studies illustrate procedures for doing this. For example, McConnell[1] sent an open-ended questionnaire to parents asking them to list from one to five items which they considered "the most important things for the teacher to tell them about their child." The returns from 745 parents of children in grades one, two, and three of the nine schools in a large urban community gave the following items:

Personal and classroom behavior	27 per cent
Academic progress	26 per cent
Social behavior	22 per cent
Home-school relations	13 per cent

McConnell found that parents from different socioeconomic groups asked much the same questions, although there was some tendency for lower class parents to ask about personal and classroom behavior (Is he troublesome? Does he show temper?), and for higher class parents to ask about social behavior (Does he get along with other children? Is he a good sport?). In the area of home-school relations the question most frequently asked was "How can I help at home?" McConnell's technique illustrates one method of finding out what parents want to know as a starting point for initial discussions of home and school people.

Smitter[2] has also listed specific items which parents wish to know about their child's progress in school and has illustrated the importance of knowing parents' wishes for their child's school and later careers. She suggested dangers in a teacher's making judgments about a child's future success and recommends, at least in early interviews, staying closely with observable facts such as "Your boy understands certain number combinations" or "He is reading a book usually read in the second grade." As parent, teacher, and child become better acquainted, the teacher may move to causes, treatment, and prognosis of the child's behavior and learning.

Some research has also been done on the relationships of home conditions to the child's readiness to read and early progress in read-

[1] Gaither McConnell, "What Do Parents Want to Know," *Elementary School Journal*, Vol. 58, pp. 83, 87, November, 1957.

[2] Faith W. Smitter, "What Should Parents Know About Their Child's Progress in School," *California Journal of Elementary Education*, Vol. 24, pp. 112-116, November, 1955. Faith W. Smitter and R. B. Haas, "Parents' Values for Their Children," *California Journal of Elementary Education*, Vol. 23, pp. 217-222, May, 1955.

ing. Undoubtedly, parental attitudes and activities are most influential here, and it may be possible for a principal or teacher to pinpoint some of the home factors which influence further reading development. The study of Almy,[3] mentioned in Chapter 6, emphasizes the positive value of many opportunities for the child to read prior to entering first grade. For example, "Experiences such as looking at books and being read to contribute to a positive relationship between reading success and responses to opportunities for reading. Interest in words, letters and numbers are also important factors in the relationship." A study by Gates and Bond[4] found a lower correlation between reading achievement and a measure of home background than between reading achievement and total readiness test scores. They found a positive relationship, however, between early reading success and the amount of previous instruction in reading at home or in kindergarten. In another study of 133 first-graders Belshaw[5] related home conditions, early test results, and later success in grade one. She found the two highest correlations with reading achievement to be those of readiness test scores ($r = .54$) and home environment ($r = .48$). Another study by Milner[6] related reading readiness to various patterns of parent-child relationships, especially in verbal communication. Superior reading in first grade was associated with a rich verbal family environment, with considerable reading by "a personally important adult," and with many opportunities for positive emotional interaction with parents.

Although parents are often most concerned about their children's reading in the first few years in school, evidence also exists that they have definite opinions about reading instruction in the later years. In one California community Pressnall[7] found in 1955 that four-fifths of the parents were well pleased or satisfied with the reading abilities of their children. Parents were satisfied with group-

3 Millie C. Almy, *Children's Experiences Prior to First Grade and Success in Beginning Reading*. Bureau of Publications, Teachers College, Columbia University, New York, 1949.

4 Arthur I. Gates and Guy L. Bond, "Reading Readiness: A Study of Factors Determining Success and Failure in Beginning Reading," *Teachers College Record*, Vol. 37, pp. 679-685, May, 1936.

5 Marjorie W. Belshaw, *Relationship between Measures of Readiness and Achievement in Reading*. Master's thesis, University of California, Berkeley, 1952.

6 Esther Milner, "A Study of the Relationship between Reading Readiness in Grade One School Children and Patterns of Parent-Child Interaction," *Child Development*, Vol. 22, pp. 95-112, June, 1951.

7 Hugo E. Pressnall, "Parents' Opinions of Reading Instruction," *Elementary English*, Vol. 33, pp. 29-33, January, 1956.

ing methods according to skill in reading. They favored more emphasis on phonic and oral reading and believed that a child whose reading achievement is low should be given an easier book but kept in his own grade. They believed they could best help their children at home by "listening to him read," "helping him recognize and understand difficult words," and "having him sound out words." As expected, Pressnall found somewhat different attitudes to the reading program among parents whose children were successful and those whose children were having some difficulty.

In another study Blitz[8] reported parents' ideas about promotion and grouping policies in relation to reading and other achievements. He found that parents favored a conference by teacher, principal, and parent in placing a retarded pupil, that promotion should be largely by age, that children should be grouped for reading on the basis of a combination of factors, and that grouping should be flexible. Such studies can be profitably repeated in different communities to determine what a certain group of parents believe and recommend for a specific school or school system.

Although adults' opinions may change with changing conditions, the results of a nation-wide poll taken in 1954 by the American Institute of Public Opinion[9] are of interest. The following replies were given by a sample of parents and of adults without children:

1. Do you think the study of reading is more important or less important than other school subjects?

More important	67%	About same	25%
Less important	4%	Undecided	4%

2. If a pupil is having trouble with reading, do you think he should spend extra time catching up, if it means taking time away from other subjects?

Extra time	74%	Undecided	4%
Should not	22%		

3. Instead of grouping pupils according to their scores on intelligence tests some public schools group them according to their skill in each particular subject. Do you think this is a good idea, or a poor idea?

Good idea: 71% Poor idea: 14% Undecided: 15%

4. If your child had trouble learning to read, would you prefer that

[8] Theodore F. Blitz, *Parents' Opinions on Grouping and Promotion.* Master's thesis, University of California, Berkeley, 1957.

[9] "Let the Parents Speak," *Ladies Home Journal,* Vol. 71, pp. 5-7, October, 1954. © 1954 The Curtis Publishing Company.

he study reading with other slow readers, or in a class where most of the other pupils read better and faster?

With slow: 67% With better: 26% Undecided: 7%

5. Do you think very poor readers should be admitted to high school, or should they be kept back until they have caught up in reading?

Thirty-two per cent said they should be kept in school till they reach the legal age limit, as at present. But 72 per cent said a different kind of training program should be provided for such pupils, and another 10 per cent believed they should be released a year or two earlier if they wish. Five per cent were undecided.

These results indicate belief in the importance of reading, and approval of some forms of grouping and of remedial work. Some inconsistency may be noted in the replies to the fourth and fifth questions. Parents approve of grouping their own children who are having difficulty with other slow-learners in reading but favor keeping the poor readers out of high school rather than continuing groups. In other questions the parents also favored non-promotion for pupils who have failed to learn—a device which has not usually proved adequate in careful studies of effects of non-promotion. (See Chapter 13.)

PARENTS AND EARLY LANGUAGE DEVELOPMENT

As outlined in Chapter 3, a child's language development before he enters school is typically enormous and a most important factor in his early progress in reading. The school can rarely hope to influence parents of two- and three-year-olds when language development is so rapid, unless older siblings are in school or a nursery-school liaison is maintained. Some of the activities of this period for which parents can plan have been listed by Schonell[10] as suitable for older subnormal children, but they apply equally to the third and fourth years of normal childhood:

1. Imitating sounds.
2. Naming things in pictures from books and magazines.
3. Giving simple directions which the child carries out without help.
4. Reading from easy, well-illustrated books and then talking over what you have read.
5. Teaching nursery rhymes and songs.

[10] Fred J. Schonell, J. A. Richardson, and Thelma S. McConnel, *The Subnormal Child at Home.* Macmillan, London, 1958.

6. Recognizing by touch and naming familiar articles in a box.
7. Speaking on a toy or real telephone.

Because children learn much language by listening to it attentively, some parents may want to encourage a few simple listening games. Some games and devices suitable for kindergarten and younger children are contained in the booklet, *Listening Aids Through the Grades*.[11] Examples are "Near and Far" (discriminating between noises close and those far away), "What Animal am I?" (associating names with traditional sounds such as "meow," "peep peep," and "chug-a-rug"), and the "Echo Game" (for exact repetition of words).

Other language games and devices may be used at home with young children. A bulletin from school to home concerned with such activities might include brief directions for such games as the following:

Categories: Go round the circle or take turns in naming animals, vegetables, sports, etc., as given by a leader or one who is "It." The person missing becomes "It" and starts a new category.

Rhymes: One person says, "I am thinking of a word that rhymes with pain and is part of our weather." "I am thinking of a word that rhymes with cat and is part of our clothes," etc. Two may play, or a family group, which is even better.

Directions: The adult asks children to listen carefully and then gives directions for doing two or three tasks, which must be performed in the correct order. "Please close the drawer, then carry the plate to the shelf, and then bring me the book. You do these, Jane," etc.

Signs: Older pre-school children may be ready to try recognizing signs such as Danger, Keep to the Right, Men, Women, Stop, and Bus Stop. Realistic copies of signs may be used.

Abstract Words: Older children at home may be ready to practice ideas involving abstract words by applying them to concrete objects which can be moved, lifted, and observed. These words may include: long, short; top, bottom; heavy, light; near, far; left, right, etc.

Charts: Some children will enjoy cutting pictures from magazines and placing them on simple charts. For example, a chart may show

[11] David H. Russell and Elizabeth F. Russell, *Listening Aids Through the Grades*. Bureau of Publications, Teachers College, Columbia University, New York, 1959.

such fruits as apple, orange, banana, pear, etc., with their names printed beside them in manuscript writing.

Besides language games many young children will enjoy playing "School" at home, particularly if they have older siblings to introduce them to certain school routines. Under the direction of the "teacher" the children may engage in drawing, water play, finger painting, simple construction, play with blocks, and other activities. Discussion of these activities will give an opportunity to develop meaningful relations to language usage.

FIRST ADVENTURES WITH BOOKS

Of all the language activities related to reading, experiences with books may be most helpful in developing interest in reading and some beginning skills in using books. An excellent guide for the use of books at all age levels from infancy through early adolescence is Larrick's *A Parent's Guide to Children's Reading*,[12] a result of the co-operation of The National Book Committee and eighteen other organizations representing children, parents, teachers, librarians, and youth organizations. *A Parent's Guide* lists books suitable for different age levels and gives hints on coping with comics and television. It has good chapters on the various kinds of reading, on how to select books for children, and on how reading is taught in most schools. It starts with a list of books for children under four years, classified as nursery rhyme books, bedtime stories, animal stories, and the child's world. Every child and every parent may have other favorites, but here is a good list for parents who have not seen children's books since they were young themselves.

In sharing these "read aloud" books, parents can help build an interest in books, provide sheer pleasure in words and stories, and aid children in understanding what reading means. Many parents encourage children to use words heard in the story, thus extending their vocabularies. Because young children especially learn through activity, many parents encourage children to participate in the story-reading in such ways as pointing out parts of pictures and repeating refrains or phrases as they occur in a classic such as Wanda Gág's *Millions of Cats* or in a modern book such as Margaret Wise Brown's *The Important Book*. Sometimes even young children will repeat

12 Nancy Larrick, *A Parent's Guide to Children's Reading*. Doubleday, Garden City, N.Y., 1958. Also Cardinal edition, Pocket Books, New York, 1958.

animal talk or use part of a well-known story in their dramatic play. Teddy bears become "Pooh" bears and a rabbit toy becomes Peter Rabbit. At three and four years, most children are not passive listeners. Then and later they "learn" a story by living it in different ways. Like primary teachers, parents can encourage children to use stories in a variety of behaviors.

As children grow older, their interests in books broaden. Four- and five-year-olds still enjoy nursery rhymes and simple home stories, but they are often ready for longer stories, which may take them away from familiar environments and ideas. The city child may be interested in *The Little Red Hen* or *The Three Little Pigs.* Stories of machines and airplanes become part of their world. At this stage children like to help in choosing the next book and may exercise this choice in a supermarket with the simpler books of a series such as the Little Golden Books. For not only do the four- and five-year-olds like to help choose books, but they are also beginning to want some books they can call their very own. Thus, even before a child enters school, a foundation of good reading habits and attitudes may be built.

SPECIFIC TEACHING AT HOME?

The above sections have emphasized the importance of a broad background of experiences, of many opportunities for the use of language, and of an introduction to the delights of literature for preschool children. In addition, parents sometimes ask school people if they should teach specific reading skills to their children. Such questions are asked because parents today have available to them materials about the reading program which fall into three main categories:

1. Magazine and newspaper articles and a few books criticizing typical reading programs.
2. Material suggesting how parents can assist the school (as given in this chapter).
3. Learn-to-read books and equipment designed for parental use and sold by drugstores, supermarkets, variety stores, and some book shops. Most of the questions about home teaching relate to the use of some of the devices in this category. Some easy-to-read books are in

a separate category and are included in the appendixes at the end of Chapter 13. This section is concerned with workbook materials, boxes of word cards, and similar devices. Examples of workbooks intended for home use are:

Horn, Gladys M., *Stories to Read, Pictures to Color, Games To Play*. Albert Whitman, Chicago 1954.

McEathron, Margaret, *Your Child Can Learn to Read,* rev. ed. Grosset & Dunlap, New York, 1952. Correlated with this are two workbooks, *I Learn to Read,* I and II.

Parke, Margaret B., *My First Book to Read* and *My Second Book to Read*. Grosset and Dunlap, New York, 1957.

Winters, Mary K., *Teach Me to Read,* rev. ed. Hart, New York, 1957.

Examples of kits of materials are the following items:

The Dolch Play-Way Learning Games, distributed by Gelles-Widner Co., St. Louis.

11 games with titles such as: *Picture Readiness Game, Look, Sentence Game, Consonant Lotto,* etc.; *Phonetic Word Builder* and *Picture Word Builder,* Milton Bradley Co.

Reading Kit, by W. F. Dearborn and P. W. Johnston. Simon and Schuster, New York, 1955. 4 books, 4 games, and word-picture cards.

These workbooks and kits are listed, not because they are recommended systems of teaching children to read, but because they illustrate the materials now being prepared to help parents who wish to teach their children at home. In general, the workbooks and kits may be criticized as covering only a very small part of the complex of skills needed in learning to read. They tend to be isolated practice materials rather than well-rounded means of developing perceptual and comprehension abilities in an organized way, over a period of years. Perhaps their chief advantage is that they can be used in the home in a situation where the child gets the individual attention of the adult, in contrast to many beginning reading situations in schools where he is taught in a group. On the other hand, many parents are unskilled in teaching specific reading techniques, and emotional tensions may arise which affect both parent and child.

The point of view expressed in this chapter is that (1) some exceptional children may learn to read at home; (2) all homes can provide a general background of experience and emotional support for learning to read; and (3) the specific jobs of learning the many phases of the reading process are best guided by the professionally trained person, the teacher.

THE FIRST WEEKS IN SCHOOL

If a child has attended nursery school, he may have attained some habits of independence and of working beside others which will help him in his first days in kindergarten or first grade. Excellent suggestions for helping a child adjust to nursery school and kindergarten have been made by the Franks.[13] Even with this background of experience, the child will face problems in a typical first grade. He is in the process of becoming a member of a group which is larger than he was used to and in which there must be established certain routines of behavior and learning. At this stage it is crucial that home and school work together to make the transition a pleasant one. As suggested above, parent-teacher conferences, bulletins from school to home about the first-grade program, and parents' visits to the classroom may all help. One bulletin sent to parents of first-graders, is given, somewhat adapted, on page 581. This bulletin suggests activities to avoid and many positive types of encouragement, both general and specifically related to reading.

A school staff can find a number of helps in planning a series of parent-teacher conferences about children in first grade or higher grades. Most of the references describe desirable procedures rather than giving research results about the methods and results of such conferences. For example, an early reference by d'Evelyn[14] contained short descriptions of interviews with comments on their successful and unsuccessful features. A later publication by Langdon and Stout[15] gave many practical suggestions for successful conferences. More general helps are given in booklets by Osborne[16] and by Stout

[13] Mary Frank and Lawrence K. Frank, *How to Help Your Child in School.* New American Library, paperbound, New York, 1954.

[14] Katherine E. d'Evelyn, *Individual Parent-Teachers Conferences.* Bureau of Publications, Teachers College, Columbia University, New York, 1945.

[15] Grace Langdon and Irving W. Stout, *Teacher-Parent Interviews.* Prentice-Hall, Englewood Cliffs, N.J., 1954.

[16] Ernest G. Osborne, *Parent-Teacher Partnership.* Parent-Teacher Series, Bureau of Publications, Teachers College, Columbia University, New York, 1959.

How to Help Your Child in First Grade

General Help

1. Be sure of your child's health and vision and see that he attends school regularly.

2. Provide experiences in the community--the playground, trips, market, railroad, museum, etc.--so he will have many ideas about things found in books.

3. Give him a chance to know and to play with other children.

4. Show interest in school life by asking him about people and events of the day--but avoid specific questions. (See Don'ts).

5. See that children's books are available at home.

6. Read and enjoy stories and poems with your child.

7. Encourage your child to begin a small library of his own.

A Few Don'ts

1. Don't put pressure on your child for quick results--just getting used to school may take a few weeks.

2. Don't ask specific questions like "Do you know your A B C's?" or "What did you learn today?" Your child may be embarrassed to say "NO," and it is easier to say what one did than what one learned.

3. Don't try to teach reading yourself--this is a skilled job for a trained teacher which must be related to other school activities.

4. Don't try to teach letter names or letter sounds. Your child will learn these at school as two small parts of a large, carefully planned program of developing reading skills.

5. Don't expect your child to read different story books or workbooks in the first few months at school, even if they are easy. He may be working hard to master one set of ideas and one basic vocabulary.

Direct Help

1. Listen with approval as your child reads short letters, exercises, or stories that he brings home.

2. Encourage visits to the public library.

3. Discuss current books, magazines, and newspaper articles of family interest.

4. Look over written work brought home and encourage discussion of this and other creative activities.

5. Plan to have a conference with his teacher before difficulties arise.

6. Your child will bring home announcements of demonstrations or talks. Be sure to notice these.

List of do's and don't's to help your child read

and Langdon.[17] Other general treatments such as the yearbook, *Parents and the Schools*,[18] contain suggestions for conducting parent-teacher interviews.

One research study by Maves[19] analyzed the characteristics of "high-level" and "low-level" parent-teacher conferences as tape-recorded in sixty meetings. The "high-level" conferences were marked by such procedures as early establishment of rapport through such devices as starting with the child's strong points or expressing appreciation because the mother had gotten time off from her employment. They gave approximately equal place to parent and teacher, instead of being dominated by one person. They concentrated on a few items instead of mechanical coverage of a whole list on a check sheet. They contained more specific illustrative incidents of the child's behavior in school or home. They included some interpretations of the school program in relation to the child's present status and more commendation by the teacher of the child and by the parent of the teacher's work.

Some suggestions from the above sources may be summarized as follows:

Parent-teacher conferences must be carefully planned.

Conferences should be scheduled some weeks in advance when teacher and parent are free of other responsibilities.

A letter suggesting times for interviews should go to all parents of children in a class.

Records of a child's work and test results, if available, should be made accessible before an interview begins.

The teacher should ordinarily take the initiative in beginning the conference on some positive aspects of the child's development or behavior.

The parent should be encouraged to discuss freely any of the child's problems from the parental point of view.

The teacher should report carefully the school's impression of the child and his work.

[17] Irving W. Stout and Grace Langdon, *Parent-Teacher Relationships*, What Research Says to the Teacher, No. 16. National Education Association, Washington, D.C., 1958.

[18] Department of Elementary School Principals, *Parents and the Schools*, Thirty-sixth Yearbook, National Education Association, Washington, D.C., 1957.

[19] Harold J. Maves, "Contrasting Levels of Performance in Parent-Teacher Conferences," *Elementary School Journal*, Vol. 58, pp. 219-224, January, 1958.

The interview should end with a few specific suggestions of ways the parent can help, such as in providing books, and encouraging use of materials sent home.

Some schools try to use the teacher's time more efficiently by answering in a school bulletin some of the questions which parents ask most frequently. This bulletin goes to all parents before a series of interviews begins. Sometimes parents may use one or two of the questions as starting points for more complete answers to be obtained in the conference or after a demonstration. Such questions as the following may be answered briefly:

What is the reading readiness program?
Why don't children learn phonics (sounds) when beginning to read?
Should I teach my child the A B C's?
Does a look-say method mean much guessing?
Why do primers contain such "baby" stuff?
How should I correct mistakes in words?
Should I read to my child after he begins to read for himself?
Does television interfere with reading?

The answers to these questions may vary somewhat according to practices in different school districts. Suggested answers are found in this book, especially in Chapters 6, 7, and 13.

HOW DOES A PARENT HELP OLDER CHILDREN?

Some parents feel that their responsibility for the child's reading is over by the time he is becoming an independent reader, somewhere around third-grade level of achievement. As suggested in Chapter 7, the second- and third-grade periods often have a significant influence on the child's total reading attitudes and achievements. In these years he must perfect some of his skills in phonetic analysis, in structural analysis, in using context clues, and in broadening his reading interests. These first three specific skills require the direct help of the professionally trained teacher and a carefully graded program of essential skills leading to more complex skills. The fourth area is one to which both home and school can contribute. If the child has acquired the necessary skills, by the third or fourth grade he may have interests which drive him to be a regular, even an insatiable, reader. As all parents know, children by this time vary widely in their abilities and interests, and not all can be expected to be doing the same thing. This is one reason why they can be encouraged to become independent readers.

Around the third- and fourth-grade levels, research suggests that children often reach some sort of maximum time spent in reading the comics and looking at television. For many children, interest in these activities is high for several years, until it begins to decrease around twelve or thirteen years of age. Accordingly, such topics as the relation of reading to comics and to television are good ones for meetings of parents of children in the third to sixth grades. Typical programs include talks by school people who are acquainted with some of the research, panels of parents and teachers, and sometimes reports by children themselves on what they are doing about such problems as television and reading. Larrick[20] has indicated why comics are appealing and has suggested ways of finding substitutes for them. Since children under ten often choose animal comics, a list of short but exciting animal stories may be a first bridge to book reading. Children from ten to twelve or thirteen seem to prefer comic books of adventure and crime, so a different collection of books related to such topics may be needed at these ages. A school program may introduce specific books available in school or public library.

Sometimes children are interested in telling a Parent-Teacher Association meeting or other group how they have improved their choices of television programs. One culmination to studies of habits of televiewing is to have pupils compare some of the advantages and disadvantages of televiewing and reading. This may be done in upper elementary or junior-high-school classes as an informal debate. A few advantages for television might include: (1) its up-to-the-minute approach in current events, (2) excitement in the stories told, (3) the fact that it can be shared by a group and then discussed, and (4) the compactness with which a story is told or ideas presented in an hour or half-hour. Some of the advantages of reading to be presented might include: (1) in reading you can go at your own rate and can review what you have read; (2) reading gives a chance to stop and think—to be critical, to take notes, etc.; (3) reading is inexpensive—

20 Nancy Larrick, *op. cit.*, Chap. 7.

a book or a newspaper does not need a call to a repair man; (4) libraries contain a range of information or fun unmatched by television; and (5) reading is best for the learning of difficult ideas. To reverse the customary saying, a thousand words can tell much more, in greater depth, than a picture.

Another type of children's program for a parents' meeting is the presentation of a collection of books or stories related to the television programs seen over the previous two or three months. Sometimes dramatic excerpts may be read from the books and the filmed program compared in some ways with the original. Some schools send out advance lists of good programs so that parents and children may enjoy them together. A parent-study group may itself work on the question of the disadvantages and advantages of television in relation to reading and other school work. Programs and studies such as these give parents information which will enable them to help older boys and girls with problems in reading and related communication fields.

Another way in which parents can help the pre-adolescent and early adolescent group is to make a number of different reference books available in the home. An article in *The Saturday Review*[21] recommended fifteen basic classes of reference books for a well-informed family: The Bible (a version based on the family's religious affiliation), an adult encyclopedia, a children's and young people's encyclopedia, an adult dictionary, a young people's dictionary, a manual on first aid, *Infant Care* from the United States Government Printing Office, a book on household repairs, a cookbook, a book of etiquette, a garden encyclopedia, an atlas, an encyclopedia yearbook, an almanac, and newspapers and magazines. Shorter and relatively inexpensive reference materials are also found nowadays in the large number of single volume books available in bookstores on non-fiction topics and in books which stand alone but are part of a series such as the Childhood of Famous Americans (Bobbs Merrill), the First Books (Watts), the Landmark Books (Random), and the Real Books (Garden City). Suggestions for evaluating such books are given in Chapter 16. Having such reference materials accessible will not only be useful in such homework but will help develop the habit of checking facts when some subject is in dispute. Especially before

[21] Louis Shores, "To Be Truly Informed," *The Saturday Review*, pp. 34, 35, February 3, 1951.

Christmas, the school can be a help to parent purchasers by having a display of new books for children as well as suitable classics. This display may be accompanied by a brief talk on what to look for when buying a book for a child or adolescent. Other suggestions for getting acquainted with children's literature are given in Chapter 13.

PARENTS' MEETINGS ON READING INSTRUCTION

Most parents want help in understanding a modern school program. They like to be informed about changes in the methods and materials of teaching. Some thoughtful parents are pleased to learn about part of the research in child growth and development and in children's learning, which has become increasingly important in the last forty or fifty years of educational practice. These parents are grateful to know that school practices are based, not on the whim or the personal experience of teacher or principal, but on a long history of experimenting with materials and methods and on several thousand scientific studies of reading instruction found in the research literature. Sometimes teachers need to show that their methods are not something hastily put together by themselves or some other individual but that they are the product of much expenditure in work, time, and money by teachers and researchers over many years. However, because parents are most interested in their own children and the concrete materials and events of the school day, these should also be used in a parents' meeting.

Parent-teacher conferences are perhaps the most valuable ways of assessing one child's progress, but they are expensive in terms of time and energy, and the explanation of what the school is doing in reading is probably best accomplished by parents' meetings. Such meetings should consist not only of a talk by teachers, principal, or other school person, but also of an actual demonstration of materials and methods used with children. Usually the talk should follow a demonstration. The topic for the meeting should deal with some genuine concerns of parents. If they are parents of beginning grade one pupils, they may be most interested in a topic such as "How is Beginning Reading Taught?" or "What is a Reading Readiness Program?" If their children have been in school for some time they may be interested in topics such as "The Place of Phonics in Reading," "Getting Meaning from Reading," or "Getting Acquainted with Children's Literature." Whatever the topic, some of the same steps in preparation and conduct of a meeting are applicable. Nine of these, slightly adapted from Robison[22] may be stated as follows:

1. Give parents a cordial invitation extended in ample time for them to arrange to come to school on the specified day. Make careful plans for all details of the meeting. Sometimes a cup of tea sets a friendly atmosphere. Provision for the care of the accompanying babies is usually a great convenience.
2. Discuss with parents the specific objectives of the demonstration lesson so that they know what to look for before the children take their places. Sometimes the objectives may be written in advance on the chalkboard.
3. Have a very short demonstration with children, using a basal reader, or with older children, using some other text. The demonstration should usually include specific work on new vocabulary skills.
4. Excuse the children. Plan for their care elsewhere in the school.
5. Discuss the demonstration, encouraging the parents to ask questions and to comment freely.
6. Allow parents to inspect the books of the children. Show the primers or other readers which they will use later.
7. Encourage parents to ask questions.
8. Suggest to parents that they visit a reading group at a higher level to see the direction in which the children are going and their future attainments.
9. Invite the parents to return to school to observe the progress of the group. If possible, set a date for the future meeting.

These nine steps illustrate the fact that parents must be prepared for what they are going to see in a demonstration and need the opportunity to follow up the demonstration with further discussion. Most parents are not skilled observers and need help in focusing their attention on important parts of the children's learning activities, such as how the teacher directs left to right eye movements, how a child works at long and short vowel sounds, how auditory and visual skills are combined, or what different types of comprehension may be involved in the reading of a paragraph. Similarly, some things they saw in the demonstration may be puzzling, and the opportunity to ask questions and discuss ideas is essential.

Although parents of intermediate and upper grade children are not always so actively concerned, a reading demonstration can be equally valuable at this level. The nine steps outlined above apply to the planning and conduct of the meeting. Topics will reflect the

[22] Eleanor G. Robison, "Helping Parents Understand the Modern Reading Program," Contributions in Reading, No. 3. Ginn, Boston, reprinted, 1957.

questions of parents and the purposes of the reading program in the intermediate grades. They may include such themes as the following:

Becoming Independent Readers
Developing Good Study Habits
How Children Use Reference Books
Getting the Most Out of a Dictionary
Developing Permanent Interests in Reading
What About Comics?
Television and Reading

The first topic might include a demonstration of how the children work out new words in context, by phonetic analysis, by structural analysis, by using the dictionary, and by a combination of these methods. The second topic might include examples of reading from basic books, from supplementary readers, from textbooks, and from library books, and using books for reading aloud, dramatization, story-telling, and other activities. The corresponding chapters of this book give many suggestions for the treatment of other topics in preparing short outlines to be placed in parents' hands and in planning actual procedures with a group.

The approach used in parents' meetings will depend upon the parents' problems such as suggested above and the backgrounds they bring to school affairs. One fairly high-level type of program is to bring actual copies of old readers, to read from them, and to show how methods in reading have changed over the years. Some old books, even replicas of Noah Webster's *Blue-back Speller* and copies of the McGuffey readers, are available in some school districts and libraries. Texts using extreme phonics methods ("The fat cat sat on the mat" school of literature) and more modern books may be shown and discussed. One other high-level type of program may be entitled "Reading Research that Makes a Difference," in which one or more people report on classic researches in reading that have affected practice down through the years. Possible studies to be included will be found in research summaries or in the volume *Research in the 3 R's*[23] which contains actual excerpts of scientific reports in reading and other fields. Such discussions may be technical or abstract for some lay groups and should be accompanied by more concrete demonstrations or collections of materials.

[23] Clarence W. Hunnicutt and William J. Iverson, eds., *Research in the 3 R's.* Harper, New York, 1958.

CONCLUSION

The school's most effective communication with parents is through happy and progressing pupils, but teachers and other school people can take additional steps to ensure parent interest and understanding of the reading program. Teachers must be able to explain what they do in classrooms and to deal with comments of parents reasonably and objectively. Co-operative activities help teachers learn from parents as well as spreading information about school procedures. Some of the ways of improving the two-way process of communication have been listed above, and two of them, the parent-teacher conference and the parents' meeting at the school, have been developed in some detail. The chapter has attempted to provide answers to the frequent parent's question, "What can we do to help our child read better?" Both general and specific activities have been suggested.

These suggestions lead to the final question of the respective roles of parent and teacher in helping children read better. Obviously, the roles are overlapping. One difference, however, seems clear. Parents are concerned most with general development and the background of experiences of the child. Teachers are concerned most with some of the specific skills and habits which must be mastered by children and which are best taught in careful sequence by professionally trained persons. Both can encourage children in developing a range of reading interests, but parents must assume responsibility for early experiences which enable the child to interpret printed pages, and teachers must assume responsibility for the development of word-recognition skills, comprehension abilities, and specific techniques involved in study habits with books and other materials.

This book has been concerned chiefly with how children learn to read in school. Especially in its first and last chapters, however, it reflects the reality that much school learning is affected by home and community conditions and becomes effective only in terms of lifetime reading behavior. Schools are concerned, first, with language habits developed in early childhood and, later, with reading skills, interests, and habits which should equip a person for a life-time of reading activities. The present chapter has suggested that the teacher gets much help from parents, especially in the early grades, if he or she can empathize and lead. The insightful teacher realizes that a parent frequently identifies with his own child, projecting his deepest sense of success and failure, his most intimate hopes and fears, into the daily experiences of the child. The teacher realizes that the parent, knowing only a few children well, may have different standards for his child than the teacher holds, with her perspective of longer and more varied experiences with children. The teacher realizes, finally, that the parent has an image of the school and its work before he enters a classroom door. The parent may see the teacher as a hard-working individual with too many children to look after or as a person in charge of a day uninterrupted by household duties, well supplied with materials and equipment, and devoted to children's needs. Such beliefs may seem unrealistic to the teacher, but they are genuinely held by the parent and the starting point from which the teacher must work.

The teacher, accordingly, is sensitive to the characteristics and needs of the child and to the parent's ambitions for the child, his hopes and fears for him in the days ahead. As suggested in Chapter 1 and throughout this book, the teacher is also conscious that the modern complex world makes many demands on us and will make many more on our children. For the years to come we must help them to read much more efficiently and delightedly than they have in the past. Perhaps this book can help them and their teachers in the dual responsibility.

SUPPLEMENTARY READINGS

A. Materials for Parents

Artley, A. S. *Your Child Learns to Read.* Scott, Foresman, Chicago, 1953.

Association for Childhood Education. *Adventuring in Literature with Children.* Portfolio of leaflets by various authors. Association for Childhood Education, 1953.

Bond, G., and Wagner, Eva. *Child Growth in Reading.* Lyons and Carnahan, Chicago, 1955.

California State Department of Education. *The Preparation of Teachers for Home-School-Community Relations.* Bulletin of the California State Department of Education, Vol. 22, No. 8, October, 1953.

Fea, Henry R. "The Meaning of Reading," *College of Education Record,* University of Washington, Vol. 21, pp. 42-45, March, 1955.

Frank, Lawrence K., and Frank, Mary. *How to Help Your Child in School.* Viking, New York, 1950.

Gans, Roma. *Reading is Fun.* Bureau of Publications, Teachers College, Columbia University, New York, 1949.

GATES, DORIS. *Helping Children Discover Books.* Science Research Associates, Chicago, 1956.

Growing Up With Books. Annual booklists, Bowker, New York.

HEWITT, RUTH B., and HEWITT, C. E. *Help Your Child be Ready for Reading.* Monographs for Elementary Teachers, No. 97. Row, Peterson, Evanston, Ill., 1960.

LARRICK, NANCY. *A Parent's Guide to Children's Reading.* Doubleday, New York, 1958. Also Cardinal Edition, Pocket Books, New York, 1958.

MACKINTOSH, HELEN K. *How Children Learn to Read.* Superintendent of Documents, U. S. Government Printing Office, Washington, D.C., 1952.

NATIONAL EDUCATION ASSOCIATION. *Janie Learns to Read.* The Association, Washington, D.C., 1954.

NATIONAL EDUCATION ASSOCIATION. *Sailing into Reading.* The Association, Washington, D.C., 1956.

ROBISON, ELEANOR G. *A Letter To Parents.* Contributions in Reading, No. 8. Ginn, Boston, 1958.

STRANG, RUTH. *Helping Your Gifted Child.* Dutton, New York, 1960.

WITTY, P. A. *How to Become a Better Reader.* Science Research Associates, Chicago, 1953.

WOLLNER, MARY H. B. "What Parents Should Know About the Retarded Reader," *Education,* Vol. 78, pp. 14-21, September, 1957.

B. Professional References for Teachers

BETTS, E. A. "Parents and Teachers Want to Know About Reading," *Education,* Vol. 78, pp. 289-299, January, 1958.

DEPARTMENT OF ELEMENTARY SCHOOL PRINCIPALS. *Parents and the Schools,* Thirty-sixth Yearbook, National Education Association, Washington, D.C., September, 1957. 310 p.

FRANK, MARY, and FRANK, LAWRENCE K. *How to Help Your Child in School.* Viking Press, New York, 1950. 368 p.

GRANT, EVA H. *Parents and Teachers as Partners.* Science Research Associates, Chicago, 1952. 48 p.

HARDIMANN, RUTH N., and ROBINSON, JOHN T. "How to Utilize Favorable, and to Cope with Unfavorable, Community Influences in Improving Reading." Supplementary Educational Monographs, No. 72, pp. 68-77. University of Chicago Press, Chicago, 1950.

HYMES, JAMES L. *Effective Home-School Relations.* Prentice-Hall, Englewood Cliffs, N.J., 1953. 264 p.

HYMES, JAMES L. *Before the Child Reads.* Row, Peterson, Evanston, Ill., 1958.

LANGDON, GRACE, and STOUT, IRVING W. *Helping Parents Understand Their Child's School.* Prentice-Hall, Englewood Cliffs, N.J., 1957. 508 p.

LONSDALE, BERNARD J. "Parent-Teacher Conferences—An Experience in Human Relations," *California Journal of Elementary Education,* Vol. 24, pp. 78-90, November, 1955.

MAVES, H. J. "Contrasting Levels of Performance in Parent-Teacher Conferences," *Elementary School Journal,* Vol. 58, pp. 219-224, January, 1958.

MCSWAIN, ELDRIDGE T. "Problems in the Parent-Teacher Relationship," *National Parent-Teacher,* Vol. 44, pp. 28-30, September, 1949.

MILNER, ESTHER. "Study of the Relationship between Reading Readiness in Grade One Children and Patterns of Parent-Child Interaction," *Child Development,* Vol. 22, pp. 95-112, June, 1951.

MORRISON, N. C. "Parent Readiness for Today's Reading Methods," *Education Digest,* Vol. 18, pp. 16-18, December, 1952.

NATIONAL SCHOOL PUBLIC RELATIONS ASSOCIATION. *It Starts in the Classroom.* National Education Association, Washington, D.C., 1951.

OJEMANN, RALPH H. "Parent-Teacher Relationships," in C. W. Harris, ed., *Encyclopedia of Educational Research,* 3rd ed., pp. 938-941. Macmillan, New York, 1960.

OJEMANN, RALPH H., and FATLAND, LUELLA. "Parents and Teachers as Partners," *National Parent Teacher,* Vol. 40, pp. 20-23, September, 1945. Condensed, *Education Digest,* Vol. 11, pp. 1-4, November, 1945.

OSBORNE, E. G. *Parent-Teacher Partnerships.* Parent-Teacher series. Bureau of Publications, Teachers College, Columbia University, New York, 1959.

OTTO, HENRY J. "Methods of Reporting Elementary School Children's Progress to Parents," *Bulletin of Texas Congress of Parents and Teachers.* University of Texas Press, Austin, 1957.

POTTER, W. N. "Role of the Parent in Relation to Pupils' Reading Progress," *California Journal of Elementary Education,* Vol. 18, pp. 135-144, February, 1950.

PRESCOTT, DANIEL. *A Child in the Educative Process.* McGraw-Hill, New York, 1957. 502 p.

PRESSNALL, H. E. "Parents' Opinions of Reading Instruction," *Elementary English,* Vol. 33, pp. 29-33, January, 1956.

SMITTER, FAITH W. "What Should Parents Know About Their Child's Progress in School?" *California Journal of Elementary Education,* Vol. 24, pp. 112-116, November, 1955.

SMITTER, FAITH W., and HAAS, R. B. "Parents' Values for Their Children," *California Journal of Elementary Education,* Vol. 23, pp. 217-222, May, 1955.

STOUT, IRVING W., and LANGDON, GRACE. *Parent-Teacher Relationships.* What Research Says to the Teacher, No. 16. National Education Association, Washington, D.C., 1958.

STOUT, IRVING W., and LANGDON, GRACE, "What Parents Want to Know About Their Child's School," *Nation's Schools,* Vol. 60, pp. 45-48, August, 1957.

INDEX

PRINTED IN THE UNITED STATES OF AMERICA